Pharmaceutical Industrial Management

Second Edition

Pharmaceutical Industrial Management

Second Edition

Prof. Dr. G. Vidya Sagar

M.Pharm., Ph.D., PGDMM., DIH., FIC., FES

Dean and Director,

Veerayatan Institute of Pharmacy

Kutch, Gujarat-370 460.

PharmaMed Press

An imprint of Pharma Book Syndicate

A unit of BSP Books Pvt. Ltd.

4-4-309/316, Giriraj Lane

Sultan Bazar, Hyderabad - 500 095.

Published by

PharmaMed Press

An imprint of Pharma Book Syndicate

A unit of BSP Books Pvt. Ltd.

4-4-309/316, Giriraj Lane, Sultan Bazar, Hyderabad - 500 095.

Phone: 040-23445605, 23445688; Fax: 91+40-23445611

E-mail: info@pharmamedpress.com

ISBN: 978-93-52300-25-9 (HB)

Foreword

It is my privilege to pen about Dr. G. Vidya Sagar's textbook **"Pharmaceutical Industrial Management"**. This book has claimed a good readership in the last 10 years since its publication in 2004. The revised Second edition has a enlarged content and is written strictly in accordance with the AICTE recommended model syllabus for the subject of 'Industrial Management'.

Management in business and organizations is the function that coordinates the efforts of people to accomplish goals and objectives by using available resources efficiently and effectively. The four basic functions of any management are planning, organizing, influencing and controlling.

The textbook consists of two major parts. 1. Principles and Practices of management in Pharmaceutical industry. 2. Basic tenets of accountancy and book keeping. All the chapters have been repositioned in a lucid language. The contents which merit attention are given in the form of points at the starting of each chapter. At the end of each chapter, important questions have been provided. The book is a modest attempt by the author to present various Pharmaceutical management principles ought to be known by a pharmacy graduate in a platter at one place.

In this second edition, according to the author, the book has been revised some of the contemporary issues of the management practice to make the book more exhaustive. The units have been subdivided into various sections for ease of study. Emphasis has been laid in explaining the terms and topics in a simple and scientific way easily understandable by students.

I strongly recommend this textbook to every pharmacy student for learning the tenets of management principles. I am confident that the book will have a wider readership among the fellow pharmacist brethren.

Prof. Dr. B. Suresh
Vice Chancellor, JSS UNIVERSITY,
Mysore, Karnataka. &
President, Pharmacy Council of India, New Delhi.

Preface to Second Edition

All organizations depend upon group efforts. Group action and joint efforts have become necessary in every walk of life. Management is required wherever two or more people work together to achieve common objectives. The success in group efforts depends upon mutual cooperation among the members of the group. Management creates teamwork and coordination among specialized efforts.

Management is indispensable in all organizations whether a business firm, a government, a hospital, a college, a club, etc. Management is a creative force which helps in the optimum utilization of resources.

This revised second edition has been written keeping in view the syllabus of various Indian universities on the subject and is strictly in accordance with the syllabus prescribed by the AICTE for the subject. The author has made attempts in simplifying the topics and presenting them in a simple and easily graspable manner by the students.

Several new and contemporary management topics like manufacturing management, pharmaceutical industry, organization of distribution and marketing have been incorporated in the book. Several chapters have been revised suiting the need of the day.

For every chapter, salient features are presented at the beginning of the chapter for knowing the contents easily. Language has been given importance and simple terms and words have been used. Revision questions are given at the end of each chapter to enable the students to test their own comprehension on the topics they have studied in the book.

The book may not serve as a reference but is informative and exhaustive to the extent required for a Pharmacy Student pursuing management subject. In this text book, an attempt has been made by the author to explain the tenets of management in a simple and lucid style.

I sincerely presume that this textbook will be a handy book for Pharmacy students and the efforts of the author will be successful if the book finds utility for which it has been written.

I solicit constructive criticism and suggestions for the improvement of quality and content of the textbook.

Dr. G. Vidya Sagar
August, 2015.

Preface to Second Edition

Acknowledgement

It is my moral duty to thank all those people who were behind me in inspiring and giving moral support for revising the first edition and bringing a more elaborate version. I am beholden to the following persons for their constant patting and encouragement.

Prof. (Dr.) B. Suresh, President, Pharmacy Council of India, New Delhi.

Prof. (Dr.) K. R. Mahadik, Principal and Dean, College of Pharmacy, Bharati Vidyapeeth University, Pune.

I am thankful to Sri Anil Shah of Pharma Book Syndicate in bringing out this book in such a nice manner. The work was truly a co-operative effort and I appreciate the services of Mr. Naresh of PBS in solving out some issues for the successful launch.

Finally, I am indebted to my wife, Mrs. G. Swapna Sagar who helped me in preparing and revising the manuscript and to my daughter G. Hasitha who bore the brunt of my preoccupation with the book.

Prof. Dr. G. Vidya Sagar

Contents

1 Management

1.1 | Definition

LEARNING OBJECTIVES

- *Meaning of Management*
- *Characteristics of Management*
- *Importance of Management*
- *Strata (levels) of Management*
- *Functions of Management (Elements of Management)*

Management is a process of conducting and coordinating various human activities. It is a method of optimizing results with minimum efforts so as to secure maximum efficiency and growth for both, the employer and the employee. Management is a subject which comes under the purview of both science and art. It can be called a science because it proves, defines, measures and uses knowledge. It is an art because it communicates, expresses, describes and practices. Management can also be called a profession because knowledge, skill and aptitude are required and also a positive work nature.

> "Management is a multipurpose organ that manages a business, manages managers and manages workers and work."
>
> **– *Peter Drucker***

> "Management is getting things done by developing people and not directing people."

> "Management is a process of planning, organizing, actuating and controlling performance to determine and accomplish the objectives by the use of people and resource."
>
> **– *George Terry***

> "Management is a process of doing and managing various activities."

Management is adoption of congenial and coherent atmosphere within the internal environs of an organization where people work in teams and groups for fulfilling the goals and objectives of an organization in a efficient way.

Basically management consists of planning, controlling, coordinating, motivating, directing and channelizing the group efforts for a specific objective.

1.2 | Meaning of Management

The term "Management" has different connotations. It is an activity, a process and it is also interpersonal achievement of goals. In one context, it means a group of individuals and in another context it is a process.

- ***Management as an activity*:** It is an art of getting work done through organized effort of individuals and groups by informal and motivational way. It is carried out by a manager who coordinates and directs the group of individuals in their work. A manager usually performs several functions in this regard. He is a conduit between his superiors and subordinates and people outside the organization.
  He is also a decision initiator. He decides about the new projects, work distribution, resources distribution and other important decisions.
- ***Management as a process*:** It is a process because it consists of several interlinked functions. It helps in fixing the objectives and taking steps to achieve the objectives. It is a process of directing, controlling and coordinating the activities of people in a unidirectional way of achieving the preset goals.
  Management as a process involves the interaction between the people, bringing people together and channelizing their energies. It is also a never ending process which involves continuous planning and solving of problems.
- ***Management as a discipline*:** It is a well organized branch of science which consists of organized body of knowledge which can be used for training and teaching. It can be called a discipline because people are learning the principles, preaching and practicing them universally.
  Management is a recently developed branch which is gaining popularity very fast. There is no place where these principles cannot be applied.
- ***Management as a group*:** Generally management means people who are on the top rung of the ladder. They are the individuals who are responsible for formulating the policies of the organization.

Characteristics of Management

- ***Management as a science and art*:** It has a pool of systematic knowledge which has to be applied skillfully to the practical situations. Scientific principles help to improve the art of management.

- ***The multi disciplinary nature of management*:** It is a branch of science that has evolved from other subjects like anthropology, sociology, public administration and psychology. These subjects are interlinked with the issues of management.
- ***Management as integrated process*:** It is the sum total of human effort with money and machine effort. It creates an environment where people can discharge their duties in a best possible way.
- ***Management as a totality*:** The basic role of management is to achieve certain goals. They are called organizational goals. As a totality, it involves the fulfillment of these goals.
- ***Unobservable nature of Management*:** Management is a force which cannot be seen. The results are very clear but we cannot see it functioning. The effectiveness of the management will be judged by the end results but we cannot see the management operations.
- ***Management towards goal orientation*:** Every organization has certain goals and objectives. These are fulfilled by means of the management. The basic objectives of management are to ensure optimum utilization of men, machinery and monetary resources for fulfilling the goals of the organization. The success of management is measured by the extent to which the established goals are achieved.
- ***Management is a human activity*:** Management consists of interrelated human activities. It requires knowledge and skill for correct utilization to obtain good results.
- ***Management as a collective effort*:** It is a group effort where several people work together in coordination and cooperation in fulfilling the goals. There are different levels of management. But usually management refers to all those individuals who perform managerial functions.
- ***The universality of management*:** Management is all pervading. Every sphere of human activity requires management. Any organization irrespective of the size or type, careful planning and organization is required which is nothing but management. All types of organizations like house, university, college, commercial enterprises, business organizations, hospitals and charity homes require management. Hence management is universal.

Importance of Management

Management is a part and parcel of any organized human activity. Optimum utilization of human and material resources is necessary for achievement of pre-determined objectives of any organization. It is the process of formulation of thoughts and passing them into action. The significance of it can be summed up in the following points.

1. It determines the objectives of a firm
2. It helps in achieving the stated objectives

3. It helps in organizational development
4. It helps in optimum utilization of resources
5. Virtually, progress and development of an organization or country depends on careful planning and management of various issues.

"Management is utilization of all available resources to the maximum in attaining all the objectives of the organization and the individual goals as well."

***Resources (6 M)*:**

INPUT			**OUTPUT**
MEN			
MATERIALS		*	ORGANIZATIONAL OBJECTIVES
MACHINERY		*	RESULTS
MONEY	------ ⇒⇒ ⇒⇒	*	PRODUCTIVITY
METHODS		*	EMPLOYEE SATISFACTION
MARKET		*	SALES PROMOTION

Strata (levels) of Management:

In any organization, there are 3 levels of management. They are :

- Top Level Management
- Middle Level Management
- Lower Level Management

Top Level Management: It consists of the Managing Director, Board of Trustees, Board of Directors and advisers. It is the ultimate source of planning and authority of the organization. The top level management performs the following important functions:

- It designs and formulates the vision and goals of the organization.
- It lays down the objectives and policies of the organization.
- It is responsible for organizing the business activity into departments and revisions.
- It appoints the personal required for the organization.
- It performs the functions of directing and coordinating the activities of the departmental heads of the organization.
- It reviews the progress of various departments and evaluates the performance in relation to the laid down objectives of the organization.

Middle Level Management: It consists of managers and heads of the departments. These people report to the top level management. They coordinate the work of supervisors and junior staff and workers and they provide necessary leadership, direction and initiative to the lower rung of management.

Lower level Management: It consists of supervisors, employees and field staff. These people are responsible for carrying out day to day activities. They solve the problems of the workers and represent the grievances to the higher authorities.

The important functions of lower level management are :

- Planning of work daily
- Assigning tasks and supervising the work
- Giving necessary guidelines and directions to the workers regarding the work to be done
- Maintaining discipline and decorum in the organization
- Maintaining cordial relationship with the work force
- Improving the morale and motivation of work force
- Evaluation of the work done
- Fixing the targets and fixing the compensation for the workers

***Functions of Management (Elements of Management)*:** The Management has several important functions. The success of an organization depends upon the efficient discharge of these functions.

The important functions are :

- Planning
- Organizing
- Staffing
- Directing
- Controlling
- Co-ordination

***Planning*:** Planning is an organized approach for accomplishment of pre-determined objectives. It is decision–making in advance regarding what to do, when to do, where to do, how to do, who has to do and methods of result evaluation.

The process of planning involves the following steps :

(a) Determining the objective
(b) Forecasting
(c) Search for alternatives
(d) Evaluation of alternative course of actions and designing of plans
(e) Formulation of plans and procedures
(f) Preparation of programmes and schedules
(g) Financial including budgeting

***Organizing*:** It is a grouping of similar activity together with a view to attain the planned objectives defining the responsibilities of the people in the organization, delegating, suitable authority to them to discharge their respective responsibilities and establishing relationship of coordinating the individual efforts to fulfill the objectives of the enterprise.

The process of organization involves the following steps :

(a) Finding the objectives and locating the main activities
(b) Division of act and creation of jobs
(c) Filling individuals into jobs developing norms, for delegating authorities and responsibilities.

Staffing: It involves placing the right people into the organizational structure by means of effective selection and appraisal procedure. A right person should be selected for a right type of job. A staffing function includes selection, communication, counseling, training, compensation, dismissals etc.

The board of directors of a company take-up the staffing functions by selecting and appraising a chief executive who in turn perform these functions in relation to the heads of various divisions or departments of the enterprise.

Direction: A management function also involves giving proper direction to its employees to work efficiently and effectively to fulfill the objectives of the organization. To do this function, manager must have leadership qualities and he should be able to influence, motivate and persuade the people. Then only he will be in a position to command or control a group of persons.

This function consists of 3 important sub functions:

(a) Communication
(b) Leadership
(c) Motivation

(a) ***Communication*****:** Communication is a process of downward and upward movement of information among the employees. A manager should be able to tell his subordinate what to do, how to do, which to do in his job.

(b) ***Leadership*****:** It is the process of giving guidance and influencing the work of sub-ordinates in the designed direction.

(c) ***Motivation*****:** It is the process of creating enthusiasm to do work among the employees. Different people are motivated by different means, financial incentives motivates some people. Whereas freedom to work, recognition etc., motivates some other. It is the responsibility of the manager to recognize this factor and he should motivate the sub-ordinates to work harmoniously towards the achievement of organizational objectives.

Controlling: It is the process of checking whether the proper progress is made or not to fulfill the objectives and goals of the organization.

Controlling involves the following elements:

- Creating standards of performance

- Measuring the actual performance.
- Comparison of the actual performance with the standard performance.
- Taking corrective steps if the performance is not up to the standard level.

Coordination: It is essential that everybody in the organization understands the main objectives of the business and work towards the common goal of the organization with active cooperation of other employees. The objectives of an organization should be clearly laid down and all the employees should work hand in glove to achieve these objectives.

The important features of coordination areas are as follows:

1. It is a continuous process.
2. Its purpose to creation of uniform action for a common goal
3. It is the unification of group efforts
4. It is the activity of a manager. It is required at all levels of hierarchy in the organization.
5. It coordinates, harmonizes, synchronizes and unites individual efforts for better action and for the achievement of business objectives.

Review Questions

Short Answer Questions

1. Explain the term management
2. Explain the different levels of Management
3. State the importance of management

Long Answer Questions

1. What are the different levels of Management? Explain the role of different people at each level of management
2. Name the fundamental functions of management and explain each of them briefly?
3. Explain the term management? Describe its main characteristics

2 Manufacturing Management

Manufacturing is the use of *machines*, *tools* and labor to make things for use or sale. The term may refer to a range of human activity, from *handicraft* to *high tech*, but is most commonly applied to *industrial* production, in which *raw materials* are transformed into *finished goods* on a large scale. Such finished goods may be used for manufacturing other, more complex products, such as *household appliances* or *automobiles*, or sold to *wholesalers*, who in turn sell them to *retailers*, who then sell them to end users - the "*consumers*".

Manufacturing takes turns under all types of *economic systems*. In a free market economy, manufacturing is usually directed toward the *mass production* of *products* for sale to *consumers* at a profit. In a *collectivist economy*, manufacturing is more frequently directed by the state to supply a centrally planned economy. In free market economies, manufacturing occurs under some degree of government *regulation*.

Modern manufacturing includes all intermediate processes required for the production and integration of a product's components. Some industries, such as *semiconductor* and *steel* manufacturers use the term *fabrication* instead.

LEARNING OBJECTIVES

- *History and Development of the concept of management*
- *Production Management concept*
- *Measurement of Work*
- *Organization of Production Planning Department*
- *Planning Methods*
- *Plant Layout*
- *Plant Layout Tools and Techniques*
- *Production Methods*
- *Production Planning and Control*
- *Factors Affecting Production Planning and Control*
- *Production Planning and Control Organization*
- *Measurement of Effectiveness*
- *New Product Development*
- *Method Study and Work Statement*
- *Statistical Quality Control*

History and Development

In its earliest form, manufacturing was usually carried out by a single skilled *artisan* with assistants. Training was by *apprenticeship*. In much of the pre-industrial world the *guild* system protected the privileges and trade secrets of urban artisans.

Before the *Industrial Revolution*, most manufacturing occurred in rural areas, where household-based manufacturing served as a supplemental subsistence strategy to *agriculture* (and continues to do so in places). Entrepreneurs organized a number of manufacturing households into a single enterprise through the *putting-out system*.

Toil manufacturing is an arrangement whereby a first firm with specialized equipment processes raw materials or semi-finished goods for a second firm.

2.1 | Production Management

Production management, alternatively referred to as manufacturing management, is required for transforming raw materials and partly, fabricated materials into finished products. Production management does not imply management of productive process alone, but it covers all there activities which go into the making of production. To make production a concrete reality, one, must pay heed to the factors of production like land, labor, capital and organization, or to speak in the language of business, materials, men, money, machines and methods. Production management thus calls for the work of planning and control pertaining to each of these factors of production.

Production management does not involve a mechanical assemblage of relevant factors. In contrast to mere transformation of raw materials into finished products, it aims at transmuting and permuting resources of higher productivity so that the greatest outputs are obtained from the least inputs. With its end in views, production management embraces the productive process too and involves planning, directing and controlling operations till their successful completion. Quality, quantity, cost and time of production have an important bearing on productivity of the manufacturing enterprise. Accordingly, it is the task of production management to see that effective utilization of resources is made, time is shortened, wastes and scrapings are avoided, and harmonious working is made to prevail in the plant.

For effective managerial performance, the work of production department is required to be organized on sound lines. All the principles and practices of organizing are to be applied in building a sound structure for improving the result of production management. Successful production management is not practicable without the existence of an appropriate organization structure. Consequently, managerial efforts are to be directed in designing an organization structure that conforms to the needs of the product, size of the enterprise and availability of production facilities. Organizing for production may be conceived in broader sense to include some aspects of works engineering or works organization like plant layout and factory building.

The problems of production management from case to case and are mainly related to the system of production. There are several systems of production which determine the magnitude of production work and the problems to be tackled in manufacturing operations. Hence, a familiarity with the different systems of production is required for understanding the intricacies of production management. Of course, the system of production is dictated in a particular case by the volume of sales and the nature of product. The quantity to be produced is nothing but an answer to the question of 'what can be sold". In the ultimate analysis, therefore, sales are the regulator of a system of production.

The management of transformation process of inputs into output is the essence of production management. In present competitive world the production process in every enterprise needs some effective and scientific planning as well as proper control. Thus production management can be defined as "Management which by scientific planning and regulation sets into motion the part of an enterprise to which it has been entrusted the task of actual transformation of inputs into output". In the words of Mr. E.L. Brech, "Production Management then becomes the process of effectively planning and regulating the operations of that part of an enterprise which is responsible for the actual transformation of materials into finished products".

This definition appears to be incomplete as it does not include the human factors involved in a production process. It lays stress only on the materialistic features.

In broader sense, production management actually deals with decision making related to production processes, so that the resulting goods and services are produced in accordance with the quantitative specifications and demand schedule with minimum cost. To attain these objectives the two main activities of Production Management are the Design and Control of production systems.

In production management effective planning and control are essential. In the absence of effective planning and regulation of any production activity the goals cannot be achieved, the customers may not be satisfied and ultimately certain activities may be closed which may lead to social evil.

Measurement of Work

In an engineering sense efficiency can be simply stated as the ratio of useful energy obtained to energy applied. We can all understand that. Put succinctly, that is what is really meant by efficiency of production, but the difficulty is to see the relationship between input and output of production, or to measure performance. Which brings us right to the heart of the problem of efficiency of production: how to measure performances.

There is usually some difficulty about measuring the comparative performance of several departments in a Company or different companies. If two factories are turning out the same product which is measured in tons or feet, then overall cost per ton or per foot is a measure of performance which can be obtained readily and used for comparison. But how does one compare the costs or efficiency of two factories or departments making dissimilar products? Cost per ton or unit is no good. As between two different firms, only the percentage net profit is any measure, and that is affected by the type of market and selling cost which are not production costs. And between different departments in the same firm there would seem to be, at first sight, no measure of efficiency on a common and therefore comparable basis.

If, however, the amount of "effort" (or cost-material, labor and overhead services) which should have been used to make a given quantity of a product is known and also the amount actually used, then surely the correct amount as a proportion of the actual amount is a measure of performance of efficiency. It is in reality an efficiency formula again, output over input. The real value of output, in efforts or hours is the amount of cost which goes out of the factory or department in a useful form, i.e., it does not include all wastage and excess costs, avoidable, and of no benefit to customer or company. And input is the total of all effort and costs absorbed. Including excess costs.

Organization of Production Planning Department

The work of a Production Planning Department generally falls into three sections, dealing with three stages of the sequence of operations. They are:

(i) Compiling and recording facts.

(ii) Developing plans.

(iii) Putting plans into operation and controlling results.

In the first stage and section, information is gathered together, recorded and filled in a way which is suitable for use by planners, and so that reference to it is easy and rapid. The information is of three kinds, relating to:

(a) Customers' orders and requirements;

(b) Stocks of materials and components;

(c) Plant available, capacities, operations and times.

Unless the organization is of such a size that each kind of information is dealt with in a separate section, it is advisable for all of it to be handled by one section under the supervision of a person skilled in the work. Its organization is mainly a problem of filling and entering-up figures or records form vouchers, i.e., transferring information and striking balances. It can usually be staffed with Juniors, female, or relatively unskilled labor, but must be carefully supervised and checked by very reliable people. The absolute accuracy and therefore double checking required in banks is not essential, but inaccuracies can be troublesome and costly.

The second stage and section comprises the vital part of planning. It is here that the effectiveness or indifference of results is ensured. And where the ability to scheme, think ahead and take all factors into account is so essential. It is a job mainly done on paper, juggling as it were with figures and charts. Sales budgets must be broken down into or integrated with long-term production plans, factory and departmental plans formulated, and weekly or daily or even hour-by-hour loads prepared. In small factories a few simple charts or schedules suffice, but in very large organizations a vast amount of detailed information, in the form of masses of figures, flows into the section, and must be rapidly and regularly collated and reissue for action. Extreme tidiness is essential, and if those concerned are not to be bogged down by a continuous stream of insistent inquiries demanding attention, much of the work must so be organized as to be dealt with in a routine manner by juniors.

The third stage consists of translating the plans into instructions and can be mainly of a clerical nature. In practice, however, it is at this stage that a certain amount of decentralization is advisable, and the hour-by-hour machine or operation loading and the actual issue of jobs to operators is done either in or adjacent to the Forman's office, or in a shop office. Progress work, that is, checking performance against plans and reporting results (with recommendations for corrective action and requests for urgent actions) to foremen or other supervisors, which is really an aspect of control, is frequently carried out from the same of and even by the same persons.

The complexity of an organization structure for production planning depends on the type of industry or manufacture rather than its scale. In mass-production and continuous-process manufacture, production planning consist of balancing the flow of materials (or components) from outside or component manufacturing departments, with consumption by the factory or assembly departments. Particularly is this so in the automobile or similar industries, where a good deal of preliminary work on materials in subcontracted, no large stocks of materials are kept (or could be for the immense consumption rate) and a small interruption to production affects a large part of the factory and is very expensive. In those factories engaged on batch production of partly standardized products there is the added complexity of setting-up (time and cost), varying batch sizes, and the synchronization of finishing dates for parts and sub assemblies when batches vary so much. It is predominantly a question of continual adjustment in order to maintain balanced loads on departments and to correct for unforeseen delays. When the product is designed to customers' requirements, the total process time is increased by the time required for design or preparation for each order, and consequently the period over which planning must extend is greater, making the problem more complex. Production planning is most complex when the product is mainly to customers' requirements, but is designed to incorporate many standard parts kept in stock. When the number of orders exceeds something like 50 per week, the amount of information to be handled becomes large and the department correspondingly so.

Planning Methods

The purpose of production order is to provide information about various operations involved in a production process. Once a production order is formulated, there arises the necessity to determine that when and where each operation is to be done. The reasons in that the operations described in a production order may be executed in several ways to get the final product and one may like to use a production strategy which makes most effective use of and machine and material in the system. The best strategy is planned through the methods of Routing and Scheduling. Thus scheduling and routing is the final stage in production planning and have the following objectives:

(i) to prescribe where and by whom each operation necessary to manufacture a product is to be executed. This is known as routing.

(ii) the establishment of times at which to begin and/or complete each even or operation. This is termed as scheduling.

Plant Layout

Layout problems are fundamental to every type of organization/enterprise and are experienced in all kinds of undertakings. Housewife must arrange her kitchen, retailer must arrange his counters and display the items in such a manner which facilitates movement and attract the attention of customers, office management positions the desks, tables and other equipment in such a way that it facilitates the flow of work. The manufacturing organizations must arrange their facilities, not only the department within the factory but also the plant, stores and services so as to achieve smooth flow of products.

The adequacy of layout affects the efficiency of subsequent operations. It is an important perquisite for efficient operations and also has a great deal in common with many of the problems.

The simplest of situations with comparatively fewer items to arrange have many alternatives available. Import the layout decisions were based merely on intuition, experience, judgment and some sort of improvisation but with increase in the complexities of organizations the layout problems are solved scientifically.

Once a decision about location of the plant has been taken, next important problem before the management is to plan suitable layout for the plant. Efficiency and performance of good machines and sturdy building depend to a great extent on the layout of a plant. Plat layout is the method of allocating machines and equipment, various production processes and other necessary services involved in transformation process of a product with the available space of the factory so as to perform various operations in the most efficient and convenient manner providing output of high quality and minimum cost.

In the words of James Lundy, "layout identically involves the location of space and the arrangement of equipment in such a manner that overall operating costs are minimized." Alternately, plant layout is an effort to arrange machines and equipment, and other services within a pre-designed building ensuring steady, smooth and economical flow of material.

Planning the layout of a plant is a continuous process as there are always chances of making improvements over the existing arrangement specially with shifts in the policies of management of techniques of production.

The disposition of the various parts of a plant along with all the equipment used is known as plant layout. It should be so designed that the plant functions most effectively.

Layout problems are common to all kinds of organization. A retailer must arrange his counter, display of items etc., office management must position desks, tables etc. in such a way that it facilitates the flow of work. A manufacturing organization must position its machinery and other equipment so as to achieve smooth flow of products through their factories.

A good layout results in comforts convenience, safety, efficiency, Compactness and profits. A poor layout results in congestion, waste, frustration and inefficiency.

Thus after plant location the proper design of plant layout is most significant for smooth functioning and success of the organization.

These three aspects of works planning and organization, viz., the production system, plant layout and factory building, are interrelated and go to decide the shape of things to come into existence. Correct layout has an important contribution towards efficient running of production affairs, because it increases the speed of in-process work, reduces the manufacturing time, lowers the cost of handling materials, and secures an integrated working of all sequential operations. Besides planning for storage of materials and finished products, service facilities like repairs, maintenance, power generation and others, different sectional offices for managerial, supervisory or inspection work, areas for canteens, crèches and parking as well as for future expansion of the plant. In addition, a number of mechanical aids are used for handling materials and finished products. For the operation of mechanical equipments like chutes, conveyor belts, elevators, high-lift fork trucks, crane trucks, overhead cranes, trolleys, etc., sufficient spaces must be provided for the operation of equipment in making the layout of a plant.

There are two distinct types of layout that are to be found in different systems of production. Group layout or process layout is adopted in job production as well as in batch production to some extent, while line layout or product layout is the rule in the case of mass production and process production.

Under group layout, machines or operators of alike. Type is grouped into a unit for discharging a particular operation in the production run. For examples, all lathe machines, drilling machines, grinding machines, or milling machines are grouped into so many different units or sections of the plant. Similarly, operators are classified into specialized units like molding, assembling, painting, etc., on the other hand, line layout is based on the sequence of operations required for manufacturing a particular product or part. Under the layout, manufacturing operations are analyzed and sequenced in such an order that work in-process moves in one direction with no backtracking or retracting of the path. In line layout, materials are worked out into finished products through a series of integrated operations that is arranged in a straight line fashion. Line layout is the only choice available to mass production and process-production.

There are several advantages of line layout, and it should be used in preference to group layout wherever practicable. Line layout eliminates cross-handling of materials, conserves floor space, assures steady flow of production, improves co-ordination between operations, economizes the use of materials, reduces the cost and time of manufacture, and increases the volume of production. However, line layout has two defects. The possible breakdown of machines in open operation may stop the working of the entire plant. Furthermore, line layout is of inflexible type and cannot be adjusted to the requirement of manufacturing other parts or products. On the contrary, group layout is effective in job production under which a variety of products is manufactured in small quantities at irregular intervals and through a varying sequence of operations by the use of the same machines. Group layout imparts flexibility to the use of machines, facilitates the work of supervision and inspection, and reduces servicing charges for repairs and maintenance. But the defect of group layout lies in poor co-ordination between operations excessive materials handling and backtracking of work in-process. It also damages the machines and equipments because of their frequent resetting and readjustments. Briefly, it makes for a higher cost of production.

Plant Layout Tools and Techniques

1. Process charts
   (i) Operation Process Charts
   (ii) Flow process Chart
2. Process Flow Diagrams
3. Machine data cards
4. Visualization of Layout
   (i) Two-dimensional plan or Templates
   (ii) Three-dimensional Plan or machine models

Plant Location

Introduction to Production

The performance of an enterprise is considerably affected by its location. The location of an industry is as important as the choice is for the location of a business or a shop in a city or locality. Unscientific and unplanned industrialization is harmful not only to the industrial unit but also to the social and economic structure of the country as a whole.

Nearly sixty years before, much importance was not given to the selection of appropriate location and the decisions in this regard were mainly governed by the individual preferences of the entrepreneurs and social customs. This resulted in failure of any organization which otherwise could have been successful. Government also with the objective of establishing socialistic pattern of society became instrument all in the selection of site for various industries in undeveloped areas by providing various investment benefits and other incentives. All this encouraged a large number of industrialists to follow a more scientific and logical approach towards the selection of site for establishing their industries.

The degree of significance for the selection of location for any enterprise mainly depends on its size and nature. Sometimes, the nature of the product itself suggest some suitable location. A small scale industry mainly selects the site where in accordance with its capacity the local market for the product is available. It can easily shift to other place when there is any change in the market. But for large scales industries requiring huge amount of investment there are many considerations other than the local demand in the selection of proper plant location. These plants cannot be easily shifted to other place and an error of judgment in the selection of site can be very expensive to the organization.

Production Methods

One activity of the administrative side of production is concerned with finding and stating the one best way to do all jobs. No longer is this left to the skilled and interested operator, proceeding by trial and error, successive operators making the same, or sometimes a different result. As more machines, tools and equipment, some of them highly specialized, have been designed and become available, and new materials and process materials and process developed, it has become increasingly a skilled technical job to keep abreast of developments and always to know the up-to-date or best way to do a job. It would be quite impossible today for the craftsman at the bench or machine to keep himself so informed and do a job of producing. Skilled men are still required, but increasingly today they become setters, minders, or maintenance men.

The old type of foreman is apt to think that the appointment of a production engineer, process engineer, or chemist, reduces his usefulness, his value to the Company, or his status. It does nothing of the kind, of course. It is true that, before the development of production engineering, and the use of chemists in the works as well as in the analytical laboratory, the Work Manger and his foreman supplied the production “know-how”, and decided how a job should be done. But it is now recognized that the training and supervising of person is a much more complex job than it once was, and to relive a foreman of a large amount of administrative work makes a higher general performance possible and his job more valuable, not less. It is essential to separate planning form doing, administration from execution.

When a new material is developed or a new product designed, the method of production is obviously either known or worked out. But form then onwards all is change. Better method of production are being discovered continually. Furthermore, in many factories, particularly those engaged in engineering, the detailed method of production for each part to be manufactured, the machines to be used and equipment required, is decided subsequent to design. The task of deciding the best method of production, of saying how a job shall be produced, and of finding new and better ways of doing so, should be the responsibility of a Method of Production Engineering Department. Similarly, in a company where the technical knowledge is supplied by chemists, production method would be the responsibility of the works laboratory.

In deciding the one best way of doing a job, the production engineer or chemist must have regard for the costs of production, and therefore for the time to do the job. He must have some say also in new tools or equipment required. These are the three divisions into which the activities of the production or methods engineer usually fall that is to say, work study or methods, work measurement or time study and tool design.

These three aspects all call for close collaboration with the designer and works departments. The design of jigs and tools might be thought to be a logical development of the Design or Drawing Office work and in some works it is done in the Drawing Office. But it cannot be effectively developed without detailed study of methods and work being done in the factory, and, as will be shown later, this study forms the basis of standards for time, and hence for payment by results, production planning and costs. This study work calls for a specialized technique and training quite different form Drawing Office work. The outlook required is different too. It is more successful in practice if it is recognized as a separate activity, and combined with the design of tools and equipment. To avoid it becoming too remote from or independent of the Drawing Office, Design Department, or Technical Department, new drawings, designs, or technical developments should always be referred to, and discussed with, the production engineers before final issue.

The development of production engineering as a special skill and the extensive use of specially designed tools and equipment have contributed largely to the very much greater output per man-hour. There is no doubt that it is through such development, adding horse-power to man-power, and taking out the manual efforts from jobs, that the way lies to reduce man-hour requirements.

Because production engineers tend to get machine or gadget minded, they are apt to forget or neglect the human factor. Machines cannot yet operate without human agency, and men should not be made into robots. The foremen may have something to say if the division of labor, for example, is carried too far, or if new methods are forced on them without consultant. Continued and close co-operation between the production engineers and works departments is absolutely essential.

The function of the production Engineering or Methods Department is to determine, in collaboration with the Design and Works Departments, the most effective, economical and suitable method of production, today down standards for material and time, and to design special tools and equipment required.

2.2 | Production Planning and Control

In any manufacturing enterprise production is the driving force to which most other functions react. This is particularly true with inventories; they exist because of the needs of production.

Objectives of Production Planning Control

The ultimate objective of production planning and control, like that of all other manufacturing controls, is to contribute to the profits of the enterprise. As with inventory management and control, this is accomplished by keeping the customers satisfied through the meeting of delivery schedules. Specific objectives of production planning and control are to establish routes and schedules for work that will ensure the optimum utilization of materials, workers, and machines and to provide the means for ensuring the operation of the plant in accordance with these plans.

2.3 | Production Planning and Control Functions

All of the four basic phases of control of manufacture are easily identified in production planning and control. The plan for the processing of materials through the plant is established by the functions of process planning, loading, and scheduling. The function of dispatching puts the plan into effect; that is, operations are started in accordance with the plant. Actual performance is then compared to the planned performance, and, when required, corrective action is taken. In some instances re-planning is necessary to ensure the effective utilization of the manufacturing facilities and personnel.

Process planning (Routing): The determination of where each operation on a component part, subassembly, or assembly is to be performed results in a route for the movement of a manufacturing lot through the factory. Prior determination of these routes is the job of the manufacturing engineering function.

Loading: Once the route has been established, the work required can be loaded against the selected machine or workstation. The total time required to perform the operation is computed by multiplying the unit operation times given on the standard process sheet by the number of parts to be processed. This total time is then added to the work already planned for the workstation. This is the function of loading, and it results in a tabulated list or chart showing the planned utilization of the machines or workstations in the plant.

Scheduling: Scheduling is the last of the planning functions. It determines when an operation is to be performed, or when work is to be completed; the difference lies in the detail of the scheduling procedure. In a centralized control situation - where all process planning, loading, and scheduling for the plant are done in a central office- the details of the schedule may specify the starting and finishing time for an operation. On the other hand, the central schedule may simply give a completion time for the work in a given department.

Combining Functions: While it is easy to define "where" as process planning, "how much work" as loading, and "when as scheduling, in actual operations these three functions are often combined and performed concurrently. How far in advance routes, loads, and schedules should be established always presents an interesting problem.

Obviously, it is desirable that a minimum of changes be made after schedules are established. This objective can be approached if the amount of work scheduled for the factory or department is equal to or slightly greater than the manufacturing cycle. For optimum control, it should never be less than the manufacturing cycle.

Dispatching: Authorizing the start of an operation on the shop floor is the function of dispatching. This function may be centralized or decentralized. Again using our machine-shop example, the departmental dispatcher would authorize the start of each of the three machine operations – three dispatch actions based on the foreman's routing and scheduling of the work through his department. This is decentralized dispatching.

Reporting or follow-up: The manufacturing activity of a plant is said to be "in control" when the actual performance is within the objectives of the planned performance. When jobs are started and completed on schedule, there should be very little, if any, concern about the meeting of commitments. Optimum operation of the plant, however, is attained only if the original plan has been carefully prepared to utilize the manufacturing facilities fully and effectively.

Corrective Action: This is the keystone of any production planning and control activity. A plant in which all manufacturing activity runs on schedule in all probability is not being scheduled to its optimum productive capacity. With an optimum schedule, manufacturing delays are the rule, not the exception.

Re-planning: Re-planning is not corrective action. Re-planning revise routes, loads, and schedules; a new plan is developed. In manufacturing this is often required. Changes in market conditions, manufacturing methods, or many other factors affecting the plant will often indicate that a new manufacturing plan is needed.

Factors Affecting Production Planning and Control

The factors that affect the application of production planning and control to manufacturing are the same as the factors we have already discussed that affect inventory management and control.

Type of product: Again, it is the complexity of the product that is important, not what the product is, except as this may in turn relate to the market being served. Production control procedures are much more complex and involve many more records in the manufacture of large steam turbine generator sets or locomotives to customer orders then in the production of large quantities of a standard product involving only a few component parts, such as electric blankets, steam irons, or similar small appliances.

Type of manufacturing: This is probably the most influential factor in the control situation. For a large continuous manufacturing plant producing a standard product, we have already indicated that the routing was included in the planning of the plant layout.

2.4 | Production Planning and Control Procedures

Planning and control practices will vary widely from plant to plant. Further the many ways in which of the functions might be carried out in practice. Though no production control function can be entirely eliminated, the least control that results in effective operation of the factory is the best control. It must be remembered that production planning and control systems should be tools of management. The objective is not an elaborate and detailed system of controls and records, but rather, the optimum operation of the plant for maximum profits.

Production planning and control systems: Because production planning and control places an emphasis on the control of work-in-process, the system will in effect tie together all previous records and forms developed in all planning for the manufacture of the product.

***Market forecast*:** Its value to production planning and control is that it will indicate future trends in demand for manufactured product. Work shift policies, plans for an increase or decrease in manufacturing activity, or possible plant expansions may often be based upon the market forecasts and in turn affect the planning of the production planning and control group.

***Sales order*:** This is the second of the five classes of orders. It is a rewrite of the customer' order specifying what has been purchased – product and quantity and authorizing shipment of the goods to the customer. Multiple copies are prepared and all interested functions are furnished a copy. Sales orders may be written by marketing, inventory control, or production control.

***Stock order*:** This third class of order is not always used. In the preceding paragraph we indicated how it may be used after sales order accumulate to an economical manufacturing lot. It is, of course, the principal order when manufacturing to stock. It will authorize production in anticipation of future sales.

***Shop order*:** This fourth class of order deals with the manufacture of component parts. Customer orders, sales orders, and stock orders are for the finished product. In the preceding chapters we discussed how, by product explosion, the requirements are established for component parts to build assembled products.

***Standard process sheet*:** This form is prepared by process engineering and it is the source of basic data as to the type of machine to be used, the time required for processing and the sequence of operations in the manufacture of the product. Routing and scheduling of shop orders, as well as loading of workstations in advance of scheduling, depend on up-to-date standard process sheets being available to the production planning and control group.

***Engineering specifications*:** Blueprints and bills of materials are used by production planning and control when they become a component part of the packaged instructions issued to the shop through the control office. One good planning procedure is to accumulate all necessary data for a shop order in a single package the standard process sheet, the blueprint, the bill of material (if an assembly operation is involved), the route sheet, and possibly the schedule for the production of the order.

***Route sheet*:** This is the form on which the route of a shop order is indicated. In practice, this form is generally combined with one of the other forms in the system. For example, the shop order, the standard process sheet, and the route sheet are often one piece of paper- usually called the shop order or the manufacturing order.

***Load charts*:** These charts are prepared to show the productive capacity that has been "sold" and at the same time the available productive capacity. These charts may be prepared for each workstation or machine in the plant, or they may be for groups of machines or departments.

***Job tickets*:** This is the fifth and last type of order in a manufacturing situation. Job tickets authorize the performance of individual operations in the manufacturing process.

***Project planning methods*:** The production planning and control methods discussed thus far in this chapter deal primarily with the production of consumer or industrial products which could be considered to fall within the area of "repetitive manufacturing". The products to be produced are often manufactured in quantities of more than one, and their total processing time can be measured in hours, or at most, days.

The best known methods that have been developed are CPM (for Critical Path Method) and PERT (for Program Evaluation and Review Technique). The original PERT technique is now considered, more accurately, PERT TIME, whereas a later development is known as PERT COST. From the optimistic, most likely, and pessimistic times, the expected elapsed time (t_e) can be obtained by statistical techniques.

System analysis: As with other manufacturing control systems and procedures, production planning, and control ends itself to modern mechanization techniques such as machine accounting and use of computers. Careful study of the control system through procedure analysis will indicate the savings that may be effected by the utilization of modern equipment. These savings may be in the clerical help required in the administration of the system or in the advantages of quick compilation of data, which in turn results in up-to-date control data.

Production Planning and Control Organization

It should be obvious that there is no single pattern for the organization of the production planning and control activity. In many small plants the routing, loading, and scheduling functions may well be included in the duties of the operating line; the shop manager, superintended, and foremen. But it is difficult to combine day-to-day work with adequate planning, and as a result it is often more feasible to break away the production planning and control functions and assign them to qualified specialists. These groups should be organized as staff sections normally reporting to the top manufacturing executive.

Centralized production planning and control: Centralization or decentralization of duties of the production control staff depends upon the design of the production planning and control system. In a completely centralized setup, determination of shipping promises; analysis of sales, stock, and shop orders; preparation of routes, load charts, and schedule charts; and dispatching of work to the shop complete with job tickets and all other necessary paper would be accomplished by a central production planning and control unit. In addition, as work is completed, a careful analysis of the actual performance would be made, and if corrective action were required, it would be initiated by this group.

Decentralized production planning and control: We have discussed at great length that no matter how general the planning may be in a central office, the plan must eventually be developed into a detailed plan on the shop floor. Some companies are now endeavoring to make each foreman a manager of his own departmental operation. In these cases the foreman is furnished with a complete staff for the production planning and control of the activities in the department.

Planning phase: We have already indicated in some details the duties involved in the production planning phase. Working from the basic data mentioned earlier, the personnel in this part of the activity routes and load and schedule charts.

Control phase: The completed job ticket, or its equivalent, is the key to this phase of the production planning and control system. It is the means of reporting back from the shop floor that indicates that a job is completed; or if daily job tickets are turned in, the daily progress of a job can be determined.

Relation to other functions: Good relationships with all the other functions in the enterprise are essential to effective production planning and control. Full cooperation with the marketing group is necessary, particularly in view of the importance of market conditions and the goodwill of customers. Both product engineering and process engineering must keep production planning and control informed as to their plans to avoid the manufacture of goods either to incorrect specifications or by an improper method.

Measurement of Effectiveness

In determining the effectiveness of a production planning and control system, there are quite a few problems. The key criterion might well be whether or not shipping promises are being kept the percentage of the order shipped on time. This, however, would not be a true criterion if excessive overtime of expediting costs were involved in getting any of these orders shipped. The cost of the control system in relation to the value of goods shipped is another possibility.

Again, however, this may not be sound: if markets slump, a bad ratio will develop. Many good production planning and control systems have been discontinued because of "high costs" under these conditions- and have never revived after business picket up.

In a study of benefits and costs of computerized production planning and control systems, Schroeder et al. list the following performance criteria by which production planning and control systems might be judged:

1. Inventory turnover
2. Delivery lead time

3. Percent of time meeting delivery promises
4. Percent of orders requiring "splits" because of unavailable material.
5. Number of expeditors
6. Average unit cost

New Product Development

In business and engineering, **new product development** (NPD) is the term used to describe the complete process of bringing a new product or service to market. There are two parallel paths involved in the NPD process: one involves the idea generation, *product design* and detail engineering; the other involves market research and *marketing analysis*. Companies typically see new product development as the first stage in generating and commercializing new products within the overall strategic process of *product life cycle management* used to maintain or grow their market share.

The Process

1. **Idea generation** is often called the "fuzzy front end" of the NPD process
   - Ideas for new products can be obtained from basic research using a SWOT analysis (Strengths, Weaknesses, Opportunities & Threats), Market and consumer trends, company's R&D department, competitors, focus groups, employees, salespeople, corporate spies, trade shows, or Ethnographic discovery methods (searching for user patterns and habits) may also be used to get an insight into new product lines or product features.
   - Idea Generation or Brainstorming of new product, service, or store concepts - idea generation techniques can begin when you have done your OPPORTUNITY ANALYSIS to support your ideas in the **Idea Screening Phase.**
2. **Idea Screening**
   - The object is to eliminate unsound concepts prior to devoting resources to them.
   - The screeners should ask several questions:
   - Will the customer in the target market benefit from the product?
   - What is the size and growth forecasts of the market segment/target market?
   - What is the current or expected competitive pressure for the product idea?
   - What are the industry sales and market trends the product idea is based on?
   - Is it technically feasible to manufacture the product?
   - Will the product be profitable when manufactured and delivered to the customer at the target price?
3. **Concept Development and Testing**
   - Develop the marketing and engineering details
   - Investigate *intellectual property* issues and search *patent* data bases

- Who is the target market and who is the decision maker in the purchasing process?
- What product features must the product incorporate?
- What benefits will the product provide?
- How will consumers react to the product?
- How will the product be produced most cost effectively?
- Prove feasibility through virtual computer aided rendering, and rapid prototyping
- What will it cost to produce it?
- *Testing the Concept* by asking a sample of prospective customers what they think of the idea. Usually via Choice Modelling.

4. **Business Analysis**
   - Estimate likely selling price based upon competition and customer feedback
   - Estimate sales volume based upon size of market and such tools as the *Fourt-Woodlock equation*
   - Estimate profitability and breakeven point
5. **Beta Testing and Market Testing**
   - Produce a physical prototype or mock-up
   - Test the product (and its packaging) in typical usage situations
   - Conduct focus group customer interviews or introduce at trade show
   - Make adjustments where necessary
   - Produce an initial run of the product and sell it in a test market area to determine customer acceptance
6. **Technical Implementation**
   - New program initiation
   - Finalize Quality management system
   - Resource estimation
   - Requirement publication
   - Publish technical communications such as *data sheets*
   - Engineering operations planning
   - Department scheduling
   - Supplier collaboration
   - Logistics plan
   - Resource plan publication
   - Program review and monitoring
   - Contingencies - what-if planning

7. **Commercialization** (often considered post-NPD)
   - Launch the product
   - Produce and place *advertisements* and other *promotions*
   - Fill the *distribution* pipeline with product
   - Critical path analysis is most useful at this stage
8. **New Product Pricing**
   - Impact of new product on the entire product portfolio
   - Value Analysis (internal and external)
   - Competition and alternative competitive technologies
   - Differing value segments (price, value, and need)
   - Product Costs (fixed and variable)
   - Forecast of unit volumes, revenue, and profit

These steps may be iterated as needed. Some steps may be eliminated. To reduce the time that the NPD process takes, many companies are completing several steps at the same time (referred to as **concurrent engineering** or **time to market**). Most industry leaders see new product development as a *proactive* process where resources are allocated to identify market changes and seize upon new product opportunities before they occur (in contrast to a *reactive strategy* in which nothing is done until problems occur or the competitor introduces an innovation). Many industry leaders see new product development as an ongoing process (referred to as *continuous development*) in which the entire organization is always looking for opportunities.

For the more innovative products indicated on the diagram above, great amounts of uncertainty and change may exist, which makes it difficult or impossible to plan the complete project before starting it. In this case, a more flexible approach may be advisable.

Because the NPD process typically requires both engineering and marketing expertise, cross-functional teams are a common way of organizing projects. The team is responsible for all aspects of the project, from initial idea generation to final commercialization, and they usually report to senior management (often to a vice president or Program Manager). In those industries where products are technically complex, development research is typically expensive, and product life cycles are relatively short, strategic alliances among several organizations helps to spread the costs, provide access to a wider skill set, and speeds the overall process.

Also, notice that because engineering and marketing expertise are usually both critical to the process, choosing an appropriate blend of the two is important. People respond to new products in different ways. The adoption of a new technology can be analyzed using a variety of diffusion theories such as the Diffusion of innovations theory.

A new product pricing process is important to reduce risk and increase confidence in the pricing and marketing decisions to be made. Bernstein and Macias describe an integrated process that breaks down the complex task of new product pricing into manageable elements

Fuzzy Front End

The Fuzzy Front End is the messy "getting started" period of new product development processes. It is in the front end where the organization formulates a concept of the product to be developed and decides whether or not to invest resources in the further development of an idea. It is the phase between first consideration of an opportunity and when it is judged ready to enter the structured development process It includes all activities from the search for new opportunities through the formation of a germ of an idea to the development of a precise concept. The Fuzzy Front End ends when an organization approves and begins formal development of the concept.

Although the Fuzzy Front End may not be an expensive part of product development, it can consume 50% of development time and it is where major commitments are typically made involving time, money, and the product's nature, thus setting the course for the entire project and final end product. Consequently, this phase should be considered as an essential part of development rather than something that happens "before development," and its cycle time should be included in the total development cycle time.

Koen et al.distinguish five different front-end elements (not necessarily in a particular order):

1. Opportunity Identification
2. Opportunity Analysis
3. Idea Genesis
4. Idea Selection
5. Concept and Technology Development

The first element is the opportunity identification. In this element, large or incremental business and technological chances are identified in a more or less structured way. Using the guidelines established here, resources will eventually be allocated to new projects. which then lead to a structured NPPD (New Product and Process Development) strategy. The second element is the opportunity analysis. It is done to translate the identified opportunities into implications for the business and technology specific context of the company. Here extensive efforts may be made to align ideas to target customer groups and do market studies and/or technical trials and research. The third element is the idea genesis, which is described as evolutionary and iterative process progressing from birth to maturation of the opportunity into a tangible idea. The process of the idea genesis can be made internally or come from outside inputs, e.g., a supplier offering a new material/technology, or from a customer with an unusual request. The fourth element is the idea selection. Its purpose is to choose whether to pursue an idea by analyzing its potential business value. The fifth element is the concept and technology development. During this part of the front-end, the business case is developed based on estimates of the total available market, customer needs, investment requirements, competition analysis and project uncertainty. Some organizations consider this to be the first stage of the NPPD process (i.e., Stage 0).

The Fuzzy Front End is also described in literature as "Front End of Innovation", "Phase 0", "Stage 0" or "Pre-Project-Activities".

A universally acceptable definition for Fuzzy Front End or a dominant framework has not been developed so far. In a glossary of PDMA, it is mentioned that the Fuzzy Front End generally consists of three tasks: strategic planning, concept generation, and, especially, pre-technical evaluation. These activities are often chaotic, unpredictible, and unstructured. In comparison, the subsequent new product development process is typically structured, predictable, and formal. The term *Fuzzy Front End* was first popularized by Smith and Reinertsen. R. G. Cooper describes the early stages of NPPD as a four step process in which ideas are generated (I), subjected to a preliminary technical and market assessment(II) and merged to coherent product concepts(III) which are finally judged for their fit with existing product strategies and portfolios (IV). In a more recent paper, Cooper and Edgett affirm that vital predevelopment activities include:

1. Preliminary market assessment.
2. Technical assessment.
3. Source-of-supply-assessment: suppliers and partners or alliances.
4. Market research: market size and segmentation analysis, VoC (voice of customer) research.
5. Product concept testing
6. Value-to-the customer assessment
7. Product definition
8. Business and financial analysis.

These activities yield vital information to make a Go/No-Go to Development decision.

In the in-depth study by Khurana and Rosen the front-end activities include:

- product strategy formulation and communication,
- opportunity identification and assessment,
- idea generation,
- product definition,
- project planning, and executive reviews.
- Economical analysis, benchmarking of competitive products, and modeling and prototyping are also important activities during the front-end activities.
- The outcomes of FFE are the

- mission statement
- customer needs
- details of the selected concept
- product definition and specifications
- economic analysis of the product
- development schedule
- project staffing and the budget, and
- a business plan aligned with corporate strategy.
- In a paper by Husig, Kohn and Huskela proposed a conceptual model of Front-End Process which includes early Phases of Innovation Process. This model is structured in three phases and three gates:
- ***Phase* 1:** Environmental screening or opportunity identification stage in which external changes will be analysed and translated into potential business opportunities.
- ***Phase* 2:** Preliminary definition of an idea or concept.
- ***Phase* 3:** Detailed product, project or concept definition, and Business planning.
- The gates are:
    - Opportunity screening;
    - Idea evaluation;
    - Go/No-Go for development.

The final gate leads to a dedicated new product development project. Many professionals and academics consider that the general features of Fuzzy Front End (fuzziness, ambiguity, and uncertainty) make difficult to see the FFE as a structured process, but rather as a set of interdependent activities. However, Husig et al. argue that front-end not need to be fuzzy, but can be handled in a structured manner. Peter Koen argue that in the FFE for incremental, platform and radical projects, three separate strategies and processes are typically involved. The traditional Stage Gate (TM) process was designed for incremental product development, namely for a single product. The FFE for developing a new platform must start out with a strategic vision of where the company wants to develop products and this will lead to a family of products. Projects for breakthrough products start out with a similar strategic vision, but are associated with technologies which require new discoveries. It is worth mentioning what are incremental, platform and breakthrough products. *Incremental products* are considered to be cost reductions, improvements to existing product lines, additions to existing platforms and repositioning of existing products introduced in markets. *Breakthrough products* are new to the company or new to the world and offer a 5-10 times or greater improvement in performance combined with a 30-50% or greater reduction in costs. *Platform products* establish a basic architecture for a next generation product or process and are substantially larger in scope and resources than incremental projects.

2.5 | Method Study and Work Statement

Work Study is the systematic examination of the methods of carrying out activities such as to improve the effective use of resources and to set up standards of performance for the activities carried out.

Work Study

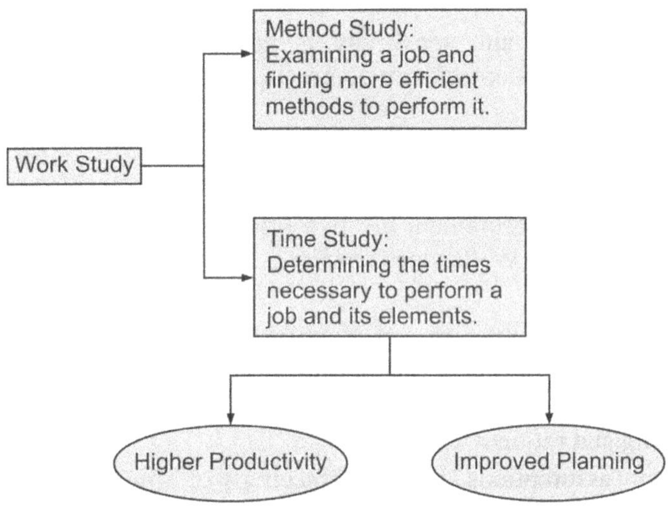

Figure 2.1 |

Components of Work Study

Another definition of Work Study could be: A generic term for those techniques, particularly method study and work measurement, which are used in the examination of human work in all its contexts, and which lead systematically to the investigation of all the factors which affect the efficiency and economy of the situation being reviewed, in order to effect improvement. This has to do with Productivity Improvement, but also improvement of Quality and Safety.

Managing people within operations involves actual design decisions about jobs, methods, relationships between jobs and machines and systems of control and communication. Work design involves complex "people" relationships between operative staff, supervisors and specialists e.g., engineering managers and staff who commission new machines and maintain them. Other specialists may co-ordinate health and safety systems or monitor performance and plan maintenance.

People are not mere extensions to machines or horsepower to be switched on and off. A worker's performance may be better than a machine's capability - yet a machine may outstrip the human being for many tasks.

People can be *hurt/injured physically by operating environments* or trapped socially and psychologically in them/by them. How operational systems are designed and the jobs and performance relationships within them are of great operational, economic and social importance. In this context then work study is

a collection of techniques used to examine work - what is done and how it is done - so that there is systematic analysis of all the elements, factors, resources and relationships affecting the efficiency and effectiveness of the work being studied.

Considerable diplomacy and sensitivity is needed by the industrial engineer or operation manager who becomes involved in work study (or business process improvement) investigations.

In the Path of F. W. Taylor

Method study and work measurement are two principal activities of work study which originated in the work of F. W. Taylor (*see Rose: 1978*). FW's "scientific management" imperatives are:

- investigate the work situation and identify weaknesses - where and why is poor performance happening? The "scientific" title for this approach to management means placing emphasis on
- data gathering and rational analysis
- certain narrow assumptions about the objectivity of efficiency criteria
- the existence of direct, deterministic relationships between worker performance and incentive payments and
- consideration of the worker to some extent as a machine. Thus we can evaluate and introduce improvements in operating methods. This includes type of equipment, its use, layout of operations, supply and use of materials, materials handling, work organization, effectiveness of planning procedures and so on.
- Productivity improvement is the aim.
- we can select staff with characteristics that fit the job, train and reward them using payment schemes the offer particular economic incentive by linking payment to measured performance.

Such propositions are commonly the stuff of managerial populists and "how-to" texts on human resource management.

Method Study

- It is an analysis of ways of doing work. The mnemonic SREDIM (a common-sense heuristic or general problem-solving strategy) represents the method study stages
    1. *select* the tasks to study
    2. *record* the facts about it

3. *examine*
4. *develop* a new method
5. *install/implement* it
6. *maintain* it

Work Measurement

- involves assessing the time a job should take to do. Similar steps are involved as to method study
  1. select the tasks
  2. record the facts
  3. analyze them
  4. calculate basic and standard times for the task
  5. *agree* the method and its related time

In the 1950's and 1960's the work study officer or O&M Person (organization and methods) gathered the data and gave advice. In the 1970's the titles evolved e.g. to that of management services officer. Work-study and methods study came within the scope of the industrial engineer. Today the techniques of method study are inclusive within the tool-kits and applications of the business systems analyst. The most modern application of some of the techniques of work study is the early 1990's managerial recipe; "*business process re-engineering*" i.e., re-designing business processes which have developed to the extent that they mismatch the needs of the situation today.

However having said this-the scope for work study definition and evaluation is useful for operations managers in a general sense. Such roles require data on operational capacities and effectiveness and the use of time and resources. Methods need regular re-evaluation. Some may have evolved and changed over time to become disjointed, patch works that no longer fully serve requirements. The case may need to be put for more staff or new methods and equipment. Such arguments call for data and measurement.

How many extra hours/people are needed? Why? What will the new method offer? Is it possible to change methods? What will be the costs/benefits?

Thus the techniques, assumptions and weaknesses of work study reflect important know-how for the operations manager generally - and not just those working in engineering or manufacturing environments. However the assumptions, difficulties and limitations of the claims must be understood.

Efficiency Indices

Using data on measured work, unmeasured work and idle time we can attempt to derive effectiveness indices. Constable and New exemplify efficiency and effectiveness indices

(a) ***Efficiency:*** While performing measured work (ratio of standard/measured hours of work produced and the actual time taken)

(b) ***Effectiveness*****:** Which includes accounting for work done for which no measured time exists. Such work is typically paid for by an agreed hourly/day rate i.e. there is no direct, measured relationship between pay and how much work is actually completed in that hour. Of course a supervisor may pass a judgment or state that the amount of work and its quality are inadequate. Recognition of possible idle time caused e.g. by management not allocating any work, supplier/materials delays, machine breakdowns etc.

Method Study

It is an analysis of ways of doing work. The mnemonic SREDIM (a common-sense heuristic or general problem-solving strategy) represents the method study stages

- select the tasks to study
- record the facts about it
- examine these
- develop a new method
- *install/implement* it
- *maintain* it

Method study is the process of subjecting work to systematic, critical scrutiny to make it more effective and/or more efficient.

It was originally designed for the analysis and improvement of repetitive manual work but it can be used for all types of activity at all levels of an organization.

The process is often seen as a linear, described by its main steps of:

- Select (the work to be studied);
- Record (all relevant information about that work);
- Examine (the recorded information);
- Develop (an improved way of doing things);
- Install (the new method as standard practice);
- Maintain (the new standard proactive).

Although this linear representation shows the underlying simplicity of method study, in practice the process is much more one of repeated passes through the sequence of steps with each dominating at a different stage of the investigation.

The cyclic process often starts with a quick, rough pass in which preliminary data are collected and examined before subsequent passes provide and handle more comprehensive and more detailed data to obtain and analyze a more complete picture.

Select

Work selected for method study may be an identified problem area or an identified opportunity. It may be identified through a systematic review of available data, normal monitoring or control processes, high levels of dissatisfaction and complaint or as part of a change in management policy, practice, technology or location, and usually because it meets certain conditions of urgency and/or priority.

Define

Before any method study investigation is begun, it is necessary to establish clear terms of reference which define the aims, scale, scope and constraints of the investigation. This should also include an identification of who "owns" the problem or situation and ways in which such ownership is shared. This may lead to a debate on the aims of the project, on reporting mechanisms and frequencies, and on the measures of success. This process is sometimes introduced as a separate and distinct phase of method study, as the "Define" stage. It leads to a plan for the investigation which identifies appropriate techniques, personnel, and timescale.

Record

The Record stage of method study involves gathering sufficient data (in terms of both quality and quantity) to act as the basis of evaluation and examination. A wide range of techniques are available for recording; the choice depends on the nature of the investigation; the work being studied; and on the level of detail required. Many of the techniques are simple charts and diagrams, but these may be supplemented by photographic and video recording, and by computer based techniques.

Especially with "hard" (clearly defined) problems, method study often involves the construction and analysis of models, from simple charts and diagrams used to record and represent the situation to full, computerized simulations. Manipulation of and experimentation on the models leads to ideas for development.

Examine

The recorded data are subjected to examination and analysis; formalized versions of this process are critical examination and systems analysis. The aim is to identify, often through a structured, questioning process, those points of the overall system of work that require improvements or offer opportunity for beneficial change.

Develop

The Examine stage merges into the Develop stage of the investigation as more thorough analysis leads automatically to identified areas of change. The aim here is to identify possible actions for improvement and to subject these to evaluation in order to develop a preferred solution.

Sometimes it is necessary to identify short-term and long-term solutions so that improvements can be made (relatively) immediately, while longer-term changes are implemented and come to fruition.

Install

The success of any method study project is realized when actual change is made 'on the ground' - change that meets the originally specified terms of reference for the project. Thus, the Install phase is very important. Making theoretical change is easy; making real change demands careful planning - and handling of the people involved in the situation under review. They may need reassuring, retraining and supporting through the acquisition of new skills. Install, in some cases, will require a parallel running of old and new systems, in others, it may need the build-up of buffer stocks, and other planning to manage the change. what matters is that the introduction of new working methods is successful. There is often only one chance to make change!

Maintain

Some time after the introduction of new working methods, it is necessary to check that the new method is working, that it is being properly followed, and that it has brought about the desired results. This is the Maintain phase. Method drift is common - when people either revert to old ways of work-in, or introduce new changes. Some of these may be helpful and should formally be incorporated; others may be inefficient or unsafe. A methods audit can be used to formally compare practice with the defined method and identify such irregularities.

Conclusion

In simple terms work study measures work and defines (some) performance standards. There are many uses for time estimates for tasks. Operations managers can guess or assume that a job is done in the correct time (whatever that is!) or they can be systematic and use time data gathered by a systematic technique which has reasonable accuracy. Whether or not the worker likes it - pushed hard in trying to complete a job with very tight measured work standards which don't anticipate the knotty problem encountered with a particular task - is another matter.

Work study/industrial engineers need time, data to plan and evaluate production/transformation processes. Rewards systems need such data for performance related bonuses. Cost calculations need to incorporate operative and machine job times Costing systems reference work study data. Work study data contributes to:

Improved methods to raise output, quality, reduce wastage, enhance reliability and ensure safety.

Standard time data contributes to capacity planning, scheduling, control of staff, asset utilization and quality improvement. Service and after-sales method improvements may be obtained as well as process improvement and better raw materials usage.

Implementation planning for product/service and process design requires a detailed understanding of methods and timings. In a distribution/transport system we can evaluate logistical efficiencies.

We need to remember always that performance inefficiency may arise from many reasons outside of worker control - a cumbersome planning system, a slow computer system with heavy overheads, lack of investment or uninformed, disorganized management. It is crass to assume that the problems will only be due to staff inefficiencies or inappropriate methods.

2.6 | Statistical Quality Control

Introduction

It has been the constant endeavor of Pharmacists to strive at higher and higher accuracy but absolute accuracy is unattainable. No two things can be made exactly alike. In Pharmaceutical production, no attempts are made to attain absolute perfection but to control the degree of variability of production so that the variation is within the prescribed statutory tolerance limits. There are two types of causes responsible for the variation of Pharmaceutical product manufactured.

(i) Inherent source of variation (Indeterminate or accidental variation)

(ii) Assignable causes of variation (determinate or constant variation)

Inherent Source of Variation

These variations or errors manifest themselves by the slight variations that occur in successive measurements by the same observer with the greatest care under as nearly identical conditions as possible. This natural variability can't be controlled and it occurs even under the best of methods and circumstances. These variations cannot be predicted and hence cannot be eliminated.

Assignable Causes of Variation

These are the variations which can be avoided or whose magnitude can be determined and hence can be checked and controlled. The assignable variations if present must be detected and corrected before defective results and products are produced. Some of the determinate errors are:

1. ***Operational and personal errors***: Mostly physical in nature. These errors are due to factors for which the individual is responsible and are not connected with the method or procedure. These errors may arise from the constitutional inability of an individual to make certain observations accurately. An example for this kind is some persons are unable to judge color changes sharply in visual titrations which may result in slight overlapping of the end point.

2. ***Instrumental and reagent errors*:** These variations arise due to defective instruments and improper chemicals.
3. ***Errors of method or variations due to the process*:** These arise from the incorrect sampling and from the incompleteness of the reaction.
4. ***Additive and proportional variations*:** The absolute value of an additive error is independent of the amount of the constituent present in the determination. Some examples of additive errors are loss in weight of a crucible in which a precipitate is ignited and errors in weights. The absolute value of a proportional error depends upon the amount of the constituents. An example of proportional error is impurity in a primary standard which leads to an incorrect value for the normality of a standard solution.

The science of quality control is largely statistical in nature. The statistical quality control technique is based on the theory of probability and sampling and is extensively used in Pharmaceutical industries and quality control labs. Quality control is a powerful productivity technique for effective diagnosis of lack of quality or conformity to settled standards in any of the materials, processes, machines or end products. Statistical quality control is a key factor in process validation and the manufacture of Pharmaceutical products. The technique attempts to locate the variability or error while the Pharmaceutical work is in process or progress.

In statistical quality control techniques, the actual physical measurements are first secured by inspection. Then the degree of variation among the measurements is analysed by statistical methods in terms of a standard value of variation among acceptable limits. By such comparisons, quality control is made to predict the significance of the variation analysed. This type of prediction can then be used to exert a positive influence over the control of product quality by studying the assignable causes. The quality control is thus directly associated with inspection and for statistical quality control, control charts are maintained. In order that things may be economical and quick, 100% inspection is not desirable. Rather 100% inspection leads to fatigue of human brain and faulty results are likely to be accepted. Control charts tell immediately whether the product is satisfactory or not.

The important objectives of statistical quality control in Pharmaceutical practice are as follows:

(i) Better quality level
(ii) Better uniformity of quality
(iii) Better utilization of raw materials
(iv) Most efficient utilization of equipments.
(v) Less scrap and rework
(vi) Better inspection
(vii) Improved producer consumer relations and
(viii) Better specifications

Attributes and Variables

Attributes

Those measurements in which a quality characteristic is present or absent or falls into a limited number of discrete categories are referred to as attribute measurements. Here the examination leads to the result being satisfactory or unsatisfactory. Measurements by attributes are generally less expensive but many more measurements have to be taken in such cases as there is no way of telling to what extent an item fails to meet the desired quality level when it is rejected on a attribute basis.

Variability

Two things are said to be alike when the differences among them are so small that we do not care about them. But generally two things are considered to be identical vary from each other when sufficiently precise measuring equipment or process is available. Measurement by variable involved the use of a scale which can be theoretically subdivided infinitely and the results of the quality can be expressed quantitatively i.e. in numbers. The measures of size, weight, surface etc. are the examples of measurement by variables.

Control Charts

The statistical quality control is mainly classified into Process Control & Product Control. The aim of process control is to maintain satisfactory quality level in production. The process control should ensure that the product confirms to specified quality standards. The process control is achieved through the technique of control charts. Controlling the quality of product by critical examination at strategic points is known as product control and is achieved through sampling inspection plans. Random samples of work in process are taken and inspected data collected are then presented graphically in chart form and chart method is an essential part of quality control systems.

A control chart is a statistical device principally used for the study and control of repetitive processes. It is a device to measure the extent of variation or defects in a process and to identify where there is an assignable cause for the variation. Dr. Walter A. Shewhart, its originator suggested that control chart may serve, first to define the goal or standard for the process that the management might strive to attain and secondly it may be used as an instrument to attain that goal and thirdly it may serve as a means of judging whether the goal is being achieved. The charts provide a very simple but powerful graphic method or finding whether a process is in statistical control or not. The control charts are simple to construct and easy to interpret and they tell the manager at a glance whether the process is in control or not. It is a graphic device for presenting data so as to directly reveal the frequency and extent of variations from established standards of goals.

The control charts help to easily identify the assignable causes of quality variation and these should be controlled or eliminated economically whenever detected. In gathering data for preparation of control chats the following points should be borne in mind:

1. We should be sure that we are measuring the thing we want to measure.
2. Measuring equipment and computing equipment should be operated properly.
3. The operator should be properly trained and instructed and free from bias.
4. Transcription errors should be avoided by adequate checking.
5. At least 40 to 100 observations should be taken.

It is necessary that the control chart limits be based on only the variability that is inherent in the process. If the standard deviation is computed on the basis of individual measurements, it will include the determination of all the assignable causes as well as chance causes of variation.

Important Points to be Observed in Drawing the Quality Control Chart

As the quality control charts form important documents and have to be examined by senior personnel, these should be drawn in convenient manner and the following points should be considered:

1. The size of the chart should be handy one.
2. The chart should be as neat as possible.
3. There should be provision for accommodating additional information on the charts in future.
4. The chart should be labeled properly and sufficiently.
5. When it becomes necessary to draw revised control chart limits on the basis of additional data, they should not be drawn over the original limits but after these.
6. Plotted point should be legible.
7. The average lines are drawn by solid and control limits by dotted lines.
8. There should be minimum number of background lines on the graph paper selected for drawing the control charts. Such charts are often plotted on rectangular cross section paper. Some times profile paper may also be used. The vertical scale is used for the statistical measures and the horizontal scale is used for subgroup numbers, dates, hours or lot numbers etc.

Objectives of Control Charts

1. To determine whether a process can meet the specifications or to collect further information for establishing or changing the specifications.
2. To get information for changing the production procedures.
3. To get information for changing the inspection techniques or acceptance procedures.

4. Determination as to when to find causes of variation and take action to correct them and when to leave the process alone.
5. To take decision on acceptance or rejection of manufactured or purchased products.

Types of Quality Control Charts

Broadly speaking, control charts can be divided under two heads:

(i) Control Charts for attributes
(ii) Control Charts for Variables

(i) ***Control charts for attributes:*** Control charts for attributes can be used for quality characteristics which can be observed only as attributes by classifying an item as defective or non defective, i.e. confirming to specifications or not. The following are the three main attribute charts:

1. p-chart or chart for fraction defectives
2. np-chart or chart for number of defectives
3. c-chart or chart for number of defects per unit

(ii) ***Control charts for variables:*** Control charts for variables are used for any quality characteristic that is measurable. Usually X and R charts used to control the mean (location) and standard deviation (dispersion) respectively of the quality characteristics.

Control charts for attributes

1. *The shewhart control chart for fraction defective*: This is also described as p-chart in technical language. In most of the routine inspection work (either 100% inspection or sampling inspection), the products are classified as either accepted or rejected. In such inspection it is a common practice to make a record of the number of items rejected. The ratio of the number of items rejected to the number of items rejected to the number of items inspected is the fraction of defective which is commonly expressed as a decimal fraction. The control limits of the chart which easily detect the presence of assignable and chance causes are set by simple statistical calculations. The p-chart is somewhat less sensitive than X and R charts and it does not have a great diagnostic value, but it serves to point out those situations needing diagnosis of trouble by the control chart for variables.

   Nevertheless, it is an extremely useful and to production supervision in giving information as to when and where to exert pressure for quality improvement. It results in the reduction of the average fraction defective and in the improvement of inspection practices by disclosing erratic fluctuations in the quality of inspection. The p-chart serves as a very good tool in dealing with outside vendors by pointing our whether the vendors differ in quality level or in the variability of quality level.

2. *The Shewart control chart for number of defectives*: This chart is also described as np-chart or the chart for the number of defectives in the sample. The control chart for this is drawn by taking *m* samples, each of size *n* are drawn at regular intervals of time from a production process and for each sample the number of defectives *d* is found out. *d* follows the binomial distribution with parameters *n* and *p*, where *n* is total the total number of items in the sample and *p* is the fraction defectives of the sample.

   The control limits for np-chart:

   CL = n p

   LCL = n p – 3 [n p (1 – p)] $^{1/2}$

   UCL = n p – 3 [n p (1 – p)] $^{1/2}$

3. *The Shewhart control chart for defects per unit*: In technical language of the subject, it is described as c-chart. This type of chart applies to a limited number of manufacturing situations involving quality, e.g., inspection of a fairly complex assembled unit in which there are a great many opportunities for occurrences of defects of various types, and the total number of defects or all types found by inspection are recorded for each unit.

   In c-chart also, the control limits are set in a way to detect the presence or absence of assignable causes of variations; thereby telling when to take action on the process and why.

(Control Charts for variables (X Chart and R Chart): These charts help in trouble shooting of the manufacturing process by providing information on three matters all of which need to be known as a basis for action.

(a) Basis variability of the quality characteristic.

(b) Consistency of Performance.

(c) Average level of the quality characteristic.

No production process can produce identical objects. Some variability is unavoidable which depends upon the various characteristics of the production process such as the machines, the materials, the operators. When both upper and lower values (e.g., dimensional tolerances) are specified and control chart shows that the process variability is great, then it is necessary to make change the process or to take the trouble of sorting good product from bad. Sometimes it may be observed that tolerances are tighter than necessary for the functioning of the product and they can be widened instead of choosing a very precise and costly process.

The control limits on the charts are so placed as to disclose the presence or absence of the assignable causes. The control charts tell when to leave process alone and when to take action to correct trouble. The elimination of assignable causes of erratic fluctuation is described as bringing a process under control and is responsible for many of the cost savings resulting from statistical quality control.

In some instances the process variability is such that the natural tolerance range is narrower than the specified tolerance range, still the products are unsatisfactory because the average level of the quality characteristic is too high or too low. This will also be disclosed by control charts and correction of the average level can be taken by changing machine setting or taking some suitable action.

Once the control chart shows that a process is brought under control at a satisfactory level and with satisfactory limits of variability, one may feel confident that the product meets specifications. This suggests the possibility of basing acceptance procedures on the control charts and thereby result in substantial savings in costs related to inspection.

$\overline{X}$ chart is used to show the quality averages of the samples drawn from a given process. Let X denote the quality characteristic of a manufactured product. *m* samples each of size *n* are drawn form the production process at regular intervals of time.

Let $\overline{X_i}$ be the mean and R_i be the range of the ith sample, $(I = 1, 2, \ldots, n)$.

Calculate $\overline{\overline{X}}$ and $\overline{R}$ using

$$\overline{\overline{X}} = \frac{\Sigma \overline{X}_i}{m} \text{ and } \overline{R} = \frac{\Sigma \overline{R}_i}{m}$$

The control limits of $\overline{X}$ chart are set at

Central line (CL) = $\overline{X}$

Lower control limit (LCL) = $\overline{\overline{X}} - A_2 \overline{R}$

Upper control limit (UCL) = $\overline{\overline{X}} - A_2 \overline{R}$

The values of the constant A_2 are computed and tabulated for different values of *n*.

The control limits for R – Chart are set at

Central line (CL) = $\overline{R}$

Lower control limit (LCL) = $D_3 \overline{R}$

Upper control limit (UCL) = $D_4 \overline{R}$

Here D_3 and D_4 are constants which depend on the sample size n.

For $\overline{X}$ chart the sample numbers are taken on the X – axis and the values of $\overline{X}$ are taken on the Y – axis. The central line and both the control limits are drawn parallel to the X – axis. The value of $\overline{X}$ for each sample is plotted on the graph paper. On joining these points in order, $\overline{X}$ chart is obtained.

For R – chart the sample numbers are taken on the X – axis and the values or R are taken on the Y – axis. The central line, LCL and UCL for R – chart are drawn parallel to the X – axis. The values of R obtained from each sample are plotted on the graph paper. On joining these points in order, R – chart is obtained.

Acceptance Sampling

Acceptance sampling is an important field of statistical quality control that was popularized by Dodge and Romig and originally applied by the U.S. military to the testing of bullets during World War II. If every bullet was tested in advance, no bullets would be left to ship. If, on the other hand, none were tested, malfunctions might occur in the field of battle, with potentially disastrous results.

Dodge reasoned that a sample should be picked at random from the lot, and on the basis of information that was yielded by the sample, a decision should be made regarding the disposition of the lot. In general, the decision is either to accept or reject the lot. This process is called *Lot Acceptance Sampling* or just *Acceptance Sampling*.

Acceptance sampling is "the middle of the road" approach between no inspection and 100% inspection. There are two major classifications of acceptance plans: by *attributes* ("go, no-go") and by *variables*. The attribute case is the most common for acceptance sampling, and will be assumed for the rest of this section.

A point to remember is that the main purpose of acceptance sampling is to decide whether or not the lot is likely to be acceptable, not to estimate the quality of the lot.

Acceptance sampling is employed when one or several of the following hold:

- Testing is destructive
- The cost of 100% inspection is very high
- 100% inspection takes too long

It was pointed out by Harold Dodge in 1969 that Acceptance Quality Control is not the same as Acceptance Sampling. The latter depends on specific sampling plans, which when implemented indicate the conditions for acceptance or rejection of the immediate lot that is being inspected. The former may be implemented in the form of an Acceptance Control Chart. The control limits for the Acceptance Control Chart are computed using the specification limits and the standard deviation of what is being monitored.

In 1942, Dodge Stated:

....basically the "acceptance quality control" system that was developed encompasses the concept of protecting the consumer from getting unacceptable defective product, and encouraging the producer in the use of process quality control by: varying the quantity and severity of acceptance inspections in direct relation to the importance of the characteristics inspected, and in the inverse relation to the goodness of the quality level as indication by those inspections."

To reiterate the difference in these two approaches: acceptance sampling plans are one-shot deals, which essentially test short-run effects. Quality control is of the long-run variety, and is part of a well-designed system for lot acceptance.

An individual sampling plan has much the effect of a lone sniper, while the sampling plan scheme can provide a fusillade in the battle for quality improvement

According to the ISO standard on acceptance control charts *(ISO 7966, 1993)*, an acceptance control chart combines consideration of control implications with elements of acceptance sampling. It is an appropriate tool for helping to make decisions with respect to process acceptance. The difference between acceptance sampling approaches and acceptance control charts is the emphasis on process acceptability rather than on product disposition decisions.

According to the ISO standard on acceptance control charts *(ISO 7966, 1993)*, an acceptance control chart combines consideration of control implications with elements of acceptance sampling. It is an appropriate tool for helping to make decisions with respect to process acceptance. The difference between acceptance sampling approaches and acceptance control charts is the emphasis on process acceptability rather than on product disposition decisions.

LASPs Fall into the Following Categories:

- ***Single sampling plans:*** One sample of items is selected at random from a lot and the disposition of the lot is determined from the resulting information. These plans are usually denoted as (n,c) plans for a sample size n, where the lot is rejected if there are more than c defectives. *These are the most common (and easiest) plans to use although not the most efficient in terms of average number of samples needed.*
- ***Double sampling plans:*** After the first sample is tested, there are three possibilities:
    1. Accept the lot
    2. Reject the lot
    3. No decision

If the outcome is (3), and a second sample is taken, the procedure is to combine the results of both samples and make a final decision based on that information.

- ***Multiple sampling plans:*** This is an extension of the double sampling plans where more than two samples are needed to reach a conclusion. The advantage of multiple sampling is smaller sample sizes.

- ***Sequential sampling plans:*** This is the ultimate extension of multiple sampling where items are selected from a lot one at a time and after inspection of each item a decision is made to accept or reject the lot or select another unit.
- ***Skip lot sampling plans:*** Skip lot sampling means that only a fraction of the submitted lots are inspected.

Deriving a plan, within one of the categories listed above, is discussed in the pages that follow. All derivations depend on the properties you want the plan to have. These are described using the following terms:

- ***Acceptable quality level (AQL)***: The AQL is a percent defective that is the base line requirement for the quality of the producer's product. The producer would like to design a sampling plan such that there is a *high probability of accepting* a lot that has a defect level less than or equal to the AQL.
- ***Lot tolerance percent defective (LTPD)***: The LTPD is a designated high defect level that would be unacceptable to the consumer. The consumer would like the sampling plan to have a *low probability of accepting* a lot with a defect level as high as the LTPD.
- ***Type I error (Producer's risk)***: This is the probability, for a given (n,c) sampling plan, of rejecting a lot that has a defect level equal to the AQL. The producer suffers when this occurs, because a lot with acceptable quality was rejected. The symbol α is commonly used for the Type I error and typical values for α range from 0.2 to 0.01.
- ***Type II error (Consumer's risk):*** This is the probability, for a given (n,c) sampling plan, of accepting a lot with a defect level equal to the LTPD. The consumer suffers when this occurs, because a lot with unacceptable quality was accepted. The symbol β is commonly used for the Type II error and typical values range from 0.2 to 0.01.
- ***Operating characteristic (OC) Curve:*** This curve plots the probability of accepting the lot (Y-axis) versus the lot fraction or percent defectives (X-axis). *The OC curve is the primary tool for displaying and investigating the properties of a LASP.*
- ***Average outgoing quality (AOQ):*** A common procedure, when sampling and testing is non-destructive, is to 100% inspect rejected lots and replace all defectives with good units. In this case, all rejected lots are made perfect and the only defects left are those in lots that were accepted. *AOQ*'s refer to the long term defect level for this combined LASP and 100% inspection of rejected lots process. If all lots come in with a defect level of exactly p, and the OC curve for the chosen (n,c) LASP indicates a probability p_a of accepting such a lot, over the long run the *AOQ* can easily be shown to be:

$$AOQ = \frac{p_a p(N-n)}{N}$$

where N is the lot size.

- ***Average outgoing quality level (AOQL):*** A plot of the *AOQ* (Y-axis) versus the incoming lot p (X-axis) will start at 0 for $p = 0$, and return to 0 for $p = 1$ (where every lot is 100% inspected and rectified). In between, it will rise to a maximum. This maximum, which is the worst possible long term *AOQ*, is called the *AOQL*.
- ***Average total inspection (ATI):*** When rejected lots are 100% inspected, it is easy to calculate the *ATI* if lots come consistently with a defect level of p. For a LASP (n,c) with a probability p_a of accepting a lot with defect level p, we have

  $$ATI = n + (1 - p_a)\ (N - n)$$

  where N is the lot size.
- ***Average sample number (ASN):*** For a single sampling LASP (n,c) we know each and every lot has a sample of size n taken and inspected or tested. For double, multiple and sequential LASP's, the amount of sampling varies depending on the number of defects observed. For any given double, multiple or sequential plan, a long term *ASN* can be calculated assuming all lots come in with a defect level of p. A plot of the *ASN*, versus the incoming defect level p, describes the sampling efficiency of a given LASP scheme.

Making a final choice between single or multiple sampling plans that have acceptable properties is a matter of deciding whether the average sampling savings gained by the various multiple sampling plans justifies the additional complexity of these plans and the uncertainty of not knowing how much sampling and inspection will be done on a day-by-day basis.

A single sampling plan, as *previously defined*, is specified by the pair of numbers (n,c). The sample size is n, and the lot is rejected if there are more than c defectives in the sample; otherwise the lot is accepted.

There are two widely used ways of picking (n,c):

1. Use tables (such as *MIL STD 105D*) that focus on either the AQL or the LTPD desired.
2. *Specify 2 desired points* on the *OC curve* and solve for the (n,c) that uniquely determines an OC curve going through these points.

The next two pages describe these methods in detail

Sampling plans are typically set up with reference to an acceptable quality level, or AQL. The *AQL* is the base line requirement for the quality of the producer's product. The producer would like to design a sampling plan such that the *OC curve* yields a high probability of acceptance at the *AQL*. On the other side of the OC curve, the consumer wishes to be protected from accepting poor quality from the producer. So the consumer establishes a criterion, the *lot tolerance percent defective* or LTPD. Here the idea is to only accept poor quality product with a very low probability. Mil. Std. plans have been used for over 50 years to achieve these goals.

Standard military sampling procedures for inspection by attributes were developed during World War II. Army Ordnance tables and procedures were generated in the early 1940's and these grew into the Army Service Forces tables. At the end of the war, the Navy also worked on a set of tables. In the meanwhile, the Statistical Research Group at Columbia University performed research and outputted many outstanding results on attribute sampling plans.

These three streams combined in 1950 into a standard called Mil. Std. 105A. It has since been modified from time to time and issued as 105B, 195C and 105D. Mil. Std. 105D was issued by the U.S. government in 1963. It was adopted in 1971 by the American National Standards Institute as ANSI Standard Z1.4 and in 1974 it was adopted (with minor changes) by the International Organization for Standardization as ISO Std. 2859. The latest revision is Mil. Std 105E and was issued in 1989.

These three similar standards are continuously being updated and revised, but the basic tables remain the same. Thus the discussion that follows of the germane aspects of Mil. Std. 105E also applies to the other two standards.

This document is essentially a set of individual plans, organized in a system of sampling schemes. A sampling scheme consists of a combination of a normal sampling plan, a tightened sampling plan, and a reduced sampling plan plus rules for switching from one to the other.

The foundation of the Standard is the acceptable quality level or *AQL*. In the following scenario, a certain military agency, called the Consumer from here on, wants to purchase a particular product from a supplier, called the Producer from here on.

In applying the Mil. Std. 105D it is expected that there is perfect agreement between Producer and Consumer regarding what the *AQL* is for a given product characteristic. It is understood by both parties that the Producer will be submitting for inspection a number of lots whose quality level is typically as good as specified by the Consumer. Continued quality is assured by the acceptance or rejection of lots following a particular sampling plan and also by providing for a shift to another, tighter sampling plan, when there is evidence that the Producer's product does not meet the agreed-upon *AQL*.

Mil. Std. 105E offers three types of sampling plans: single, double and multiple plans. The choice is, in general, up to the inspectors.

Because of the three possible selections, the standard does not give a sample size, but rather a sample code letter. This, together with the decision of the type of plan yields the specific sampling plan to be used.

In addition to an initial decision on an *AQL* it is also necessary to decide on an "inspection level". This determines the relationship between the lot size and the sample size. The standard offers three general and four special levels.

The steps in the use of the standard can be summarized as follows:

1. Decide on the *AQL*.
2. Decide on the inspection level.
3. Determine the lot size.
4. Enter the table to find sample size code letter.
5. Decide on type of sampling to be used.
6. Enter proper table to find the plan to be used.
7. Begin with normal inspection, follow the switching rules and the rule for stopping the inspection (if needed).

We start by looking at a typical *OC curve.* The OC curve for a (52, 3) sampling plan is shown below.

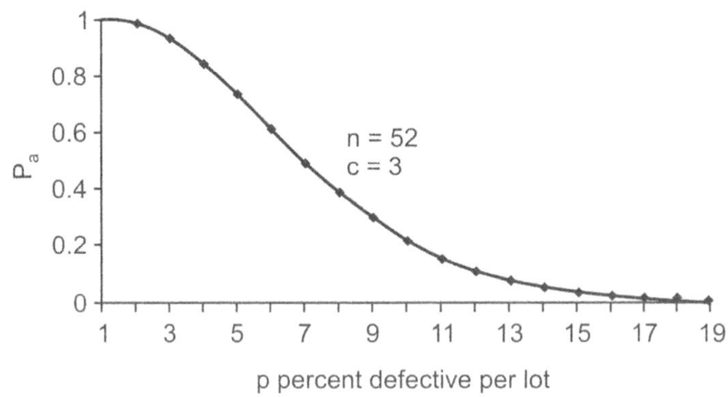

Figure 2.2|

It is instructive to show how the points on this curve are obtained, once we have a sampling plan (n,c) - later we will demonstrate how a sampling plan (n,c) is obtained.

We assume that the lot size N is very large, as compared to the sample size n, so that removing the sample doesn't significantly change the remainder of the lot, no matter how many defects are in the sample. Then the distribution of the number of defectives, d, in a random sample of n items is approximately binomial with parameters n and p, where p is the fraction of defectives per lot.

The probability of observing exactly *d* defectives is given by

$$P(d) = f(d) = \frac{n!}{d!(n-d)!} p^d (1-p)^{n-d}$$

The probability of acceptance is the probability that *d*, the number of defectives, is less than or equal to *c*, the accept number. This means that

$$P_a = P\{d \le c\} = \sum_{d-0}^{c} \frac{n!}{d!(n-d)!} p^d (1-p)^{n-d}$$

Using this formula with $n = 52$ and $c = 3$ and $p = .01, .02, ...,.12$ we find

P_a	P_d
.998	.01
.980	.02
.930	.03
.845	.04
.739	.05
.620	.06
.502	.07
.394	.08
.300	.09
.223	.10
.162	.11
.115	.12

Solving for (*n*, *c*)

In order to design a sampling plan with a specified OC curve one needs two designated points. Let us design a sampling plan such that the probability of acceptance is 1-α for lots with fraction defective p_1 and the probability of acceptance is β for lots with fraction defective p_2. Typical choices for these points are: p_1 is the AQL, p_2 is the LTPD and α, β are the *Producer's Risk (Type I error)* and *Consumer's Risk (Type II error)*, respectively.

If we are willing to assume that binomial sampling is valid, then the sample size *n*, and the acceptance number *c* are the solution to

$$1 - \alpha = \sum_{d-0}^{c} \frac{n!}{d!(n-d)!} p_1^d (1-p_1)^{n-d}$$

$$\beta = \sum_{d-0}^{c} \frac{n!}{d!(n-d)!} p_2^d (1-p_2)^{n-d}$$

These two simultaneous equations are nonlinear so there is no simple, direct solution. There are however a number of iterative techniques available that give approximate solutions so that composition of a computer program poses few problems.

Average Outgoing Quality (AOQ)

We can also calculate the AOQ for a (n,c) sampling plan, provided rejected lots are 100% inspected and defectives are replaced with good parts.

Assume all lots come in with exactly a p_0 proportion of defectives. After screening a rejected lot, the final fraction defectives will be zero for that lot. However, accepted lots have fraction defective p_0. Therefore, the outgoing lots from the inspection stations are a mixture of lots with fractions defective p_0 and 0. Assuming the lot size is N, we have.

$$AOQ = \frac{p_a p(N-n)}{N}$$

For example, let $N = 10000$, $n = 52$, $c = 3$, and p, the quality of incoming lots, = 0.03. Now at $p = 0.03$, we glean from the OC curve table that $p_a = 0.930$ and

$AOQ = (.930)(.03)(10000 - 52) / 10000 = 0.02775$

Setting $p = .01, .02, ..., .12$, we can generate the following Table

AOQ	p
.0010	.01
.0196	.02
.0278	.03
.0338	.04
.0369	.05
.0372	.06
.0351	.07
.0315	.08
.0270	.09
.0223	.10
.0178	.11
.0138	.12

A plot of the AOQ versus p is given below.

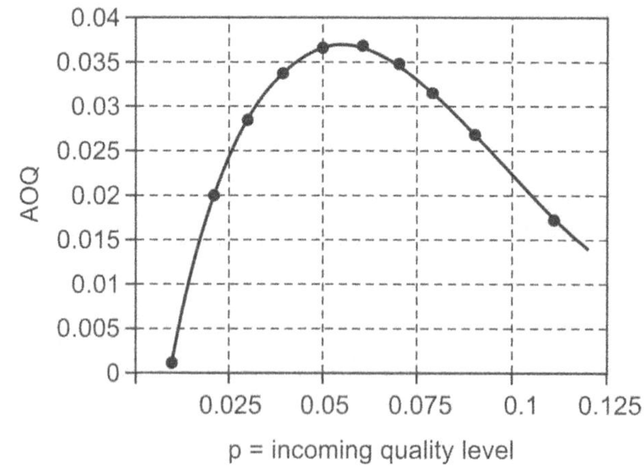

Figure 2.3|

From examining this curve we observe that when the incoming quality is very good (very small fraction of defectives coming in), then the outgoing quality is also very good (very small fraction of defectives going out). When the incoming lot quality is very bad, most of the lots are rejected and then inspected. The "duds" are eliminated or replaced by good ones, so that the quality of the outgoing lots, the AOQ, becomes very good. In between these extremes, the AOQ rises, reaches a maximum, and then drops.

The maximum ordinate on the AOQ curve represents the worst possible quality that results from the rectifying inspection program. It is called the **average outgoing quality limit, (AOQL).**

From the table we see that the $AOQL = 0.0372$ at $p = .06$ for the above example.

One final remark: if $N >> n$, then the $AOQ \sim p_a p$.

What is the total amount of inspection when rejected lots are screened?

If all lots contain zero defectives, no lot will be rejected.

If all items are defective, all lots will be inspected, and the amount to be inspected is N.

Finally, if the lot quality is $0 < p < 1$, the average amount of inspection per lot will vary between the sample size n, and the lot size N.

Let the quality of the lot be p and the probability of lot acceptance be p_a, then the ATI per lot is

$$ATI = n + (1 - p_a)\,(N - n)$$

For example, let $N = 10000$, $n = 52$, $c = 3$, and $p = .03$. We know from the OC table that $p_a = 0.930$. Then $ATI = 52 + (1 - .930)\,(10000 - 52) = 753$. (Note that while 0.930 was rounded to three decimal places, 753 was obtained using more decimal places.)

Setting *p*= .01, .02, ... .14 generates the following table

ATI	P
70	.01
253	.02
753	.03
1584	.04
2655	.05
3836	.06
5007	.07
6083	.08
7012	.09
7779	.10
8388	.11
8854	.12
9201	.13
9453	.14

A plot of *ATI* versus *p,* the Incoming Lot Quality (*ILQ*) is given below.

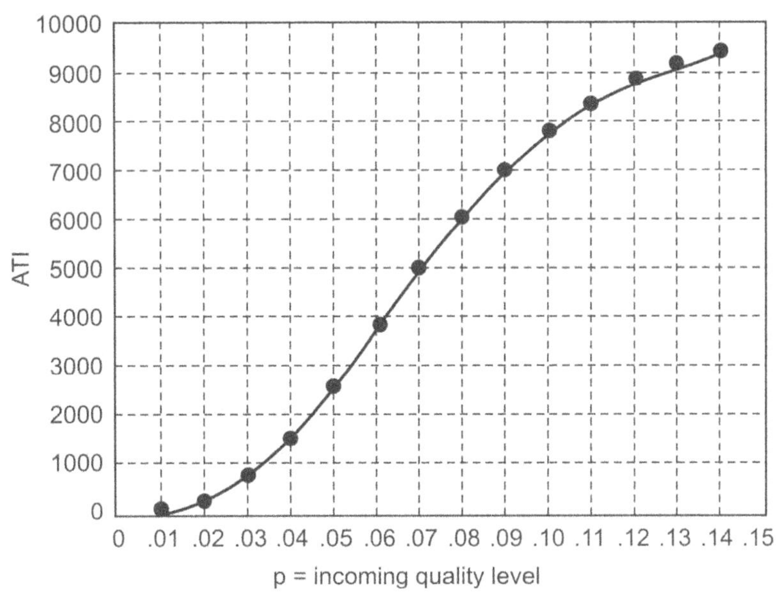

Figure 2.4|

Double and multiple sampling plans were invented to give a questionable lot another chance. For example, if in double sampling the results of the first sample are not conclusive with regard to accepting or rejecting, a second sample is taken. Application of double sampling requires that a first sample of size n_1 is taken at random from the (large) lot. The number of defectives is then counted and compared to the first sample's acceptance number a_1 and rejection number r_1. Denote the number of defectives in sample 1 by d_1 and in sample 2 by d_2, then:

If $d_1 \leq a_1$, the lot is accepted.

If $d_1 \geq r_1$, the lot is rejected.

If $a_1 < d_1 < r_1$, a second sample is taken.

If a second sample of size n_2 is taken, the number of defectives, d_2, is counted. The total number of defectives is $D_2 = d_1 + d_2$. Now this is compared to the acceptance number a_2 and the rejection number r_2 of sample 2. In double sampling, $r_2 = a_2 + 1$ to ensure a decision on the sample.

If $D_2 \leq a_2$, the lot is accepted.

If $D_2 \geq r_2$, the lot is rejected.

The parameters required to construct the OC curve are similar to the single sample case. The two points of interest are (p_1, $1 - \alpha$) and (p_2, β, where p_1 is the lot fraction defective for plan 1 and p_2 is the lot fraction defective for plan 2. As far as the respective sample sizes are concerned, the second sample size must be equal to, or an even multiple of, the first sample size.

There exist a variety of tables that assist the user in constructing double and multiple sampling plans. The index to these tables is the p_2/p_1 ratio, where $p_2 > p_1$. One set of tables, taken from the *Army Chemical Corps* Engineering Agency for $\alpha = .05$ and $\beta = .10$, is given below:

Tables for $n_1 = n_2$				
	Accept		**Approximation values**	
***R* =**	**numbers**		**of pn_1**	**for**
p_2/p_1	**c_1**	**c_2**	**P = .95**	**P = .10**
11.90	0	1	0.21	2.50
7.54	1	2	0.52	3.92
6.79	0	2	0.43	2.96
5.39	1	3	0.76	4.11
4.65	2	4	1.16	5.39
4.25	1	4	1.04	4.42
3.88	2	5	1.43	5.55

Contd...

Tables for $n_1 = n_2$				
	Accept		**Approximation values**	
R **=**	**numbers**		**of** pn_1	**for**
p_2/p_1	c_1	c_2	**P = .95**	**P = .10**
3.63	3	6	1.87	6.78
3.38	2	6	1.72	5.82
3.21	3	7	2.15	6.91
3.09	4	8	2.62	8.10
2.85	4	9	2.90	8.26
2.60	5	11	3.68	9.56
2.44	5	12	4.00	9.77
2.32	5	13	4.35	10.08
2.22	5	14	4.70	10.45
2.12	5	16	5.39	11.41

Tables for $n_2 = 2n_1$				
	accept		**approximation**	**values**
R =	**numbers**		**of** pn_1	**for**
p_2/p_1	c_1	c_2	**P = .95**	**P = .10**
14.50	0	1	0.16	2.32
8.07	0	2	0.30	2.42
6.48	1	3	0.60	3.89
5.39	0	3	0.49	2.64
5.09	0	4	0.77	3.92
4.31	1	4	0.68	2.93
4.19	0	5	0.96	4.02
3.60	1	6	1.16	4.17
3.26	1	8	1.68	5.47
2.96	2	10	2.27	6.72
2.77	3	11	2.46	6.82
2.62	4	13	3.07	8.05
2.46	4	14	3.29	8.11
2.21	3	15	3.41	7.55
1.97	4	20	4.75	9.35
1.74	6	30	7.45	12.96

We wish to construct a double sampling plan according to

$$p_1 = 0.01 \quad \alpha = 0.05 \quad p_2 = 0.05 \quad \beta = 0.10 \quad \text{and} \quad n_1 = n_2$$

The plans in the corresponding table are indexed on the ratio

$$R = p_2/p_1 = 5$$

We find the row whose R is closet to 5. This is the 5th row (R = 4.65). This gives $c_1 = 2$ and $c_2 = 4$. The value of n_1 is determined from either of the two columns labeled pn_1.

The left holds α constant at 0.05 ($P = 0.95 = 1 - \alpha$) and the right holds β constant at 0.10. ($P = 0.10$). Then holding α constant we find $pn_1 = 1.16$ so $n_1 = 1.16/p_1 = 116$. And, holding β constant we find $pn_1 = 5.39$, so $n_1 = 5.39/p_2 = 108$. Thus the desired sampling plan is

$$n_1 = 108 \quad c_1 = 2 \quad n_2 = 108 \quad c_2 = 4$$

If we opt for $n_2 = 2n_1$, and follow the same procedure using the appropriate table, the plan is:

$$n_1 = 77 \quad c_1 = 1 \quad n_2 = 154 \quad c_2 = 4$$

The first plan needs less samples if the number of defectives in sample 1 is greater than 2, while the second plan needs less samples if the number of defectives in sample 1 is less than 2.

ASN Curve for a Double Sampling Plan

Since when using a double sampling plan the sample size depends on whether or not a second sample is required, an important consideration for this kind of sampling is the Average Sample Number (*ASN*) curve. This curve plots the ASN versus p', the true fraction defective in an incoming lot.

We will illustrate how to calculate the ASN curve with an example. Consider a double-sampling plan $n_1 = 50$, $c_1 = 2$, $n_2 = 100$, $c_2 = 6$, where n_1 is the sample size for plan 1, with accept number c_1, and n_2, c_2, are the sample size and accept number, respectively, for plan 2.

Let p' = .06. Then the probability of acceptance on the first sample, which is the chance of getting two or less defectives, is .416 (using binomial tables). The probability of rejection on the second sample, which is the chance of getting more than six defectives, is (1–.971) = .029. The probability of making a decision on the first sample is .445, equal to the sum of .416 and .029. With complete inspection of the second sample, the average size sample is equal to the size of the first sample times the probability that there will be only one sample plus the size of the combined samples times the probability that a second sample will be necessary. For the sampling plan under consideration, the ASN with complete inspection of the second sample for a p' of .06 is

$$50(.445) + 150(.555) = 106$$

The general formula for an average sample number curve of a double-sampling plan with complete inspection of the second sample is

$$ASN = n_1P_1 + (n_1 + n_2)(1 - P_1) = n_1 + n_2(1 - P_1)$$

where P_1 is the probability of a decision on the first sample. The graph below shows a plot of the ASN versus

P_1 is the probability of a decision on the first sample. The graph below shows a plot of the ASN versus p'.

The ASN curve for a double sampling plan

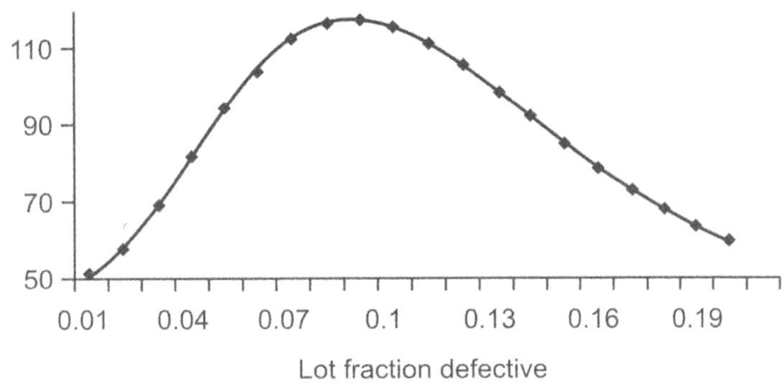

Figure 2.5|

Multiple sampling is an extension of double sampling. It involves inspection of 1 to *k* successive samples as required to reach an ultimate decision.

Mil-Std 105D suggests $k = 7$ is a good number. Multiple sampling plans are usually presented in tabular form

The procedure commences with taking a random sample of size $n_1$from a large lot of size *N* and counting the number of defectives, d_1.

if $d_1 \leq a_1$ the lot is accepted.

if $d_1 \geq r_1$ the lot is rejected.

if $a_1 < d_1 < r_1$, another sample is taken.

If subsequent samples are required, the first sample procedure is repeated sample by sample. For each sample, the total number of defectives found at any stage, say stage *i*, is

$$D_i - \sum_{j=1}^{i} d_j$$

This is compared with the acceptance number a_i and the rejection number r_i for that stage until a decision is made. Sometimes acceptance is not allowed at the early stages of multiple sampling; however, rejection can occur at any stage.

Efficiency for a multiple sampling scheme is measured by the *average sample number (*ASN*)* required for a given *Type I* and *Type II* set of errors. The number of samples needed when following a multiple sampling scheme may vary from trial to trial, and the *ASN* represents the average of what might happen over many trials with a fixed incoming defect level.

Sequential sampling is different from single, double or multiple sampling. Here one takes a sequence of samples from a lot. How many total samples looked at is a function of the results of the sampling process.

The sequence can be one sample at a time, and then the sampling process is usually called *item-by-item* sequential sampling. One can also select sample sizes greater than one, in which case the process is referred to as *group* sequential sampling. Item-by-item is more popular so we concentrate on it. The operation of such a plan is illustrated below:

Sampling. Item-by-item is more popular so we concentrate on it. The operation of such a plan is illustrated below:

Diagram of Item-by-Item Sampling

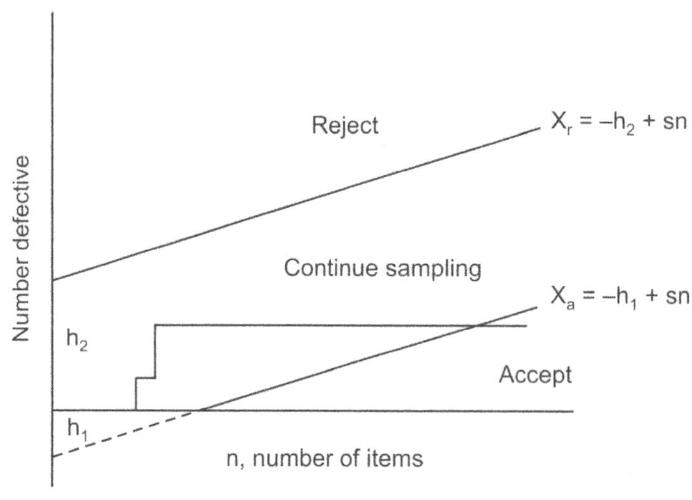

Figure 2.6 |

The cumulative observed number of defectives is plotted on the graph. For each point, the x-axis is the total number of items thus far selected, and the y-axis is the total number of observed defectives. If the plotted point falls within the parallel lines the process continues by drawing another sample. As soon as a point falls on or above the upper line, the lot is rejected. And when a point falls on or below the lower line, the lot is accepted. The process can theoretically last until the lot is 100% inspected. However, as a rule of thumb, sequential-sampling plans are truncated after the number inspected reaches three times the number that would have been inspected using a corresponding single sampling plan.

The equations for the two limit lines are functions of the parameters p_1, α, p_2, and β.

$$x_a = -h_1 + sn \text{ (acceptance line)}$$

$$x_r = h_2 + sn \text{ (rejection line)}$$

where

$$h_1 = \left(\log\frac{1-\alpha}{\beta}\right)\Big/k_i$$

$$h_2 = \left(\log\frac{1-\beta}{\alpha}\right)\Big/k_i$$

$$k_i = \log\frac{p_2(1-p_1)}{p_1(1-p_2)}$$

$$s = \left(\log\left[\frac{1-p_1}{1-p_2}\right]\right)\Big/k$$

Instead of using the graph to determine the fate of the lot, one can resort to generating tables (with the help of a computer program

As an example, let $p_1 = .01$, $p_2 = .10$, $\alpha = .05$, $\beta = .10$. The resulting equations are

$$x_a = -0.939 + 0.04n$$

$$x_r = 1.205 + 0.04n$$

Both acceptance numbers and rejection numbers must be integers. The acceptance number is the next integer less than or equal to x_a and the rejection number is the next integer greater than or equal to x_r. Thus for $n = 1$, the acceptance number = –1, which is impossible, and the rejection number = 2, which is also impossible. For $n = 24$, the acceptance number is 0 and the rejection number = 3.

The results for n =1, 2, 3... 26 are tabulated below.

n inspect	*n* accept	*n* reject	*n* inspect	*n* accept	*n* reject
1	x	x	14	x	2
2	x	2	15	x	2
3	x	2	16	x	3
4	x	2	17	x	3
5	x	2	18	x	3
6	x	2	19	x	3
7	x	2	20	x	3
8	x	2	21	x	3
9	x	2	22	x	3
10	x	2	23	x	3
11	x	2	24	0	3
12	x	2	25	0	3
13	x	2	26	0	3

So, for $n = 24$ the acceptance number is 0 and the rejection number is 3. The "x" means that acceptance or rejection is not possible.

Other sequential plans are given below.

n inspect	*n* accept	*n* reject
49	1	3
58	1	4
74	2	4
83	2	5
100	3	5
109	3	6

The corresponding single sampling plan is (52,2) and double sampling plan is (21,0), (21,1). For a sequential sampling scheme is measured by the *average sample number* (ASN) required for a given *Type I* and *Type II* set of errors. The number of samples needed when following a sequential sampling scheme may vary from trial to trial, and the *ASN* represents the average of what might happen over many trials with a fixed incoming defect level. Good software for designing sequential sampling schemes will calculate the *ASN* curve as a function of the incoming defect level.

Skip Lot sampling means that only a fraction of the submitted lots are inspected. This mode of sampling is of the cost-saving variety in terms of time and effort. However skip-lot sampling should only be used when it has been demonstrated that the quality of the submitted product is very good.

A skip-lot sampling plan is implemented as follows:

1. *Design a single sampling plan* by specifying the alpha and beta risks and the consumer/producer's risks. This plan is called "the reference sampling plan".
2. Start with normal lot-by-lot inspection, using the reference plan.
3. When a pre-specified number, *i*, of consecutive lots are accepted, switch to inspecting only a fraction *f* of the lots. The selection of the members of that fraction is done at random.
4. When a lot is rejected return to normal inspection.

The parameters *f* and *i* are essential to calculating the probability of acceptance for a skip-lot sampling plan. In this scheme, *i*, called the *clearance number,* is a positive integer and the sampling fraction *f* is such that $0 < f < 1$. Hence, when $f = 1$ there is no longer skip-lot sampling. The calculation of the acceptance probability for the skip-lot sampling plan is performed via the following formula

$$P_a(f,i) = \frac{fP + (1-f)P^i}{f + (1-f)P^i}$$

where *P* is the probability of accepting a lot with a given proportion of incoming defectives *p*, from the *OC curve* of the single sampling plan.

The following relationships hold:

for a given *i*, the smaller is *f*, the greater is P_a for a given *f*, the smaller is *i*, the greater is P_a

An illustration of a a skip-lot sampling plan is given below.

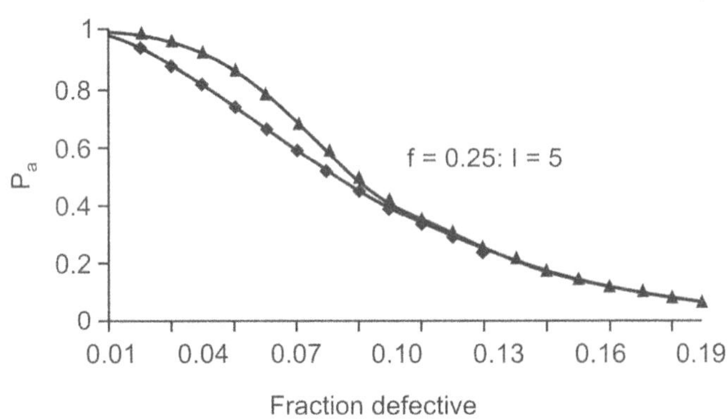

Figure 2.7|

An important property of skip-lot sampling plans is the average sample number (ASN). The *ASN* of a skip-lot sampling plan is

$$ASN_{skip\text{-}lot} = (F)(ASN_{reference})$$

where F is defined by

$$F = \frac{f}{(1-f)P^i + f}$$

Therefore, since $0 < F < 1$, it follows that the *ASN* of skip-lot sampling is smaller than the *ASN* of the reference sampling plan.

In summary, skip-lot sampling is preferred when the quality of the submitted lots is excellent and the supplier can demonstrate a proven track record.

Control charts are used to routinely monitor quality. Depending on the number of process characteristics to be monitored, there are two basic types of control charts. The first, referred to as a univariate control chart, is a graphical display (chart) of one quality characteristic. The second, referred to as a multivariate control chart, is a graphical display of a statistic that summarizes or represents more than one quality characteristic.

A single quality characteristic has been measured or computed from a sample, the control chart shows the value of the quality characteristic versus the sample number or versus time. In general, the chart contains a center line that represents the mean value for the in-control process. Two other horizontal lines, called the upper control limit (UCL) and the lower control limit (LCL), are also shown on the chart. These control limits are chosen so that almost all of the data points will fall within these limits as long as the process remains in-control. The figure below illustrates this.

Demonstrating basis of control chart

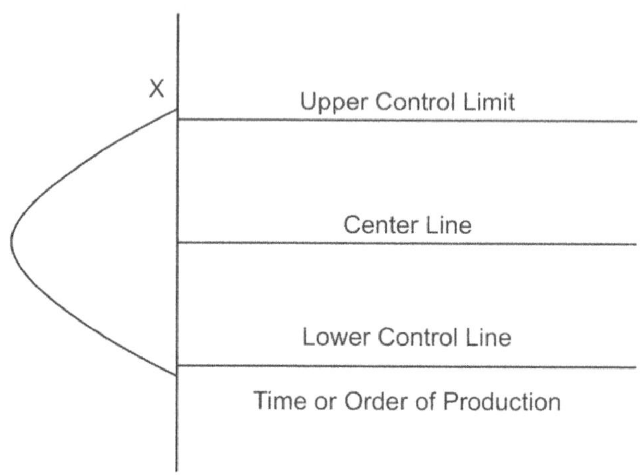

Figure 2.8 |

The control limits as pictured in the graph might be .001 *probability* limits. If so, and if chance causes alone were present, the probability of a point falling above the upper limit would be one out of a thousand, and similarly, a point falling below the lower limit would be one out of a thousand. We would be searching for an assignable cause if a point would fall outside these limits. Where we put these limits will determine the risk of undertaking such a search when in reality there is no assignable cause for variation.

Since two out of a thousand is a very small risk, the 0.001 limits may be said to give practical assurances that, if a point falls outside these limits, the variation was caused be an assignable cause. It must be noted that two out of one thousand is a purely arbitrary number. There is no reason why it could not have been set to one out a hundred or even larger. The decision would depend on the amount of risk the management of the quality control program is willing to take. In general (in the world of quality control) it is customary to use limits that approximate the 0.002 standard.

Letting X denote the value of a process characteristic, if the system of chance causes generates a variation in X that follows the normal distribution, the 0.001 probability limits will be very close to the 3σ limits. From normal tables we glean that the 3σ in one direction is 0.00135, or in both directions 0.0027. For normal distributions, therefore, the 3σ limits are the practical equivalent of 0.001 probability limits.

In the U.S., whether X is normally distributed or not, it is an acceptable practice to base the control limits upon a multiple of the standard deviation. Usually this multiple is 3 and thus the limits are called 3-sigma limits. This term is used whether the standard deviation is the universe or population parameter, or some estimate thereof, or simply a "standard value" for control chart purposes. It should be inferred from the context what standard deviation is involved. (Note that in the U.K., statisticians generally prefer to adhere to probability limits.)

If the underlying distribution is skewed, say in the positive direction, the 3-sigma limit will fall short of the upper 0.001 limit, while the lower 3-sigma limit will fall below the 0.001 limit. This situation means that the risk of looking for assignable causes of positive variation when none exists will be greater than one out of a thousand. But the risk of searching for an assignable cause of negative variation, when none exists, will be reduced. The net result, however, will be an increase in the risk of a chance variation beyond the control limits. How much this risk will be increased will depend on the degree of skewness.

If variation in quality follows a Poisson distribution, for example, for which $np = .8$, the risk of exceeding the upper limit by chance would be raised by the use of 3-sigma limits from 0.001 to 0.009 and the lower limit reduces from 0.001 to 0. For a Poisson distribution the mean and variance both equal np. Hence the upper 3-sigma limit is 0.8 + 3 *sqrt* (.8) = 3.48 and the lower limit = 0 (here *sqrt* denotes "square root"). For $np = .8$ the probability of getting more than 3 successes = 0.009.

If a data point falls outside the control limits, we assume that the process is probably out of control and that an investigation is warranted to find and eliminate the cause or causes.

Does this mean that when all points fall within the limits, the process is in control? Not necessarily. If the plot looks non-random, that is, if the points exhibit some form of systematic behavior, there is still something wrong. For example, if the first 25 of 30 points fall above the center line and the last 5 fall below the center line, we would wish to know why this is so. Statistical methods to detect sequences or nonrandom patterns can be applied to the interpretation of control charts. To be sure, "in control" implies that all points are between the control limits and they form a random pattern.

During the 1920's, Dr. Walter A. Shewhart proposed a general model for control charts as follows:

Shewhart Control Charts for variables

Let w be a sample statistic that measures some continuously varying quality characteristic of interest (e.g., thickness), and suppose that the mean of w is μ_w, with a standard deviation of σ_w. Then the center line, the UCL and the LCL are

$$\text{UCL} = \mu_w + k\sigma_w$$

$$\text{Center Line} = \mu_w$$

$$\text{LCL} = \mu_w - k\sigma_w$$

where k is the distance of the control limits from the center line, expressed in terms of standard deviation units. When k is set to 3, we speak of 3-sigma control charts.

Historically, k = 3 has become an accepted standard in industry.

The centerline is the process mean, which in general is unknown. We replace it with a *target* or the average of all the data. The quantity that we plot is the sample average, $\overline{X}$. The chart is called the $\overline{X}$ chart.

We also have to deal with the fact that σ is, in general, unknown. Here we replace σ_w with a given standard value, or we estimate it by a function of the *average standard deviation*. This is obtained by averaging the individual standard deviations that we calculated from each of m preliminary (or present) samples, each of size n. This function will be discussed shortly.

It is equally important to examine the standard deviations in ascertaining whether the process is in control. There is, unfortunately, a slight problem involved when we work with the usual estimator of σ. The following discussion will illustrate this

If σ^2 is the unknown variance of a probability distribution, then an unbiased estimator of σ^2 is the sample variance

$$s^2 = \frac{\sum_{i-1}^{n}\left(x_i - \overline{x}\right)^2}{n-1}$$

However, s, the sample standard deviation is *not* an unbiased estimator of σ. If the underlying distribution is normal, then s actually estimates $c_4\,\sigma$, where c_4 is a constant that depends on the sample size n. This constant is tabulated in most text books on statistical quality control and may be calculated using

C_4 factor

$$c_4 = \sqrt{\frac{2}{n-1}}\frac{\left(\frac{n}{2}-1\right)!}{\left(\frac{n-1}{2}-1\right)!}$$

To compute this we need a *non-integer factorial,* which is defined for $n/2$ as follows:

So the mean or expected value of the sample standard deviation is $c_4\,\sigma$.

The standard deviation of the sample standard deviation is

$$\sigma_s = \sigma\sqrt{1-c_4^2}$$

What are the differences between control limits and specification limits?

Control Limits are used to determine if the process is in a state of statistical control (i.e., is producing consistent output).

Specification Limits are used to determine if the product will function in the intended fashion.

How many data points are needed to set up a control chart?

Shewhart gave the following rule of thumb:

"It has also been observed that a person would seldom if ever be justified in concluding that a state of statistical control of a given repetitive operation or production process has been reached until he had obtained, under presumably the same essential conditions, a sequence of not less than twenty five samples of size four that are in control."

It is important to note that control chart properties, such as false alarm probabilities, are generally given under the assumption that the parameters, such as μ and σ, are known. When the control limits are not computed from a large amount of data, the actual properties might be quite different from what is assumed (see, e.g., *Quesenberry, 1993*).

When do we recalculate control limits?

Since a control chart "compares" the current performance of the process characteristic to the past performance of this characteristic, changing the control limits frequently would negate any usefulness.

So, only change your control limits if you have a valid, compelling reason for doing so. Some examples of reasons:

When you have at least 30 more data points to add to the chart and there have been no known changes to the process

- you get a better estimate of the variability

If a major process change occurs and affects the way your process runs.

If a known, preventable act changes the way the tool or process would behave (power goes out, consumable is corrupted or bad quality, etc.)

What are the WECO rules for signaling "Out of Control"?

General rules for detecting out of control or non-random situations

WECO stands for Western Electric Company Rules

Any Point Above +3 Sigma

---+3 σ LIMIT

2 Out of the Last 3 Points Above +2 Sigma

---+2 σ LIMIT

4 Out of the Last 5 Points Above +1 Sigma

---+1 σ LIMIT

8 Consecutive Points on This Side of Control Line

=================================== CENTER LINE

8 Consecutive Points on This Side of Control Line

--- – 1 σ LIMIT

4 Out of the Last 5 Points Below – 1 Sigma

--- – 2 σ LIMIT

2 Out of the Last 3 Points Below – 2 Sigma

--- – 3 σ LIMIT

Any Point Below –3 Sigma

Trend Rules

6 in a row trending up or down. 14 in a row alternating up and down

The WECO rules are based on probability. We know that, for a normal distribution, the probability of encountering a point outside ± 3σ is 0.3%. This is a rare event. Therefore, if we observe a point outside the control limits, we conclude the process has shifted and is unstable. Similarly, we can identify other events that are equally rare and use them as flags for instability. The probability of observing two points out of three in a row between 2σ and 3σ and the probability of observing four points out of five in a row between 1σ and 2σ are also about 0.3%.

Note: While the WECO rules increase a Shewhart chart's sensitivity to trends or drifts in the mean, there is a severe downside to adding the WECO rules to an ordinary Shewhart control chart that the user should understand. When following the standard Shewhart "out of control" rule (i.e., signal if and only if you see a point beyond the plus or minus 3 sigma control limits) you will have "false alarms" every 371 points on the average (see the description of *Average Run Length or ARL* on the next page). Adding the WECO rules increases the frequency of false alarms to about once in every 91.75 points, on the average (see *Champ and Woodall, 1987*). The user has to decide whether this price is worth paying (some users add the WECO rules, but take them "less seriously" in terms of the effort put into troubleshooting activities when out of control signals occur).

With this background, the next page will describe how to construct Shewhart variables control charts.

Samples are Individual Measurements

Moving range used to derive upper and lower limits

Control charts for individual measurements, e.g., the sample size = 1, use the *moving range* of two successive observations to measure the process variability.

The moving range is defined as

$$MR_i = |x_i - x_{i-1}|$$

which is the absolute value of the first difference (e.g., the difference between two consecutive data points) of the data. Analogous to the Shewhart control chart, one can plot both the data (which are the individuals) and the moving range.

For the control chart for individual measurements, the lines plotted are:

$$\text{UCL} = \bar{x} + 3\frac{\overline{MR}}{1.128}$$

Centre line = $\bar{x}$

$$\text{LCL} = \bar{x} - 3\frac{\overline{MR}}{1.128}$$

where $\overline{X}$ is the average of all the individuals and $\overline{MR}$ is the average of all the moving ranges of two observations. Keep in mind that either or both averages may be replaced by a standard or target, if available. (Note that 1.128 is the value of d_2 for $n = 2$).

The following example illustrates the control chart for individual observations. A new process was studied in order to monitor flow rate. The first 10 batches resulted in

Batch Number	Flow rate x	Moving Range MR
1	49.6	
2	47.6	2.0
3	49.9	2.3
4	51.3	14
5	47.8	3.5
6	51.2	3.4
7	52.6	1.4
8	52.4	0.2
9	53.6	1.2
10	52.1	1.5
	$\overline{X} = 50.81$	$\overline{MR} = 1.8778$

This yields the parameters below.

$$UCL = \bar{x} + 3\frac{\overline{MR}}{1.128} = 50.81 + 3\frac{1.8778}{1.128} = 55.8041$$

Centre line $\bar{x} = 50.81$

$$LCL = \bar{x} - 3\frac{\overline{MR}}{1.128} = 50.81 - 3\frac{1.8778}{1.128} = 45.8159$$

The control chart is given below

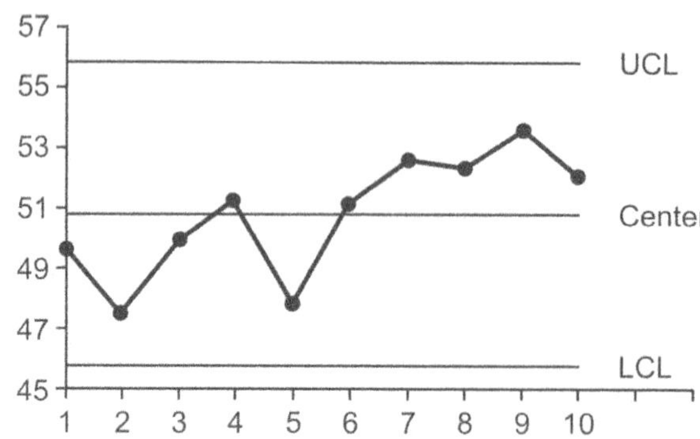

Figure 2.9|

The process is in control, since none of the plotted points fall outside either the *UCL* or *LCL*.

Alternative for constructing individuals control chart

Note: Another way to construct the individuals chart is by using the standard deviation.

Then we can obtain the chart from

$$\bar{x} \pm 3s / c_4$$

It is preferable to have the limits computed this way for the start of Phase 2.

Dr W. Edward Deming's 14 Principles

Deming's Principles of Quality Improvement

Constancy of purpose: Create constancy of purpose for continual improvement of products and service to society, allocating resources to provide for long range needs rather than only short term profitability, with a plan to become competitive, to stay in business, and to provide jobs.

1. ***The new philosophy:*** Adopt the new philosophy. We are in a new economic age, created in Japan. We can no longer live with commonly accepted levels of delays, mistakes, defective materials and defective workmanship. Transformation of Western management style is necessary to halt the continued decline of business and industry.
2. ***Cease dependence on mass inspection:*** Eliminate the need for mass inspection as the way of life to achieve quality by building quality into the product in the first place. Require statistical evidence of built in quality in both manufacturing and purchasing functions.
3. ***End lowest tender contracts:*** End the practice of awarding business solely on the basis of price tag. Instead require meaningful measures of quality along with price. Reduce the number of suppliers for the same item by eliminating those that do not qualify with statistical and other evidence of quality. The aim is to minimize total cost, not merely initial cost, by minimizing variation. This may be achieved by moving toward a single supplier for any one item, on a long term relationship of loyalty and trust. Purchasing managers have a new job, and must learn it.
4. ***Improve every process:*** Improve constantly and forever every process for planning, production, and service. Search continually for problems in order to improve every activity in the company, to improve quality and productivity, and thus to constantly decrease costs. Institute innovation and constant improvement of product, service, and process. It is management's job to work continually on the system (design, incoming materials, maintenance, improvement of machines, supervision, training, retraining).
5. ***Institute training on the job:*** Institute modern methods of training on the job for all, including management, to make better use of every employee. New skills are required to keep up with changes in materials, methods, product and service design, machinery, techniques, and service.
6. ***Institute leadership:*** Adopt and institute leadership aimed at helping people do a better job. The responsibility of managers and supervisors must be changed from

sheer numbers to quality. Improvement of quality will automatically improve productivity. Management must ensure that immediate action is taken on reports of inherited defects, maintenance requirements, poor tools, fuzzy operational definitions, and all conditions detrimental to quality.

7. Drive out fear: Encourage effective two way communication and other means to drive out fear throughout the organization so that everybody may work effectively and more productively for the company.
8. ***Break down barriers:*** Break down barriers between departments and staff areas. People in different areas, such as Leasing, Maintenance, Administration, must work in teams to tackle problems that may be encountered with products or service.
9. ***Eliminate exhortations:*** Eliminate the use of slogans, posters and exhortations for the work force, demanding Zero Defects and new levels of productivity, without providing methods. Such exhortations only create adversarial relationships; the bulk of the causes of low quality and low productivity belong to the system, and thus lie beyond the power of the work force.
10. ***Eliminate arbitrary numerical targets:*** Eliminate work standards that prescribe quotas for the work force and numerical goals for people in management. Substitute aids and helpful leadership in order to achieve continual improvement of quality and productivity.
11. ***Permit pride of workmanship:*** Remove the barriers that rob hourly workers, and people in management, of their right to pride of workmanship. This implies, among other things, abolition of the annual merit rating (appraisal of performance) and of Management by Objective. Again, the responsibility of managers, supervisors, foremen must be changed from sheer numbers to quality.
12. ***Encourage education:*** Institute a vigorous program of education, and encourage self improvement for everyone. What an organization needs is not just good people; it needs people that are improving with education. Advances in competitive position will have their roots in knowledge.
13. ***Top management commitment and action:*** Clearly define top management's permanent commitment to ever improving quality and productivity, and their obligation to implement all of these principles. Indeed, it is not enough that top management commit themselves for life to quality and productivity. They must know what it is that they are committed to-that is, what they must do. Create a structure in top management that will push every day on the preceding 13 Points, and take action in order to accomplish the transformation. Support is not enough: action is required

PDCA Cycle

From problem-faced to problem-solved

The PDCA Cycle is a checklist of the four stages which you must go through to get from `problem-faced' to `problem solved'. The four stages are Plan-Do-Check-Act, and they are carried out in the cycle illustrated below.

The concept of the PDCA Cycle was originally developed by Walter Shewhart, the pioneering statistician who developed statistical process control in the Bell Laboratories in the US during the 1930's. It is often referred to as `the Shewhart Cycle'. It was taken up and promoted very effectively from the 1950s on by the famous Quality Management authority, W. Edwards Deming, and is consequently known by many as `the Deming Wheel'.

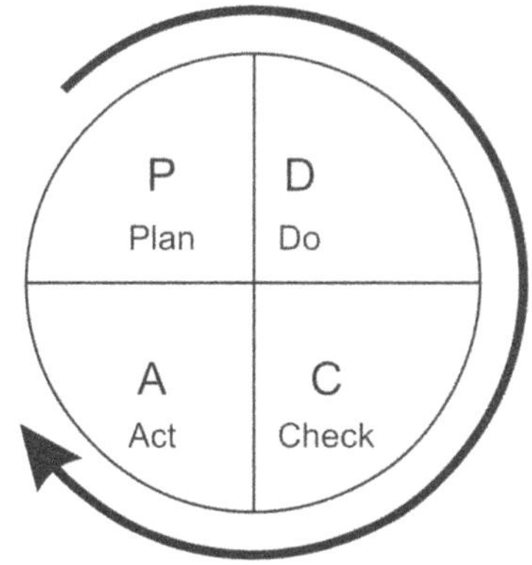

Figure 2.10|

Use the PDCA Cycle to coordinate your continuous improvement efforts. It both emphasises and demonstrates that improvement programs must start with careful planning, must result in effective action, and must move on again to careful planning in a continuous cycle.

Also use the PDCA Cycle diagram in team meetings to take stock of what stage improvement initiatives are at, and to choose the appropriate tools to see each stage through to successful completion.

Plan-Do-Check-Act

Here is what you do for each stage of the Cycle:

Plan to improve your operations first by finding out what things are going wrong (that is identify the problems faced), and come up with ideas for solving these problems.

Do changes designed to solve the problems on a small or experimental scale first. This minimises disruption to routine activity while testing whether the changes will work or not.

Check whether the small scale or experimental changes are achieving the desired result or not. Also, continuously Check nominated key activities (regardless of any experimentation going on) to ensure that you know what the quality of the output is at all times to identify any new problems when they crop up.

Act to implement changes on a larger scale if the experiment is successful. This means making the changes a routine part of your activity. Also Act to involve other persons (other departments, suppliers, or customers) affected by the changes and whose cooperation you need to implement them on a larger scale, or those who may simply benefit from what you have learned (you may, of course, already have involved these people in the Do or trial stage).

You have now completed the cycle to arrive at `problem solved'. Go back to the Plan stage to identify the next `problem faced'.

If the experiment was not successful, skip the Act stage and go back to the Plan stage to come up with some new ideas for solving the problem and go through the cycle again. Plan-Do-Check-Act describes the overall stages of improvement activity, but how is each stage carried out? This is where other specific quality management, or continuous improvement, tools and techniques come into play. The diagram below lists the tools and techniques which can be used to complete each stage of the PDCA Cycle.

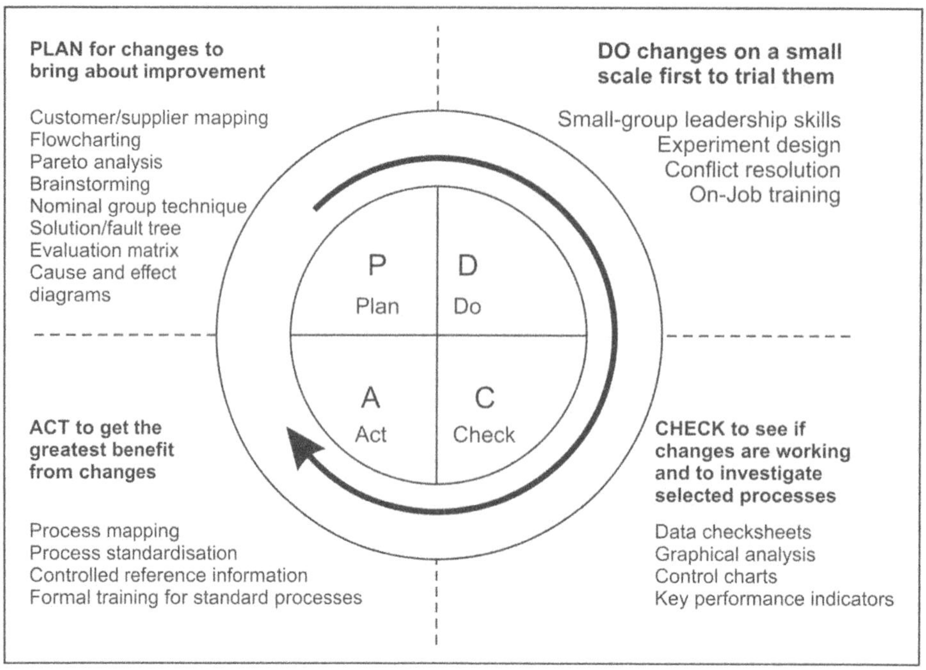

Figure 2.11 |

This classification of tools into sections of the PDCA Cycle is not meant to be strictly applied, but it is a useful prompt to help you choose what to do at each critical stage of your improvement efforts.

Review Questions

1. Explain the concept: manufacturing management?
2. Explain manufacturing and production with suitable examples?
3. Discuss the steps involved in the production control?
4. What are the different components of facility location planning?
5. Explain the different methods of production?
6. What is production planning and control? Discuss its significance in the context of manufacturing management?
7. Explain the various factors to be taken into consideration while taking a decision on factory location?
8. What do you understand by statistical quality control?
9. Explain Edward deming's 14 points of improving quality?
10. What is control chart? Explain the different types of control charts?
11. Describe deming's pdca cycle and state its significance?
12. Define work study, method study and work measurement? Explain their significance?
13. State the applications of work study? Describe the procedure for work study?

13. State the applications of work study? Describe the procedure for work study?

3 Pharmaceutical Industry

3.1 | Indian Pharmaceutical Industry

LEARNING OBJECTIVES

- *Indian Pharmaceutical Industry*
- *Advantage India – Current Status and its Role in National Economy*
- *Steps to Strengthen the Pharm.Industry*
- *Indian Pharm. research and development – Challenges*
- *Indian Patents and TRIPS*
- *Indian Pharmaceutical Landscape – Post TRIPS*
- *Clinical Trials*
- *Current Scenario*

Introduction

The **Indian Pharmaceutical Industry** today is in the front rank of India's science-based industries with wide ranging capabilities in the complex field of drug manufacture and technology. A highly organized sector, the Indian Pharma Industry is estimated to be worth $ 4.5 billion, growing at about 8 to 9 percent annually. It ranks very high in the third world, in terms of technology, quality and range of medicines manufactured. From simple headache pills to sophisticated antibiotics and complex cardiac compounds, almost every type of medicine is now made indigenously.

Playing a key role in promoting and sustaining development in the vital field of medicines, **Indian Pharma Industry** boasts of quality producers and many units approved by regulatory authorities in USA and UK. International companies associated with this sector have stimulated, assisted and spearheaded this dynamic development in the past 53 years and helped to put India on the pharmaceutical map of the world.

The Indian Pharmaceutical sector is highly fragmented with more than 20,000 registered units. It has expanded drastically in the last two decades. The leading 250 pharmaceutical companies control 70% of the market with market leader holding nearly 7% of the market share. It is an extremely fragmented market with severe price competition and government price control.

The pharmaceutical industry in India meets around 70% of the country's demand for bulk drugs, drug intermediates, pharmaceutical formulations, chemicals, tablets, capsules, orals and injectibles. There are about 250 large units and about 8000 Small Scale Units, which form the core of the pharmaceutical industry in India (including 5 Central Public Sector Units). These units produce the complete range of pharmaceutical formulations, i.e., medicines ready for consumption by patients and about 350 bulk drugs, i.e., chemicals having therapeutic value and used for production of pharmaceutical formulations.

Following the de-licensing of the pharmaceutical industry, industrial licensing for most of the drugs and pharmaceutical products has been done away with. Manufacturers are free to produce any drug duly approved by the Drug Control Authority. Technologically strong and totally self-reliant, the pharmaceutical industry in India has low costs of production, low R & D costs, innovative scientific manpower, strength of national laboratories and an increasing balance of trade. The Pharmaceutical Industry, with its rich scientific talents and research capabilities, supported by Intellectual Property Protection regime is well set to take on the international market.

Advantage India – Current Status and its Role in National Economy

***Competent workforce*:** India has a pool of personnel with high managerial and technical competence as also skilled workforce. It has an educated work force and English is commonly used. Professional services are easily available.

***Cost-effective chemical synthesis*:** Its track record of development, particularly in the area of improved cost-beneficial chemical synthesis for various drug molecules is excellent. It provides a wide variety of bulk drugs and exports sophisticated bulk drugs.

***Legal and Financial Framework*:** India has a 53 year old democracy and hence has a solid legal framework and strong financial markets. There is already an established international industry and business community.

***Information and Technology*:** It has a good network of world-class educational institutions and established strengths in Information Technology.

***Globalization*:** The country is committed to a free market economy and globalization. Above all, it has a 70 million middle class market, which is continuously growing.

***Consolidation*:** For the first time in many years, the international pharmaceutical industry is finding great opportunities in India. The process of consolidation, which has become a generalized phenomenon in the world pharmaceutical industry, has started taking place in India.

The Growth Scenario

India's US$ 3.1 billion pharmaceutical industry is growing at the rate of 14 percent per year. It is one of the largest and most advanced among the developing countries.

Over 20,000 registered pharmaceutical manufacturers exist in the country. The domestic pharmaceuticals industry output is expected to exceed Rs. 260 billion in the financial year 2002, which accounts for merely 1.3% of the global pharmaceutical sector. Of this, bulk drugs will account for Rs 54 billion (21%) and formulations, the remaining Rs 210 billion (79%). In financial year 2001, imports were Rs 20 billion while exports were Rs. 87 billion.

As per WTO, from the year 2005, India will grant product patent recognition to all new chemical entities (NCEs) i.e., bulk drugs developed then onwards. The Indian Government's decision to allow 100 percent foreign direct investment into the drugs and pharmaceutical industry is expected to aid the growth of contract research in the country. Technology transfer to 100 percent Indian subsidiaries of MNCs is expected only in 2005.

Indian pharmaceutical interests in making a mark on the global scene got a boost when Dr. Reddy's licensed two of its anti-diabetic molecules to Novo Nordisk and when Ranbaxy licensed its Novel Drug Delivery System (NDDS) of ciprofloxacin to Bayer. MNCs in India faced the problem of having a very high DPCO coverage, weakening their bottom lines as well as hindering their growth through the launch of new products. DPCO coverage is expected to be diluted further in the near future benefiting the MNCs. New legislation is also expected in the OTC segment increasing the number of brands in the Over the Counter (OTC) segment.

The Indian pharmaceutical industry is also getting increasingly U.S. FDA compliant to harness the growth opportunities in areas of contract manufacturing and research. Indian companies such as Ranbaxy, Sun Pharma, and Dr. Reddy's are increasingly focusing on tapping the U.S. generic market, projected to be around $180 billion by 2015.

Steps to Strengthen the Industry

Indian companies need to attain the right product-mix for sustained future growth. Core competencies will play an important role in determining the future of many Indian pharmaceutical companies in the post product-patent regime after 2005. Indian companies, in an effort to consolidate their position, will have to increasingly look at merger and acquisition options of either companies or products. This would help them to offset loss of new product options, improve their R & D efforts and improve distribution to penetrate markets.

Research and development has always taken the back seat amongst Indian pharmaceutical companies. In order to stay competitive in the future, Indian companies will have to refocus and invest heavily in R & D.

The Indian pharmaceutical industry also needs to take advantage of the recent advances in biotechnology and information technology. The future of the industry will be determined by how well it markets its products to several regions and distributes risks, its forward and backward integration capabilities, its R & D, its consolidation through mergers and acquisitions, co-marketing and licensing agreements.

Research and Development is the key to the future of pharmaceutical industry. The pharmaceutical advances for considerable improvement in life expectancy and health all over the world are the result of a steadily increasing investment in research. There is considerable scope for collaborative R & D in India. India can offer several strengths to the international R & D community. These strengths relate to availability of excellent scientific talents who can develop combinatorial chemistry, new synthetic molecules and plant derived candidate drugs.

R & D in the pharmaceutical industry in India is critical to find answers for some of the diseases peculiar to a tropical country like India and also for finding solutions for unmet medical needs. Industrial R & D groups can carry out limited primary screening to identify lead molecules or even candidate drugs for further *in vivo* screening, pre-clinical pharmacology, toxicology, animal and human pharmacokinetics and metabolic studies before taking them up for human trials. In such collaborations, harmonized standards of screening can be assured following established good laboratory practices. The R & D expenditure by the Indian pharmaceutical industry is around 1.9% of the industry's turnover. This obviously, is very low when compared to the investment on R & D by foreign research-based Pharma companies. They spend 10-16% of the turnover on R & D. However, now that India is entering into the Patent protection area, many companies are spending relatively more on R & D.

When it comes to clinical evaluation at the time of multi-center trials, India would provide a strong base considering the real availability of clinical materials in diverse therapeutic areas. Such active collaboration will be mutually beneficial to both partners. According to a survey by the Pharmaceutical Outsourcing Management Association and Bio/Pharmaceutical Outsourcing Report, pharmaceutical companies are utilizing substantially the services of Contract Research Organizations (CROs).

Indian Pharmaceutical Industry, with its rich scientific talents, provides cost-effective clinical trial research. It has an excellent record of development of improved, cost-beneficial chemical syntheses for various drug molecules. Some MNCs are already sourcing these services from their Indian affiliates.

The Pharmaceutical and Biotechnology Industry is eligible for weight deduction for R & D expense up to 150%. These R & D companies will also enjoy tax holiday for 10 years. A promotional research and development fund of Rs.150 crores is set up by the

Government to promote research and development in the pharmaceutical sector. The Indian pharmaceutical industry is highly regulated. The Government controls prices of a large number of bulk drugs and formulations. Profit margins of players vary widely in both domestic and export sales due to many factors.

Domestic Trade

More than 85% of the formulations produced in the country are sold in the domestic market. India is largely self-sufficient in case of formulations. Some life saving, new generation under-patent formulations continue to be imported, especially by MNCs, which then market them in India. Overall, the size of the domestic formulations market is around Rs 160 bn and it is growing at 10% p.a.

Exports

Over 60% of India's bulk drug production is exported. The balance is sold locally to other formulators. India's pharmaceutical exports are to the tune of Rs. 87 bn, of which formulations contribute nearly 55% and the rest 45% comes from bulk drugs. In financial year 2000, exports grew by 21%. India's pharmaceuticals imports were to the tune of Rs. 20.3 billion in FY2001. Imports have registered a CAGR of only 2% in the past 5 years. Import of bulk drugs have slowed down in the recent years.

3.2 | Indian Pharma Research and Development - Challenges

Pharmaceutical R & D management is braving unprecedented challenges. Drug Research and Development (R & D) costs have rocketed 23 fold in 28 years, touching an all time high of $1.25 billion per new molecular entity (NME). Drug development time has gone up from 11.6 years in the 1970s to 14.9 years in 2001 reducing patent protected market life and saving billions off potential revenues. And the output does not justify the increasing time and cost. The pharmaceutical R & D pipeline is thinning, with more blockbusters set to go off patent than to emerge from the R & D pipeline. Blockbusters are now not only desirable for success, but essential for survival. However future blockbusters are more likely to emerge from outside traditional chemistry based pharmaceutical industries (Pharma) or from innovative small biotech startups scattered around the world. As a result, Big Pharma companies historic high valuation is being questioned – it was based on steady and measurable income from patent protected drugs and rich R & D pipelines with potential blockbusters.

Background

"India meets Doha, a white paper from Deloitte, focused on the recent strengthening of the patent laws in India (Indian Patent (Amendment) Act 2000) and mentioned several new opportunities for one of the most Intellectual Property (IP) sensitive industries of our time - the pharmaceutical industry – emphasizing increased R & D productivity by outsourcing drug research and development to India. This paper, as a sequel, presents an overview of the Indian pharmaceutical landscape, and studies the opportunities for outsourcing clinical trials - the most cost and time intensive phase of the R & D process today.

Indian Patents and TRIPS

India could not have stepped into the limelight at a more opportune time. From January 2005, the country became TRIPS compliant and formally recognized product patents. Patent protection in India is now on levels comparable to developed nations (caveat). For any Intellectual Property (IP) sensitive industry India is now a destination to be considered – both as a market and for manufacturing and research and development (R & D).

Patent Progress

The Indian Patents and Designs Act (1911) recognized product patents but the goals of patent protection - to promote and protect innovation – did not materialize. To encourage investments and promote development. The Indian Patent Act, 1970 (with amendments) removed product patents in pharmaceutical, agro-chemical and food processing sectors, where only process patents were admissible. This legalized copycat drug making Indian entrepreneurs could reverse engineer patent protected drugs, tweak the manufacturing process to bypass patent infringement suits, and market the drugs at a fraction of the price of the original drug, having no R & D costs to recover.

The effects of this law were predictable. Between 1970 and 2004, Pharmaceutical Transnational companies (TNCs) saw their market-share fall from 85 % to 15%. TNCs could not compete against local manufacturers on price, and local ingenuity and process chemistry skills saw many patented products launched in the local markets even before the patent owners (TNCs) could launch them. As a result TNCs lost interest in India and either stopped supporting their local subsidiaries or withdrew altogether. The local pharmaceutical (Pharma) manufacturing industry, on the other hand, grew to over 20,000 manufacturing units, including around 300 in the organized sector and a few large publicly traded companies.

As one of the founding members of the World Trade Organization, India committed to bring its patent protection laws to internationally acceptable minimum TRIPS levels in 10 years. Accordingly, from January 01, 2005, product patent was recognized in the pharmaceutical sector and the patent period increased from the earlier seven years to 20 years.

Indian Pharmaceutical Landscape – Post TRIPS

The Indian pharmaceutical industry is the worlds 13th largest in terms of value and the 4th largest in terms of volume. With over 60,000 brands in over 60 therapeutic categories, the total market size is approximately USD 5 billion. India has world class facilities and expertise in manufacturing with the largest number of US FDA approved manufacturing units in the world outside the US. Ancillary industries are well developed with support available locally. Quality bulk drugs at competitive prices are assured. In R & D, basic research and biology skills are weak, a legacy of the lax patent regime where basic research was neglected. But process chemistry skills – honed over decades of reverse-engineering – are strong. The Indian pharmaceutical industry accounts for at least 35% of bulk drug filings in the US.

Post-TRIPS, the Indian pharmaceutical landscape is set to change permanently. Local pharmaceutical majors are moving up the international value chain, focusing on generics marketing in Europe and the US to complement their already-strong presence in bulk active pharmaceutical ingredient (API) supply, and to capitalize on the record number of drugs set to go off-patent over the next five years.

To leverage their experience in manufacturing, local companies are scouting for contract manufacturing opportunities. And to leverage their country-wide network of skilled marketing personnel they are actively seeking in-licensing and marketing opportunities.

Local pharmaceutical majors do not have the finances to take a product to market. With annual sales of a billion - less than the R & D budgets of Big Pharma companies – they are out licensing their NME innovation, and focusing on cheaper Abbreviated New Drug Applications (ANDAs). And to 'learn and earn', they are positioning themselves as willing partners in global pharmaceutical knowledge networks. With cost and process skills working to their advantage, local companies are also scouting to grab a share of the international R & D outsourcing market.

Of all the opportunities for global pharmaceutical companies in this scenario, outsourcing the clinical development phase of the R & D process appears the most promising. With a large population and world class medical skills, this outsourcing service segment is developing rapidly and with patent protection no longer a hurdle, a fresh look at this segment is warranted. Including India in the clinical development outsourcing network presents a fourfold benefit – it is the most immediate opportunity with the greatest potential benefit in the shortest possible time addressing the most pressing issue today.

Clinical Trials

Clinical studies take up between 30 to 50% of the time spent in R & D, and within this, a third of the time (in clinical trials) is taken in patient recruitment. With patent protection being limited to 20 years including the R & D stage, every year saved here can bring in additional revenues of a billion dollars for a blockbuster. As drugs targeting smaller segments of therapeutics are discovered, the clinical development stage can present a serious bottleneck. It is conceivably difficult to find the adequate study population in time, particularly in smaller geographies with small population densities, particularly in the west, with highly treatment experienced patients causing a delay in 80% of clinical trials.

Advantage - India

The duration of clinical trials can be greatly reduced in India. India is the second most populous country in the world with a large pool of naïve patients and the fourth largest pool of medical professionals in the world. Rapidly improving support industries such as labs and hospitals, and a world respected IT industry capable of picking up domain expertise to support R & D and clinical trials are further advantages. Pharma giants are also attracted by the heterogeneity of the billion plus population, the fact that the country offers nearly 700,000 specialty hospital beds at about a tenth of the price in developed nations, 221 medical colleges and skilled English-speaking medical personnel In India, the contract research and clinical business in India during FY 2003-04 was USD 59.4 million (INR 275 crores) as against USD 29.16 million (INR 135 crore) in the previous year, a growth of 104 percent, and is projected to grow 8-10 times by 2010 to $ 250-300 million .

Optimistic estimates put the figure between $500 million and $1 billion by 2010. University and other diploma courses in biotechnology, bioinformatics, and clinical trials are beginning to become fashionable just as IT was in the 1990s and a reverse brain drain from the west is beginning and can help greatly in scientific and accurate clinical trials. It is easier to do multi-centric large-scale trials in India for many diseases, since the patients' enrollment rate for phase III studies can be up to six times higher in India than US or Europe. Because of the god-like status traditionally accorded to doctors, patient compliance and commitment is extremely high.

But the size of the industry is very small by global standards. In the US, for example, the number of GCP trials is 60,000 and the number of GCP trained investigators is over 40,000. According to Center Watch 2.8 million US subjects completed initial screening in 1999, of which 5 per cent (140,000) completed the trial and 2005 projections for screening are19.8 million subjects. In comparison, the estimated number of ICH-GCP clinical studies was 40-50 and the number of GCP trained investigators was 200-250. Most studies are carried out in 20-25 major public hospitals in capital cities. However, because of global pressures on industry to recruit patients faster and make the trials economic, large numbers of clinical trials are likely to be placed in countries like India. This is expected to explode the Indian clinical trials market over next 5 years.

Disadvantage - India

However, India faces quite a few challenges, before it can claim to be the world class status like the IT industry. Unlike IT, healthcare requires more specialized, less transferable competencies. Furthermore, the IT industry in India flourished, it can be argued, because it was under-regulated and did not hamper entrepreneurship, in contrast to the overregulated pharmaceutical industry. Pharmaceutical products and services from India may also be stonewalled in other overregulated markets, all these are probable barriers to entry and growth. Though the doctors have excellent skills and patient coverage, their lack of experience in GCP trials is undeniable. Furthermore, it is unclear whether an international company cannot carry out concurrent phase I trial. After submission of phase I data generated outside India, sponsors may be permitted to repeat phase I trials. Phase II, III, and IV trials can be concurrently done with other global trials for that drug.

Imports of body fluids/test samples from India have been another bottleneck hampering the industry. Companies that have global testing labs for sample testing have had failures in the entire outsourcing strategy due to this and a lack of world class GLP labs further incapacitated these companies from successfully completing their trials.

Ethical trials are another issue that is hard to ignore. There are instances of litigation for unethical trials without requisite permissions, or on ill-informed patients. A recent survey of 200 health researchers globally that was commissioned by the former US National Bioethics Advisory Commission and published in February's edition of the Journal of Medical Ethics revealed that a quarter of clinical trials conducted in developing countries did not undergo ethical review.

Local disinformation campaigns can also mar clinical studies and damage company reputation. A TNC runs the risk of being labeled an exploiter of local poverty or ignorance for carrying out cheap clinical trials.

Current Scenario

There has been an overall positive effect of India complying with TRIPS norms on product patents. Even before January 2005, a number of MNCs have set up R & D centers in India. Around 25 contract research organizations (CROs) and almost all multinational pharmaceuticals companies have started full-fledged clinical trials there in the last three years. This move accelerated from up to January 2005 and afterwards. To prepare for the opportunity, reputed institutions for training such as the Academy for Clinical Excellence and Institute of Clinical Research have been established over the last decade to train physicians in ICH-GCP guidelines and ethical trial requirements. The Clinical Data Interchange Standards Consortium (CDISC), USA, an NPO committed to the development of clinical research organizations' standards the world over, is looking at setting up a chapter in India. The Indian Society for Clinical Research launched in August 2005, aims to bring world-class clinical research organizations in India together, advise the government on clinical trials issues and foster the highest levels of ethics in the industry.

The Bottom-line

Outsourcing clinical development to India generates benefits in terms of time and cost savings that are too significant to be ignored. Some estimates we made to analyze the dollar benefits of outsourcing showed that the average saving per commercialized drug can be up to an optimal $ 363 million to a desirable first target of $40 million.

Conclusion

Of the several new opportunities created by India's compliance with WTO levels of patent protection, clinical research outsourcing has the most significant impact. Moreover clinical trials outsourcing fits the classic requirements of outsourcing a process – it is standard, increases efficiencies of time and costs, and improves organizational flexibility. Finally, India has country specific factors that favor outsourcing of this part of the R & D process. From 2005, patent protection is no longer a barrier to outsourcing and the way is clear for global pharmaceutical companies to include Indian clinical research organizations in the global R & D network.

While there seems to be an exciting time ahead, a few challenges still remain. As in all cases of successful outsourcing, three things are necessary – commitment, compliance and quality. The right partner selection can eliminate the hazards of outsourcing and the potential pitfalls of a well intentioned venture.

From the host country perspective, the government initiatives need to be clear cut and quick and more educational institutions need to offer specialized courses to tackle the impending shortage of ICH-GCP trained doctors. On the other hand Indian CROs need to be more aggressive in their marketing of their skills externally, and combat potential disinformation campaigns internally. If high ethical standards are adhered to, clinical research studies help the poor in the country by giving them free access to the newest drugs and the highest levels of health care that even the middle class cannot afford to have access to. This should always be remembered and portrayed.

Two approaches can be taken to estimate the savings by time and cost by outsourcing clinical trials to India.

In the first approach widely accepted estimates that a clinical trial costs an average $ 30,000 a day and lasts an average 6.6 years, and that outsourcing to India could save half the time and cost.

In the second approach a more generic view that bringing a molecule to market has crossed a billion dollars in recent times, and that overall half the costs of clinical trials can be saved by outsourcing to India.

The calculation table is presented below.

		Phase - Clinical Trials		
Row	**calculation**	**Method – I**	**US$**	**Source**
		Present Clinical trials costs		
a		Cost per day	30,000	
b		Average Duration	2,409	Tufts Center for the study of drug Development 2001
c	(a*b)	Total Costs	72,270,000	
		Clinical trials costs in India		
d	(a/2)	Cost per day	15,000	
e	(b/2)	Average Duration	1,205	
f	(d*e)	Total Costs	18,067,500	
g	(f*10%)	Add offshoring costs	1,806,750	
h	(f+g)	Total costs of outsourced trials	19,874,250	
i	(c-h)	Direct Savings	52,395,750	
j	(b-e)*20%	dded Margins (20%)	316,783,500	CenterWatch (assuming avg. annual sales of $ 480 mn)
i		TOTAL IMPACT	369,179,250	
		If only 25% of the work outsourced	92,294,813	
Row	calculation	Method – II	US$mn	Source
a		Cost of Drug R&D	1,000	PhRMA
b	(a*32%)	Clinical Trials phase	320	Business Insights
c	(b*50%)	Overview of 50% savings	160	Interviews, Reports
d	(c*50%)	If only 25% of the work outsourced	40	Conservative outsourced

3.3 | Globalization and its Impact on the Indian Pharmaceutical Industry

Globalization is a process which involves economic inter-dependence of countries world-wide removing all barriers for economic integration as if the whole world is a single village. Obviously, in this process, the rich nations with their superior financial power, control the scenario and the poor and the developing nations are forced to integrate surrendering their economic independence knowing fully well what they are forced to accept is really prejudicial to their own interest. In this process the world financial institutions like the World Bank, IMF and now the WTO advance the interest of the rich countries alone. The draconian policies of the World Bank and the IMF under the structural adjustment Programme resulted in the net transfer of $178 billion between 1984 and 1990 from the poor countries to the commercial banks of rich nations. (UNDP Human Development Report, 1994). The Transnational Corporations (TNCs) of the rich nations are practically controlling the world finances. Today, the whole world is colonized by global finance and the TNCs supported by the neo-colonial structure including the World Bank, IMF and WTO are controlling the financial situation world-wide. The governments of third world countries are powerless against global finance and are unable to control its movement within their own national boundaries.

The situation of the world drug industry is no different. 'Operating at the behest of the Pharmaceutical Research and Manufacturers' Association (PhRMA) for a decade and a half, the U.S. Government has waged a ruthless crusade to force third world countries to adopt strait jacketing intellectual property rules at the expense of protecting public health', says the editorial comment in the June 1998 issue of *Multinational Monitor*, a journal published from Washington.

The structural adjustment Programme introduced by the government of India at the behest of the IMF, World Bank and WTO created a serious impact on India's drug industry, health care system, on the workers engaged in the industry and ultimately on the people of the country. These reform policies are mainly the reduced role of the Government, cut in subsidy in the social sector, increase in administered prices, liberalization of trade by increasing tariff rates providing incentives for foreign investment, privatization of the public sector, equating foreign companies with Indian companies, de-regulating the labor market etc. This is aimed at the withdrawal of the state initiative from the social and welfare sectors like health, education, public distribution etc.

Drug Industry situation prior to the Indian Patent Act, 1970

At the time of independence, the total drug production in our country was around Rs. 10 *crores*. At that time the MNCs taking the help of the colonial Patent and Designs Act, 1911 exploited the drug market of our country. They were engaged mainly in the import of drugs from their country of origin. Between 1947-57, 99% of the 1704 drugs and pharmaceutical patents in India were held by foreign MNCs. During that time the MNCs who were controlling 80% of the market did not come forward with financial investment and technological help to establish drug production centres in India. Drug prices in India were amongst the highest in the world. In 1954, the first public sector drug company Hindustan Antibiotic Ltd. (HAL) was established with the help of WHO and UNICEF. The Indian Drugs and Pharmaceutical Limited (IDPL) was established in 1961 with help from the Soviet Union. The establishment of these two public sector units and the coming into force of the Drug Policy of 1978 had been mainly responsible for the availability of drugs and medicines at relatively lower prices in India. The country became almost self-sufficient in the production of drugs.

Indian Patent Act 1970

The Patent Bill was first introduced in Parliament in 1967, but the Patent Act, 1970 came into force only in 1972. The Indian Patent Act 1970 which is in operation in our country does not allow product patents on medicines, agricultural products and atomic energy. This is the most suitable patent act for the developing world. Here, process patents are allowed for 5-7 years. Mainly with the help of the Indian Patent Act 1970 India is today self-sufficient in the production of basic drugs covering various groups of drugs. Indian scientists developed new processes for 107 drugs. Indian companies are now among the world leaders in the production of bulk drugs from basic stages. At present, the prices of drugs in India are comparatively cheaper than many other countries. As per UNIDO, India is identified to produce its own drug needs with its own technology and manpower indigenously. After 1970, many new drug firms were established by Indian businessmen. At present, around 23 thousand small, big, and medium factories are producing drugs in India.

Attempts to change the Indian Patent Act 1970 are a part of this globalization Programme. The imposition of an unequal trade treaty like the World Trade Organization (WTO) is a step towards globalization in favor of the MNCs of rich nations. With its help, the market of the developing nations is forced open for the developed countries. Most of the developing countries were forced to sign the WTO agreement without realizing its implication: as a result, the developed countries are the gainers. Already, at the dictates of the IMF, World Bank and WTO, the Government of India is slackening all checks and controls to invite the MNCs in all industries including the pharmaceutical industry. FERA and MRTP Acts have been amended. Customs duties and corporate taxes have been lowered. Relief, concessions and facilities have been extended to the MNCs as to Indian companies. All these, already, had an adverse impact on the indigenous drug industry. As per the requirement of WTO guidelines for the product patent regime, the availability of new drugs in our country may be delayed depending on the desire of the patent holders. As per the guidelines, a product patent is granted for 20 years and a process patent for another 20 years. At present, newer drugs are made available in our country within a 4-6 years period. Prices of drugs will go up by 5 to 10 times as it is evident from the prices of drugs in India and other countries like Pakistan, U.K. and U.S.A. where product patents are in force. Ranitidine is sold by Glaxo in India at Rs. 7.20. The same product is sold by the same company in Pakistan at Rs. 65 and in the U.S.A. at Rs. 545. Similarly, the anti-viral drug Aciclovir costs Rs. 33.75 in India while the same drug is sold in Pakistan at Rs. 363. There are many such examples. The drug prices in the U.S.A., U.K. and other developed countries have gone up so high that the health care expenditure in those countries is predominantly funded by insurance companies at a very high premium. In those countries people cannot think of treatment without insurance coverage. Product patent regime will definitely hamper India's drugs exports as countries will be forced to purchase from patent holders only.

Dilution of Drug Policy and Drug Price Increase

Unlike consumer goods, drugs are not purchased by the preference of a person, but on a doctors' prescription. Consumers have no choice of their own on this matter.

Prices of drugs are increasing by leaps and bounds along with the prices of other commodities in recent times. The drug manufacturers are flouting the Drug Price Control Order (DPCO). The DPCO was first introduced in 1970. In 1970 most of the drugs were under price control. In 1987 this was diluted and the number of drugs which were restricted declined to 347, in 1987 it was brought down to 163 drugs and in 1994 only 73 drugs were under DPCO. Even then industry is not happy; they want the control to be abolished totally. They have already demanded decontrol of 17 bulk drugs and further recommended full decontrol within 3 years time. Many developed countries of Europe control drug prices directly. In the U.K., the government determines the profit level of drugs supplied by individual companies. A company has to reimburse excess profits to the Department of Health.

A recent study shows that the prices of many life-saving bulk drugs have gone up steeply. Drugs policies in our country are decided not by the need of our people, the pattern of diseases or by the purchasing capacity of the people, but by the profit motive of the industry and the Central Government is playing the role of a silent onlooker.

The prices of twelve essential drugs before the liberal decontrol of DPCO in 1995 and today are given below.

Table 3.1 |

Name of drug	For treatment	Packing	Price 1995	1998	Percentage increase
Diazepam	Depression	10	3.13	9.50	204%
Ampicillin	Antibiotic	4	12.85	23.15	80%
Cephalexin	Antibiotic	10	45.07	113.15	151%
Ethambutol	Anti T.B.drugs	10	5.92	33.00	457%
Rifampicin	-do-	10	24.00	64.00	167%
Pirazinamide	-do-	10	17.01	46.95	176%
Lignocaine Hcl	Anaesthetic	30 ml	4.16	12.40	198%
Promethaxine Hcl	Anti allergic	10	1.25	3.23	158%
Antacid liq.	Gastritis	200 ml.	13.00	23.00	77%
Oxyfedrine Hcl	Angina pectoris	10	10.44	21.41	105%
Discopyramide Phosphate	Cardiac problems	10	16.50	50.46	206%
Dipyridamole	Anti angina	10	2.00	4.73	137%

The above list is only indicative. Hundreds of such examples can be given.

Further, under the WTO agreement and the imposition of a products patent regime, the prices of all new drugs (patented) will go up without any control of domestic law. The DPCO will become further irrelevant and Indian people's accessibility to newer drugs will be restricted only to the rich of the country. Given below are the high prices of some of the new drugs introduced in 1997 in the Indian market.

Table 3.2 |

Drug	Company	Strength	Pack	Price
Sporanox	Ethnor	100 mg	4 tablets	173.00
Lumicil	Novertis	250 mg	14 capsules	1247.00
Spariex	Sun Pharma	200 mg	6 tablets	154.00
Rispid	Panacea	50 ml	1 mg/ml capsule	141.00
Livial	Infar		28 tablets	1225.00
Pipracil	Cyanamid	2 G	Vial	215.78
Amate	Mesco Pharma	50 mg	12 tablets	180.00
Adnoject	Inca	3 mg	2 ml vial	210.00
Roxisara	Sarabhai	300 mg	6 tablets	165.00
Celex	Glaxo	250 mg	4 tablets	140.00

World-wide concern has been expressed about the sharp rise of drug prices. The WHO's goal of Health for All by 2020 will remain a distant dream.

Moreover, with the rapid development in technology, a greater number of new drugs are being introduced. Experts say that very few of them are having therapeutic advantages over the existing drugs. 'Out of 348 new drugs introduced by 25 big US companies during 1981 to 1988 only 3 per cent made important potential contribution while 84 percent made little or no potential contribution' said the US federal authority. Hence the introduction of new costly drugs should be properly monitored by the central government.

Mass Ending of Jobs

With the reduction of the customs duties on foreign imports many drugs manufactured in India have become unviable compared to the foreign goods in the Indian market. As a result, the owner of these factories are closing down their units and throwing the workers out of employment. Messrs. Boehringer Mannheim, and Parks Davis who were the lone producers of Chloramphenicol in India stopped their production as its prices in the international market were cheaper than the cost of production in India. M/s. Sarabhai Chemicals closed their Vitamin 'C' plant for a similar reason. Like Chloramphenicol and vitamin 'C' many other drugs like paracetamol, metronidazole, ampicillin, amoxycillin etc., are available at a cheaper price in our country from abroad because of the lowering of the customs duties so that Indian factories have closed and workers are on the streets. For the above drugs our country has became dependent on foreign supply.

In their attempt to shift the production to the third party manufacturing already, Hindustan Ciba Geigy, Roche, Abbot, Boehringer Mannheim, Boots, Park Davis, Unichem etc., have closed their factories and offered a voluntary retiring scheme to workers and they have sold the land of their factory premises at a premium price. Apart from these closures, Pfizer, Rhone Poulenc, Hoechst, Glaxo etc., have reduced their work force. *Crores* of rupees have been spent to give VRS. These companies are manufacturing their products with the help of loan licenses. Some of the companies have opened new smaller factories in new places and appointed workers with lower wages and more workload. More casual workers are being appointed. In the last two years in the Mumbai Thane region of Maharashtra around 30,000 workers have lost their jobs in the pharmaceutical industry.

Apart from the factory workers the distribution workers are gradually being replaced by Cost and Freight agency system. In this system, the original company does not have any responsibility for the workers. They are employed by agents with more workload and lower wages. In the last decade around 15 thousand distribution workers have lost their jobs in the pharmaceutical industry. Moreover, through the agency system the Government is deprived of sales tax.

In marketing also the field workers or the sales promotion employees are facing tremendous attacks in the name of franchise, co-marketing, appointment of communicators etc., many permanent sales promotion employees are losing their jobs. Many others are appointed in the name of so-called executives to remove them from the fold of the union. More casual and contractual workers are being recruited.

Table 3.3 |

Company	Year	Reduction of work force
Glaxo	1995	1564
Hoechst	1996	1049
Knoll Pharma (Boots)	1995	600 (All workers)
Smith Kline Beecham	1995	208
E. Merck	1995	194
Rhone Poulenc	1996	700
Hindusthan Ciba Geigy	1993	907
Duphar Interfran	1996	154
Bayer	1996	590
Abbott	1996	All workers
Roche	1996	All 320 workers
Boehringer Mannheim	1997	All 335 workers
Park Davis	1997	All 650 workers
Pfizer	1995	215
Unichem	1997	All workers

(*Source:* Annual reports of respective companies and interaction with the office bearers of Unions).

Thus, the total payment on voluntary retirement schemes by firms like Glaxo, Hoechst, Pfizer, Knoll Pharma, Rhone Poulenc, Park Davis, Smith Kline Beecham, Duphar, Bayer etc., are more than Rs. 200 crores in the last three years. The main important thing is that employment opportunities in these units have been reduced for ever.

Impact on Public Sector

With the reduced role of the state under globalization the public sector drug companies are faced with serious problems including imminent closures. Public sector drug companies like Indian Drugs and Pharmaceuticals Ltd. (IDPL), Hindustan Antibiotics Ltd. (HAL), Bengal Chemicals and Pharmaceuticals Ltd. (BCPL), Bengal Immunity (BI) and Smith Stanistreet Pharmaceuticals Ltd. (SSPL) played an important role in the production of essential drugs at affordable prices. Under the globalization process the role of the public sector has been marginalized and they have been made sick. Attempts have been made to either privatize or close them. The Penicillin Plant in HAL, the biggest in the country, has been handed over to private hands. Its Streptomycin plant also has been leased to a private company for manufacture of other drugs. IDPL which is having the biggest pharmaceutical plant in Asia is closed from 1996 for want of proper financial assistance from the government. The public sector drug companies used to supply raw materials to the small scale sector companies. Now, these companies are facing difficulties in procuring raw materials. Similar is the fate of BCPL, B.I. and SSPL. These three units were taken over by the government after they were made sick by the private owners. Proper utilization of their capacity could not be made due to lack of will on the part of the government, mismanagement at the administrative level and high level corruption.

With the pharmaceutical industry taking a leap towards biotechnology development world-wide, only the public sector drug companies, with the backing of the Central Government, could have faced the challenge effectively from the MNCs in the new situation.

Mergers and Acquisitions

International and national level mergers, acquisitions and takeovers have now become a common phenomenon in the pharmaceutical industry. Internationally American Home Product merged with Cyanamid, SKB with Sterling, Rhone Poulenc took over Fashions, BSF with Boots, Glaxo with Burroughs Welcome, Ciba Geigy with Sandoz, Warner Hindustan with Parke Davis, Hoechst with Rhone Poulenc etc., are some of the examples of big take overs. By mergers and acquisitions these companies became even larger with more financial power at their disposal over their competitors.

In the future, with the help of international financial companies the MNCs will capture and take control of Indian companies to control the Indian market.

To match the situation created by international mergers and takeovers, Indian companies are adopting the same path. For example Wockhardt took over Merind and Tata Pharma, Ranbaxy took over Croslands, Nicholas Piramal took over Roche, Boehringer, Sumitra Pharma. The inevitable results are job loss of workers. Because of overlapping of jobs large numbers of workers are declared surplus. After merger Glaxo-Welcome and Ciba-Sandoz announced a reduction of 15 thousand and 10 thousand of their work force respectively world-wide. Upjohn and Pharmacia decided to close 24 of their 57 plants in different countries after their merger.

Some countries are adopting the 'buy and grow' method. They are taking over some popular brands and increasing their business. SKB took over Crocin from Duphar, Ranbaxy took over 7 leading brands from Gufic, Dr. Reddy's Lab purchased 6 products of Dolphin and two each from Pfimex and SOL Pharma. Sun pharma purchased all leading brands of NATCO, after selling the popular brands the companies are becoming sick and closing their shutters throwing the workers on the street.

The governments permission to the MNCs to come to India with 100% equity have threatened the existing companies with the same origin and their workers.

Through the process of mergers, acquisitions and takeovers MNCs will gradually perpetuate their grip on the Indian industry by the creation of a limited number of mega companies having monopoly control and domination world wide. In the absence of competition people will have to pay any price as it happens in the sellers market.

Conclusion

The present government at the centre is bringing a bill in the winter session of Parliament to change the Indian Patent Act 1970. The change in the Act is not in the interest of the people of the country. Now patents have become an object of business instead of development. Considering the wide gap of industrial and technological development between developed and developing countries monopoly rights through the patent system should not be allowed to the rich nations. Today 85% of the patents are being controlled by the TNCs of the rich nations. 'Globalization is hurting poor people, not just the poor countries. In this process poor countries and poor people will become increasingly marginalized', says the 1997 world development report of UNDP.

The main aim is to impose the conditionality of WTO and to change the Indian Patent Act as MNCs need more markets and are eyeing Asia which is the largest continent of the world where 60% of the world population lives but contributes only 20% of the world pharmaceuticals business. With a high rate of population growth it is expected that the need of drugs will tremendously increase in the third world countries including India in the next millennium. India contributes 16.1% of the world population, but it produces only 1.2% of world drug production. Hence the MNCs are trying to have more control over the pharmaceutical markets of the developing nations.

Developed countries are backing their own big companies to capture markets in other countries even at the cost of the interest of the people there. The United States has successfully battled for the inclusion of strict intellectual property rules in international trade agreements such as NAFTA and GATT. Often the U.S. position has literally been drafted by PhRMA. These trade agreements disregard public health considerations and have forced dramatic changes in the intellectual property rules the world over. Still PhRMA is not satisfied. And when PhRMA is not happy the office of U.S. Trade Representative (USTR) is not happy, says the editorial comment of *Multinational Monitor*.

Table 3.4 | Some top Pharma company mergers in the world

Company	Merger	Year of merger	Value of merged company
Dow Chemicals	Marion Labs	1986	$ 6.21 bn.
Bristol Myers	Squibb Corp	1989	12.09 bn.
Beecham group	Smith, Kline & French	1989	7.9 bn.
American Home Products	American Cynamide	1994	9.7 bn.
Hoffman La Roche	Syntex Lab.	1994	5.3 bn.
Eli Lyly	PCS Health System	1994	4 bn.
Sandoz	Gerber	1994	3.7 bn.
Smith Kline Beecham	Sterling	1994	2.9 bn.
Glaxo	Burroughs Wellcome	1995	14.2 bn.
Hoechst	MMD Roussel	1995	7.2 bn.
Pharmacia	Upjohn	1995	7 bn.
Rhone-Poulenc Rorers	Fison	1995	2.7 bn.
BASF	Boots	1995	1.3 bn.
Ciba Geigy	Sandoz	1996	30.1 bn.
Hoffman la Roche	Comage Ltd.	1997	11 bn.
Hoechst A.G.	Rhone Poulenc	1998	
Astra	Zeneca	1998	67 bn.

Table 3.5 | Percentage of drug production and world population in some countries

Country	% of world drug production	% of world population
USA	28.2%	4.7%
Germany	7.7%	1.5%
France	7.1%	1.1%
U.K.	3.4%	1.1%
Brazil	1.7%	2.8%
India	1.2%	16.1%

3.4 | Indian Pharmaceutical Industry Trends 2010

Indian domestic pharmaceutical market has seen growth at a CAGR of about 12% in the last 5 years. About 67 million Indians are expected to reach the age of 67 years by 2011. People of this age group spends around 3 to 4 times more on drugs than people in younger age groups. This indicates substantial growth of Indian pharmaceutical industry. Patented drugs are expected to have a 10% market share of pharmaceutical industry in 2010. Incomes of people in rural India are on a rise and the distribution network of drugs is also very strong. These factors are contributing to a high growth of India's rural pharmaceutical market. The positive approach towards product patent product has encouraged the Indian pharmaceutical companies to invest more in Research and Development. Indian pharmaceutical market is expected to have compound annual growth rate of 9.5 per cent by 2011.

Indian Pharmaceutical Industry - Future Perspectives

Future trends of Indian pharmaceutical industry seems to be in positive tone. Consumer spending on healthcare services and products has increased in India due to the increasing affordability, shifting disease patterns and modest healthcare reforms. Healthcare budget of an average Indian household is expected to grow from 7% in 2005 to 13% in 2025. The future trends of Indian pharmaceutical industry can be listed as under.

- By 2015, India will probably open a US$ 8 billion market for multi national pharmaceutical companies selling expensive drugs as predicted by the FICCI-Ernst & Young India study.
- The domestic India Pharma market is likely to reach US$ 20 billion by 2015.
- A whopping amount of US$ 6.31 billion will be invested in the Indian pharmaceutical industry as per the estimates of the Ministry of Commerce, Government of India.
- Indian pharmaceutical off-shoring industry is predicted to be a US$ 2.5 billion opportunity by 2012 all because of low cost of R & D.
- Patented drugs are predicted to capture up to a 10% share of the total Indian pharmaceutical industry by 2015 with a market size of US$ 2 billion.
- The branded generics market will continue to dominate the Indian pharmaceutical industry. Sixty one drugs worth US $ 80 billion will go off patent at the US Patent and Trademark Office between 2011 and 2013. Indian pharmaceutical industry is all set to gain from the patent expiry of some blockbuster drugs by producing their generic equivalents. However, the influence of physicians will remain high that will ensure fair competition on the basis of product quality and scientific detailing.
- By 2015, the specialty and super-specialty therapies will account for 45% of the Pharma market. The growing lifestyle disorders, particularly metabolic disorders like diabetes and obesity as well as coronary heart disease and hypertension, cardiovascular, neuropsychiatry and oncology drugs will gain considerable significance.
- Although there will be a shift towards specialty therapies, mass therapies will remain important in the Indian pharmaceutical industry. This will be, primarily due to the gap between the prevalence of common diseases and their treatment rates. Diseases

like anemia, diarrhea, gastro-intestinal & respiratory problems, acute pain, infections etc., is suffered by a large number of population. The growing income levels will also increase spending on basic healthcare and the consumption of mass therapy drugs for acute ailments.

The Indian pharmaceuticals industry has grown reasonably during the past decade and has the potential to transform itself over the next decade too. The domestic Pharma market of India will play a crucial role in fighting the growing diseases. However, the full potential of Indian pharmaceuticals can only be achieved through sustained, progressive and collaborative efforts by the government and the pharmaceutical industry as a whole.

Export and Import of Drugs and Pharmaceuticals

The Indian pharmaceutical industry, now a $17 billion (over Rs 68,000 crore) Industry, has shown tremendous progress in terms of infrastructure development, technology base creation and a wide range of products. It has established its presence and determination to flourish in the changing environment. The industry now produces bulk drugs belonging to all major therapeutic groups requiring complicated manufacturing technologies. Formulations in various dosage forms are being produced in GMP compliant facilities. Strong scientific and technical manpower and pioneering work done in process development have made these possible. The country now ranks 4th worldwide accounting for 8% of world's production by volume and 1.5% by value. It ranks 17th in terms of export value of bulk actives and dosage forms. Indian exports are destined to more than 200 countries around the globe including highly regulated markets of US, Europe, Japan and Australia.

The country is also showing excellent performance on the Pharma export front. The figures of exports under this category during the current decade have been:

(Figures in Rs. Crores)

2001-02	2002-03	2003-04	2004-05	2005-06	2006-07
9751	12826	15213	17857	22116	24942

Technological Strengths

The following attributes constitute the basis of the technological strengths of the Indian Pharmaceutical Industry:

Self-reliance displayed by the production of 70% of bulk drugs and almost the entire requirement of formulations within the country

- Low cost of production
- Low R & D costs
- Innovative Scientific manpower

- Excellent and world-class national laboratories specialising in process development and development of cost effective technologies.
- Increasing balance of trade in Pharma sector.
- An efficient and cost effective source for procuring generic drugs especially the drugs going off patent in the next few years.
- An excellent centre for clinical trials in view of the diversity in population.

Restricted Items for Import

Import of most of the bulk drugs, intermediates and formulations under the rules is free except for a quite a few narcotic drugs & psychotropic substances, that were restricted as per Exim Policy 2002-2007 at the instance of the Department of Revenue. On account of structural similarities and non availability of specific codes for many narcotic drugs & psychotropic substances, a large number of organic chemicals including vital bulk drugs & intermediates required by the Pharma industry were also put under restricted category by virtue of their coverage under 9 residual categories of "Others". Keeping in view the difficulties of a large number of genuine actual users of these substances, at the instance of this Department import restrictions on the narcotic drugs & psychotropic substances including those under "others" were lifted. At the same time a new regime for import of narcotic drugs & psychotropic substances has been brought in by DIRECTOR GENERAL OF FOREIGN TRADE. Import of all Drugs & Pharmaceuticals is subject to registration and other requirements as administered by Drug controller General of India under the provisions of Drugs & Cosmetics Act.

Small Scale Units in Drugs and Pharmaceuticals

As per the guidelines issued by the Ministry of Micro, Small & Medium Enterprises, the investment limit for units to qualify as a small-scale unit is Rs. 5 crore. After latest amendments in the list of items reserved for SSI units in March 2007 only following four items having relevance to the drugs & pharmaceutical industry are left as reserved for exclusive manufacture by the small-scale units:

1. Niacinamide
2. Pyrazolones
3. Lanolin anhydrous
4. Potassium Citrate- industrial grade

Pharmaceutical Advisory Forum

Though Drug Policies announced from time to time, Government of India has been trying to ensure abundant availability of good quality essential pharmaceuticals of mass consumption at reasonable prices. At the same time strengthening the indigenous capability for cost effective quality production of medicines has been an important objective. To help realize this and in order to provide a Forum for a meaningful dialogue amongst all the stakeholders on various issues concerning the drug policy, it was decided to constitute a Pharmaceutical Advisory Forum in the Department of Chemicals & Petrochemicals

The Pharmaceutical Advisory Forum was constituted in July 2004 having following composition:

1. Hon'ble Minister for Chemicals & Fertilizers (Chairman)
2. Hon'ble Minister of State for Chemicals and Fertilizers (Member)
3. Health Ministers of All States/UTs (Members)
4. Secretary, Dep't. of Chemicals & Petrochemicals Government of India. Member)
5. Secretary, Dep't. of Health Government of India. (Member)
6. Chairman, NPPA (Member)
7. Drugs Controller General of India (Member)
8. Joint Secretary (Pharmaceuticals), Department of Chemicals & Petrochemicals (Member Secretary)
9. Member Secretary, NPPA (Member)
10. Director (Pharmaceuticals), Department of Chemicals & Petrochemicals (Convener)
11. Drugs Controller of all States/UTs (Member)
12. Joint Secretary (Drugs), Dept. of Health, GOI (Member)
13. Two representatives of Consumer to be nominated by Dept. of Chemicals & Petrochemicals from each States/UTs. (Member)
14. One representative of Chemist Associations from each States/UTs. (Member)
15. One representative each of Drug Industry Association viz., IDMA, BDMA, OPPI, IPA and AISSPMA. (Member)

Till date three meetings of the Pharmaceutical Advisory Forum have been held at Vigyan Bhavan, New Delhi on 11.02.2006, 23.09.2006 and 15.5.2007 respectively. Important suggestions emanating from the deliberations of these meetings have already received serious consideration and steps are being taken to act upon them.

Pharmaceutical Export Promotion Council

Pharmaceutical Export Promotion Council (Pharmexcil) having its Headquarters at Hyderabad and Regional offices at Mumbai and Delhi, was set up by the Ministry of Commerce and Industry, Government of India vide Notification No 64 dated the 12th May, 2004. Under Para 3.12.1 of Export and Import Policy 2002-2007, Pharmexcil is the only Designated Agency for issue of Registration and Membership Certificates for Pharmaceutical Exports dealing in products/services like:

Bulk Drugs (APIs), Drug Intermediates, Drug Formulations, Biotechnology, Biological Products, Herbal Products (Ayurveda, Siddha & Unani), Medicinal Plants, Homeopathy, Nutraceuticals and Physiochemical, Diagnostics, Contact Research; contract Manufacturing, Clinical Research, Surgical, Collaborative Research and Technologies/ Consultancy.

Objectives: The objectives of the Council (Pharmexcil) are to extend all assistance to the pharmaceutical industry in India to explore their opportunities. Towards achieving this aim, the Council is taking delegations to various countries, organizing Business meets etc., encouraging export activities by arranging fund support under MAI programmes of the Government.

Services: This Council is a Government sponsored single window contact to the world of Pharmaceuticals from India and an only authorized agency for issue of Registration cum Membership Certificate (RCMC) for pharmaceutical exports under Foreign Trade Policy of Government of India. Apart from this, the Council is also providing following

(a) Trade Enquiries received from foreign Embassies /Buyers
(b) Market Development assistance as provided by Ministry of Commerce for business tours to foreign countries.
(c) Arrange one to one Buyer/Seller Meets in India/Abroad.
(d) Arrange Exhibitions in India and Abroad for market promotion.
(e) Assist in Regulatory matters with domestic and Foreign Government agencies.
(f) Provide financial assistance for Product Registration charges, Research and Development, Product showcasing etc., as per rules.
(g) Arrange Conferences/Seminars in domestic and foreign countries - for market and technical up-gradation of information

Working Groups/ Joint Working Groups / Sub-Groups

India-EU Joint Working Group

Under India-EU Sub-Commission on Trade, India-EU Joint Working Group (JWG) on Pharmaceuticals and Biotechnology was set up under the Co-Chairmanship of Joint Secretary (Pharma) since 2006. D.G. Enterprises is the counterpart from the EU side. The first meeting of the said JWG was held on 18th July 2006 at Brussels wherein the Terms of Reference for the JWG was finalized. Its 2nd meeting was held on 30th and 31st May 2007 at New Delhi.

Indo Tunisia Joint Working Group

A Joint Working Group on Drugs & Pharmaceuticals under the Aegis of the Indo-Tunisian Joint Commission has been constituted since 2004. Three meetings have since been held. The Tunisian Government has given permission to 5 Indian Companies for registering their products in Tunisia.

Sub Group on Pharmaceuticals under the aegis of Indo-Russian Working Group on Trade and Economic Cooperation (IRWGTEC)

Under the Indo-Russian Working Group on Trade and Economic Cooperation (IRWGTEC) a sub group on pharmaceuticals is functioning under this Department and provides inputs to IRWGTEC.

Under the said JWG the issues discussed were various areas of cooperation like promotion of Trade and exports of pharmaceuticals to these countries, Joint Venture Cooperation in manufacture as well as R & D, regulatory cooperation, HRD and Training taking part in Exhibitions and Trade Fairs.

Working Group on Drugs and Pharmaceuticals

The report includes a number of measures aimed at accelerating the growth of Indian Drugs and Pharmaceuticals Industry in the globalize scenario and at the same time benefit the common man in line with the Common Minimum Programme of the Union Government. Some of the important measures for the welfare of common man and ensuring growth of the domestic Drugs and Pharmaceuticals Industry as envisaged in the Report include:

(i) Creation of 5 new NIPER like institutions to generate requisite HR in this field.

(ii) Interest subsidy to Pharma Industry for Schedule M compliance.

(iii) Setting up 10 Pharma Parks to provide global environment to the Pharma industry.

(iv) Creation of District Drug Banks for BPL families.

(v) Provision for Price and availability of Cancer medicines Fund.

(vi) Measures for Pharma PSUs welfare including revival of sick PSUs.

(vii) Strengthening and up gradation of infrastructure at NPPA and NIPER and Pharmexcil.

Pharmaceutical Export Promotion Cell

An Export Promotion Cell in the Pharmaceutical Division has been functioning with the objective of boosting pharmaceutical exports and to act as a nodal center for all queries/issues regarding pharmaceutical exports.

In order to give adequate attention to day-to-day problems faced by the exporters, there were interactions with various Ministries/Departments and our Missions abroad. The Cell collects statistical data on export and import of pharmaceuticals in the country and provides commercially useful information for developing and increasing drugs and pharmaceutical exports. It is acting as nodal center for all queries and issues regarding Pharma exports. The Cell also undertakes promotional activities for acceleration of pharmaceutical exports and considers suggestions for modifications in EXIM POLICY from the industry. The Cell has also been entrusted with the organization of seminars and workshops on standards, quality control requirements of important countries so as to prepare the domestic companies for exporting their products. Database on the status of pharmaceutical industry in many countries is available in the cell for the benefit of Indian exporters.

The Department has been associated with Department of Commerce in the promotion of exports and various events by way of GCC Africa and Latin America meets at Hyderabad and CIS meeting in Mumbai were organized. In these events there were interaction between Indian exporters and foreign buyers and regulatory officials.

Pharma exports touched a level of over Rs. 24942 crores during 2006-07. Exports constitute a substantial part of the total production of Pharmaceuticals in India. Another note worthy feature of export is more of dosage form export to advanced markets like Europe, US, CIS Africa etc. The trend of exports is as follows:

Year	Export (Rs. in Crores)
1998-1999	6256.06
1999-2000	7230.16
2000-2001	8757.47
2001-2002	9751.20
2002-2003	12826.10
2003-2004	15213.24
2004-2005	17857.80
2005-2006	22578.98
2006-2007	24942.00

Licensing and FDI Policy

Industrial Licensing for all bulk drugs cleared by Drug Controller General (India), all their intermediates and formulations has been abolished, subject to stipulations laid down from time to time in the Industrial Policy. 100% FDI is also permissible for the manufacture of Drugs and Pharmaceuticals.

Indian Pharmaceutical Industry Strong Medium Term Visibility in Regulated Market Generics and Domestic Growth

- Global generic opportunities over the medium term are supported by large patent expiries and growing generic penetration backed by government initiatives in the regulated markets.

- The domestic formulations business continues to report strong growth aided by increasing expenditure on healthcare; changing disease profile on account of lifestyle related diseases and growing penetration in tier II & III markets.
- For most large Indian pharmaceutical companies, the domestic formulations business has been a core earnings contributor even as other segments face challenges either from increased competition or weak economic scenario globally.
- Globally generics players continue to face competitive environment with increasingly crowded space for filing ANDAs (abbreviated new drug application) challenges as well as aggressive defense by innovators including patent extensions and market authorization. Certain Indian generic majors are pursuing differentiated model with target on niche and "difficult-to- manufacture" molecules. Cost control, however, remains the key to success in the generic business.
- Increasing generic penetration in relatively untapped developed markets such as Japan however offers strong long-term potential as generic companies scout for investment opportunities to establish a foothold in these markets.
- Focus on establishing presence in the branded segment (domestic/semi-regulated markets) through in-organic investments or in-licensing route continues.
- Contract Research & Manufacturing (CRAMS) segment is affected by weak economic environment forcing companies to rationalize inventory levels. Slowdown in investments in new molecule research also affected business for contract research providers. There are, however, early signs of recovery.
- Patent expiries and increasing focus by Governments to reduce healthcare costs continue to put pressure on big pharmaceutical companies to pursue cost reduction including through outsourcing of non-core activities - supporting long-term prospects for CRAMS business. Upfront investments on infrastructure and establishing a diversified clientele, however, remain as challenges facing this segment.
- On the export front, companies are facing increasing working capital engagement in certain semi-regulated markets.
- Exports to the regulated markets would remain a strong growth driver for Indian companies.
- However, in spite of the sheer size of the opportunities, there are significant challenges in this business such as margin pressure; legal issues; parallel launch of authorized generics; access to distribution channels, increasing compliance costs and Government mandated changes in business environment in several countries.
- R & D investments in product development (for generic fillings) and Novel Drug Delivery System (NDDS) research continue to increase. However, investments in New Chemical Entities (NCEs) have generally been curtailed by several players on the back of lackluster response in the initial phase and funding challenges.

- Overall, investments in capital expenditure and acquisitions are likely to remain buoyant in the medium term. Balance sheets of major pharmaceutical companies remain strong providing some room for debt rising.

Growth prospects for Domestic Branded Formulations remain Favorable

The Indian pharmaceutical industry continues to witness 12-14% growth year-on-year driven by increasing expenditure of healthcare; changing disease profile; rising disposable income levels and growing penetration of health insurance besides regulatory reforms. New product introductions contribute to around 6-8% of the total growth, with the rest being contributed by a combination of volume and price increase. Amongst therapeutic areas, chronic segments such as anti-diabetics, CVS, CNS and oncology have been growing at fairly strong rates owing to changing lifestyle patterns and have been the key drivers of growth. The key acute infective, which were affected in the past owing to pricing pressure (as a result of drug pricing control), resulting in lower growth for the industry have also in the recent period reported stable growth. Expanding reach in under-penetrated markets has also supported the growth of companies with a large field force presence. It is estimated that only 35% population has access to modern medicines in the aforementioned under penetrated tier II/III markets.

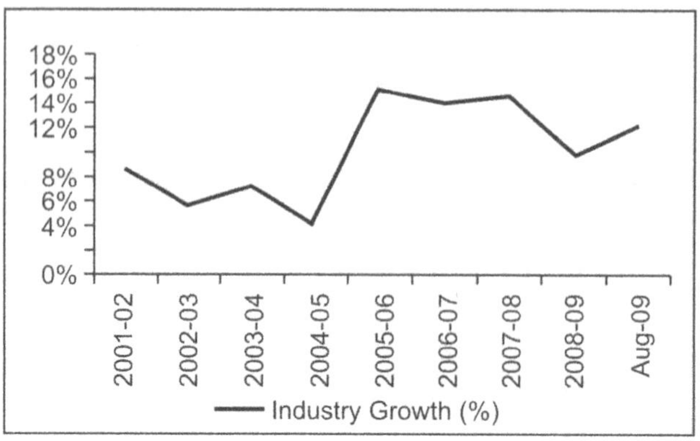

Figure 3.2 |

Source: Industry Research; ICRA Estimates

The industry structure remains highly fragmented, with top ten pharmaceutical companies accounting for only ~35% of total pharmaceutical sales. However, the leading players continue to retain their market share owing to their strong distribution reach, strong field force and new product launches. While the domestic branded formulations business continues to offer high gross margin, many of the innovator companies are now aggressively targeting this segment, which is likely to increase the competitive pressures. Also, potential changes in price control mechanism remain an area of uncertainty for the industry. If the scope of price control is expanded, there could be significant adverse impact on the profitability of domestic branded business.

Profitability indicators remain stable for Formulation Entities

The profitability indicators of leading formulations companies have remained fairly stable over the past six quarters except for marginal fluctuation during October-March 2009. As evidenced below (Fig. 3.3), slight contraction in margins during the aforementioned period was largely on account of spike in input material prices and foreign currency fluctuations during the same period. In spite of competition, profitability in the domestic branded business remains healthy supported by new product launches; investments on branding; increasing presence in chronic segments and above all an efficient operating cost structure.

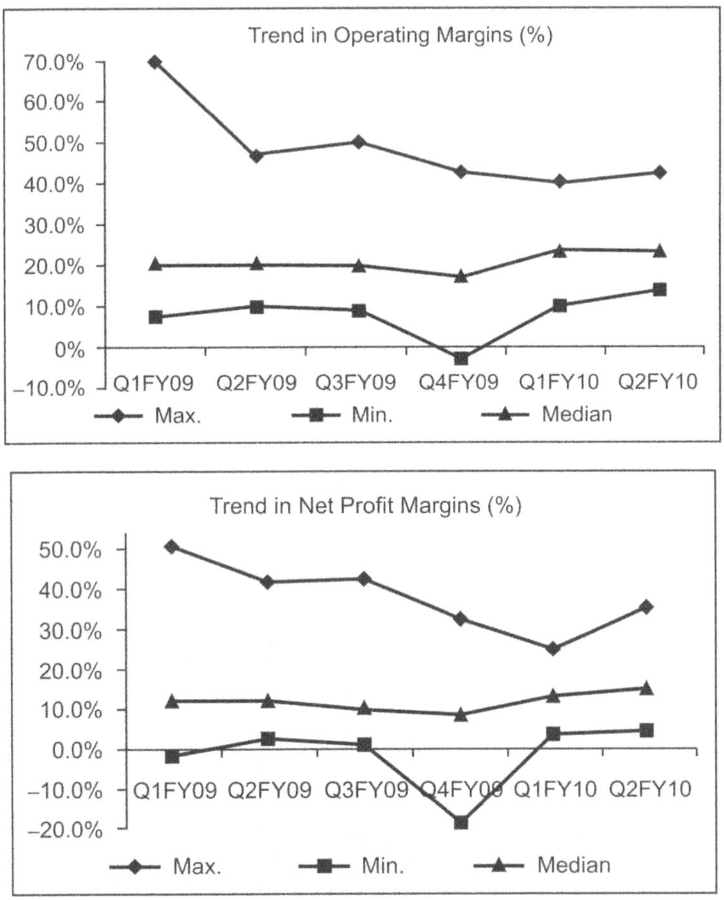

Figure 3.3 | Trend in operating and net margins for formulation companies

Bulk Drug players faced margin contraction during the last fiscal

The sample of Active Pharmaceutical Ingredients (APIs)/Bulk Drugs companies also reported a similar trend with fluctuation in OPBDIT margins during H2 FY09. In terms of return indicators, bulk drug manufacturers typically generate lower return on capital employed as compared to formulation companies owing to higher capital investments. With bulk drug business being completely driven by scale of operations, most Indian companies barring a few large ones are relatively small companies, which results in high product concentration and pricing related vulnerabilities.

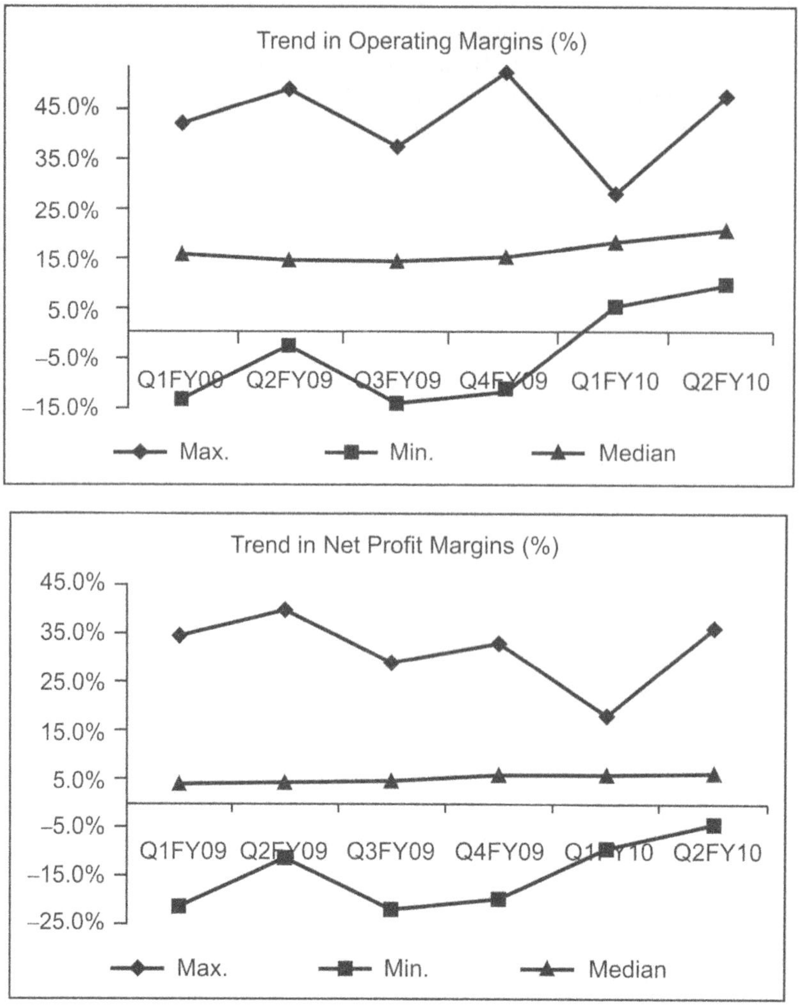

Figure 3.4 | Trend in operating and net margins for API companies

Many small companies in the API segment have been struggling for survival and offer room for consolidation within the industry. The bulk drug companies also remain dependent on Chinese companies for certain key intermediates and there have been instances of disruption in supplies leading to significant adverse impact on their profitability. The Indian generic companies, traditionally a key client segment for API manufacturers, have also backward integrated into bulk drugs (especially for critical APIs for products targeting the developed markets) to have better control on cost and quality, thereby limiting business for pure API players. Amongst Indian companies, entities like Lupin, Aurobindo Pharma, and Matrix Laboratories (acquired by Mylan) have created a meaningful presence in API segment worldwide. Lupin for instance commands a leadership position in the Anti-TB space and a strong position in cephalosporin API/ intermediates and cardiovascular API.

Global trends in generics – moving away towards unbranded generics and tender business

The prospects of the generic business worldwide is supported by large expected patent expiries in developed markets (estimated at ~$235 billion in the period from 2010 to 2015) and growing generic penetration supported by initiatives from Governments and Insurance Companies to control healthcare costs. While the United States remains the largest generic market in the world with a fairly high (~65-70%) generic penetration, the growth potential in some of the smaller developed markets remains higher due to rapid growth in penetration expected over the medium term.

Table 3.6| Some developed markets, their current generic penetration and growth potential

Country	Estimated generic potential	Comments on penetration
Japan	19%	Growing, large market
France	20%	Growing, large market
Spain	18%	Growing
Italy	10%	Growing
USA	~ 65-70%	Mature, large market
Germany	70%	Mature, large market
U.K.	60-65%	Mature, large market
Netherlands	50%	Mature
Poland	70%	Mature
Czech Republic	55%	Mature

Note: *Even mature markets remain lucrative due to potentially large patent expiries and the large size of some of the markets*

A key concern in the developed markets is the rapid increase in healthcare costs, which is aggravated by an ageing population. Some of these markets are shifting away from branded generics to unbranded generics or tender market; in the process, the pricing power of generics companies is getting rapidly eroded. Government legislation and insurance companies are increasingly incentivizing pharmacists/ medical practitioners and patients with lower copayments to prescribe/ substitute branded medicine with cheaper generic alternatives. In addition, the rising bargaining power of large distributors, retailers and insurance companies are potential dampener to pricing power of generic companies. The generic companies also face challenges from adoption of aggressive product life cycle management strategies such as patent extensions, switching to OTC category, product substitution and launch of authorized generics, which can significantly erode attractiveness of the Para I[1] exclusivities. All these have significantly increased the costs and capped potential upsides from patent challenges for generic companies. In the last two years, there has been greater emphasis on patent settlements by Indian generics, which significantly reduces launch uncertainties and litigation costs and hence is a positive. These however are likely to come under greater regulatory scrutiny in the future.

Cost-effectiveness and superior quality remains the key drivers for success in the generics business. However first to file (FTF) opportunities and Para IV related exclusivities continue to provide significant profit upsides in developed markets because of limited competition during these periods. In the absence of a healthy pipeline of FTF/ exclusive products, these one-off upsides could lead to significant volatilities in performances. Most of the large Indian companies in the past have displayed large swings in their performance in developed markets depending on the availability of such one-off upsides in a particular year. This volatility could be corrected only through a strong pipeline of products to ensure steady flows of one-offs over the years. Also, patent settlements help reduce uncertainties in costs and timing of inflows from product launches.

Service levels and product pipelines remain extremely critical in developed markets, especially as these markets are dominated by large distributors/retailers that enjoy tremendous bargaining power. Clearly while low cost is a necessary condition, it does not provide sufficient enough differentiation in the business. Strong management focus on legal and R & D skills is necessary to ensure emphasis on product development of FTF/ exclusive products, which remains a key success factor. A portfolio that includes products beyond commodity generics is necessary to maintain healthy profitability, as competitive pressures drive down prices by up to 99% + post patent expiry in many products. A strong product pipeline can go a long way in sustaining interest of large

[1]The US market offers 180-day exclusivity to successful patent challenges through Para IV fillings, which can potentially offer a large profitable entry in this market

distributors/retailers and capturing of market share. A fewer products with reasonable market share is a more profitable strategy than having large number of products with insignificant market share. Further, generic companies need to develop strong relationships with the channels to ensure an adequate market share. Also in recent periods regulatory compliance for developed markets has been a cause of concern for a number of companies. While most Indian manufacturers have been able to resolve 483s/ regulatory concerns flagged by international regulatory agencies, our discussion with industry indicates that there is likely to be some increase in compliance cost over the near term to meet the quality norms in these markets.

The global generics companies like Teva, Mylan etc., are scaling up rapidly, while Indian companies continue to be relatively small in comparison. The global generics business has been undergoing steady consolidation. In the US generic market, the top four players now account for ~61% market share as compared to around ~35% share 10 years back. Large generic companies like Teva, Sandoz, and Mylan have widely diversified products and a much bigger pipeline as compared to Indian companies. The largest Indian generic players are currently around $1.5 billion in revenues – this is against $5-11 billion range for the three largest players globally. The sheer scale of these entities and the resultant advantages may necessitate some consolidation in the Indian generics business over the longer term.

Japanese market offers new growth avenue for Indian Generic Players

Amongst the key markets outside the United States and Europe, the Japanese market offers potential to drive significant growth in the medium term. With healthcare reforms aimed to reduce healthcare budgets and generic friendly policies being adopted by the Japanese Government, the pharmaceutical market is gradually opening up to generics. The current generic penetration in Japan, estimated at 6-7%, is amongst the lowest in the world. As a result, despite being the second largest pharmaceutical market in the world, the Japanese market ranks only as the sixth largest generic market. The Japanese Government has set a target of reaching a generic penetration of 30% by 2012, implying strong growth potential in the market.

The Japanese pharmaceutical market is characterised by a complex regulatory framework, thereby creating a high entry barrier. Thus, partnerships with local generic companies and/or acquisitions of local companies are emerging as the likely route to gain presence. Indian generic players have also made inroads in the Japanese market. The generic pricing in the market however remains favourable as compared to markets in Europe and the United States. Lupin, Ranbaxy and Cadila Healthcare are amongst the front runners. While Lupin gained access in the Japanese market through the acquisition of Kyowa Pharmaceuticals in 2007. Ranbaxy is exploring opportunities of marketing its generic products through Daiichi's distribution network post its acquisition by the latter.

Table 3.7| Indian generic companies in the Japanese pharmaceutical market

Lupin	Acquired Kyowa Pharmaceutical (generic company) in Japan in FY 08; actively pursuing integration with Indian operations in terms of product launches and material sourcing
Ranbaxy	Aims to leverage its wide-product basket with Daiichi Sankyo distribution network
Cadila Healthcare	Acquired Nippon Universal in 2007. Plans to increase presence through generic launches
Dr. Reddy's Lab.	Plans to establish presence in the Japanese market; Inorganic investment could be a possible route
Torrent Pharmaceutical	Established subsidiary

Aggressive brand defense by Innovators remains a Challenge

Generic business by its nature grows at the expense of branded products on patent expiry, bringing in potential conflict of interest between the two. While generic companies continue to seek ways to accelerate entry into the market through development of non-infringing processes/ patent challenges, innovator companies seek to extend their product life through effective patent defense. In recent times, the pressure on innovator companies has increased due to large impending patent expiries and shrinking new product pipelines. Aggressive product lifecycle management by innovators includes filing new patents; changing product benefit claims and labeling; switching to OTC products and launching of authorized generics. All these have effectively either delayed the entry of generics in the market or reduced benefits from patent challenges, thus restricting potential upsides for generic companies. With rising complexity of brand defense, evaluating likely response by innovator companies to patent challenges remains a critical input in pipeline planning for generic companies.

Strategic Alliances by Innovator Companies

As mentioned earlier, potentially large patent expiries over the next five years and weak pipeline quality have increased the pressure on innovator companies to explore other avenues including generic business. While the global pharmaceutical business is expected to register moderate single digit growths, the growth in generic business is likely to be in double digits, reflecting the attractive potential of the business. Some of the global innovator companies already have their generic arms which are aggressively pursuing the business in all markets. In recent periods, a number of innovator companies have explored alliances and M & A in the generic space. Some examples include the acquisition of Ranbaxy by Daiichi; Zentiva by Sanofi; Glaxo's tie-up with Aspen. In recent periods some of the innovator companies have entered into alliances with Indian generic companies. These alliances are designed to exploit the low-cost manufacturing skills of Indian players with the reach of innovator companies in the branded generic space across world markets.

Table 3.8| Collaborations by Indian companies

Companies	Partner	Comment
Aurobindo Pharma	Pfizer	100 plus oral dosages across NA, Europe, LA and Asia across CVS, CNS and anti-infective space
Dr. Reddy's Limited	GlaxoSmithKline Plc	To market its portfolio of products across emerging markets outside India, including co-marketing arrangements
Strides Arcolab	Pfizer	Generic oncology products, primarily injectibles for the US market
Claris Life sciences	Pfizer	Sterile injectibles covering anti-infective, antibiotics and other critical care products

M&A activities by Indian Companies

Acquisitions have played a vital role for Indian companies in establishing their presence in international markets. Most acquisitions have either been in the generic or CRAMS space. Only a handful of acquisitions have been in the $200 million plus range, with a majority being small-sized acquisitions in value terms. Investments in generic space have been aimed at gaining presence in newer markets and acquiring marketing and distribution front-end. In the CRAMS space, access to new clients and technologies has been key rationale for acquisitions. The initial phase of investments has been in regulated markets (European Union and North America). However, the focus is now shifting to semi-regulated markets in Africa, Latin America, and South-East Asia. These markets offer potential for profitable growth with relatively easier regulatory pathways. Except for certain transactions, most acquisitions have in relatively small sized.

The performance of the investments by Indian companies overseas has so far been a mixed bag. Unanticipated change in market dynamics, inability to move sourcing to low-cost locations and contract cancellation have been some of the factors affecting performance. Certain companies have also faced challenges in securing new contracts, particularly in the CRAMS space. Unanticipated changes in market dynamics like those in Germany (market moved rapidly from branded generics to tender market) have also eroded value for some acquisitions. Indian companies are also looking at in-licensing opportunities to enter into the branded segment in regulated markets through patent acquisitions.

Biogenerics space offers strong long-term potential; Indian Companies Stepping up Investments

In addition to strong potential offered by patent expiries, generic companies are also eyeing the dissimilar space as a key long-term growth potential avenue. As per industry estimates, nearly 41 molecules worth US$ 57 billion in sales in the biopharmaceutical space are expected to go off patent over the in the future.

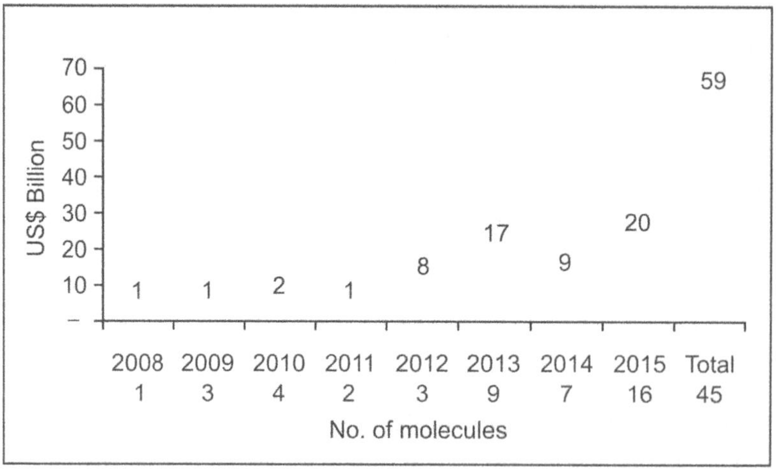

Figure 3.5 | Worldwide sales (in US $ billion) of biologics by patent expiration

Generic majors as well Indian generic companies have stepped up investments in this space and expect to tap the emerging opportunity. While the segment does offer strong potential, uncertainties related to clear regulatory pathway for bioequivalence studies act as a restraint. Moreover, the biologics space is also characterized by technology barriers in terms of complex product development & production process besides being highly capital intensive segment. Strategic alliances between generic and biotech companies are likely to strengthen in the future. Generic major – Teva has collaborated with Lonza to capitalize on biologics development & manufacturing expertise and infrastructure. Amongst Indian companies, Dr Reddy's, Biocon and Lupin are amongst the front runners in this space and are at present in the investing in product development.

Significant up-front investments and client relationships is the key in CRAMS

With innovator companies focusing on cost rationalization, outsourcing opportunities across the value chain - from low volume drug discovery activities to higher volume commercial scale manufacturing - have emerged over the past few years. Within the CRAMS segment, Indian companies such as Piramal Healthcare, Jubilant Organosys, Dishman Pharmaceuticals, and Divi's Labs have invested significantly in establishing expertise and infrastructure across contract research and manufacturing space. While contract research largely involves providing drug discovery and development services, contract manufacturing includes outsourcing manufacturing of intermediates and APIs as per the specific requirements of innovator/generic companies. Establishing relations with several innovator companies is a necessary precursor in scaling up this business, which also entails significant investments in manufacturing and R & D capabilities. Innovator companies typically look for strong R & D capabilities and human resources as the key criteria while selecting contract research companies, while the ability to ensure low-cost manufacturing is seen as their key strength.

CRAMS affected by inventory rationalization measures and tight fund raising environment

The CRAMS space witnessed subdued performance during the last 12-18 months as global pharmaceutical companies adopted inventory rationalization as one of the cost reduction initiative in view of the tight credit conditions. The contract research space was also affected by lower contract research orders from smaller innovator R & D and biotech companies that faced funding constraints as risk aversion to fund new projects increased. During the earlier period, several contract research players faced significant slowdown in orders from key clients. Given such a scenario, players such as Piramal Healthcare gradually moved part of its business from international assets to Indian facilities. While performance of key CRAMS players has been lackluster in the current fiscal as well, our recent discussion with industry players suggest that inventory de-stocking is nearing completion and fund raising for small and medium-sized innovator companies appears to be easing. This trend is early to assess, but could lend some stability to the business environment.

Players focusing on collaborations in the Drug Discovery Space

Besides providing pure vanilla contract research services, leading Indian contract research led companies have also been targeting collaborative approach in the drug discovery space with leading innovators companies, demonstrating their importance within the overall drug discovery and development value chain. Companies such as Biocon and Jubilant Organosys have been that front run of such transactions.

Outlook

In 2008-09, while most sectors have faced some challenges emerging from global economic slowdown, the pharmaceutical industry world-wide and generic business in particular has been relatively recession proof except for certain specific segments. Some large players in India witnessed significant financial stress during 2008-09 – most of it was related to impact of forex fluctuations on derivatives exposure and foreign currency liabilities. The other areas involving some stress included large acquisitions – some of the large overseas acquisitions by Indian companies failed to deliver in expected lines due to reasons ranging from unexpected changes in the business environment to contract cancellations (in CRAMS business). In third-party API business there have been sharp fluctuations in performance, contributed by a large fluctuation in raw material costs. Also, many of these API units remain vulnerable due to relatively high product and/or client concentration.

Table 3.9| Key collaborations for leading companies

Company	Association with	Comments
Jubilant Organsys	Eli Lilly	Targeting multiple therapeutic areas; functional outsourcing across
		all discovery functions with joint venture for drug development
	Forest Labs	Collaboration in the area of metabolic disorder
	Astra Zeneca	To deliver steady streams of discovery programmes; eligible forresearch funding spanning over five years
Biocon	Bristol Myers Squibb	Research partnership
	Mylan	Collaboration to develop and manufacture generic biologics
	Amylin	Collaboration to develop and manufacture novel peptide therapeutic for potential treatment of diabetes
Zydus Cadila	Eli Lilly	Collaboration for drug discovery and development in the cardiovascular space
	Kara Bio	Collaboration for drug discovery and development for treatment of inflammatory disorders

Exports to the regulated markets would remain a strong growth driver for Indian companies. However, there are multiple challenges such as margin pressure; legal issues; parallel launch of authorized generics; access to distribution channels, increasing compliance costs and Government mandated changes in business environment in several countries. Margin pressures continue in the regulated generics markets because of a host of factors, such as increasing competition from India and other low-cost manufacturing locations; more aggressive brand defense by innovator companies (through authorized generics, for instance); increasing bargaining power of large distributors in these markets and pressure from Government and insurance companies to cut costs. Further, the attractiveness of the US market has suffered some setback, especially for the large generics targeting exclusivity. The reasons include, among others, legal challenges by patent holders, which delays and increase the cost of launch; and authorized generics taking away a large market share and profit from the generic patent challenger during exclusivity periods. These factors have sharply impacted the exclusivity-related profits that generic players seek from the US market. The attractiveness of relatively fragmented European market and new markets like Japan however has increased as generic penetration continues to rise rapidly in these markets.

While the supply-side environment for the generics business in major export markets appears to have turned adverse, the same is partly mitigated by the favorable outlook for the demand side. An ageing population and increase in healthcare costs continue to put pressure on all major Pharma markets like the United States, Europe and Japan, thereby encouraging higher penetration of generics through a mix of legislation and incentives to doctors and pharmacies.

For formulations companies, the domestic branded generics business has traditionally been the cash cow, providing steady cash flows that serve as a buffer against the uncertainties of international ventures. The growth prospects continue to remain strong on back of increasing healthcare awareness, rising penetration in semi-urban and rural markets and changing disease profile. Most MNC Pharma majors have also stepped up their focus on Indian market exploring opportunities of expanding their product portfolio. Uncertainty related to potential changes in the scope of price control, however, remains a negative. Regulatory price controls are however an integral part of the Pharma business world-wide. The risks of adverse developments in the domestic market also highlight the importance of geographical diversification as a risk mitigating measure in the Pharma industry.

On the CRAMS front, Indian players are focusing on providing services across the value chain spanning from development stage to commercial scale production. Relatively lower exposure to small biotech companies has been a risk mitigant during the downturn for these entities. With several drugs going off-patent and big Pharma increasing exposure to cost efficient sourcing locations, opportunities remain favorable for CRAMS players to provide developmental services and subsequently graduate to commercial scale production.

ICRA currently has 46 entities with long-term ratings (excluding 'SO' ratings) in the pharmaceutical sector. About 17% of these entities are rated in the 'AA' category. Most of these entities have a fairly strong and profitable domestic branded formulations business, which has been a stable source of cash flows over the years. Around 22% of the entities are rated in the non-investment graded. Most of these entities are relatively small entities, often in API business and suffer from high product and or client concentration.

Financials of Formulation Companies

Table 3.10| Median of formulation companies – annual audited numbers

In Million	2009	2008	2007	2006
Revenue	15,427	13,016	12,273	9,752
Gross profit	6,032	4,827	4,668	3,846
OPBDIT	3,048	2,497	2,545	1,594
Net profit	780	1,766	1,699	1,024
Net cash accrual	818	1,436	1,600	820
OPM (%)	19.9%	19.0%	18.7%	16.9%
NPM (%)	9.8%	12.0%	12.7%	10.3%
RoCE (%)	21.7%	21.9%	20.6%	15.5%
TD/ OPBDIT	1.6	1.8	1.7	2.6
TD/ TNW	0.8	0.6	0.6	0.6
FFO/TD	0.4	0.2	0.3	0.2
Debtors	76	86	81	76
Inventory	112	128	114	129
NWC/OI (%)	30.1%	36.2%	29.5%	33.2%

Note: Year ending 2009 include audited year ending Mar-09 and Dec-08 and so on

List of ICRA (industrial credit rating agency) Rated Entities

Table 3.11| List of ICRA rated formulation companies

S. No.	Company Name	Long-Term Rating	Short-Term Rating
1	Amneal Pharmaceuticals Limited	LBB	
2	Biological E Limited	LBB+	A4+
3	Bliss GVS Pharma Limited	LBBB	A3+
4	Cadila Pharmaceuticals Limited	LBBB+ (stable)	A2+
5	Dr. Reddy's Laboratories Limited	LAA+	A1+
6	Fresenius Kabi Oncology Limited	LBBB+	A2+
7	Ind Swift Limited	LBBB	A3+
8	Indoco Remedies Limited	LA+ (stable)	A1+
9	Intas Pharmaceuticals Limited	LAA	A1+
10	Khandelwal Laboratories Private Limited	LBBB- (stable)	A3

Table 3.11 *Contd...*

S. No.	Company Name	Long-Term Rating	Short-Term Rating
11	Lupin Limited	LAA+	A1+
12	Merck Limited	LAA	A1+
13	Natco Pharma Limited.	LA+	A1
14	Piramal Healthcare Limited	LAA	A1+
15	Ranbaxy Laboratories Limited		A1+
16	Tablets (India) Limited	LBBB-	A3
17	Torrent Pharmaceuticals Limited	LAA	A1+
18	Troikaa Pharmaceuticals Limited	LBBB-	A3
19	Twilight Litaka Pharma Limited	LBBB	A2
20	Unichem Laboratories Limited		A1+

Table 3.12| List of ICRA rated bulk drug companies

S. No.	Company Name	Long Term- Rating	Short Term- Rating
1	Aarti Drugs Limited	LBBB+ (stable)	A2
2	Anu's Laboratories Limited	LBBB	A3+
3	Apex Drugs & Intermediates Limited	LBBB-	A3
4	Arch Pharmalabs Limited		A1
5	Biocon Limited	LAA+	A1+
6	Dhanuka Laboratories Limited	LBB+	A4+
7	Elam Pharma Private Limited	LB+	A4
8	Enaltec Labs Private Limited	LBB-	A4
9	Hikal Limited	LB+	A4
10	Ind Swift Laboratories Limited	LBBB+	A2+
11	Megafine Pharma (P) Limited	LBBB- (stable)	A3
12	Novodigm Limited	LA-	A1
13	Sara Exports	LBB+	A4+
14	Shasun Chemicals & Drugs Limited	LBBB- (negative)	A3
15	Shodhana Laboratories	LBBB	A2
16	Sri Krishna Pharmaceuticals Limited	LBBB-	A3
17	SR Drugs &Intermediates Pvt. Limited	LBBB-	A3
18	Surya Pharmaceutical Limited	LBBB-	A3
19	Unimark Remedies Limited	LBBB+	A2
20	Vamsi Labs Limited	LB-	A4

Table 3.13 | List of Other Pharmaceutical Companies rated by ICRA

S. No.	Company Name	Long-Term Rating	Short-Term Rating
1	Akums Drugs & Pharma Limited	LBBB+	A2+
2	Aurigene Discovery Technologies Limited	LAA+ (SO)	A1+ (SO)
3	Biocon Biopharma Private Limited	LAA (SO)	
4	Clinigene International Limited	LAA(SO)	A1+(SO)
5	Enem Nostrum Remedies Private Limited	LB+	A4
6	Medreich Limited	LBBB	A2
7	Merck Specialities Private Limited		A1+
8	Next Wave India	LBB+	A4+
9	RFCL Limited	LA-	A1
10	Rusan Pharma Limited	LBBB-	A3
11	Syngene International Limited	LAA-	A1
12	Sai Advantium Pharma Limited	LBBB-	
13	TIL Exports Private Limited	LBBB-	A3

Note- Other Pharmaceutical Companies mainly include contract research and manufacturing companies

Key Acquisitions by Indian Companies

Table 3.14 | Key acquisition concluded/announced by major pharmaceutical companies during the last two year

Company	Acquisition	Details	Rationale/Key Benefits
Dr. Reddy's Laboratories	Dow Pharma's small molecule business in the UK	**Region** – Europe (two sites in the UK) **Area** – CRAMS **Investment** – US$ 32.1 million	Complements DRL's existing custom pharmaceutical business through access to relevant customers, process technology, associated products and R & D team; Contributed Rs. 1,021 million to DRL's turnover in FY09.
	BASF's formulation manufacturing unit in the US	**Region** – USA **Area** – CRAMS **Investment-** US$ 40,466	Access to contract manufacturing of generic prescription and OTC products in the US market through customer contracts, related ANDAs and NDAs and a manufacturing facility.

Table 3.14 *Contd...*

Company	Acquisition	Details	Rationale/Key Benefits
	Jet Generici SRL	**Region** – Europe (Italy) **Area** – Generics **Investment** – Euro 2.34 million	Establish presence in the Italian generic market; provides access to product portfolio, a pipeline of registration applications and a marketing set-up.
Piramal Health care	Minrad International Inc. & RxElite	**Region** – USA **Area** – Generic Inhalation Anesthetics **Investment** – US$ 52 million (including US$ 12 million for working capital)	Strengthen presence in the global inhalation anesthetics segment through access to process-based intellectual property for two main products i.e., sevoflurane and desflurane. RxElite's acquisition allows access to sales & distribution network for Minrad in the US.
Lupin Limited	Kyowa Pharmaceuticals	**Region** – Japan **Area** – Generics **Investment** – US$ 63 million*	Establish a strong foothold in a relatively complex & highly regulated Japanese market; Kyowa is positioned as the tenth largest generic company in Japan.
	Harmason Pharma	**Region** – Germany **Area** – Generics **Investment** – Rs. 311 million	Access to German market through an approved product pipeline and an established field force
	Pharma Dynamics	**Region** – South Africa **Area** – Generics **Investment** – Rs. 901 million**	Access to South African generic market through an established distribution and marketing set-up
Ranbaxy	Zenotech Laboratories	**Region** – India **Investment** – Rs. 1,385 million***	Strengthen presence in the areas of biosimilars and oncology (injectibles)
	Vectra Pharma		
Jubilant Organsys	Draxis Pharmaceuticals	**Region** – North America **Area** – CRAMS **Investment** – US$ 253 million	Strengthens Jubilant's CRAMS business in North America with capabilities to manufacture sterile and non-sterile products and provides access to the niche radiopharmaceuticals market.

Table 3.15 | Key acquisition concluded/announced by major pharmaceutical companies during the last two years

Company	Acquisition	Details	Rationale/Key Benefits
Jubilant Organsys	Hollister Stier Laboratories LLC	**Region** – North America **Area** – CRAMS **Investment** – US$ 140.7 million	Strengthens Jubilant' CRAMS business with addition of contract manufacturing of sterile injectibles
Zydus Cadila	Etna Biotech	**Region** – Italy **Area** – Vaccines **Investment**	Access to a highly evolved research platform for developing new vaccines and technology
	Quimica e Farmaceutica Nikkho do Brasil Ltda. (Nikkho)	**Region** – Brazil **Area** – Generics **Investment** – US$ 26 million	Entry into the Brazilian branded generics market through established therapeutic products and sales network
	Simayla Pharmaceuticals	**Region** – South Africa **Area** – Generics **Investment**	Entry into the South African generics market through the well established product portfolio and marketing setup of the acquired company
	Laboratorios Combix	**Region** – Spain **Area** –Generics **Investment**	Strengthens the company's presence in Europe through an entry into the Spanish generics market
Wockhardt	Negma Laboratories	**Region** – France **Area** – Generics **Investment** – US$ 265 million	Access to a portfolio of patents and help establish the company as the biggest Indian pharmaceutical player in Europe with an entry into the French generics market
	Morton Grove	**Region** – USA **Area** – Generics **Investment** – US$ 38 million	Strengthens the company's position in the US market through an established portfolio of 31 products
Dishman Pharma	Vitamins & fine chemicals businesses of Solvay Pharmaceuticals, BV	**Region** – Netherlands **Area** – Vitamins **Investment**	Provides an opportunity to the company to bring fine chemical expertise to India
Sun Pharma	TaroPharmaceutical Industries Ltd.	**Region** – North America **Area** – Generics **Investment** – US$ 454 million	Strengthens the company's position in North America by leveraging on Taro's strong product portfolio and manufacturing facilities

Table 3.15 ***Contd...***

Company	Acquisition	Details	Rationale/Key Benefits
	Chattem Chemicals, Inc.	**Region** – USA **Area** – API **Investment** Undisclosed	Strengthens the company's presence in the controlled (narcotic) substance API business
Glenmark	Seven Formulation brands of Actavis and Biovena	**Region** – Poland **Area** – Generics **Investment**	Strengthens company's presence in the European generics market through entry into Poland
	Medicamenta	**Region** – Europe **Area** – Generics **Investment**	Provides entry into two of the fastest growing European markets viz. Czech Republic and Slovakia through the established sales & marketing setup and EU GMP approved manufacturing facility
Aurobindo Pharma	TAD Italy	**Region** – Italy **Area** – Generics **Investment**	Entry into the highly regulated Italian generic market through more than 70 ready-to-market products

Review Questions

1. Explain the progress of Pharma Industry in the last 3 decades in India?
2. Explain the future trends and prospects of Pharma Industry in India?
3. Discuss the role of Pharma Industry in Indian economic progress and nation building?
4. Explain export and import potential of pharmaceuticals in India?
5. Explain the basic drug research progress in the country?
6. Add a note on the following (a) strengths and weakness of Indian Pharma. Industry.
7. Explain the role of public sector units in Pharma. sector in India?
8. Write short notes on the following:
   (a) global Pharma industry challenges.
   (b) Hindustan antibiotics Ltd.
9. Explain the market share of different therapeutic categories in India?
10. Write short notes on the following
    (a) structure of Pharma industry in India
    (b) export and import trade.

4 Organisation of Distribution and Marketing

4.1 | Marketing and Functions of Marketing

LEARNING OBJECTIVES

- *Marketing and Functions of Marketing*
- *Marketing Mix*
- *Product Life Cycle*
- *Strategies for the different stages of the Product Life Cycle*
- *Channels of Distribution*
- *Role of middlemen in the distribution of goods*
- *Sales Promotion*

What is Marketing?

Marketing is defined as the process of determining the needs and wants of consumers and being able to deliver products that satisfy those needs and wants. Marketing includes all of the activities necessary to move a product from the producer to the consumer. *Think of marketing as a bridge from the producer to the consumer.*

Marketing starts with market research, a learning process in which marketers get to know everything they can about the needs and wants of consumers, and it ends when somebody buys something. Many companies feel that services provided to customers after the purchase also are an important part of marketing. All of these enterprises -- production, advertising, transportation, processing, packaging, and selling -- are included in the marketing process.

The Nine Functions of Marketing

In order for the marketing bridge to work correctly -- providing consumers with opportunities to purchase the products and services they need -- the marketing process must accomplish nine important functions.

The functions are:

Buying: People have the opportunity to buy products that they want.

Selling: Producers function within a free market to sell products to consumers.

Financing: Banks and other financial institutions provide money for the production and marketing of products.

Storage: Products must be stored and protected until they are needed. This function is especially important for perishable products such as fruits and vegetables.

Transportation: Products must be physically relocated to the locations where consumers can buy them. This is a very important function. Transportation includes rail road, ship, airplane, truck, and telecommunications for non-tangible products such as market information.

Processing: Processing involves turning a raw product, like wheat, into something the consumer can use, for example, bread.

Risk-Taking: Insurance companies provide coverage to protect producers and marketers from loss due to fire, theft, or natural disasters.

Market Information: Information from around the world about market conditions, weather, price movements, and political changes, can affect the marketing process. Market information is provided by all forms of telecommunication, such as television, the internet, and phone.

Grading and Standardizing: Many products are graded in order to conform to previously determined standards of quality. For example, when you purchase No.1 Potatoes, you know you are buying the best potatoes on the market.

The Four Utilities of Marketing

The marketing process must also add "utility" to the products consumers want. Utility is the use or satisfaction a person gets from a product. If you purchase a chain saw you anticipate that you will receive a certain amount of utility from it. You will be able to use the saw to cut fire wood, prune trees, and take care of a variety of jobs around your home. There are four types of utility.

Form Utility: a product must be processed into a form that the customer wants or needs. For example, wheat is processed into bread, trees are processed into lumber, and potatoes are processed into french fries. If you ordered french fries with your lunch and the waiter brought you a raw potato, you probably wouldn't be too happy.

An example of ***Form Utility.*** involves transporting products to the location where consumers can buy them. If you live in HYDERABAD, you certainly wouldn't want to have to drive to kurnool to buy oranges. Thanks to our modern transportation systems you don't have to; you simply drive to the local grocery store and oranges are there ready to add to your shopping cart -- place utility.

Trucking is one form of transportation that helps add **Place Utility** to products.

Possession Utility: Possession utility establishes legal ownership of a product. When you purchase something you normally receive a receipt; this provides legal ownership and the right to use the product. Some products, computer software, for example, also provide a user license. A license of this kind gives you the right to use the product within certain guidelines. *Stock certificates are proof of ownership.*

Stocks prove that you own part of a company. This is an example of **Possession Utility.**

Time Utility: This could be described as being in the right place at the right time when a customer is ready to purchase a product. Creating and keeping customers means having products available for when they want them, and often this requires some type of storage facility. Wheat is one example of a commodity that must be stored after it is harvested. It is stored in silos until processors are ready to convert it into food products such as bread or cereals.

Silo is used to store grain products like wheat. This allows the product to be used by people when they need it; an example of ***Time Utility.***

4.2 | Marketing Mix

Introduction

The basic task of marketing is the delivery of product(s) to consumers so that their needs are fulfilled and organisational objectives are also achieved. This involves several important decisions, e.g. deciding about the product or products which should be offered for sale, price of the product, markets where products may sell and the means of communication with the consumer for the sale of the product. All these decisions form part of marketing-mix.

Concept and Characteristics of Marketing Mix

The process of marketing or distribution of goods require particular attention of management of business because production has no relevance unless products are sold. Marketing mix, simply stated, is the process of designing and integrating various elements of marketing in such a way as to ensure the achievement of enterprise objectives

The elements of marketing mix have been classified under four heads - product, price, place and promotion. That is why marketing mix is said to be a combination of 4 P's.

Decisions relating to the product include product designing, packaging and labelling and varieties of the product. Decision on 'Price' is very important because sales depend to a large extent on product pricing. Whether uniform price will be charged or different prices will be charged for the same product in different markets are examples of decision pertaining to the price of the product.

The third important element is 'place', which refers to decision regarding the market where products will be offered for sale. 'Promotion' involves decisions bearing on the ways and means of increasing sales.

Different tools or methods may be adopted for this purpose. The relative importance to be attached to the various methods is decided while concentrating on the element of 'promotion' in marketing mix, lastly, the marketing manager has to take into account the impact of external factors like consumer behaviour, competitors' strategy, and Government policy on each element of marketing mix.

In short, marketing mix involves decisions regarding products to the made available, the price to be charged for the same, the incentives to be provided to the consumers in the markets where products would be made available for sale. These decision are taken keeping in view the influence of marketing forces outside the organisation.

Characteristics of Marketing Mix

(i) ***Marketing-mix is the crux of marketing process:*** Marketing mix involves many crucial decisions relating to each element of the mix. The impact of the mix would be the best when proper weightage is assigned to each element and they are integrated so that the combined effect leads to the best results.

(ii) Marketing mix has to be reviewed constantly in order to meet the changing requirements.

(iii) The marketing manager is required to constantly review the mix and conditions of the market, and make necessary changes in the marketing mix according to changes in the conditions and complexion of the market.

(iv) Changes in external environment necessitate alterations in the mix:

(v) Changes keep on taking place in the external environment. For many industries, customer is the most fluctuating variable of environment. Customers' tastes and prefrances change very fast. Brand loyalty and purchasing power too change over a period of time. The marketing manager has to carry out market analysis constantly to make necessary changes in the marketing mix.

(vi) Changes taking place within the firm too necessitate changes in marketing mix:

(vii) Changes within the firm may take place due to technological changes, or changes in the product line, or changes in the size and scale of operation. Such changes call for correspondent changes in the marketing mix.

(viii) Marketing mix should be so planned that it fulfills the needs of the consumer as well as the organisation.

Elements of Marketing Mix

As mentioned earlier the elements or constituents of marketing mix may be grouped broadly under four heads:

(i) Product (ii) Price (iii) Promotion (iv) Place

(i) Product: Product refers to a physical product or a service or an idea which a consumer needs and for which he is ready to pay. Physical products include tangible goods like grocery items, garments etc. Services are intangible products which are offered and purchased by consumers. Services may involve also an innovative idea on any aspect of operation.

Products is the key element of any marketing mix. The decisions concerning product may relate to –

(a) Product attributes
(b) Branding
(c) Packaging and labelling
(d) Product support service
(e) Product mix.

Product attributes refer to the quality, features and design of the product. A product should serve the purpose for which it is made, in terms of utility and quality. In a competitive market, products are differentiated on the basis of certain features or design. For example, in the whirlpool washing machine. 'Agitate wash' is the distinctive feature.

Branding is a crucial decision. In a competitive market, many products are sold by brand names. You might have come across Indian brand names, like Maruti, HMT, Godrej, TATA. Amongst foreign brand names Sony, Samsung are well known. Brand is an identification of product. It plays an important role in creation of demand while branding a product, it should be ensured that the name is simple, easy to read and pronounce and if possible, it should have an appeal.

Packaging and labelling of product are quite important decisions Packaging means putting the products in suitable containers or packets such as tin, plastic jar or card board box, etc. Packaging should be such that product is protected and easily handled. Sometimes, the container may have its own usefulness. For instance Baidyanath chyawanprash (pack) is available in a plastic jar which can be reused after consuming the chyawanprash. Certain polythene and plastic are not considered good as packaging material from the environment point of view. Their usage should be avoided.

Labelling serves the purpose of indicating the contents, weight or measure, instructions for use, price, name of the producer, date of manufacture and expiry, etc. The information on the label is essential for various reasons. For example, the date of expiry in case of medicines, and date of manufacture in the case of eatables prevent the sale of products which may prove harmful.

Product support service is another important element of product decision. It includes decision pertaining to the type of service and availability of the service. Service may be by way of installation service, training in product use, after sale service, credit and financing service, etc. It should be decided whether services would be provided free or against separate charge. Secondly, how the services would be made available by the producers or agencies, are also important decisions to be made particularly with respect to durable consumer goods like TV, washing machines electric fans, etc.

The markets in which products will be offered is yet another important decision. A company may decide to a single or a variety of products, add new products, or withdraw certain products. Relevant decisions are made keeping in view the scope of marketing. Such decisions are called product line or product mix decisions. Product life cycle is a guiding factor while decisions are made.

***Product Life Cycle*:** Product life cycle denotes different stages through which the sale of any product changes over a period of time. Generally, there are four stages in the life of each product–introductory stage, growth stage, maturity stage, and declining stage. When any product is introduced in the market, heavy expenditure is incurred on advertising and other methods of increasing the sale. This is known as introductory stage.

During the growth period, sale of the product increases fast and cost of production comes down due to increase in scale of production. Profits earned increase substantially. During the maturity stage, the growth in sale of the product slows down. Profits also start declining. After the maturity stage there is a stage of decline, when the product starts losing its acceptance. There is a pressure for price cut. Firms generally start withdrawing the product after maturity stage. Some firms start preparing for introducing alternative product at the end of growth stage. Product life cycle, thus, helps in deciding about the product or products which should be offered in different markets.

(ii) Price: Price is the amount charged for a product or service. It is the consideration paid by consumers for the benefit of using any product or service. Price fixation is an important aspect of marketing. Pricing decisions of a company are affected by both internal as well as external factors.

Internal Factors External Factors

- Cost of the product – Nature of market
- Marketing objectives Pricing or demand for product
- Marketing mix strategy Decision – Competitors' costs and strategy price offers.
- Organisation for pricing – Other environmental factors like economy, government's policies, etc.

***Internal factors*:** Internal factors, affecting the price of a product, are many. Cost of the product sets the floor. Any company would like to charge a price which covers the cost of the product and a fair rate of return. Cost of the product means total cost i.e., fixed plus variable costs. Fixed costs do not change with the change in volume of production upto a certain level. Variable costs change proportionately. In the period of recession, companies continue to supply at a rate which covers variable costs and as much of costs as possible.

The Company's marketing objective is yet another important variable for price fixation. If it is survival, the company would stay in the market as long as it covers variable costs fully and fixed costs partly. In case it is market leadership, a low price will be fixed initially. After wards prices may be enhanced. 'Surf Excel' is an example. At the time of introduction, its price was just equal to other close substitutes, but today it has its own market. It is bought by consumers without comparing its price with other substitutes.

The relative importance of pricing decision in marketing mix, also affects price fixation. Sometimes pricing decision is the control decision and all other decisions are taken afterwards. It may also happen that other variables of marketing mix like promotion become more important. Price is fixed after considering other variables. Who will fix the price is yet another important decision. In small organisations, top management sets the price. In large companies, product line managers perform this job. For industrial markets, sales managers are permitted to negotiate prices within a specified range. These days many companies set up a separate department to handle pricing decision.

***External factors*:** Besides internal factors, external factors also influence the pricing decision of a company. These factors are called environmental factors. Nature of demand, competitors' costs, price offers and government policy are very important factors to be considered while fixing prices. The relationship between price and demand should be analysed properly. No company can ignore the costs, prices and offers of substitute items from competitiors. Economic factors, like rate of interest, state of industry (boom or recession), inflation, etc. affect the price-fixing decision. In case of certain products, e.g. products which fulfil basic needs, government may impose price control. Thus, it would also affect price of the product.

There may be two methods of price-fixation:

Business Studies

1. Cost-based approach
2. Competition-based approach

***Cost-based approach*:** This is the simplest method of pricing. Generally companies add a certain percentage of Profit, to the total cost of the product. The total cost of the product is calculated after taking all types of costs into consideration. While following this approach, no other factors e.g. prices of substitute goods, nature of demand, etc. are considered.

***Competition-based approach*:** In competitive market, cost-based approach is not always practicable. The prices are determined on the basis of conditions in the market. Companies may follow any one of the following three approaches.

(a) Price-in-line (b) Market-plus (c) Market-minus

Price-in-line means prices fixed nearly equal to the prices of close alternatives. Generally this happens under free market conditions i.e. when the number of buyers and sellers is so large that they cannot affect the prices. Prices are decided by the market forces of demand and supply.

When companies charge (fix up) a price which is more than the price of existing substitutes, it is called market plus pricing. This approach is adopted when the quality of a product is better, or it has a popular brand name, or its packaging is attractive and useful. Consumers will pay more only when they find distinctive differences in the product and its substitutes.

Sometimes business enterprises get ready to supply products at a price lower than the market price. It may be adopted to grab a larger market share or to make a newly introduced product more popular. This approach is called market-minus approach. Companies having shorter channels of distributions or direct selling facilities can afford to fix a price lower than the prevailing market price.

(iii) Promotion: Promotion refers to using methods of communication with two objectives : (i) informing the existing and potential consumers about a product, and (ii) to persuade consumers to buy the product. It is an important element of marketing mix. In the absence of communication, consumers may not be aware of the product and its potential to satisfy their needs and desires. Various tools of communication form part of promotion mix. Companies must decide which tool(s) should be used for larger sales and in what proportion. The tools should be combined. These decisions are known as promotion-mix decisions.

There are four components of promotion-mix i.e., advertising, personal selling, sales promotion and public relations. Thus, promotion mix is a company's total communication programs which consists of different blends of its components and which is used to achieve the company's marketing objectives.

***Tools of Promotion-mix*:** Advertising, personal selling, sales promotion and publicity are the major tools. The marketing manager must recognise the characteristics of each tool and costs involved while deciding on the promotion-mix.

Advertising: Advertising is an impersonal form of communication for which the seller pays in order to promote a physical product or service. It may be in print form as in newspapers and magazines, or in audio form as on the radio and other similiar methods, or in audio-visual forms as on the Television, cinema screen, etc.

The merits of advertising is that it reaches a larger number of people, the message can be repeated, its cost is not high, and with the development of art and computer graphics, simple statements can be transformed into forceful messages.

The other side of advertising is that it doesnot provide any feed back, it is not as forceful as personal selling, it is not flexible, and good advertisements cost a lot.

Personal selling: Personal selling is a personal communication with one or more prospective buyers for the purpose of selling a product or service.

These days, personal selling is considered to be the most effective tool because of various characteristics which are listed below:

- It involves personal interaction, hence feed back is received immediately;
- It is quite flexible, salesman can adjust communication according to the level of customer's under-standing.
- It is more persuasive; buyers can be convinced about the utility of the product;
- Impressive salesman leaves an impression on the prospective buyer; it may increase sales in the future.

Personal selling suffers from a few drawbacks too. It is the most expensive tool of promotion. Secondly, it requires too much dependence on sales force.

Sales Promotion: Sales promotion means the use of short-term incentives which are designed to encourage immediate purchase of a product or service by the buyer. It may includes offer of discounts, free gifts, free sample, coupons, demonstration, store display, etc. One tooth brush free with one 100gm. Close-up dental cream is an example of sales promotion.

Generally this tool supplements the efforts made through personal selling and advertisement. Most of the sales promotion activities come in the form of some incentive for the buyer; hence sales generally increase immediately. Big business enterprises use sales promotion tools while introducing a new product. It adds to the effectiveness of total promotional efforts of a company.

Sales promotion has certain demerits e.g. it does not leave a lasting effect. Some customers also feel that sales promotion schemes are launched to clear old stocks.

Publicity: Publicity takes place when a favourable presentation is made through mass media about a product or service. People believe more on such news than in advertising. It covers people who do not entertain personal selling and sales promotion approaches. It is a non-paid form of communication but sometimes it is not regarded as a promotional tool within the reach of a company. Very few products or services are covered by publicity.

Packaging is also considered as a powerful sales promotion tool these days. It immediately attracts the buyer and makes him buy the product. This tool has produced good results in case of consumer goods. To some extend, packaging has replaced the counter salesman.

You have now learnt about the various tools of promotion. Each tool has certain merits and demerits. It is very important that promotion mix is so devised that it achieves marketing objectives optimally. It is not an easy task. There are no hard and fast rules of promotion mix.

Hence every factor should be paid due attention while deciding on the promotion mix.

Factors governing Promotion-mix

1. *Nature of product*: Different types of products require different promotion mix. In case of consumer goods, advertisement is considered to be the most important because the goods are non-technical and produced on a large scale. But for industrial goods personal selling is regarded as the most important tool because the products are technical in nature, costly and persuasion is considered essential for their sale.
2. *Type of the market*: If the number of customers is quite large and they are spread over a vast area, advertisement is more helpful because it can reach people everywhere. However if number of customers is not very large and they are concentrated geographically, personal selling and sales promotion may be more effective.
3. *Stage of the product life cycle*: The promotional mix depends upon the stage of the product in product life cycle. During introduction, heavy expenditure is incurred on advertisement followed by personal selling and sales promotion. During the growth stage, customers are aware of the benefits of product. Hence advertisement along with personal selling will be more effective. At the maturity stage, competition is more intense. Sales promotion becomes the most important tool to boost sales.
4. *Budget*: Funds available for promotion also decide promotion mix, e.g. advertisement is a costly tool. If sufficient funds are not available this tool may not be adopted. Personal selling involves continuous spending. Thus, budget is a deciding factor for promotion-mix.
5. *Push vs. Pull Strategy*: When the firm pushes the product to the middlemen they in turn push it to the consumers, it is known as 'push' strategy. In this case, personal selling or display should be more effective.

Pull strategy refers to the policy of a company to strive to build up consumer demand without recourse to middlemen. Generally advertising is considered more important in case of pull strategy.

To sum up, it may be said that all promotional tools are complementary and not competitive. The degree of emphasis on each tools will differ depending upon the influence of certain factors. A proper combination of promotional tools should be designed to attain better results.

(iv) Place: Place is another important element of marketing mix. Once the goods are manufactured, packaged, priced and promoted, they must be made available to the consumers. Activities related to placing the products are covered under this element of marketing-mix. It consists of decisions relating to channels of distribution and physical distribution. Channels of distribution refer to the individuals and organisations which facilitate moving the goods from manufactures to consumers. It is important that regular and smooth flow of goods is maintained so that products are not spoiled and supplies are not delayed. To ensure this, various facilitating services need to be arranged like transportation, warehousing, inventory control, and order processing. These are known as components of physical distribution. Let us now study the two sub-elements of 'place'-

(a) Channels of distribution (b) Physical distribution

(a) ***Channels of Distribution*****:** Channel of distribution denotes the intermediaries involved in the process whereby a product passes from the manufacturer to consumers. It is very important for the producers to involve middlemen in order to reach consumers. Middlemen reduce the problems of both producers and consumers. Secondly, middlemen help in distributing the products over a large area. Middlemen also supply useful market information to the producer for improving the product. Involvement of middlemen adds to the convenience of consumers because they are able to lay many items from a single store. Some people feel that by involving more middlemen in the process of distribution, the final price of a products is considerably raised which is ultimately paid by the consumer. Therefore the number of middlemen involved should be limited, if at all necessary: There can be various levels of channel. It is for the producer to decide which level would suit the sale of his product.

Number of Channel Levels: Distribution channel starts from the producer and ends with the consumer. Each layer of middleman that performs some work in bringing the product closer to the final layer is a channel level. The diagram given below shows the various channel levels.

Channel 1 Manufacturer-Consumer

Channel 2 Manufacturer-Retailer-Consumer

Channel 3 Manufacturer-Wholesaler-Retailer-Consumer

Channel 4 Manufacturer-Wholesalers-Jobers-Retailer-Consumer

Channel 1 is called a direct marketing channel. It has no intermediary level. Producers sell products directly to the consumers. Channel 2 includes one intermediary which is generally a retailer. Retailers buy products directly from the manufacturer and sell these to the consumers. Generally electronic goods like televisions, computers, are sold through this channel level. Channel 3 consists of two levels, typically a wholesaler and a retailer. This channel is often used by small manufacturers of food items, and other products. Channel 4 contains three middlemen levels. Jobbers usually come between wholesalers and retailers. They buy from wholesaler and sell to small retailers who generally are not served by wholesalers. There can be even more levels in distribution channel but from producers point of view, greater number of levels means less control and greater complexity of channel.

Choice of channel of distribution: There are a number of factors which govern the choice regarding channel of distribution. These are listed below:-

(i) *Nature of product:* For perishable goods, shorter channel is preferred whereas for durable goods channel 3 is more popular. If goods are made to order, direct selling may be effected. For technical products and costly products, manufacturers generally go for direct selling through agents specially hired for this purpose.

(ii) *Nature of market:* If the market is concentrated and not scattered, producers may go for direct selling but for scattered market, middlemen are involved. If there are more buyers, there may be a need to include more middleman. For consumer product market retailers are essential but in case of industrial products a shorter channel is preferred, hence middlemen may be eliminated.

(iii) *Middlemen:* Middlemen who can provide desired marketing services are given preference. The availability of middlemen also affect channel decision. The middlemen must be co-operative and honest. The channel which generates largest sales volume at lower unit cost will be given priority.

(iv) *Size and Policy of the Company:* There are many factors related to company which influence channel decision. A big size company with broader product line can afford to have shorter channel. New companies heavily rely on middlemen. A company with sufficient financial resources can spend heavily on advertisement and its own outlets.

Hence need for middleman is reduced. Companies desiring efficient control over channel members will always prefer shorter channel.

(v) *Marketing Environment:* During recession or depression shorter channels are preferred because of being less costly. In times of prosperity a wide choice is available. Technological inventions also have an impact e.g., distribution of perishable goods to distant places has become possible due to cold storage facilities in warehousing and transporting. Such facilities have expanded the role of intermediaries.

(vi) *Competitors:* Channels of distribution used by competitors also influence this decision. Some organisation may like to follow the same chains as used by competitors. On the other hand, some organization may avoid channels already customary. They may have their own decisions.

Thus after visualising the impact of the factors mentioned above a company adopts the best channel from among the available alternatives.

(b) ***Physical Distribution*****:** Physical distribution comprises all those activities which deliver customer satisfaction by supplying right type of products at right place and at right time regularly. Economical and satisfactory customer service is the primary goal of physical distribution. Providing the right type of goal at right place and at right time is the ultimate goal of any marketing department. These goals may be conflicting, sometimes, e.g., for meeting sudden and unforeseen demand for goods, maintenance of large inventory is suggested but this involves cost as well as risk. This means that a proper balance between the cost and service should be achieved.

Components of physical distribution:

(i) *Order Processing:* Physical distribution begins with customers' order. Both the company and customer are benefitted if order processing is carried out quickly and accurately. These days computers are used which establish a link between retailers and producers. Producers keep a watch on the stock position at retailers' place retailers may also place orders through computer. This facility speeds up the process.

(ii) *Warehousing:* Every company must store goods to maintain a proper flow. Storage facilities are important because production and consumption cycles generally do not match. Companies need to decide the number, space and location of warehouses. The cost of these should be in balance with customer service. Companies may own warehouses or take them on rent.

4.3 | Product Life Cycle

The Product Life Cycle (PLC) is based upon the biological life cycle. For example, a seed is planted (introduction); it begins to sprout (growth); it shoots out leaves and puts down roots as it becomes an adult (maturity); after a long period as an adult the plant begins to shrink and die out (decline).

In theory it's the same for a product. After a period of development it is introduced or launched into the market; it gains more and more customers as it grows; eventually the market stabilises and the product becomes mature; then after a period of time the product is overtaken by development and the introduction of superior competitors, it goes into decline and is eventually withdrawn.

However, most products fail in the introduction phase. Others have very cyclical maturity phases where declines see the product promoted to regain customers.

Strategies for the different stages of the Product Life Cycle

Introduction

The need for immediate profit is not a pressure. The product is promoted to create awareness. If the product has no or few competitors, a skimming price strategy is employed. Limited numbers of product are available in few channels of distribution.

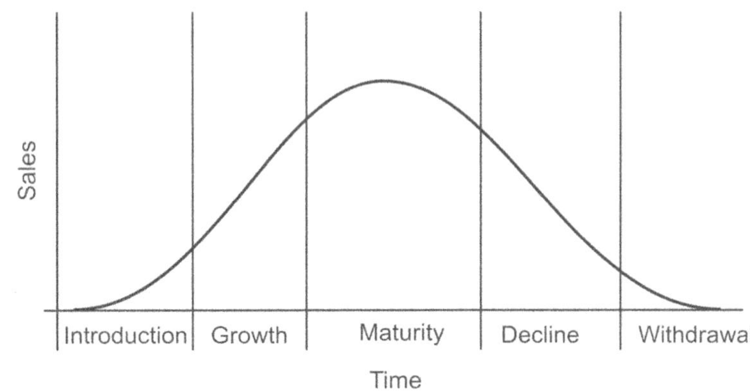

Figure 4.1 |

Growth

Competitors are attracted into the market with very similar offerings. Products become more profitable and companies form alliances, joint ventures and take each other over. Advertising spend is high and focuses upon building brand. Market share tends to stabilise.

Maturity

Those products that survive the earlier stages tend to spend longest in this phase. Sales grow at a decreasing rate and then stabilise. Producers attempt to differentiate products and brands are key to this. Price wars and intense competition occur. At this point the market reaches saturation. Producers begin to leave the market due to poor margins. Promotion becomes more widespread and use a greater variety of media.

Decline

At this point there is a downturn in the market. For example more innovative products are introduced or consumer tastes have changed. There is intense price-cutting and many more products are withdrawn from the market. Profits can be improved by reducing marketing spend and cost cutting.

Problems with Product Life Cycle

In reality very few products follow such a prescriptive cycle. The length of each stage varies enormously. The decisions of marketers can change the stage, for example from maturity to decline by price-cutting. Not all products go through each stage. Some go from introduction to decline. It is not easy to tell which stage the product is in. Remember that PLC is like all other tools. Use it to inform your gut feeling.

4.4 | Product Life Cycle – Stages

There are 4 stages in a product's life cycle.

Stage	Characteristics
1. Market introduction stage	Costs are high slow sales volumes to start little or no competition demand has to be created customers have to be prompted to try the product makes no money at this stage
2. Growth stage	Costs reduced due to economies of scale sales volume increases significantly profitability begins to rise public awareness increases competition begins to increase with a few new players in establishing market increased competition leads to price decreases

Contd...

Stage	Characteristics
3. Maturity stage	Costs are lowered as a result of production volumes increasing and experience curve effects sales volume peaks and market saturation is reached increase in competitors entering the market prices tend to drop due to the proliferation of competing products brand differentiation and feature diversification is emphasized to maintain or increase market share Industrial profits go down
4. Saturation and decline stage	Costs become counter-optimal sales volume decline or stabilize prices, profitability diminish profit becomes more a challenge of production/distribution efficiency than increased sales

Request for deviation

In the process of building a product following defined procedure, an RFD is a request for authorization, granted **prior** to the manufacture of an item, to depart from a particular performance or design requirement of a specification, drawing or other document, for a specific number of units or a specific period of time.

Market identification

A "micro-market" can be used to describe a *Walkman,* more portable, as well as individually and privately recordable; and then Compact Discs ("CDs") brought increased capacity and CD-R offered individual private recording...and so the process goes. The "technology lifecycle" is a most appropriate concept in this context.

In short, termination is not always the end of the cycle; it can be the end of a micro-entrant within the grander scope of a macro-environment. The auto industry, fast-food industry, petro-chemical industry, are just a few that demonstrate a macro-environment that overall has not terminated even while micro-entrants over time have come and gone.

Lessons of the product life cycle (PLC)

It is claimed that every product has a life period, it is launched, it grows, and at some point, may die. A fair comment is that - at least in the short term - not all products or services die. Jeans may die, but clothes probably will not. Legal services or medical services may die, but depending on the social and political climate, probably will not.

Even though its validity is questionable, it can offer a useful '*model*' for managers to keep at the back of their mind. Indeed, if their products are in the introductory or growth phases, or in that of decline, it perhaps should be at the front of their mind; for the predominant features of these phases may be those revolving around such life and death. Between these two extremes, it is salutary for them to have that vision of mortality in front of them.

However, the most important aspect of product life-cycles is that, even under normal conditions, to all practical intents and purposes they often do not exist (hence, there needs to be more emphasis on model/reality mappings). In most markets the majority of the major brands have held their position for at least two decades. The dominant product life-cycle, that of the brand leaders which almost monopolize many markets, is therefore one of continuity.

In the criticism of the product life cycle, Dhalla & Yuspeh state:

...clearly, the PLC is a dependent variable which is determined by market actions; it is not an independent variable to which companies should adapt their marketing programs. Marketing management itself can alter the shape and duration of a brand's life cycle.[1]

Thus, the life cycle may be useful as a description, but not as a *predictor*; and usually should be firmly under the control of the marketer. The important point is that in many markets the product or brand life cycle is significantly longer than the planning cycle of the organisations involved. Thus, it offers little practical value for most marketers. Even if the PLC (and the related PLM support) exists for them, their plans will be based just upon that piece of the curve where they currently reside (most probably in the 'mature' stage); and their view of that part of it will almost certainly be *'linear'* (and limited), and will not encompass the whole range from growth to decline.

Limitations

The PLC model is of some degree of usefulness to marketing managers, in that it is based on factual assumptions. Nevertheless, it is difficult for marketing management to gauge accurately where a product is on its PLC graph. A rise in sales *per se* is not necessarily evidence of growth. A fall in sales *per se* does not typify decline. Furthermore, some products do not (or to date, at the least, have not) experienced a decline. *Coca Cola* and *Pepsi* are examples of two products that have existed for many decades, but are still popular products all over the world. Both modes of cola have been in maturity for some years.

Another factor is that differing products would possess different PLC "shapes". A fad product would hold a steep sloped growth stage, a short maturity stage, and a steep sloped decline stage. A product such as Coca Cola and Pepsi would experience growth, but also a constant level of sales over a number of decades. It can probably be said that a given product (or products collectively within an industry) may hold a unique PLC shape, and the typical PLC model can only be used as a rough guide for marketing management. This is why its called the product life cycle.

4.5 | Channels of Distribution

Introduction

As you know, the primary objective of all business enterprises is to earn profit by selling goods and services to ultimate consumers or users. In order to bring goods from the place of manufacture to the place of consumers, the goods have to follow a path or route which is known as channel of distribution or trade channel. A trade or marketing channel consists of producer, middlemen, and consumers or users. The channel serves as a link between the producer and consumers. In the present lesson we shall discuss the various aspects of channels of distribution.

Direct Sale
Retailer
Wholesaler Retailer
Agent Retailer
Agent Wholesaler Retailer
Agent/dealer Retailer
Agent/dealer Wholesaler Retailer

Channel of distribution – importance

A channel of distribution or trade channel is the path or route along which goods move from producers to ultimate consumers or industrial users. In other words, it is the distribution network through which a producer puts his product in the hands of actual users. The channel of distribution includes the original producer, the final buyer and any middlemen-either wholesaler or retailer. The term middleman refers to any institution or individual in the channel which either acquires title to the goods or negotiates or sells in the capacity of an agent or broker. But facilitating agencies who perform or assist in marketing function are not included as middlemen in the channel of distribution. This is because they neither acquire title to the goods nor negotiate purchase or sale. Such facilitating agencies include banks, railways, roadways, warehouses, insurance companies, advertising agencies, middleman. But that is very rare.

The producer may sell goods to retailer who may then sell the same to consumers. The producer may sell goods to wholesalers who may in turn sell to retailers and the retailer may sell to consumers. The fourth alternative channel of distribution is when any agent/dealer intervenes between the producer and retailers and acts as a middlemen. The agent is appointed by the producer for the sale of goods to the retailers. Another alternative channel is there when producer's agent sells goods to wholesalers who sell to retailers. Agent/dealer is an independent person/firm buying goods and selling them to retailers. Agent/dealer may also sell to wholesalers who may then sell to retailers and goods are thus made available to consumers. In the channel of distribution there may be more than one agent/dealer and wholesaler.

Role of middlemen in the distribution of goods

The middlemen perform the following marketing functions which are listed in sequence.

(i) Searching out buyers and sellers (contacting & Merchandising), matching goods to the requirements of market.
(ii) Offering goods in the form of assortments or packages.
(iii) Persuading and influencing the prospective buyers to favor a certain product and its maker (personal selling/sales promotion).
(iv) Implementing pricing policies in such a manner that would be acceptable to buyers and ensure effective distribution.
(v) Providing feed back information, marketing intelligence and sales forecasting services for the regions to their suppliers.
(vi) Looking after the process of distribution where necessary.
(vii) Participating actively in the creation and establishment of a market for a new product.
(viii) Offering pre and after sale services to consumers.
(ix) Communicating the use of technique of the product to the users.
(x) Offering credit to retailers and consumers.
(xi) Risk bearing with reference to stock hoarding/transport.

Desirability of eliminating the middlemen

You have already learnt the role of middlemen above, which indicates the significance of middlemen in the channel of distribution. Indeed without the existence of middlemen goods produced on a mass scale could not have reached the consumers at right time and place. However the existence of middlemen may lead to several short comings. The elimination of middlemen is based on the following grounds.

(i) ***Excessive number:*** Often there are too many middlemen between the manufacturers and consumers. As every middleman charges some commission or profit, the ultimate consumer has to pay a very high price for goods. They are social parasites thriving at the cost of the consumer and their ultimate elimination will reduce prices and burden on consumers.

(ii) ***Superfluous:*** Most middlemen do not render any useful service in lieu of profit or commission. They act as only transfer agents and unnecessarily cause delay in the flow of goods. Their elimination will result in quick and smooth flow of goods.

(iii) ***Limited risk taking:*** Middlemen do not bear the producers' risk such as loss due to strikes, lockouts, depression and change in fashions and habits, etc.

(iv) ***Anti-social activities:*** They take undue advantage of adverse conditions in business. Some businessmen (middlemen) indulge in anti-social activities like hoarding and adulteration to earn huge amount to profits.

(v) ***Limiting consumers' choice:*** The middlemen often promote products which are inferior in quality and get high margin of profit. Thus they exploit consumers and limit their choice.

Role of wholesaler and retailer in distribution of goods

Role of Wholesaler: Wholesaler acts as a middlemen in the channel of distribution as he buys goods in large quantity from the manufacturer and sells these to retailers in small quantities. His role in distribution of goods is discussed below:

(i) ***Buying and assembling:*** A wholesaler forecasts the demand for goods and assembles different varieties of goods from several manufacturers. Some wholesalers also import goods from foreign countries.

(ii) ***Selling and dispersing:*** A wholesaler breaks the bulk so that retailers and users can buy them in small lots. His representatives regularly call on retailers and industrial users/buyers to distribute the goods among widely scattered people.

(iii) ***Transportation:*** A wholesaler arranges transportation of goods from producers to his godowns and from there to retailers.
Sometimes he has his own transport arrangement for this purpose.

(iv) ***Storage:*** He holds large stocks and serves as a reservoir and supplies to retailers. He helps in establising prices by adjusting supply of goods to their demand.

(v) ***Packing and grading:*** A wholesaler packs and repacks goods in convenient lots. He sorts out goods in different grades. He also gives brand names to the products packed and graded by him.

(vi) ***Advertising and sales promotion:*** A wholesaler performs advertising and sales promotion activities to increase the sale of products. He also takes the services of experts for this purpose.

(vii) ***Financing:*** Sometimes the wholesaler buys goods on cash basis from manufacturers and sells them on credit to retailers. In this way he provides financial help both to the producers and retailers. If necessary, the wholesaler also provide financial help by way of advance payment to producers.

(viii) ***Risk-taking:*** A wholesaler bears risks of changes in demand and prices, bad debts and damage to goods in the course of transportation and storage. By undertaking various risks he simplifies the process of distribution.

Role of Retailers

Retailers buys goods from wholesaler and sells them directly to consumers. Thus he acts as a direct link between the wholesaler and consumers. His role in distribution of goods is enumerated below:

(i) ***Wide choice to consumers:*** The retailer anticipates needs of consumers. He assembles goods from different sources and stocks different varieties of products. Thus, he offers a wide choice to consumers. They can buy according to their purchasing power and requirements.

Availability of goods in small quantities and at convenient locations: A retailer provides ready supply of goods so that consumers can buy conveniently and quickly in small lots without any inconvenience of placing advance orders and waiting for supplies. By ensuring uninterrupted and fresh supply of goods, he saves consumers from the botheration of buying goods in bulk and storing them.

(ii) ***Home delivery:*** A retailer transports goods from wholesalers to ultimate consumers. Some retailers provide free home delivery service to their consumers. Thus they create place utility.

(iii) ***Assurance of regular supply:*** He maintains adequate supply of goods so that consumers are sure of getting regular supply at the time of their need.

(iv) ***Credit facility:*** Although retailers mostly sell goods for cash, they also supply goods on credit to their regular customers.

(v) ***Close interaction with customers:*** A retailer brings new products to the notice of customers and educates them in their uses. A retailer thus, acts as a friend and guide to his customers. Indeed his interaction with customers is of intimate personal nature and thus he is able to provide feed back to wholesalers and manufacturers about consumers' preferences.

Role of specialized retail outlets e.g., departmental stores, multiple shops and mail order business house

A retailer is the final link in the distribution channel between a manufacturer and the consumers. He is directly and continuously in touch with people of varied tastes and preferences. Retailers may be divided into two categories, namely institutional and non-institutional. The institutional retailers (retail outlets) include departmental stores, multiple shops and mail order houses. Non-institutional retailers include the floating population of street sellers, pedlars, and hawkers.

(a) ***Departmental Stores:*** A departmental Store is a big retail store with many departments under one roof. It offers a wide range of products so as to suit different consumer tastes and preferences. All the departments are centrally controlled but each department forms a complete sales unit in itself. The examples of such stores in metropolitan cities are Akbarally's and Sahakari Bhandar in Bombay and Spencers in Madras.

(b) ***Multiple shops or chain stores:*** Manufacturers often use their own retail shops for direct sale of their products to consumers. These retail shops are established as multiple shops operating in the same city or different parts of the country. These shops have identical product display. Bata India Ltd and DCM provide typical examples of multiple shops system. In this type of retail selling manufacturers have control over distribution channel and have first hand information regarding customers' preferences.

(c) ***Mail-order business:*** These are retail outlets which sell goods by mail only. The mail order house centrally procures products, advertises them and expect perspective buyers to send offers/orders. The products are sent through value-payable post. Mail Order Sales Ltd, Bombay, the seller of 'Bull worker' health aid, is a typical example of such mail order business in India. It is through these retail outlets that manufacturers often by pass the wholesalers in trade route or path.

Choice of a channel of distribution

The factors to be considered before choosing a suitable channel of distribution are listed below:

1. ***Product considerations:*** The nature and type of product have an important bearing on the choice of distribution channels. For examples, perishable goods need speedy movements and hence shorter channel or route of distribution; For durable goods, longer and diversified channels may be used; Similarly, for technical products requiring specialized selling and serving talents, the shortest channel should be used.
2. ***Market considerations:*** The nature and type of customers and size of market are important considerations in the choice of a channel of distribution. For example, if the market size is large, there may be long channels, whereas in a small market direct selling may be profitable. The nature and type of consumers include factors such as desire for credit, preference for the stop shopping, demand for personal services, amount of time and effort the customer is willing to spend. It also includes factors like age, income group, sex, and religion of customers.
3. ***Company considerations:*** The nature, size and objectives of the business firm also play an important role in the selection of distribution channel. It includes financial resources, market standing, volume of production, desire for control of channel, services provided by manufacturers', etc. For example a company with substantial financial resources need not rely too much on the middlemen and can afford to reduce the levels of distribution. Similarly a company desiring to exercise greater control over channel will prefer a shorter channel.
4. ***Middlemen considerations:*** The cost and efficiency of distribution depend largely on the nature and type of middlemen. It includes characteristics of middlemen such as availability, attitudes, services, sales potential, costs etc. For example, if the terms

and conditions of engaging wholesalers are unfavorable, a manufacturer may like to channelise his products through wholesalers or retailers, thereby, bypassing wholesalers. However, the determining factor would be the differential advantage involved in the choice.

To conclude, the channel generating the largest sales volume at lower unit cost will be given top priority. This will minimize distribution costs.

4.6 | Sales Promotion

Sales promotion is one of the four aspects of *promotional mix*. (The other three parts of the *promotional mix* are *advertising, personal selling*, and *publicity/public relations*.) Media and non-media marketing communication are employed for a pre-determined, limited time to increase consumer demand, stimulate market demand or improve product availability. Examples include:

- *Contests*
- Point of purchase displays
- *Rebate (marketing)*
- Free travel, such as free flights

Sales promotions can be directed at either the *customer*, sales staff, or *distribution* channel members (such as *retailers*). Sales promotions targeted at the *consumer* are called **consumer sales promotions**. Sales promotions targeted at retailers and *wholesale* are called **trade sales promotions**. Some sale promotions, particularly ones with unusual methods, are considered *gimmick* by many.

Consumer sales promotion techniques

- ***Price deal*:** A temporary reduction in the price, such as *happy hour*.
- ***Loyal Reward Program*:** Consumers collect points, miles, or credits for purchases and redeem them for rewards. Two famous examples are *Pepsi Stuff* and *Advantage*.
- ***Cents-off deal*:** Offers a brand at a lower price. Price reduction may be a percentage marked on the package.
- ***Price-pack deal*:** The packaging offers a consumer a certain percentage more of the product for the same price (for example, 25 percent extra).
- ***Coupons*:** Coupons have become a standard mechanism for sales promotions.
- ***Loss leader*:** The price of a popular product is temporarily reduced in order to stimulate other profitable sales.
- ***Free-standing insert (FSI)*:** A coupon booklet is inserted into the local newspaper for delivery.

- ***On-shelf couponing***: Coupons are present at the shelf where the product is available.
- ***Checkout dispensers***: On checkout the customer is given a coupon based on products purchased.
- ***On-line couponing***: Coupons are available online. Consumers print them out and take them to the store.
- ***Mobile couponing:*** Coupons are available on a mobile phone. Consumers show the offer on a mobile phone to a salesperson for redemption.
- ***Online interactive promotion game***: Consumers play an interactive game associated with the promoted product. See an example of the *Interactive Internet Add* for tomato ketchup.
- ***Rebates***: Consumers are offered money back if the receipt and *barcode* are mailed to the producer.
- ***Contests/sweepstakes/games***: The consumer is automatically entered into the event by purchasing the product.
- ***Point-of-sale displays***:
    - *Aisle interrupter:* A sign that juts into the aisle from the shelf.
    - *Dangler:* A sign that sways when a consumer walks by it.
    - *Dump bin:* A bin full of products dumped inside.
    - *Glorifier:* A small stage that elevates a product above other products.
    - *Wobbler:* A sign that jiggles.
    - *Lipstick Board:* A board on which messages are written in crayon.
    - *Necker:* A coupon placed on the 'neck' of a bottle.
    - *YES unit:* "your extra salesperson" is a pull-out *fact sheet.*
- Kids eat free specials: Offers a discount on the total dining bill by offering 1 free kids meal with each regular meal purchased.

Trade sales promotion techniques

- ***Trade allowances***: Short term incentive offered to induce a retailer to stock up on a product.
- ***Dealer loader***: An incentive given to induce a retailer to purchase and display a product.
- ***Trade contest***: A contest to reward retailers that sell the most product.
- ***Point-of-purchase displays***: Extra sales tools given to retailers to boost sales.
- ***Training programs***: Dealer employees are trained in selling the product.

- ***Push money***: Also known as "spiffs". An extra commission paid to retail employees to push products.

Trade discounts (also called functional discounts): These are payments to distribution channel members for performing some function.

4.7 | Pharma Marketing Process and its Challenges

Introduction

The pharmaceutical industry is the world's largest industry due to worldwide revenues of approximately US$2.8 trillion. Pharma industry has seen major changes in the recent years that place new demands on payers, providers and manufacturers. Customers now demand the same choice and convenience from pharma industry that they find in other segment. Indian Pharmaceutical Industry is poised for high consistent growth over the next few years, driven by a multitude of factors. Top Indian Companies like **Ranbaxy, DRL, CIPLA** and **Dabur** have already established their presence. The pharmaceutical industry is a knowledge driven industry and is heavily dependent on Research and Development for new products and growth. However, basic research (discovering new molecules) is a time consuming and expensive process and is thus, dominated by large global multinationals.

Indian companies have only recently entered the area. The Indian pharmaceutical industry came into existence in 1901, when Bengal Chemical & Pharmaceutical Company started its maiden operation in Calcutta. The next few decades saw the pharmaceutical industry moving through several phases, largely in accordance with government policies. Commencing with repackaging and preparation of formulations from imported bulk drugs, the Indian industry has moved on to become a net foreign exchange earner, and has been able to underline its presence in the global pharmaceutical arena as one of the top 35 drug producers worldwide. Currently, there are more than 2,400 registered pharmaceutical producers in India. There are 24,000 licensed pharmaceutical companies. Of the 465 bulk drugs used in India, approximately 425 are manufactured here. India has more drug-manufacturing facilities that have been approved by the U.S. Food and Drug Administration than any country other than the US. Indian generics companies supply 84% of the AIDS drugs that Doctors without Borders uses to treat 60,000 patients in more than 30 countries.

Therapeutic Area wise Total Pharma Market

Category	***Value Market Share%***
Anti-Infective	16.4
Gastrointestinal	10.9
Cardiac	10.3
Respiratory	10.2
Vit./Minerals/Nutrient	9.6
Pain/Analgesics	9.5

Dermatologics	5.4
Gynecology	5.3
Neuro psychiatry	5.3
Ant diabetics	4.4
Opthologicals	1.7
Others	11.0
Total	100.00

It is very much evident that chronic therapy area (Gastro Cardiac, Respiratory, Neuro Psychiatry and Ant diabetics) is dominating the market in long run.

Pharma Marketing Process and its Challenges

While many pharmaceutical companies have successfully deployed a plethora of strategies to target the various customer types, recent business and customer trends are creating new challenges and opportunities for increasing profitability. In the pharmaceutical and healthcare industries, a complex web of decision-makers determines the nature of the transaction (prescription) for which direct customer (doctor) of Pharma industry is responsible. Essentially, the end-user (patient) consumes a product and pays the cost.

Use of medical representatives for marketing products to physicians and to exert some influence over others in the hierarchy of decision makers has been a time-tested tradition. Typically, sales force expense comprises an estimated 15 percent to 20 percent of annual product revenues, the largest line item on the balance sheet. Despite this other expense, the industry is still plagued with some very serious strategic and operational level issues.

From **organizational perspective** the most prominent performance related issues are enlisted below:

(a) Increased competition and unethical practices adopted by some of the propaganda base companies.
(b) Low level of customer knowledge (Doctors, Retailers, Wholesalers).
(c) Poor customer (both external & internal) acquisition, development and retention strategies.
(d) Varying customer perception.
(e) The number and the quality of medical representatives.
(f) Very high territory development costs.
(g) High training and re-training costs of sales personnel.
(h) Very high attrition rate of the sales personnel.
(i) Busy doctors giving less time for sales calls.
(j) Poor territory knowledge in terms of business value at medical representative level.

(k) Unclear value of prescription from **each doctor** in the list of **each sales person.**

(l) Unknown value of revenue from each retailer in the territory

(m) Absence of ideal mechanism of sales forecasting from field sales level, leading to huge deviations

(n) Absence of analysis on the amount of time invested on profitable and not so profitable customers and lack of time-share planning towards developing customer base for future and un-tapped markets.

Patents

Patents are a vital aspect of the global Pharma industry. Patent protection is essential to spur basic R&D and make it commercially viable. But, only the developed nations endorse product patents. Most third world countries have patent laws but enforcement is totally lax.

New Drug Approval (NDA)

Prior to launching its products in any country, a Pharma company undertakes patent registration to protect its own interests. To protect the interests of the consumers, it is necessary that the product be approved by the drug authorities in that country. Mostly the process for seeking approval is initiated alongside the patent registration process.

WTO

Due to pressure from the developed countries, across the world uniformity in patent laws is being implemented under WTO (World Trade Organization - earlier GATT i.e., General Agreement on Tariffs & Trade). Presently, different countries have different patent types and life period. WTO has decided upon a product patent life of 20 years in all countries.

Research and Development (R & D)

The pharmaceutical industry is characterized by heavy R&D expenditure. It is only the large pharmaceutical companies who can allocate significant resources for R&D to introduce new products. As the products are an outcome of significant R&D expenditures incurred by these companies, they have their products patented. The patent allows the companies concerned to wield immense pricing power for their new products.

The Competition

The level of competition on day-to-day basis in very **high** in **Acute segment,** however the degree of competition is not as much as high in **Chronic therapy** area. As doctor has to prescribe drug for a long time in chronic cases and patient is suppose to consume it without any change of brand. While in acute cases doctor is changing brands on day to day basis. In acute area however there is a large competition from local and propaganda companies.

Pharmaceutical Company Business Strategies

What's the secret behind successes? For one, the company operates in niche formulations (**chronic**) segments such as psychiatry, cardiovascular, gastroenterology and neurology. While most of the top Indian companies have focused on antibiotics and anti–invectives (**acute**), Sun Pharma focused on therapeutic areas such as depression, hypertension and cancer. The company has introduced the entire range of products and has gained leadership position in each of these areas. Being a specialty company insulates Sun Pharma from the industry growth. The first quarter results for FY02 explain this to some extent. While the industry was affected to a large extent by a slowdown in the domestic formulations market, Sun Pharma logged a growth of 26% in revenues. Over the years Sun has also used the strategy of acquisitions and mergers to grow quickly. It acquired Knoll Pharma's bulk drug facility, Gujarat Lyka Organics, 51.5% in M. J. Pharma, merged TamilNadu Dadha Pharma & Milmet Labs and acquired Natco's brands. Post Merger with TamilNadu Dadha Pharma the company gained presence in gynecology and oncology segments.

The bases of marketing strategies can be best described in these two models in both acute and chronic segments:

(i) **Super Core Model** involving the search for, and distribution of a small number of drugs from **Chronic Therapy Area** that achieve substantial global sales. The success of this model depends on achieving large returns from a small number of drugs in order to pay for the high cost of the drug discovery and development process for a large number of patients. Total revenues are highly dependant on sales from a small number of drugs. This model incorporates highly specialized approach in all the manner. Initially the competition is seems more at entry level but since growth is stable and more in this area; every company is striving very hard to enter in this area. The major strategy in this model involves right focus to highly specialized customer by well trained team.

(ii) **Core Model** in which a larger number of drugs from **Acute Therapy Area** are marketed to big diversified markets. The advantage of this model is that its success is not dependant on sales of a small number of drugs. Here presenting a large number of product and taking the advantage of opportunity cost is one of the important strategy.

Marketing approaches of Super Core Model

In pharmaceutical market there has been a significant shift from Acute towards Chronic Therapy area. Chronic segments are driving the growth of the market as leading prescribes in these segments are specialists as opposed to general practioners. This is evident from high growth rates achieved by firms like Sun Pharma, Dr.Reddy.

Laboratories and Dabur Pharma Ltd. Who have focused on these segments The doctor's prescription has become just the starting point in determining what drug the retailer dispenses. During last five years Pharma companies have started identifying the hidden potential of oncological market also. A number of drugs have been launched into the oncological market by pharmaceutical companies, including new biological drugs and drugs that can be used as a support for patients undergoing cytotoxic chemotherapy. As a matter of fact, pharmaceutical companies are merging, and, through the merging process, the portfolio of the new companies changes.

Medical representatives are rearranged throughout the new companies. Some of the sales representatives are now afraid of losing their job, due to the changing scenario and the possible lay offs. On the other hand, the new, bigger, pharmaceutical companies are competing more and more with one another, and, in order to stress their products, might adopt a more aggressive sales strategy. For example, sometimes in the same geographical area there are eight to ten representatives for just one company, or different representatives for the same drug in different settings. As a result of the new, aggressive strategy, the aggressiveness of representatives has also been increasing, since the larger stress exerted by their companies might affect their stay in the company. Therefore, they tend to have more frequent visits to encourage doctors to prescribe drugs and thus increase sales.

In this model medical representatives are the key actors for example in a small cardiology unit almost 40 sales representatives interacting with doctors, and most of them are coming for a visit on a regular once-a-month basis as this is the restriction put by doctors of meeting only once in a month that to on a fix time only, in order to stress the usefulness of their products and push clinicians towards the use of their drugs. This means that, basically, there are at least two representatives every day in busy clinic asking for a 'short' meeting to support their product.

Pharmaceutical marketing is a specialized field where medical representatives form the backbone of entire marketing effort. Pharmaceutical companies also appoint medical representatives and assign them defined territories. Medical representatives meet doctors, chemists and stockiest as per company norms. Medical representatives try to influence prescription pattern of doctors in favor of their brands.

The pharmaceutical distribution channel is indirect with usually three channel members i.e. depot/C&F, stockiest and chemist. Pharmaceutical companies appoint one company depot or C&F agent usually in each state and authorized stockist(s) in each district across the country. Company depot/C&F sends stocks to authorized stockists as per the requirement. Retail chemists buy medicines on daily or weekly basis from authorized stockiest as per demand. Patients visit chemists for buying medicines either prescribed by a doctor or advertised in the media. Here patient is end customer and doctor is direct customer for any pharmaceutical company. But for doctor customer (patient) is more important so he wants an effective supply chain management from prescribed company. And for pharmaceutical companies their customer that is doctor is more important that's why they emphasize more on supply chain management. Ultimately end customer is benefited out of this.

For marketing of these type of products companies require more and more skilled field force to develop good rapport with their direct customer (doctor). Moreover field force should have good product knowledge and USP of their products over other so as to convince doctors and **PULL** the demand for their products i.e. from Doctor to Retailer to Stockist to CFA to company.

CORE CUSTOMER
(Doctor)
END-CUSTOMER
(Patient)
NONCORE
CUSTOMER
(Retailer)
CUSTOMER
(Stockist)
CUSTOMER
(C & FA)
Marketing & Sales
Team

In this system, doctors are the core customers and the major thrust is given to build and retain these customer because they are pulling the demand for products hence companies also give main emphasis in building and retaining these customers. All efforts are being put for generating **secondary sales i.e.** from stockist to retailer. Ensuring of auto demand with limited availability and maximum liquidation of the products is the main characteristic of this approach.

For retaining and developing customers, the companies normally provide gifts like sponsorship for various conferences like RSSDI, FOGSI, APICON, UPCON etc. For example Dabur having PASS (Professional Academic and Scientific Services) activities for promoting its chronic therapy range.

Also it is interesting to note that since this is a pull system demand is being pulled in to the market so generally representatives calculate product orders i.e. **primary sales** from their stockist on the basis of following formula:

Normally there are absolutely no chances of dumping of goods at stockist and retailer level is yet reported also payment recovery of companies is also very good.

Marketing Approaches of Core Model

In present scenario companies are focusing more and more on the availability of products so as to enjoy good image in their customer's (doctors) chamber. Many companies such as Glaxo, Pfizer, Dabur, FDC, Aventies, and Cipla etc. are known for their availability of products.

For marketing of these types of products companies require more and more field force to remind their products on daily basis to their direct customer (doctor). Moreover field force should have good knowledge of product schemes and offers. Also field force is required to have a good rapport with retailers. Field force also required to ensure good availability of their products to convince doctors and **PUSH** their products i.e. from to Stockist to Retailer to Doctor.

It has been observed that sometimes there are more than fifteen or sixteen representatives in a day are meeting with their customer and requesting for same type of products. Although field force visits are important for an update on drugs and their use. The doctors are, in general, sneaking away, trying to hide from sales representatives, since there are too many and they are too pushy and there is too little time, and the representatives probably have noticed that the reluctant doctors have always less time for short meetings and less interest and tend to reduce the time of the visit.

SECONDARY SALES * 2 – OPENING STOCK= ORDER

The relationship between clinicians and representatives has always been good and pharmaceutical companies have provided, and still provide, the major economical support for customers' continuous medical education. Something needs to be done to find a solution to this problem that takes into account the needs of both pharmaceutical companies and their representatives on one side and physicians on the other, for a better professional interaction.

Push System Working in Acute Therapy Segment

In this system, doctors and retailers are the core customers and the major thrust is given to build and retain these customers. Here retailers are also core customer as most of the times they are substituting the products based on their own discretion.

For retaining and developing customers, the companies normally provide utility gifts to remind the products on daily basis.

Also it is interesting to note that since this is a push system products are being pushed in to the market so generally representatives place product orders from their stockist on the basis of SKUs sold and schemes. In this pumping the goods in the market and ensuring

CORE CUSTOMER
(Doctor)
END-CUSTOMER
(Patient)
CORE CUSTOMER
(Retailer)
CORE
CUSTOMER
(Stockist)
Marketing & Sales

Team more and more **primary sales i.e. from CFA to Stockist and availability of goods are major strategies.**

Normally the chances of dumping of goods at stockist and retailer level are reported also payment recovery of companies is also not very good.

Here the role of supply chain managers can be to provide considerable value to their companies by understanding the customers' delivery requirements. A very powerful tool for understanding these requirements is account segmentation. A company can use account segmentation to identify market segments Such as Acute & Chronic therapy market. which is well positioned to serve and then organize its product range and even SKU's and service in a superior way.

Companies are fighting (for customers) like never before and if anything is certain then it is further intensification of this war, and because of this companies are increasingly looking at Logistics, as a weapon to gain Competitive Advantage and it is true that Logistics has the potential to do so. and corporate cases associated with them are given below:

Conclusion

There can be various ways through which a business organization can achieve success in the market, but all those ways can be comprised into as above, then it can be rightly said that it revolves specifically around three parties or more; the triangular linkages or the relationship between these three parties (company, customers and competitors) determine the success and failure of business organization. In the medium to long run, the domestic pharmaceutical market will be largely driven by the increasing prevalence of chronic segment. The domestic industry is principally being driven by the chronic segment which has grown by **17.8%** this year. Against the backdrop up- take of acute segments has been slow and has grown by **10.1%** only. The basis of success in any competitive context can be, at the most, elemental level commercial success; and commercial success can be derived either from a cost advantage or a value advantage or ideally from a combination of both. In other words, the organization with Competitive Advantage tends to be the cost leader in the industry or a seller of most differentiated products amongst all the players. At last the role of supply chain is very prominent in both the phases (in acute as well as in chronic). But the successes of any pharmaceutical industry; when a company changes its concentration from "Acute" to "Chronic" therapy market depend on competitiveness of supply chain. Supply Chain Managers can provide considerable value to their companies by understanding the customers' delivery requirements. A very powerful tool for understanding these requirements is account segmentation. A company can use account segmentation to identify market segments Such as Acute & Chronic therapy market. which is well positioned to serve and then organize its product range and even SKU's and service in a superior way. The company must tailor its supply chain offerings to meet the needs of each of the market segment it serves. For example, **Dabur Pharma** has started launching of its products which were G.P.(**Acute Threapy**) oriented latter it enter in to specialists oriented (**Chronic Threapy**) products.

Review Questions

1. Define sales promotion? Explain the different methods of sales promotion?
2. What is product life cycle? Explain strategies to extend the product life cycle with examples?
3. What is sales organization"? What are the different types of sales organization available in the marketing process?
4. Explain marketing mix? What significance does marketing mix has in Pharma. Industry?
5. Explain the concepts 'market" and 'marketing' with suitable examples? add a note on social marketing and multi level marketing?
6. What are channels of distribution and explain its importance in market building?
7. Add note on the following: (a) window display (b) e-marketing.
8. What are the different factors to be considered while deciding about a suitable channel of distribution?
9. Explain the major differences between general marketing and Pharma marketing?
10. Explain the various functions of marketing?

5 Principles of Management

5.1 | Management – A Dynamic Science

Management is a dynamic science. According to need, time and circumstances it has undergone significant changes time and again. It is said that in future too it would adjust and embody in itself the changes which would be necessitated.

Industrial and other economic activities are becoming complex day by day. These are creating numerous problems which are to be tackled as per the dictate of the situations arising from time to time. The management has to cope up with such complexities. With technological advancement management services are also becoming complex every day. All these have given rise to more researches and new generalizations and principles have since been evolved in order to make the management up to date and helpful in coping up the problems which the industrial and commercial world is facing today. These have also revealed the dynamic character of the management sciences which has stood up the test of the time and which has shown the enormous capacity of adaptability.

LEARNING OBJECTIVES

- *Principles of Management*
- *Management Thoughts (Theories of Management)*
- *Scientific Management Theory*
- *Management Process Theory*
- *Comparison between Management of F.W.Taylor and Henry Fayol*
- *Coordination*
- *Communication*
- *Motivation*
- *Morale*
- *Leadership*
- *Qualities of a good leader*
- *Decision Making*
- *Steps in decision making*
- *Advantages of workers' participation in decision making*
- *Authority*

5.2 | Principles of Management

Principles are fundamental truths applicable to a given set of circumstances and having value in predicting results. A management principle is a statement of a general truth about organization or management. 'Principles of Management are the guiding rules of laws for managerial action.' They are designed primarily to provide a better understanding of business circumstances and improving the organizational performance.

A number of principles of management have been developed to aid managers in performing their functions well. The growth of modern management techniques began with the industrial revolution in England during the 18th and 19th centuries. The development and inventions during industrial revolution led to the emergence of different schools of thought of management. The divergent directions of management thoughts have caused one management writer, Harold Koontz, to call the resulting array "Management Theory Jungle." Starting with the oldest school of management theory, the different approaches can be summarized as follows:

5.3 | Management Thoughts (Theories of Management)

1. Scientific Management School
2. Management Process School
3. Human Relations School
4. Behavioral Sciences School
5. Quantitative Approach to Management
6. Systems Approach to Management
7. Contingency Approach to Management
8. Operational Approach to Management

5.4 | Scientific Management

F.W. Taylor is regarded as the father of Scientific Management. Taylor's chief contribution was not in the field of higher management. He devoted mainly at the shop-floor level. The idea he brought to the Science of Management include the following:

- Planning of work in advance
- Selecting the best man for identified jobs
- Timing of jobs in its minute possible points
- Determining the standard time required for the accomplishment of a given job

- Standardizing of tools and equipment and right training, motion for the use of such tools and equipments
- Eliminating unnecessary movement in and outside the workshop
- Dividing the work, and
- The scientific approach to all the problems in management.

Regarding scientific approach Taylor himself summed up his combination of principles in the following terms:

- Science, not rule of thumb
- Harmony, not discord
- Cooperation, not individualism
- Maximum output, in place of restricted output

The development of each man to his greatest efficiency and prosperity.

For industries the scientific approach to the problems in management yield the following results:

- Reduction in labour trouble due to harmony, co-operation and development of each person according to his greatest efficiency which in turn helps the labour to earn more and more.
- Increase in productivity due to maximum utilization of labour resources to the extent it is humanly possible with maximum possible co-operation and greatest degree of harmony.
- Improvement in the quality of products due to efficient working and scientific production.
- Promptness in meeting the orders.

The labour with the help of Taylor's scientific management derives the following main advantages:

- Easier work
- High pay
- Steady movement
- Job satisfaction

Taylor's scientific management was criticized on grounds that Taylor's intention was to give all gains to the labour out of his principles of scientific management. At that time Taylor's critics did not realize that with the help of scientific approach to the problems of management, efficiency would be brought at all levels. The fruits from scientific approach to managerial problems at all levels would certainly be shared by both the workers and the management.

5.5 | Management Process Theory

The advocates of this school perceive management as a process of getting things done through and with people operating in organizational groups. "It aims to analyse the process, to establish a conceptual framework for it, to identify principles underlying it, and to build a theory of management from them. It regards management as a universal process, regardless of the type of the enterprise, or the level in a given enterprise. It looks upon management theory as a way of organizing experience so that practice can be improved through research, empirical testing of principles and teaching of fundamentals involved in the management process." This process school is also called the 'traditional or universalist' school as it believes that management principles are applicable to all the group activities. Henry Fayol is regarded as the father of this school. Oliver Sheldon, J.D. Mooney and Chester I. Barnard are the other important contributors to this approach.

Henry Fayol (1841-1925)

Henry Fayol was almost a contemporary of F.W.Taylor who worked quite independently and in different circumstances though on the same branch of knowledge and discipline. Unlike Taylor, Fayol started from the top of the management as a technical process, of course, subject to certain generalizations based on empirical analysis.

Fayol divided all industrial activities into the following six groups:

1. Technical – production, manufacture and adaption
2. Commercial – buying, selling and exchange
3. Financial – search for optimum use of capital
4. Security – protection of property and person
5. Accounting – stock-taking, balance sheets, costing and statistics.
6. Managerial

His main theory was that with every group of activities there exists a corresponding special ability. He advocated that respective special ability required by every group of activities must necessarily be in sufficient amount at the top also. He believed that technical ability at higher level is not of much significance as compared to administrative ability without which the interest of the enterprise may not be served well. He also advocated that technical ability curve goes up while the curves of other abilities slopes down from higher to lower hierarchy.

He sub-divided the key functions of management (he called it as administration) into five groups which are given below:

1. Prevoyance (forecasting and planning)
2. Organization
3. Co-ordination

4. Command
5. Control

He reviewed the principles of management also. According to him there are fourteen principles which an effective management usually follows. The principles as given by Fayol are enumerated as under:

- Division of Work
- Authority and Responsibility
- Discipline
- Unity of Command
- Unity of Direction
- Subordination of individual interest to general interest
- Remuneration of personnel
- Centralization and De-centralization
- Scalar Chain (Line of Authority)
- Order
- Equity
- Stability of the tenure of personnel
- Initiative
- Esprit de corps (Team Spirit)

5.6 | Comparison between Management of F.W.Taylor and Henry Fayol

F.W. Taylor	Henry Fayol
1. Taylor's philosophy of Management is known as "Scientific Management"	1. Fayol's approach to management is known as "General Theory of Administration"
2. His concept was to improve labour productivity and eliminating all types of waste through standardization of the theory	2. Fayol developed an universal theory of management. He laid more stress or teaching work and tools and practice of management.
3. Taylor's management was from the supervisory point of view and he tried principles to improve efficiency at the shop floor.	3. Fayol laid more concentration on the functions of managers and his of management is applicable to all spheres of human activity.
4. Taylor looked at management from the supervisory point of view and tried to improve efficiency at the operating level	4. Fayol analysed management from the angle of top management downward emphasis on co-ordination.

5.7 | Coordination

Coordination is harmonization of all the activities of a concern in order to facilitate its working and its success. It is the orderly arrangement of a group effort, to provide unity of action in persuasion of common goal. It is the effort to ensure a smooth interplay of the functions and forces of all different component parts of an organization to the end that its purposes will be realized with a minimum of friction and a maximum of collaborative effectiveness.

Nature of coordination

1. Coordination is the responsibility of the top executive which is related with the qualities of his leadership.
2. Coordination is a process the need of which is felt in all the activities. The managers, however, should be conscious of "the coordinating efforts".
3. Coordination is an orderly arrangement of group activities which is a necessity in all activities. It is important particularly in a group related activity.
4. Coordination's success largely depends on unity of action.
5. Coordination aims at the attainment of common purpose as defined by the objectives of the enterprise.

***Characteristics of Coordination*:** "Good coordination," according to Koontz and O'Donnel, "is that which solves the problems when it comes to the fare." However, according to them the best coordination is that which forecasts the problems and takes necessary preventing measures so that it may not arise at all.

Every effort should be made to have best coordination system. But efforts should always be made for a good system of coordination. A good system of coordination should satisfy the following characteristics:

1. Coordination should not be made through orders. It should not come from the above. Instead it should come through cooperation and willingness. Coordination through cooperation and willingness ensures better results.
2. Coordinating activities must respond to time, policies, programmes and objectives. They should always be in tune.
3. Coordinating approach should be balanced and as far as possible it should be of both the types – vertical as well as horizontal.
4. Coordination should be based on personal contact, mutual cooperation, mutual confidence, good human relations and above all on the continuity principles.
5. Coordination should aim at morale boosting of the workers.

***Advantages of Coordination*:** The following are the advantages of a good coordination system:

Increases the Efficiency: If there is an effective coordination of all the activities of the enterprise, then there is no reason why efficiency of the business enterprise cannot increase. Overall and effective coordination results in the following benefits to the organization in general:

1. It increases the productivity
2. It economizes the various processes
3. It helps in economizing the activities and interrelated economy
4. It reduces the cost of production
5. It reduces the cost of distribution and marketing
6. It results in increased profitability.

Improves the Morale: Effective leadership makes the coordination effective and thereby successful. An effective coordination helps in increasing the efficiency of the business enterprise which brings growth and prosperity to the enterprise. A growing and prosperous enterprise not only secures the job of those who are working with the enterprise but future promotion, expected higher income and further incentives encourages the workers to come out with their best to help their enterprise to achieve success. This naturally boosts the morale of the workers. Hence they work with a common aim to achieve the pre-determined objectives.

Develops and Retains Good Personnel: Coordination helps in evaluation of work and conduct of all those who are working for the enterprise. Evaluation in its turn helps in rewarding the good worker. If workers are being suitably rewarded it is natural for them to remain with their organization and serve it better. They, therefore, would not like to leave the organization. Instead they would like to stick to it. An effective and successful coordination attains the objective of developing its working force and retaining them with the organization as long as they are fit to render their valuable services to their organization.

Types of Coordination

There are two types of coordination. 1. Internal Coordination and 2. External Coordination.

1. ***Internal Coordination***: Internal coordination is the establishment of relationship with a view to coordinate the activities of all the departments, divisions, sub-divisions, branches, managers, executives and other workers.

   It is classified into two types (a) Vertical Coordination and (b) Horizontal Coordination

   (a) *Vertical Coordination*: Vertical coordination refers to that coordination in which a superior authority coordinates with his subordinates and vice-versa. Production manager coordinates the activities of production superintendent.

Similarly production superintendent is required to have a coordination and cordial relation with his superior(s).

(b) *Horizontal Coordination*: Horizontal Coordination refers to coordination of relations and activities between the authorities and employees of same status e.g., coordination between different departmental heads, foremen of different workshops, superintendents of different sections etc.

2. ***External Coordination***: External Coordination refers to the establishment of relationship with a view to coordinate the activities of those who are not the part of the organization and hence are not internally connected with each other. The enterprise has to establish relations and coordinate their activities for the benefit of the enterprise as a whole.

   The following are the outside agencies with which an enterprise has to establish relationship for the benefit of the enterprise:

   - Market Agencies
   - Competitors
   - Union Government, State Government(s), Local Self Government(s) and

   Other Government Agencies:

   - Technological Agencies
   - Different commercial organizations
   - Different Industrial Organizations
   - Different Institutions rendering auxiliary services
   - Customers
   - General Public

The function of external coordination is assigned to a person who is specially appointed for the purpose. He is generally designated as Public Relations Officer.

Principles of Coordination: The following are the principles of coordination with the help of which an executive ensures integrated efforts in an organization with a minimum of friction and a maximum of collaborative effectiveness

Principles of Early Beginning: The success of coordinating activities depends on the beginning itself. If it has started at the early stage it will prove fruitful. Planning is the beginning of an enterprise. Coordination should be from this very stage.

Principle of Direct Contact: Instead of issuing orders and instructions it is rewarding if the coordinating parties meet personally and talk over the matter. This helps in mutual understanding and creates mutual confidence. A respect for each other develops between the personnel at the same level and also at different levels which is helpful in future also.

Principle of Reciprocity: A situation can be easily visualized where all elements are influenced by doing and undoing of each one. For example, in an industrial undertaking production department is as much linked with purchase department as the personnel department or vice versa. Principle of reciprocity help in coordinating the efforts of each other thus help in establishing an effective and harmonious relations between each other.

***Principle of Continuity*:** Coordination is a continuous process. It goes on relentlessly from the very beginning. If anywhere it either stops or slackens, a derailment is the only possibility which in that case will harm the whole enterprise.

***Techniques of Coordination*:** The following are the six techniques which adopted in coordinating the efforts of different individuals and groups of individuals working for an enterprise to attain a common purpose:

Coordination

1. by Command
2. by Personnel Leadership
3. by Communication
4. by Committee
5. by Group meeting
6. by Special Appointee

***Coordination by Command*:** Managerial order is the first stage in coordination which is also regarded as an important method of coordinating the efforts. A manager keeps an eye over the work and conduct of his subordinates. The work and conduct are regulated, directed, guided and controlled through order either in the form of advice or in the form of do's and don'ts or in any other suitable form.

In principle coordination by command is good. But modern thinkers don't consider this as good method since in the technique human relations are pushed to the background which in the long run may not prove to be fruitful either for the management or for the enterprise.

***Coordination by Personnel Leadership*:** Coordination expects a high class leadership. According to E.F.L. Breach 'Coordination is a human effort in which the character temperament and morals of the manager are very important. His personal example may have a lasting effect on his subordinates who may emulate him. If this happens the self-coordination attitude may develop among subordinates.

Limitations of span of control however, limit the utility of this technique of coordination.

***Coordination by Communication*:** Communication efforts, if effective and properly channelized go a long way in establishing a good system of communication. What is required here is that communication should be complete, properly channelized and fully effective. Circulars, Bulletins, Code of Conduct, Rules and Regulations, Bye-laws are a few of the communicative documents which are adopted in coordinating the efforts of an enterprise.

***Coordination by Committees*:** Committee form of organization is on increase these days. With the help of departmental heads and conveners of committee and sub committees, the Chief Executive coordinates the activities of an enterprise. It is easy for him to coordinate with the help of committee. It is less time consuming and less efforts are involved in coordinating the activities according to this technique of coordination.

***Coordination by Group Meetings*:** Where committee form of organization is not in existence coordination through group meeting is advantageous. Here also it is easy to coordinate. Cooperation usually comes of its own from subordinates who feels elevated when attending a meeting called by the executive.

***Coordination by Special Appointee*:** For coordinating the activities in the enterprise an independent coordinator may be appointed. He may be made in charge of his cell and may be asked to look after the coordinating activities. This is regarded as a very sound and satisfactory technique of coordination. The coordinator appointed to look after the coordinating activities may have to be made master of all which is neither possible nor various executives would like such an arrangement. The appointed coordinator will be then deprived of the active cooperation of all the personnel in the enterprise which undoubtedly is essential for any coordinating efforts. Moreover the coordinator so appointed may not be master of all. At best he can be jack of all. This naturally will not be a good arrangement because the coordinator may not be able to do justice to the job entrusted to him, in such a situation.

Choice of technique of coordination depends on the size, time, purpose and technicalities of the job in an enterprise. There may be a combination of techniques which may be adopted by an enterprise.

5.8 | Communication

Any business organization is a human group constituted for certain specified objectives. The achievement of these objectives largely depends upon the fact that all human efforts are properly coordinated and integrated. Individuals in the organization performing different activities are functionally interrelated. The working and maintaining of these relationships is possible only through communication. It provides for exchange of information. No business organization can work without communication network. It is an important human skill.

Communication is to tell, to inform, to show or to spread information. It is an inter exchange of thoughts and information. Communication thus is a (i) Two-way traffic and involves more than one person, (ii) Continuous process, (iii) Short-period process (as long as messages etc., are being made understood or received) (iv) Process of conveying messages etc. (v) It deals with the transmission of facts and feelings or both (vi) Media of communication may be numerous (vii) The process of communication is a continuous one and (viii) The effectiveness of communication depends upon the proper understanding of what is being communicated and what is being received and then responded.

Communication Process: Communication has been defined as a process. The process is a concept of changing rather than static existence. Events and relationships are seen as dynamic, continuous and flexible and are strutted only in a relative sense. Communication process, as such, must be considered, as a whole, a continuous and dynamic interaction both effecting and being affected by many variables.

The events of communication process

A communication process involves the following elements:

Sender □ Ideas □ Encoding □ Channel □ Receiving □ Decoding □ Feedback

Thus the above illustration shows the following elements:

1. ***Sender***: The person, who intends to make contact with objective of passing information and ideas to other persons, is known as sender.
2. ***Ideas***: This is the subject matter of communication. This might be an opinion, attitude, feelings, views, orders or suggestions etc.
3. ***Encoding***: Since the subject matter of communication is abstract and intangible, its transmission requires the use of certain symbols such as words, actions or pictures, etc. Conversion of the subject matter into these symbols is the process of encoding.
4. ***Channel***: These symbols are transmitted to the receiver through certain channel or medium.
5. ***Receiver***: Receiver is the person to whom message is meant for.
6. ***Decoding***: Receiver converts the symbols received from the sender to give him the meaning of the message.
7. ***Feedback***: Feedback is the process of ensuring that the receiver has received the message and understood in the same sense as sender meant it.

Objectives of Communication

The following are the main purposes of a communication:

1. ***Conveying the right message***: The fact is that communication is meant for conveying the message which should be a right one to the right person. The message conveyed should be well understood and accepted. The message is not

only meant for simple understanding or acceptance. It has to be translated into practice as well. The receiver should therefore understand it correctly and may, then, he will be able to carry out the message effectively.

2. ***Coordination*:** To co-ordinate the efforts of all who are involved in running a business is the important and a necessary activity of the management. Communication serves as a tool for coordinating activity. Coordination without communication is a remote possibility.
3. ***Good industrial relations*:** To have a good industrial relation it invites every success at your doorsteps. Success is considered to be in the bag of an industrial enterprise. Communication aims at such a good industrial relation.
4. ***Development of managerial skill*:** Communication is a learning process of facts, information, ideas, etc., which enriches the knowledge of the executive. He tries to make use of the acquired knowledge which results in an increase in his wisdom and skill.
5. ***Effectiveness of policies*:** Policies and programs of the enterprise need communication to those who are to execute them. Effective communication translates the policies into effective instrument of seeing through the organization on the rail of its progress. Effectiveness of the policies can be judged from its success which surely depends on effective communication system.

Fundamentals of Communication

The following are the important fundamentals of communication which are the guiding force for an executive of a business and industrial organization.

1. Specific purpose of communication for which it is meant.
2. Study of the receiver of the communication who is to accept and comply with the message he receives.
3. Organization of an idea so that it may be properly arranged and correctly understood.
4. Interesting transmission so as to make it readily acceptable. Communication is an art. This art is to be practiced. The interest of the receiver is to be aroused, sustained and assured for the bare statement or narration of bare facts, howsoever tasteful it may be, does nor pay dividends. Comparison analogies etc., naturally help.
5. Personal touch, sympathy and comparison on the part of the communication help in better understanding. Before communicating for an effective compliance the communicator must think of the receiver's attitude and response. As far as possible the communicator should avoid official attitude. This may be responded by the receiver and thus may ensure effective compliance.

Principles of Communication

The factors which make a communication in an industrial concern are the principles of communication which may be enumerated as under:

1. ***Principles of clarity***: The message should be clear. It should be communicated in simple, easy and commonly understood language. The words do not speak themselves. They convey. It is the speaker who makes them meaningful and it is the receiver who interprets them. Therefore whatever is conveyed should be conveyed in unambiguous clear words.
2. ***Principles of attention***: The recipient's attention to the message communicated must be drawn in order to make the communication effective. The communication is always meant for action. Words may not help. Dale Breach has rightly put it that "People think with their heart, not with their mind." Human heart is the controller of emotions and it is the emotion which decides the degree of our attention which he may be inclined to pay to the communication received by him.
3. It is not possible to assess every time the emotions and moods of individuals in an organization. However, a good manager has to decide time of communication. This decision of time helps him in reducing the effect of man's emotions and moods.
4. ***Principle of consistency***: The communications should be consistent with the plans, policies, programs and objectives of the enterprise. Among themselves also communications should be consistent communications.
5. ***Principle of adequacy***: Communications should be adequate and complete. It should not be broken neither in any way incomplete. Inadequate communication delays action and spoils understanding as well as good relations. Efficiency of both the communicator and recipient is also affected.
6. ***Principle of time***: Information should be communicated at the proper time. When it is to be communicated, it is of course the prerogative of the communicator but wrong choice of time may not have the desired impact on recipient.
7. ***Principle of Integration***: Communication is a means and not an end itself. It is a means to attain the objectives of the enterprise. Communication tries to get cooperation of all with a view to see that the work is accomplished satisfactorily. Therefore, it should as far as possible be based on the policy of integration of efforts in order to avoid confusion and help in better understanding. It should be such that it may help in achieving a genuine spirit of co-operation among the personnel of the organization.
8. ***Principle of Informality***: Informality in any sphere of life is a good principle and the executive should try to remain informal in his behavior with his subordinates. But in a certain situation, of which the individual executive is the sole and best judge, he may bid good bye to informality and become formal in his relations and conduct.

9. ***Principle of feedback*:** Communication is a two-way traffic. Messages, policies, programs, directions, opinions etc., are communicated downward. Grievances, complaints, suggestions etc., are communicated upward. Both are necessary in an organization. It is because of this reason that communication is also termed as two-way process. Communication follows the principle of 'give and take'. Communications are meant for being communicated. But reaction of the communication is also to be known and judged. The reactions should be calmly watched, sympathetically received and incorporated wherever and whenever necessary.

Methods (Types) of Communication: The important types of communications in industry are as follows:

1. According to Organizational Structure
   - (a) Formal
   - (b) Informal
2. According to Expression
   - (a) Oral
   - (b) Written
3. According to the direction
   - (a) Upward Communication
   - (b) Downward Communication
   - (c) Horizontal Communication

1. *According to Organizational Structure*:

***(a) Formal Communication*:** Formal Communication is possible in formal type of organizational structure. In this type of communication the status or position in the hierarchy of the communicator as well as receiver is important. Formal communication establishes a relationship between the two positions. The General Managers communicate with superintendents, superintendents with supervisors and so on. A formal communication derives its support from scalar chain system of organization

***Merits of formal communication*:** The formal communication or communication through channels of command has the following advantages:

- ***Maintenance of authority of the officers*:** The formal communication helps the maintenance of authority of the line officers. Subordinates respect their superiors. It helps in exercising control over subordinates and fixation of responsibility in respect of activities to be carried on by a person in the organization.

- ***Sound and proper communication*:** An immediate superior has a direct contact with his subordinates. He understands their attitudes, wants, level of intelligence and capacity as well. He can determine it efficiently as to how, what and at what time the information is to be communicated and to whom. It is easy to maintain and orderly in nature.
- ***Other advantages*:** Formal communication offers certain other advantages too. The formal organization moulds the communication process along certain lines. It receives the support of line authorities and closeness of superior subordinates reduces the chances of misunderstanding.

***Demerits of formal communication*:** Formal communication is not an unmixed blessing. It has the following disadvantages too:

- ***Overload of work*:** In modern business organizations, there is a lot of information, messages and other things to be communicated and that if transmitted through formal lines of authority only, it will increase the workload on line officers. They will not be able to perform their other functions well.
- ***Decay in accuracy*:** It provides bottlenecks in the flow of information. It enhances the organizational distance also and the chances of more transmission errors are likely to incur there. Screening of information at various positions reduces the accuracy of the message.
- ***Overlook by line officers*:** Communication through chains of command is not suitable for upward communications at all. Line officers do not take any interest in the grievances of their subordinates. They do not like to forward the suggestions to the top management given by their subordinates. They naturally introduce their own views into information. This bias changes the nature and characteristics of information when it reaches its final destination.

***(b) Informal communication*:** This type of communication is based on informal relationship that grows up in an organization informally. It is generally referred to as the grapevine system of communication. A nod, a glance, a gesture, a smile, a silence may be the way to convey the message in this system of communication. Informal communication as distinguished from formal communication is more indirect, less explicit, mostly unofficial, spontaneous and flexible. Gossip and rumor may become a part of communication under informal method though it may never be intended to.

***Merits of informal communication*:** Informal channels of communication perform a positive service to the organization. It operates with much greater speed. Moreover, there might be certain subject matter of communication which do not require their transmission through the formal channel. The formal network of communications is often relatively static, while the organization it seeks to act is dynamic and react quickly to its changing environment. Consequently, the informal non-stable network of communications comes into frequently plain in every organization. The informal communication needs of the various persons in the organization, more particularly those persons who freely mix up with others and rely upon informal relationships. A typical informal communication network involves people within the same hierarchy level of an organization, for example, among various departmental managers. Such communication enhances the ability of the organization to meet sudden problems.

***Demerits of informational communication*:** Informal communication has certain basic limitations also. It is less orderly and less static also. Sometimes, messages communicated through the informal channel are so erratic that any action based on these may lead to difficult situation to the organization. Often, it carries inaccurate information, half truths, rumors and distorted information. In this case, the irresponsibility of the persons communicating through the informal channel is the most important factor. Since origin and direction of the flow of information is hard to pinpoint, it is difficult to assign responsibility for false information or morale lowering rumors. Moreover, each person conveying the message may add, or subtract or change the original message according to his motive, information communication problems multiply. There is chance that by the time a communication completes a complex journey it may be completely distorted.

The informal communication is the part and parcel of the organizational process. The only thing management can do in this respect to take suitable actions to minimize the adverse effects of such channels. Proper analysis of informal communication and a suitable classification in this respect would be helpful in making its use towards organizational efficiency.

2. ***According to Expression*:** There are two types of communications in this category:

   (a) Oral or Verbal Communication

   (b) Written Communication.

   ***(a) Oral or verbal communication*:** When face-to-face conversation is resorted to and for every communicator and recipient is in verbal contact then it is termed as oral or verbal communication. Verbal orders, address, discussions, conferences, table talks, interviews, radio talk, telephonic conversation, ringing the bell etc., are a few of the examples of verbal communication.

***Advantages of oral or verbal communication*:**

The following are important advantages of a verbal communication:

- It saves time and money. There is absolutely no shortcut to verbal communication.
- It gives a personal touch. It, therefore, is more effective. Gestures, tones, facial expressions make communication effective and efficient.
- It helps in greater understanding. Doubts are spontaneously cleared. Queries answered and clarified making the communication easy and simple. Give and take spirit makes the willing acceptance possible.
- The communicator knows immediately the reaction of the recipient.
- The spoken words are more flexible and certainly because of this quality it proves to be the best way of communication even in modern management also. "The fact that the spoken word appeared first both in the history of man and in the conduct of management does not mean that it is primitive medium. On the contrary we can look for an increased application and refinement of oral media in the large and complex organization of today and tomorrow," say Redfield.

***Disadvantages of Oral or Verbal Communication*:** It does not mean that verbal communication is all good. It suffers from certain disadvantages also. The disadvantages are as enumerated below:

- In most of the cases the impact of verbal communication is temporary.
- If long and clear communication is intended to them the verbal communication becomes fairly unsuitable.
- No thinking is possible in this type of communication. Spontaneous decision is to be taken by the recipient.
- Own interest of the recipient is always uppermost in his mind at the time of conversation with the communicator. He usually takes less interest in communication.
- The past relationship between the communicator and recipient comes in the way of effective verbal communication.

***(b) Written Communication*:** When face-to-face conversation is avoided and communication of ideas, orders, instructions etc., are resorted to writing then it is designated as written communication.

***Advantages of written communication*:** The following are the advantages of a written communication:

- The written communication is the only means of communication where the communicator and recipient are at a distant place and even telephonic conversation is neither convenient nor very much possible.

- Written communication is the only way out where the communication is lengthy and is meant for larger number of persons.
- Policy matters, service conditions, secret orders, instructions etc., can only be satisfactorily and effectively communicated through written communication.
- Written communications have permanent effect on the recipient.
- Written communications are helpful in reducing dispute, jurisdictional fractions, buck passing etc.
- Written communications give time to the recipient to think, analyze and then decide their own course of action.

***Disadvantages of written communication*:** Written communication though appears to have more advantages is certainly not free from disadvantages. The following are the main disadvantages of written communication:

- It is time consuming. It cannot be as brief as possible. Neither can it be communicated as quickly as a verbal communication can.
- Everything cannot be put in black and white, anticipation of everything at the time of writing is obviously the greatest handicap.
- It cannot remain as confidential as it might be intended to.
- It is seldom flexible.
- Red-tapism is the result of every written communication.

Verbal v/s Written Communication a Comparative Account

Oral	Written
1. Personal Instructions	1. Rules and Instructions
2. Lecture, Conferences, Meetings.	2. Letters, Circulars and Memos.
3. Interviews	3. Bulletin and Notice Boards
4. Grapevine, rumors	4. Posters
5. Face-to-face conversation	5. Handbooks and Manuals.
6. Telephone, etc.	6. Annual Reports
7. Union Channels	7. House Magazines
8. Union Publications	
9. Personal letters and suggestions	
10. Complaint Procedure	

5.9 | Motivation

Human motives are based on needs. Some of our needs are primary and some of them are secondary. Food, cloth, shelter, water, air, sleep, sex are some of the primary needs and affiliation, status, love and affection, self-assertion are some of the secondary needs of human being. These needs may vary in intensity and according to situation and time, but certainly these are the motivating factors about which a manger must know.

Performance of a group of individuals depends on the needs of the group as well as of individuals who are forming the group. Group's needs may not be the same as that of individuals but given a common goal, the individuals who are forming the group may come to identify themselves with the group's needs. The sole responsibility of the manger is to recognize the group's need without unduly and unimaginately compromising the needs of individuals who as a group have extended their helping hand for the accomplishment of given task. The manager creates and then maintains necessary environment for the accomplishment of the objectives. This he does by motivating – inducing the people to work for the attainment of the objectives.

Motivation is an act of energizing and activating the people to satisfy their needs. If their energies are channelised then certainly it is going to satisfy their needs – human needs and social needs. Social needs if satisfied leads to a safe conclusion that the objectives are being achieved. The efforts are thus being directed towards right channels in a right direction. This means that the management is making the people to work. If work is going on smoothly then it means that people at work have properly been induced, in other words, effectively motivated. Knoontz and O'Donnell are of the view that "motivation is a general term applying to the entire class of drives, desires, needs, wishes and similar forces that induce an individual or a group of people to work".

Definition: Motivation is a process consisting of three important parts.

1. The Motive
2. The Needs, drives, desires, aspirations etc. and
3. Attainment of the objectives. Motivation is the process of attempting to influence others to do your will through the possibility of gain or reward.

Elements of sound motivation system: The following are the important elements of sound motivation system.

- ***Productivity***: A good motivational system is that which helps in increasing efficiency and productivity of the labour.
- ***Competition***: An inducement to work hard and compete with each other is a sound proof of the good motivational system. Of course, one has to see that the cost of production does not go up because of such inducements.
- ***Comprehensiveness***: A good motivational system should help the working force to satisfy primary, social and personal needs. It should be applicable to all types of workers and as far as possible in equal proportion.

- ***Flexibility***: A motivation system should be such which is able to adopt itself according to circumstances and situations since different individuals or group of individuals has different needs and thus can be induced differently. Rigidity in any system is not good. Flexibility helps in adjustments; hence advocated.

Importance of motivation: If the members of an organization are effectively motivated then from such motivation the expected results are that:

- All the members will try to cooperate and coordinate their activities with a view to achieve the goals which they are required to achieve.
- All the members will do their best to carry out the plans in accordance with the policies and programmes laid down by the organization.
- All the members will also try to be as efficient as possible. And will try to improve upon their skill and knowledge so that they may be able to contribute to the progress of the organization as much it is possible.

These results will accrue to the organization because all the members are known of the fact that in return they will get what have been promised to them. And ultimately they will be able to satisfy their needs – personal as well as social.

Methods of motivation: Motivation is a planned inducement to the employees offered by an organization. It may be of monetary nature or of non-monetary nature.

Monetary motivation

1. Personal 2. Group

1. ***Personal***: Different financial incentives to individual workforce.
2. ***Group***:
   (a) Participation in management
   (b) Profit sharing plan
   (c) Equal wage rate for equal work
   (d) Pensions
   (e) Dividends and Bonus.

Non-monetary motivation

1. Personal 2. Group 3. Organizational

1. ***Personal***
   - Dignity of work
   - Security and stability of job
   - Future promotions
   - Motivation and reward for constructive work

2. ***Group***
   - Team work
   - Healthy competition
   - Loyalty
   - Societal recognition for hard work
   - Honest and sincere work for attainment of the objectives
3. ***Organizational*:**
   - Good discipline
   - Development of morality
   - Improvement in human relations
   - Participation in management
   - Better and effective communication

***Advantages of motivation*:** A good motivation plan offers the following advantages:

1. Increasing the productivity and efficiency of operation
2. Decreasing the tardiness and absentism
3. Decreasing the opposition to changes being effected for better organizational results
4. Decreasing the friction between workers themselves and between the management and workers. Instead it improves the relations
5. Decreasing the wastage and accidents
6. Decreasing the number of complaints and grievances thereby reducing the loss in man-hour.
7. Increasing the possibility of reduced cost of production and distribution
8. Increasing the overall efficiency in the organization.

5.10 | Morale

The satisfaction or dissatisfaction from the job gives to the psychological problem of morale. Morale is an individual or group feeling of competence and confidence reinforced by job satisfaction and need fulfillment. It may precede or follow performance and productivity. Morale is a total attitude towards oneself, one's work and one's colleagues. In work situations, it is a product of need satisfaction and job satisfaction level.

Definition: "Morale is a feeling of togetherness. There is a sense of identification with an interest in the elements of one's job, working conditions, fellow workers, supervisors, employers and the company".

Measurement of morale: According to John M. Pfiffner there are two ways of measuring the morale

1. ***Result method*:** Checking the extent to which the organization is achieving results. The extent of increase or decrease in profitability, productivity or any other direct benefit to the enterprise.
2. ***Attitude–gain method*:** The extent to which sentiments and attitude of an employee has developed for the betterment of the organization and the work has gained momentum can be a measuring rod. Attitude surveys help in measuring the morale in quantitative terms.

Importance: Morale, productivity of workers and their level of motivation are directly correlated. As we know, motivation is an intrinsic ability and desire for positive efforts towards performance. The word 'motivation' is derived from 'motive' which is defined as an inner state that activites a man to do some work or channelise his behavior towards goals. So, it is clear that if the level of morale is high, the motivation degree will also be high. If these both are high, the quantity of work and level of performance will also be high. Consequently, positive efforts and sound performance in job will also lead to high morale and motivation. Thus, we can say that the level of morale of an efficient and capable worker will be high, simultaneously, he will be highly motivated too. But research studies have been unable to establish a conclusive and consistent correlation between motivation and morale. Sometimes, it happens that the morale is high but productivity is low or vice versa. Similarly, in some cases, high morale and low motivation may also co-exit. It is also possible to witness situations in which people suffering from low morale do neverthless perform the assigned tasks rather well. But theoretically, we may say that motivation, productivity and morale move together.

Essential steps for building morale: The following are a few of the steps which may be taken by the Manager to build the morale of his employees:

1. Right job to right person under right knowledgeable, skilled and intelligent supervisor.
2. Proper and adequate training
3. Expansion of work
4. Change of work whenever possible
5. Improvement in working system
6. Proper division of work
7. Unbiased work analysis
8. Good work evaluation system
9. Development of good communication system
10. Provision of incentives – both monetary and non-monetary
11. Promotion channel

12. Provision for suggestions and actions thereon
13. Institution of awards for work and suggestion, if original and beneficial to the organization.

5.11 | Leadership

Leadership is a quality in human beings to induce his followers to do whatever he is directed to do with zeal and enthusiasm. Literally the term 'leadership' has come from the word 'lead'. The verb 'to lead' has meanings – 'to excel or to be in advance' and 'govern' and command other or to head an organization. Leadership is the ability to secure desirable actions from a group of followers voluntarily, without the use of coersion.

Managers at all levels act as leaders because they have subordinates (followers) whose efforts have to be channalised in a definite direction. It is only the leadership of management that guides, inspires and directs organization members for achieving common purposes. It is the quality of leadership that usually determines the failure or success of a business enterprise. As a matter of fact, no organizational unit can function effectively without effective leadership.

The following are the four important primary functions of a leader.

1. To represent the organization and its mission.
2. To initiate steps which are necessary for healthy and progressive growth of the organization.
3. To administer the undertaking.
4. To interpret the reasons for everything to everybody, particularly the reasons for the changes demanded by those who help him in administration.

The differences between a boss and a leader are as follows:

The Boss	The Leader
1. He drives and orders.	1. He coaches and advises
2. He depends on his authority	2. He depends on his confidence and enthusiasm.
3. He engenders fear.	3. He inspires enthusiasm.
4. He fixes blames and finds faults.	4. He solves problems.
5. He knows all the problems	5. He knows all the answers.
6. He makes the work drudgery.	6. He makes the work a game
7. He believes in "I".	7. He believes in "we" and "you"

Characteristics of leadership: The important traits of Leadership are as follows:

1. Leadership is a personal quality of character and behavior in man which enables him to exert internal personal influence.

2. Leadership helps others in choosing and attaining specified goals to the maximum satisfaction of both the leader and the follower.
3. The leader leads his group with authority and confidence.
4. The leader unifies his group and motivates the group to work for the attainment of a goal.
5. The leader establishes relationship between an individual and a group around some common interest.
6. Leadership is the process of
   (i) directing
   (ii) guiding and
   (iii) influencing the people to do their best for the attainment of a specified goal.

Qualities of a good leader: The essential qualities of a good leader can be grouped into the following four categories.

1. Physical qualities
2. Psychological qualities
2. Intellectual qualities
4. Character qualities.

1. ***Physical qualities*:** These are the qualities related to a physical personality of a leader.
   - Good Health to work for fulfilling the obligations of the organization
   - Vigor, vitality and endurance to face hardships and difficulties.
2. ***Psychological qualities*:** These are the qualities related to the mental psyche of a leader
   - Personnel magnetism
   - Enthusiasm
   - Co-operation
   - Ability to inspire and integrate
   - Resourcefulness
   - Exerting
   - Tact and skillful handling
3. ***Intellectual qualities*:** These are the qualities related to his intelligence quotient and personality related traits :
   - A high degree of intelligence
   - A capacity to deal in every situation courageously
   - A sound judgment
   - A scientific approach to the problem
   - An open mind
   - An astute diplomat
   - A best teacher.

4. ***Character qualities***: These are the qualities related to the social aspects of his behavior.
    - Integrity
    - Self-discipline
    - Good nature
    - Willingness to work hard
    - Willingness to accept and share responsibilities
    - Good mannered and courteous
    - Courageous
    - Initiative
    - Humanist.

Importance of leadership: Leadership plays a vital role in management. Good leadership is an integral part of effective direction. It provides the vital to morale of human beings. Morale has its roots in good human relations, which, in turn, can be fostered and toned up by leadership. Whole part of a manager's job involves getting things done through people is undoubtedly made easier when the manager is a skillful leader.

The importance of leadership function in a modern organization can be very well understood by reviewing the various functions which are generally performed by managers as a leader. The main functions of a leader manager are as follow:

- He formulates objective for his group
- He gives orders and instructions to do work
- He maintains discipline in the organization
- He maintains communication in the organization
- He listens to subordinates and responds to their needs
- He takes important decisions for the group
- He maintains unity and cohesiveness in the organization
- He inspires and motivates the various members of his group
- He represents the group to the outside world.

5.12 | Decision Making

Decision making is a blend of thinking, deciding and acting. It consists of 3 processes – the process of thinking, deciding and acting. Decision making permeates almost all the fundamental functions of the management. It is present in every part of an organization and it deals with every possible subject.

Decisions are countless. A manager firing his subordinate is taking a decision. When he motivates his subordinates he takes a decision. While setting a plan he is making a bundle of decisions. A manger right from the start of his work starts taking decision. It is an inescapable function to him. A manager's main job is to take important decisions. Decisions are to be acted upon which is more important than taking a decision. Decision making is choosing one out of many all possible alternatives.

Characteristics of decision making: The important characteristics of decision making process are as follows:

1. Exploring all possible alternatives, analysis and evaluations and choosing between different available alternatives.
2. It is a selection process and the best possible decision is chosen.
3. Decisions are outcome of logical discussion. Hence it is a mental process.
4. Every decision affects the past, present and the future. Past cannot be amended by the present decision. But it has a bearing on the historical conclusions which affect the present. Present decision is taken for the present as well as for the future. So it affects both in its natural course.
5. Decisions have wide ranging, long-term and lasting effect.
6. Decisions are the tools of management. On them depends the success and failure of the enterprise.

Steps in decision making: The decision making process consists of the following 6 steps:

1. Perception
2. Conception
3. Investigation
4. Deliberation
5. Selection
6. Implementation or promulgation

***Perception*:** A state of awareness is known as perception. Out of perception a consciousness of being arises. This consciousness of being given tilt to the decision making process. The executive first perceives and then moves on to choose one of the alternative and thus takes a decision. Perception is, therefore, an important and first step without which decisions relating to any of the problems of the organization cannot be taken. Other steps follow. "Perception" is the first step in decision making.

***Conception*:** Conception relates to that power of mind which develops ideas out of what has been perceived. Designs for action or programme for action may be known as conception.

***Investigation*:** Perception is a sort of location of the problem whereas conception is the preparation of design or programme for solving the problem. But only perception and conception cannot offer the solution. For solution investigation is to be carried out. Informations relevant to a particular concept is to be sought, acquired and then analyzed. Relative merits and demerits of a different analyzed concepts are to be measured. Alternative course of action is to be thought, analyzed and compared to. This needs investigation with which the manager should be armed. The investigation provides an equipment with the help of which he tries to go ahead with a debate either in his mind independently or with his co-workers.

***Deliberation*:** Deliberations are strictly debates. Weighing the consequences of possible course of action is called deliberation. The manger may either weigh the relative merits and demerits and the following consequences in his own mind or share his mental exercise with others to equip himself better. The deliberations remove bias, equip the manger with different ideas and alternatives and help him in arriving at a decision which may safely be ascribed as a good decision.

***Selection*:** After deliberations one of the alternatives, the best possible in the circumstances, is selected. Selection is thus an act of choice which in management terminology is known as decision.

***Promulgation*:** Perception, conception, investigation, deliberation and lastly selection will carry weight only when the selected the chosed alternative, that is, the decision is properly and timely communicated to all those who are concerned and for whom the decision is meant. Only proper promulgation will help its execution.

***Advantages of workers' participation in decision making*:** Advantages of workers' participation in decision making are numerous, provided the principle has been acted upon seriously both in letter as well as in spirit. The advantages accrue to an organization by following the principle of participation are as given below:

1. The participants feel that the business is their own of which they are important parts.
2. Opposition to a decision is considerably reduced, instead those who are to carry the decision gladly accept even if any change is being introduced.
3. Guidance and direction functions of management are easily performed.
4. Decisions are the result of best possible selection of the alternatives, therefore decisions may yield results to the advantage of the organization on the expected lines.
5. Increase in the efficiency of workers
6. Development of coordinated efforts
7. Development of good human relations
8. Development of team spirit and better understanding because of good human relations
9. Assurance of growth and prosperity to both the organization as well as the whole working force – managerial, supervisory and operating.

The managers today are interested in eliciting the participation of workers with their decision with a view to get more cooperation and to exercise effective control over them in the accomplishment of the tasks assigned by the objectives of the organization.

5.13 | Authority

Authority is the power to make decisions which guide the action of others. It is a right and power to influence the behavior or efforts of other persons. It involves the 3 basic elements – power to use discretion and making decisions, the right to compel for its obedience and the power to influence the behavior or actions of the subordinates. Authority is a binding force and hence it can be called as the cement of the organization.

Definition: Authority is the right to give orders and the power to extract obedience. It is the right that a manger has to request a subordinate to do something in accomplishing the organizational objectives and goals. It principally consists of the right to decide and command. The person who exercises authority by taking decisions to guide the activities of others is called the superior or boss and the person who is guided and accepts authority is called the subordinate.

Sources of authority: There are three recognized sources of authority. They are:

1. Formal Authority 2. Acceptance Authority 3. Competence Authority

1. ***Formal authority***: The formal authority stems from his superior within the organizational structure. It is a traditional concept which assumes that authority is a right based on natural law or on the sanction of legislation. Hence the authority by this method flows from the top to down through the organization. Such authority may be expressed or implied.
2. ***Acceptance authority***: This authority is the relationship that is there between individuals when one accepts the directive of another. A communication carries authority if it is accepted by the recipient as authoritative. Thus this expression of the source of authority of the manager is the acceptance by his subordinates. This concept is based on behavioral approach of management. It shows that the manager has no real authority unless the individual subordinate confers it upon him. A subordinate accepts the authority of his superior because of the duly constituted authorities, obtaining rewards and incentives from his superior, contribution to the realization of the organizational objectives. Acceptance authority is the legal and social basis for authority. It depends to a large extent on the personal traits of leadership, ability to persuade others to work for accomplishing organizational goals.
3. ***Competence authority***: This is based on the competence of the managerial personnel. A person gets authority from his managerial position and in addition to it the authority is derived from the technical competence or personal qualities of a manager. His authority is accepted not because of any position he holds in the organization but because of his authority of knowledge. In each organization there are certain persons who do not possess any formal authority but they command respect and authority on account of their personality influence and technical competence.

***Limits to authority*:** There are many limitations to the concept of authority. Authority is never absolute like responsibility. It changes with time, position and group behavior of the subordinates, etc. While exercising authority, the manager must keep the following limitations in his mind. It will help him in successful utilization of his authority. They are as follows

1. ***Regard for the mores and folkways of the group*:** Authority when used commands reactions from individual as well as groups. It may be favorable or unfavorable. So a manager must keep in his mind, while using authority, the reaction of his orders on employees, shareholders and customers, etc.
2. ***Legal limitations*:** A manager's authority is restricted by the enterprise goals, objectives, policies, programmes and procedures, etc. These all are governed by the Articles and Memorandum of Association, which are governed themselves by the commercial and industrial laws of the country. Every manager, at any level in the organization, must respect these laws, traditions and restrictions, etc.
3. ***Natural or biological limitations*:** No subordinate can be ordered to do a job which is impossible to be performed due to biological limitations. For example, one can hardly order a person to walk up to side of a building or do such impossible things.
4. ***Physical limitations*:** Physical limitations such as climate, geography, chemical elements and so on put limits on authority. For example, an order to make gold from copper will be ineffectual.
5. ***Technological limitations*:** There are technological limits on authority too. Until and unless any performance is technically possible, an order to do any such work would be futile.
6. ***Economic limitations*:** Sometimes, a manager may not get the work done from the subordinate if the wages to be paid are not according to his expectations. The competition, prices of the product and other economic factors also affect the authority.
7. ***Authority delegation limitations*:** The extent of delegation of authority also restricts the authority of a manager. Generally, the authority to make decisions or the right to command decrease as it proceeds from the highest to lowest level of any organization.

Review Questions

Short Answer Questions

1. Is productivity affected by Employee Morale? How ?
2. Distinguish between motivation and morale.
3. Define Authority.
4. Explain with suitable examples the limitations of an Authority.
5. Distinguish between the Fayol's concept and Taylor's version of Management.
6. "Functions of management is to manage workers and work" comment.
7. Explain the significance of communication.
8. Differentiate between oral communication and written communication.
9. Explain the steps involve in decision making.
10. List out the traits of a good leader.

Long Answer Questions

1. "The Principles of scientific management makes the beginning of management movement". Discuss the statement bringing out clearly the broad principles of scientific management.
2. Attempt a critical note on Fayol's contribution to management.
3. What is the sources of authority in management? Are there any limitations to such an authority?
4. Give a critical appraisal of various methods of communications used in Business Management.
5. What are the qualities a leader should possess to become an effective leader?
6. As a management leader what problems would you face in motivating your work force? What measures would you adopt to overcome them?
7. Define communication? What is the purpose of communication in an enterprise? Write a note on principles which should guide managers towards establishing good communication network.
8. Define coordination. Discuss its importance in a business organization. Briefly explain the important characteristics of coordination.
9. Define the term 'Management'. Compare and contrast the concepts of management as proposed by F.W.Taylor and Henry Fayol.
10. Explain the term 'Decision Making'. Discuss the steps involved in decision making. Write its salient features.

6 Administrative Management

6.1 | The Management

Management is a technique by means of which the purposes and the objectives of a particular human group are determined, classified and effectuated. Management is forecasting, planning, organizing, commanding, coordinating and controlling. It is a social process entailing responsibility for the efficient planning and regulation of the operations of an enterprise.

LEARNING OBJECTIVES

- *Elements of Management*
- *Planning*
- *Organizing*
- *Staffing*
- *Directing*
- *Order*
- *Supervision*
- *Controlling*

6.2 | Elements of Management

These are the sole source of power and inspiration with the help of which all activities of the enterprise move and remain in purposeful positive action.

The six management elements are as follows:

(a) Determine objectives - Planning

(b) To setup an organization and assign responsibility – Organizing

(c) To interrelate and direct activities – Command

(d) To set standards and effect control accordingly – Controlling

(e) To motivate and socialize the employee groups- Motivation

(f) To cause cooperation among various factors of production and organized groups of personnel – Coordination

6.3 | Planning

Definition: Planning is an intellectual process, conscious determination of courses of action, basing the decisions on purpose, facts and considered estimates. Planning is deciding in advance what is to be done, when, where, how and by whom it is to be done. Planning is a determined course of action. It is a mental process requiring the use of intellectual faculties, foresight, imagination and sound judgment. It is concerned with the setting of organizational goals or objectives and determining the approach by which the goals and objectives are to be accomplished.

Elements of planning: Planning coordinates the activities of the organization towards defined and agreed upon objectives. The following are the important elements of planning:

(a) Objectives (b) Policies (c) Procedure (d) Program and
(e) Budget

(a) ***Objectives*****:** Objectives determine the goals on the basis of which the action of an enterprise is projected. Goals are the foundation over which the whole structure of plans is built.

(b) ***Policies*****:** Policies provide guidance to subordinates and enlist their cooperation on the guided lines. Policies may either be written or oral but they must be stated in clear terms so that nothing should be left for interpretations which sometimes create a very funny situation. Policies are mini-plans since they also set out certain course of action to be followed for the attainments of the objectives.

(c) ***Procedure*****:** Procedure charts out specific manner in which actions are to be taken and work accomplished. Procedures thus provide a charted course of action, deviation from which may be termed as setting up of an unhealthy trend and undisciplined action on the part of subordinates. Procedures are generally rigid and gain a permanency during a course of time. Policies are flexible and are subject to change according to the demand of situation and time.

(d) ***Program*****:** For a complete and orderly course of action programs are meant for assembling all plans into one in a workable form. Programs may both be for repetitive and non-repetitive actions. Repetitive action programs are termed as routine planning while non-repetitive action programs are classed as creative planning.

(e) ***Budget*****:** Budgets too are part of plans. Budgets are said to be the statement of numerical facts designed to attain desired results. Man-hours, finances, production units etc., are a few of the items which can only be stated in numbers. They are analyzed and then plans are formulated with an aim to attain expected results.

Importance of Planning: Planning is the foundation of most successful action of an enterprise. Without effective planning it is difficult to anticipate future uncertain events.

Planning brings efficiency, stability and orderliness in managerial actions and decisions. It is a rational approach for all the activities of a manager.

The important benefits of planning are:

1. ***Improves competitive strength***: By proper planning the organization has a competitive edge. Planning enables to anticipate the tastes and fashions of people, technological changes, changes in work methods etc.
2. ***Improves motivation***: It improves the motivation of workers because the workers know what exactly is expected of them.
3. ***Encourages innovations and creativity***: It generates thinking among the managers because new ideas come to the mind when we plan something. It creates a positive looking attitude among the mangers.
4. ***Planning offsets future uncertainty and change***: Without planning a manger is forced to react to situations or problems. Planning permits a manger to act with initiative and to create situations to the organization's advantage.
5. ***Planning helps in management by objectives***: Once the objectives are laid out, all efforts are directed towards desired and well-defined objectives.
6. ***Better coordination***: Well-defined objectives, well developed programs and procedures lead to better coordination.
7. ***Economy in operation***: Planning paves the way for proper utilization of resources. It develops one best way of doing things which is economical to the organization.
8. ***Helps in control***: Due to good control, effectiveness and smoothness is achieved.
9. **Helps in executive development.**

Steps in Planning: The following are the important steps in the process of planning.

1. ***Determination of objectives***: The first step in planning work is to determine the enterprise objectives. These objectives set the pattern of the proposed course of action and shape the future policies.
2. ***Establishment of planning premises***: The second step in planning is to establish planning premises. Premises are planning assumptions, the future setting in which planning takes place. Thus, it is a forecast of those business conditions under which a plan is to operate.
3. ***Determination of alternative courses***: The third step in planning is to search for and examine alternative courses of action. There is hardly a plan for which a number of alternatives cannot be found out. In business, there exist a number of alternative courses of action for achieving the desired objectives. All possible alternatives should be found out for their comparison and analytical evaluation.
4. ***Evaluation of alternatives and selection of course of action***: The next step is the evaluation of alternative courses of action and selecting a suitable and best course of action.

5. ***Preparation of derivative plans*:** The next step in the planning process is to formulate the derivative plans in support of the basic plan. There are sub-plans or departmental plans. The basic plan prepared for the whole enterprise cannot be effectively operated in the absence of such plans. So within the framework of a primary or basic plan, derivate plans are developed.
6. ***Timing and sequence of operations*:** Timing is an essential consideration in planning. After developing the plan, sub-plans, the starting and finishing times should be fixed for each plan. Scheduling is very useful not only in sales and production areas but in other functional areas also.
7. ***Securing participation of employees*:** The execution of a successful plan depends to a large extend upon the loyalty and sincerity of the subordinates. It can be secured only when in planning their proper participation is secured. Plans must be communicated, explained and consulted thoroughly.
8. ***Considering the strategy*:** Strategy has a significant contribution towards the execution of a plan. So, consideration of different strategies becomes an integral part of the planning process. A suitable strategy should be planned and followed for the success of planning.
9. ***Providing follow–up to the proposed course of action*:** In the last, a provision for follow up measures should be made for the time when a plan is put into action. In the context of current problems and situation, necessary adjustment in plans become imperative, so necessary provision should be made for it before hand.

Limitations of planning: The following are the obstacles to the process of planning.

1. A costly proposition 2. Planning fails with big and regular changes 3. Inelastic administration 4. Unreliable estimates and 5. Initiative, originality and individuality yield to planned efforts.

1. ***A costly proposition*:** Planning involves cost. It involves a loss of time, money and labor.
2. ***Planning fails with big and regular changes:*** Usually plans are made as flexible as possible so that they are adaptable to changes. But still the possibility of flexibility is very limited. Regular changes may convert the plan into a waste and nothing else.
3. ***Inelastic administration:*** A planning beforehand makes the administration inelastic to a certain degree as people's imagination is taken away and they are made to work just like a machine and no chance for them to think and rethink beyond a certain limit.
4. ***Unreliable estimates:*** Estimates are based on facts, data and information. Human prejudices cannot be ruled out while planning. Hence this leads us to a conclusion that estimates based on so called reliable data really are not reliable.

5. ***Initiative, originality and Individuality yield to planned efforts:*** Well planned out programs, policies and procedures lead to loss of initiative and original approach to the problem on the part of the employees. Individuality of the employees is lost because they are not a part of planning.

6.4 | Organizing

Definition: Organizing is a process of dividing and combining efforts of a working group for making such joint efforts more productive and fruitful. Organizing establishes a pattern of relationships among efforts to be put, jobs to be done and work to be performed. Organizing creates teamwork. It is a framework for the fulfillment of common objectives.

An effective and efficient organizing process increases managerial efficiency and facilitates coordination. It ensures an optimum use of human efforts balancing various activities. It provides for adequate training and helps in identifying the defects. It consolidates growth and expansion of the enterprise and discourages corrupt practices.

Organizing includes activities like grouping, assigning activities, allocation of duties and responsibilities and delegation of authority in order to facilitate the smooth functioning of the organization.

Elements of Organization: Organizing involves sharing the duties and responsibilities within a broad frame work. There are 3 important elements of an organization:

1. Division of Work 2. Interrelationship and 3. Individual Performances

1. ***Division of work:*** An effective division of work between personnel selected to do a particular job(s) is the foremost function of an organization. If it is effective it will bear fruits and desired results may be achieved.
2. ***Interrelationship:*** Establishment of inter-relationships between jobs, duties, responsibilities and authority either in a formal or in an informal way is also a primary function of an organization without which nothing tangible could be achieved.
3. ***Performance by individuals:*** Individuals do the assigned jobs. Whether an individual or a group of individuals is doing the assigned duties and carrying out the responsibilities in accordance with the instructions or not is to be observed and any deviation should have to be reported on for adequate action against the erring group or individual. The organization ensures it by preparing a scheme of inspection and supervision. It also make one answerable for his work and conduct. It also aims at the strict adherence of the rules etc. framed for the purpose. Unless it is done the very purpose of organization will be defeated.

Types of organization (patterns): There are certain patterns of organizing the personnel in the organization. They are as follows:

1. Line Organization (a) Pure line organization (b) Departmental line organization
2. Functional Organization

1. ***Line Organization*:** It is also known as vertical organization or departmental organization or scalar organization. This organization is based on the superior-subordinate relationship. A superior delegate's authority to a subordinate who in turn delegates authority to another subordinate and thus forming a line from the top to bottom of the organizational structure. The line of authority is known as "Line Authority."

   (a) *Pure line organization:* This type of organization is simple in form and seen in small units producing only one item where activities can be grouped according to their nature. In this organization, the activities at any one level are the same with each man performing the same type of work and the division is only for direction and control.

   (b) *Departmental line organization:* In this type the business unit is dividing into departments which are headed by departmental heads. These heads enjoy equal status and work independently. A departmental head receives order from the general manager and passes them on to his immediate subordinate. The whole organization is under the charge of a general manager.

   Advantages of line organization: It is easy to establish and very simple for the employees and leads to better coordination and stability. It ensures strong discipline because of unity of command. The authorities of various personnel are well defined hence no conflict in their powers and authority. This type of organization is elastic and changes can be easily incorporated in the organization. Due to the unification of authority and responsibility, quick decisions can be taken.

   Disadvantages of line organization: All the decisions are taken by the single boss and the success and the growth of whole department depends on his abilities only. The boss is over loaded with work and he may not direct the efforts of his subordinates properly. This type of organization suffers from lack of specialized skill of experts and inadequacy of a communication. There is a scope of favoritism by the boss. It is not suitable for large-scale organization. Creating so many departments becomes a problem.

2. ***Functional Organization*:** In this type of organization the whole task of management is classified according to the type of work involved. The normal operations performed in a business house are production, research, personnel, purchasing, finance etc. These activities are assigned to various departments and functional experts are appointed to look after those activities.

Advantages of functional organization: It ensures higher degree of efficiency as the workers get instructions from experts and they have to perform a limited number of tasks. It ensures a greater division of labor. This type of organization is flexible and changes can be incorporated without disturbing the whole organization. It facilitates mass production through specialization and standardization of operations.

***Disadvantages of Functional Organization*:**

- ***Conflict in authority:*** This authority relationship violates the principle of 'unity of command'. It creates several bosses instead of one line authority. It creates conflict in the minds of workers to whom they should obey and to whom they should ignore. Their loyalty is divided.
- ***Discipline is slackened:*** Due to decentralization of control and division of loyalty of subordinates, the discipline of the enterprise becomes loose.
- ***Lack of coordination:*** Use of several functional experts in organization creates the problem of coordination.
- ***Complication procedure:*** It is too complicated in operation because it entails the division of functions into a number of sub-functions.
- ***Conflict in foremen:*** It may also lead to conflict among foremen or bosses of equal rank. This conflict mars their zeal and initiative. They work only as a machine in a routine manner. It harms the efficiency of sub-ordinates also.
- ***Impracticable and expensive:*** This pattern of organization is quite impracticable and expensive also. So small organizations cannot follow it.

Importance of organization: The success of an organization depends upon how the organizing process has been carried out. The whole structure of management is built on the foundation of well planned organization. A well-planned organization has the following benefits.

1. It makes the management simple and efficient and accelerates the progress.
2. It encourages specialization and promotes constructive thinking among the employees.
3. It increases productivity and boosts the confidence of the employees.

6.5 | Staffing

Definition: The staffing is the procurement of efficient people for the organization. It is a process of matching the jobs with individuals. It is a function of manning the jobs. After organizing the enterprise, management is in a position to know the actual manpower requirement. Then by means of staffing, the management recruits, selects and trains the employees.

Staffing is continuous process because existing employees may leave the organization and new employees may join it. Hence business organization has to recruit additional manpower to meet the growing requirements of the organization. Staffing is related to the following functions:

1. Forecasting the manpower requirements
2. Establishing job specifications and job descriptions
3. Determining the sources of recruitment
4. Recruitment
5. Selection and Placement
6. Training and educating the employees
7. Coordinating, promotions, Transfers etc.
8. Maintenance of necessary records for the efficient manpower management
9. Developing and following sound personnel policies

Importance of Staffing:

1. Staffing injects life into the organization by providing right person for every job. The effectiveness of directing and control functions also depends upon staffing.
2. Employees in the organization are the most valuable asset of an organization. The quality of human assets largely determines the success and growth of the organization. Hence staffing helps to built up the human resources as assets.
3. Staffing helps to build up a healthy organization in which the job performance and satisfaction of every employee can be high. Staffing identifies people with necessary skills and attitudes, induces them to join the organization and ensures their continuous co-operation and association with the organization.

6.6 | Directing

Directing is a managerial function performed by manager at all the levels of the organization. Managers have the responsibility of not only planning and organizing the operations but also of guiding and directing the subordinates.

Definition: Directing consists of the process and techniques utilized in issuing instructions and making certain that operations are carried on as originally planned. In simple words, directing is guiding the subordinates in doing their work. Direction is a complex function that includes all those activities which are designed to encourage subordinates to work effectively and efficiently in both the short and the long run.

The function of direction has 3 essential components.

1. ***Function of command:*** It is issuing of instructions and orders.

2. ***Guiding the people:*** It is the responsibility of a manager to guide and teach the subordinates in the proper methods of work.
3. ***Supervising the people:*** The management has to supervise the subordinate to ensure that their performance conforms to the plans. Directing is an executive function of guiding and observing subordinates.

Directing is the inter-personal aspect of managing by which subordinates are led to understand and contribute effectively to the attainment of enterprise objectives.

Nature of direction: The function of directing has the following characteristics :

1. It is an executive function and extends from top to the bottom of the organization. It involves in framing the scope, giving orders and instructions and providing dynamic leadership.
2. Directing is a continuous activity. It is the basis of all future activities.
3. Directing is all pervading. It is not only concerned with issuing orders and instructions but also communication, supervision, motivation and involves how a employee can contribute to the common objectives of the organization.
4. Directing is to have direct contact with the people. Direction relates to the direction of subordinates and hence it requires a direct contact with them.

Principles of Direction: There are certain principles of direction which should be observed by the management in directing its subordinates. These principles can be dividing into two parts.

Principles of Direction

	Principles relating to the purpose of organization		**Principles relating to the process of organization**
1.	Principle of maximum individual Contribution.	1.	Principle of unity of command
2.	Principle of harmony of objectives	2.	Principle of direct supervision
3.	Principle of efficiency of direction	3.	Appropriateness of direction techniques.
		4.	Principle of managerial communication.
		5.	Principle of comprehension
		6.	Principle of flow of information
		7.	Principle of strategic use of informal organization.
		8.	Principle of leadership
		9.	Principle of follow through.

6.7 | Order

Order is a basic tool utilized by a manager to direct his subordinates. It is also called as commanding. An order initiates, modifies or stops an activity. A manager can by his order motivate, inspire or discourage his subordinates in doing their duties.

Definition: An order is a command by a superior requiring a subordinate to act or refrain from acting in given circumstance. It is usually an instruction given by a superior to his subordinate. A direct line of command is required for giving orders. An order implies to do or not to do a certain thing in given circumstances. An order is enforceable. A subordinate can be punished by his boss for not carrying out his orders.

Characteristics of a good order:

1. The order must be reasonable and capable of immediate compliance by the subordinates.
2. Order must be compatible with the purposes and objectives of the enterprise.
3. The order should be intelligible, complete and clear.
4. The tone of the order should be appropriate. It should stimulate ready acceptance.
5. It must specify the time within which the instruction should be carried out and completed.

Techniques of orders: The following are the important techniques of issuing orders.

1. ***General or specific orders*:** An order can be related to a general matter or specifically on particular issue. An order should be specific or general depends upon the preference of superior, his ability to foresee the circumstances.
2. ***Written or oral orders*:** The written orders are more accurate, intelligible and well considered. The subordinates get sufficient time to understand the order. It fixes the responsibility and accountability also. But written orders cannot be revised as oral orders. Moreover they are expensive and time consuming and they are inflexible. For routine matters oral orders serve the purpose. In emergencies also, oral orders can be used.
3. ***Conformality*:** The orders should be normal, informal and courteous. This type of orders motivates the subordinates to do their best.
4. ***Timing*:** The orders should be timely and suiting the situation and circumstances. Then only the enterprise and the subordinates will achieve good results.
5. ***Follow-up orders*:** After the orders have been issued, a manager should find out whether his orders have been carried out or not. If necessary he may cause some changes to his instructions.

6.8 | Supervision

Supervision is overseeing the subordinates at work. It is an important part of direction function of every manager. It is the observation to see if the subordinates are working according to the plans and policies of the organization and keeping the time schedule and to help them in solving their problems.

Definition: Supervision refers to the direct and immediate guidance and control of subordinates in the performance of their task. Thus supervision is direction, guidance and control of work force to see they are working according to plan, policy, program, and instruction and keeping up the time schedule and helping subordinates in their working and if they are need of help of any kind in accomplishing their assigned tasks.

Functions of a supervisor: The supervisor has to perform the following important functions:

1. To schedule work for its even and steady flow
2. To assign work to different workers according to their abilities.
3. To provide proper working environments to the workers
4. To provide leadership to the workers
5. To elicit their willingness to work for the achievement of group objectives.
6. To control the performance of workers.
7. To motivate the workers by giving them various incentives.
8. To take corrective action, whenever necessary.

***Qualities of a good supervisor*:** A good supervisor should possess the following qualities:

1. He should have human approach to human problems. His attitude towards his subordinates should be sympathetic in dealing with their problems.
2. He should be alert mentally and at no time, he should be caught unaware.
3. He should be competent to take quick decisions.
4. He should be honest in dealing with the subordinates so as to leave no scope in the minds of his subordinates about his integrity.
5. He should have patience and should not lose temper easily.
6. He should not depend upon his formal authority too much.
7. He should be a good leader so as to guide the subordinates towards organizational goals.
8. He should have sufficient technical skill to perform the jobs, to be supervised and to get output of better quality from the subordinates.

Requisites (essential qualities) of effective supervision: The following are the essential requirements of effective supervision.

1. ***Knowledge of work and techniques of the supervision*:** A supervisor to be effective must have knowledge of different techniques of supervision, knowledge of machines, equipments, tools and materials that are under his control

2. ***Knowledge of rules and regulations***: A supervisor should be familiar with the organizational rules and regulations which are related to his organization. He should possess the knowledge of various labor laws that affect his organization.
3. ***Skill in instructing***: A supervisor should have knowledge to issue instructions to his subordinates. Hence he should have good communication skills.
4. ***Skill in leading***: A supervisor should be a good leader. He should be able to guide the subordinates and promote harmonious relationship among them.
5. ***Skill in dealing with current problems***: The supervisor is expected to make the best possible use of resources available to him – men, material, machine and money.
6. ***Human orientation***: A supervisor should treat his subordinates in a equitable manner and motivate them to achieve good results. He should adopt a helping attitude towards his subordinates.

Importance of supervisor: The ability of the workers and the success of an organization depend upon the supervisor's ability to plan and schedule within the framework of the organization. A position of a supervisor is very important in an organization because he is a conduit between the management and the workers. He functions as a specialist in human relations in the whole of the organizational structure. Because of his peculiar but significant position, he influences the work environment. He also influences the attitude, behavior, conduct and even cooperative efforts of the workers in the organization. He is a morale booster. Hence it is well said that "even the best supervisor is no substitute for poor principles and practices in managing workers." Hence it is the supervisor who brings success or failure to the organization.

6.9 | Controlling

Definition: Control is checking current performance against the pre-determined standards contained in the plans with a view to ensuring adequate progress and satisfactory performance. The objects of control are to point out the weakness and error in order to rectify them and prevent occurrence. It operates on everything i.e., things, people and action.

The important features of controlling are:

1. It is an important managerial function
2. It is a step to ensure the performance according to the plans.
3. It involves the management of actual performance and recording the deviations.
4. It involves the preparation of plans, setting goals and objectives and setting the standards.
5. Controlling is positive and corrective, providing guidance for future steps. It is neither an order nor giving a command.

Salient features (characteristics) of controlling: The following are the salient features of control.

1. ***An end itself*:** Control is an end function of the process of management. It judges the performance of different factors engaged in the attainment of the said objectives.
2. ***A forward looking process*:** Even though it lives in the present, it is related to future. It is the present over which control is exercised with a view to guard against future. Loss, deviation from plans, policies, programs and schedules etc., are to be guarded against.
3. ***A dynamic process*:** Control is a dynamic process. Since the management functions are flexible and are required to adjust according to the needs and situations arising from time to time, the controlling process also acquires a flexible character.
4. ***A continuous process*:** Control is a continuous activity. It does not stop. A business manager should continuously monitor his organization for a steady development.
5. ***Operation at all levels*:** Controlling is done at all the levels of management. The chain of control is pre-determined which runs through the whole organization.
6. ***Identified with individuals*:** The individuals in an organization are in charge of various operations and they are held responsible for any short comings and thus control is exercised over individuals performing their duties in an organization.

Steps in the process of control: The process of control can be split into various well-defined steps. The important elements of this process are as follows:

1. ***Well defined objectives and goals*:** The organization has to define its objectives and goals first. The goals should be split into sub-goals at the departmental level. The planned goals or objectives of an organization serve as a standard for performance measurement.
2. ***Determination of strategic point of control*:** The responsibility centers should be selected and fixed. In order to make the control process effective, the management should concentrate upon strategic point only.
3. ***A pre-determined criterion*:** In this stage, standards are established against which the actual results can be measured. Standards provide a way of stating what should be accomplished. These standards can be in the terms of money, time, physical units or some index. But there should be specific units so that comparison between the standard and the actual performance can be judged.
4. ***Determination of controllable cost and control period*:** A good control is the one which establishes strategic points where corrective action will be cheapest, easiest and most effective.

5. ***Strengthening the organization*:** The process of control should be such that it over comes the weakness and deviations and establishes corrective steps which strengthen the organization.
6. ***Measurement of performance*:** It is the evaluation of actual performance. It involves the management of performance in respect of a work in terms of control standards and communicating to the person concerned for reason for deviations and taking corrective actions. The measurement of performance must be clear, simple, rational, relevant and reliable. It must be understandable and inviting attention.
7. ***Comparison of actual performance with standards*:** This step helps to determine the extent of mistakes and enable a manager to predict future results. Since all activities yield some variation, it is necessary to determine the limits within which this variation can be held and still be considered to be in control. When adequate standards are developed, it is very simple to compare the results of any major variations. Comparison of the performance can be done by means of control charts, pictorial presentation of data, ratios, indices and averages.
8. ***Correction of deviations*:** The final step is to correct deviations. The purpose of comparison of the planned with the actual performance is to make necessary corrections. The corrective measures may be based on any one of the following :
   (a) Review of plans and goals (b) Change in the assignment (c) Change in the existing techniques of direction and control (d) Change in the organizational structure and (e) Incorporating new facilities.
9. ***Review of control system*:** It is necessary that periodically the process and procedure of control should be re-examined and modifications made according to the new plans and goals to fit realities as conditions change.

Elements of a good control system: The necessity, size and nature of the enterprise decide the control system on which depends the element of control. The following are the elements of a good management controlling system:

1. The control system should be according to the (a) requirement (b) Size (c) Nature and (d) necessity of the enterprise.
2. The system should be capable of detecting the deviations etc. quickly and correctly.
3. The system should be flexible enough to incorporate the future changes, improvements etc., in the system without much of dislocation.
4. The system should be such which is capable of defining the exceptions, if any, as clearly as possible.
5. The system should be objective oriented and should be in accordance with the organizational structure, plan, policies and programs.
6. It should be simple and easy to follow.
7. It should be economical.

Review Questions

Short Answer Questions

1. Define the term 'Control'?
2. Explain the steps involved in planning process?
3. Define 'Order'? Explain the Characteristics of a good order?
4. Explain the limitations of 'planning'?
5. Explain the requirements of an 'adequate control system'?
6. Explain the term 'organization'? Why it is regarded as the foundation upon which the whole structure of management is built?
7. Explain the benefits of 'organizing'?
8. Explain the scope of 'staffing'?

Long Answer Questions

1. Explain the direction function Management? What are the elements of the direction process?
2. 'Plans are selected courses along which the management desires to coordinate group action' – Discuss?
3. What do you mean by 'supervision'? Discuss the position and importance of a supervisor in an industrial organization?
4. 'Managerial planning seeks to achieve a coordinated structure of operations' – Discuss?
5. What are the basic elements of 'Control'? Discuss its elements? How do managers exercise control?
6. Explain the concept 'Staffing'? State its salient features and significance?

7 Production Management

7.1 | Introduction

Production is main activity of an enterprise. Primarily two functions are accomplished by every business organization, namely production and marketing. Acquisition of essential resources and the effective and economical use is important and it is performed by production management. So, production management is that part of management process which begins from acquisition of the production resources (men, materials, machinery and equipment) and ends with manufacture of goods or providing services.

LEARNING OBJECTIVES

- *Introduction and definition of Production Management*
- *Importance of Production Management*
- *Functions of Production*
- *Organization for Production Management*
- *Production Planning and Control*
- *Elements of Planning and Control*
- *Production forecasting*
- *Quality Control*

7.2 | Definition

Production management comprises of two words: 'Production' and 'Management'. 'Production' means creation of utility. In a manufacturing concern production is the *transformation of raw materials by factory methods into finished goods wanted by society.*

Production is the process of transforming raw materials or purchased components into finished products for sales.

Management is the second word in 'production management'. Management in the context of production means planning and organizing the production process and effective utilization of production facilities.

Its main object is to transform the shape and nature of raw materials at a minimum cost with an object to produce as much as possible. Thus, 'production management' means planning of different production process, directing and regulating them, with the result that all diverse activities could be performed successfully.

Production management is a process of decision-making regarding production. 'Production Management' and 'Production Function' are two different activities. Production management is a decision-making challenge whereas production function is discharged by the employees working in the organization. Production management is related with organization, planning, directing, and controlling the production activities.

It includes production, planning, acquisition of production resources, directing, regulating and controlling of production process.

The elements essential for production are men, materials and machines. Production management is an important functional areas of business management which provides goods by coordinating all the above said elements. In these days production process has become very complex. Technical development like standardization, specification, simplification and automation all have made it a topic of detailed investigation and research.

Production is an important functional area of management and interrelated with marketing, selling and finance functions. Main object of production management is to produce, the goods and service at a minimum cost, with fine methods at the right time, production of quality goods so that the resources of the enterprise can be used effectively and efficiently.

7.3 | Importance of Production Management

All programs whether – marketing, research and development, financing, go on smoothly with the help of production. Production management is essentially inter-related with marketing management, financial management and personnel management.

The main object of production management is to produce goods and services at a possible minimum cost of a good quality and with a simple and fine method, with a view to increase the profits.

(a) ***Customer services*:** Stability with growth and profits can be sustained by providing the goods and services. When goods are produced as per orders it must be delivered as per date agreed upon, of a right quality. If production is for the satisfaction of further demand there must be sufficient stock in stores. Production department contributes to the organizational objective by providing goods of a right quality.

(b) ***Uninterrupted material flow*:** Production department maintains the essential stock of raw materials so that production becomes possible as per schedule. If production schedules are ignored, the result would be dangerous *e.g.,* increase in costs, less sales and finally decreasing the profits of the organization.

(c) ***Optimum inventory level*:** Production planning department maintains the stock of raw materials at an optimum level. As a result production-program goes on as per schedule; secondly it results in decrease in costs.

(d) ***Increased productivity*:** The production management department utilize the capacity of allied department, like purchasing, stores etc., and contributes to the organizational efficiency. The contribution of various activities relating to production is essential. The production control aspect of production function makes the coordination feasible. Thus, production function becomes mainly a coordination activity.

(e) ***Production and employment stabilities*:** Production manager through production planning and adjusting violent fluctuations in demand of goods, makes the production program in such a way that organization can face these ups and down efficiently and effectively. Lastly, stabilization of production increases the employment and decreases the cost of production.

***Functions of production*:** The prime responsibility of production management is to produce goods at a right time, of right quality and of required quantity.

Quantity of production is determined on the basis of forecasts made by marketing division or research branch and time of production is determined by the order and delivery date mutually agreed upon with customer.

Production manager performs the following functions in order to discharge his responsibilities:

(a) ***Production planning*:** It is an inaugurator activity and is the soul of production management. It involves projection of sales, determination of production resources, quantity, quality and determination of standards of production, labor force, raw materials requirements, plant layout, inventory control and managements of internal transportation facilities. In another words production planning is the function of setting the limits on levels of manufacturing operation in the future. Consideration be given to sales forecasts and the requirements and availability of men, machine, materials and money.

(b) ***Regulation and control of production*:** Regulation and control of production means centralization of powers and liabilities related with production which begins with the first step of production and extends up to the beginning of distribution. It involves – routing, scheduling, dispatching work orders and instructions follow up, quality control, cost control and budgetary control etc.,

(c) *Other functions*: It includes all these:

1. ***Method analysis*:** It is an important responsibility of a production manager to study various production methods and to develop or select good, suitable and economically variable methods. To develop a suitable and economical method it becomes essential for a manager concerned to study various alternatives.
2. ***Cost control*:** Cost of production must be controlled; for this he has to study internal transportation system and plant layout, etc., so that the movement of raw material is the minimum and cost is reduced.
3. ***Economy in labor costs*:** For this purpose it is essential for a production manager to carry out work study and to determine the quantity, quality and standard of work. If labor efficiency increases labor cost is sure to decline.
4. ***Inventory control*:** It involves the determination of raw material requirements considering the sales forecasts in order to maintain their optimum level. It will contribute to the organizational profitability. Inventory control has become the part and parcel of over-all control system.

***Organization for production management*:** The production of quality goods at a reasonable price is essential for the successful working of an enterprise. To discharge this function effectively, efficient and sound production department is indispensable which can coordinate, direct and control the production activities efficiently.

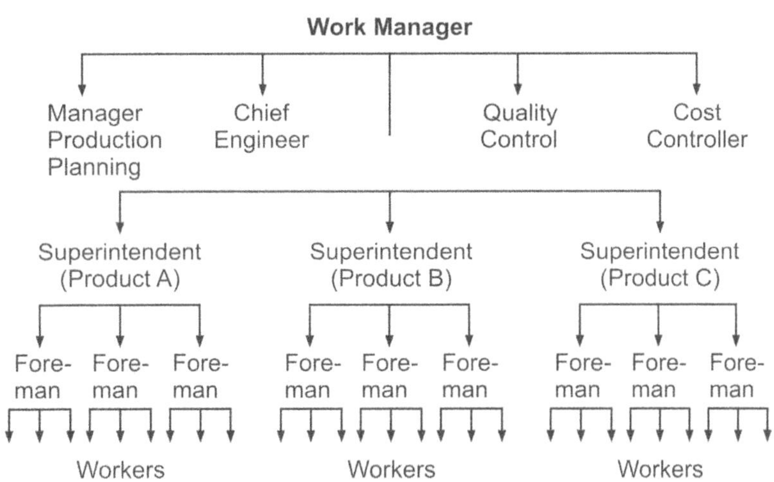

Works manager is generally the Chief authority of production department. Different staff personnel work under him in advisory capacity. The superintendents can be appointed for different products separately. They all implement the program as per planning schedule.

Superintendents delegate the authority to the foreman working under them. Thus, foremen are first line supervisors. They come in the direct contact with the workers.

Production planning manager performs scheduling and routine functions while superintendents perform dispatching, etc. Quality controller looks after the quality control, standards and inspection. Chief engineer looks after product-development, product research, designing and work-methods, etc.

***Production Planning and Control*:** The word 'Production Planning and Control' is a combination of the two terms: production planning and 'Production control'. The term 'Production Planning' comprises the planning of production process such as routing, scheduling, dispatching and follow-up function in the process so organized so that the movement of materials, performance of machines, operations of labor may be planned. These are, sub-divided, directed and coordinated as to quantity, quality, time and place. Thus, production planning provides management with the information necessary to plan and schedule work in the plant so that the minimum expense and optimum efficiency can be achieved, both of which make for greater profits. The other word, 'Production Control' refers to ensuring the work according to plans. In production terms, it assures a more positive and accurate completion of product by delivery date.

***Elements of production planning and control*:** The PPC can be scientifically sub-divided into three Parts:

PPC

- Production planning
  1. Production forecasting
  2. Determing production methods
  3. Plant layout
  4. Material management
  5. Product designing
  6. Internal transportation system
- Regulation of production
  7. Routing
  8. Scheduling
- Production control
  9. Dispatching
  10. Follow-up
  11. Quality control
  12. Cost control

1. ***Production forecasting*:** Demand of any product is the basis of its production. Hence, future demand is estimated before actual production. Though basically demand forecasting is the function of marketing management but it is also an integral part of PPC. After demand forecasting, the actual requirement of production can be determined. In deciding it a note must be taken of these things: closing stock of finished goods, opening stock of finished goods, number of machines and labor force, etc., equipments, tools and facilities, etc.
2. ***Determining production methods*:** A standard and a right type of quality of the product can be produced only after careful study of manufacturing process. Manufacturing can be classified as either continuous or intermittent. Continuous production is characterized by a relatively constant flow of a product and an

extensive use of special purpose machines. Petroleum refining, cement manufacturing, flour milling, and cigarette manufacture and typical of continuous manufacturing operations. Intermitted manufacture as its name implies, is characterized by an interrupted flow of material through a plant with general purpose rather than special purpose machines used. In such method, various products in differing quantities and manufactured at diverse intervals for many customers, e.g., automotive repair shops and machine shops before planning for the production.

3. ***Plant layout***: Plant layout is also a decision relating to physical production facilities. For the efficient working of production process arrangement of plant and machinery in a desirable manner should be made. An efficient plant layout brings down the cost of production and increases the efficiency of the system.
4. ***Materials Management***: The term Material Management is a very wide term. As we know, no product can be manufactured without raw-material. The quality, price and supply of raw material at right time determine the quality, standard, price and timely shipment of finished products in a factory. Hence, the importance of raw material is quite obvious. It includes the determination of material specification, determining economic order quantity, scientific purchasing, scientific storing of raw materials, exercising effective control on the stores, applying various techniques of inventory control like ABC control, etc., and finally, good warehousing of finished product till the time of their shipment and so on.
5. ***Product Development and Designing***: Law of variety in economics provides a guideline to modern business community to produce goods of various varieties with slight modification as it will contribute a lot to the organization objectives of earning handsome profits. In order to capture the more and more market, continuous efforts should be made in this direction.
6. ***Internal Transportation System***: Generally, internal transportation system of many concerns is ill equipped, mis-organised but it is dangerous for the growth of the organization. It must be quick, dynamic, economical, distinct, simple and finally suitable to organization needs.
7. ***Routing***: Routing includes, "Planning of where and by whom work shall be done, the determination of path that work shall follow, and the necessary sequence of operations." Hence routing is activity of deciding about the most economical way of production. Thus, it is a comprehensive pre-planning of manufacture activity.
8. ***Scheduling***: It is the determination of the time that should be required to perform the entire series, as planned, making allowance for the factors concerned. For this purpose, a master schedule is prepared. In the words of S. Ellen "Scheduling is perhaps the toughest job facing a production manager because it determines the utilization of equipments and manpower and hence the efficiency of plant."

9. ***Dispatching***: Production function, in fact, starts from here. Implementation of manufacturing policies, plans adopted by Production Planning Dept. and providing required tools, equipments, instructions, work-orders, record-keeping of time taken at a machine comes under it. "The duty of dispatcher is to see that order are issued to the shop, materials are at the work-place, that the tools are produced, that job cards are issued and in general that all necessary steps are taken to ensure that the schedules will be properly carried out."
10. ***Follow-up***: Deciding about producing and giving orders for it is not sufficient but evaluation of work performed, and sending progress report is also imperative. It is part and parcel of follow-up or chasing, and the superior concerned should keep his fingers on the pulse of worker's performance by continuously observing it.
11. ***Quality Control***: It is necessary to ensure quality of the products on a continuous basis at all stages of the production process to forestall defective process and production to take only connective action. Maintenance of quality of product does not increase the goodwill of the firm but increases its sale and profits also. Various statistical techniques like-probability and sampling have greatly economized the quality control efforts. The term 'Statistical Quality Control' has become very popular these days.
12. ***Cost Control***: Cost control is also an important aspect of production control. During the course of production, data are collected on the consumption of materials, stores and consumables, man hours and machine hours, etc. The wastage and slack are recorded. The actual costs are compared with standard cost in order to discover deviations and to set in motion corrective action.

Review Questions

Short Answer Questions

1. What do you understand by Production Planning and Control?
2. State the objectives of Production Planning

Long Answer Questions

1. Explain the various techniques of production control.
2. Define Production Management? Add a note on importance of production planning and control?

8 Personnel Management

8.1 Introduction

LEARNING OBJECTIVES

- *Introduction and definition of Personnel Management*
- *Aims and Objectives of Personnel Management*
- *Functions of Personnel Management*
- *Principles of Personnel Management*
- *Necessity of a separate Personnel Management Department*

Labor is a major constituent of any production process. In the early stages the factory system dealt only with the physical organization of the manufacturing unit. No attention was paid to labor, its organization and management. In the initial days, production was a privilege of few people and labor had no place in the production scheme. But today, there is a drastic shift in the thinking. Today employers have realized the importance of workers in the growth and progress of industry, trade and commerce. Today labor is considered as a social and an economic entity.

8.2 Definition of Personnel Management

Personnel Management is a distinctive part of management and it is concerned with people at work and their relationship within the enterprise seeking to bring together into effective organization, the men and women who staff the enterprise, enabling each to make his/her own best contribution to its success, both as an individual and as a member of a working group.

Personnel Management knits together the personnel working in an organization into a high potentiality team in such way that the following are achieved.

(a) Objectives for which the company is established are attained economically and effectively

(b) Objectives of all levels of personnel are served to the highest possible degree

(c) Objectives of the community are duly considered and served.

Personnel administration is a code of the ways of organizing and treating individuals at work so that they will get the greatest possible realization of their intrinsic abilities, thus attaining maximum efficiency for themselves and their group, and thereby giving to the enterprise of which they are a part in determining competitive advantage and its optimum results.

8.3 | Salient Features of Personnel Management

Personnel Management is a well established branch of management and has the following distinctive features.

1. It is a staff function
2. It is a line responsibility
3. It is an instrument to attain the established objectives of the organization
4. It is a means to serve all personnel at all levels to the highest possible degree and to realize the intrinsic worth of the personnel serving the organization.
5. It is a process of (a) planning (b) organizing (c) building a team (d) executive action, and (e) controlling the personnel with a view to attain maximum efficiency and to get best results.
6. It is a technique of handling men at work and also a point of view to be served and realized.
7. It paves a way for the realization of maximum individual satisfaction
8. It is an aim to personnel development
9. It is the basic function of management
10. It provides means of getting effective results as desired and planned

8.4 | Aims and Objectives of Personnel Management

Usually the field of work of personnel department is limited and its activities are confined to the following :

1. Recruitment of labour force
2. Guidance and placement of labour force
3. Arrangement for compensation

4. Job description, analysis and evaluation
5. Merit rating
6. Arrangement for employee's training
7. Maintenance of Personnel records
8. Arrangement of Personnel welfare
9. Provision for better industrial relations
10. Creation of industrial psychology.

8.5 | Functions of Personnel Management

From the above activities there emerges the following broad functions of personnel management:

1. Recruitment of personnel
2. Placement of labour force : the right man on the right job
3. Providing training to those who need such a training for improving their efficiency and skill
4. Improving the job performance
5. Soliciting creative cooperation from the labour force
6. Developing better coordination and good cordial industrial relations
7. Providing explanation and interpretation of the policies and procedure of the organization
8. Controlling labour cost creating soothing work atmosphere.

8.6 | Functions of Personnel Department based on Organization, Implementation and Coordination of Personnel Policies of the Organization

Category	Functions
1. Recruitment	• Find out sources of supply • To have a liaison with available sources of supply • Calling for applications from the prospective applicants • Selection and screening of the candidates as per the policy of the organization • Prepare, update and properly maintain the personnel statistics • Ranking the personnel

Contd...

Category	Functions
2. Placement and training	• To place right person in the right job based on the training and aptitude • To give counseling and guidance to the employees • Training for fresh employees • Continuing education and refresher training • Motivation and boosting the interest of the employees by providing incentives etc.
3. Internal Management of salary	• To frame rules and regulations of promotion and take a wages and decision on promotion of the employees • To effect transfer of employees • To punish the employees – demotion, suspension, termination etc.
4. Administration of wages and salary	• To analyze the job • To evaluate the job • To prepare wage and salary structure and carry on surveys for the betterment of the structure already in existence • To carry on merit rating • To prepare incentive schemes. • To prepare profit sharing schemes. • To prepare schemes for workers' participation in management • To see that the labour-oriented scheme prepared by the department gets approved from the management and get implemented properly.
5. Industrial Relation	• To boost workers' morale • To discipline the workers • To interprete the legislations pertaining to labour • To settle labour disputes • To solicit workers cooperation • To attend the labour problems including grievances and arbitration
6. Welfare and social security	• To make provisions of welfare schemes and to see they are implemented by the management in right earnest and accepted by the labour without hesitation • To see that labour welfare scheme results in real welfare of the labour • To see that all legal provisions in relation to welfare schemes are implemented in both letter and spirit • To see that social security legislations are implemented honestly by the management • To manage the statutory social security provision such as provident fund, pension, insurance etc.

8.7 | Personnel Policy

Personnel policy is the statement of objectives and predetermined course of action for the guidance of management and the subordinates in its relation with employees. It constitutes guide to action. The personnel of an organization sets the general standards or basis on which the organizational decisions are made. The genesis of a personnel policy of an organization lies on values, philosophy, concepts and principles of the industrial organization.

The real intentions of the management can be known by the personnel policies. They are the directives to the management with the help of which it strives to accomplish the task assigned to it. Personnel policies indicate objectives. They are not objectives in themselves but they are formulated to achieve personnel and organizational objectives.

8.8 | Principles of Personnel Management

Personnel management has certain principles which are required for the sound functioning of the organization and for building a good team of workers and for giving a boost to the morale and motivation to employees. The important principles are given below:

- ***Careful selection***: Great caution, proper care and a good amount of skill should be exercised while making selection of personnel for the organization.
- ***Satisfactory introduction of the employee to the job***: The personnel recruited to do job is to be introduced to the job without which it may be difficult for him to involve himself in the job honestly and with satisfaction. For this introduction is a must which in all the circumstances should be (i) friendly, (ii) skillful, (iii) absorbing and (iv) adequate.
- ***Appreciation***: Punishments are correctives but appreciation is morale-boosting and interest arousing. A word of appreciation may take more work from the worker than an incentive or a bureaucratic thrashing. Each employee should be made to feel that he is the most important organ of the organization and his every effort is not only being appreciated at proper level and by appropriate personnel but his contribution is praise worthy.
- ***Feelings of employees should be taken care of***: While framing rules, governing policies, issuing orders and notification and giving practical shape to all these the feeling of each employee should be carefully considered.
- ***Participation***: Workers' participation should be carefully planned and an atmosphere should be created in which every worker should be made to feel that his role is not that of only to work and earn his livelihood. He should be made to feel that he is very much part of the organization. He should be assured that at least in planning the future course of action within the broad framework of policies,

programs and objectives of the organization he will be consulted and due weight to his role, his activities and his thinking will be given.

- ***Social security and freedom to work*:** There should be a sense of security of his job and personnel well-being. The labor should also be given reasonable freedom to work.
- ***Fairness of policies*:** The management should be fair in its policies and programs. Constant and intelligent effort should be made to do justice and avoid biased and unjust decisions. The policies should be such which may be implemented with fair amount of justice, which may be clearly explained and understood. Every employee should have a feeling of pride in working with the organization.
- ***Simple organization*:** The organizational set-up should clearly bring out the duties and responsibilities of all concerned. Accountability should be clearly spelled out and no confusion as to authority, power, delegation, area of supervision, and control should be there in the mind of the personnel.
- ***Satisfaction*:** Working conditions should be such which may be socially satisfying and should prove an idle means of livelihood.

8.9 | Necessity of a Separate Personnel Department

A separate personnel department in true sense of term is an insurance against falling labor efficiency and less labor productivity. It is because a separate personnel department holds the labor of personnel. It analyses, evaluates, trains and establishes a relation which satisfies both the labor as well as the management. Hence a separate personnel department. The following are the arguments in support of personnel department as a separate wing:

- Personnel department carries extensive as well as intensive job analysis, job-evaluation, and merit-rating and tries to place right man on right job. All these are an aid to the management.
- The above duties if performed in right earnest goes a long way in reducing the cost of production. A proper control, reduced wastages and leakage and work stoppage due to acceptable or reasonable personnel policies help the maximization of profit and minimization of production cost.
- Personnel department on its own tries to build a reasonably contented labor force. The obviously increase production and labor efficiency thereby paves a way to reduction in production cost.
- A separate personnel department takes proper care of the personnel. Scientific selection, adequate training and systematic promotion, demotion, transfer rules create a proper atmosphere in which one likes to do his best in order to achieve best results.

- A cordial relation between the personnel on the one hand and employee on the other helps in smooth growth of the organization.

All the above add to the efficiency of labor which not only satisfy him but it also satisfy the whole organization and the society which in its turn bring social and economic prosperity.

Review Questions

1. "Personnel Department of an industrial undertaking ensures labor efficiency" Elucidate the statement.
2. "Labor in an industrial house must be given a social and economic entity. This can ensure better industrial relations and higher labor productivity." Discuss.
3. What is a personnel policy? Does it help in achieving the objectives of the organization?
4. What do you understand by Personnel Management? Discuss its importance in an industrial house.

9 Pharmaceutical Marketing

9.1 | Introduction to Market

LEARNING OBJECTIVES

- *Introduction and definition of Market*
- *Classification of Market*
- *Definition of Pharmaceutical Marketing*
- *Objectives and Importance of Pharmaceutical Marketing*
- *Major differences between General Marketing and Pharmaceutical Marketing*
- *Marketing Functions*
- *Functions of Exchange*
- *Transport and its different types*
- *Storage and Warehousing*
- *Financing and Sources of Capital*
- *Types and causes of Risks*

Marketing is a human commercial activity which involves buying and selling of goods and services and thus facilitating exchange of commodities. Market is a place or area where buyers and sellers function. Market in an economic point of view is not any particular place of business where goods and services are exchanged. It refers to a commodity which is sold and purchased at competitive prices. In other words, market means "The demand for a commodity". Thus market implies a set of conditions and forces which determines prices. Putting it in a nutshell, the meeting of buyers and sellers, price determination and transfer of title, are the activities essential to the existence of a market.

9.2 | Definition of Market

Marketing is designing of products acceptable to the consumers and conduct of those activities which facilitate the transfer of ownership between buyer and seller. It is the sum total of the situation or environment in which the resource activities and attitudes of buyers and sellers affect the demand for products in a given area.

The American Marketing Association suggested the following definition for the term 'market'.

1. The place or area where buyers and sellers function
2. The center in which certain business activities are undertaken to direct the flow of goods and services from the producer to the consumer or user.

9.3 | Classification of Market

Markets are classified in different ways by approaching the definition from different standpoints.

A. ***According to geographical area***

(a) Local Markets
(b) Regional Markets
(c) National Markets
(d) World or International Markets

B. ***On the basis of the position of sellers***

(a) Primary Market – Primary producers to wholesalers or their agents.
(b) Secondary Market – Wholesalers to retailers
(c) Terminal Market – Goods purchased for final consumption. It is a market where the journey of a commodity comes to an end.

C. ***On the basis of the volume of business transacted***

(a) Wholesale Market
(b) Retail Market

D. ***On the basis of the nature of transaction***

(a) Spot Market: Where goods are physically transferred from sellers to the buyers.
(b) Future Market: It is a part of the product exchange where sellers and buyers enter into future contract which do not require actual delivery of goods from sellers to buyers.

E. ***From the standpoint of the buyer's and seller's ability to dictate terms***

(a) Seller's Market: It is a market where sellers can part with their goods at high prices owing to shortage in market supplies.
(b) Buyer's Market: Due to abundant supplies in the market, buyers can dictate terms to the sellers owing to a keen competition among the sellers.

F. ***On the basis of the goods transacted***

(a) Commodity Market
(b) Capital Market: Long-term funds are made available.
(c) Money Market: Short-term funds are made available.

G. ***Classification from economic standpoint of view***

(a) Perfect competition markets: Market where demand and supply factors are in perfect harmony. Due to lopsided development and inequality in distribution such markets remain a myth.

(b) Imperfect Competition Market: This is a market where some kind of maladjustment in demand and supply exists. In a way, all markets are imperfect only.

H. ***On the basis of time***

(a) Very short period market: In this market, the supply is fixed and the demand plays an important role in price fixation.

(b) Short period market: In this market, the supply can be adjusted with demand up to the existing capacity. No new plant, new equipment can be constructed.

(c) Long period market: In this market the period is sufficiently long so as to adjust the demand with the supply.

I. ***On the basis of goods***

(a) Commodity Market: 1. Product Exchange 2. Manufacture Goods Market 3. Bullion Market – Valuable Metals like Gold and Silver.

(b) Capital Market: 1. Money Market 2. Foreign Exchange Market 3. Stock Market or Security Market or Stock Exchange

J. ***On the basis of regulation***

(a) Regulated Markets – These markets are regulated by statutory measures

(b) Un-regulated or free markets – These Markets are un-controlled. They are left free and mostly operate according to demand and supply.

9.4 | Definition of Pharmaceutical Marketing

Marketing of pharmaceuticals or fine chemicals and raw materials related to the production of medicines is known as Pharmaceutical Marketing. It is the sum of all the business activities that are related to the flow of pharmaceutical goods and services from the pharmaceutical manufacturer to the ultimate consumer, the patient.

9.5 | Objectives and Importance of Pharmaceutical Marketing

The following are the important objectives of pharmaceutical marketing :

- To provide guiding policies for marketing of drugs and pharmaceuticals.

- To study the problems associated with the marketing of drugs and pharmaceuticals and to suggest solutions.
- To enable successful distribution of drugs, pharmaceuticals and medicinal products.
- To analyze the shortcomings in the existing pattern of pharmaceutical marketing.

The importance of pharmaceutical marketing is as follows :

Drugs and pharmaceuticals are required by rich and poor alike for removing diseases and disabilities. Hence drugs should be available at a cheaper rate and accessible to everyone. Simply producing quality medicines is not sufficient. Their distribution and making them available when required is also very important. Hence pharmaceutical marketing is a potential force that commands high significance for the country as a whole.

The Importance of pharmaceutical marketing is revealed by the following points:

1. Drugs and pharmaceuticals are related to Nation Health Care Policy. An increase in the efficiency of pharmaceutical marketing results in a lower cost of distribution. Lower prices to patients means a real increase in the National income.
2. Due to efficient pharmaceutical marketing activity, a decrease in the prices of drugs and pharmaceuticals will make even a poor man too afford for purchase of medicines.
3. Pharmaceutical marketing makes available life saving drugs and medicines which enhance the life span of people thereby rising the standard of living of people.
4. In our Country, a total of 75,000 crores of drugs and pharmaceuticals are produced. This activity gives job opportunities and livelihood to several thousand people.

9.6 | Major Differences between General (Consumer) Marketing and Pharmaceutical Marketing

General (Consumer) Marketing	Pharmaceutical Marketing
1. Consumer is the ultimate decision maker.	1. The Doctor or Physician is the decision maker
2. No control of Government on quality of items	2. The quality of Medicines is stringently controlled by the Government
3. Audio visual media is used for advertising the products	3. Advertising of Drugs and Medicine is strictly prohibited by Law.
4. General Marketing strategies are used.	4. It is usually done by personal approach

Contd...

General (Consumer) Marketing	Pharmaceutical Marketing
5. General Marketing sales personnel not require qualified people.	5. Only science and Pharmacy Graduates utilized as representatives.
6. No shelf-life and no expiry date for general goods	6. Shelf-life and expiry date is fixed and legal control is there over the issue
7. Obsolescence is very fast (change in the trend and fashions)	7. No such Obsolescence
8. Prescription is not required for purchasing consumer goods	8. A prescription from a qualified physician is mandatory for purchase of medicines
9. Consumer has several options and choices	9. Consumer does not have a choice
10. Licenses are not mandatory except for sales license	10. Licenses are required for distribution and selling of drugs

9.7 | Marketing Functions

Marketing is concerned with the movement of goods from the point of production to the point of ultimate human consumption or use. In this movement, goods pass through several essential processes. These processes are known as Marketing Functions.

Various Marketing Functions are commonly grouped into following 4 classes

1. Functions of Exchange – This includes buying, assembling and selling
2. Functions of Physical Supply – Transportation and storage.
3. Facilitating Function – Financing, Risk bearing and Marketing Information.
4. Equalization Function – Grading and dividing.

A classification of Marketing Process based on the flow of goods from the producer to the consumer is given below:

Marketing Process

Concentration	Equalization	Dispersion
1. Buying	1. Storage	1. Selling
2. Assembling	2. Grading	2. Transporting
3. Transporting	3. Transporting	3. Grading
4. Financing		4. Financing
5. Risk-bearing		5. Risk-bearing
6. Storage		

Another model of classification of Marketing Functions from the economist's point of view

All business functions are essentially economic activities is provided hereunder.

Marketing Function

Creating time and place utility (Physical movement)	Creating possession utility (movement of title or ownership)	Creating form utility
1. Transporting	1. Determining needs	1. Formulating policies
2. Storing	2. Creating demand	2. Financing
3. Packing	3. Finding buyers and sellers	3. Supervising
4. Dividing	4. Negotiating	4. Accounting
5. Grading	5. Transporting title	5. Securing information
6. Order assembly	6. Equalization	6. Risk-bearing

9.8 | Functions of Exchange

Exchange means the transfer of goods and services for money or money's worth. It results in the change in the ownership of goods. It is a two way process. Whenever the ownership of the goods changes the transferor is called seller, and the transferee, a buyer. Thus, changes in the ownership of goods actually involve two separate but supporting functions called buying and selling.

***Buying and assembling*:** Buying is the first step in Pharmaceutical Marketing. It is concerned with the selection of raw materials to be used in the process of manufacture of Pharmaceuticals on the basis of price, service rendered by the seller and the quality of goods. The Pharmaceutical manufacturer has to buy the raw materials necessary for the manufacture of Pharmaceuticals in sufficient quantity and of required quality to be able to run his factory efficiently and profitably.

Similarly, merchants have to purchase goods or products from various sources of supply to meet the demands of their consumers to earn profit. For this purpose, goods of the best possible quality are to be purchased at the most favorable price, from sellers offering best terms. To ensure buying which may combine all these benefits – lists of specific requirements are prepared and suppliers are contacted. Terms of sale, mode of delivery, etc., are negotiated with the suppliers. On the basis of the negotiation purchase orders are prepared and goods are received and inspected.

Thus buying involves taking the following decisions:

(a) What kind of goods is required?

(b) In what quantity these goods are to be bought?

(c) When are they to be bought?

(d) From whom are these goods to be bought?

***Methods of buying*:** There are 4 methods of buying

1. Inspection
2. Sample
3. Description
4. Grade

1. ***Buying by inspection*:** This implies physical presence of the goods which are inspected by the buyer or his agent in the presence of the seller or his agent. Purchases are made after the buyer is satisfied with regard to the quality of the goods on actual examination.
2. ***Buying by sample*:** This method of buying is very common. It avoids the physical presence of the goods to be purchased. Only a sample of goods is given to the buyer. Buyer examines the sample and decides to purchase or not to purchase. While taking decision he ensures that the whole lot of the goods to be purchased will be of the same quality as that of the sample.
3. ***Buying by description*:** It refers to the purchase of goods made on the basis of description of goods in a catalogue. Popularity of this method of buying depends upon the reputation of the seller in regard to his honesty and integrity of character. This method saves the cost of sample. But this method presumes that the buyer has a technical knowledge of the product.
4. ***Buying by grade*:** Goods which are standardized and graded are purchased in required quantity simply by mentioning their grades. Cotton, Ghee, Eggs, etc., have been divided into certain grades based on the quality etc. They are bought by mentioning the grade of the required quality.

Assembling

It is an important aid to the function of buying. Assembling starts with the goods have already been purchased. It is a function different from buying. Assembling implies collection of goods required at a central place. This is also known as 'concentration'. Buying involves transfer of ownership of goods where as assembling involves creating and maintaining of stock of goods purchased from different sources. Usually goods are not purchased from one seller only. When they are purchased from different sellers, they have to be collected and assembled at one place making available when and where they are wanted.

The goods are required to be kept at centrally located places because of four reasons.

1. Goods are usually produced in small quantities at different parts of the country which cannot be processed by the manufacturer economically unless they are made available at one place.
2. Transportation of the goods will be economical if the goods are moved in bulk.
3. For meeting the immediate demand of the buyer.
4. To provide sufficient volume of business to business intermediaries like retailers and wholesalers.

Assembling is a specialized function and it is required for the following types of goods:

1. When the producers are widely scattered and geographically apart.
2. Non-standardized goods (Goods which vary widely in quality)
3. Seasonal goods.

Advantages of Assembling

1. Standardization and grading of goods are made possible.
2. Seasonal goods are made available throughout the year.
3. Scope of marketing of goods is enhanced.
4. Economical because saving in the repeated handling of goods is avoided.

Selling

Selling is an important function of marketing which involves transfer of the title of goods to the buyers. Nothing happens unless goods are sold by somebody. It is through selling that a business firm achieves its objectives and consumers obtain the goods for their needs. Mass production has created the need for mass selling. It is easy to produce goods but it is very difficult to sell them. Demand creation is one of the difficult job that a sellers has to face.

Sales are the lifeblood of business and selling is the heart of marketing. Selling comprises of all personal and impersonal activities like creating demand, locating buyers, negotiating terms of sale, transferring title, credit, collection, servicing sales planning, marketing research, price fixing, product development and administration of sales force etc.

In Pharmaceutical Marketing, the sale of Pharmaceuticals and medicines, depend to a large extent on the prescribing patterns of physicians. Hence the Pharmaceutical manufacturers, by utilizing the personal selling efforts through medical representatives, try to influence the physician's prescribing trends.

9.9 | Functions of Physical Supply

The Marketing results in the creation of place and time utilities. Physical supply means the actual movement of products to the customer with the help of transportation and warehousing facilities. The principal economic basics for transportation is in enhancing the value of goods by the creation of place utility.

A. ***Transportation*:** It is an integral part of the process of marketing. Transportation is carrying of goods and people from one place to another by means of different modes of conveyance. Goods are produced at different places far away from the place of consumption or use. It is by means of transport that production and consumption are linked together. By moving goods and persons over long distances, transport creates place utility. Mass selling and mass production are impossible without efficient and economical transport. It makes for geographical specialization. Improvement in the means of transport has resulted in lower prices and better services to consumers. Increases in the speed of various modes of transport have helped in reducing price fluctuations.

   The movement of equipment, raw materials, the shipment of the finished goods and their subsequent delivery to consumers indicates the importance of transportation. Transportation has an important influence on other marketing functions. Goods must be financed and insured in the course of transit.

   Railways, roads, waterways and airways are the chief modes of transport. Modern transport is capable of creating time utility with the increase in the speed of various modes of quotation. Transportation provides the following advantages to the functions of marketing.

   - Created opportunities for optimum utilization of capital and labor.
   - Helped in the growth and distribution of wealth.
   - Promotes division of labor and specialization.
   - Creates new markets and widening the scope of existing markets.
   - Helps in the stabilization of prices of goods by movement of supplies from surplus to the shortage areas.
   - Helps the trade within and between the countries.
   - It helps in the promotion of several industries producing perishable items like fishing, dairy farming, poultry farming, vegetables and food items.
   - It is indispensable for the assembling and distribution of raw materials required for production of goods regularly.

Rail transportation is the common medium for transporting Pharmaceutical goods from one place to another within the country. Goods are carried from Pharmaceutical industries to the railway station by road transport and loaded into wagons of goods train. Big Pharmaceutical companies have their own fleet of motor vehicles like trucks, tempos and lorries to transport their goods from one place to another.

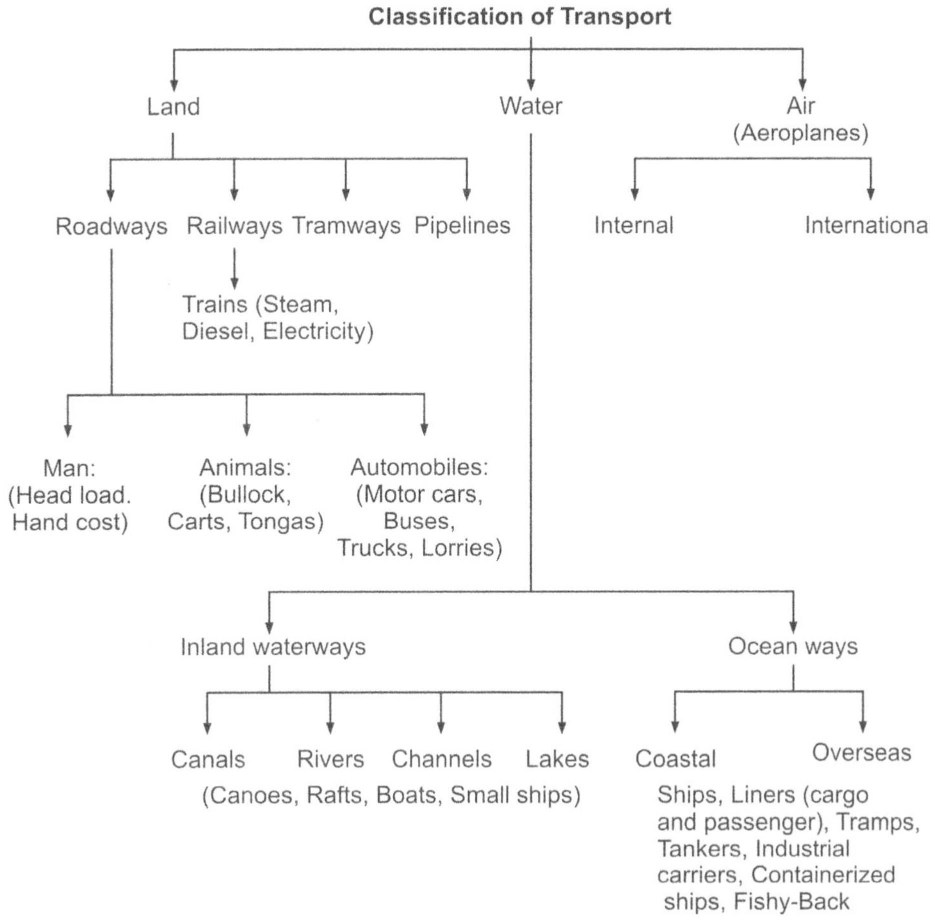

B. ***Storage and warehousing*:** Storage becomes necessary under two conditions: When production is seasonal but consumption is perennial and also when production is continuous but consumption is seasonal. In other words, storage involves holding and preserving of goods between the time of their production and the time of their use. It facilitates a steady flow of commodities to markets throughout the year.

***Needs for storage*:** Need for storage arises due to the following reasons:

1. Goods are produced in anticipation of demand and must be stored until they are sold.
2. Some goods are produced regularly but consumed only during particular season, e.g., wool, rain-coats, umbrellas, heaters, etc.
3. Certain products are demanded throughout the year but produced in certain season, e.g., crops.
4. Perishable goods are needed to be stored for preservation.
5. Raw materials and products produced at distant places have to be stored near the point of consumption to overcome delays and uncertainties of transport and possible shortage.
6. Goods may be stored in anticipation of rise in prices. Goods like rice, tobacco, etc., become more valuable with the passage of time. Warehousing helps reduce price fluctuations.
7. Small quantities are stored to make large lots which are economical to transport.
8. Large-scale buying is economical and goods have to be stored.
9. Certain products have to be conditioned or processed to make them fit for human use, e.g., meat, coffee, cheese, tobacco, etc.
10. Demand for certain goods is irregular and storage is necessary for regular production. Jewellery, utensils, toys, etc. are purchased on special occasions.

***Warehousing*:** The storage function is made effective through the establishment of warehouses. Warehouses also help in having a central place for keeping goods from where the distribution could be made easily and according to needs. Storage can be regarded as a function of equalization. Ultimately, it tends to adjust the supply to demand so as to equalize them in the interest of the manufacturers, middlemen and consumers. Moreover, it creates time and place utilities.

There are three types of warehouses :

1. Private warehouses
2. Public warehouses
3. Bonded warehouses

1. ***Private warehouses*:** Private warehouses are owned and operated by manufactures. Wholesalers and retailers to fulfill their own storage requirements.
2. ***Public warehouses*:** A Public warehouse is a specialized business firm which provides storage facilities to the general public for a certain charge. It may be owned and operated by an individual, a co-operative society, a dock authority, etc. It has to work under a license from the Government and under prescribed rules and regulations. It is also known as commercial or duty paid warehouse.
3. ***Bonded warehouses*:** These warehouses are licensed to accept imported goods for storage until the payment of custom duties are made. These are situated at

ports. These warehouses are either owned or operated by the Government or work under its control. The warehouse is required to give an undertaking or 'Bond' that it will not allow the goods to be removed without the consent of the customs authorities. The goods are held in bond and the owner cannot interfere with them without the permission of the customs authorities.

Further a broader classification of warehouses is as follows:

1. ***On the basis of place of necessity***: (a) In-plant warehousing (b) Field warehousing (Custodian warehousing) (c) Bonded warehouses.
2. ***On the basis of ownership***: (a) Private warehouses (b) Public warehouses (c) Co-operative warehouses
3. ***On the basis of specialty*** : (a) General merchandise warehouses (b) Special commodity warehouses (c) Refrigerated warehouses (Cold storage) (d) Household warehouses (e) Grain elevators (f) Yard and ground storages
.

9.10 | Facilitating Function

This function is an indirect function and remains as an undertone. Hence it is treated as auxiliary or ancillary function of marketing. But its importance and necessity cannot be ignored. It is helpful in minimizing various lags between production and consumption created by time, place, quantity and quality elements. The facilitating function of marketing is

1. Financing
2. Risk bearing and standardization
3. Market Information

1. ***Financing***: Finance is the life-blood of any industrial or commercial undertaking and is an essential element for every kind of business activity. It is the provision of money at the time it is wanted. Money is like an arm or a leg. You either use it or loose it. Money or credit is the lubricant that facilitates the operation of marketing machine.

   A business requires finance for many purposes. From the moment an organization is born till its death, finance is required for varied purposes. One of such purposes is marketing, a process which requires adequate and enough finance. The process of arranging the necessary finance for marketing activity is a branch of business finance and is termed "Marketing Finance".

***Need of Finance*:** The need for finance in marketing arises due to the following factors:

1. To regulate production and storage of goods demanded during particular seasons.
2. To maintain a minimum level of inventories in anticipation of demand.
3. To meet buying, selling and transport expenses.
4. To meet changes in style, fashion and competitive products.
5. To meet temporary needs during depression, low sales, etc.
6. To grant credit to customers.

   Credit extended to consumers is known as consumer credit. Mercantile credit, on the other hand, represents credit extended by one business enterprise to another.

Enterprises engaged in marketing, such as wholesaler, retailer, commission merchant, broker, cooperative undertakings or the sales department of a manufacturer need relatively large amount of capital for the purchase of goods for resale, for paying wages and salaries and other operating expenses and for extending credit to customers. Capital required for these purposes is called working capital. Also they require some fixed capital for land, building, furniture and other office appliances. But the amount required for such purposes is usually small. Generally, land and buildings are rented and not owned by the marketing concerns.

***Source of Capital*:** Funds to meet all the requirements mentioned above are obtained from the following sources:

1. Investment of own money by the owners of the concerns.
2. Borrowings for short-term ranging from one to four months from commercial banks.
3. Borrowings from friends and relatives.
4. Loan from finance companies on the security of merchandise or bills receivable.
5. Credit extended by sellers.

There are 2 important sources of capital. They are 1. Fixed Capital 2. Working Capital.

***Fixed Capital*:** The finance required for acquiring fixed assets such as land, plant and machinery is known as fixed capital. It is a long term investment and not recurring in nature. It is for satisfying the needs of fixed or permanent nature of a business. Generally it is not converted into cash.

***Working Capital*:** It is the capital required for purchasing raw materials, stores (Inventories), finished and partly finished products and for day to day expenditure which consists of wages, salaries, rents, rates, advertisements etc. Goods are not sold immediately after the manufacture and there exists a gap between production and ultimate use. It takes time for the goods to reach the consumer and the replenishment of the capital invested is delayed. The capital raised temporarily to meet this situation is called as working capital. It is also called as circulating capital or revolving capital or floating capital or liquid capital. This type of capital is more liquid in nature than the fixed capital which is more static. Working Capital is for short duration and recurring in nature.

***Kinds of working capital*:** Working capital is flexible and its requirement is permanent. The different types of working capital are :

1. Regular or permanent working capital
   (a) Primary working capital
   (b) Normal working capital
2. Variable working capital
   (a) Seasonal working capital
   (b) Cyclical working capital
   (c) Special or emergency working capital

The sources of working capital can be broadly divided into two main categories.

1. External sources
2. Internal sources

1. *External sources*

- Public
- Bankers and money lenders
- Financial institutions
- Commercial banks

2. *Internal sources*

- Trade credit: (a) Mercantile credit - 1. Cycle billing 2. Revolving credit plan
- Retail credit - (a) Installment system (b) Hire purchased system
- Accounts receivable financing
- Customer advance

2. *Risk bearing*: Risk means the possibility of loss likely to be caused by some unforeseen events like fire, floods, cyclones, earthquakes, sea-wreck, theft, etc.

In the case of liquids, loss is likely to occur owing to leakage or evaporation. Again, loss may arise because of price fluctuations; fall in demand due to changes in fashion or style, unforeseeable competition, bad debts, etc. Thus, the loss may be either actual loss or loss of 'Potential profit' to the owner as well as to the purchaser of goods. Some of these risks like loss arising out of fire, floods, theft, burglary and other losses in transit can be insured against by securing protection through insurance contracts.

But certain other risks like leakage, spoilage, bad debts, and fluctuations in prices, tastes, habits, fashion, etc., cannot be insured and hence, the entrepreneur himself will have to bear the losses arising from such risks.

Types and causes of risks: Prof. Clark has classified the risks as under:

1. ***Economic risks***: These risks arise from changes in market and other economic conditions. They are of following types:
   - Time Risks – Such risks arise due to the time gap between purchase and sale of commodity. During this period, demand and prices may fall, due to changes in style, fashion, tastes, etc. The round about methods of production and distribution has increased time risks. Besides price fluctuations, goods may deteriorate with the passage of time or assets may become obsolete.
   - Place Risks – These arise due to differences in prices of the same commodity at different places. They are also caused by spoilage, breakage, leakage, etc., in the course of transit. Modern means of transportation have reduced such risks.
   - Risk of Changes in Demand – Goods are produced in present in anticipation of demand. If the actual demand comes to be lesser than expected, some of the goods remain unsold and result in loss.
   - Risk of Competition – This risk refers to the loss of demand due to the activities of competitors. Competitors may improve their quality or reduces costs and prices. A competitor may improve the method of production and marketing that result in reduction of costs. This may reduce the sales and profits of competitors who are unable to take such advantage. Competitors may also adopt unfair trade practices.
2. ***Natural risks***: These risks arise due to unforeseen natural events, such as fire, flood, earthquake, storm, death of key personnel, lightning, hailstorm, disease, etc. These are largely beyond the control of man.
3. ***Human risks***: These risks arise due to social hazards and man-made factors, such as theft, dishonesty, pilferage, fire, accidents, riots, strikes, lockouts, war, bad-debts, etc. Risks may also arise due to technological changes.
4. ***Political risks***: These risks are caused by changes in Governments and Government policies. Changes in taxation, licensing, industrial and tariff policies and changes in labor and other laws are important cause of business risks. Risks may also arise due to adverse public opinion, disputes between nations, etc.

Thus, a marketing concern is exposed to risk, that is, the possibility of future loss.

Protection against risk

Usually, there are five methods of protection against risk

1. Prevention of risk
2. Reduction of risk
3. Self-assumption of risk
4. Shifting of risk
5. Spreading over of risk through insurance

1. ***Prevention of risks***: Prevention of risk is considered to be the best solution of the problem of risk. Risk of fire can be prevented by the construction of fire-proof buildings. Industrial machinery may be thoroughly examined before it is operated so as to prevent the accident. Refrigerators may be used to prevent loss by spoilage.
2. ***Reduction of risks***: Prevention of risk may prove very costly. For example, construction of a fire-proof building involves locking-up of a large amount of capital. Reduction of risk is more feasible. Risk of fire may be reduced by introducing 'automatic sprinkler system' and proper training in fire-fighting. Market research may help in reducing the risk of price changes and reduction in value.
3. ***Self-assumption of risks***: Self-assumption usually means making provisions for the occurrence of the loss by setting aside a reserve fund to meet a particular loss. In its ultimate analysis this method amounts to shifting the risks to the consumer by way of increased prices.
4. ***Shifting of risks***: It simply means to transfer the risk to others who specialize in assuming the risk.
5. ***Spreading of risks***: Risk is spread over through the use of insurance. This method is by far the most important method of protecting against risk of fires, accidents, theft, burglary, etc.

Thus, the risks involved in marketing activities will have to be either shouldered by the business entrepreneurs themselves or shifted to others with the help of insurance companies or commodity (or produce) exchanges.

3. ***Market information***: Marketing function can be very efficient and highly successful only when it is possible to take correct and timely decisions. The marketing policies can be formulated and the plans of production and marketing of goods can be quickly finalized only if accurate and up to date information of market conditions is readily available. All those who participate in the marketing activities can do their jobs very successfully only when they possess thorough and up to date knowledge of conditions prevailing in the various related markets. A marketer will have to collect information relating to the following:

1. Places where prospective buyers exist.
2. Quantity of goods that can be marketed.
3. Quality of goods desired by consumers, their tastes, habits, fashions, preferences, etc.
4. Price at which goods can be sold.
5. Possibilities of introducing new products and creation of new demand in the potential markets.
6. Types of products to be collected and stocked and in probable quantities.

The information can be collected first by conducting the market survey and then by interpreting such facts and data so collected. This is called 'market research'.

But it is very essential to ensure that the market information is accurate, adequate, correct, useful and up to date so that it will be easy to take correct decisions and formulate proper and reliable marketing strategy. The various sources of marketing information may be classified as under:

1. ***Internal sources*:** A lot of valuable information is available within the firm. Main internal sources are records of the concern and salesmen's report. The data with regard to sales, costs and profits can be analyzed in terms of different products and sales territories. Such data is very convenient and economical provided records are kept systematically and up to date.
2. ***External sources*:** All the required information is often not available internally. Internal records often provide the clue to further information. External sources are of two types:
   - **(a)** ***Primary sources*:** Primary data is obtained directly from first hand sources through direct market research or field investigation. Data may be collected from consumers, dealers and competitors or through business trips and questionnaires. Observation, survey and experimental methods are used. Collection of information in this manner is quite inconvenient and expensive. It requires a separate organization and work force or use of the services of specialized marketing agencies. However, the data collected is likely to be more accurate and up to date.
   - **(b)** ***Secondary sources*:** These refer to collection of data from the published or unpublished reports of the Government, trade associations and other relevant agencies. Marketing research does not consist only of field research or collection of data directly from the market. Various economic and financial journals published by different trade bodies like Chambers of Commerce, Government agencies like RBI, professional bodies like AIMA and independent research organizations like NCAER, are a perennial source of marketing information.

9.11 | Equalization Function

***Standardization and Grading*:** Standards are models which are the basis for comparison with identical products. Standards convey the idea of uniformity and identity in respect of quality or quantity. Standard is a measure which is accepted to have a fixed value. It may be in units of quality or characteristics of a service. Standards are classified into positive standards and negative standards. The standards which express the good qualities of a product are called positive standards. The standards which express positively the qualities absent in the product are called negative standards.

Standards are also classified as general standards and private standards. General standards refer to similar commodities irrespective of the producer. Private standards are the limits laid down by a manufacturer for his own products.

Standardization is the determination of basic qualities to which the article must conform and it improves the process of fixing such standards. It is considered to be an ancillary function of marketing because it helps in the efficient performance of the various marketing functions.

***Grading*:** Grading is the process of sorting out individual specimens of a given product to the standard grades or classes to which they belong. Grading uses a set of standards for sorting ungraded products. It involves the division of products into classes made up of units having similar quality and size. There are two kinds of grades:

1. Fixed grades
2. Variable grades

1. ***Fixed grades*:** Fixed grades have fixed limits within which more or less all the grading factors are present. This is some what closely resembles a standard.
2. ***Variable grades*:** The grading factor or limits fluctuate widely and no permanency in quality is found.

   Grading is separating products into groups of uniform kind, quality and size. Standardization is the establishment of a certain standards based upon the intrinsic physical properties and qualities of a product. Standards are permanent and this factor is extended to grades. Hence established standards are grades.

***Advantages of standardization and grading*:** Standardization and grading are useful marketing functions and they offer the following advantages:

1. They protect the goods during transportation from damage and reduce the cost of marketing by achieving economy in freight and handling.
2. They help to remove the element of speculation.
3. They help the manufacturer to use the brand names effectively.
4. They facilitate buying and selling and help to increase the market for particular product.
5. They provide the ethical basis for marketing standards.

6. They provide a measure of quality control and help in economical production on a large scale.
7. They help the consumers in getting good quality goods at a reasonable price.
8. They reduce the costs of advertising and sales promotion.
9. They help in valuation of products. This helps in making insurance claims.
10. Standardized goods sell better. Uniformity of quality eliminates uncertainty in purchasing and fetches a better price to the seller.
11. Standardized goods required less storage area. This reduces storage charges.

***Disadvantages of standardization and grading*:** Standardization and grading have some inherent disadvantages. They are as follows:

1. Individual skill and ingenuity is destroyed.
2. Workers are treated as machinery and their personal skill in the evaluation of the product is not there.
3. They retard progress and introduction of new ideas.
4. They limit markets and destroy the foreign trade.
5. They afford an atmosphere where even the low quality goods are sold under certain special standards or grade.

Review Questions

Short Answer Questions

1. Differentiate between time risks and place risks?
2. What are the methods through which risks may be avoided or minimized?
3. Discuss about fixed and working capital.
4. Write a note on standardization as an aid to increase market.
5. Define the concepts – Buying and Selling.

Long Answer Questions

1. Mention the various marketing functions? Discuss in detail marketing risks and marketing finance.
2. What are the various sources of meeting the current financial needs of a marketing concern?
3. What is working capital? Explain how a marketing firm estimates its working capital requirements?
4. State the importance of Standardization and grading in marketing?
5. What is marketing risk? What are the different types of marketing risks? Explain their causes?

10 Channels of Distribution

10.1 | Introduction and Definition

LEARNING OBJECTIVES

- *Meaning of channels of distribution*
- *Factors to be considered-selection of channel of distribution*
- *Different channels of distribution*
- *Wholesalers and Retailers*
- *Advantages of Wholesalers and Retailers*
- *Departmental store*
- *Multiple shops or Chain store*
- *Mail Order Business*
- *Consumer Co-operative stores.*

Channels of distribution are the route taken by goods as they move from the producer to ultimate consumer. It is the last component of total marketing process. The ultimate aim of every producer is to get the goods delivered to the consumers. He manufactures the goods. The customer comes to know about the product through advertising and next step is to see that the goods are available to the consumers. The 'trade channels' or 'channels of distribution' signifies various trade links connecting the producer and the ultimate consumer.

It includes producers, wholesalers and retailers and sometimes mercantile agents are also included. But channels of distribution does not include transport agencies, insurance companies, banks, warehouses and other non-middlemen institutions though they perform very important functions in aid of trade but they do not play any major role in negotiating purchase and sale of products.

Advantages of channels of distribution

1. Time utility and place utility. Consumers can get the goods at the place and at the time they require the goods.
2. Marketing costs are less.

3. Due to financial pooling from different sources, financial burden on producer is less.
4. Due to large net-work, more promotional efforts by each category, hence more advertisement for the product.
5. Creation of more employment potential and standard of living.

The distribution channels my be grouped under two major heads :

(i) Direct selling (ii) Indirect selling

(i) ***Direct selling:*** Manufacturer sells goods directly to the customer. (No Intermediaries). It is called as zero stage marketing channel. It is the simplest form of channel of Distribution.

(ii) ***Indirect selling:*** The manufacturer sells to intermediaries and they sell the products to consumers. There is no direct contact between the manufacturer and the customer. Depending upon the number of intermediaries present, the channels of distribution are classified as follows:

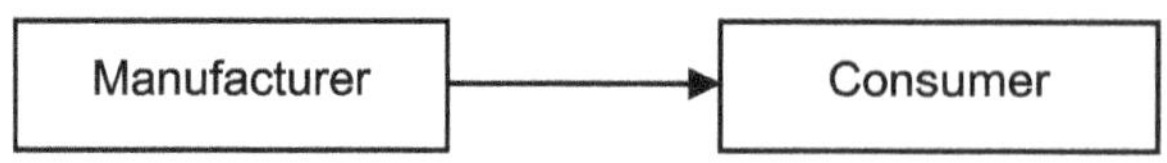

Table 10.1 | Channels of distribution

One Stage	-	Manufacturer → Retailer → Consumer
Two Stage	-	Manufacturer → Wholes → Retailer → Consumer
Three stage	-	Producer → Distributor → Wholesaler → Consumer

(a) Producer and consumer or direct sale (Zero stage marketing): Direct selling of goods and services by the manufacturer to the consumer. The producers establish connection with the consumers directly through door to door salesmen, direct mail or by its own retail outlets.

Direct Selling is gaining ground Now-a-days because of exorbant distribution costs through sale-intermediaries like retailers and wholesalers. This method is usually adopted to sell industrial goods of high value and also goods like perishable commodities. In this type of selling, the marketing activities are performed by the producer himself.

(b) Producer, retailer and consumer: This is single phase distribution where the manufacturer sells the goods to retailer who in turn sells to the consumer. This is a popular method of distribution because of emergence of super markets and big departmental stores. The retailer procures the goods in large quantities from the manufacturer and sells them to the consumers.

(c) Producer-wholesaler-retailer and consumer: This is called two stage marketing where two intermediaries are involved. This is the traditional channel of distribution for the sale of consumer goods. This channel is most suitable for widely scattered Markets.

(d) Producer-distribution-wholesaler-retailer and consumer: This type of distribution network is required when large number of retailers and wholesalers are present. Hence it becomes difficult for the producer to keep contact with such a large sales agencies. Hence the producer employs few distributors.

Usually the consumer goods are produced in large scale and everyone requires these goods. Hence a big channel of distribution is required whereas industrial goods are costly and few requirements are there. Hence a short channel of distribution.

Choice of channels of distribution or

Factors to be considered in the selection of channels of distribution:

- The selection of a right channels of distribution is the most powerful element in the selling of products.
- Even the best goods cannot be sold-out, if correct channel of distribution is not selected and vice versa.
- While taking a decision in this matter, the organization should consider carefully the following factors.

1. Market factors
2. Product factors
3. Organization factors
4. Market intermediaries factors

1. *Market Factors*

(a) *Type of market*: The manufacturer should first decide about his product, whether it is meant for consumer market or industrial market. If it is for industrial market, there is no need of middle man, because industrial users secure goods in large quantities directly from the producer. If it is a consumer market, retailers and wholesalers will be included in the channel of distribution.

(b) *Consumer potential*: If the product is intended for very large number of people, it will become difficult for the producer to distribute the goods efficiently whereas if the numbers of customers are small, the manufacturer can sell the goods directly to customers.

(c) *Quantum of goods*: Direct selling is convenient for large quantity of goods where as when the products are sold in smaller quantities, retailers, wholesalers are there to distribute the product.

(d) *Tastes and preferences of consumers*: The buying behavior of the consumer, credit facility, single stop shopping etc., is some of the factors useful in the choice of distribution of channels.

2. ***Product Factors*:** The nature and the category of the products also has a good influence on the selection of a suitable channel of distribution. The important product considerations are
   (a) *Value of goods*: If the products manufactured are very costly like diamonds, super computers etc., they are directly sold. For cheaper goods like tooth paste, stationary, soaps etc., the consumption is very high. Hence a very long channel of distribution is required.
   (b) *Product of category*: A manufacturer producing several products of same category requires a small channel of distribution like for example soaps, tooth paste and tooth brushes etc., can be moved in the same channel of distribution where as products falling in the varied category requires more number of channels of distribution.
   (c) *Popular products*: Popular products having good brand identify and because of their popularity can be sold through longer channel of distribution. Whereas un standardized products can be sold directly by the producer to the customer.
   (d) *Nature of the product*: If the product is of highly technical nature it is usually distributed directly to the user. This usually happens in case of industrial goods. Products of non-technical nature like consumer goods are usually sold through a chain of outlets.
   (e) *Size and weight*: If the goods are heavy in order to minimize physical handling of the goods and cost factor, they are usually distributed directly to the customer.
   (f) *Spoilage*: If the goods are perishable items and if they are subsected physical or fashion perishability they have to be sold as early as possible directly to the consumers. Non-perishable items usually have a longer channel of distribution.
3. ***Organization Factors*:** The nature and the size of the manufacturer also have an important impact. Some of the important aspects to be considered in this category are :
   (a) *Financial capability*: A strong financial company can distribute products on its own employing its own sales force and retail outlets where as financially weaker company can't do this and has to use services of retailers and wholesalers for this purpose.
   (b) *Control of distribution*: If the channel of the distribution is under the control of the manufacturer, it has to be a shorter one. By having control it is possible to have aggressive promotion of the product.
   (c) *Scale of operation*: If the scale of (operation) production is small, it is not possible to sell directly. Hence wholesalers and retailers are required to sell the products. For a big manufacturer, if he is

manufacturing wide variety of products he can sell the products directly to the customers by opening retail outlets in different parts of the country.

4. ***Market Intermediaries Factors***: There should be good co-operation and assistance between the middlemen and the manufacturer. Sometimes the middle man does not want to sell the manufactures because the processing of the manufacturers will not suit them or sometimes the retailers asked for a more credit period. The manufacturer will select a channel offering good sale potential in the long run. Similarly the large manufacturers usually select middle man, who are financially sound and can offer long standing credit facility to the customers.

10.2 | Different Channels of Distribution

Channels of distribution are broadly classified into 2 groups. (See chart)

1. Direct selling   2. Indirect selling

1. ***Direct selling***: In direct selling the manufacturer sells his products directly to the customers by employing his own salesmen or middle man who contact the consumer.

   Direct selling is advantageous because the middle men are eliminated and hence the goods utility became cheap, moreover the incentives can be directly given to the customers. It is also possible for the manufacturer to give information regarding the products to the customer and also get feedback directly. Now a day's direct selling is gaining wide popularity and many manufacturers are adopting this technique for selling the products.

2. ***Indirect selling***: This method adopts middles men who acts as a link between the producer and the consumer. They are engaged in the marketing and help in purchase and sale of goods and services.

   Middle man usually charge for the services they have rendered to manufacturers and the consumers.

   In the absence of middle man the manufacturers will have to perform all the functions for selling the products, Middle-men are also useful for the manufacturers in knowing the tastes and preferences of the customers and giving a feed back to the manufacturer regarding the requirements of the customers pertaining to the goods.

   Types of middle men: Middle men can be mainly classified into 2 kinds :

   1. Mercantile agents or agent middle man or functional middle man
   2. Merchant middle man or merchants

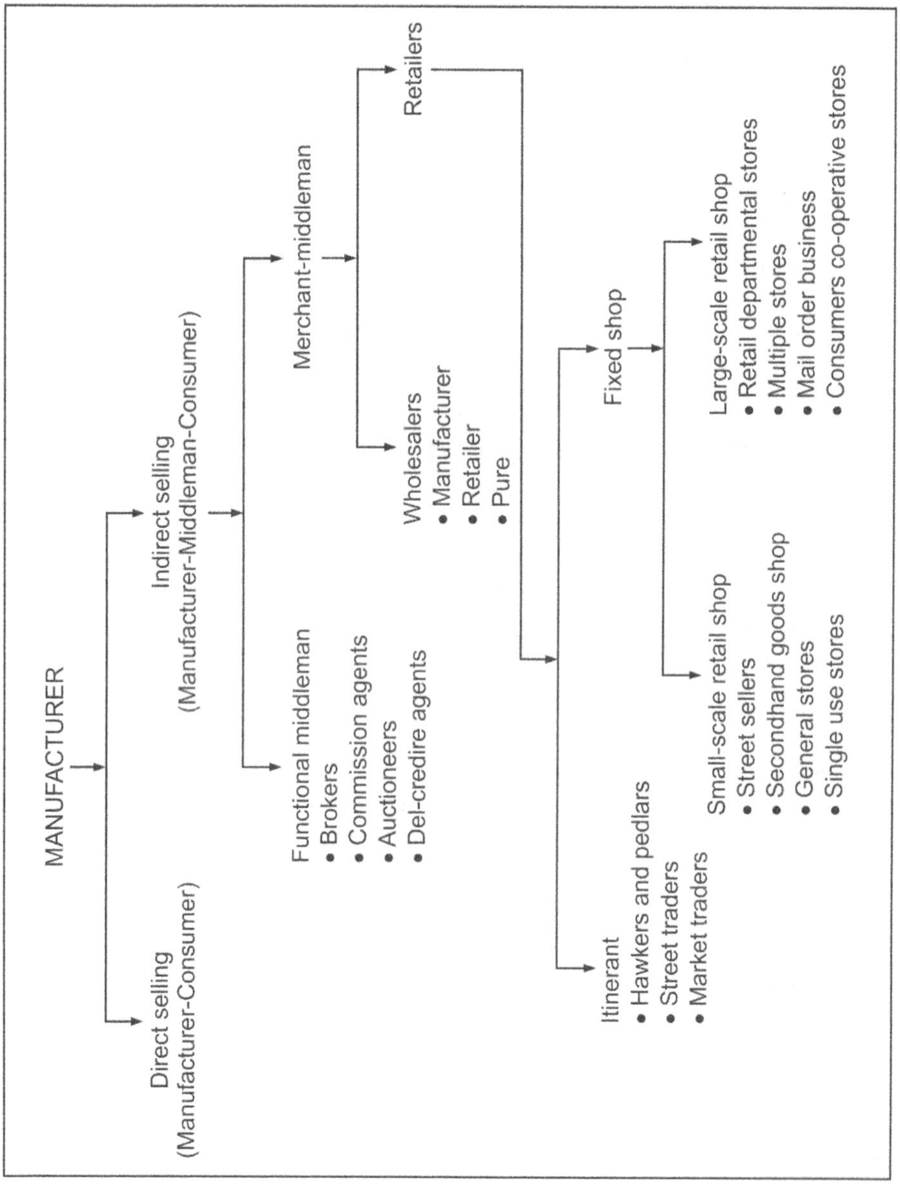

1. ***Mercantile agents***: These are the intermediaries who perform important services for the exchange of the goods but do not handle the goods in the capacity of owners. They assist in the buying and selling of the goods by taking part in the negotiations. They do not sell the products; hence they do

not earn profits. They charge remuneration for the services undertaken in the form of commission or brokerage.

Mercantile agents are of the following types:

1. Commission agents
2. Auctioneer
3. Brokers
4. Factor or del-credire agents

1. *Commission agents*: They sell goods on behalf of the seller. They physically possess the goods, negotiate the sale of goods and make necessary arrangements for the transfer of title of the goods to consumers. They also perform the associated function of the marketing like warehousing, assortments and assembling of goods and final disposal. A certain percentage of commission is paid to them for their services.
2. *Auctioneers*: They are the mercantile agents to sell goods on behalf of their principals by under taking auction of goods. They take physical possession of goods from the sellers, put for display before the prospective buyers and receive bids from the purchasers (Bid means the price which the buyer is willing to pay for the goods being auctioned). The bidder gets the goods provided for the highest bid is at least equal to the minimum reserved price fixed for the purpose. If the highest bid happens to the lower than the minimum reserved price fixed, then the auctioneers can cancel the auction. Auctioneer gets a certain percentage for the services rendered by him.
3. *Brokers*: A broker is a mercantile agent to negotiate, purchase or selling of goods on behalf of other parties, he neither takes the physical possession of goods nor change of title of goods on his name but only facilitates the exchange of goods by bringing buyer and seller together. He gets brokerage which is a percentage of the value of the transaction involved.
4. *Factors or Del-credire agents*: A Del-credire agent locates the prospective buyers and also guarantees the payment of the prices of the goods on their behalf. In case any buyer fails to pay, he pays on the behalf of the buyer. For this additional responsibility an extra commission is charged.

2. *Merchant middle man or merchants*: Also known as traders or dealers in goods and services who carry out buying and selling on their own name for profit. They take possession and become owner of the products and transfer title of ownership to the buyer when the goods are sold. The middle man belonging to this category are:

1. Wholesaler
2. Retailer

1. *Wholesalers:* They are the merchants to buy and sell the goods in large quantities and generally deal in a narrow range of goods. They provide an important link between the manufacturer and retailer.

   He possesses the title to the goods and he takes up several marketing risks in the process of distribution of goods.

   He purchases goods in large quantity and sells them in smaller quantities to the retailers.

   The wholesalers are usually located far away from the ultimate consumers.

   The wholesalers handling pharmaceutical products required a drug Licence from the drug control department of the concerned State. He sells the products to the pharmacist and physicians. A wholesaler is called a stockist if he handles the products of a single manufacturer.

Classification of wholesalers: The wholesalers can be classified into 3 types namely:

1. Manufacturer-wholesaler
2. Retail wholesaler
3. Wholesaler proper (Or) Pure wholesaler.

1. ***Manufacturer wholesaler*:** He undertakes the manufacturing of goods along with distribution to retailers. They may not only sell their own products to the retailers, but also make large scale purchases from other manufacturers to meet the demand of the materials. In this way their turnover is increased and sale price and over head expenses are reduced by eliminating the wholesalers.

2. ***Retailer wholesaler*:** A wholesaler combines his business of wholesale with the function of retail trade. They purchase goods in large quantities directly from the producers and sell them both to the producers and as well as to the consumers.

3. ***Pure wholesaler*:** He is a merchant who deals only in business relations. He neither manufactures, nor sells the goods directly to the consumers.

   Sometimes they are also known as distributors wholesaler. He purchase goods from number of manufacturers in large quantities and sells to the retailers in small quantities. He has warehousing facility and also arranges for transportation of goods to the retailers.

   The wholesalers specialising only in a particular line of product is known as "Single line Wholesaler".

Functions of wholesalers

1. **Assembly of goods:** He places orders to various producers and collect different types of goods at one place and resells them to the retailers.

2. **Distribution:** The wholesalers distribute the goods to the retailers, who are generally widely scattered.
3. **Storage:** Wholesalers help the goods to assemble in the warehousing to supply them to retailers whenever they order. They relieve the manufacturer and retailers from the burden of making storage arrangement.
4. **Transportation:** He moves the goods from the place of production to his own warehouse and from there to the retailers. Usually he has his own lorries for the purpose of transportation of goods.
5. **Financing:** Wholesalers provide financial assistance in the form of credit to manufacturers and the retailers.
6. **Risk taking:** Bulk buying and storage of goods involves several risks like accidental damage to goods, vagaries of nature, change of demand etc. These risks are born by the wholesaler.
7. **Pricing:** The price fixed by the wholesaler is based on the price at which the retailer charges from its customers.
8. **Grading and packaging:** Grading of goods into different categories based on the quality and packing the goods in smaller containers.
9. **Market research:** The wholesaler is close to the retailers and hence he gets information regarding the preferences and tastes of the customer. Hence he is in a position to advice the manufacturer regarding the product and price fixations to fit the customer needs.
10. **Promotion:** He also performs several advertising and promotional activities to increase the sales of the products. He also assist the retailers in dispersal of goods.

Advantages of wholesale trade

A. To producers

1. Financial help to producers by giving advance.
2. Assistance in marketing functions like sales promotions and advertisement.
3. Feed back information (marketing research)
4. Facilitates large scale production by placing advance orders of the goods.
5. Shares the risk with producer by bulk buying and storage.
6. Helps in adjusting demand and supply and hence in stabilising the price of goods.

B. To Retailers

1. Provision of transportation to retailers.
2. Help in promoting the products to retailers.
3. Retailers get discount on bulk purchasing from the wholesaler.
4. Gives advance information to the retailers regarding the new products of the manufacturer.

5. Provides credit facilities to the retailers.
6. He helps the retailers free from the risk of large stock.

C. Services to the consumers and society

1. Provides latest information regarding the products.
2. Prevents price fluctuation of the products by constantly suppling enough goods to the market.

Disadvantages of wholesalers

1. Price of the product is increased due to increase in the margin of profit by wholesalers.
2. Some times they create artificial scarcity of goods by hoarding the goods.

10.3 | Retail Trade

Retailers: A retailer sells the goods to the customers and maintenance good liaison with the wholesaler, manufacturer and consumer. He is a middle man between a wholesaler and actual consumer. He collects various kinds of goods from numerous sources and sells them to the consumers in small quantities. They are generally located at the popular residential areas. Retail business is organised on proprietorship or partnership basis.

Functions of retailers

1. ***Wide variety of goods:*** Various items according to the needs of consumers are kept by him. He should know the potential of the goods and he should know the tastes of the consumers.
2. ***Transport:*** Retailers usually have their own facilities for transportation of goods from the godowns of wholesalers.
3. ***Financing***: He provides credit facility to the consumers.
4. ***Market research***: He is in close contact with the customers. Hence he knows the tastes and preferences of the customers. This information will be useful to the manufacturers.
5. ***Sales promotion***: He exhibits the goods in his counters and helps in promotion and sale of goods.

Services performed by retailers

He performs number of services not only to the wholesaler and manufacturer but also to the actual consumer.

Services to the producer - wholesaler

1. They are the best link between the producer and the customer and helps in the distribution of goods.
2. They take over the function of dealing with large number of persons and selling goods in very small quantities, thus resolve the wholesalers from his job.
3. Without the service of the retailers, it is not possible to introduce a new product in the market.
4. They provide the latest information with regard to tastes, fashions and demand of the consumers to the wholesalers who in turn transmit the same to the producers.
5. Sometimes they make advance payments for the goods to be received, this helps in financing the wholesalers.

10.4 | Services to Consumers

1. They sell goods to the consumers in the smallest possible quantities according to the needs of the customers.
2. They keep large variety of goods and thus offer a wide choice to the customers.
3. The retailers keeps personal contacts with the customers, listen to their complaints and tries to satisfy them. He passes these genuine complaints to the manufacturer/wholesalers for rectification or substitution of goods.
4. They advice the customers regarding the suitability, use and maintenance of the products.
5. They also provide free home delivery and after sales services to regular customers.
6. The retailers often grant credit facility to the needy customers thereby helping them in times of difficulty.
7. They allow cash discount to the consumers on the product sold.
8. They provide fresh and latest products to the consumers.
9. Since the retail shops are generally situated near the residential areas so it is convenient to the customers to meet their daily requirements.
10. Some of the retailers render day and night services which are very helpful in emergency time.

Types of retailers

Based on the size of operation retailing activity is classified into small scale retailing and large scale retailing.

Small scale retailing includes mobile retailers and fixed shopkeepers.

***Mobile retailers*:** No fixed premises. They move from place to place for selling the goods. They are also known as 'Itinerant retailers'. Hawkers, market traders and pavement-sellers come under this category.

***Fixed shop retailing*:** They operate from fixed premises. Small scale fixed retail shops are located near residential areas. They deal in all category of consumer goods. Some shops also provide free home delivery and services also.

***Large scale retailing*:** Large retail outlets have become the current practice in big towns and cities. They cater well to the fast changing needs of urban population. These include super-markets, shopping malls etc. Several advantages of large scale retailing are effective sales promotion, creative selling, increased turn over and employment of skilled people for better co-ordination and control. These outlets provide 'one stop shopping', for customers and are usually centrally located and offer convenience of purchasing all the requirements of consumers under one roof.

Small Scale Retailers

1. ***Street hawkers and peddlars*:** This concept is as old as civilisation. In this type, vendors carry all the household requirement of the customers and sell them moving from one house to another. They do not have fixed premises. Much capital is not required and majority do business based on borrowing. Since it is convenient for the customer to get the goods at his house, hawkers do good business. The quality of goods is not superior.
2. ***Street traders*:** These traders offer a wide assortment of items of common use. They sell their products at relatively low prices. They pick up small shops temporarily. These traders sell their goods at pavements of busy roads, near railway stations, temples, cinema halls etc.
3. ***Market traders*:** These type of trading activity can be seen at weekly, fortnightly or monthly fairs. They move from place to place. During holidays, when big shops are closed, traders put up their tents and sell goods. The goods sold by them are usually cheap and related to domestic and household items.
4. ***Street stalls*:** These can be seen at street crossings or near the junction of the main roads. They usually consist of a Kiosk having elevated platform and a table to keep the items. The street stalls usually sell inexpensive goods like cigarettes, matches, ball pens, tooth pastes etc.
5. ***General stores*:** These are usually set up in residential areas. They maintain all kinds of items required by the families residing in the colony for the daily use. They provide a great service to the consumers because several required items of daily use are made available in an earshot distance.

   A general store is usually managed by single proprietor who establishes good rapport with the local residents of the colony. A general store may be a single line store or a multi-line store. A single line store sells only items of a single category. For example cloth store or a medical store.

6. ***Second hand goods store***: They deal with seconds or items once used such as books, clothes, furniture, electrical-appliances. These stores collect their items during auctions and from also customers directly by striking a bargain.

10.5 | Retail Departmental Store

A departmental store is a big store or retail organisation engaged in retail trade of wide assortment of goods under one roof. The store is divided into well defined departments for better co-ordination and control. Every department is related to a particular line of products. The organisation is centrally controlled. Each department confines its activities to a particular line of business. The departmental store deals in a very wide range of products. The main object of a departmental store is to satisfy consumer needs at one place, to save trouble for consumers from going pillar to post to purchase everyday necessities.

Advantages

1. Convenience of shopping.
2. Large assortment of goods – wider choice for customers.
3. Centrally located. Easily accessible.
4. Provision of television, recreation for children, home delivery etc.
5. Economy of large scale operations.
6. Better promotional and ad-campaigns to educate the consumers.
7. Employment of competent sales persons. Increased customers satisfaction and services.
8. Due to large purchase in bulk, better discounts can be given to customers.

Disadvantages

1. The cost of running the business is very high.
2. High operational costs, hence goods become costlier.
3. Since centrally located, traffic congestion and not easily accessible to people living in city outskirts.
4. Since many employees are working, difficult for the owner to achieve better co-ordination and supervision.
5. There is lack of 'personal touch' with the customers. The paid salesman may fail to give personal attention to a large number of customers of the store.

Multiple shops or chain stores

Multiple shops are the group of shops in the same branch of retail trade under a centralised management and dealing in similar lines of product. A single business firm opens a number of branch shops which are situated at different locality in the city and different parts of the country. The main objective is providing shoping facilities to the customers near their residence. The multiple shops are centrally controlled and received supply from the central office and remit the sales proceeds regularly to the central office. They have uniformity of operation and each branch deals in a similar line of goods. The price of all items is fixed by head office and the same is charged at every branch. Purchasing, pricing and advertising are done centrally. There is only decentralisation of selling. They display goods in an identical manner and sell the same type of goods. Generally, they deal only in a limited variety of products and all the goods are usually consumer goods. They generally sell goods on cash and carry basis and do not allow credit and free delivery services to customers. When organised by manufacturers, multiple shops aim at eliminating both sellers and retailers; Examples of multiple shops are Bata, Reymonds, DCM, MTC, Usha appliances, Dabur, Hamdard etc.

Advantages

1. The prices are fixed and no bargaining is done.
2. Multiple shops can easily be identified because uniform pattern of design and decoration of the shops.
3. Generally quality goods are sold.
4. Due to lower operational costs, the prices of goods are generally lower.
5. Common advertisement is done from a centralised place which covers the entire national network.
6. In multiple shop system, there is direct contact between producer and customer so middle men's profit are eliminated.
7. In multiple shops, sales are made strictly on cash payment. So there is practically no loss due to bad debts.
8. The fixed price and standard quality of the good helps in winning the confidence of customer.
9. There is a considerable increase in sale because majority of the branches of multiple shops are located in important locality of the city for the convenience of the customer.
10. Better market research can be done because of direct contact with consumer.
11. Multiple shops are run under the control of head office which shows uniform policies in regard to all important matters. This makes it easy for the head office for exercising effective control and supervision of its attached branches.

12. The shortage of supplies at one branch can easily be met by transfer from another branch having a surplus stock.
13. Under multiple stock system all purchases of the branches are made by the central office. This results in bulk buying which reduces cost of the product.
14. There is a diversification of risks. Unsold stock can be transferred to other branches to prevent loss or damage.
15. Greater flexibility in operation because it is easier to shift a store from one place to another.

Disadvantages

1. It can not offer a wide variety of products to customers because the range is limited.
2. There is lack of free home delivery service and credit facility to customers.
3. The owner of shops cannot make personal contacts with these customers. The success of organisation depends on the branch manager.
4. The head office of the multiple shops is generally located at a far away place so there is generally no effective supervision on the staff working in its branches.
5. Since the products are of standardised nature, they cannot be adjusted to suit the needs of the local market.
6. To run chain stores, heavy investments and faithful persons are required to look after business.
7. Since only the staff employed run the shops they may not give full attention towards customer's satisfaction and as well they may not be faithful to owner.

10.6 | Mail Order Business

Mail order business is a type of retail trade which involves activities taking place through post. The orders are received by post and the goods are send to the customers by post. Mail order business is also known as "Selling through Post" for the retailer and shopping by the post. The manufacturers establishes contact with the customers by means of advertisements in leading newspapers, magazines and TV, radio etc. The manufacturers send their price lists, samples, circulars etc., giving details of the product by post. The customer places order for supply of goods after they go through an advertisement. Generally, the goods are sent by VPP [value payable post]. The goods are delivered to the addresses on the payment of the price to the post office which remits it to the owner of goods. Sometimes the goods are also send by railway or transport agencies. The bills are sent to respective places and customers are informed accordingly. After paying the amount to the bank, the bill is released. After presenting the bill to the delivery office of railway or transport agencies the goods are handed over to the customers.

The important characteristic of mail order business are:

1. There is no need of middle men.
2. Goods are sold without any personal contact between buyer and seller.
3. There is no need of large capital.
4. There is no need of keeping goods in godowns, moreover shop is not required because business can be carried on without it.
5. It is purely based on advertisement.
6. The orders are placed by post only.

Mail order business has become successful because of the following factors :

1. Development of better communication facilities and better transportation facilities.
2. Large number of newspapers and magazine circulation among the people.
3. Change in the taste of the people and their preference for a wide variety and quality of goods.

This business has become successful in developed countries like US and UK. But in India it is still in infancy because of low poverty and literacy rate, lack of effective advertising media, lack of standard products and fraudulent practices adopted by the traders.

For mail order business to become popular or successful, the following criteria are to be fulfilled:

1. Goods should enjoy good demand by large number of customers.
2. Goods should have recognisation and should be of standard quality.
3. Goods should not require skills in handling.
4. Goods should not be perishable items and should not get destroyed during transportation. For e.g., Books, cosmetics, medicines, sports goods etc., are some of the good examples.

Advantages

1. The customer need not travel long distance to procure the goods.
2. The business can be located in less expensive localities.
3. The buyer is generally given a money back guarantee.
4. It is economical operation since overhead expenses like showroom rent, salesmen's salary, commission to middle men etc., are not required.
5. There is no need of appointing middle men.
6. There is no need for storing of goods. The same may be procured as and when the order is received.
7. The system is very useful for those customers who live in remote areas of the country. They get their requirement while staying in their home.

8. There is no danger of bad debts since the price of goods is received either in advance or collected from post office and goods sent by VPP.
9. The seller gets a very wide market to sell his products.
10. Advertisement and other promotional efforts can be optimised depending upon the quantum of orders obtained.

Disadvantages

1. Risk of goods getting damage during transportation.
2. There is lack of personal contact and the buyer cannot examine the goods before its purchase.
3. The credit facilities are not available to the customer.
4. Goods send by post are costlier because postal expenses are met by the customer.
5. Seldom, postal delay and strike cause inconvenience to the buyer.
6. The price of goods increases because a large chunk of money is spent on advertisement, correspondence and packing of goods.
7. Fraud can be committed on innocent customer.
8. There is no after sales services to the customers.
9. This system is suitable only to educated people.
10. This system can be used for specific type of goods. This facility is not suitable for perishable items.
11. Advertisement requires large amount of money.
12. The customers who like to make enquires have to waste time and money in correspondence.
13. Inspection of goods by the customer before purchase is not possible.
14. Customer loyalty cannot be developed because there is no personal rapport between manufacturer and customers.

10.7 | Consumer's Co-operative Stores

The consumer's co-operative stores is owned and operated by the consumers themselves under the co-operative society's Act. The shareholders provide the capital. Membership is voluntary. The basic purpose is to eliminate middlemen and provide service oriented benefits to the members without any profit motive. The members provide capital by purchase of shares of small denominations.

Hence even poor consumers can become members of such society. The society purchases its requirements in bulk from the wholesalers at wholesale rates, and sell them to their member's at the market rate. A part of the profit earned in the business is given to the members as bonus on purchases and also they get a dividend on their shares. Since there are no middlemen, the consumers get products of good quality at cheaper rate.

Sometimes certain percentage of profit is utilised for benevolent purposes.

Advantages

1. The consumers get good quality products because the chances of adultration by retailers is not there.
2. The overall cost of product is reduced because large quantities are directly purchased from the manufacturer, moreover the middlemen profit is eliminated.
3. The liability of the members of a co-operative stores is limited.
4. A co-operative society can be formed easily. Large number of members join it because the value of the shares is very low.
5. The government gives good patronage to the co-operative society.
6. The society is managed on democratic norms because every member has only one vote irrespective of the number of shares held by him.
7. It promotes thrift among members and increases their economic security.
8. Unnecessary expenditure on advertisements and decoration of store is not required.

Disadvantages

1. All the members of the society may not be co-operative and responsible, hence the society suffers financial losses.
2. The society has very limited resources and hence it cannot be run on large scale.
3. There is lack of ability, experience and business training on the part of members who are running the stores.

Supermarket

It is also known as 'Super-Bazar' or 'Self Service Store'. It has several separate units under one roof. It is a large retailing institution selling mainly food items, items of grocery and household requirements.

A supermarket is generally located in central shopping areas. They do not employ salesmen in large number. Only singleton shop assistants will be present for supervision. Goods are displayed on the well designed racks and consumer has a wider choice in picking up goods according to his tastes. He can touch, feel and smell the items. He has to place the selected items in a trolley and then bring items to cashier for billing the goods. As supermarkets follows the principle of 'Self Choice' and there is no pressure from salesman. These markets operate strictly on cash and carry principle and do not provide any after sales service to the clientele.

Advantages

1. Due to large scale buying and selling, operating costs are low.
2. Customer choice is the advantage. He is free to inspect physically various items leisurely and take decision. Packaging of the goods is given importance.
3. Goods at cheaper rates because lack of sales force.
4. No chances of bad debts because of cash and carry principle.
5. All items under one roof, no need for customer to go to several shops for purchasing his requirements.

Disadvantages

1. Individual persuasion by salesman is not there. Some people do not like this technique of selling.
2. Mishandling and carelessness attitude of customers spoil the goods.
3. Expenditure for maintenance is high and the turn over should be high to keep the overhead expenditures under check.

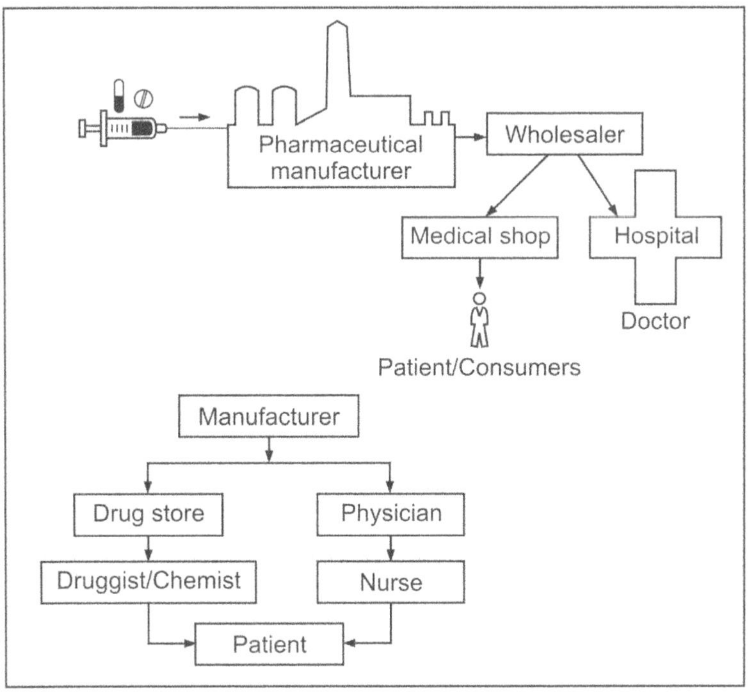

Review Questions

Short Answer Questions

1. Write the main features of multiple shops.
2. Give a comparative account of Retail and wholesale trade.
3. Describe briefly functional middlemen.
4. Give the salient features of retailing.
5. Give a brief account of consumer co-operative stores.

Long Answer Questions

1. Distinguish between the following:
   (a) Multiple shops and departmental stores.
   (b) Retail and wholesale.
2. Define the concept wholesale? Explain the general functions of it ?
3. Explain by means of a chart, the channels of Distribution.
4. Discuss in detail a retail departmental store? What are its advantages and disadvantage ?

11 Salesmanship

11.1 | Adverstising

LEARNING OBJECTIVES

- Definition and objectives of Advertising
- Media of Advertising
- Phases of Scientific Advertising
- The Advertisement Copy
- Themes of Advertisement
- Personal Selling and Salesmanship
- Qualities of a Successful Sales man
- Sales Promotion

Advertising is an art of creating public awareness or favorable attitude towards a product, brand, idea or service through dissemination of information regarding the product or service in accordance with the wishes of the advertiser. It consists of all the activities involved in communicating non-personal, oral or visual, openly sponsored message regarding a product, service or idea.

Definition

Advertising is defined as any paid form non personal presentation and promotion of ideas, goods or services by an identified sponsor.

The message is the advertisement and it is communicated through one or more media and is paid by the identified sponsor. The message is known as advertisement.

Advertisement is a non-personal form of promotion and there is no direct contact with the customer. It is a paid form of communication. The advertiser has to pay for the space or time hired by him for communicating the message.

Objectives of Advertising

The important objectives of advertising are:

1. To create primary demand.

2. To introduce a new product by creating awareness about it among the customers.
3. To inform about a product, its availability and its price.
4. To support personal selling program.
5. To reach people who are in accessible to salesmen.
6. To help salesmen to get orders from retailers easily.
7. To create a reputation for the company.
8. To create a brand image for the product.
9. To increase market share.
10. To increase the frequency in usage of a product.
11. To enter a new market and to attract a new group of customers.
12. To warn the public against imitation of an enterprise's products.
13. To improve dealers relations. Advertising support the dealers in selling the product.
14. To effect immediate buying action.
15. To develop overseas market.
16. To fight competition in the market and increase the sales.

Advantages of advertising

To manufacturer

1. It helps in marketing goods produced on a large scale through the method of mass persuasion.
2. It inculcates a sense of pride in employees, improved performance of workers, inspiration in executives and boosts up the morale of men working in the manufacturer's organization.
3. It helps in lowering average cost of production per unit. This is because of high turnover due to advertising which demands higher volume of production.
4. It helps easy introduction of product into the market.
5. It helps to establish a direct contact between manufacturer and customer.
6. It helps to create the reputation of the product and the manufacturer.
7. It helps salesmen by familiarizing the prospective customer with the product.

To wholesalers and retailers

1. It supplements the merchant middlemen's activity.
2. It provides information regarding the products. Hence provides brand identity. Hence items become well noticed.
3. It increases the sales turnover.

To Consumers

1. Advertising gives information about quality and price of the product.
2. It helps the consumers to know where and when the products are available. This reduces their shopping time.
3. Purchasing becomes easy due to selective choice and fixed resale price of the advertised products.
4. Consumers get good quality products.
5. Direct contact between the customer and manufacturer. Hence it widens the margin of profit to the manufacturer and lowers the cost of production for the consumers.

To Society

1. Advertising supports and helps to sustain the print media.
2. It encourages industrial research.
3. Advertising educates the public.
4. It provides a view of country's way of life style.
5. It leads to large scale production creating more employment opportunities.
6. It provides job potential for professional artists.

Drawbacks of Advertising

1. It involves huge wasteful expenditure; people usually don't give attention to them.
2. It does not increase demand for the product. It helps in shifting demand from one seller to another.
3. People are induced to buy items which they really do not need or afford to pay.
4. It increases the cost of production.
5. Advertisements usually misrepresent the facts.

11.2 | Advertising Techniques in Marketing or Media of Advertising

The channel or means utilized for transmitting the message from the advertiser to the public is known as advertising medium or media. The following are the important media of advertising:

1. Direct advertising or postal advertising or literature advertising
2. Indoor advertising
3. Outdoor advertising or external advertising
4. Point of purchase advertising
5. Specialty advertising

1. ***Direct advertising***: In direct advertising, the manufacturer informs the customers about their goods through leaflets, folders, booklets and catalogues etc.

   In this method, a mailing list of customers is prepared. Leaflets, folders etc., prepared by the company are sent to customers regularly through mail to inform them of the details of the products manufactured by the firm. This type of advertising is commonly seen for pharmaceutical products. The company sends the information directly to registered medical practitioners, pharmacists and chemists about the product range, new product introduction etc.

   Advantages

   1. It has a personalized appeal since it is directly addressed to a customer.
   2. Flexibility of advertising.
   3. Detailed information about the product can be furnished.
   4. Selected medium of advertising. Advertisement is sent to selected customers only, no wastage.
   5. Maintains confidentiality.

   Disadvantages

   1. It is not suitable for all range of products.
   2. Collecting mailer's list is a difficult proposition.

2. ***Indoor advertising:*** When the advertisements are seen or heard inside the premises, then it is known as indoor advertising. It is carried out through the following media.

   1. Press Advertising

      e.g.: Newspapers
      Magazines
      Journals

   2. Audio-Visual Advertising

      e.g. : Cinema, Radio and Television

   3. Exhibitions (indoor display)

   1. ***Press advertising:*** This is the popular method of advertising. There are two forms of press advertising namely, 1. News papers and 2. Magazines and Journals.

      Newspapers: A Newspaper is a daily publication which consists of news related to current events and feature articles. Newspaper is read by a large section of the society and it has become a part and parcel of life of many people. Now a days, newspapers reach remote villages also because of improved transport facilities.

      Hence newspapers serve as a good vehicle for advertising while selecting this medium, the advertiser has to keep in mind the circulation strength, geographical area covered by it and cost of space etc.

Advantages

1. Due to large circulation, many people can see the advertisements.
2. Continuously the advertisement can be seen because the newspapers are published daily and continuously.
3. Due to large revenue from advertisements, newspapers are sold at reduced prices.
4. Flexible in operation. Advertisements can be stopped and initiated quickly.

Limitations

1. People usually spend very less time reading the newspapers. Hence newspaper has a short life.
2. Highly glossy and attractive advertisements cannot be printed.

Magazines: Magazines are excellent medium which gives glossy and colorful printing. It can be directed towards the required segment of the people, thus waste full expenditure is avoided. Now days a wide variety of magazines are available catering to every need and every type of customer. Hence it is a convenient method of advertising when it is target oriented.

Advantages

1. Magazines are usually read leisurely and carefully. Hence advertisements have more effect on the customer.
2. Magazines are usually preserved for a long period and read again and again. Hence the life span of the magazine advertisements is more.
3. Since attractive colors are used in printing of magazines, the product can be advertised in a better way.

Limitations

1. Magazine advertisements is costly.
2. Circulation of magazine is small.
3. Well prepared advertisements need to be sent to magazines well in advance. Hence last minute changes in the advertisements are not possible.

3. ***Radio advertising:*** Advertisements of various products are broadcast from transmission stations of the All India Radio and messages reach the public through their radio sets. The radio advertisement or commercials are broadcast along with popular programs of music.

   Merits

   1. It is a mass media and even the customers who are illiterates can understand it.
   2. It is well suited for mass scale consumer goods because the messages reach nook and corner of the country.
   3. Cost of advertising is less. Hence economical.

Demerits

1. Visual impact is not there. Hence good illustration of the product visually cannot be done.
2. Lengthy messages can't be broadcast. It is difficult to remember the long messages.
3. Usually customers get-bored by continuous monologue of advertisements and hence they switch off the radio.

Cinema advertisements: Advertisements of products can be effectively achieved through film advertising. It is done through two methods. The simplest method is through slides on the screen. Another form of advertising is to show a short film on the screen.

Film advertisements are very effective because it has both spoken message and visual impact. Selectivity can also be achieved by going for advertising only in required areas. The major drawback of the system is people go out of theatre when advertisements are presented. Hence messages are not taken seriously by the customers.

Television advertisements: Television is the fastest and latest medium of advertisement. The presentation can be heard and seen. Hence eye as well as ear contact is there. The products usage can be demonstrated. Advertisements are in the form of commercials and sponsored programs.

Advantages

1. Selectivity of the message can be achieved.
2. Audio-visual effect. Hence customers remember the products for a long period.
3. Directly customers can watch T.V. sitting in their houses.

Disadvantages

1. It is a very costly medium of advertising.
2. Once it is presented, back reference is not possible.

11.3 | Outdoor Advertising or External Advertising

Outdoor advertising is useful when people move from one place to another. Hence people see the advertisement and product will be remembered by the customer. The various media in this method are posters, electric neon signs, travelling displays, sky advertising, vehicular car cards etc.

Poster Advertising

Messages and promotional idea is printed on a paper and is pasted on the walls or other places of public visibility. They are useful and put up where there is a large movement of people like bus stands, railway stations, busy cross roads etc.

Travelling Display

Posters of required dimensions containing promotional messages are displayed on the outer and inner sides of vehicles like buses, vans and trains. Such advertisements are called vehicular display. People while boarding and alighting, read these messages, vehicles provide mobility to the message. This method is useful for consumer products promotion since it attracts the attention quickly and customer can very easily grasp the message without much effort. It is also a flexible medium of advertising and a low cost method.

11.4 | Electric Light or Neon Signs

It is a very attractive method of advertising. These are glass tubes or signs with electric wiring made in the form of letters or design to exhibit the names of the products with brief advertising message. Neon signs are effective because in the darkness of night, they are bright and catch attention quickly.

Sky Advertising

Display of messages and figures is done on the sky using laser lights, smoke messages and balloons etc.

Advantages of outdoor advertising

1. Flexible medium and a least cost method.
2. Advertisements can be displayed at crowded places. Hence useful for advertising consumer products.
3. Pictures of the products and short messages can be displayed.
4. It immediately draws attention and the messages are easy to understand without difficulty.

Disadvantages

1. It causes road accidents and distracts the attention of customers while walking or travelling.
2. Customers devote less time in reading messages while moving. Hence less retention value.

Point of Purchase Advertising

In this type, the products are displayed prominently in the shops premises. The customers and passersby are made and compelled to look at it and tempted to go for a purchase. Different methods in this type are :

1. ***Window display:*** The products are displayed in the exterior of shops by glass paneling art transparent well dressed windows to attract the passersby.
2. ***Counter display:*** The products are displayed on the counter and inside the shops. This method is adopted when a new product is introduced.
3. ***Showrooms:*** Here the goods are displayed and allowed for inspection by the customers, e.g., Mixies, Washing machines etc. The products are purchased only after close scrutiny and personal inspection.

   Specialty advertising: Specially crafted items like diaries, pen stands, desk trays, key chains, calendars with the name and addresses of the advertiser are engraved on the items and these items are distributed to the customers and prospective customers. Since the articles of daily use, they are remembered for a longer period by the customers.

   Principles of window display: In this method, the products are displayed in front of the shop in an artificially laid out windows where they would be prominent so that passer by cannot escape the display. This type of advertising also can be seen in busy centers like railway stations, bus stops, underground pass ways etc. Big scale organizations utilize show rooms to display their products.

   Objectives of window display

   1. To create attention of the public and to induce interest about the product displayed in the customer.
   2. Brand identify is created.
   3. Products should contain price tags
   4. Brand image and loyalty among the customers.

   The following fixed units must be arranged to produce a pleasing effect to increase the sales:

   Position of the window: The products positioned inside the window should be well-decorated. The price of product should be tagged. Artificial flowers and leaves of suitable color enhance the appearance of show window and helps in introducing personal atmosphere especially for products like cosmetics, lotions etc. The background of the window display should be in obstructive. Back ground walls may be permanent wood finish. Temporary or movable back ground panels are used for drug store windows. Dark backgrounds should not be used unless the product is light colored.

Window frame and glass should be neat and clean. The size of the window should be correct. Window space should be appropriate. Proper lighting and illumination in the window display attracts more people. The lighting should be free from glare. In case of interior window lighting, only shaded light should be used.

For a pharmacy store (retail), the following principles of window display should be kept in mind.

1. Pharmacy insignia should be displayed. (Green cross +)
2. OTC products and seasonal products should be displayed
3. Products should contain price tags
4. Frequently, the items displayed in the window should be changed to give an aura of freshness and novelty
5. The window should be illuminated during nights.
6. Background should be decorative and display can be made attractive using coloured papers, Satin cloth etc.

The colors also play an important role. Dark and light shades usually attract the attention of customers. It is advisable to use a dark color in harmony with light shades.

11.5 | Choice of Advertising Media

There are several factors which are to be taken into account while selecting a suitable advertising media. The important factors are:

1. Nature of the product
2. Market area
3. The purpose of advertising
4. Type of audience
5. Financial propositions
6. Media circulation
7. Life span of advertisement
8. Competitor's method or choice of media

1. ***Nature of the product:*** If consumer goods are to be promoted, the media required is mass media like TV, Radio, and Newspapers etc. Industrial goods should be advertised in scientific and technical periodicals and journals.
2. ***Market area:*** Market factors like demographical profile, geographical area, purchasing power of customers etc., are to be considered. Similarly if the product is for local market, film-advertising, Cable TV ads and outdoor advertising are suitable. If the product is sold throughout the country, then TV and Newspapers, magazines are the best bet.

3. ***The purpose of advertising:*** The objectives of advertising are also an important factor in selecting a suitable media of advertising. Some of the purposes are introduction of a new product, sustaining the existing market for the product, to counter the competition of the rivals etc. Each purpose requires a separate-advertising strategy.
4. ***Type of audience:*** If the advertisement is meant for illiterate people, it will always be better to use audio visual media like Radio, television and Cinema Advertisement and if the message is for urban elite, Newspapers, Magazines, and direct mail can be used as Media of Advertisement. Since different languages are popular in different regions, advertisements in different languages should be given to popularize the product.
5. ***Financial propositions:*** The financial implications involved in the advertising depend on the funds at the disposal and the circulation of the media. The cost benefit analysis of different media of advertising will give the manufacturer a choice with regard to the selection of the advertising media.
6. ***Media circulation:*** If the advertisement should reach a large number of people throughout the country, then mass media like T.V and Newspapers have to be selected. But other media like journals and outdoor advertising have limited circulation.
7. ***Life span of advertisement*:** Life span of television, radio and newspaper advertisements is very short where as the life of magazines, direct mail, and outdoor advertisements have longer life. Hence it is necessary that the duration for which the advertisement should create an impression on the audience is also an important criterion.
8. ***Competitors methods or choice of media:*** The media selected by the competitor for advertising the product is also an important criterion. If the competitor advertises his product in television, the producer of the substitutes will also find it convenient to advertise his product in T.V. only. This is the order of the day and common practice adopted to fight competition.

Phases of scientific advertising:

Well planned scientifically designed advertising usually consist of 4 important phases.

I. Preliminary investigation
   (a) Market identification
   (b) Product analysis
   (c) Consumer research or Motivation Research
II. Budgeting and media planning
III. Execution
IV. Testing of results

I. *Preliminary investigation:* An advertiser should investigate beforehand the following aspects to prepare a logical plan of advertising

(a) *Market identification:* The advertiser has to carefully identify the following:

1. Climatic conditions, traditions, habits, customs etc., of the market.
2. Age groups, income groups, sex, occupation and literacy rate of the consumers.

(b) *Product analysis*

1. Type of commodity
2. Different uses of the product
3. Nature and quality of the product
4. Packaging trends and their possible effects
5. The common unit of sale.

(c) *Consumer research:* The factors that motivate consumer to buy a product should be identified.

These factors such as desires, emotions, impulses, attitudes etc., bridges the gap between the producer and the consumer.

II. *Budgeting and media planning:* The producer determines the budget of the advertising program with direct reference to the clearly defined objectives and targets. Further depending on the comparative effectiveness of media in reaching the consumers, cost, the length of the sale message etc., the medium of advertising should be selected.

III. *Execution:* The producer should follow the pattern set out in the advertising plan formulated as the basis of research

IV. *Testing of results:* This is the phase of scientific advertising which evaluates the performance in the light of plans. The results of advertising are tested by using any of the established methods. Most popularly used method is to insert different advertisements for the article in different number of copies. The medium selected keying helps to find out the following:

1. The medium inviting the large number of enquiries.
2. The medium read by the largest number of prospective consumers.

The above method is known of 'split on method with keying'. Its results can be used in the formulation of further advertising programs.

11.6 | The Advertisement Copy

An advertisement copy must win Attention, create Interest, produce a Desire and lead the prospective consumer to Action (AIDA). The creator of advertisement should formulate it keeping the psychological profile of the customer in view. He should device themes and concepts in such a way that the customer should be persuaded and convinced to go for a buy. An advertisement copy is prepared to achieve the following

Objectives

1. To Attract Attention
   (a) Use of Pictures
   (b) Use of display types
   (c) Borders etc.
   (d) Price Quotation
2. To give suggestions
3. Repetition for the memory
4. To create conviction value
5. To create sentiments
6. To appeal to instincts
7. To create demand

1. **To attract attention:** The advertisement copy must be catchy. Hence for making it noticeable, the following techniques can be adopted
   (a) ***Use of pictures:*** Colorful pictures of the products attract attention of the prospective customers. It is a better way of telling about the product.
   (b) ***Use of display type:*** Bold and crossing headlines consisting of three to four words about the product or message.
   (c) ***Borders:*** Under lying the key words and giving good borders to the messages also makes the message readable and attractive to the customer.
   (d) ***Price quotation:*** Mentioning the price on the product (if it is lower than other competitor's product) invite the attention of the readers.
2. **To give suggestion:** Continuous suggestions, slogans and banners create a positive impact on the minds of the customers and will be able to have an impact on cognitive mind of the readers.
3. **Repetition for the memory:** Repeated usage of brand names, use of suggestions for remedies and display of empathy create 'Auto suggestion' and remain in the minds of the customer for longer periods.
4. **To create conviction value:** The message should be simple, convincing and relevant regarding the product.
5. **To create sentiments:** The message should appeal to the sentiments of people. People give much value to the emotions and sentiments.
6. **To create demand:** An advertisement must be able to appeal to the psyche of people and introduce new habits in the customer to make use of the product. It should educate people about the use of new products.
7. **To appeal to instincts:** An advertisement should motivate the customers by appealing to the instincts like beauty, honesty, comfort etc.

11.7 | Themes of Advertisements

The advertisements employ different ideas to influence the instincts of people. Some of the themes are:

1. **Parental affection:** Theme is used to advertise for children toys, baby foods, household items like pen, suit cases etc.
2. **Beauty:** Cosmetics, perfumes, soaps etc.
3. **Health:** Food stuffs, Health, drinks.
4. **Comfort:** For products like air conditioners, fans, sofas, cushion beds etc.
5. **Prestige:** Luxurious items like personal computers and DVD's etc.
6. **Achievement:** Foreign exchange earned, awards received.
7. **Fear:** Insurance companies appealing to customers about future disability, death etc., Earth quakes to promote their products.
8. **Patriotism:** Products made in India only
9. **Economy:** For mass selling as the issue of reduced prices.

11.8 | Personal Selling and Salesmanship

The ultimate aim of any business organization is to generate profits and to develop the organization. The profit usually depends upon the volume of sales. Sales are the life blood of any business. The ultimate objective of all production is finally consumption by consumers. In order to achieve higher sales businessmen has to adopt several techniques to generate the momentum of sales. Salesmanship or personal selling is one of the most important techniques of promoting sales. It is an important method of selling. It increases profitable sales by offering want, satisfying needs to the people over the long run. It is the process of creating demand and promoting sales by assisting and persuading the prospective buyer to buy a commodity in a face to face situation. It involves direct line personal contact between the seller and buyer.

In personal selling the basic objective is winning regular and permanent customer. It is persuasive in nature. It is not to induce innocent people to buy which they do not require but to educate the customers about the good qualities of the product, remove their misunderstandings and to create a permanent demand and good will of product.

Personal selling helps in understanding the need, motives and behavior of the people. They are also useful in knowing the habits, tastes and attitudes of customers. The information is useful for the manufacturer in designing the new products and also improving the already existing product.

Significance of personal selling

1. It generates large employment opportunities to young people.
2. It helps in creating a demand for new product.
3. It helps in maximizing the sales and profits to the business men.
4. It generates urge in the buyers to buy a particular product by fine art of persuasion.
5. It increases the living standards of the people by creating demand for new and novel products.
6. It provides speedy back information regarding the customer's tastes and preferences to the manufacturer which is helpful in regulating the production.
7. Customer can select a product among the large lot available to suit his pocket.
8. It is flexible in operation. Salesman can modify their sales presentation to suit the needs of individual customers.

Types of salesmen

Depending on the type of employer the salesman represents. The salesmen are classified into three types 1. Manufacturer's salesman. 2. The wholesaler's salesmen 3. The retailer's salesmen.

1. ***Manufacturer's salesman*:** They deal only in a limited number of products manufactured by the producer. They possess specialized and thorough knowledge about the products. Generally they deal directly with the middle men and collect bulk orders from them and pass on the same to the manufacturer. In this type we come across 3 categories.
   - **(a)** ***Specialty salesman:*** Is the representative of a manufacturer who meets the customer and sells household goods or office appliances, shows the usage of the product by demonstration and clears the doubts of the customers. He should be well trained, alert, persistent and capable of working without direct supervision.
   - **(b)** ***Dealer servicing salesman:*** He is in regular touch with the dealers of his products. He keeps them well in contact and well informed about products selling points and also trains the dealer's salesman in effective selling methods.
   - **(c)** ***Promotional salesman or pioneer products salesman:*** He is entrusted with the responsibility of creating new demand for a new product. This type of salesman should be aggressive and imaginative. He should be highly skillful and should be able to generate the desirability of the product which never existed before.
2. ***Wholesaler's salesman*:** He works for the wholesalers and deals with retailers or industrial consumers. These salesmen may be outdoor salesmen or indoor salesmen. The outdoor salesman go out in the market and explain the information about the products, new techniques of sales promotion, types of concessions and book orders from the retailers.

The indoor salesmen remain in the shop and supply the products required by the retailers. They also assist the wholesaler in the activities like counting and checking the articles, bank work etc.

Second type of classification of salesmen is on the basis of products and services which they sell. In this category there are two types:

(a) Salesmen selling tangible goods

(b) Salesmen selling intangible goods

***Tangible goods*:** The products which can be seen, felt and handled physically.

***Intangible goods*:** Goods which relate to mind. For example pushing up the sale of tickets for a movie.

Third type of classification of salesmen is (a) creative salesmen (b) service salesman.

(a) ***Creative salesmen:*** He is responsible for introducing a new brand or a new product in the market for generating sales. For such a task generally a salesman should be dynamic and full of energy.

(b) ***Service salesman:*** The person who sells already existing products but having less demand. He has to create more demand for products or maintain the existing demand.

11.9 | Methods of Remuneration for Salesman

Salary is an important component which influences the quality and the amount of effort put on by an employee on his job. A good remuneration package should provide good income, security, incentives, flexibility and fairness.

Types of plans: There are two schemes of remuneration.

1. ***Straight salary plan*:** It provides fixed remuneration.
2. ***Commission Plan*:** This gives information which changes as the volume of sales change.

   (a) Fixed remuneration. Straight salary

   (b) Fixed and variable remuneration

      (i) Salary and commission

      (ii) Drawing account and commission

      (iii) Salary and bonus

      (iv) Salary, commission and bonus

      (v) Variable compensation

         (a) Commission (b) Commission and bonus (c) Bonus

Straight salary: A salesman is paid a fixed amount of salary. The salary component is based on the market rate and internal job evaluation irrespective of their achievements, the amount of remuneration payable to him is same. This plan has the following advantages and disadvantages.

Advantages

1. This is simple and involves no complex calculations on the part of clerk.
2. Sales force has a feeling of security and confidence and hence they are motivated to work hard.
3. The remuneration of a salesman is not affected by the factors beyond his control.
4. It minimizes clash of interests between the management and salesman.
5. No necessity of salesmen's aggressive promotion to increase the sales.

Disadvantages

1. No incentive for the salesmen who increases sales by additional efforts.
2. Plan is inflexible because it pays the same remuneration to hard working and under working salesmen.

Commission plans

This plan is a different system in which remuneration is given on the basis of pre-determined ratio or in comparison with the results obtained pertaining to sales volume or measure of performance.

Commission plans are flexible and are incentive oriented. They ensure efficiency and economy and place value for higher productivity and punish inefficiency. But they are complex and sometimes unjustified particularly due to some factors which are beyond the control of salesman. These are based on aggressive-Promotional strategies. Several disputes arise in this system and management also has hassles with the system.

Combination plans

These plans combine the positive features of straight salary plan and commission plan. Some important systems are

(a) Salary and commission
(b) Salary and bonus
(c) Drawing account and commission

(a) ***Salary and commission:*** The salesman gets a fixed salary every month and based on sales volume he gets a commission. As he is getting salary, his life is secured and depending upon his hard work and increased productivity, he gets commission.

(b) ***Salary and bonus:*** In addition to salary regularly drawn, he gets a certain percentage of salary as bonus earnings, e.g., 20% or 30% of the salary. This is less attractive than incentive plan because it is not directly related to more productivity.

(c) ***Drawing account and commission:*** A drawing account is a prepaid commission. It is an advance paid to the salesman. The commission earned by salesman is adjusted against the drawing account.

Steps in personal selling process: The process of personal selling consists of the following steps:

1. Pre sale preparation
2. Prospecting
3. Approaching
4. Presentation
5. Demonstration
6. Dealing with objections
7. Closing the sale
8. Follow up

1. ***Pre sale preparation:*** The selection, training and motivation of the sales personnel is the first step. He should be trained to possess a thorough knowledge of the products, customers, competitor's products and techniques of selling.
2. ***Prospecting:*** The salesman must identify the potential buyers and recognize their needs. They should examine the records of the past and present customers to find out the nature and attitude of potential buyers.
3. ***Approaching:*** The salesman should introduce himself. He should be polite and courteous while approaching the customers. He should greet them and behave in a friendly manner. He should make the customer feel that he is getting undivided attention from the sales-person. If the sales person is busy with some other customers, he should assure new customers that he would be attended very soon. Before making any presentation, the sales person should try to understand the nature, need and the spending capacity of the customer.
4. ***Presentation:*** The salesmen should attract the attention of the customer and his presentation should be in such a manner that the customer does not loose interest. The salesman should enthusiastically describe the various features of the product and benefits of the products and need of the customer which will be fulfilled by the particular product. There is no universal approach which suits practically all the situations. The success of a sales person will depend upon his orientation and aptitude in matching the needs and attitude of the customer.
5. ***Demonstration:*** It is frequently used to hold the customer's interest and generate urge for the product. Through demonstration, the prospect can be made to realize the

suitability of the product or satisfaction of his wants. Demonstration also creates certain queries in the mind of the customer.

6. ***Dealing with objections:*** Usually after presentation the customer raises certain doubts and objections, which should be welcomed. Usually these doubts are regarding the product, price, quality and design. The salesman should not loose his cool if the customer is persistent and asks too many questions and takes time in coming to a decision. The main aim of a salesman should be to clear the objections of the customer, so that the customer is satisfied with the product.
7. ***Closing the sale:*** Once the customer has come to a conclusion to buy a product, the salesman should close the deal in a cordial manner. Customer should make to feel that he has taken a right decision in buying the product.
8. ***Follow up:*** Next step is noting down the details of the product sold and informing the details to the manager.

Requisites of successful salesmanship: In order to achieve good results in personal selling, the business enterprises should develop good caliber to salesman to promote its products. The following are the general requirements to be fulfilled for achieving good personal selling

1. Personal qualities
2. Training and motivation
3. Sound knowledge
   (a) Self
   (b) Employer
   (c) Product
   (d) Competitor's products
   (e) Customers

1. ***Personal qualities:*** He should posse's sound physical, mental and social qualities.
2. ***Training and motivation:*** The training programs are designed in such a manner, keeping in view the requirements of the business. The training program should provide knowledge required for effective selling and he should be able to motivate the sales persons.
3. ***Sound knowledge:*** The salesman should have the following information with him.
   (a) *Self:* He should be able to adapt himself to the selling role. If he has any short comings in presentation skills, he should make necessary amends through training.
   (b) *Employer:* The salesman should have thorough knowledge towards employer, clear objectives of the organization and organizational structure. He should have an idea of the origin and growth of employer's business.

(c) *Product*: He should possess sufficient details about the product in selling, what are its unique selling propositions [USP], process adopted for the manufacture of the product etc., so that he can give sufficient information to the customers during sales presentation.

(d) *Competitor's Products*: He should possess knowledge about the competitor's product, their merits and demerits so that he can convince the customer regarding superiority of his product while presentation.

(e) *Customers*: Customer's patronage is very important for achieving good sales. Hence he should possess sound knowledge towards the nature of customers, their habits and their buying motives. He should understand why customers buy certain products and why they buy the goods from specific dealers only.

11.10 | Qualities of a Successful Salesman

The essential qualities of a good salesman are:

1. Physical attributes or personal qualities
2. Mental abilities
3. Moral and social qualities
4. Vocational or job related skills

1. *Physical attributes or Personal qualities*

(a) He should have a charming and attractive personality

(b) Good habits, well dressed, Good voice, Good tone of speech etc.

(c) He should be physically fit and should possess good health

(d) He should have good stamina for working hard for sustained periods of time.

2. *Mental abilities*

(a) A good salesman should possess a sound memory and should recognize his customers even if he meets after a long time

(b) He should have good presence of mind, imagination, sound judgment, foresightedness and initiation

(c) He should be imaginative and tactful

(d) He should have good presentation skills and good ability to convince the customers

(e) He should have thorough knowledge of the product.

3. *Moral and social qualities*

(a) A good salesman should be customer friendly and he should have a liking for people and the ability to mix with them

(b) He should be able to deal with people of all types, nature and temperament
(c) He should not be shy and should not be an introvert
(d) He should be sincere, dependable, honest, loyal and cooperative
(e) He should maintain friendly relations with fellow salesmen and be helpful to customers
(f) He should have capacity to speak in different languages particularly the local dialect.

4. ***Vocational or job related skills***
   (a) He should have sound general education and specialized knowledge of selling techniques
   (b) He should have ambition, knowledge and enthusiasm to become a good salesman.
   (c) He should have thorough knowledge of the products, customers and products of same category of other manufacturers already available in the market.

11.11 | Medical Representatives as Salesmen or Salesmanship in Pharmaceutical Industry

Selling consumer goods is different from selling pharmaceutical products. Ordinary consumer goods are sold by the retailers and pharmaceutical products are sold by the chemist and pharmacists on the written prescription of a physician. Hence salesmanship in pharmaceutical industry is a totally different setup. The salesman in pharmaceutical industry is known as medical representatives or sales officers or detailed-men or Brand Officer.

A medical representative approaches the doctors and person to person, explain the details about the products of their manufacturer. They provide information regarding various aspects of the products.

Hence every pharmaceutical manufacturing house has its own marketing department for promoting the sales of the company products. This method of personal selling is very costly but normally adopted by all pharmaceutical companies because it has the following advantages.

1. A medical representative can pay a personal visit to the physician and can explain the pros and cons of the product and he can also answer the questions raised by the doctors.
2. Frequently the representative visits the physician and informs him about the introduction of new products and also about the existence of old products. From the talks with the physician the representative can understand the prescribing patterns of the doctors and information can be passed on to the manufacturer.

Training of Medical Representatives

The success of any pharmaceutical company usually depends on its sales force. Hence the sales force should be well trained to carry on their tasks effectively. For training purpose a separate department is created and this department takes up the difficult responsibility of training newly appointed science or pharmacy graduates, sometimes experienced representatives from other companies. The sales training department consists of pharmaceutical and medical research faculty who train and give information to trainees regarding the various facets of pharmaceutical products.

The training is imparted on three fronts

1. ***General training***: In which the fundamental craft of selling is taught.
2. ***Specialized training***: Where they are taught about the products manufactured by their company, details about the formulation, standardization and testing procedures adopted by them and other companies etc. They also inform about the company corporate policy and overall information like technology adopted in the production etc.
3. ***Continuous training***: This is given at specific intervals of time to update the knowledge of medical representatives regarding the product of the company and the continuous trends of the market. Hence training is a continuous process for sales personnel.

11.12 | Sales Promotion

Sales promotion is the promotional activity other than personal salesmanship, advertising and publicity, which stimulate consumer purchasing and dealer effectiveness.

E.g. Displays, exhibitions and showrooms, demonstrations, free samples, coupons, premiums, contests and various non-recurrent selling efforts.

Definition: Sales promotion consists of short-term incentives to encourage purchase or sales of a product or service.

In short, sales promotion is a bridge or a connecting link covering the gap between advertising and personal salesmanship, the two wings of promotion.

Objectives of sales promotion: Sales promotion has the following objectives:

(a) To increase buying by consumers

(b) To increase selling efforts and intensity by dealers as well by sales personnel

(c) To supplement and co-ordinate efforts of advertising / personnel selling

Need for sales promotion

(a) Calling attention to new products and product improvement

(b) Informing buyers of new brands and new package

(c) Improving market share

(d) Increasing usage rate by present customers
(e) Maintaining customer interest and brand loyalty
(f) Obtaining dealer outlets
(g) Securing additional shelf space and added display
(h) Creating selling points for sales personnel
(i) Meeting market competition effectively

Roles of advertising in sales promotion: Advertising is one of the wings of sales promotion along with personal salesmanship. It promotes sales by:

(a) Persuading by direct or openly to consumer to try the product immediately
(b) It promotes an immediate job of boosting sales
(c) Advertising usually has long-term goals. E.g. to build awareness image or loyalty, or repositioning of a brand
(d) Sales only alter price-value relationship of the product. Advertising adds some value to the product.

Kinds of sales promotion: There are two kinds of the sales promotion

(a) Activities intended to educate or inform the consumers and those intended to stimulate the consumers. These are called **"Consumer sales promotion".**
(b) Activities to increase the interest and enthusiasm of dealers and distributors. These are called **"dealer/distributor sales promotion"**.

Consumer sales promotion

These methods are:

Samples: Usually in consumer sampling, free samples are given to consumers to introduce a new product or to expand the market. The consumer can try the product and assess it.

Demonstrations: These include instructions or educating the customers in the usage of the product.

Coupon system: A coupon is a certificate devise that reduces a price. When a buyer gives a coupon to a dealer, he gets the product at the lower price.

e.g. If a regular price of a product is Rs. 20, with a coupon it would be Rs. 18 only

Money-refund orders: These are the temporary offers regarding price reductions, which appeal to bargain instinct.

e.g. Instant coffee sold in cafeteria by one company was very successful.

Liril gave a soapbox with the purchase of two toilet soaps.

Price off: Brooke bond gave Rs. 2 off on 500 grams pack-encouraging consumers to buy half kilo packs, Festive offers offered by cloth brand also come under this category.

Fashion shows: Fashion shows and parades are good promotion aids in men's and women's clothing, cosmetics and varied products.

Contests/quiz: The advent of private channels has thrown open to business corners the possibilities of brand promotion via the countless Quizzes and contests.

Sponsor companies on the TV are adapting the quiz and contest route a profitable means of establishing brand equity over a period of time.

e.g. In programs like Phillips top - 10, bourn vita, close up antakashari, Bajaj ke tarane and Lux kya scene hai brand equity has been used as a format. These programs have gained popularity and would be remembered for a long time.

The basic strategy in contest is to provide an extra incentive to the consumer for buying the product.

11.13 | Dealers / Distributor Sales Promotion

1. In this case there is provision of free display material either at the point of purchase or point of sale. Depending on one's viewpoint display reaches consumers when they are buying and actually spending their money.
2. Retail demonstrators are supplied by manufacturers for preparing and distributing the product as a retail sample.

   e.g.: Nescafe (instant) to customers for trying the sample on the spot or demonstration regarding the method of using the product.
3. Trade deals are offered to encourage retailers to give additional selling support to the product.

   e.g.: Toothpaste sold with 30% to 40% margin.
4. Sellers give buying allowance of a certain amount of money for a product brought.
5. Buy back allowance is given to encourage repurchase of a product immediately for another trade deal.
6. Seller gives free goods

   e.g.: One free with 11 or 2 free with 10 is common free deals.
7. Advertising and display allowance may be given.
8. Sales contests for salesman are held.
9. Dealer and distributor training is given to salesman to give him better knowledge.

Various Means of Promoting Sales

- Cost sharing and joint promotion is an attractive benefit for advertising and promoters.
- A very great advantage, the exclusive showrooms offer to a company is the ability to impress the consumer with whole range of its products, at a time when all companies are going for diversification and expansions.

Publicity

- Publicity comes from news reporters, columnist and journalists. It comes to the receiver as a truth rather than a commercial. The firm having a poor public image will have lower sales and lower profits.
- It is important because consumerism is altering consumer attitudes not only towards products but also towards the firm and dealers selling the products of the firm.

Public Relations

- The total process of building goodwill towards a business enterprise and securing a bright public image of the company is called as public relations. It creates favorable atmosphere for conducting business.
- Marketers in the joint promotion game claim that such strategies can reduce media spend by as much as 70%.

  e.g. Joint promotion between two brands that pose no threat to each other aim at the same target audience and belong to the same usage category (e.g. : Washing machine and detergent).

Exhibition and Trade Fairs

A successful stand in the exhibition or trade fair gives three services to the owner.

- It provides entirely new business, which cannot be secured by any other method.
- Will on their own account do a lot of purchase in trade fairs. These buyers are usually resellers.
- The conservative buyer can compare the competitive products displayed in close distance to each other.

The Fashion Shows

A series of glamorous fashion shows are held in all metros. It is the best medium of advertising to reach the target audience.

TV now commands a viewership of 12 crore.

Exclusive show rooms

- generally show rooms idea is used as a tool of distribution. Exclusivity plays the role of Unique Selling Proposition (USP) to increase the sales.

  There are four groups of public:

  Customers

  Share holders

  Employees

  The community

Effective marketing communication is not possible without establishing and maintaining mutual understanding between the company and its products and its consumers. Bright image created is maintained only by public relations. Liberal aid in all social welfare projects enhances the public image of the marketer.

Advantages of Sales Promotion

- It stimulates positive attitudes towards the product
- It gives extra incentive to the customer to make a purchase
- It gives direct inducement to make immediate action now rather than later.
- It has flexibility and it can be used at any stage of new product introduction

Sales promotions are very Effective

(a) When a new brand is introduced.
(b) When we have to communicate a major improvement in our product.
(c) When we want to amplify the results of advertising.
(d) When we want to increase the number of retail sellers to sell our products.

Limitations of Sales Promotion

- Sales promotions have temporary and short life not exceeding three months. Sales promotion alone cannot build up brand loyalty.
- Sales promotion is only supplement devices to supplement selling efforts of other promotion tools.
- They are non-recurring in their use. They have seldom refuse values.
- Too many sales promotions may have adverse affects on the brand image suggesting its lack of popularity or over stocking by a company.
- Advertising agencies accord low status to sales promotion and usually employ junior staff for sales promotion

Sales Promotions are Effective

- When established brands have declining market.
- There are no product improvements.
- When there is intensive competition on consumer sales promotion

Review Questions

Short Answer Questions

1. Write a note on window-display?
2. Define Advertising? Explain its objectives?
3. What are the various kinds of advertisements?
4. Write short notes on TV and radio as media of advertising.
5. Explain the benefits of advertisements.
6. Define the following terms:
   (a) Salesman
   (b) Medical detail men
7. Explain the types of salesmen
8. What are the objectives of sales promotion?
9. Explain the major draw backs of sales promotion technique.

Long Answer Questions

1. Outline the different media of advertising?
2. State and explain different methods of indoor advertising?
3. Explain the objectives of an advertisement copy?
4. Explain the different themes of advertisement.
5. Write an essay on window display?
6. What is salesmanship? Describe the importance of salesmanship?
7. Describe the qualities of a salesman?
8. What do you understand by the word "medical representative'? Explain the training given to him?
9. Describe the salesmanship in pharmaceutical industry? How it differs from salesmanship of ordinary goods?
10. Explain briefly the various techniques of sales promotion.

12 Marketing Research

LEARNING OBJECTIVES

- *Introduction and definition of Marketing Research*
- *Marketing Research Process*
- *Marketing Research Reports*
- *Questionnaire*
- *Guidelines for designing a good Questionnaire*
- *Methods of data collection*
- *Survey Techniques*
- *Types of Survey*
- *Experimental research*
- *Data analysis*
- *Report Writing and report preparation*

12.1 | Introduction and Definition

Marketing research is defined as the objective and formal process of systematically obtaining, analyzing and interpreting data for actionable decision making in marketing.

Market research is the process of systematic gathering, recording and analyzing information data about problem related to the marketing of goods and services. The information/data can be concerned with performance, attitude and behavior.

Marketing concept emphasizes the determination of consumer wants and needs and then only deploys resources to match these wants and needs. Hence marketing research is an invaluable technique in decision making process to solve any marketing problem as well as in the evaluation of decisions when these are implemented to accomplish the customer satisfaction and welfare.

Marketing research under customer oriented marketing can offer current, adequate and accurate information about potential customer and all other aspects of market environment such as dealer's needs and preferences, consumer expectations, competition, marketing conditions etc.

Marketing research is a field where experts having special training are required. We need a group of specialists such as economists, management scientists (OR = Operational Research analyst), statisticians, mathematicians, psychologist, ecologists, sociologists and computer experts offerings staff services to marketing executives.

Marketing research process

Definition: Marketing research is the application of the systems approach to the task of *collecting, organizing, analyzing and interpreting desired marketing information.*

This definition indicates that each step in the research process must be carefully planned, effectively co-ordinated with all other related steps so that all steps are properly integrated and executed as specified at the proper time and in the desired sequence. Each important division or segment of the process of investigation and analysis plays a vital role in the efforts of the records team to achieve the stated goals.

Marketing researcher is directly concerned with all *three operations: input, process and output.*

Input is usually data i.e., facts and figures and values often quantified.

The collected data is processed by researchers. In data processing we have the operations of editing, classification and analysis and output is the result of processing.

Output is in the form of information - information power.

Characteristics of good output (Information):

1. It should be timely.
2. It should be current or up-to-date.
3. It should be accurate.
4. It should be sufficient.
5. It should be relevant/making for decision.
6. It should be reliable.
7. It should be economical.
8. It should be understandable and acceptable to marketing executives, in charge of decision-making and solving marketing problems.
9. It should be viable without further modification.
10. Output should not be data but information (Information is the processed data in the form of interpretations).

Marketing research process provides information, not data to marketing executives. Marketing decisions are based on information and not on data.

Marketing research process involves the following seven steps in sequence.

1. Situation Analysis
2. Preliminary Investigation
3. Research Design
4. Sources of Data
5. Data Analysis
6. Report Preparation
7. Follow-up Recommendations

1. ***Situation analysis*:** Define and analyze the marketing problem to be solved. Determine clearly the purpose of inquiry. State the immediate as well as ultimate objectives. You should have familiarity of situation surrounding the problem. Personal interviews, company records, library material and trade papers are the sources.

2. ***Preliminary investigation*:** It is an investigation to secure minimum acquaintance or feel for the problem. The researcher may meet consumers, dealers, marketing executives, competitors to get background information which can elucidate some critical issues for study and investigation. This investigation must be economically feasible.

3. ***Research design*:** A research design is a master plan or model for conducting formal investigation. A research design is the specification of methods and procedures for acquiring the information needed for solving the problem. Data gathering forms are prepared. Questionnaires and other forms are tested. Samples for investigations are planned.

4. ***Sources of data*:** A research study may require both primary and secondary data. Primary data must be assembled by the researcher for the first time. Secondary data is already available for processing.

   Primary data may be collected through a number of methods such as survey, experimental method or observation method.

5. ***Data analysis*:** Collected data must be edited, tabulated and analyzed.

6. ***Report preparation*:** Conclusions and recommendations supported by necessary analysis are submitted in the form of a written report and it is submitted to marketing executives.

   ***Marketing research report*:** Report usually has: 1. Title page 2. Table and contents 3. A brief outline of research and it's findings 4. A concise statement of the marketing problem and its translation into a research problem 5. Aims and objectives of research 6. An outline of research design or plan describing the methodology used in research 7. Data analysis and result with an abstract of the relevant data 8. Limitations imposed on the research 9. The findings, conclusions and recommendations 10. Appendices E.g., Questionnaire copy, glossary of terms used, sample design, detailed tables etc.

7. ***Follow up recommendations*:** The report presented to the management must be followed up to ensure the implementation of recommendations. An excellent report may be simply wasted when management takes no steps in the implementation of the recommendations of the research report.

***Sampling*:** Sampling is based on the law of statistical regularity and the law of inertia of large numbers.

A sample is a selection of unit from the entire group called the population or universe of interest. In marketing a sample of a particular segment or a part of market and it is the focus for taking marketing decisions, which can be applied to the entire market.

Questionnaire: A questionnaire is a set of questions with or without a blank space for recording answers. The questions can secure the relevant facts or opinions from informed and interested respondents included in sample survey. Questionnaire is used to obtain data on almost any type of marketing problem.

Rules or guideline for designing a good questionnaire

1. Questions should be short, simple, easily understandable, direct and have one interpretation or meaning.
2. Every questionnaire must explain the purpose of inquiry in order to stimulate interest, and request the respondent to offer full cooperation in giving answers.
3. There should be no misleading and ambiguous questions.
4. Questions that cannot/would not/need not be answered must not be used.
5. Develop a logical sequence in questionnaires and interviews. (Ask easy questions first, save the most difficult and sensitive questions and questions about age, income, marital relations etc. at the last stage).
6. Objective questions are preferable.

Methods of Data Collection

All marketing researches can tap two sources of data for investigation

1. Internal Sources   2. External Sources

Internal sources are the company's own records, registers, documents etc., sales records. Invoices provide valuable information regarding sales by products/territories/customers/preliminary sources.

All others are external sources of data.

Another way of classifying the sources of information is:

1. Primary data   2. Secondary data

Two major types of data

Primary data

1. Information obtained from original sources by researcher. The important sources are (a) Consumers (b) Orders (c) Salesmen (d) original sales records (e) Invoices, Credit slips etc.
2. Primary data can be gathered slowly at a high cost. But it offers much greater accuracy and reliability.
3. It is personally developed. It gives latest information.

4. It is not a published source of data.
5. It has to be accurate.

Secondary data

1. It is compiled by someone other than the researcher (not personally developed).
2. It already exists.
3. It must be relevant to the research under study.
4. Unit cost of information is less but lacks reliability.
5. It may have bias. It must be sufficiently current. It is published/semi published data.

Secondary data

There are numerous sources of secondary data:

1. Published surveys of markets
2. General library research sources
3. Govt. Publications and reports
4. All advertising media, particularly newspapers, magazines, trade journals etc.
5. Trade association and other technical and foundation organization
6. Universities
7. Specialized market intelligence services such as advertising agencies, market research firms, stock exchanges, banks etc.
8. Specialized libraries.

Limitations of secondary data

1. It must be sufficiently current.
2. It must be relevant and valid
3. It must be accurate and reliable
4. It must be impartial.

Merits

1. It is much cheaper to use
2. It is quicker to obtain
3. It is available on all subjects, particularly where primary data may be impossible and causes variation.
4. Its unit costs are low.

Primary Data

The following are the methods of obtaining primary data.

1. **Survey Technique or Approach**
   (a) Mail (Questionnaire) Survey or postal enquiry.
   (b) Personal interview/field survey
   (c) Telephonic survey
2. **Panel Research.** Consumer panel or dealer panel – for testing and comments.
3. Observation Approach
4. Experimental Research

12.2 | Survey Techniques (Questionnaire or Survey Method)

The information is recorded in the form of a Questionnaire or a Schedule or a Blank form of enquiry. As data is gathered by asking questions to persons who are thought to have desired information, it is called 'questionnaire technique'.

Survey method is the most widely used technique in marketing research because:

1. It can secure information directly from respondents.
2. It is the only method to measure attitudes and motives directly.
3. It is quite flexible in terms of types of data to be assembled, method of collection or the timing of research.

Uses of Survey Method

There are 3 main uses

1. We can have factual survey together with facts. e.g.: "what brand of tea/soap do you use?"
2. We can have opinion survey to secure personal opinions or thinking on a particular matter. e.g.: "which design of ornaments do you think is the most beautiful."
3. Interpretative survey can be conducted to probe into personal feelings, motives, attitudes etc., of the respondent. e.g.: "Why do you use Brand X detergent?"

Types of Survey

We can have communication with the informant in three alternative ways:

1. Through mail or post office
2. Through Telephone
3. Through personal interview

1. ***Mail Survey by Questionnaire***: It is very effective and cheap method of conducting surveys. An up-to-date mailing list is prepared. Printed copy of the questionnaire along with the covering letter and stamped reply paid envelope will

be posted to the respondent on the mailing list. Reply letter should be stamped, so that the respondent need not pay.

The covering letters as a silent salesman, should create interest, and motivate or induce informant to send prompt and quick replies.

Gift/Incentive is provided to get co-operation and quick return of duly completed questionnaire.

Mail survey has no geographic limitation. It can secure information from hard-to reach respondents. Higher rate of refusal and lower degree of accuracy are major weakness of mail survey.

2. ***Telephone Survey***: In urban areas we can interview the respondent through telephone. This method is very suitable to obtain factual answers to few questions.

   On phone people are unwilling to give personal information/may give non committed answers.

   Detailed investigation is not possible on telephone.

3. ***Personal Interview/Field Survey***: It is the direct form of investigation involving face-to-face communication with free feedback of information. It offers a sense of participation. It is more flexible form of data collection as refusal rate is low.

   We need trained, experienced and competent interviewers. It is costly and time consuming method. Interviewer must be honest and loyal.

Observation Approach

Here no questions are asked in data collection. It is more objective and accurate.

In this method, we have the observation of overt or obvious behavior of consumers/buyers using trained observers or some mechanical or electronic devices.

In order to evaluate the effectiveness of window display, an investigator may observe a special display of foam rubber pillows in a big store by checking the number of persons passing by, the number who stopped to look at the display, the number who handled the product, and the number who bought it. An audiometer may also be used.

Observation method can be used to study:

1. Sales technique 2. Customer movement 3. Customer responses in retail stores 4. Stock audit in retail stores for brands brought 5. Pantry check in the kitchen of house wife for brands brought 6. Dust-bin check at customer's house 7. Poster research, country cars and people passing by the poster.

Panel Research

When research analyst interviews the sample group of respondents two or more times or secures data from them on two or more occasions it is called Panel research.

Respondents may be individual consumers, retailers, wholesalers etc. Panel research enables researcher to measure small changes in habits or other activities over a time purchase habits.

This is in contrast to non panel type surveys where an entirely different group is measured each time a study is conducted. Panels are made up of respondents who regularly and routinely report their buying behavior. They keep a diary of purchases, advertising exposure, shopping activity or any other item under research.

Uses of Consumers Panel

1. To find out consumer attitudes, preferences, changes in demand relating to particular brand from time to time.
2. To assess market trends.
3. To get consumer reaction to prices and to advertising.

Experimental Research

Experimental method is an important tool to find out causal relationship (cause-effect). For example, effect of price change up on sales, effect of advertisement on roles, of promotion or package changes and so on.

What would be the level of sales, if that variable has not been introduced etc.

In the test market, attempt is made to establish a causal relationship by introducing the variables factor. *e.g.* seller wants to know the effect of price change upon his product.

1. Sample stores/market is selected.
2. One store/market will acts as a control
3. Prices are changed in test markets stores. Sales are carefully checked.
4. Effect of price changes on sales can be evaluated and reference to sales in the control market where price is not changed.

Uses

This technique of experimental method (test marketing) can evaluate different kinds of sales promotion, premiums, package designs or advertising levels in the same way.

Controlled experiment gives small scale experience which is useful to determine the large scale action in any branch of marketing.

Data Analysis

Once the data is collected, the data has to be processed, analyzed and interpreted.

Tabulation of Data

The objective is to organize the information and prepare a summary that highlights its salient features. Tabulation comprises sorting of the data into different categories and counting the number of cases that belong to each category.

The simplest way to tabulate is to count the number of responses to one question. This is also called **Univariate tabulation**.

The analysis based on just one variable is called monovariate tabulation. When two or more variables are involved in tabulation, it is called bivariate or multivariate tabulation.

Editing: Tabulation of data should simultaneously carry out an editing function. It is the process by which data collected is scrutinized so as to ensure consistency, unambiguity and accuracy.

Coding: It is the process by which response categories are summarized by certain symbols to carry out subsequent operations of data analysis.

Frequency Table

Having obtained a set of response categories, frequency table shows the counts or occurrence of individual categories among the sample.

e.g: How many injections are sold in the last week? For a sample of say, 60, respondents the tabulation may be as shown below:

Category of injections	Group I	Group II
a	IIII IIII	9
b	IIII IIII	10
c	IIII	5
d	IIII IIII IIII	15
e	IIII IIII III	13
d	IIII III	8
	60	60

Interpretation

It is remarkable that the importance to the various attributes is almost the same for the two groups listed.

e.g. for attributes – color, size, flavor, Brand name, Symbol, Advertisements. Further, data is analyzed or interpreted with mathematical/statistical techniques. Some of the statistical techniques are

Parametric and non-parametric tests

Z test	Binomial
t test	Sign
T test	Chi-square
Paired test	Comparison

Multivariate test. Correlation, Regression, Variance etc.

The interpreted data is also explained in the report with groups. Diagrams, trend analysis to understand the data in a better way.

12.3 | Report Writing/Report Preparation

This is one of the most important stage of marketing research. The report is prepared for effectively communicating the research findings.

Written Research Report

The content of a research report will certainly depend on the nature of the study, requirements of managers acting on the study results, and the philosophy, back ground of the researchers involved. But even so, one should take the following precautions.

Research report format should contain the following:

(i) Title Page
(ii) Table of Contents
(iii) Introduction
(iv) Statement of objectives
(v) Research methodology
(vi) Results/findings
(vii) Conclusions and recommendations
(viii) Appendix

(i) ***Title page***: The major function of the title page is that of research report identification. The title page should indicate the subject of the report, for whom it is prepared and by whom it is prepared.

(ii) ***Table of contents***: A table of contents outlines how the study report is organized. It divides the whole report into several parts (sections, chapters etc.) which facilitates in locating different components of the report.

(iii) ***Introduction***: It serves to present the background of the research study and particularly highlights the major issues which are examined in the project. The main purpose of writing an introduction is to lay down the perspective of the study.

(iv) ***Statement of objectives***: An explicit statement of marketing research objectives clarifies the issues covered in the study.

(v) ***Research methodology***: It states how the research study is undertaken. This includes specification of research design, sources of data, method of primary data collection, the sampling decisions, analysis procedures employed to carry out the research study.

(vi) ***Results/findings***: These are basically the outcome of the study. Researchers usually try to display data through summary tables and graphs along with some textual commentary on the interpretation of the data.

(vii) ***Conclusions and recommendations***: Based on the research results, a separate paragraph under this heading is often added. To some extent it shows researchers opinions on the issues examined. Under conclusions, sometimes, researchers state the potential short comings of the study and also throw light on future avenues of study.

(viii) ***Appendix***: The purpose of an appendix is to provide supporting documents in the form of technical details *e.g.* statistical tests used or information schedule (questionnaire) which reader may go through at a later point of time. Bibliography is a list of books and journals used as a source of data in the report.

Review Questions

Short Answer Questions

1. What is mail survey?
2. Explain the differences between primary data and secondary data.
3. Explain consumer panel marketing research.
4. What is telephone survey?

Long Answer Questions

1. Explain the various steps involved in marketing research.
2. Explain different techniques adopted to collect primary data.

13 Personnel Management Functions

Introduction

Personnel management is the management of personnel working for an organization. Every organization hires people to carry out its organizational objectives.

LEARNING OBJECTIVES

- *Scope of Personnel Management Functions*
- *Recruitment of employees*
- *Selection of employees*
- *Training of employees*
- *Evaluation of employees*
- *Compensation of employees*

13.1 | Definition

Personnel Management can be defined as planning, organizing, directing and controlling, procurement, development, maintenance, integration and separation of human resources so that individual, organizational and societal goals can be achieved.

Personnel management has the following essential components:

(a) Recruitment (b) Selection
(c) Training (d) Evaluation
(e) Compensation

(a) Recruitment: It is the process of identifying different avenues of man power requirements. It involves the generation of applications for specific positions. It is the process of searching prospective workers and stimulating them to apply for jobs in the organization. Hence it is a positive process of prospecting. The process of recruitment involves:

1. Identification of different areas of employment of manpower.

2. Examines their suitability
3. Choosing the best sources matching its objectives
4. Inviting the prospective candidates to apply for the said jobs

Sources of recruitment: There are two major sources.

(a) Internal sources of recruitment (b) External sources of recruitment

(a) ***Internal sources of recruitment:*** Internal sources refer to the present working force of a company. When vacancy arises, people within the organization are chosen. Outside recruitment is resorted to only when requirements cannot be met from within. Two important sources of internal recruitment are:

1. Transfer, and
2. Promotions

1. *Transfer:* It involves the shifting of an employee from one spot to another. Proper assessment beforehand should be done regarding the suitability of person in the new job. There is no change in the responsibilities and official position of the employee.

   Transfer is defined as "a lateral shift causing movement of individuals from one position to another usually without involving any marked change in duties, responsibilities, skills needed".

2. *Promotions:* It is shifting an employee to a higher placement which has more responsibility, salary and status.

   According to Paul Pigors and Charles A. Myers, "Promotion is advancement of an employee to a better job - better in terms of greater responsibility, more prestige or status, greater skill and especially increased rate of pay or salary".

   Arun Monappa defined promotion as, "the upward reassignment of another level job to an internal employee individual in an organization's hierarchy, accompanied by increased responsibilities and enhanced status".

Merits of internal recruitment

1. Morale and motivation of employees is increased.
2. No problems with worker's organizations.
3. Industrial peace prevails
4. It is economical to fill the post from within the organization.
5. It absorbs people already acquainted with the company culture.
6. Job training is reduced.
7. Cost of selection can be minimized.

Demerits of the system

1. Time bound promotions makes employees lazy.
2. No scope for new people with better talent.
3. Efficiency of the organization is hampered because of frequent change in positions.

(b) ***External sources of recruitment:*** It is essential that excessive inbreeding should be avoided and infuses new blood into the organization to broaden the present ideas, knowledge and enthusiasm. Hence recruitment can also be done from external atmosphere to the organization. The important sources of external recruitment are:

1. ***Direct employment at factory gate:*** This type of employment is usually done for casual labor and lower level jobs. In this method, the hands required and no. of vacancies available is mentioned on the notice board or at factory gate.

Every day large number of people comes to factory for job and the manager will select and scrutinize the workers required and pick up the required number.

Advantages

1. Simple and easy method of recruitment
2. Cheapest method of recruitment.

Unsolicited Applications: In a routine manner, good organisations receive large no. of uncalled applications for jobs. This stockpile also serves as a source of manpower requirement. Even if there are no particular openings when the applicant makes contact with the organization, the application can be kept on file for later needs.

Application from individuals who already employed can be referred to many months later and can provide applicants who 1. Are interested in considering other employment opportunities and 2. Regard the organization as a possible employer.

2. ***Advertisements:*** When an organization desires to communicate to the public that it has a vacancy, advertisements are one of the most popular methods used. What type of advertisement is placed is determined by the type of job.

The higher the position in the organization, the more specialized the skills, the more widely dispersed the advertisement will be. The search for a top post includes advertisements in national dailies whereas for local level jobs, the advertisement is given in local daily newspaper or trade journals.

A well-thought of and planned advertisement for an appointment reduces the possibility of unqualified people applying. Organizations often spend large amounts of money and time in sifting and processing applications. If an advertisement is clear and to the point, candidates can assess their abilities and suitability for the position and then apply for the job.

Advertisement are given in three different ways: First method is the company selects an advertisement agency and this agency advertises positions in leading newspapers without disclosing the name of the client company. The applications received from the candidates by the agencies are duplicated and mailed to the clients.

Second method is some companies give only numbers. Box numbers advertisements generally do not draw good candidates who feel that it is not worthwhile to apply without knowing employer's name.

Third method is the company will give its profile and mentions the requirement for the positions offered.

Advantages

1. Comprehensive information about the organization, job designing and job specifications can be given
2. The management has option of wide range of candidates to choose from.

Disadvantages

1. Large number of applications and many a time, a large chunk of unsuitable candidates apply.

3. ***Employment Agencies:*** Employment agencies managed by the Govt. are a good source of recruitment of workers and employees but not the managerial staff. However in higher job operational arena, private and professional agencies are co-coordinating in a better way. Employment exchanges are open to all citizens and every one can utilize the services of employment exchange for obtaining a job. But Government employment exchange does not have functional efficiency and hence most of the private organizations search for some other sources for potential employees. Moreover the employment exchanges are not well equipped to screen various candidates but they provide only the list of registered candidates having required qualifications for a particular job. For most of the government jobs, notifications of vacancies to employment exchange are required by law.

4. ***Educational institutions and campus interviews:*** Many big organizations like Hindustan lever, Glaxo etc., are increasingly adopting this popular practice. There is a tie up by the organizations with the universities, vocational institutes and management institutes for recruitment to various technical and management jobs. The employer visits the campus and conducts interviews and screening of the candidates is done.

5. ***Recommendations:*** Friends and relatives of existing employees may prove to be good source of recruitment. Similarly applicants introduced by friends and relatives are also a good source. Employers prefer to take such persons because their back-ground is known to certain extent. It may be provided that other conditions being equal, preference will be given to children and relatives of the existing employees.
6. ***Websites and internet:*** The order of the day is internet. Employer Service Providers have their own web pages in which the data of the subscribing prospective employees is displayed. All organizations requiring man-power can browse through the bank for job hands. Good examples of this category are Naukri.com and jobs.com.
7. ***Labor Contractors:*** Labor contractors are an important source of recruitment in many industries in India. Workers are recruited through labor contractors who are themselves employees of the organizations. There are labor ministry approved labor contractor organizations. They advertise for various jobs in local newspapers and recruit people for overseas employment. Good examples are labor contractors in Bombay and metropolitan cities supplying manpower to Gulf-countries.
8. ***Management Consultants*:** They are also known as 'head hunting' firms which look out for executive search. Agencies of this type are specialized private employment agencies. They specialize in middle level and top level executive placements. Their uniqueness is fees, their nation, wide contacts and perfectness of investigation. Executive search firms canvass their contacts and do preliminary screening. They seek out highly effective executives who have the skills to do the job, can effectively adjust to the organization and willing to consider new challenges and opportunities. The executive search firm can act as a buffer for screening candidates and also keep prospective employer anonymous.
9. ***Deputations*:** Another source of recruitment is deputation from other organizations. Since the person possesses certain abilities useful to another organization, he is deputed to it for a specified duration. Deputation is useful because it provides ready experience. However, because of the short duration, the deputed employees often fail to become part of the organization.
10. ***Field trips*:** An interviewing team makes trips to towns and cities which are known to contain the kinds of employees required. Arrival dates and the time and venue of interview are advertised in advance.

11. ***Temporary help services***: When individuals are needed on a temporary basis, temporary help services are of good use. Temporary employees are valuable in meeting short term fluctuations in personnel needs. While traditionally developed in the office administration area, the temporary rental service has expanded its coverage to include a broad range of skills. Hence it is possible to hire a temporary pharmacist or a stop gap-nurse.

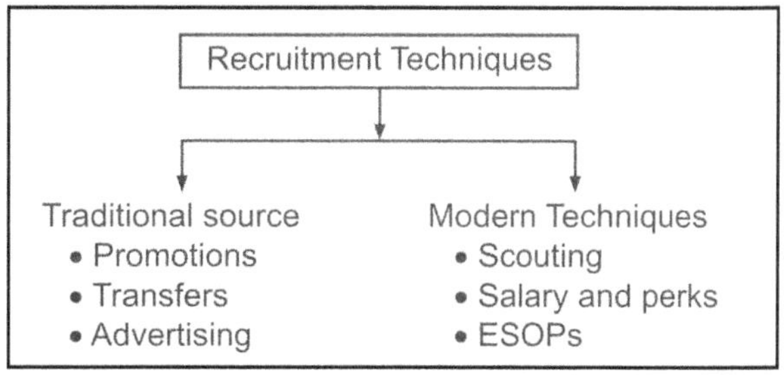

Techniques of recruitment: Recruitment techniques are the means by which management contacts prospective employees and provides necessary information.

Traditional techniques

Promotions: Promotions are shifting an employee to higher placements which will increase responsibility, authority, power, salary and status.

Transfers: Transfer involves shifting of employee from one job to other in the same level. This is done so in the organization with the help of management.

Advertising: Advertisements can be given through agencies, consultants or company itself gives a notification in newspapers, magazines or T.V etc., to attract the prudent and intelligent candidates.

Modern Techniques

(i) ***Scouting***: It means sending the representative to the organization with a view to persuading or stimulating the candidates by answering and clarifying their doubts.

(ii) ***Salary and perks***: Companies stimulates the prospective candidates by offering higher level salary, more perks and also provides better facilities for their career development.

(iii) ***ESOPS:*** It means Employees Stock Ownership programs.

The bases on which decision can be made concerning promotion are:

Basis for Promotion: Many complex and interrelated factors enter into the decision in a promotion system. The basis on which decision can be made concerning promotion are:

(i) Merit (ii) Seniority (iii) Seniority cum merit.

Promotion Policy: Considering the need for promotion, every organization should formulate its promotion policy which should be linked to overall human resource policy and consistent to organizational policies.

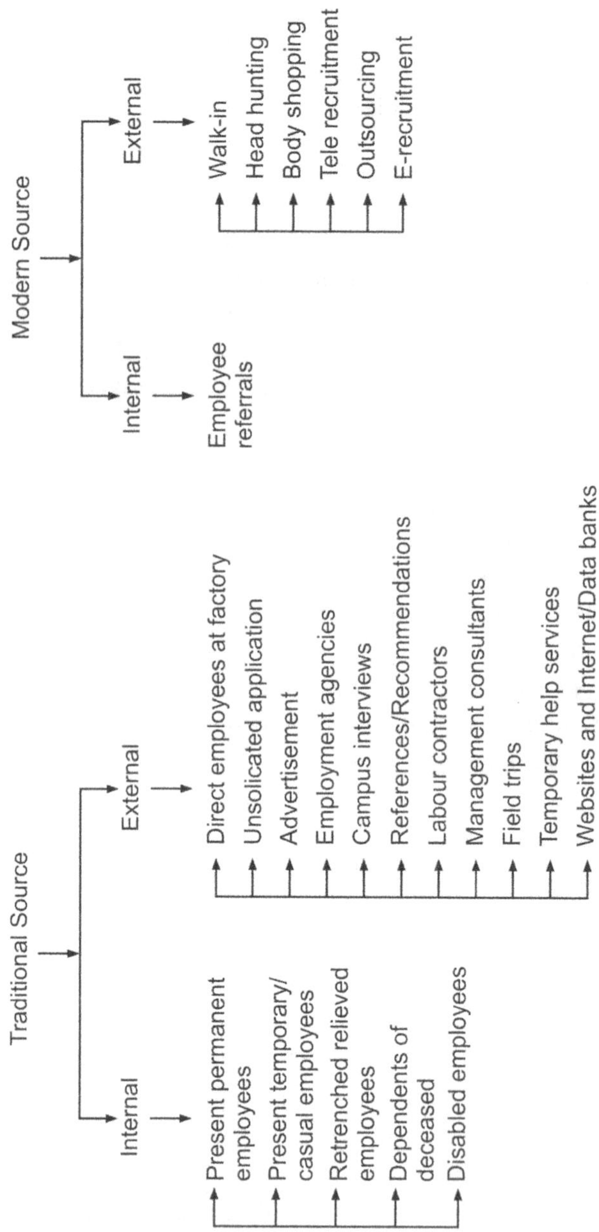
Traditional Source
Internal
Present permanent employees
Present temporary/casual employees
Retrenched relieved employees
Dependents of deceased
Disabled employees
External
Direct employees at factory
Unsolicated application
Advertisement
Employment agencies
Campus interviews
References/Recommendations
Labour contractors
Management consultants
Field trips
Temporary help services
Websites and Internet/Data banks
Modern Source
Internal
Employee referrals
External
Walk-in
Head hunting
Body shopping
Tele recruitment
Outsourcing
E-recruitment

A sound Promotion Policy should consist the following Points

1. ***Consistency*:** The policy should be consistent. It should be linked with career planning of individuals.
2. ***Fair and impartial*:** Policy should be fair and impartial to the personnel at all the levels.
3. ***Promotion rules*:** The routes of promotion to be clearly mentioned, this is to be provided in advance.
4. ***Promotion procedure*:** Top management has to review the system regularly. The methods or basis for promotion to be made clear.

Transfer Policy: In every organization, transfer of employees is a frequent phenomenon. While framing such policy, the following principles are to be kept in mind, such as:

1. The policy should be fair, impartial and practicable.
2. Objectives of different types of transfer should be spelled out clearly to avoid any misgivings.
3. The policy should lay down the basis on which transfer are to be given.
4. There should be specification of authority which will either transfer by their own authority or in consultation with other officials / consultants.

13.2 | Employee Selection

Definition: Based upon the ability and qualifications to perform the job which is vacant in the organization, employment of persons to the jobs is selection. Selection is a negative process because it divides the candidates into two categories, those offered employment and those who are not appointed.

Selection is a process which helps in choosing right type of candidate to right position in the organization. A well organized selection procedure involves many steps and in each step more information is obtained about the candidates.

Importance of Selection

Selection of employees for an organization is an important task of personnel department. Right selection procedure has to be adopted while selecting the candidates for various posts. If the selection process is faulty, absenteeism will be too high and the efficiency of the organization will go down. If the right candidate is not selected, it will lead to wastage of time, energy and money in hiring such employees. The training expenses spent on such employee will also go waste.

Selection Procedure

A well organized selection procedure has to be adopted to select suitable candidates for various jobs.

1. ***Scrutiny of applications***: The applications received up to the due date are carefully scrutinized. The incomplete applications and applications of candidates who do not fulfill the required eligibility conditions are rejected.
2. ***Preliminary interview***: The candidates considered suitable on the basis of their applications are called for a preliminary interview. This is generally a brief interview and its purpose is to eliminate those candidates who are either unqualified or unsuitable for the job.
3. ***Selection test***: It may be written or an oral test. The technical knowledge and administrative capability can be judged from these tests. The psychological tests are very popular these days to judge human behavior in actual work situations. The following tests are commonly used in the selection process.
   (a) *Intelligence tests:* These tests are used to estimate the IQ or mental alertness of the candidate.
   (b) *Aptitude tests:* These tests help to measure a candidate's capacity to learn and his potential abilities.
   (c) *Trade tests:* These tests help to measure a candidate's capacity to learn particular trade related skills and his acumen.
   (d) *Personality tests:* These tests are employed to find out the emotional balance, maturity, temperament etc., of the candidate.
4. ***Selection interview***: A face-to-face dialogue between the employer or his representatives and the interested candidate is the most popular tool of selection. The main purpose of a selection interview is:
   (a) To find out the stability of the candidate.
   (b) To cross check the information revealed in the application and the tests.
   (c) To give to the candidate an accurate picture of his job and the enterprise.

   An interview is a time-consuming and expensive process and its conclusions may be distorted due to the bias of the person conducting the interview.

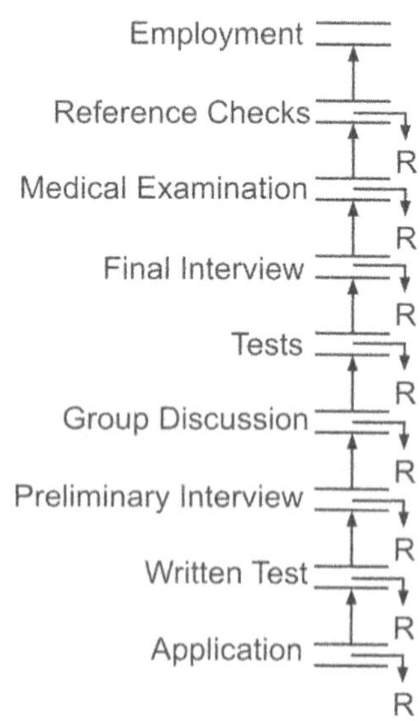

5. ***Physical examination***: Physical examination of the candidate is conducted to ensure that he is physically fit for the job. If he is suffering from any disease or disability, he is rejected.
6. ***Reference check***: Usually the candidates are required to write in their application form the names and address of two important persons who know the candidate. These persons are contacted to collect the information about the character, ability and background of the candidate. But the information supplied by them may be biased in favor of the candidate.
7. ***Final selection and placement***: The candidates who have been found suitable in all respects are appointed by issuing appointment letter to them. They are generally

appointed on probation for one or two years. After successful completion of the probationary period, they are made permanent employees. The selected candidates are assigned specific jobs. This is known as placement.

13.3 | Personnel Management Training

Purpose of giving training: The selected candidates should be given training in order to acquire knowledge of the product, knowledge of the company, knowledge of the customers, knowledge of the techniques of selling and knowledge about market conditions.

1. ***Knowledge of the product*:** A salesman must have detailed knowledge regarding (i) nature of product (ii) method of production (iii) ingredients used (iv) method of packing and (v) uses of the product. These knowledge could be gained only through properly organized training by the company.
2. ***Knowledge of the company*:** A salesman must have a detailed knowledge regarding (i) history of the company (ii) achievements (iii) sales policies (iv) distribution policies and (v) customer services provided by the company.
3. ***Knowledge of the customers*:** A salesman must have perfect prior knowledge of the customers to whom the products are to be sold in order to overcome sales resistance.
4. ***Knowledge of the technique of the selling*:** Like the consumers are different, the products are also different. For example, the selling technique adopted for a consumer product will not be applicable to the industrial products. This knowledge should be acquired only through training.
5. ***Knowledge about market conditions*:** Knowledge about market conditions is also necessary for the salesman. Salesman should know about the competition of similar products in the market.

Methods of training

The salesmen are given the following methods of training : (i) Apprenticeship method (ii) Part time instruction method (iii) Evening school work method (iv) Correspondence method (v) Sales conference method (vi) Lectures method (vii) Sales demonstration method (viii) Round table method (ix) Sales dramatization method and (x) Display of films, charts and picture method.

The above methods of training given to the salesmen may be grouped into :

1. ***Individual Training*:** Under this method, every salesman is given training individually. He is given training of theoretical and practical aspects of salesmanship. Apprenticeship method and correspondence method are examples of individuals training.

2. ***Group Training***: Under this method, the training is given collectively (in groups). Lectures method, sales conference method, round table method, audio-visual method (display of films, charts and picture method) are examples of group training.
3. ***On-the-job method***: In this method, the salesmen are given practice-oriented training instead of giving the theoretical training.
4. ***Follow-up training method***: Under this method, training is given for long period (i.e. continuous training). In order to know all the developments up to date, even the trained salesman is also given periodic training under this method. This is known as follow-up training or refresher training.

Advantages of training

1. ***Advantages to the firm (Company)***:
   (i) A trained salesman sells more than an untrained salesman.
   (ii) A trained salesman can show increase in sales than untrained salesman.
   (iii) The customers are satisfied with trained salesman. If the customers are satisfied, the products move quickly in the market.
   (iv) More goods are sold easily by trained salesman.
2. ***Advantages to the salesman***:
   1. Training program improves the personality of the salesman and they become more efficient in their work.
   2. Whenever they leave the service from one firm it will be easier for a trained salesman to get other job in another firm.
   3. The trained salesman receives higher commission and other benefits from the firm if he shows increased volume of sale.
3. ***Advantages to the customers***: The trained salesman satisfies the customers more efficiently. Moreover he gives suggestions to the customer in selection of goods. So the greatest advantage to the customers is that they are fully satisfied with what they purchase through trained salesman.

13.4 | Personnel Management Evaluation

After the initial training (on job) of the trainee is complete, an appraisal of performance, i.e., evaluation must be done. For fair and unbiased evaluation, standards of performance must be established. Based on these, periodic appraisals of employees are undertaken and their work is evaluated fairly. This aspect is very important because:

1. It helps in identifying abnormally low level of performance displayed by the employee.
2. It assists in fair compensation of the pharmacist according to the degree of accomplishment of set standard (estimated by evaluation).
3. The weaker points of pharmacist can be detected and improvement can be done in the same.

4. Employees with good performance are motivated by giving promotion as an incentive.
5. It helps in increasing the productivity of pharmacist for the risk of being fired if found inefficient.

Basic features of good evaluation system

1. Should be based on 'Complete Employee Record' for comparison with the expected standards. This helps in avoiding confused judgments.
2. Should be coupled with surprise inspection at regular intervals. It should be neither too infrequent nor too frequent. Since in both the cases it will hinder the smooth running of the drug store.
3. Should have predetermined standards of performance for the employees. A good evaluation system should encourage employees towards above average performance.
4. Should be circulated among all the employees concerned, so that they strive towards better performance to achieve high achievement rating.
5. Should be based on simple and consolidated records.

***Evaluation systems*:** Two primary means of evaluating employees are

1. ***Achievement measurements*:** These are more objective, easy to formulate and make use of. Basically, in a drug store, the pharmacists are evaluated by measuring annual or a combination of the following achievements.
    1. ***The total sales by each salesman:*** A better performing salesman is expected to attract the total sales at least at par or above the set targets.
    2. ***Number of patrons attended and served by salesman:*** Number of patrons served by sales-person during a target time period is directly proportional to the total sales and hence profit of the drug store. Hence those with a record number of patrons served should receive high rating and hence recognition.
    3. ***Average sales made by sales person:*** Average sale made by a sales person during a period

       Average sales made by a sales person should be well above target sales to earn good profits.
    4. ***Unit Cost of selling of Sales Person:*** Unit cost of selling to a customer

       A sales person who lowers down this unit cost of selling gets the higher achievement rating. Such sales persons are a boon to a drug store since they maximize sales but minimize running expenses. This serves as a guide to the employees also. Thus with a high unit cost of selling gets a lower rating and should enhance and serve more and more number of people.
    5. ***Sales Volume of Store:*** Sales person who achieve exceptional targets (whether daily/weekly/fortnightly/monthly/annually) should be given high achievement ratings so that the less efficient also get motivated to achieve the same standards.

2. ***Rating Scales:*** Though rating scales are a matter of opinion only yet in some cases, simply their introduction acts as a motivator to employees. Moreover these are helpful in activating the employees towards improvement upon the weaker area of their performance. The drug store owner can approximately arrange the employees in the order of their performance.

13.5 | Compensation of Pharmacists

The compensation to the pharmacists who are involved in sales is vital part to the companies where they work in. When they are low paid, their efficiency will be affected and they do not work with interest and enthusiasm. When they are highly paid, it costs the exchequer. Thus it is essential that proper remuneration and compensation should be paid to them. Adequate compensation helps in retaining good employees and encourages them to work efficiently. The compensation includes salary and other benefits such as house rent allowance or free residential accommodation, city compensatory allowance, medical allowance, group insurance scheme, provident fund scheme, leave travel concession, bonus, travelling allowance and other benefits.

Essentials of a good scheme of remuneration and compensation

A good remuneration should be offered to the pharmacists who are involved in sales so that they will work efficiently with interest and enthusiasm. To increase the sales, the companies should offer good incentive and other compensatory allowance. The following points may be considered as a good remuneration plan :

1. The remuneration and compensation may be fixed on the basis of qualifications and qualities of work.
2. The remuneration and other compensatory allowances may be according to their sales efforts.
3. The rate of remuneration may be in proportion to volume of sales.
4. The remuneration should be sufficiently enough to maintain a living standard.
5. The remuneration plan must be in such a way that pharmacists improve their qualities.

Methods of compensation or remuneration

The following are some of the methods of compensation.

1. Fixed salary or straight salary method.
2. Straight commission method.
3. Salary, commission and allowance method.
4. Profit sharing method
5. Salary and bonus method.
6. Promotion in service

1. ***Fixed salary or straight salary method*:** In this method, the pharmacists (as a salesman) are paid salary per month. The salary is fixed at the time of appointment. The annual increment is granted on successful work and sometimes two or more increments are granted for good work.
2. ***Straight commission method*:** Under this method the remuneration paid to the pharmacists depends upon the sales made by them. The remuneration under this method entirely depends upon the skill and efforts of the pharmacists or salesman. This method provides good incentive for the pharmacists who involve in sales.
3. ***Salary, commission and allowance method*:** Under this method, the pharmacists (as salesman) are paid allowance along with salary and commission. The main purpose of giving allowance and commission is to compensate the expenses incurred by the salesman on sales efforts and activities.
4. ***Profit sharing method*:** Under this method, the pharmacists are allowed to share in the profits of the firm or company. This method realizes the importance of pharmacist's efforts for the progress of the firm. Generally profits are shared by the pharmacists on the basis of sales in their areas.
5. ***Salary and bonus method*:** Under this method, pharmacists are paid salary as well as bonus. The purpose of giving bonus is to increase the efficiency of pharmacists on sales efforts and activities.
6. ***Promotion in service*:** A provision should be made in the compensation plan to provide promotion for continuous, long and devoted service of the employees.

Review Questions

Short Answer Questions

1. What is the significance of selection?
2. Write in brief about the evaluation of a pharmacist?
3. What are the purposes of training a pharmacist?
4. Explain the types of recruitments?
5. Name the various steps in the selection of a pharmacist?

Long Answer Questions

1. What is recruitment? What are the different methods of recruitment?
2. Define selection? What steps are involved in selection of employee?
3. Define the term 'training'? Why is it necessary? Explain the various types of training?
4. Discuss the various plans of compensating an efficient employee to continue with his job?

14 Accounting and its Principles

14.1 | Introduction to Accounting

LEARNING OBJECTIVES

- *Introduction to Accounting*
- *Branches of Accounting*
- *Functions of Accounting*
- *Accounting Concepts and Conventions*
- *Definition and Objectives of Book Keeping*
- *Differences between Book Keeping and Accountancy*
- *Different kinds of Accounting*

Definition: Accounting or accountancy is an art of recording, classifying, summarizing and analyzing the business transactions to ascertain the financial position of the company.

Objectives of accounting or accountancy (Necessity of accounting): The main objectives of accounting are as follows:

1. To record all business transactions in a ledger regularly with a view to prepare the financial statements as and when required.
2. To prepare the Profit and Loss Statement. By means of preparing Profit and Loss Statement, the profit and loss of the organization can be calculated.
3. To prepare Balance Sheet. By means of preparing Balance Sheet, the financial position of the organization can be ascertained.
4. To know the progress and growth or downfall of business.
5. To know as to what amount is due to a person (creditor) or what amount is due from a person (debtor) on a particular date.
6. To know the quantity and value of goods.
7. To know the position of cash in hand and at bank.

8. To know the errors and frauds committed by the employee.
9. To know the requirements of business at a particular time.

Advantages of accounting

1. If proper accounts are maintained, the final accounts are prepared at the end of every year. From this final account, the financial position of the business can be compared with previous year's position.
2. If proper accounts are maintained, profits and losses, assets and liabilities, purchases and sales, opening and closing stocks etc., can be compared.
3. If proper accounts are maintained, then it may be a good proof in case of any litigation.
4. The share of a retired / deceased partner can be settled easily.

Branches of accounting

There are three branches of accounting namely:

1. Financial accounting 2. Cost accounting 3. Management accounting

1. ***Financial accounting***: It is mainly concerned with preparation of Profit and Loss Account and Balance Sheet.
2. ***Cost accounting***: It is the process of accounting for cost. The main function of cost accounting is to find out the cost of product and to help the management in controlling its cost.
3. ***Management accounting***: It is mainly concerned with providing information which is useful to the management to take decisions for smooth and efficient running of their business.

Functions of accounting

1. ***Recording business transaction***: The main function of accounting is to maintain systematic record of business transactions.
2. ***Preparation of final accounts***: Another important function of accounting is to prepare final accounts such as Trading account, Profit and Loss Account and Balance Sheet. This final account is the basis for finding out the financial position of the company.
3. ***Complying legal requirements***: The function of accounting is to satisfy the government authorities (*e.g.*, Income Tax Department, Sales Tax Department)
4. ***Assisting Management***: Accounting provides important information to the management which is useful for the development of business.

Common terms used in accounting

1. ***Debtor:*** Debtor is a person who received money as a loan from the business. (Receiver is a debtor)
2. ***Creditor:*** Creditor is a person who gives money as a loan to the business. (Giver is a creditor)
3. ***Account:*** It is the record of business transaction. It gives information about the quantity and value of goods, the financial position of the business organization etc.
4. ***Goods:*** It includes all merchandise and commodities.
5. ***Assets:*** Assets are properties belonging to a trader, *e.g.* cash, stock, furniture, building etc.
6. ***Liabilities:*** Liabilities are debts payable by the trader to others.
7. ***Capital:*** Capital is the amount with which a trader starts the business.
8. ***Solvent:*** A person is said to be solvent when his assets exceed his liabilities. If the liabilities exceed his assets he is called insolvent.

14.2 | Accounting Concepts and Conventions

Definition: There are some assumptions on which accounting are based. These assumptions are natural but not forced one. They are called as accounting concepts. The following concepts are most popular in accounting:

1. Accounting period concept
2. Dual aspect concept
3. Money measurement concept
4. Revenue realization concept
5. Cost concept
6. Going concern concept
7. Matching concept
8. Accrual concept.

1. ***Accounting period concept*:** It is necessary to ascertain the performance and financial position of the company once in a year. According to the Companies Act, accounts are to be checked once in 12 months (either from January 1 to December 31; or April 1 to March 31). This period is called 'Accounting Period'. This concept is useful to compare the financial position of one year to that of another year.
2. ***Dual aspect concept*:** Whenever any business transaction takes place, it has to be recorded in two aspects namely credit aspect and debit aspect. This concept of

recording transactions is called “double entry system’ (i.e., dual aspect concept). All business transactions are recorded on the basis of this concept. Without this dual aspect concept, no business transaction is complete. So the whole of book-keeping and accounting is based on this concept.

3. ***Money measurement concept***: According to this concept, business transaction is recorded if money is involved. If money is not involved in business transaction, it is not recorded as per this concept. For example, if a business organization has a cash balance of Rs. 50,000/-, a three storied building, three acres of land, 20 machines, 1000 kg of raw materials, 50 working tables, 50 chairs etc., it is not possible to record all the items in the accounting book because money is not involved to account for all these assets. But if these items are expressed in terms of money i.e., Rs. 50,000/- cash, Rs. 20,00,000/- worth of building, Rs. 60,00,000/- worth of land, Rs. 3,00,000/- worth of machines, Rs. 1,00,000- worth of raw material, Rs. 50,000/- worth of working tables and chairs, they should be recorded in the accounting book because they are in terms of money. The major disadvantage of this concept is that if there is any change in the value of the above assets in future, these changes are not considered and recorded in the accounting book.
4. ***Revenue realization concept***: When a sale of goods is completed, the revenue is realized (i.e., the amount is collected). There will not be any income or profit without sales. Therefore, under this concept only those revenues or incomes which have been realized in cash are recorded. Without realization, no earning can be taken into account by the business organization.
5. ***Cost concept***: According to this concept, the actual cost of assets at the time of purchase should be entered in the accounting book. For example if a land was purchased for Rs. 20,00,000/- but now the market value of the same land is approximately around Rs. 50,00,000/-. The actual cost of land at the time of purchase i.e., Rs. 20,00,000/- should be entered in the accounting book but not the present market value Rs. 50,00,000-. The present market price is ignored due to cost concept. This concept is applicable to fixed assets only (*e.g.*, building, land, furniture etc.).
6. ***Going concern concept***: According to this concept, it is assumed that the business will continue to exist for a long period. Most of the business organizations continue their business profitably for indefinite periods and are considered as going concerns. On the basis of this concept, the other parties enter into long term contracts with the business organization by giving loans, purchasing bonds or investing funds in long-term securities.
7. ***Matching concepts***: It is the aim of every businessman to earn maximum profit at minimum cost. So in an accounting period (i.e., in one year), he tries to earn maximum profit. Then he compare the profit with that of previous year and he can come to conclusion about the progress or downfall of the business. By this

matching concept, the proprietor can easily find out the profit or loss. He can also make effort to improve the economy, efficiency and increase the profit.

8. ***Accrual concept***: While preparing the financial statements, all the revenue earned during a particular period (i.e., in one year or in two years) and all the expenses incurred during the same period are to be recorded in the accounting register. Then only the proprietor can find out the actual financial position of his business. The revenue earned but not yet received is considered to be "accrued and receivable". The expenses incurred but not yet paid in cash are considered "accrued and due". These "accrued income" and "accrued dues" are to be entered in the accounting book while preparing financial statements. Under this concept, cash and credit transactions are recorded. This concept is helpful in finding out the earning capacity of the business during the particular period i.e., in one year.

Accounting conventions

The term "Convention" means the traditional practice followed to prepare accounting statements. The following conventions are commonly used in accountancy:

1. Conservatism 2. Disclosure 3. Consistency 4. Materiality

1. ***Conservatism***: The principle of recording the actual facts of the business is called as "Convention of Conservatism". It is not proper to hide the actual position of the business. In other words, secret reserves are not permitted. The statements written in the accounting register should disclose the true and fair position of the business. On any account a false impression should not be created.
2. ***Disclosure***: Under this convention 'Disclosure', all information relating to business transactions must be disclosed and the accounts are prepared honestly. As far as possible, each item of expense and income should be disclosed independently and separately. Thus full disclosure of all relevant facts in accounts is necessary in order to make accounting record useful.
3. ***Consistency***: If one accounting method is followed in one year, the same method should be followed in subsequent years. Thus continuances of one method in number of years indicate the 'Convention of Consistency'. The important advantage of this Convention of Consistency is that the account of one year can be easily compared with the account of other years. It gives reliable results and helps to the management in the matter of planning.
4. ***Materiality***: The term "Materiality" refers to material facts which are capable of influencing decisions. As per this convention only material facts or important facts are to be recorded in a register through financial statements. So the financial statements are expected to disclose all the material items.

14.3 | Book Keeping

Definition: Book keeping is an art and science of recording business transactions.

Objectives of book keeping:

1. To have a permanent record of all business transactions carried out during a particular period.
2. To know the actual result of the business, i.e., whether the business is either in profit or in loss.
3. To know the amount of assets, liabilities and capital in the business on any particular date.

Difference between book keeping and accountancy

Book Keeping involves only the recording of business transactions which is just one part of the accounting process. Accountancy involves the entire accounting process i.e., recording, classifying, summarizing and analyzing the business transaction.

Books of accounts used in book-keeping: There are several books of accounts used in Book Keeping. They are as follows:

1. Primary books of accounts: (a) Journal (b) Ledger
2. Subsidiary books of accounts:
   (a) Cash book
   (b) Purchase book
   (c) Sales book
   (d) Purchase returns book
   (e) Sales returns book
   (f) Bills receivable book
   (g) Bill payable book.

Primary books of accounts

(a) ***Journal:*** It is known as book of original entry. Journal is a record in which all business transactions are analyzed and recorded under the heads of Debits and Credits.

(b) ***Ledger:*** Ledger is the chief book of accounts. In this book all the business transactions are recorded under their respective heading such as cash account, capital account, personal account, furniture account, building account etc.

***Subsidiary books of accounts*:** Subsidiary books are also known as 'Daily Records'. All transactions are recorded.

(a) ***Cash book*:** It is a journal in which the cash and bank transactions are recorded

(b) ***Purchase book*:** It is a journal in which all purchases of goods are recorded

(c) ***Sales book***: It is a journal in which all the sales of goods are recorded

(d) ***Purchase returns book***: It is a journal in which all the transactions regarding return of goods by the retailers to the wholesalers are recorded.

(e) ***Sales returns book***: It is a journal in which all the particulars regarding return of goods by customers are recorded.

(f) ***Bills receivable book***: The Bills received are recorded in this book.

(g) ***Bills payable book***: The bills accepted are recorded in this book.

14.4 | Different Kinds of Accounts

An account is a summarized statement, recording transactions regarding asset, a liability or capital. It has two sides namely left hand side (Debit side) and right hand side (Credit side). The different kinds of accounts are Personal Accounts, Real Accounts and Nominal Accounts.

1. ***Personal accounts***: It deals with the individual person (*e.g.* an account of Mr. Prasad), firm (*e.g.* account of M/s. Gopi Medical Hall), individual Company (*e.g.* account of Andhra Bank or individual institution (*e.g.* account of A.S.N. Pharmacy College).

   A person or firm which supplies the goods to the person who is doing business is a creditor and entries are made on credit side of his account. A person or firm who receives money or goods from a person who is doing business is a debtor and the entries are made on debit side of his account.

2. ***Real accounts***: It deals with transactions related to building, cash, furniture, land, machinery, stock etc. A separate account is maintained for each item. When an item is purchased or received, the transaction is recorded on the debit side.

3. ***Nominal accounts***: These accounts deal with discounts, insurance, rent, wages, salaries, interest, commission, cost of stationary items, amount spend on advertisements etc. A separate account is maintained for each type of expenditure. The entries of profits or gains are made on credit side and the entries of expenses or losses are made on debit side.

General rules: Generally there are three rules are followed to make entries in the Journal Book:

Name of the Account	Debit	Credit
1. Personal	The receiver	The giver
2. Real	What comes in	What goes out?
3. Nominal	All expenses and losses	All gains and incomes

Review Questions

Short Answer Questions

1. Write the history of book keeping
2. Give two definitions of book keeping
3. Give the meaning of book keeping
4. Discuss the meaning of accountancy
5. What is accounting cycle?
6. Discuss the objects of book-keeping
7. What are the advantages of book-keeping & accountancy?
8. Discuss the limitations of accounting
9. Explain the following terms:
   (a) Capital
   (b) Drawings
   (c) Trade discount
   (d) Cash discount
   (e) Assets
   (f) Liabilities
   (g) Turnover
   (h) Proprietor
   (i) Accounting equation
10. Give the meaning of accounting principles
11. Explain the meaning of 'accrual concept' of accounting.
12. What is meant by convention of materiality?
13. Explain the money measurement concept
14. Describe the separate entity concept.

Long Answer Questions

1. Define book keeping and accountancy and point out the difference between them.
2. Discuss the advantages of book keeping and accountancy.
3. What is an accounting cycle? Describe the limitation of accounting.
4. What do you mean by 'basic accounting concepts and conventions'? Discuss in brief some of the important concepts and conventions of accounting.
5. Explain accounting principles.

15 Recording of the Business Transactions

15.1 | Double Entry System of Book-Keeping

LEARNING OBJECTIVES

- *Double Entry System of Book Keeping*
- *Rules for Debit and Credit*
- *Journal*
- *Cash book*
- *Petty Cash book*
- *Purchase Return Journal*

Book-keeping is the art of recording business transactions in books of accounts maintained for the purpose. A transaction has been defined as that which involves the transfer of money or money's worth. Hence every business transaction involves a transfer and hence consists of two aspects, 1. The Receiving aspect and 2. The giving aspect. It is necessary to note that these aspects go together. The record of any business transaction will be complete only when both of these aspects are recorded. This recording of the two aspects of each transaction is known as 'Double Entry' and the system called "Double Entry System".

Double Entry System is the only scientific system of book-keeping. Every business transaction affects two accounts and according to double entry system entries will be made in both of them – on the debit side in one account and on credit side in the other. Hence for every debit there must be a corresponding credit for an equal amount and vice versa. This is known as the 'Principle of Double Entry'.

The fundamental rule of double entry system of book keeping is "Debit the Account which receives the benefit and Credit the Account which gives the benefit".

Double Entry system of book-keeping is simple and has Universal Applications. It is being used for several hundred years and a worthy system for adoption by a business man.

General principles: The basic principles of double entry system are as follows :

1. Debiting one account and crediting another account is the basic principle of double entry system.
2. In every business transaction, there are two aspects, one is giving aspect and another is receiving aspect. The giver is called 'Creditor' and the receiver is called 'Debtor'. The giver is credited the worth of goods whatever he gives. The receiver is debited the worth of goods whatever he receives.
3. In double entry system of book-keeping, both aspects are recorded. For every debit there must be a corresponding credit. So each account is divided into two parts i.e., 1. Left hand side is known as debit side and is denoted by 'Dr'. 2. Right hand side is known as credit side and is denoted by 'Cr'.

***Advantages of double entry system of book-keeping*:** The main advantages of Double Entry system of Book Keeping are as under:

1. It brings into record both the aspects of every transaction.
2. The correctness of all entries can be verified.
3. It is easy to find out the Assets & Liabilities, Income & Expenditure, Purchase & Sales etc., for a particular period.
4. It helps in ascertaining the arithmetical accuracy of the books by means of trail balance.
5. It is easy to find out Gross Profit, Net Profit or Loss with the help of Complete Double Entry System of Book-Keeping.
6. The exact state of affairs is verified by preparing the Balance Sheet.
7. The comparison between the previous & current years sale, purchases, opening & closing stock, Income & Expenditure can be made.
8. The books maintained under this system are more scientific.
9. The errors can easily be located under this system. However, there are some errors which Double Entry System fails to discover such as a mistake or omission into Double Entry, A double or equivalising error in the transfer to The Ledger & Posting an account to the wrong account.

***Disadvantages of double entry system of book keeping*:** This system of book-keeping though very scientific and accurate is not free from defects. The defects/ disadvantages of this system are as follows :

1. If any business transaction is not recorded in any book of original entry, it may remain undetected.

2. If the amount of any business transaction is wrongly recorded in any book of the original entry, it may not be discovered by this method.
3. A compensating error may not be detected by this method. For example, instead of Rent Account, Gopi Account may be debited. This error may not be detected as both the sides of Trial Balance will tally.

***Stages of double entry system*:** The following are the three stages of a complete system of double entry :

1. All transactions are first recorded in Journal or Subsidiary Books as and when they take place.
2. All entries in the Journal or Subsidiary Books are posted in the Ledger.
3. All the accounts are closed or balanced and final accounts are prepared. When these steps are completed, the cycle begins again for the next year.

***Rules for debit and credit*:** Every transaction affects two accounts and this effect will have to be entered in both the sides, on the debit side in one account and on the credit side in the other account. Therefore, it is necessary to find out which of the two accounts is to be debited and which is to be credited. For this purpose, one has to first identify the class to which these two accounts belong, i.e., personal, real or nominal, and then certain rules known as 'rules of debit and credit' are applied.

1. ***Personal Accounts :*** The account of the person receiving the benefit (Receiver) of the transaction is debited and the account of the person giving the benefit (giver) of the transaction is credited.

   Rule : 'Debit the receiver, Credit the giver'

   Ex : G pays Rs. 1,000 to K. In this transaction G is the giver and K is the receiver. Hence, in the Books of G, the account of K (the receiver) is to be debited, and in the books of K, the account of G (the giver) is to be credited.

2. ***Real Accounts :*** When an asset is coming into the business, the account of that asset is debited. When an asset is going out of the business, the account of that asset is credited.

   Rule : ' Debit what comes in, Credit what goes out'.

   Ex : In (1) above, cash comes in to the receiver K, and cash goes out from the giver G. Accordingly, K in his books debits cash and G in his books credits cash. Thus, the double entry for the aforesaid transaction will be completed in K's books by debiting Cash Account and crediting G's as shown below :

Books of K

Dr.	**Cash Account**	**Cr.**	**Dr.**	**G's Account**	**Cr.**
	Rs.				Rs.
To G	1,000			By Cash	1,000

In G's books, the double entry would be completed by debiting K's Account and Crediting Cash Account as under:

Books of G

Dr.	**K's Account**	**Cr.**	**Dr.**	**Cash Account**	**Cr.**
	Rs.				Rs.
To Cash	1,000			By K	1000

3. ***Nominal accounts*:** When an expense is incurred or loss is suffered, the account representing the expense or the loss is debited. When any income is earned or gain made, the account representing this income or the gain is credited.

   Rule: 'Debit all expenses and losses, Credit all incomes and gains'.

   Ex: If Rent of Rs. 2,000 is received by landlord from tenant, the former will credit rent Accounts as it is his income, and the latter will debit Rent Account as it is an expense to him.

   In the books of landlord, the double entry would be completed as shown under :

Dr.	**Cash Account**	**Cr.**	**Dr.**	**Rent Account**	**Cr.**
	Rs.			Rs.	
To Rent	2,000		By Cash	2,000	

   In the tenant's books, the double entry would be completed as shown below :

Dr.	**Rent Account**	**Cr**	**Dr.**	**Cash Account**	**Cr.**
	Rs.				Rs.
To Cash	2,000			By Rent	2,000

The three types of accounts and their respective rules for debit and credit can be shown as below:

15.2 | Types of Accounts

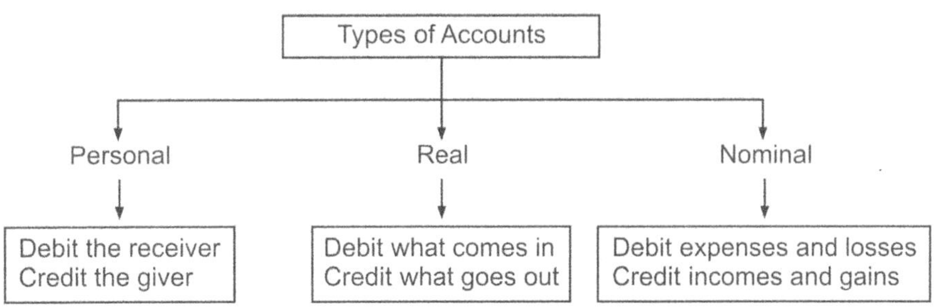

The expressions 'receiver' and 'giver' in personal account, 'coming in' and 'going out' in real account, and 'expenses and losses' and 'incomes and gains' in nominal account, are considered from business view point.

The student is now familiar with the rules of debit and credit. Now we can take the following transactions and mention which accounts are involved in each case and which of them is to be debited or credited :

April 2	Bought goods from Prasad, Rs. 8,000
April 10	Paid Cash to Prasad Rs. 5,000
April 21	Sold goods to Srinivas, Rs. 3,000
April 25	Received cash from Srinivas, Rs. 20,000
April 30	Paid salaries to Office Staff, Rs. 500
April 30	Received commission, Rs. 250

In the following table, we show the accounts to be debited and credited in the case of each transaction.

Date of Transaction	Account to be debited	Account to be credited	Type of Account	Reason for debit
April 2	Goods A/c.	......	Real	Goods come in
	.....	Prasad A/c.	Personal	Prasad is the giver.
	April 10	Prasad A/c	......	Personal Prasad is the receiver
	....	Cash A/c	Real	Cash goes out.
April 21	Srinivas A/c	....	Personal	Srinivas-receiver
	....	Goods A/c	Real	Goods go out
April 25	Cash A/c	....	Real	Cash comes in.
	....	Srinivas A/c	Personal	Srinivas-giver
April 30	Salaries A/c	....	Nominal	Expense
	....	Cash A/c	Real	Cash goes out.
April 30	Cash A/c	....	Real	Cash comes in
	....	Commission A/c	Nominal	Income

***Books of accounts*:** The books used in book keeping are called Books of Accounts. They are mainly two types

1. Books of Original Entry or Books of Prime Entry
2. Books of Final Entry or Ledger Accounts

Books of Original Entry are again of two types

1. General Journal or Journal
2. Subsidiary Journals or Subsidiary Books

Ledger Accounts are again of two types

1. Personal Ledger
2. Impersonal Leger

Personal Ledger is of three types

1. Debtor's Ledger
2. Creditor's Ledger
3. Private or Self Ledger

***Journal*:** A journal is a book in which transactions are recorded in the order of their occurrence i.e., in chronological order. A Journal is called a book of prime entry because all business transactions are entered first in this book. The process of recording a transaction in the journal is called journalizing. The format of a Journal is shown as follows :

15.3 | Journal

Date	Particulars	Ledger Folio Debit (Rs.)	Credit (Rs.)

1. **Date column:** In this column the date on which transaction is undertaken is recorded.
2. **Particulars column:** In this column the names of the accounts to be debited and credited are shown followed by narration (brief explanation of the transaction).
3. **Ledger folio column:** Ledger Folio Column presents ledger page number of each account in the ledger in which entry is posted.
4. **Debit column:** In this column the amount to be debited is entered against debit aspect.
5. **Credit column:** In this column, the amount to be credited is entered against credit aspect.

***Steps in journalizing*:** In order to journalize the transactions the following steps are to be adopted.

Step I: Analysis of transaction to identify whether given transaction is cash or credit transaction.

Step II: Ascertaining the accounts involved in the transaction worth recording.

Step III: Ascertaining the nature of accounts to which the accounts identified through Step II belong i.e., Personal, Real or Nominal

Step IV: Ascertaining which account is to be debited and which account is to be credited.

Step V: Recording the transaction in Journal in the form of an entry

***Note*:** Cash transactions are those which involve cash flows i.e., either inflow or outflow. Credit transactions are those which include neither inflow of cash nor outflow of cash. In these transactions personal accounts are to be identified and recorded.

Example : Analyze the following transactions and identify the accounts to be debited or credited in a tabular form by identifying also their nature and rule applicable.

1. Kiran started his business with cash
2. Borrowed from Andhra Bank
3. Purchased goods for cash
4. Purchased goods from Srinivas
5. Purchased Machinery for Cheque
6. Sold goods to Ram on Credit
7. Received cash from Ram
8. Deposited into Bank
9. Withdrawn cash for personal use
10. Withdrawn cash from bank for office use
11. Goods withdrawn for personal use
12. Received cheque from Sarada Deposited into Bank
13. Sarada's Cheque dishonored as intimated by the Bank
14. Paid interest on Loan
15. Paid installment of loan

Analysis of Transactions

Transaction No	Accounts involved	Nature	How affected Accounts	Whether Debited/ Credited
(1)	Cash A/c	Real	Cash is coming in	Debit
	Capital A/c	Personal	Kiran is the giver	Credit
(2)	Cash A/c	Real	Cash is Coming in	Debit
	Andhra Bank A/c	Personal	Andhra Bank is giver	Credit
(3)	Purchases A/c.	Real	Goods are coming in	Debit
	Cash A/c	Real	Cash is going out	Credit
(4)	Purchases A/c	Real	Goods are coming in	Debit
	Srinivas A/c	Personal	Srinivas is the giver	Credit
(5)	Machinery A/c	Real	Machinary is coming in	Debit
	Bank A/c	Personal	Bank is the giver	Credit
(6)	Ram A/c	Personal	Ram is the receiver.	Debit
	Sales A/c	Real	Goods are going out	Credit
(7)	Cash A/c	Real	Cash is coming in	Debit
	Ram A/c	Personal	Ram is the giver	Credit
(8)	Bank A/c	Personal	Bank is the receiver	Debit
	Cash A/c	Real	Cash is going out	Credit

Contd...

Transaction No	Accounts involved	Nature	How affected Accounts	Whether Debited/ Credited
(9)	Drawings A/c	Personal	Kiran is the receiver	Debit
	Cash A/c	Real	Cash is going out	Credit
(10)	Cash A/c	Real	Cash is coming in	Debit
	Bank A/c	Personal	Bank is the giver	Credit
(11)	Drawings A/c	Personal	Kiran is the receiver	Debit
	Purchases A/c	Real	Goods are going out	Credit
(12)	Bank A/c	Personal	Bank is the receiver	Debit
	Sarada A/c	Personal	Sarada is the giver	Credit
(13)	Sarada A/c	Personal	Sarada is the receiver	Debit
	Bank A/c	Personal	Bank is the giver	Credit
(14)	Interest on loan A/c	Nominal	Interest on loan is expense	
	Cash A/c	Real	Cash is going out	Credit
(15)	Loan A/c	Personal	Lender is the receiver	Debit
	Cash A/c	Real	Cash is going out	Credit

Ledger: After recording a transaction in the journal, the next stage is the transfer of transactions into the respective accounts opened in the ledger. This process of transfer is called posting. A ledger is a book containing accounts of various aspects. These accounts relate to any one of the accounts viz., personal, real or nominal etc.

Format of a ledger account: A ledger account can be prepared in the following form.

Name of the Account

Date	Particulars	L.F	Amt (Rs.)	Date	Particulars	L.F	Amt (Rs.)

Steps in posting: The following are the steps to be adopted in posting the journal entries in to the relevant accounts.

Step I: Enter the date of the transaction in date column on relevant side of the account.

Step II: Write the name of the account with which the present account has transacted with in the particulars column on the side i.e., Debit or Credit, based on the journal entry, whether the said item of account debited/credited. Name of the account recorded on debit-side should start with 'To' and credit-side with 'By'.

Step III : Record the page number of the journal in the 'L.F Column' in which the present entry is recorded.

Step IV: Enter the relevant amount in the "Amount Column" of the side on which the entry is posted.

Step V: Ascertain the net balance of the account at the end every fortnight or every month. The balancing of account is called casting.

Example: Enter the following transactions in the Journal of Sagar and post them into Ledger.

1999		Rs.
Jan 1	Sagar started Business with Cash	1,00,000
2	Purchased goods	40,000
10	Sold goods	50,000
15	Purchased goods from Suresh	30,000
20	Sold goods to Narayana	50,000
24	Paid to Suresh on account	20,000
28	Interest paid on Loan	2,000
29	Returned goods to Suresh	10,000
30	Paid Salaries	5,000
31	Purchased Furniture	10,000
31	Drawn goods for personal use	2,000
31	Received dividends on Shares	500
31	Papers, Pens, Pencils etc. purchased	150

Journal of Sagar

Date	Particulars	L.F	Debit (Rs.)	Credit (Rs.)
1999	Cash A/c Dr.		1,00,000	
Jan 1	To Capital A/c		1,00,000	
	(Being the Capital introduced)			
Jan 2	Purchases A/c Dr.		40,000	
	To Cash A/c			40,000
	(Being the goods purchased)			
Jan 10	Cash A/c. Dr.		50,000	
	To Sales A/c			50,000
	(Being the goods sold)			
Jan 15	Purchases A/c Dr.		30,000	
	To Suresh A/c.			30,000
	(Being goods purchased on credit)			
Jan 20	Narayana A/c. Dr		50,000	
	To Cash A/c			50,000
	(Being the goods sold on credit)			

Contd...

Date	Particulars	L.F	Debit (Rs.)	Credit (Rs.)
Jan 24	Suresh A/c Dr.		20,000	
	To Cash A/c			20,000
	(Being the amount paid on A/c)			
Jan 28	Interest A/c Dr.		2,000	
	To Cash A/c.			2,000
	(Being interest paid on loan)			
Jan 29	Suresh A/c Dr.		10,000	
	To Return outwards A/c			10,000
	(Being the goods returned to Suresh)			
Jan 30	Salaries A/c Dr.		5,000	
	To Cash A/c			5,000
	(Being the salaries paid)			
Jan 31	Furniture A/c Dr.		10,000	
	To Cash A/c			10,000
	(Being the furniture purchased)			
Jan 31	Drawings A/c Dr.		2,000	
	To Purchases A/c			2,000
	(Being goods drawn by the owner)			
Jan 31	Cash A/c Dr.		500	
	To Dividends A/c			500
	(Being the dividends received on shares)			
Jan 31	Stationary A/c Dr.		150	
	To Cash A/c			150
	(Being Papers, Pens and Pencils purchased)			

Ledger of Sagar

Cash A/c

Dr **Cr**

Date	Particulars	L.F	Amount (Rs.)	Date	Particulars	L.F	Amount (Rs.)
1999				1999			
Jan 1	To Capital A/c		1,00,000	Jan 2	By Purchases A/c		40,000
10	To Sales A/c		50,000	24	By Suresh A/c		20,000
31	To Dividends A/c		500	28	By Interest A/c		2,000
				30	By Salaries A/c		5,000
				31	By Furniture A/c		10,000
				31	By Stationary A/c		150
				31	By Balance C/d		73,350
			1,50,500				1,50,500
Feb 1	To Balance b/d		73,350				

Capital A/c

Dr **Cr**

1999			1999		
Jan 31	To Balance c/d	1,00,000	Jan 1	By Cash A/c	1,00,000
		1,00,000			1,00,000
			Feb 1	By Balance b/d	1,00,000

Purchases A/c

Dr **Cr**

1999			1999		
Jan 2	To Cash A/c	40,000	Jan 31	By Drawings A/c	2,000
15	To Suresh A/c	30,000		By Balance A/c	68,000
		70,000			70,000
Feb 1	To Balance b/d	68,000			

Sales A/c

Dr **Cr**

Date	Particulars	L.F	Amount (Rs.)	Date	Particulars	L.F	Amount (Rs.)
1999			1999				
Jan 31	To Balance c/d	1,00,000	Jan 10		By Cash A/c		50,000
			20		By Narayana A/c		50,000
		1,00,000					1,00,000
			Feb 31		By Balance b/d		1,00,000

Suresh A/c

Dr **Cr**

Date	Particulars	L.F	Amount (Rs.)	Date	Particulars	L.F	Amount (Rs.)
1999		1999					
Jan 31	To Cash A/c	20,000		Jan 15	By Purchases A/c		30,000
	To Return out-wards A/c						10,000
		30,000					30,000

Narayana A/c

Dr | Cr

Date	Particulars	L.F	Amount (Rs.)	Date	Particulars	L.F	Amount (Rs.)
1999				1999			
Jan 20	To Sales A/c		50,000	Jan 31	By Balance c/d		50,000
			50,000				50,000
				Feb 1	To Balance b/d		50,000

Interest A/c

Dr | Cr

Date	Particulars	L.F	Amount (Rs.)	Date	Particulars	L.F	Amount (Rs.)
1999				1999			
Jan 20	To Cash A/c		2,000	Jan 31	By Balance c/d		2,000
			2,000				2,000
				Feb 1	To Balance b/d		2,000

Return Outwards A/c

Dr | Cr

Date	Particulars	L.F	Amount (Rs.)	Date	Particulars	L.F	Amount (Rs.)
1999				1999			
Jan 20	To Balance c/d		10,000	Jan 29	By Suresh A/c		10,000
			10,000				10,000
				Feb 1	By Balance b/d		10,000

Salaries A/c

Dr | Cr

Date	Particulars	L.F	Amount (Rs.)	Date	Particulars	L.F	Amount (Rs.)
1999				1999			
Jan 30	To Cash A/c		5,000	Jan 31	By Balance c/d		5,000
			5,000				5,000
				Feb 1	To Balance b/d		5,000

Furniture A/c

Dr **Cr**

Date	Particulars	L.F	Amount (Rs.)	Date	Particulars	L.F	Amount (Rs.)
1999			1999				
Jan 31	To Cash A/c	10,000		Jan 31	By Balance c/d		10,000
		10,000					10,000
				Feb 1	To Balance b/d		10,000

Drawings A/c

Dr **Cr**

Date	Particulars	L.F	Amount (Rs.)	Date	Particulars	L.F	Amount (Rs.)
1999			1999				
Jan 31	To Purchases A/c		2,000	Jan 31	By Balance c/d		2,000
		2,000					2,000
				Feb 1	To Balance b/d		2,000

Dividends A/c

Dr **Cr**

Date	Particulars	L.F	Amount (Rs.)	Date	Particulars	L.F	Amount (Rs.)
1999			1999				
Jan 20	To Cash A/c	2,000		Jan 31	By Balance c/d		2,000
		2,000					2,000
				Feb 1	To Balance b/d		2,000

Stationary A/c

Dr **Cr**

Date	Particulars	L.F	Amount (Rs.)	Date	Particulars	L.F	Amount (Rs.)
1999			1999				
Jan 31	To Cash A/c	150		Jan 31	By Balance c/d		150
		150					150
				Feb 1	To Balance b/d		150

15.4 | Cash Book

All the receipts and payments of cash are recorded in a separate book known as Cash Book. A large number of Cash transactions takes place each day and as such, it is necessary to record such transactions in a separate Book. Cash can also be stolen by an employee and to detect or prevent such loss, it becomes imperative to find out the balance of Cash Book at the end of each day and to tally it with the actual cash in Hand.

Kinds of cash book

1. Simple cash book
2. Two columnar cash book
3. Three columnar cash book
4. Petty cash book.

***Simple cash book*:** A simple Cash book is itself regarded as a ledger and ruled out just like a Cash Account. Only cash transactions are recorded in Cash book. Transactions relating to Banking and Discount are not recorded in this Book. All receipts in the form of currency notes, coins, cheques, Darshani Hundis, Bank Drafts, Postal Orders etc., are recorded in debit side while all payments in credit side. 'The Ruling' of Simple Cash Book is given below:

Specimen of Simple Cash Book

Dr **Cr**

Date	Particulars	L.F	Amount (Rs.)	Date	Particulars	L.F	Amount (Rs.)

Each side has the same columns. The day of transaction is recorded in 'date' column. In 'receipt' column the account is entered on behalf of which the amount has been received by using the word 'To'. Ledger Page No. of the account is recorded in the column 'L.F'. Amount received is entered in column meant for 'Amount' on debit side. Similarly, the entries for payments are recorded in the credit side by using the word 'By".

***Balancing*:** The debit side of the Cash Book must be at all times greater than the credit side as a business can not be out more than what it has or what it receives. Thus, the cash book always shows a debit balance.

***Posting*:** The balance at the beginning of the period is not posted to any account, because it comes in the Cash Book from the opening entries while other entries appearing on the debit side of the Cash Book are posted to the credit of the concerning accounts in the ledger. The entries appearing in the credit side of the Cash Book are posted to the debit of the concerning accounts in the ledger.

***Example*:** Prepare a simple Cash Book from the following transactions and also prepare the necessary accounts in the ledger.

1994	Particulars	Rs.
Jan 1	Cash in hand	10,000
Jan 2	Purchased Machinery	4,000
Jan 2	Purchased Furniture	1,000
Jan 2	Purchased Building	4,000
Jan 6	Purchased Goods for Cash	1,000
Jan 15	Goods Sold for Cash	1,800
Jan 23	Paid Salaries	300
Jan 23	Paid Wages	200
Jan 23	Paid to Krishna	500
Jan 27	Received from Sanjiv Kumar	1,000

Cash Book

Date	Particulars	L.F	Amount (Rs.)	Date	Particulars	L.F	Amount (Rs.)
1994				1994			
Jan 1	To Balance B/d		10,000	Jan 2	By Machinery A/c		4,000
Jan 15	To Sales A/c		1,800	Jan 2	By Furniture A/c		1,000
Jan 27	To Sanjiv Kumar		1,000	Jan 2	By Building A/c		4,000
				Jan 6	By Purchases A/c		1,000
				Jan 23	By Salaries A/c		300
				Jan 23	By Wages A/c		200
				Jan 23	By Krishna		500
				Jan 31	By Balance c/d		1,800
			12,800				12,800
				Feb 1	To Balance b/d		1,800

LEDGER ACCOUNT

Machinery A/c

Dr **Cr**

Date	Particulars	L.F	Amount (Rs.)	Date	Particulars	L.F	Amount (Rs.)
1994							
Jan 1	To Cash A/c		4,000				

Furniture A/c

Dr | Cr

Date	Particulars	L.F	Amount (Rs.)	Date	Particulars	L.F	Amount (Rs.)
1994							
Jan 2	To Cash A/c		1,000				

Building A/c

Dr | Cr

Date	Particulars	L.F	Amount (Rs.)	Date	Particulars	L.F	Amount (Rs.)
1994							
Jan 2	To Cash A/c		4,000				

Purchases A/c

Dr | Cr

Date	Particulars	L.F	Amount (Rs.)	Date	Particulars	L.F	Amount (Rs.)
1994							
Jan 6	To Cash A/c		1,000				

Salaries A/c

Dr | Cr

Date	Particulars	L.F	Amount (Rs.)	Date	Particulars	L.F	Amount (Rs.)
1994							
Jan 23	To Cash A/c		300				

Wages A/c

Dr | Cr

Date	Particulars	L.F	Amount (Rs.)	Date	Particulars	L.F	Amount (Rs.)
1994							
Jan 23	To Cash A/c		200				

Krishna A/c

Dr | Cr

Date	Particulars	L.F	Amount (Rs.)	Date	Particulars	L.F	Amount (Rs.)
1994							
Jan 23	To Cash A/c		500				

Sales A/c

Dr							Cr
Date	**Particulars**	**L.F**	**Amount (Rs.)**	**Date**	**Particulars**	**L.F**	**Amount (Rs.)**
1994							
Jan 15	By Cash A/c		1,800				

Sanjiv Kumar's A/c

Dr							Cr
Date	**Particulars**	**L.F**	**Amount (Rs.)**	**Date**	**Particulars**	**L.F**	**Amount (Rs.)**
1994							
Jan 27	By Cash A/c		1,000				

Exercise: Enter the following transactions in a Simple Cash Book of M/s Rao & Co.

1994		**Rs.**
May 1	Started Business with a Capital of	6,000
May 2	Purchased Goods for Cash	2,000
May 3	Goods Sold for Cash	2,500
May 5	Purchased Good from Star Traders on Credit	1,700
May 7	Received from Gopi	400
May 9	Paid Star Traders on Account	1,500
May 15	Deposited into Bank	500
May 18	Withdrew from Bank for Office use	250
May 20	Received Interest	25
May 25	Paid to Chandu Bros.	20
May 28	Withdrew Cash for Personal use	150
May 31	Paid Cash in the Bank in excess of	2,000
(Ans. Amount Paid into Bank Rs. 30,005)		

Two columnar cash cook

As the discount is so closely related to cash being allowed or received with cash transactions only, it can conveniently be recorded in the cash book along side the relative cash receipt or payment, by ruling a double column cash book.

***Discount*:** Very often cash discount accompanies cash receipts and payments. The discount allowed shown in discount column on debit side while discount received is shown on the credit side. Two columnar cash book may be of two types (i) Cash book with Cash and discount column (ii) Cash book with bank and discount columns.

(i) *Cash book with cash and discount columns:* If a businessman receives or allows cash discount, he may keep a cash and discount columns.

Posting: The cash columns are recorded in the same way as in the simple cash book. But discount columns in each side are totaled without balancing. As regards discount, each item of discount allowed is recorded to the credit side of the concerned personal account while each item of discount received is posted to the debit of respective personal accounts.

The total of the discount column on the debit side is debited to the discount account and the total of the discount column on the credit side is credited to the discount account. The balance of cash columns are ascertained in the same manner as the balancing of simple cash book.

***Example* 1:**

1994		Rs.
Jan 1	Cash in Hand	2,000
Jan 5	Paid to Ramarao	300
	Discount Allowed by him	10
Jan 8	Cash Purchased	400
Jan 10	Received from S.P.Balu and Sons.	980
	Discount allowed	20
Jan 16	Cash Sales	900
Jan 21	Paid to Jayaraj and sons	395
	Discount allowed by them	5
Jan 26	Paid Wages	50
Jan 31	Paid to Nanaji and Bros.	395
	In full settlement of their account which shows a credit	

Balance of Rs. 420

Solution:

Cash Book (Double Column)

Date	Particulars	LF	Discount (Rs.)	Amount	Date	Particulars	LF	Discount	Amount (Rs.)
1995					1995				
Jan 1	To Balance B/d			2,000	Jan 5	By Rama Rao		10	300
Jan 10	To S.P. Balu and Sons		20	980	Jan 8	By Purchased A/c			400
Jan 16	To Sales A/c			900	Jan 21	By Jayaraj and Sons		5	395
					Jan 26	By Wages			50
					Jan 31	By Nanaji and Bros.		25	395
					Jan 31 C/d	By Balance			2,340
			20	3,880				40	3,880
	To Balance B/d			2,340					

Rama Rao's A/c

Dr **Cr**

Date	Particulars	L.F	Amount (Rs.)	Date	Particulars	L.F	Amount (Rs.)
1995							
Jan 5	To Cash A/c		300				
Jan 5	To Discount A/c		10				

Purchases A/c

Dr **Cr**

Date	Particulars	L.F (Rs.)	Amount	Date (Rs.)	Particulars	L.F	Amount
1995							
Jan 8	To Cash A/c		400				

S.P. Balu & Sons A/c

Dr **Cr**

Date	Particulars	L.F (Rs.)	Amount	Date (Rs.)	Particulars	L.F	Amount
			1995				
				Jan 10	By Cash A/c		980
				Jan 10	By Discount A/c		20

Sales A/c

Dr **Cr**

Date	Particulars	L.F (Rs.)	Amount	Date (Rs.)	Particulars	L.F	Amount
			1995				
				Jan 16			
					By Sales A/c		900

Jayaraj & Sons

Dr **Cr**

Date	Particulars	L.F (Rs.)	Amount	Date (Rs.)	Particulars	L.F	Amount
1995							
Jan 21	To Cash A/c		395				
Jan 21	To Discount A/c		5				

Wages A/c

Dr							Cr
Date	**Particulars**	**L.F (Rs.)**	**Amount**	**Date (Rs.)**	**Particulars**	**L.F**	**Amount**
1995							
Jan 26	To Cash A/c		50				

Nanaji Bros. A/c

Dr							Cr
Date	**Particulars**	**L.F (Rs.)**	**Amount**	**Date (Rs.)**	**Particulars**	**L.F**	**Amount**
1995							
Jan 31	To Cash A/c		395				
Jan 31	To Discount A/c		25				

Example 2:

2000		**Rs.**
May 1	Cash in Hand	1,500
May 6	Received from Jai Javan Enterprises	196
May 9	Discount Allowed by him	4
May 17	Goods bought for Cash	200
	Paid to Mr. Ramanadham	293
	And received discount	7
May 25	Received from Madhu	94
	And allowed him discount	6
May 29	Paid Wages	140
May 31	Paid Salaries	30
May 31	Paid Rent	20

Prepare a Two Column Cash Book and Post them into Ledger of the above transactions

Ans: Cash Balance Rs. 1107

(ii) *Cash book with bank and discount columns*: A businessman usually keeps bank account and, in so far possible, receives or makes payments through cheques. In such conditions the cash book with bank and discount columns is maintained. Balancing and posting of such Cash Book is exactly same as in the Cash Book with cash and discount columns.

***Example* 3:** Enter the following transactions in a Cash Book having bank and discount columns assuming that all receipts are banked and that all payments are made by cheques only:

1998		Rs.
Jan 1	Opened a bank A/c and deposited	20,000
Jan 4	Cash Purchases	6,400
Jan 5	Cash Sales	2,700
Jan 7	Paid office rent to landlord	300
Jan 11	Drew cheque for personal use	1,700
Jan 15	Received Cheque from Garuda Bros. Rs. 1,670 In full and final settlement of their a/c of Rs. 1,700	
Jan 18	Received Interest	220
Jan 19	Paid to imperial Medical Stores for Purchases	500
Jan 22	Paid to Srikanth	990
	Discount Allowed	10
Jan 27	A Cheque issued by the proprietor to present his wife's friend at her marriage for a gift	200
Jan 30	Cash Sales 1,200	

Solution:

Cash Book (Double Column)

Date	Particulars	LF	Discount	Amount (Rs.)	Date	Particulars	LF	Discount	Amount (Rs.)
1998			1995						
Jan 1	To Cash A/c			20,000	Jan 4	By Purchases A/c			6,400
Jan 5	To Sales A/c			2,700	Jan 7	By Rent A/c			300
Jan 15	To Garuda Bros.		30	1,670	Jan 11	By Drawings A/c			1,700
Jan 18	To Interest A/c			220	Jan 19	By Purchases A/c			500
Jan 30	To Sales A/c			1,200	Jan 22	By Srikanth		10	990
					Jan 27	By Drawings A/c			200
					Jan 31	By Balance			15,700
			30	25,790				10	25,790
					Feb 1	To Balance B/d			15,700

Enter the following transactions in the Cash Book and discount columns assuming that all receipts are banked and that all payments are made by cheques only:

1999		Rs.
April 1	Opened a bank A/c and deposited	25,000
April 2	Cash Purchases	8,500
April 4	Cash Sales	3,000
April 7	Paid office rent to landlord	500
April 11	Drew cheque for personal use	1,600
April 15	Received Cheque from R.S Bros. Rs. 1,700 In full and final settlement of their a/c of Rs. 1,700	
April 18	Received Interest	100
April 19	Paid to Andhra Paris Furniture Mart for Furniture Purchased	500
April 22	Paid to Vikranth	980
	Discount Allowed	20
April 27	A Cheque issued by the proprietor to present His wife's friend at her marriage for	300
April 30	Cash Sales	1,500

Ans: Cash Balance Rs. 18,900

Three Columnar Cash Book

When a merchant keeps a bank account, an additional column on either side of the Cash Book becomes necessary for recording the amount deposited in his banking account and the cheques that he issues on the same. In such a case, the cash book will have three columns, i.e., Discount, Cash and Bank. Such a cash book is known as "Three Columnar Cash Book" or "Triple Columns Cash Book".

How To Write Up Three Columnar Cash Book

1. When a cash book possessing bank column is in use, every time that a payment is made by cheque, the entries are made direct into bank column on the credit side and it will then be necessary to post the amount to the debit of the concerning account.
2. When cash is received and the same is sent to bank for deposit, then in the debit side bank account is debited and cash account is credited in the credit side. Similarly, when cash is withdrawn from bank for office use, the cash account is debited in the debit side and bank account is credited in the credit side. Such entries are called contra entries. The letter 'C' is recorded in the L.F. column.
3. Whenever a Cheque is received from a customer, it should be entered in the bank column straightway because the cheques will have to be sent to the bank.
4. In case the cheque is received but the same has been sent to bank for deposit on a later date, it is presumed that it is kept in the Cash box and treated as cash and can too be used like cash.

5. When crossed cheque is received, it is recorded in the debit side in the bank column, but when bearer or other cheque is received, it is recorded in the debit side in the cash column.
6. When a cheque is endorsed to a person, the entry will be just like of a cash payment.
7. If bank charges any commission or collection charges for any service rendered with due intimation, the customer should enter this item in the credit side of the cash column. If these charges are made by the bank without any intimation, then these items should be recorded in the credit side in the bank column.
8. When amount is received in cash, it is recorded in the debit side in the cash column and discount allowed to the party concerned in this connection is recorded in the discount column of debit side.
9. All cash payments are to be recorded in the credit side in the cash column and discount received from the party concerned in this respect shall be recorded in the discount column of the credit side.
10. Cash and bank accounts are not opened in ledger, these accounts in this book serve the purpose of ledger accounts. Other accounts are opened and the amount of discount is also taken to the discount account along with its related amount.

Enter the following transactions in three columner Cash Book, balance it and carry out the posting.

1999	
Nov 1	Balance of Cash in hand Rs. 4000 and in the bank Rs. 10,000
Nov 2	Received Cash from Kishan Rs. 1000 and allowed him discount 30
Nov 3	Paid in to the bank Rs. 2000
Nov 4	Paid to Pavan and Co. by cheque Rs. 320 in full settlement of their account Rs. 350
Nov 5	Received from Cash Sale, Cash Rs. 275 and Cheque Rs. 225
Nov 6	Paid for Cash purchased by cheque Rs. 645
Nov 7	Paid by Cheque to Radhika and Co. Rs. 725 in full settlemtn of Rs. 800
Nov 8	Drew for office use Rs. 900 and Rs. 100 for personal use
Nov 11	Paid Cash for advertisement Rs. 45
Nov 15	Drew a Cheque of Rs. 500 for personal use
Nov 19	Paid salaries to staff by Cheque Rs. 1,250
Nov 20	Paid Life Insurance premium Rs. 300
Nov 23	Paid rent Rs. 400
Nov 26	Purchased, by Cheque, Office Furniture worth Rs. 375
Nov 30	Received a Cheque of Rs. 580 from Nayar & Co. in full settlement of their account for Rs. 620

Cash Book
Triple Column

Date	Particulars	LF	Discount	Cash	Bank	Date	Particulars	LF	Discount	Cash	Bank
1999				1999							
Nov 1	To Balance		4,000	10,000		Nov 3	By Bank A/c	C		2,000	
Nov 2	To Kishan		30	1,000		Nov 4	By Pavan & Co.		30	320	
Nov 3	To Cash A/c	C		2.000		Nov 6	By Purchases A/c			645	
Nov 5	To Sales A/c		275	225		Nov 7	By Radhika & Co.		75	725	
Nov 8	To Bank A/c	C	900			Nov 8	By Cash A/c	C		900	
Nov 30	To Nayar & Co.		40	580		Nov 8	By Drawings A/c			100	
						Nov 11	By Advertisement A/c			45	
						Nov 15	By Drawings A/c			500	
						Nov 19	By Salaries A/c			1,250	
						Nov 20	By Drawings A/c			300	
						Nov 23	By Rent A/c			400	
						Nov 26	By Furniture A/c			375	
						Nov 30	By Balance C/d			3,430	7,990
			70	6,175	12,805				105	6,175	12,805
						Dec 1	To Balance			3,420	7990

Kishan A/c

Dr Cr

Date	Particulars	L.F	Amount (Rs.)	Date	Particulars	L.F	Amount (Rs.)
				1999			
				Nov 2	By Cash A/c		1,000
					By Discount A/c		30

Sales A/c

Dr Cr

Date	Particulars	L.F	Amount (Rs.)	Date	Particulars	L.F	Amount (Rs.)
				1999			
				Nov 5	By Cash A/c		275
				Nov 5	By Bank A/c		225

Nayar & Co A/c

Dr Cr

Date	Particulars	L.F	Amount (Rs.)	Date	Particulars	L.F	Amount (Rs.)
				1999			
				Nov 30	By Bank A/c		580
					By Discount A/c		40

Pavan & Co A/c

Dr Cr

Date	Particulars	L.F	Amount (Rs.)	Date	Particulars	L.F	Amount (Rs.)
1999							
				Nov 4	To Balance B/d		320
				Nov 4	To Discount A/c30		

Purchases A/c

Dr Cr

Date	Particulars	L.F	Amount (Rs.)	Date	Particulars	L.F	Amount (Rs.)
1999				1999			
				Nov 6	To Bank A/c		645

Radhika & Co's A/c

Dr Cr

Date	Particulars	L.F	Amount (Rs.)	Date	Particulars	L.F	Amount (Rs.)
1999							
				Nov 7	To Bank A/c		725
				Nov 7	To Discount A/c75		

Drawings A/c

Dr | Cr

Date	Particulars	L.F	Amount (Rs.)	Date	Particulars	L.F	Amount (Rs.)
1999							
				Nov 8	To Bank A/c		100
				Nov 15	To Bank A/c		500
				Nov 20	To Bank A/c		300

Advertisement A/c

Dr | Cr

Date	Particulars	L.F	Amount (Rs.)	Date	Particulars	L.F	Amount (Rs.)
1994							
Nov 11	To Cash A/c		45				

Salaries A/c

Dr | Cr

Date	Particulars	L.F	Amount (Rs.)	Date	Particulars	L.F	Amount (Rs.)
1999							
				Nov 19	To Bank A/c		1,250

Rent A/c

Dr | Cr

Date	Particulars	L.F	Amount (Rs.)	Date	Particulars	L.F	Amount (Rs.)
1999							
				Nov 23	To Cash A/c		400

Furniture A/c

Dr | Cr

Date	Particulars	L.F	Amount (Rs.)	Date	Particulars	L.F	Amount (Rs.)
1999							
				Nov 26	Bank A/c		375

Discount A/c

Dr | Cr

Date	Particulars	L.F	Amount (Rs.)	Date	Particulars	L.F	Amount (Rs.)
1999				1999			
	Nov 30 To Sundries		70	Nov 30	By Sundries		105

Example 4

Cash Book

Date 2000	Particulars	LF	Discount	Cash (Rs.)	Bank (Rs.)	Date 2000	Particulars	LF	Discount (Rs.)	Cash (Rs.)	Bank
Mar 1	To Balance B/d		400	8,000	Mar 2	By Bank A/c				5,000	
Mar 1	To Capital A/c		6,000	Mar 9	By Elect. Charges					110	
Mar 2	To Cash A/c	C	5,000	Mar 11	By Machinery A/c					1,200	
Mar 4	To Sales A/c		400	Mar 14	By Purchases A/c					2,000	
Mar 6	To Kalyan	20	1,980	Mar 17	By Srikanth A/c				10	490	
Mar 19	To Bank A/c	C	400	Mar 19	By Cash A/c					400	
Mar 26	To Maria Das	20	780	Mar 21	By Drawings A/c					600	
				Mar 22	By Rent A/c					200	
Mar 27	To Prasad	10	390	Mar 29	By Bank A/c					390	
Mar 29	To Cash A/c	C	390	Mar 30	By Bank A/c					470	
Mar 30	To Cash A/c		470	Mar 31	By Salaries C/d					600	
				Mar 31	By Balance C/d					200	12,550
		50	10,350			13,860			10	10,350	13,860
	To Balance	200	12,550								

***Example* 5:** Write the following transactions in a Cash Book with Cash, Bank and Discount Columns:

1999	
Mar 1	Balance in hand Rs. 100 and overdraft at Bank Rs. 20,000
Mar 2	Received Cash from Raju for goods sold in last month Rs. 1000
Mar 3	Sold goods for cash Rs. 19,000
Mar 4	Received two cheques from Rajesh each of Rs. 5,000. One is crossed while the other is bearer
Mar 5	Bearer cheque received from Rajesh is endorsed to Tarun in full settlement of Rs. 5,050
Mar 6	Settled Ramesh's account of Rs. 2,025 by a cheque of Rs. 2,000
Mar 7	The crossed cheque of Rajesh is returned as dishonored by the bank. The bank has debited our account with Rs. 5 as a bank charges.
Mar 8	Drew from the bank for personal expenses Rs. 200, and for office use Rs. 3,000
Mar 9	Banked all Cash, keeping a balance of Rs. 100 only in hand.

Enter the following transactions in the Cash Book with Cash, Discount and Bank Columns.

1995	
July 1	Balance of Cash in hand Rs. 1,400 Overdraft at bank Rs. 5,000
July 4	Invested further capital of Rs. 10,000 out of which Rs. 6,000 deposited in the Bank
July 5	Sold goods for Cash Rs. 3,000
July 6	Collected from debtor of last year Rs. 8,000, discount allowed to them Rs. 200
July 10	Purchased goods for cash Rs. 5,500
July 11	Paid Leela Vilas, our creditor Rs. 2,500, discount allowed Rs. 65
July 13	Commission paid to our agent Rs. 530
July 14	Rent paid Rs. 50
July 14	Electricity charges paid Rs. 10
July 16	Drew cheque for personal use Rs. 700
July 17	Cash Sales Rs. 2,500
July 18	Collection from Arjun Rs. 4000; deposited in the bank next day.
July 19	Drew from bank for office use Rs. 500
July 22	Drew cheque for petty cash Rs. 150
July 24	Dividend received by cheque Rs. 50, deposited in the Bank the same day.
July 25	Commission received by cheque Rs. 230; deposited in the bank on 28th
July 29	Drew from the bank for salary of the office staff Rs. 1,500
July 30	Cash Deposited in the bank Rs. 10,000

Ans: Cash Rs. 810(Dr) ; Bank Rs. 11,930(Dr)

***Example* 6:** Mr. Sagar, a Chemist of Jalandhar City, maintains Cash Book with bank column. Enter the following transactions of Nov 21, 1996 in the Cash Book and balance the same.

1. Balance at the beginning of the day : Cash – 150, Andhra Bank – 25,000, Bank of India (Overdraft) – 3,000
2. Received a cheque of Rs. 5,350 from Merman Bros. In full settlement of invoice for Rs. 5,500. The cheque was deposited in Bank of India, which charges Rs. 3 as collection charges.
3. Cash Purchases Rs. 10,000 paid barer cheque on Andhra Bank
4. Transferred Rs. 5,000 from Andhra Bank to Bank of India
5. Withdrew Rs. 5,000 from Andhra Bank (Rs. 3,000 for office use and Rs. 2,000 for personal use.)
6. Paid advance salary to manager Rs. 1,000 by bearer cheque on Bank of India.

Exercise 1: Prepare a Cash Book from the following trapnsactions:

1996		
March 1	Cash in hand	250
	Balance with Canara Bank	6,750
	Balance with Andhra Bank (Overdraft)	2,575
March 6	Bought furniture & issued cheque on Canara Bank	1,500
March 8	Transferred from Canara Bank to Andhra Bank	1,980
March 9	Sale of Machinery Payment recd. In cash.	2,200
March 12	New Machinery purchased and cheque issued at A.B	1,470
March 15	Deposited into Canara Bank	680
March 20	Goods sold for Rs. 9,230 out of which deposited Rs. 5,000 in Andhra Bank and Balance in Canara Bank	
March 29	Withdrew from Canara Bank for personal use	340

***Petty Cash Book*:** Every business house has to spend small amounts in several miscellaneous items. There are certain payments which cannot be made by issuing cheques such as, postage stamps, telegrams, clearing charges, octroi, rickshaw, coolie charges, cartage, etc., because they are so small in nature and the concerned recipient will hesitate for receiving the payment. Thus, it is essential to leave some cash in the office with junior cashier for such disbursements. This cash is called petty cash and the record of receipt and payment in a book is known as "Petty Cash Book" and the person handling this cash is known as "Petty Cashier".

The Petty Cash Book is usually maintained when all the cash transactions are passed through Bank but it is not a hard & fast rule. However, even if all the cash transactions are not passed through Bank, there may be a Petty Cashier in addition to the Chief Cashier.

The Imprest System: According to this system, a round sum necessary for possible needs of the business for meeting the petty cash expenses for the week or month is drawn by a cheque and handed over to the petty cashier. The petty cashier finds out the amount spent during the period and get a cheque for the exact amount expanded by him so that he may start the next period with the same amount as in the beginning of the last period. For example, Rs. 3000 are given to the petty cashier on June 1st and he has spent Rs. 260 during the month, he will be paid Rs. 260 so that he may again start next month with Rs. 3000. This system in known as imprest system of Petty Cash Book.

***Example* 7:** Record the following transactions in the petty cash book.

1995		
Feb 1	Amount received from the Head Cashier	100-00
Feb 2	Purchased Stationery	5-00
Feb 5	Postage	12-50
Feb 7	Printing Charges	6-00
Feb 10	Paid Tonga Charges	1-50
	Coolie Charges	0-50
Feb 15	Sent a Telegram to Anitha and Vanitha	1-20
Feb 25	Postage	2-10
Feb 26	Printing Charges	10-50
Feb 28	Purchased (Twine) Sutle, Sua etc.	1-00
Feb 29	Paid Cartage	0-50
Feb 30	Stationery Purchased	2-20
Feb 31	Paid for Ricksaw Charges 0-50	

Dr **Cr**

Date	**Particulars**	**V.No.**	**L.F**	**Amount (Rs.)**	**Date**	**Particulars**	**V.No.**	**L.F**	**Amount (Rs.)**
1995			1995						
Feb 1	To Cash A/c		100-00		Feb 2	By Stationery			5-00
					Feb 5	By Postage			12-50
					Feb 7	By Printing Charges			6-00
					Feb 10	By Tonga Charges			1-50
					Feb 10	By Coollie Charges			0-50
					Feb 15	By Telegram			1-20
					Feb 25	By Postage			2-10
					Feb 26	By Printing Charges			10-50
					Feb 28	By Twine			1-00
					Feb 29	By Cartage			0-50
					Feb 30	By Stationery			2-20
					Feb 31	By Rickshawcharges			0-50
					Feb 31	By Balance C/d			56-50
			100-00						100-00
Mar 1	To Balance B/d		56-50						
	To Cash A/c		43-50						

Exercise 2: Record the following transactions in a Petty Cash Book.

June 1	Amount Received from the Head Cashier	10-00
June 2	Purchased Stationery	7-00
June 5	Postage	10-50
June 7	Printing Charges	1-50
June 10	Paid Tonga Charges	1-20
	Coolie Charges	5-00
June 15	Sent a Telegram to Madhusudhan	2-20
June 25	Postage	2-10
June 26	Printing Charges	8-00
June 28	Purchase (Twine) Sutle, Sua etc.	2-00
June 29	Paid Cartage	1-00
June 30	Stationery Purchased	3-20
June 31	Paid for Rickshaw Charges	5-50

Analytical Petty Cash Book: If the petty cashier is to analyze the petty cash payment which will disclose the money spent by debiting the relevant accounts instead of petty expenses account. This book has two sides. In the left hand side records receipts of cash from chief cashier. The right hand side records payments and analysis of payments. There are several columns to record payment such as wages, cartage, postage & stamps etc. The Petty Cash Book is balanced periodically.

Posting: The posting does not differ from the posting of simple Cash Book with the exception that the item on the credit side of analytical petty Cash Book are not posted individually and date wise. However, periodical totals of the extended columns are debited to the relative accounts in the ledger. But the ledger or personal accounts are debited individually and date wise. This method is followed when the petty Cash Book forms part of the Double Entry System.

Where the Petty Cash Book is regarded only a Memorandum Book, a Petty Cash account is opened in the ledger by debiting through Cash Book entry with the original imprest amount. A journal entry is passed periodically from Petty Cash Book analysis columns, debiting the various heads of expenses and crediting petty cash account in journal proper.

Record the following transactions in Analytical Petty Cash Book. Post them into ledger and prepare Petty Cash Account.

1995		
Mar 1	Amount received from the Head Cashier	50-00
Mar 2	Purchased Stationery	5-00
Mar 5	Postage	10-50
Mar 7	Printing Charges	5-00
Mar 10	Paid Tonga Charges	1-00
	Coolie Charges	1-50
Mar 15	Sent a Telegram to Prasad & Gopi	1-20
Mar 25	Postage	2-10
Mar 26	Printing Charges	8-50
Mar 28	Purchased (Twine), Sutle, Sua etc.	1-00
Mar 29	Paid Cartage	0.50
Mar 30	Stationery Purchased	1-20
Mar 31	Paid for Rickshaw Charges	0.50

Journal Proper

Date	Particulars	L.F	Dr. Amount	Dr.Amount
1995			Rs.	Rs.
Mar 30	Postage A/c Dr.		13-80	
	Stationery A/c Dr.		6-20	
	Printing A/c Dr.		13-50	
	Coolie and Cartage A/c Dr.3-50			
	Twine Expenses A/c Dr.		1-00	
	To Petty Cash A/c			
	(For Petty Cash Expenses)		38-00	

Ledger

Postage A/c

Dr Cr

Date	Particulars	L.F	Amount (Rs.)	Date	Particulars	L.F	Amount (Rs.)
1995							
Mar 30	The Petty Cash A/c		13-80				

Stationery A/c

Dr Cr

Date	Particulars	L.F	Amount (Rs.)	Date	Particulars	L.F	Amount (Rs.)
1995							
Mar 30	To Petty Cash A/c		6-20				

Analytical Petty Cash Book

Receipt	Date	C.B Falio	Particulars	V.No	Payments	Postage and Telegram	Stationery	Printing	Coolie	Twine Exp.	Sundries
Rs.	**1995**				**Rs.**	**Rs.**	**Rs.**	**Rs.**	**Rs.**	**Rs.**	**Rs.**
50-00	Mar 1		To Cash								
"	Mar 2		By Stationery		5-00	---	5-00	---	---	---	---
"	Mar 5		By Postage		10-50	10-50	---	---	---	---	---
"	Mar 7		By Printing Charges		5-00	---	---	5-00	---	---	---
"	Mar 10		By Tonga Charges		1-00	---	---	---	1-00	---	---
"	Mar 10		By Coolie Charges		1-50	---	---	---	1-50	---	---
"	Mar 15		By Telegram		1-20	1-20	---	---	---	---	---
"	Mar 25		By Postage		2-10	2-10	---	---	---	---	---
"	Mar 26		By Printing Charges		8-50	---	---	8-50	---	---	---
"	Mar 28		By Twine Expenses		1-00	---	---	---	---	1-00	---
"	Mar 29		By Cartage		0-50	---	---	---	0-50	---	---
"	Mar 30		By Stationery		1-20	---	1-20	---	---	---	---
"	Mar 31		By Rickshaw		0-50	---	---	---	0-50	---	---
			Charges		**50-00**	**38-00**	**13-80**	**6-20**	**13-50**	**3-50**	**1-00**
	Apr 1		To Balance B/d 12-00								
			To cash 38-00								

Printing A/c

Dr | Cr

Date	Particulars	L.F	Amount (Rs.)	Date	Particulars	L.F	Amount (Rs.)
1995							
Mar 30	To Petty Cash A/c		13-50				

Coolie and Cartage A/c

Dr | Cr

Date	Particulars	L.F	Amount (Rs.)	Date	Particulars	L.F	Amount (Rs.)
1995							
Mar 30	To Petty Cash A/c		3-50				

Twine Expenses A/c

Dr | Cr

Date	Particulars	L.F	Amount (Rs.)	Date	Particulars	L.F	Amount (Rs.)
1995							
Mar 30	To Petty Cash A/c		1-00				

Petty Cash A/c

Dr | Cr

Date	Particulars	L.F	Amount (Rs.)	Date	Particulars	L.F	Amount (Rs.)
1995							
Mar 1	To Cash A/c		50-00	Mar 30	By Postage A/c		13-80
Apr 1	To Cash A/c		38-00		By Stationery A/c		6-20
					By Printing A/c		13-50
					By Coolie and Cartage A/c		3-50
					By Twine Expenses A/c		1-00

Exercise 3 : Raghavendra maintains Analytical Petty Cash Book. From Particulars given below prepare a Petty Cash Book, Posting it to Ledger direct :

1998		
Nov 1	Received Rs. 50 from the Chief Cashier	
Nov 2	Paid for Postage	0-50
Nov 3	Telegram to Chennai	2-50
Nov 4	Bus Fare to Karnataka	5-00
Nov 5	Carriage on Goods	2-00

1998		
Nov 6	Paid for traveling Expenses	2-50
Nov 10	Cartage for sending goods to stores	1-50
Nov 15	Tea and refreshment to Staff	5-75
Nov 20	Paid for stationery	4-00
Nov 25	Paid for advertisement	9-00
Nov 28	Paid for wages	8-50
Nov 31	Paid for Printing	6-75

***Advantages of petty cash book*:** The following are the advantages of Perry Cash Book:

- ***Saving of labor*:** By preparing Petty Cash Book, all the petty expenses are neither recorded in the Cash Book nor the ledger accounts are prepared. Thus it saves labor.
- ***Saving of time*:** As the petty expenses, are recorded in the Petty Cash Book, it saves the time of Head Cashier.
- ***Less chances of mistake*:** At the end of the month, the head cashier checks the Petty Cash Book and then the Petty Cashier is given imprest for meeting the expenses of next month. Thus, there are very remote chances of mistake.
- ***Simple method*:** It is very simple to maintain the petty cash book. All the expenses are shown very easily in the petty cash book. Thus the accounts of petty expenses are accurately maintained.
- ***Less chances of fraud*:** It is essential to keep the vouchers of all the petty expenses. Thus, it minimizes the chances of fraud.
- ***Easy for posting*:** While making the posting, the total amount of each account is posted in the Ledger. Thus, it is simple to post the items in the respective ledger accounts.

Other day books

In a large organization, usually there is more number of transactions of similar nature. In order to maintain a proper record of all such transactions, the organization maintains special journals for these purposes known as 'Day Books'. The commonly used day books are 1. Purchases Journal 2. Sales Journal 3. Purchases Return Journal and 4. Sales Return Journal.

***Purchases journal*:** It is also called 'Invoice Book' and is used for recording purchase of goods on credit. The cash purchases are not recorded in it. Instead of that cash purchases are recorded in the Cash Book. Other purchases such as purchase of office equipment, furniture, building (i.e., assets) are recorded in general journal if purchased on credit or in Cash Book if purchased for cash.

Purchases journal

Date 2000	Invoice No	Name of the Supplier	L.F	Amount (Rs.)
Nov 1	1254	Mercury Lab	4	6,200-00
Nov 4	2410	IBM	8	5,600-00
Nov 6	4134	Intex	10	4,700-00
Nov 15	550	Frontech	25	2,100-00
Nov 20	8102	Pharma Pulse	30	4,600-00
Nov 30	5213	Logitech	45	4,500-00
				27,700-00

The entries into purchases Journal are recorded from the invoices or bills received from the suppliers of the goods. The trade discount and other details are not recorded in the purchases journal.

The transactions which are properly recorded in purchases journal are then posted to the ledger. The posting to the individual supplier account may be done daily on the credit side of their accounts. The monthly total of the purchases book is posted to the debit side of purchases account in the ledger. The format and preparation of the purchases journal is given in above Table.

***Sales journal*:** It is also called day book and is used for recording sale of goods on credit. Cash sales are recorded in the Cash Book. If an asset is sold on credit it is recorded in the general journal. The entries into sales journal are recorded from the sales invoices or bills issued by the firm to the customers.

The transactions recorded in the sales journal are then posted to the ledger. The posting to the individual customer's accounts may be made daily on the debit side of their accounts. The monthly total of the sales journal is posted to the credit side of sales account :

The format and preparation of the sales journal is illustrated below:

Sales journal

Date 2001	Invoice No	Name of the Supplier	L.F	Amount (Rs.)
Mar 3	2160	Mahaveer, Raipur	20	700-00
Mar 5	2170	Ram Lal, Gauhati	28	1,460-00
Mar 8	2180	Sri Krishna, Mumbai	38	2,100-00
Mar 18	2190	Prasad, Delhi	25	400-00
Mar 25	2120	Shyam, Haryana	30	4,200-00
				8,860-00

Purchases Return Journal: This journal is used for recording transactions relating to return of goods purchased on credit. When the goods purchased are returned to the supplier for any reason, a debit note is prepared in duplicate. The original one is sent to the supplier for making necessary entries in his books and the duplicate copy is kept for official record. A debit note contains the name of the party to whom the goods have been returned, details of the goods returned and reason for returning the goods. Each debit note is numbered serially and dated.

The individual amounts are posted immediately by making a debit entry in the party's account. The monthly total of the purchases returns journal is credited to the purchases return accounts. The format and preparation of the purchases returns journal is illustrated below:

Purchases return journal

Date 2003	Debit Note	Name of the Supplier	L.F	Amount (Rs.)
Nov 13	28	Ramlal, Chennai		1,900-00
Nov 25	32	Essr Pharma, Delhi		4,200-00
Nov 28	35	R.K. Pharma, Hyderabad		2,100-00
				8,200-00

Sales Return Journal: This Journal is used for recording transactions relating to return of goods which were sold by the firm to customers on credit. On receipt of goods from the customer, a credit note is prepared in duplicate. The credit note contains details relating to the name of the customer, details of goods received back and the amount. Each credit note is serially numbered and dated.

The individual amounts are posted immediately by making an entry on the credit side of the party's account and the monthly total of the sales returns journal is debited to sales returns account.

The format and preparation of the sales returns journal is illustrated below :

Sales return journal

Date 2003	Debit Note	Name of the Supplier	L.F	Amount (Rs.)
Apr. 15	15	Shyam, Kolkatta		1,400-00
Apr. 20	18	Krishna, Karnataka		2,050-00
Apr. 25	20	G.K. Raghu, Mumbai		3,200-00
				6,650-00

Review Questions

Short Answer Questions

1. What is the purpose of providing L.F in Journal and J.F in the Ledger Account?
2. What is the basic principle of Double Entry Book Keeping System?
3. Explain the different types of the Accounts with examples?
4. What is posting?
5. What is the difference between Journal and a Ledger?

Essay Questions

1. What is a Journal? Give a specimen of Journal showing few entries?
2. Explain the meaning and purpose of a Ledger? How will you make posting from a Journal and Cash Book to a Ledger?
3. What do you know about Book Keeping? How does it differ from Accounting? What are the basic principles of Double Entry Book Keeping?
4. What is an Account? Explain the different types of Accounts with suitable Examples?
5. Define a Cash Book? What is the use of it? Explain the different types of Cash Books? Give the typical format for each case?
6. What is a Petty Cash Book? How will you maintain the Petty Cash Book? Explain it by giving a format of a Petty Cash Book?
7. Enter the following transactions in the Journal :

2004	Mar 1	Cash brought as Capital Rs. 10,000
	Mar 5	Goods purchased from Sagar Rs. 4,500
	Mar 9	Sold goods for Cash Rs. 1,000
	Mar 14	Paid Rent Rs. 500
	Mar 16	Received Commission Rs. 400
	Mar 25	Purchased Machinery for Cash Rs. 4,000
	Mar 30	Paid Wages Rs. 1,500

8. Journalize the following transactions:

2002	May 1	Cash brought into business Rs. 40,000 and tools Rs. 10,000
	May 2	Purchased goods from Rao Rs. 10,000.
	May 3	Paid Cash to Rao Rs. 3,000
	May 4	Sold goods to Kalyan Rs. 7,000
	May 4	Sold goods to Kalyan on Cash Rs. 2,700
	May 12	Received Cash from Kumar Rs. 2,000
	May 18	Paid in to Bank Rs. 2,500
	May 19	With drew from bank Rs. 1,900
	May 21	Purchased buildings Rs. 14,000
	May 22	Drawn Cash for personal use Rs. 300
	May 24	Interest received on Investments Rs. 140
	May 27	Bought Govt. Bonds Rs. 2,000
	May 30	Loan given to Rama Rao through Bank Rs. 400
	May 31	Mr. Murthy is appointed as a Manager for the salary Rs. 2000

9. Journalize the following transactions and post the into Kiran's Account.

1999	Jan 1	Amount owned by Kiran to the firm Rs. 3,000
	Jan 4	Sold good to Kiran Rs. 1,500
	Jan 7	Received cash from Kiran Rs. 600
	Jan 8	Returned goods by Kiran Rs. 100
	Jan 9	Bought furniture from Kiran Rs. 1,000
	Jan 10	Purchased goods from Kiran and paid cash Rs. 400
	Jan 20	Paid Cash to Kiran Rs. 600
	Jan 25	Bought Machinery from Kiran Rs. 1,200
	Jan 30	Sold goods to Kiran on Cash Rs. 700

10. Journalize the following transactions and prepare the ledger Accounts.

2000	Dec 1	Mr. Sagar brought the capital into the business Rs. 10,000
	Dec 2	Purchased goods Rs. 100
	Dec 3	Bought furniture and paid Cash Rs. 400
	Dec 5	Sold goods to Gopi & Co. Rs. 500
	Dec 6	Cash Sales Rs. 200
	Dec 6	Goods returned by Gopi & Co. Rs. 50
	Dec 10	Sold goods to Murthy Bros. Rs. 450
	Dec 12	Bought a Bike for office use and paid Cash Rs. 400
	Dec 14	Received returns from Murthy Bros. Rs. 40
	Dec 16	Sold goods on Cash to Pavan & Sons Rs. 150
	Dec 19	Commission received from Chandrika & Co. Rs. 50
	Dec 22	With drew for personal use Rs. 200
	Dec 24	Goods with drawn for personal use Rs. 100
	Dec 28	Received a Cheque from Rao & Co worth Rs. 200 in order to goods sold
	Dec 31	Paid Salaries to Office Staff Rs. 500
	Dec 31	Paid lighting charges by cheque Rs. 30

11. Prepare the necessary subsidiary books and enter the following transactions and also prepare the concerned ledger Accounts:

1998	Feb 1	Purchased goods from Ramakrishna Rs. 650
	Feb 3	Sold goods to Rajiv Rs. 300
	Feb 4	Bought goods from Srinivas Rs. 450
	Feb 5	Brahmanandam purchased goods from us Rs. 250
	Feb 5	Returned goods to Ramakrishna Rs. 20
	Feb 6	Received returns from Rajiv Rs. 20
	Feb 7	Sold goods to Shiva Rs. 280
	Feb 9	Bought goods from Vikram Rs. 540
	Feb 10	Returns by Shiva Rs. 15
	Feb 15	Returns from Brahmanandam Rs. 20
	Feb 16	Purchased goods from Prasad Rs. 350
	Feb 17	Cash Purchases Rs. 500
	Feb 18	Goods returned to Prasad Rs. 45
	Feb 19	Cash sales Rs. 1,000

12. Enter the following transactions in the necessary cash book:

1995	March 1	Balance b/d Rs. 4,000
	March 2	Received Cash from Kishan Rs. 300
	March 5	Paid Rent Rs. 200
	March 7	Cash sales Rs. 400
	March 9	Paid cash to Raghuram Rs. 700
	March 10	Bought Furniture Rs. 900
	March 11	Advertisement Rs. 50
	March 13	Received Cash from Kiran Rs. 500
	March 14	Paid to Gopi Rs. 400
	March 15	Cash Sales Rs. 300
	March 16	Cash Purchases Rs. 1,200
	March 18	Prepaid rent Rs. 50
	March 20	Purchases from Prasad Rs. 800
	March 22	Made sales to Raghuveer Rs. 700
	March 23	Returns received Rs. 50
	March 25	Travelling expenses paid Rs. 50
	March 26	Paid electricity charges Rs. 80
	March 28	Out standing wages Rs. 100

(*Ans:* Cash Balance Rs. 1,920/-)

13. Two Columns Cash Book (a) Cash Book with Discount & Cash Columns:
Record the given transactions in the Double Columns Cash Book:

1998	July 1	Cash in hand (Balance) Rs. 7,500
	July 2	Received on Account of Sudhakar Rs. 3,200 and discount allowed Rs. 50
	July 10	Sold good for Rs. 2,000
	July 15	Received on A/c of Ramanadham Rs. 2,500 and allowed discount Rs. 35
	July 18	Paid to Gokul Rs. 1,800 and discount received Rs. 35
	July 26	Paid Cash to Mohan Rs. 900 and discount received Rs. 15
	July 28	Drawings Rs. 250
	July 30	Salaries Rs. 1,000
	July 30	Paid for Petty Expenses Rs. 50

(*Ans :* Cash Balance : 11,200/- Discount Allowed (Dr) 85/-, Discount Received (Cr) 50/)

14. Compile the two columns Cash Book and Show the Discount Account in the Ledger.

2000	March 1	Cash in Hand Rs. 10,000
	March 2	Purchases Rs. 700
	March 3	Made Sales for Cash Rs. 800
	March 7	Cash Paid to Bhanu Rs. 570, and discount received Rs. 30
	March 9	Cash received from Anand Rs. 475 and discount allowed 5 %
	March 10	Received Commission Rs. 400
	March 11	Bought Stationery Rs. 200

March 14	Received Cash from Naresh Rs. 760 and discount allowed 5%
March 16	Paid Cash to Mahendra Rs. 679 and discount received 3%
March 18	Paid Wages Rs. 350
March 19	Received dividends Rs. 450
March 20	Drawings Rs. 400
March 22	Sold his own cycle for Rs. 500 and brought in to the business
March 28	Cash Purchases Rs. 200
March 30	Cash in excess of Rs. 10,000 was paid into bank.

(***Ans:*** Cash Paid into Bank Rs. 286, Discount (Dr.) 65/- and Discount (Cr.) 51/-)

15. Prepare Three Columns Cash Book from the following transactions and bring down the balance for the start of next month.

2004	Nov 1	Cash in hand Rs. 1,450, Cash at Bank Rs. 6,500
	Nov 2	Paid into Bank by Ramu Rs. 630, Discount allowed him Rs. 20
	Nov 2	Paid advertisements by Cheque Rs. 350
	Nov 3	Cash Sales Rs. 250
	Nov 3	Paid Salaries Rs. 435
	Nov 4	With drew cash from bank for office use Rs. 600
	Nov 5	Cash Drawings Rs. 200
	Nov 6	Issued a Cheque to Ramana & Sons Rs. 1,000, Discount received Rs. 25
	Nov 8	Received a cheque from Mehta & Bros, Rs. 800, Discount Allowed them Rs. 20
	Nov 9	Cash Paid into Bank Rs. 1,000
	Nov 10	Sold the Machinery and the same paid into bank Rs. 2,500.
	Nov 12	Cheque dishonored which is received for Mehta Bros.
	Nov 15	Bought Machinery and Paid by cheque Rs. 1,000, Paid installation charges Rs. 500
	Nov 17	Bank Charges defined in the Pass Book Rs. 10

(***Ans:*** Cash Balance Rs. 165, Bank Balance Rs. 7670, Dis (Dr) 40/-, Dis (Cr.) 45/-)

16. Prepare the Three Columns Cash Book from the following Particulars :

1998	May 1	Cash Balance Rs. 10,000 and Bank Balance Rs. 8,000
	May 2	Cash Paid into Bank Rs. 2,000
	May 10	Drawn Cash from Bank Rs. 1,000
	May 12	Received Cheque from Mithra for Rs. 3,000 and paid the same into bank immediately
	May 14	Received cheque from Shankar for Rs. 2,000
	May 15	Drawings by Cheque Rs. 500
	May 18	Shankar's Cheque is sent to Bank for Collection
	May 20	Issued Cheque to Sundaram Rs. 1,500

	May 28	Paid Salaries by Cheque Rs. 1,200
	May 29	Received Cheque towards commission Rs. 200 was sent to bank on the same date.
	May 30	Sold goods for Cash Rs. 500, by Cheque Rs. 700
	May 30	Balance of Cash Paid into Bank except Rs. 2,000 being in office.

(*Ans:* Cash Balance Rs. 2,000, Cash Paid into Bank Rs. 8,200, Bank Balance Rs. 19,200, Discount (Dr.) – NIL, Discount (Cr.) – NIL)

17. Prepare the Petty Cash Book of Sri Govinda Rao from the given particulars :

1996	June 1	Received a Cheque from head cashier for petty disbursements Rs. 250.
	June 2	Paid for Postage Rs. 15
	June 3	Paid for stationery Rs. 20
	June 5	Paid for traveling expenses Rs. 26
	Jun e 6	Paid for carriage Rs. 12
	June 7	Paid for Office Cleaning Rs. 9
	June 10	Paid for Printing Rs. 20
	June 12	Bought stationary Rs. 18
	June 15	Petty Expenses Paid Rs. 4
	June 16	Postage Paid Rs. 12
	June 18	Paid for Carfare Rs. 25
	June 20	Paid for Office Cleaning Rs. 8
	June 26	Paid Madhukar on Account Rs. 30
	June 28	Paid for cartage Rs. 6
	June 30	Spent for repairs Rs. 5

18. Write up the analytical petty cash book from the following and also show the necessary entries to be followed :

2004	Feb 1	Gave an imprest cheque for Rs. 250 to the petty cashier to begin with
	Feb 2	Paid for Postage Rs. 10
	Feb 3	Paid for stationary Rs. 35
Feb 6		Paid for traveling Expenses Rs. 20
Feb 8		Coolie Charges Paid Rs. 14
	Feb 9	Sent a Telegram to Mumbai Rs. 12
	Feb 10	Paid for Printing Rs. 25
	Feb 15	Auto Charges Paid Rs. 25
	Feb 18	Tea for Guests Rs. 10
	Feb 20	Paid for Stationary Rs. 15
	Feb 22	Paid for Carriage Rs. 8
	Feb 24	Wages to Office Cleaner Rs. 10
	Feb 26	Paid to Mohan on A/c Rs. 30
	Feb 28	Sent Registered Notice to Land Lord Rs. 9

(*Ans:* Cash Balance Rs. 34)

19. Rule a Petty Cash Book with suitable analysis columns and enter up the following transactions :

The Book is kept in imprest system, the amount of imprest being Rs. 200. on Oct 16, 2003.

2004	Oct 16	Paid Cartage on goods Rs. 10
	Oct 16	Taxi Hire Rs. 8
	Oct 16	Postage Expenses Rs. 12
	Oct 17	Stationary Purchased Rs. 16
		Oct 17 Bus Fare Rs. 4
	Oct 17	Refreshments to Customers Rs. 5
	Oct 18	Wages Paid Rs. 20
	Oct 18	Coolie Charges Paid Rs. 6
	Oct 19	Telegram Rs. 5
	Oct 19	Tips Paid Rs. 6
	Oct 19	Paid to Ramlal on Account Rs. 15
	Oct 20	Bus fare Rs. 5
	Oct 20	Paid Printing bill Rs. 8
	Oct 20	Cartage on goods Rs. 4
	Oct 21	Wages Paid Rs. 15
	Oct 21	News Paper bill Paid Rs. 8

(***Ans:*** Cash Balance 53/-)

16 Trial Balance and Errors

16.1 | Definition and Importance

LEARNING OBJECTIVES

- *Definition and importance of Trial Balance*
- *Rectification of Errors*
- *Problems and postings related to trial balance*
- *Rectifying Journal entries.*

"Trial Balance is a statement containing the balances of all ledger accounts, as at any given date, arranged in form of debit and credit columns placed side by side and prepared with the object of checking the arithmetical accuracy of ledger postings". The fundamental principle of double entry system of book-keeping is that every debit has a corresponding credit and vice-versa of equal amount. Therefore, the total of the debit balances must equal in aggregate to the total of the credit balances when accounts are balanced. The agreement of the trial balance signifies that both the aspects of each transaction have been recorded and that the books are arithmetically correct. If the trial balance does not agree, it suggests that there are some errors which must be detected and rectified before the final accounts can be prepared.

The main function of Trial Balance is that it acts as a device to check the arithmetical accuracy of the accounting process, it shows that ledger postings have been properly made and balance in each account is computed correctly. It acts as a starting point for the preparation of final accounts. It facilitates the preparation of Trading Profit and Loss Account and Balance Sheet by making available the balances of all the accounts at one place.

It should be noted that agreement of Trial Balance does not necessarily prove the accuracy of all the entries and postings. It is simply a proof of the total amount debited to various accounts is equal to total amount credited to other accounts in the same period. Trial Balance is a means by which only the arithmetical accuracy of the accounting work is checked. There are certain errors which are not disclosed by Trial Balance.

16.2 | Total Method

Under this method, the debit and credit totals of each account are shown in the debit and credit columns of the trial balance.

16.3 | Balance Method

Under this method, the difference of each account is extracted. If the debit side of an account is bigger in amount than the credit side the difference is put in the debit column of the trial balance and if the credit side is bigger, the difference is written on the credit column of Trial Balance.

16.4 | Points to be Noted for the Preparation of Trial Balance

1. Accounts dealing with assets, expenses & losses will show debit balance.
2. Accounts dealing with liabilities, incomes and gain will show credit balance.
3. 'Sundry Debtors' is the total amount due from various debtors and 'Sundry Creditors' is the total amount due to various creditors.
4. Opening stock will show debit balance, generally closing stock will not appear in Trial Balance.
5. Reserves and Provisions such as General Reserve, Provision for doubtful debts, Reserve for discount on debtors will show credit balance. However Reserve for discount on Creditors will show debit balance.

16.5 | Accounts Appearing in Trial Balance on Debit and Credit Side

Debit Balance	**Credit Balance**
Personal Accounts	***Personal Accounts***
Sundry Debtors	Sundry Creditors

Bank Balance	Bank Overdraft
Loan or Advance given	Loan taken or Mortgage loan
Drawings A/c	Capital A/c
Prepaid Expenses	Outstanding Expenses
Real Accounts	***Real Accounts***
(a) Dealing with goods	(Dealing with goods)
Purchases Account	Sales Account
Opening Stock	Return Outwards Account
Return Inwards	**Nominal Accounts**
(b) Assets	All Incomes & gains
Land and Building	Such as Interest received
Plant and Machinery	Rent Received
Furniture	Commission received
Investments	Discount received
Goodwill	Reserves & Provisions
Nominal Accounts	Provision for Doubtful Debts
All Expenses and Losses	Provision for Discount on Debtors
Such as Salaries, Rent & Taxes	General Reserve etc.,
Carriage, Advertising.	Bad Debts etc.

16.6 | Examples

Prepare a Trial Balance from the Following Information

	Rs.
Capital Account	1,00,000
Plant and Machinery	1,60,000
Sales	3,54,000
Purchases	1,20,000
Returns Outwards	1,500
Returns Inwards	2,000
Opening Stock	60,000
Discount Allowed	700
Discount Received	1,600
Bank Charges	150
Sundry Debtors	90,000
Sundry Creditors	50,000
Salaries	13,600

Manufacturing Wages	20,000
Carriage Inwards	1,500
Carriage Outwards	2,400
Provision for Bad Debts	1,050
Rent, Rates and Taxes	20,000
Advertisements	4,000
Cash in Hand	1,800
Cash at Bank	12,000
Closing Stock	70,000

Solution:

Trial Balance As at ---------------

	Debit Balance Rs.	Credit Balance Rs.
Capital Account		1,00,000
Plant and Machinery	1,60,000	
Sales		3,54,000
Purchases	1,20,000	
Returns Outwards		1,500
Returns Inwards	2,000	
Opening Stock	60,000	
Discount Allowed	700	
Discount Received		1,600
Bank Charges	150	
Sundry Debtors	90,000	
Sundry Creditors		50,000
Salaries	13,600	
Manufacturing Wages	20,000	
Carriage Inwards	1,500	
Carriage Outwards	2,400	
Provision for Bad Debts		1,050
Rent, Rates, and Taxes	20,000	
Advertisements	4,000	
Cash in Hand	1,800	
Cash at Bank	12,000	
	5,08,150	5,08,150

16.7 | Rectification of Errors

Error is a mistake committed in Book-Keeping. Errors can be broadly divided into:

(a) Errors of Principle and (b) Clerical Errors.

Errors of Principle are committed when a transaction is not recorded according to accounting principles. For example business expenditure treated as personal expenditure etc.

Clerical Errors are those errors which are generally committed by the clerical staff while recording the transactions in the account books. Such errors may be :

1. ***Errors of Omission***: When a transaction is either completely or partially omitted from the books it is called error of omission. Ex : Purchase of goods on credit may be omitted to be entered in the purchases book, sale of goods on credit omitted to be posted in the personal account of the customer etc.
2. ***Errors of Commission***: Such errors arise when any transaction is incorrectly recorded either wholly or partially. *Ex*: entering wrong amount in subsidiary books, posting wrong amount to an account, posting correct amount to wrong side of an account etc.
3. ***Compensating Errors***: In case of such errors one error is compensated - by other. From another point of view, errors may be divided into two categories.
    1. Errors disclosed by Disagreement of Trial Balance.
    2. Errors not disclosed by disagreement of Trial Balance.

16.8 | Errors Disclosed by Trial Balance

1. Wrong totaling of Subsidiary Books
2. Items omitted to be posted from a subsidiary books into ledger.
3. Posting of a wrong amount to a ledger account.
4. Posting an amount on the wrong side of the ledger account.
5. Wrong additions or balancing of ledger accounts.
6. An item of subsidiary book posted twice to ledger account.
7. Omission of a balance of an account in the trial balance.
8. Balance of some account wrongly entered in the trial balance.
9. Balance of some account written on the wrong side of trial balance.

16.9 | Errors not • isclosed by a Trial Balance

1. Omission of an entry altogether in a subsidiary book.

2. Writing the wrong amount in the subsidiary books.
3. Posting an item on the correct side but in the wrong account.
4. Compensating errors.
5. Errors of Principle.

16.10 | Rectification of Errors Discovered before the Preparation of Trial Balance

1. **Errors affecting one account:** Such errors can be rectified by giving an explanatory note. Ex: "The Purchases Book is under cast by Rs. 500". As the mistake involves only one account, namely Purchases Account, rectification entry cannot be passed. The correction can be made by writing on the Debit side of Purchases Account.

   "To correction of under casting of Purchases Book for the month of——
   Rs. 500"
2. **Errors Affecting Two Accounts:** Such errors can be generally rectified by passing rectification entry. Ex : "A sale of Rs. 50 to A was wrongly debited to the account of B", can be rectified by passing the following rectification entry.

	Rs.	Rs.
A's Account	50	
To B's Account		50

Sometimes even though the mistake is in two accounts, rectification entry cannot be passed. *Ex*: "Rs. 300 received from Raghuram has been debited to Sundar (Cash Book correctly entered)". In this case rectification entry cannot be passed because the accounts of both Raghuram and Sundar have to be credited. This mistake can be rectified by giving explanatory note in both the accounts.

16.11 | Rectification of Errors Discovered •fter the Preparation of Trial Balance

If the Trial Balance does not tally in spite of best efforts, the presentation of final statement of accounts cannot be postponed for a long period. In such a case the difference of the Trial Balance is placed to a Suspense Account and the Trial Balance is made to tally. If the debit side is short, the Suspense Account will be debited and if the credit is less, Suspense Account will be credited.

As explained earlier, the difference in trial balance is generally due to the mistake which effect only one account. For correcting such errors the account to be corrected will be debited or credited as the case may be and the journal entry will be completed by crediting or debiting the Suspense Account. When all the mistakes are rectified the Suspense Account will show nil balance.

If the mistake is in two accounts, the normal rectification entry should be passed and Suspense Account should not be touched. There is a wrong notion in the minds of some students that if Suspense Account balance is given in the problem, then corrections have to be made only through Suspense Account. For example, if it is stated that "Carriage on Machinery Rs. 1,000 has been debited to Carriage Account" then Suspense Account will be neither debited nor credited. The rectification entry will be:

		Rs.	Rs.
Machinery Account	Dr.	1,000	
To Carriage Account			1,000

16.12 | Corrections in Next Trading Period

If corrections are to be made in the next Trading Period, a separate account called Profit and Loss Adjustment Account should be opened and all debits and credits in respect of nominal accounts for errors committed in previous Trading Period should be passed through that account. The balance of that account should be transferred to Capital Account. This method will ensure that the correction of mistakes of last year will not affect the Profit or Loss of the current year.

16.13 | Example

The following errors were located in the books of a business concern after books were closed and suspense account was created in order to agree the trial balance.

1. An Amount of Rs. 500 paid for the repair of furniture was debited to Furniture Account.
2. Goods bought from a merchant amounting to Rs. 55 had been posted to the credit of his account Rs. 550
3. A dishonored Bill Receivable for Rs. 400 returned by the bank had been credited to Bank Account and debited to Bills Receivable Account.
4. Sales Day Book was overcast by Rs. 400
5. General Expenses Rs. 28 were posted in the ledger as Rs. 82

Pass Journal entries to rectify the above mistakes and prepare the Suspense Account.

16.14 | Problems

1. The Trial Balance of a book-keeper shows an excess of debits over credits by Rs. 577. This difference is placed in a suspense account and books are closed. Later on the following are discovered. Rectify and also prepare Suspense Accounts:
   (a) A Credit item of Rs. 249 has been debited to a personal account Rs. 429
   (b) Rs. 900 Paid for furniture bought have been charged to purchases Account.
   (c) A discount allowed to a customer has been credited to him as Rs. 145 in place of Rs. 154.
   (d) The total of Return Inward Book has been added Rs. 10 short.
   (e) A cheque for Rs. 100 for petty cash was not posted into petty cash A/c

Solution:

Journal

(Rs.)	Particulars		L.F	Debit (Rs.)	Credit
	Repairs A/c	Dr		500	
1.	To Furniture A/c				500
	(Being the mistake of debiting				
	Furniture instead of repairs rectified)				
2.	Suppliers A/c	Dr		495	
	To Suspense A/c				495
	(Being the mistake of crediting suppliers				
	A/c with excess amount rectified)				
	Acceptor A/c	Dr			
3.	To Bills Receivable A/c			400	400
	(Being the mistake of debiting B/R A/c				
	instead of acceptor's a/c rectified)				
	Sales A/c	Dr.			
4.	To Suspense A/c			400	400
	(Being rectification of overcastting of				
	sales book)				
	Suspense A/c	Dr			
	To General Expenses A/c				
5.	(Being the mistake of debiting general expenses a/c with excess amount rectified)			54	54

Suspense A/c

Dr.			Cr.
	Rs.		Rs.
To Balance b/f		By Suppliers A/c	495
(Balancing figure)	841	By Sales A/c	400
To General Expenses A/c	54		
	895		895

2. Give rectifying Journal Entries for the following errors:
   1. A Purchase of goods from X amounting to Rs. 1,250 has been wrongly passed through the Sales Book.
   2. Rs. 1,500 paid for furniture purchased has been charged to ordinary purchases Account.
   3. A Cheque for Rs. 250 received from Swaroop was dishonored and had been posted to the debit of Sales Returns Account.
   4. An amount of Rs. 1,400 due from Chandu which had been written of as a bad debt was unexpectedly recovered and has been posted to the personal account of Chandu.
   5. Rs. 2,000 paid to cash for a typewriter was charged to Office Expenses Account.

Solution:

Journal

Date	Particulars	L.F	Debit(Rs.)		Credit (Rs.)
	Purchase A/c	Dr.		1,250	
1.	Sales A/c	Dr.		1,250	2,500
		To X			
	(Being purchase of goods has wrongly passed through the sales book, now rectified)				
	Furniture A/c	Dr.			
2.	To Purchase A/c		1,500	1,500	
	(Being amount paid for furniture has been charged to ordinary purchases, now rectified)				
	Swaroop A/c	Dr.			
3.	To Sales Returns A/c		250	250	
	(Being amount received from Swaroop by cheque was dishonored and debit to Sales Returns A/c now rectified)				

Contd...

Date	Particulars	L.F	Debit(Rs.)	Credit (Rs.)
4.	Chandu Dr.		1,400	1,400
	To Bad Debt Recovered A/c (Being amount written off as Bad Debt was recovered wrongly posted to personal A/C of Chandu, now rectified)			
	Office Equipment A/c Dr.			
5.	To Office Expenses A/c		2,000	2,000
	(Being Cash Paid for typewriter was charged to Office Expenses now rectified)			

3. There was on error in the Trial Balance of Mr. Vivek on 30th April, 1990 and the difference in books was carried to Suspense Account. On going through the books, you find that:

   1. Rs. 5,400 received from Kantha Rao were posted to the debit of his account.
   2. Rs. 1,000 being purchases return were posted to the debit of Purchase A/c.
   3. Discount Rs. 2,000 received were posted to the debit of Discount A/c
   4. Rs. 3,740 paid for repairs to Motor Car A/c as Rs. 1,740
   5. Rs. 4,000 paid to G. Balu were debited to the Account of K. Balu.

   Give journal entries with complete narration, to rectify the above errors and state what amount was carried to Suspense A/c

Solution:

Journal

Date	Particulars	L.F	Debit (Rs.)	Credit (Rs.)
1990	Suspense A/c Dr.		10,800	
April 30	To Kantha Rao			10,800
	(Being a sum of Rs. 5,400 received from Kantharao were posted to the debit of his a/c, Now rectified)			
	Suspense A/c Dr.		2,000	
	To Return A/c			1,000
	To Purchase A/c			1,000
	(Being the Purchases return of Rs. 1000 were posted to the debit of purchases A/c. Now rectified)			
	Suspense A/c Dr.		4,000	

Contd...

Date	Particulars	L.F	Debit (Rs.)	Credit (Rs.)
	To Discount A/c			2,000
	To Discount Received A/c			2,000
	(Being a sum of Rs. 2,000 of discount received was posted to the debit of discount A/c. Now Rectified)			
	Motor Car Repair A/c Dr.		3,740	
	To Motor Car A/c			1,740
	To Suspense A/c			2,000
	(Being a sum of Rs. 3,740 paid for repairs to motor car was debited to Motor Car A/c as Rs. 1,740. Now rectified)			
	G. Balu's A/c Dr.		4,000	
	To K. Balu's A/c			4,000
	(Being Rs. 4,000 paid to G. Balu were debited to the account of Balu's Now rectified)			

Suspense A/c

To Kantha Rao A/c	10,800	By Difference in T.B b/d (Balancing Figure)	14,800
To Purchases Return A/c	1,000	By Motor Car Repair	2,000
To Purchase A/c	1,000		
To Discount A/c	2,000		
To Discount Received A/c	2,000		
	16,800		16,800

4. Following errors were discovered in the books of a firm at 31st March 1996.
   - Rs. 13,000 spent on extension of factory building charged to repairs account.
   - Cheque of Rs. 450 received from Gopal is dishonored but its amount has been posted to allowance account.
   - Returns of Rs. 200 from Mahendra have been included in stock but no entry has been made in books of accounts.
   - Repairs of Machinery Rs. 260 have been added to machinery account.
   - An amount of Rs. 360 withdrawn for personal use by the proprietor of the firm has been debited to traveling expenses account.
   - An amount of Rs. 150/- of a cheque received through Ramanadham has been credited to his account.

Give journal entries with complete narration, to rectify the above errors.

Solution:

Journal

Date	Particulars	L.F	Debit (Rs.)	Credit (Rs.)
1996	Factory Building A/c	Dr.		13,000
March 31	To Repairs A/c			13,000
	(Being wrong posting to repairs account, Now rectified)			
	Gopal A/c	Dr.		
	To Allowance A/c		450	450
	(Being wrong posting to allowances account, Now rectified)			
	Returns Inward A/c	Dr.		
	To Mahendra A/c		200	200
	(Being entry made for omission)			
	Repairs A/c	Dr.		
	To Machinery A/c		260	260
	(Being wrong posting of machinery account, Now rectified)			
	Drawings A/c	Dr.		360
	To Travelling Expenses A/c			360
	(Being wrong posting to traveling expenses account, Now rectified)			
	Ramanadham A/c	Dr.		
	To Concerned Customer A/c		150	150
	(Being amout of Rs. 150 of a cheque received through ramanadham wrongly credited to his account, Now rectified)			

Review Questions

Short Answer Questions

1. Name the errors which do not affect the Trial Balance?
2. Describe the method of preparing a Trial Balance?
3. What is a one sided error?
4. Explain an error of commission with a suitable example?
5. What are the limitations of a Trial Balance?
6. What are the causes of Accounting Errors?
7. Explain the error of Principle with a suitable example?
8. Write the Names of errors which do not affect a Trial Balance?

Long Answer Questions

1. Explain the various errors disclosed by a trial balance with suitable examples?
2. Explain the meaning of a trial balance? What are the different methods of preparing a Trial Balance?
3. What are the main objectives of a Trial Balance?
4. From the following balances taken from the ledger of Sri. Sagar, prepare Trial Balance.

	Rs.
Purchases	15,750
Sales	21,000
Returns Inwards	600
Carriage Inwards	50
Freight outwards	65
Salaries and Wages	1,572
Rent and Taxes	526
Traveling Expenses	387
Opening Stock	12,000
Discount Allowed	225
Discount Received	110
Commission Paid	108
Bank Account	6,027
Sundry Debtors	6,800
Trade Creditors	5,000
Capital Account	28,500
Drawings Account	4,500
Bills Receivable	8,000
Bills Payable	2,000
Closing Stock	15,800

(Ans : Total Trial Balance Rs. 56,610)

5. Rectify the following errors discovered before the preparation of Trial balance.

   1. Machinery Purchased for Rs. 10,000 debited to Purchases Account
   2. The total of Purchases Book is Rs. 1,500 short.
   3. Sales Books is overcast by Rs. 1,250
   4. An item of Rs. 58 was posted as Rs. 85 in the Purchases Account.
   5. Goods purchased from Sagar worth Rs. 500 were omitted to be entered in the Purchases Book.
   6. Total of the Returns Inward Book is undercast by Rs. 150.
   7. A sale of Rs. 235 to Sastry has been debited to his account as Rs. 352
   8. Cash received from K. Srikanth Rs. 300 posted to the account of N. Srikanth.
   9. An amount of Rs. 1,500 withdrawn by the proprietor for personal expenses has been debited to Trade Expenses Account.
   10. Salary Paid to Ramdas, a clerk, Rs. 500 stands debited to his personal account.
   11. Discount of Rs. 75 allowed by Samuel has not been entered in the Cash Book although correctly posted in the ledger in his account.

6. Correct the Following Errors

(a) Goods amounting Rs. 275 had been returned by a customer and were taken into stock, but no entry in respect thereof was made in the books.

(b) A Sale of Rs. 175 to Nagaraju was wrongly credited to his account.

(c) While posting the account of Ramakrishna from the purchases book, the purchase of Rs. 651 has been debited to him.

(d) A purchase of Rs. 785 from Prasad Bros. has been entered in the Purchases Book as Rs. 587

(e) Rs. 195 received from Sudesh has been debited to Suresh

(f) Goods taken by the proprietor Rs. 500 have not been entered in the books at all.

(g) Rs. 400 received from Dukhi against a debit previously written off has been credited to his account.

(h) A sale of Rs. 350 to Sastry has been entered in the Sales Book as Rs. 850

(i) A purchase of Rs. 600 from Gopi & Co. has been entered in the Sales Book.

(j) A sale of Rs. 900 to Sastry & Co. has been entered in the Purchases Book.

(k) A Contractor's bill for extension of Premises amounting to Rs. 5,000 has been debited to Building Repairs Account.

(l) On 26th December 1989, goods of the value of Rs. 450 were returned by Praveen Kumar and were taken into stock, but the returns were entered in the books under date 3rd January 1990, i.e. after the expiration of the financial year on 31st December 1989.

(m) A Bill Receivable for Rs. 550 received from Padma Rao had been dishonoured on maturity and was posted to the debit of "Allowances Account".

7. Write entries for the rectification of following errors

    1. Sales Book was overcast by Rs. 100
    2. A sale of Rs. 50 to A was wrongly debited to account of B
    3. General expenses of Rs. 18 was posted in the General ledger as Rs. 80
    4. A bill receivable for Rs. 155 was passed through bills Payable book. This bill was given by R
    5. Legal expenses Rs. 119 paid to Mr. Rao was debited to his personal account.
    6. Rs. 150 received from Gopi was debited to Govind.

8. Rectify the following errors by using Suspense Account

    1. Goods sold to Shyam Rs. 175 were not posted to his account
    2. Purchases Book total was overcast by Rs. 400
    3. Sales Book Total was undercast by Rs. 53
    4. Purchases Returns Book total was undercast by Rs. 16
    5. Cash received from Gopal Rs. 111 was posted to his account as Rs. 1,111
    6. Cash Paid to Ramna Rs. 770 was posted to his account Rs. 170.

17 Financial Statements

17.1 | Definition of Financial Statements

After preparation of the trial balance, the business organization prepare a statement in order to know the financial position of the firm and to find out profit or loss of the business. Such a statement is known as 'Financial Statement'.

The purpose of preparing financial statement is :

1. To know the present status of investments in the business.
2. The results achieved at the end of the year or at the end of the prescribed period.

The financial statement comprises of: 1. Profit and Loss Account (Income Statement) and 2. Balance Sheet (Statement of present financial position). These two statements Profit and Loss Account and Balance sheet together are known as "Final Accounts".

LEARNING OBJECTIVES

- *Definition and advantages of Financial Statements*
- *Profit and Loss Account*
- *Balance Sheet*
- *Preparation of Balance Sheet*
- *Grouping and recording of assets and liabilities*
- *Differences between Profit and Loss Account and Balance Sheet*
- *Differences between Balance Sheet and Trial Balance*
- *Financial Analysis*
- *Various Techniques of analyzing Financial Statements*

17.2 | Advantages of Financial Statements

1. The management can review up to date progress of the company and decide what action is to be taken to improve the business in future.

2. On the basis of financial statements, the shareholders can judge the future prospects of their investments and decide whether they can sell the shares or not.
3. From the financial statement, the employees can find out the present financial position of the company and the employees can decide whether the company is in a position to pay higher wages, bonus etc.

Limitations of financial statements

1. Financial statements reveal only the details in terms of money. Other important information like the working condition of the employees, administrative set up, sales policies of the company, quality of the product etc., are not recorded in the financial statements.
2. The profit shown in Profit and Loss Account and the financial position revealed by the Balance Sheet cannot be exactly true since these statements are only interim reports.

17.3 | Profit and Loss Account

Definition: Profit and Loss Account Statement is a financial statement. Profit and Loss Account is called as income statement.

Purpose of preparing profit and loss account: The purpose of preparing profit and loss account is to find out the net profit or net loss. If the total amount on the credit side is more than the debit side it shows 'Net Profit'. The net profit amount is added to the capital and entered in the debit side as 'To Net Profit'. If the total amount on the debit side is more than the credit side it shows 'Net Loss'. The net loss amount is deducted from the capital and entered in the credit side as 'By Net Loss'.

The net profit or net loss of the current year can be compared with that of previous years. Such comparison is helpful in controlling sale of goods and thus eliminating wastage.

Items to be entered in the debit side: The following items are to be entered in the debit side: The expenses like salaries to the employees, postage and telegram expenses, shop rent, any taxes paid by the company, repair charges, printing and stationary charges and other expenses spent by the company.

Items to be entered in the credit side: The following items are to be entered in the credit side. The incomes like gross profit, rent received, interest received, discount received, profit on sale of assets etc.

Preparation of profit and loss account: From trading account (it is an account prepared to find out gross profit or gross loss on the basis of purchases and sales), the gross profit or gross loss is determined. Then the gross profit is recorded on the credit side of the profit and loss account and the gross loss is recorded on the debit side of the profit and loss account. Afterwards the other incomes like rent received, interest received, discount received etc., are entered in the credit side. The expenses like salaries to the employees, rent paid, any taxes paid by the company, repair charges, printing and stationary charges etc., are entered in the debit side. The grand total on both debit and credit sides are obtained.

If the grand total on the credit side is more than the debit side, it shows 'Net Profit'. The net profit amount is added to the capital and entered in the debit side as 'To Net Profit'. If the grand total on the debit side is more than the credit side, it shows 'Net Loss'. The net loss amount is deducted from the capital and entered in the credit side as 'By Net Loss'.

Model form of Profit and Loss Account

Profit and Loss Account of Sagar & Co., for the year ending 31st March, 2000

Dr			Cr
Particulars	**Amount**	**Particulars**	**Amount**
To Salaries	500-00	By Gross Profit b/d	1,200-00
To Rent	100-00	By Rent received	200-00
To Taxes	50-00	By Interest received	300-00
To Repairs	50-00	By Discount received	100-00
To Printing and Stationery	100-00		
To Net Profit	1,000-00		
	1,800-00		1,800-00

17.4 | Balance Sheet

Definition: Balance Sheet is a financial statement or statement of accounts prepared to find out the exact financial position of the business on the last date of the financial year. It is called Balance Sheet because it is prepared on a sheet of ledger folio.

Purpose of preparing balance sheet: The Balance Sheet is prepared for the following purposes:

1. It shows the financial position of the business on a particular date.
2. It provides information regarding the nature and the cost of assets of the company.
3. It provides information regarding the nature and the cost of liabilities of the company.
4. It provides information about the total amount of money involved in running the business.

Preparation of balance sheet

1. Balance Sheet is prepared from the trial balance. There are two columns in the balance sheet namely Liabilities Column and Asset Column. All the liabilities are entered in the left hand side and all the assets are recorded in the right hand side.
2. The liabilities (left hand side) and the assets (right hand side) should be equal.
3. The following items are generally included in the balance sheet :
   - ***Current assets***: Current assets are temporary assets which are either in the form of cash or can be easily converted into cash within a year, e.g., cash at bank, bills, short–term securities etc.
   - ***Fixed assets***: Fixed assets are permanent assets, *e.g.,* land, building, machineries, furniture etc.
   - ***Current liabilities***: Liabilities expected to be cleared within a year or within short period are called current liabilities, *e.g.*, wages, salaries, rent, taxes etc.
   - ***Long-term liabilities***: Liabilities expected to be cleared after a period of one year or more are called long-term liabilities, *e.g.*, loans, mortgage etc.
   - ***Investments***: Investment represents funds invested in government securities, shares of companies etc.
   - ***Capital***: Capital is the amount invested by the proprietor/partners and the profit occur in the business.
   - ***Drawings***: Drawings are sums of money or goods withdrawn by the proprietor from the business.

Grouping and recording of assets and liabilities: While preparing balance sheet, the liabilities and assets are grouped and recorded. They can be grouped and recorded in the balance sheet by the following methods:

1. ***Order of Liquidity***: It means that the order in which they can be converted into cash. For example, the most liquid asset namely cash in hand is shown last in the balance sheet. Similarly the liabilities are arranged and shown in order of urgency of their repayment. For example, the most urgent repayment, *e.g.*, short term creditors are shown first and the least urgent repayment, *e.g.*, long term creditors are shown at the end. The business organizations which are run by a sole proprietor or by a group of partners follow this method.
2. ***Order of Permanence***: As per this method, the permanent assets and liabilities are shown first, followed by current assets and liabilities. Generally joint stock companies follow this method.

Model form of Balance Sheet

Balance Sheet of Mr. Suresh as on 31-03-1998

Liabilities			Assets		
Capital Account	18,000-00		Land and Buildings	10,000-000	
Add – Net Profit	2,000-00		Less – Depreciation	1,000-00	9,000
	20,000-00		Plant and Ma chinery	5,000-00	
			Less – Depreciation	500-0	4,500
Less-Drawings	6,000-00	14,000			
Sundry Creditors		4,000	Closing Stock		2,000
		1,000	Sundry Debtors		1,000
			Cash at Bank		2,000
					500
		19,000			19,000

17.5 | Difference between Profit and Loss Account and Balance Sheet

S.No	Profit and Loss Account	Balance Sheet
01	It provides information regarding profit or loss of the company.	It provides information about the financial position of the company.
02	Nominal account are recorded in Profit and Loss Account	Personal Accounts and Real Accounts are recorded in Balance sheet
03	It gives information about debits and credits	It gives information about liabilities and assets.
04	'To' and 'By' are written in Profit and Loss Account	'To' and 'By' are not written in Balance Sheet.

17.6 | Difference between Balance Sheet and Trial Balance

S.No.	Balance Sheet	Trail Balance
01	It is prepared to know the financial position of the company	It is prepared to check the arithmetical of posting of transactions to the ledger.
02	It is generally prepared at the end the accounting period or on the last date of the financial year.	It is prepared at the end of a month or once in three months or at any time.
03	It shows liabilities and assets balances.	It shows debit and credit balance
04	In Balance Sheet accounts of liabilities and assets are recorded	In Trial Balance all types of accounts are recorded.
05	Only closing stocks appear on the assets side of the balance sheet.	Only the opening stock appears on the debit side.
06	Net profit earned or net loss incurred can be known from the balance sheet	It is not possible to know the net profit or net loss from the trial balance.

17.7 | Financial Analysis and Usefulness

Financial statements should be analyzed in order to understand the financial position and performance of the company. Financial analysis is useful to different groups of people. For example (1) The proprietor can know the financial position and overall performance of the company (2) The shareholders and investors can know whether they will get dividend for their shares or not (3) By means of financial analysis, the debenture holders can know the financial as well as the earning position of the company (5) The Banks and other short-term creditors can know the current assets and current liabilities of the company.

17.8 | Various Techniques of Analyzing Financial Statements

Financial statements can be analyzed by the following methods:

- Comparative financial statements
- Common size financial statements
- Funds flow analysis
- Ratio analysis.

- ***Comparative financial statements*:** These are statements of the financial position of the company at different periods of time. The financial statements are shown in a comparative form so as to know the financial position of the company at the current year as well as the previous year. Generally two financial statements namely Profit and Loss Account and Balance Sheet are prepared in comparative form for financial analysis purpose. A comparative profit and loss account gives expenses and revenues of two consecutive years. A comparative balance sheet gives the amounts of assets and liabilities of two consecutive years.
- ***Common size financial statements*:** In this statement, the figures (amount) shown in the financial statements are converted into percentages. For example in the profit and loss account, the sale figure is assumed to be 100 and all figures are expressed as a percentage of sales. Similarly, in the Balance Sheet, the total assets or liabilities are taken as 100 and all figures are expressed as a percentage of this total.
- ***Funds flow analysis*:** Funds flow analysis reveals changes in the working capital position of the company. It indicates the sources from which the working capital was obtained and the purpose for which it was used.
- ***Ratio analysis*:** Ratio analysis is one of the most widely used techniques of financial analysis. It is very simple and more informative method. The term 'Ratio' refers to the relationship between two figures or two amounts. Ratios are derived from balance sheet and profit and loss statement.

The Accounting ratios are classified as:

- Liquidity ratios
- Solvency ratios
- Efficiency ratios
- Profitability ratios
- Miscellaneous ratios
- ***Liquidity ratios:*** Liquidity ratios are used to measure the ability of the company to meet its current expenses. Liquidity ratios are further subdivided into Current ratios and Quick ratios.
    - *Current ratios:* It is also known as working Capital Ratio. This technique is used to know the relationship between the current assets and current liabilities.

$$\text{Current Ratio} = \frac{\text{Current assets}}{\text{Current liabilities}}$$

- *Quick ratios*: It is also known as Acid Test Ratio. This technique is used to measure the ability of the company to convert its current assets into cash in order to meet out its current expenditures (i.e., current liabilities).

$$\text{Quick Ratio} = \frac{\text{Current assets}}{\text{Current liabilities}}$$

- ***Solvency ratios:*** Solvency Ratio technique is used to measure the relationship between the owner's fund and the creditor's fund. Solvency ratio is further subdivided into (a) Debt-Equity Ratio (b) Debt to total Capital Ratio.

  (a) ***Debt-equity ratio*****:** This technique is used to measure the claims of creditors and owners.

$$\text{Debt-Equity Ratio} = \frac{\text{Claims of creditors}}{\text{Claims of owners}}$$

  (b) ***Debit to total capital ratio*****:** This technique is used to measure the relationship between the long term debt and permanent capital.

$$\text{Debt to Total Capital Ratio} = \frac{\text{Long term debit}}{\text{Permanent capital}}$$

- ***Efficiency ratios*****:** It is also known as Activity Ratios. Efficiency ratio is used to measure the relationship between the sales and various assets of the company. The efficiency ratio is also used to measure the efficiency of the company. By means of efficiency ratio, the proprietor can find out the position of his business turn-over. The efficiency ratio is further subdivided into (a) Inventory turnover ratio (b) Capital turnover ratio.

  (a) ***Inventory turnover ratio*****:** It is also known as stock turnover ratio. This type of ratio is used to measure the relationship between the sale of the inventory (stock) and the replacement of inventory. This ratio reveals the number of times the stock (inventory) is replaced.

$$\text{Inventory Turnover Ratio} = \frac{\text{Sale of stock i.e., cost of goods sold}}{\text{Average stock i.e., average inventory}}$$

  (b) ***Capital turnover ratio*****:** This ratio is used to measure the relationship between the sales and the capital invested in the business.

$$\text{Capital Turnover Ratio} = \frac{\text{Net sales}}{\text{Capital invested}}$$

- ***Profitability ratios:*** These ratios are useful to measure the operating efficiency of the company. Profitability ratios are further subdivided into (a) Gross Profit Ratio (b) Net Profit Ratio and (c) Return on investment.

(a) ***Gross profit ratio*****:** It shows the relationship between the gross profit and net sales.

$$\text{Gross Profit Ratio} = \frac{\text{Gross profit}}{\text{Net sales}} \times 100$$

(b) ***Net profit ratio*****:** It shows the relationship between net income (after deduction of taxes) and net sales.

$$\text{Net Profit Ratio} = \frac{\text{Net income after deduction of taxes}}{\text{Net sales}} \times 100$$

(c) ***Return on investment*****:** It shows the relationship between net profit after taxes and capital invested. This ratio is used to know the over all profitability of the business.

$$\text{Return on Investment} = \frac{\text{Net profit after taxes}}{\text{Capital invested}}$$

Miscellaneous ratios

(a) ***Earning per share ratio*****:** This ratio is used to measure the amount of earning against each share.

$$\text{Earning per share ratio} = \frac{\text{Net profit after tax}}{\text{Total number of shares}}$$

(b) ***Earning yield ratio*****:** This ratio is used to find out the return given to share holder in lieu of the market value of the share.

$$\text{Earning Yield Ratio} = \frac{\text{Market value of the share}}{\text{Earning per shares}}$$

(c) ***Dividend per share ratio*****:** This ratio is used to measure the amount of dividend paid against each share

$$\text{Dividend per share} = \frac{\text{Total amount paid to share holders}}{\text{Outstanding number of shares}}$$

Advantages of ratio analysis

1. Ratio analysis technique is helpful to compare the financial position of one company with that of other firms. As the result the management can able to detect the weakness and strength of company.
2. Ratio analysis helps to judge whether the financial position of the company is improving or deteriorating over the years.
3. It helps in future planning.

Disadvantages of ratio analysis

1. The ratio analysis are based on the data written in the financial statements. If the data written in the financial statement is not accurate and up-to-date, the analysis ratios become unreliable.
2. Assets acquired at different periods at different prices are shown in balance sheet. Due to changes of price level at different periods, these figures cannot be compared by means of ratio analysis.
3. Ratio analysis are useful when they are compared with similar ratios of other companies. Many companies may have accounting periods of their own and different types of assets. In such case, ratio analysis may not be helpful to compare the statements of other companies.

Review Questions

1. What are Financial Statements? For what purpose the Financial Statements are prepared? What are its advantages and disadvantages?
2. What do you understand by the term 'Profit and Loss Account'? What information does it provide? How is it prepared? Write a model form of Profit and Loss Account?
3. Define the term 'Balance Sheet'? How it is prepared?
4. Discuss about grouping and recording of liabilities and assets?
5. What is Financial Analysis? Discuss the usefulness of Financial Analysis? Explain the various methods of analyzing financial statements?
6. What do you understand by Ratio-Analysis? Discuss the various methods used in ratio analysis to analyze the financial statements?
7. Explain the following terms
   (a) Profitability Ratio
   (b) Liquidity Ratio
   (c) Common Size Financial Statements

18 Bank Reconciliation Statement

18.1 | Introduction and Definition

LEARNING OBJECTIVES

- *Introduction and definition of Bank Reconciliation Statement*
- *Essentials of Bank Reconciliation Statement*
- *Causes of difference*
- *Importance of Bank Reconciliation Statement*
- *Preparation of Bank Reconciliation Statement*

Now a day's all the business organizations conduct their daily transactions with a Bank Account. Only a small amount of cash is kept in the office for immediate requirements and the remaining is deposited with the bank which helps in avoiding the risk of theft, mis-appropriation or fraud of money. The payments are also made by cheque. The bank account provides a convenient place for the cash resources of the business. Money deposited in the bank is safe. The bank account enables the business concerned to settle its debts by means of cheques. This avoids the difficulty of counting cash.

When a business organization opens an account with the bank, the bank supplies a book called 'Pass Book'. Pass Book is a bound or loose book supplied by the bank to the depositor. This book is a copy of the depositors account in the bank's ledger. Amounts paid into and withdrawn from the bank by the depositor are entered date wise from the ledger in this book by the banker. Depositor is allowed to keep this book with him but is required to send to the bank at frequent intervals for necessary entries in the pass book. On its return from the bank, the depositors check the entries therein with those in the bank columns of the cash book and ascertain their accuracy.

The business man records all the transactions relating to his bank account in the cash book. All deposits are shown in the bank column on the debit side of the cash book and all withdrawals on the credit side. The bank also maintains a separate accounts in its ledger for every customer. It credits the customers account with all deposited made by him and debits it with all withdrawals.

Thus what is shown on the debit side of the cash book appears on the credit side of the pass book (i.e., Customer's Account in the Bank's Ledger) and vice versa.

18.2 | Need for Reconciliation

Normally, entries in the Pass Book would tally with those in the Cash Book, and their balances should also be the same. But, in actual practice, they would generally differ. This may be because of some mistakes committed either by the business concern or by the bank in recording the transactions. But the main reason why, on a particular date, the balance shown in the Pass Book differs from the balance shown in the Cash Book is that many transactions are not recorded on the same date in both of these books. That is, there is always some time lag between the date of recording the transaction in the Cash Book and the date on which it is recorded in the Pass Book. So, on a particular date, the balances in these two books are bound to be different.

Hence a mechanism is required to locate the difference between the two balances and to cross check the two balances. Such a mechanism is called Bank Reconciliation Statement. Bank Reconciliation Statement is a statement prepared mainly to reconcile the difference between the bank balance shown by the pass book and the bank cash book (ledger).

Essential features of bank reconciliation statements

1. It is prepared for reconciling the difference between Cash Book balance and Pass Book balance.
2. It is prepared on a particular date.
3. It is prepared by the customer and not by the banker.

Objects

1. To detect any errors which might have been committed either in the Cash Book or in the Pass Book.
2. To ascertain the bank balance which should be shown in the Balance Sheet at the end of the period.

Advantages

1. Errors in Cash Book and Pass Book can be known and corrected.

2. Misappropriation (by the bank staff and the depositor) of cash or cheques deposited can be checked.
3. Delay in collection of cheques and also the non-payment of cheques issued can be brought to light.

18.3 | Causes of Difference

1. Transactions that appear in the Cash Book, but not in the Pass Book

(a) ***Cheques deposited but not collected*****:** When cheques are deposited, the trader debits the Cash Book (Bank Column) immediately. But in the books of the bank, the trader's account is not credited until they are actually collected by the bank. Till the time the cheques are collected, the balance appearing in the Pass Book will be less than the balance appearing in the Cash Book.

(b) ***Unpresented cheques*****:** When a trader issues a cheque, he immediately credits the Cash Book (Bank Column). This reduces the balance as per Cash Book. But the person to whom the cheque is issued may not present it in the bank immediately. The bank will debit the Customer's A/c (Pass Book) in his books only when the Cheque has been presented and paid. So long as it is not presented, the balance shown in the Pass Book will be more than the balance shown by the Cash Book (Bank Column)

(c) ***Cheques dishonored but no entry made in the cash book:*** When cheques are sent to the bank for collection, they are entered in the Cash Book immediately. But no entry appears in the Pass Book till such cheques are actually collected by the bank. Sometimes, the cheques deposited for collection get dishonored. The bank returns such cheques to the trader. On receiving the dishonored cheques from the bank, a reverse entry must be passed in the Cash Book. But, the trader fails to pass an entry for the dishonor of the cheque or does so much later. In such a situation, the Cash Book will be showing a higher balance because no corresponding entry will appear in the Pass Book

(d) ***Cheques not deposited*****:** Sometimes cheques received by the trader, though entered in the 'bank' column of the Cash Book, are not sent to the bank for collection for one reason or the other. Since, these cheques are not received by the bank, they are not credited in the Pass Book. In such cases, the balance in the Cash Book will be larger than the balance as per the Pass Book.

(e) ***Cheques not issued*****:** Cash Book (Bank Column) is credited for issue of cheques but they are not actually issued. Hence, the balance as per the Cash Book will be less than the balance as per the Pass Book.

(f) ***Errors in the cash book***: It is quite possible that while recording transactions in the Cash Book some errors have been committed.

- A transaction recorded more than once
- A transaction to be recorded on the debit side has been wrongly recorded on the credit side, or vice versa.
- Sometimes the trader maintains more than one bank account. It is possible that a cheque issued on one bank account has been wrongly recorded in another bank account. This affects both the bank accounts.
- Errors committed in balancing the cash book, or carrying forward the balance to another page.

2. Transactions that appear in the Pass Book, but not in the Cash Book

(a) ***Direct deposits***: Sometimes payments due to the trader may be made into his bank account directly by his customers. The bank credits the account of the trader in its ledger. This increases the balance of the trader in the bank. Since the trader has no intimation of the same, he does not debit the Cash Book (Bank Column). In that case, the Pass Book balance will be higher than the Cash Book balance.

(b) ***Direct collection***: Sometimes, on standing instructions, bank collects dividend on shares, interest on securities, etc., on behalf of its customers and credits their Pass Book. Since the customer has no intimation of the same, he cannot debit the Cash Book (Bank Column). This causes a difference in the two balances.

(c) ***Direct payment***: When the customer instructs his banker to make payments on his behalf to clubs, insurance company, newspaper agents, etc., the banker debits the Pass Book of the customer as soon as he makes payment. But the customer records these transactions in his Cash Book (Bank Column) on the credit side only after he receives 'advice' from the banker. Till the advice is received and Cash Book is credited, the Cash Book shows higher balance.

(d) ***Bank charges and commission***: Bank renders many services to its client and for that it levies charges. Entry for such charges is made by the bank but the corresponding entry for it does not appear in the Cash Book of the concern because it is not known to the client until he receives a statement. This causes a difference.

(e) ***Dishonored cheques***: Sometimes cheques are sent to the bank for collection and entries are made both in the Cash Book and the Pass Book of the trader. But when the cheques are dishonored and not collected, the bank will debit the trader's account in the Pass Book. The corresponding entry will not be made in the Cash Book until the trader receives the intimation to that effect. This causes a difference.

(f) ***Deposits and issues of cheques not recorded*:** The Pass Book may have credits for cheques deposited and collected, and debits for payment of cheques issued, but both have remained unrecorded in the Cash Book. This causes a difference.

(g) ***Interest allowed by bank, if any*:** The banks normally do not allow any interest on the current account balances. However, some banks may allow nominal interest. When interest is allowed, the bank credits it to the Customer's account. The trader would pass the corresponding entry in the Cash Book only when he receives the intimation from the Bank. Till that time, the Pass Book balance will be higher.

(h) ***Interest on overdraft*:** If customer is enjoying overdraft facilities with bank, the bank will charge him interest on amount given to the trader as overdraft. The interest on overdraft is debited in the Pass Book whereas the trader passes no entry in Cash Book until he receives the Pass Book. This causes difference in Cash Book and Pass Book.

18.4 | Importance of Bank Reconciliation Statement

It is essential to tally the bank balance shown by the Cash Book with the balance shown by the bank Pass Book. If there is any difference, identify the reasons for the difference. This is possible only by preparing a bank reconciliation statement. This statement ensures that the bank balance shown by the cash book is reconciled with that of the bank Pass Book. In the absence of bank reconciliation statement, the customer cannot be sure of the correctness of the bank balance depicted by the cash book. Hence, periodic preparation of the bank reconciliation statement is essential.

18.5 | Preparation of Bank Reconciliation Statement

Bank Reconciliation Statement can be prepared on the following lines :

(a) Compare the entries in the Cash Book with those found in the Pass Book and mark points of difference.

(b) Take balance either as per Pass Book or as per Cash Book as a starting point.

(c) Adjust the balance which has been taken as a starting point. This adjustment is to be made according to the other book. For example, if balance as per cash book has been taken as a starting point, then Cash Book balance is to be adjusted according to the entries passed in the Pass Book and vice versa.

The following rules are to be observed for the preparation of the Bank Reconciliation Statement.

***Favorable balance*:** In this case, the Cash Book (Bank Column) shows debit balance and the Pass Book shows credit balance.

(a) If we start from the bank balance as per the Cash Book :

1. Add to Cash Book balance if the amount is more in the Pass Book.
2. Deduct from Cash Book balance if the amount is less in the Pass Book

(b) If we start from the bank balance as per the Pass Book, the procedure mentioned above is just reversed:

1. Add to Pass Book balance if the amount is more in the Cash Book
2. Deduct from Pass Book balance if the amount is less in the Cash Book.

***Unfavorable balance or overdraft*:** In this case, the Cash Book (Bank Column) shows credit balance and the Pass Book shows debit balance. Whenever over draft as per any book is given, it is better to assume that there is an overdraft as per the other book also in order to find the effect of each entry on the starting point.

(a) If we start from the overdraft balance as per Cash Book :

1. Add to Cash Book balance (overdraft) if the overdraft is more in the pass book.
2. Deduct from the Cash Book balance (overdraft) if the overdraft is less in the pass book.

(b) If we start from the overdraft balance as per Pass Book :

1. Add to Pass Book balance (overdraft) if the overdraft is more in the Cash Book.
2. Deduct from pass book balance (overdraft) if the overdraft is less in the cash book.

Examples

1. Prepare a Bank Reconciliation Statement and find out the balance as per Pass Book on 31-12-1990.

   (a) Cash Book balance as on 31-12-1990 Rs. 1,75,000

   (b) Cheques amounting to Rs. 80,000 issued on 28-12-90 were presented for payment on 5-1-91.

   (c) A cheque for Rs. 60,000 deposited on 25-12-90 was returned dishonored on 10-1-91.

   (d) Interest on investments Rs. 4,000 was collected and credited by bank but no entry is there in the Cash Book.

   (e) Bank charges debited in Pass Book only Rs. 60.

Solution:

Bank Reconciliation Statement as on 31-12-90

	Rs.	Rs.
Bank Balance as per Cash Book		1,75,000
Add : Cheques issued but not presented		
for payment	80,000	
Interest on investment collected and		
Credited by bank in Pass Book	4,000	84,000
		2,59,000
Less : Dishonored Cheque debited in Pass		
Book	60,000	
Bank balance as per Pass Book	60	60,060
	1,98,940	

2. On 30th April 1992 the Pass Book of a trader showed as credit balance of Rs. 15,000. Cheques amounting to Rs. 3,500 were deposited in the Bank but only cheques of Rs. 1,500 were cleared up to 30th April. Cheques amounting to Rs. 5,000 were issued but cheques worth Rs. 1,700 had not been presented for payment in the Bank up to 30th April. In the Pass Book there was a credit of Rs. 100 for interest on investments and debit of Rs. 25 for bank charges. Prepare a Bank Reconciliation Statement showing the balance as per cash book.

Solution:

Bank Reconciliation Statement of a trader as on 30-4-1992

		Rs.	Rs.
Bank Balance as per Pass Book			15,000
Add : Cheques deposited but not yet cleared...		2,000	
Bank charges debited in Pass Book only		25	
			2,025
			17,025
Less : Cheques issued but not presented for			
Payment		1,700	
Interest investments credited in the			
Pass Book only.		100	1,800
Bank Balance as per Cash Book	15,225		

3. Prepare Bank Reconciliation Statement as on 30-6-1990 from the following particulars:

		Rs.
(a)	Overdraft balance as per Cash Book as on 30-6-90	3,595
(b)	Interest on overdraft was entered in Pass Book only	80
(c)	Cheques issued but not cashed before 30-6-90	635
(d)	Cheques paid into bank but not cleared	1,105
(e)	Interest on investments collected by the bank but not entered in Cash Book	250

***Solution*:**

Bank Reconciliation Statement as on 30-6-1990

		Rs.	Rs.
Overdraft balance as per Cash Book			3,595
Add : Interest on overdraft –entered in Pass Book only		80	
Cheques paid in but not cleared		1,105	1,185
			4,780
Less : Cheques issued but not cashed.		635	
Interest on investments collected and Credited by the Bank.		250	885
Bank Balance as per Pass Book	3,895		

Review Questions

1. Explain the term "Bank Reconciliation Statement"? State its significance? Give a model proforma for the Bank Reconciliation Statement?
2. Explain in detail various steps involve in the preparation of Bank Reconciliation Statement?
3. What are the causes of differences in the Cash Book and Pass Book balances? How would you reconcile them?

19 Bills of Exchange

19.1 Definition

LEARNING OBJECTIVES

- *Definition of Bills of Exchange*
- *Characteristics of Bills of Exchange*
- *Endorsement of Bills of Exchange*
- *Dishonoring the bill*
- *Definition and characteristics of Promissory Notes*
- *Differences between a Bill of Exchange and a Promissory Note*
- *Hundi, types ,advantages and disadvantages of Hundi.*

A bill of exchange has been defined as an "instrument in writing containing an unconditional order signed by the maker directing a certain person to pay a certain sum of money only to or to the order of a certain person or to the bearer of the instrument". The specimen of a properly drawn bill of exchange is given below.

Vijayawada

March 31, 1995

Rs. 500/-

Three months after date pay M/s. Sri Krishna & Sons or order the sum of Rs. 500/- for value received.

G. Avinash

To

M/s. Ramesh & Co.,

Brodipet,

Guntur.

This is known as a draft bill. This will be sent to M/s. Ramesh & Co. If this order is acceptable to them, they will write across the order as under:

ACCEPTED

Payable at Andhra pradesh

Brodiper, Guntur.

For M/s. Ramesh & Co

Ramesh Partner

After acceptance it becomes a proper bill of exchange.

19.2 | Characteristics of Bill of Exchange

The following are the important characteristics of a bill of exchange.

(a) It must be in writing

(b) It must be dated

(c) It must contain on order to pay a certain sum of money

(d) The money must be payable to a definite person or to his order or to the bearer.

(e) The draft must be accepted for payment by the party on whom the order is made.

(f) It must be unconditional

19.3 | Parties to the Bill

There are four important parties to a Bill, namely

(a) Drawer

(b) Drawee

(c) Endorser

(d) Endorsee.

(a) ***Drawer*****:** The person who writes the bill

(b) ***Drawee*****:** The person who accepts the bill

(c) ***Endorser*****:** The person who transfers the bill. Every holder of the bill has got a right to transfer the bill before its due date falls.

(d) ***Endorsee*****:** The person to whom the bill is transferred.

Apart from the above we also find another party called 'Payee'. He is the person to whom the bill amount is paid on the due date of the bill.

19.4 | Endorsement of the Bill

Bills of exchange being a negotiable instrument, it can be endorsed/transferred any number of times before its due date. The endorsement of the bill completes as and when endorser puts his signature on the back side of the bill with or without any specific remarks. Based on the remarks made, the endorsement methods can be classified into 5 major categories viz., Blank Endorsement (where the transferor of the bill just signs on the backside of the bill without making any remarks), specific endorsement (a remark regarding the person to whom it is transferred is written); Restrictive endorsement (where the person to whom the bill payment is to be made is mentioned restricting its further transfer); Facultative Endorsement (where the right to receive dishonor notice by the transferor looses) and Endorsement sans recourse (the agent who is transferring the bill on behalf of his principal disowns the responsibility of payment on the bill).

Due date of the Bill: The due date of the bill is arrived at after adding 3 grace days to the date on which the duration of the bill completes. Ex: If a 2 months bill is written on 1st January, 1999, the due date of the bill is 4th March, 1999 i.e., the date on which duration completes is 1st March, 1999 and after adding 3 grace days to it, the date that is arrived at is 4th March, 1999. The number of grace days given to each bill is same irrespective of its period of duration.

Honoring of the Bill: The bill is said to be honored if the payment on the bill is made by the drawee on its due date to the person who submits it on such date.

19.5 | Dishonoring the Bill

The bill is said to be dishonored if the amount on the bill is not paid on due date by the drawee on its presentation.

***Noting Charges*:** The charges that are paid by the holder of the bill on its dishonor to get the fact of dishonor registered with a notary are called noting charges. These charges are to be born ultimately by the drawee due to whose failure of paying the bill these expenses are incurred.

***Dishonor Notice*:** The holder of the bill in whose hands the bill is dishonored has to serve notice of dishonor to each of the endorser of such bill to make them responsible to bear the liability of that bill. In the case of facultative endorsement, the endorser of such bill need not be sent with dishonor notice to make him responsible for its payment.

***Renewal of the Bill*:** On the request of the drawee if drawer writes a new bill in the place of an old bill it is called renewal of the bill. When bill is to be renewed the drawee collects some interest on the face value of old bill from drawer for the additional time given through the new bill.

***Settlement of bill with rebate*:** When drawer pays the bill amount to drawee/ holder of the bill before its due date by claiming some discount from the former, such type of settlement is called 'retiring the bill with rebate' before the due date of such bill.

***Bankruptcy of Drawee*:** When drawer becomes bankrupt before the due date of the bill, the bill gets dishonored. It is the drawer's responsibility to pay the bill amount to the holder of the bill along with noting charges on such dishonored bill. This amount drawee, in turn collects from the estate of drawer in the proportion in which the drawer's assets are available on his insolvency. The remaining amount not recovered will be transferred to bad debts account in the books of drawee. This unpaid amount is credited to deficit account in the books of drawee.

19.6 Model Entries

The entries to be recorded in the books of Drawer and Drawee in respect of different transactions that arise on different occasion is as follows:

Nature of Transaction ***Books of Drawee***	***Books of Drawer***
1. When Bill is Drawn Drawer A/c. Dr.	Bills receivable A/c Dr.
	To Drawee A/c To Bills Payable A/c
2. When Bill is discounted or sold to bank	Cash A/c Dr. Discount A/c Dr.

	To Bills Receivable A/c
3. When Bill is endorsed Bills Receivable A/c	Endorsee A/c Dr. To -------------------
4. When Bill is sent for Collection to Bank	Bill Sent for Collection A/c Dr. To Bills Receivable A/c
5. When Bill is Honored:	
(a) If Drawer retains the Bill till its due date Bills Payable A/c Dr.	Cash A/c Dr.
	To Bills Receivable A/c To cash A/c
(b) If Drawer discounts the bill with Bank --- Do---	- - - No Entry ----
(c) If Drawer endorses the Bill --- Do---	- - - No Entry ----
(d) If the drawer sends the bill for collection --- Do---	Bank A/c Dr.
Bills sent for Collection	To

Contd...

Nature of Transaction Books of Drawee	Books of Drawer
6. When BIll is dishonored i.e.,. drawee fails to pay on due date.	
(a) When Bill is retained by drawee till its due	Drawee A/c Dr.
Bill Payable A/c Dr.	
date and noting charges paid by him	To Bills Receivable A/c
Noting Charges A/c Dr.	
To Cash A/c	
To Drawer A/c	
(b) When bill is discounted and banker pays	Drawee A/c Dr.
--- Do---	
noting charges	To Bank A/c
(c) When Bill is endorsed and endorsee pays	Drawee A/c Dr.
--- Do---	
noting charges	To Endorsee A/c
(d) When Bill is sent for collection	Drawee A/c Dr.
--- Do---	
	To Bills sent for collection A/c
	To Bank A/c
7. When Bill is renewed :.	
(a) To Cancel the Old Bill	Drawee A/c Dr.
Bills Payable A/c Dr.	
	To Bills Receivable A/c
To Drawer A/c	
(b) For interest worked out for the period of	Drawee A/c Dr.
Interest A/c Dr. extension	To Interest A/c
	To Drawer A/c.
(c) For Writing a New Bill	Bill Receivable A/c Dr.
Drawer A/c Dr.	
To Bills Payable A/c	To Drawee A/c
8. When Bill is retired under rebate	Cash A/c Dr.
Bills Payable A/c Dr.	
	Discount / rebate A/c Dr.
To Cash A/c	
To Discount / Rebate A/c	To Bills Receivable A/c

Contd...

Nature of Transaction Books of Drawee	Books of Drawer
9. When Drawee becomes insolvent	
(a) Entry for Dishonor Bills Payable A/c Dr. To Drawer A/c	Drawee A/c Dr. To Bills Receivable A/c
(b) For Partial amount received Drawer A/c Dr. Bad debts A/c Dr. To Drawee A/c	Cash A/c Dr.` To Cash A/c To Deficit A/c

19.7 | Accommodation Bills

These are the bills written and accepted by the drawer and drawee respectively without any trade transaction base or consideration. These bills are written to meet the short-term financial needs of one of the parties of the bill i.e., drawer, or both i.e., drawer and drawee. Generally these bills are discounted immediately on the date of writing the bill and the discount loss is shared in the proportion in which the net proceeds of the bill is shared. Before the due date of the bill, the amount used by the drawer for his purpose will be sent to drawee to enable him to honor the bill. As far as accounting treatment to be given to these bills is concerned the same criterion is adopted as followed in the case of trade bills.

Bills Receivable and Bills Payable Books

When the number of acceptances received or given is large, it is advisable to record them in separate subsidiary books, instead of journalizing each receipt of bill or issue of bill. The formats of these books are as follows.

Bills Receivable Book

S.No	Date of Receipt Received	From Whom	Name of the Acceptor	Where Payable Bill	Date of Term	When Due	L.F	Amount	Remarks

Bills Payable Book

S.No	Date of Remarks	Name of Bill	Name of Drawer	Term Payee	When	L.F Due	Amount	How Met

***Example* 1:** Sudhakar settles his account with Mahesh on February 1, 1999 by sending two acceptances for Rs. 3,000 and Rs. 7,000, due three months and six months after date respectively. Mahesh discounts the first bill immediately at 8% per annum. Sudhakar honors the first bill but before the due date of the second bill he approaches Mahesh to request him to write a new bill with 2 months duration at 6% interest. Sudhakar agreed to do so and writes a new bill for 2 months. On 30th September Sudhakar becomes insolvent and his creditors could get 50 paise per rupee from his estate in full settlement of their debts.

Write the Journal entries in the books of both Mahesh and Sudhakar and show important accounts in their respective ledgers.

Solution:

Journal Entries in the Books of Mahesh

Date	Particulars	L.F	Debit Amount (Rs.)	Credit Amount (Rs.)
1999	Bills Receivable A/c Dr.		3,000	
Feb 1	To Sudhakar A/c			3,000
	(Being the three months bill written)			
	Bills Receivable A/c Dr.		7,000	
Feb 1	To Sudhakar A/c			7,000
	(Being the six months bill written)			
	Cash A/c Dr		2,940	
	Discount A/c Dr.		60	
Feb 1	To Bill Receivable A/c			3,000
	(Being the 3 months bill discounted @ 6% Per Annum)			
	Sudhakar A/c Dr		7,000	
Aug 4	To Bills Receivable A/c			7,000
	(Being the 6 months bill cancelled for its renewal)			
	Sudhakar A/c Dr		70	
	To Interest A/c			70
Aug 4	(Being the interest @ 6% P.A calculated for the extension period i.e. 2 months)			
	Bills Receivable A/c Dr.		7,070	
Aug 4	To Sudhakar A/c			7,070
	(Being the new bill written with 2 months duration)			
	Sudhakr A/c Dr.		7,070	
Sep 30	To Bills Receivable A/c			7,070
	(Being the 2 months bill dishonored due to insolvency of drawee)			
	Cash A/c Dr.		3,535	
	Bad Debts A/c Dr.			3,535
Sep 30	To Sudhakar A/c			7,070
	(Being 50 Paise per 1 rupee recovered in full settlement of the debt)			

Mahesh's Ledger
Sudhakar A/c

Dr. Cr.

1999		(Rs.)	1999		(Rs.)
Feb	To Balance b/d	10,000	Feb 1	By Bills Receivable	3,000
Aug 4	To B/R A/c	7,000	Feb 1	By B/R A/c	7,000
Aug 4	To Interest A/c	70	Aug 4	By B/R A/c	7,070
Sep 30	To B/R A/c	7,070	Sep 30	By Cash A/c	3,535
			Sep 30	By Bad Debts A/c	3,535
	24,140	24,140			

Journal Entries in the Book of Sudhakar

Date	Particulars	L.F	Debit Amount (Rs.)	Credit Amount (Rs.)
1999	Mahesh A/c Dr.		3,000	
Feb 1	To Bills Payable A/c			3,000
	(Being the 3 months bill accepted)			
	Mahesh A/c Dr.		7,000	
Feb 1	To Bills Payable A/c			7,000
	(Being the 6 months bill accepted)			
	Bills Payable A/c		3,000	
May 4	To Cash A/c			3,000
	(Being the 3 months bill honored)			
	Bills Payable A/c Dr.		7,000	
	To Mahesh A/c			7,000
Aug 4	(Being the 6 months bill cancelled for its renewal)			
	Interest A/c Dr.			
	To Mahesh A/c		70	70
Aug 4	(Being the interest Payable @ 6% for the extension period)			
	Mahesh A/c Dr.			
	To Bills Payable A/c		7,070	7,070
Aug 4	(Being the new bill accepted for 2 months duration)			
	Bills Payable A/c Dr.			
	To Mahesh A/c		7,070	7,070
Sep 30	(Being the bill dishonored due to insolvency)			
	Mahesh A/c Dr.		7,070	
	To Cash A/c			3,535
	To Deficit A/c			3,535
Sep 30	(Being the partial amount paid i.e. 50 paise per 1 rupee, in full settlement of debt on account of insolvency			

Sudhakar's Ledger

Mahesh A/c

Dr.					Cr.
1999 (Rs.)		**(Rs.)**	**1999**		
Feb 1	To Bills Payable A/c	3,000	Feb 1	By balance b/d	10,000
Feb 1	To Bills Payable A/c	7,000	Aug 4	By Bills Payable A/c	7,000
Aug 4	To Bills Payable A/c	7,070	Aug 4	By Interest A/c	70
Sep 30	To Cash A/c	3,535	Sep 30	By Bills Payable A/c	7,070
Sep 30	To Capital A/c	3,535			
		24,140			24,140

***Example 2: (on Accommodation Bill)*:** Krishna draws a bill for Rs. 1,500 and Gopal accepts the same for the mutual accommodation of both of them to the extent of Krishna 2/3 and Gopal 1/3. Krishna discounts the same for Rs. 1,410/- and remits 1/3 of the proceeds to Gopal. Before the due date, Gopal draws another bill for Rs. 2,100/- on Krishna in order to provide funds to meet the first bill; the second bill is discounted for Rs. 2,040 with the help of which the first bill is met and Rs. 360 are remitted to Krishna. Before the due date of the second bill, Krishna becomes insolvent and Gopal receives a dividend of Rs. 50 paise in the rupee in full satisfaction. Pass entries in the books of Krishna and Gopal.

Solution:

Journal Entries in the Books of Krishna

S.No	Particulars	L.F	Debit Amount (Rs.)	Credit Amount (Rs.)
1.	Bills Receivable A/c Dr. To Gopal A/c (Being the bill written for mututal accomdation)		1,500	 1,500
2.	Cash A/c Dr. Discount A/c Dr. To Bills Receivable A/c (Being the bill discounted with bank		1,410 90	 1,500
3.	Gopal A/c Dr. To cahs A/c To Discount A/c (Being the 1/3 proceeds of the bill sent)		500	 470 30
	Gopal A/c Dr.		2,100	

Contd...

S.No	Particulars	L.F	Debit Amount (Rs.)	Credit Amount (Rs.)
4.	To Bills Payable A/c (Being the bill accepted for mutual accomodation)			2,100
	Cash A/c Dr.		360	
	Discount A/c Dr.		40	
5.	To Gopal A/c (Being the amount received and shared proportionate discount loss for the net benefit recived			400
	Bills Payable A/c Dr.		2,100	
6.	To Gopal A/c (Being the bill dishonored due to insolvency			2,100
	Gopal A/c Dr.		1,400	
7.	To cahs A/c			700
	To Deficit A/c (Being 50% of the due amount paid and remaining transferred to deficit account on insolvency)			700

Krishna's Ledger

Gopal A/c

Dr. Cr.

S.No	Particulars	(Rs.)	S.No.	Particulars	(Rs.)
1.	To Cash A/c	470	1.	By Bills Receivable a/c	1,500
	To Discount A/c	30	2.	By Bills Payable A/c By	360
2.	To Bills Payable A/c	2,100		By Discount A/c	40
3.	To Cash A/c	700	3.	By Bills Payable A/c	2,100
	To Deficit A/c	700			
	4,000		4,000		

Journal Entries in the Books of Gopal

S.No	Particulars	L.F	Debit Amount (Rs.)	Credit Amount (Rs.)
	Krishna A/c Dr.		1,500	
1.	To Bills Payable A/c (Being the accommodation bill accepted)			1,500
	Cash A/c Dr.		470	
2.	Discount A/c Dr.		30	
	To Krishna A/c (Being 1/3 proceeds of the bill received)			500
	Bills Receivable A/c Dr.		2,100	

Contd...

S.No	Particulars	L.F	Debit Amount (Rs.)	Credit Amount (Rs.)
3.	To Krishna A/c			2,100
	(Being the second bill written)			
	Cash A/c Dr.		2,040	
4.	Discount A/c Dr.		60	
	To Bills Receivable A/c			2,100
	(Being the bill discounted)			
	Bills Payable A/c Dr.		1,500	
5.	To Cash A/c			1,500
	Krishna A/c Dr.		400	
	To Cash A/c			360
6.	To Discount A/c			40
	(Being Part of the proceeds of bill sent with proportionate discount)			
	Krishna A/c Dr.		2,100	
7.	To Cash A/c			2,100
	(Being the dishonored bill paid)			
	Cash A/c Dr.		700	
8.	Bad debts A/c Dr.		700	
	To Krishna A/c			1,400
	(Being 50% of the amount received in full settlement of the amount due to insolvency)			

Gopal's Ledger

Krishna A/c

Dr. Cr.

S.No	Particulars	(Rs.)	S.No.	Particulars	(Rs.)
1.	To Bills Payable A/c	1.500	1.	By Cash A/c	470
2.	To Cash A/c	360	2.	By Discount A/c	30
3.	To Discount A/c	40	3.	By Bills Receivable A/c	2,100
4.	To Cash A/c	2,100	4.	By Cash A/c	700
			5.	By Bad debts A/c	700
	4,000	4,000			

Note : Krishna's share of discount loss in respect of 2nd bill is be calculated as under :

Net benefit received by Krishna = Benefit enjoyed in 1st bill.

The benefit shared from 2nd bill = 1000 + 360 = 1,360/-

$\therefore$ Discount loss to be borne by Krishna = $\frac{1360}{2040} \times 60$ = Rs. 40/-

19.8 | Promissory Notes

(a) Definition: When the purchaser has to pay the seller a certain sum of money on account of goods purchased, he can execute a promissory note. Promissory note is an unconditional promise in writing to pay a certain sum of money. It is usually made payable on demand and sometimes at a specified future date. The promissory note is defined as "an instrument in writing containing an unconditional undertaking signed by the maker, to pay a certain sum of money only to, or to the order of a certain person, or to the bearer of the instrument."

(b) Characteristics: The essentials of a promissory note are the following:

1. It must be in writing
2. It is an unconditional promise to pay
3. The promise is to pay a certain sum of money only
4. It must be signed by the maker
5. The name of the payee must be mentioned in the instrument.
6. It must be stamped

***Parties to a promissory note*:** There are two parties to a promissory note :

1. *Maker*: The person who makes a promissory note is called the maker.

2. *Payee*: The person to whom the money is to be paid is called the payee.

(c) Kinds of promissory notes:

1. *Demand promissory note:* In this, the amount of the promissory note is payable on demand.

2. *Time promissory note:* In this, the amount is payable after the fixed period mentioned in it.

There is another way of classifying the promissory notes.

(i) ***Single promissory note:*** It is promissory note, made and signed by one individual.

(ii) ***Joint promissory note:*** It is one, made and signed by two or more persons. They are jointly responsible for payment. In case of dishonor, all the makers should be sued together in one legal action. The holder has only one right of action.

(iii) ***Joint and several promissory note:*** It is also made and signed by two or more persons. In the case of dishonor, the payee can proceed against all or any one of them, as he likes.

According to the Indian Negotiable Instrument Act, a joint pro-note is in effect the same as a joint and several pro-note.

(d) Differences between a bill of exchange and a promissory note

S.No.	Point of Difference	Bill of Exchange	Promissory Note
1.	Promise or Order	It is an unconditional order to pay money	It is an unconditional promise to pay money.
2.	Number of Parties	There are three parties to it parties, viz., maker and payee.	There are only two viz., drawer, drawee and payee.
3.	Acceptance by the (Acceptance is already	It is to be accepted by the drawee	It need not be accepted maker there)
4.	Party making Payment	Acceptor makes the Payment.	Maker makes the Payment
5.	Liability maker is secondary and conditional	The liability of the drawer is only	The liability of the primary and unconditional.
6.	Conditions for Payment any or conditional	Acceptance may be general condition.	Maker cannot attach
7.	Drawer (Maker) and Payee	Drawer and payee may be the be the same person	Maker and payee cannot same person
8.	Status	Drawer is a creditor.	Maker is a debtor
9.	Circulation	It is widely circulated	Not so common in circulation
10.	No. of Copies	It may be drawn in sets	It cannot be drawn in sets
11.	Purpose as a form	It is usually employed for financing of personal security for raising trade.	It is usually employed loans.
12.	Notice of Dishonor	Notice of dishonor must be given required to be given to the maker.	Notice of dishonor is not to all persons liable to pay.

19.9 | Hundi

A 'Hundi' is a negotiable instrument written in a vernacular (local) language in accordance with local customs. It is not governed by the Negotiable Instruments Act, but by customs and practices. It is a credit instrument generally used in our local and regional markets. The word 'Hundi' is said to be derived from the Sanskrit word 'Hundi' which means 'to collect'. They are quite popular among the Indian merchants from very olden days.

Types of Hundies

1. ***Darshini hundi*:** A darshini hundi is one payable at sight. It is similar to demand bill.
2. ***Muddati hundi*:** A hundi payable after a specified period of time from the date of the hundi is called muddati hundi. It is the equivalent of a time bill.
3. ***Shahjog hundi*:** "Shah" means a respectable person well-known in a place. The amount on the bill is paid to a Shah or on endorsement by Shah. If there is any fraud or if the hundi is stolen or forged, the drawee can recover the loss from the Shah. It is similar to a crossed cheque. It does not require acceptance or endorsement.
4. ***Namjog hundi*:** A hundi payable to the party named in the hundi.
5. ***Firmonjog hundi*:** A hundi payable to order.
6. ***Dhanijog hundi*:** A hundi payable to the owner or bearer.
7. ***Dekhander hundi*:** A hundi payable to bearer.
8. ***Zikri chit*:** It is a letter written by the drawer or any other party and given to the holder of hundi.
9. ***Jokhami hundi*:** Seller or Consignor of goods calls upon the buyer or consignee to pay the value of the goods to the holder of the hundi.
10. ***Jawabee hundi*:** It is a hundi through which money is remitted from one place to another with the help of a bank.

Advantages of Hundies

1. It is a good proof of indebtedness
2. It has got all the qualities of a bill of exchange
3. It enjoys all the legal privileges of negotiable instrument.
4. By writing a hundi, the purchaser is bound to pay a specific amount after a specific period.
5. The time of payment of hundi is fixed.
6. Hundi can be discounted if he needs the amount earlier.

Disadvantages of Hundies

1. It is written in local language only.
2. It is not useful for external trade
3. It is not a negotiable instrument.

Review Questions

Short Answer Questions

1. Explain the essential features of Promissory Note?
2. Explain the Advantages of Promissory Note?
3. What is the difference between Bills of Exchange and Promissory Note?
4. Write the Characteristics of bill of exchange?
5. Explain the different types of hundies?

Long Answer Questions

1. What do you understand by bill of exchange? Write its main characteristics? How does it differ from a promissory note?
2. Explain a Promissory Note? Write a note on different types?
3. Why do majority of businessmen prefer making payment by bill of exchange? Prepare a specimen of bill of exchange?

20 Treatment of Cheques

20.1 | Definition

A cheque is an instrument in writing containing an un-conditional order, signed by a customer, directing his banker to pay on demand a certain sum of money only to or to the order of a certain person or to the bearer of the instrument.

LEARNING OBJECTIVES

- *Essential features of a Cheque*
- *Parties to the Cheque*
- *Specimen form of Cheque*
- *Precautions necessary while drafting a cheque*
- *Crossing of Cheque and types of crossing*
- *Bearer and Order Cheques*

20.2 | Essential Features of a Cheque

The important characteristics of a cheque are

1. It must be in writing
2. It must contain an unconditional order
3. It must be an order to pay a certain sum of money only
4. It must always be drawn on a specified banker
5. It must be signed by the customer of the bank
6. It must always be payable on demand
7. It is payable either to a specified person or to the bearer.

20.3 | Parties to the Cheque

There are three parties to a cheque. They are:

1. ***Drawer***: The drawer is the person who issues the cheque. He is customer of the bank.

2. ***Drawee*** **:** The drawee is the banker on whom it is issued. The drawee is always a bank.
3. ***Payee*****:** The payee is the person to whom the cheque is made payable.

20.4 | Specimen Form of Cheque

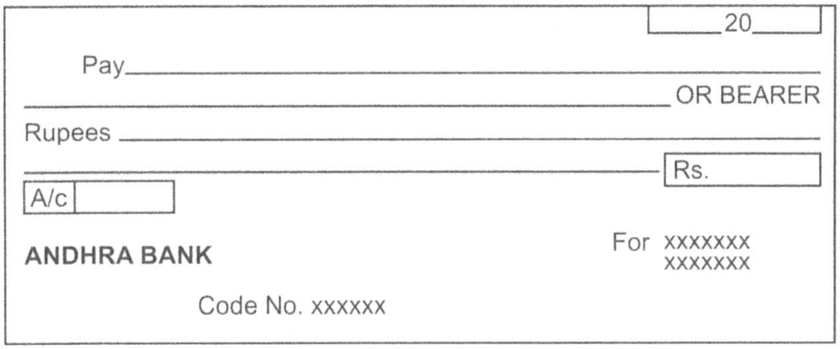
20

Pay

OR BEARER

Rupees

Rs.

A/c

ANDHRA BANK

For xxxxxxx
xxxxxxx

Code No. xxxxxx

20.5 | Precautions Necessary While Drafting a Cheque

The following are the important precautions which are to be taken while writing a cheque:

1. ***Date*****:** *A cheque should be properly dated.* Write in legible hand writing the date on the top right-hand corner. If a cheque carries a future date, it is called a post-dated cheque. The banker does not honour post-dated cheques. A stale cheque i.e., a cheque older than six months is also not honoured by the bank.
2. ***Drawer's signature*****:** *Cheques are signed by the drawer or account holder on the bottom right-hand corner.* He should sign the cheque in such a manner that his signature on the cheque should tally with the specimen signature in the bank's record. If the signature of the drawer on the cheque differs from the specimen signature, the banker refuses to pay money to the payee.
3. ***Amount*****:** *The cheque must contain the amount both in words and in figures.* Both the amount in words and figures must be identical. If there is any difference between the words and figures, the banker will refuse to pay the money.

   A caution should also be adopted by the drawer of the cheque that no space should be left between the figures; otherwise somebody may cheat by writing the increased figures.
4. ***Name of the payee*****:** *The cheque must contain the name of the payee.* The person who is entitled to receive the amount is called payee. Payee's name should be properly written, including the initials or "Company Limited" or whatever is the

full style. If you are drawing money for yourself out of your own account, write "self" on the payee line.

5. ***Counterfoil***: In cheque book, an additional slip is also perforated with the cheque. The cheque is written and given to the other party and other slip is to be filled in by the drawer for his own records.
6. ***Bearer and order cheques***: When the contents of the cheque are payable to a person or bearer, it is called a "Bearer cheque".

   Ex: Pay to Mr. Anand or bearer.

   These cheques can be negotiated by mere delivery. They can be passed from hand to hand. The transferee gets the contents of the cheque.

   When the contents of the cheque are payable to a person or to his order, it is called an 'Order Cheque'.

   Ex : Pay to Mr. Raghuram or bearer.

   Order cheques can be negotiated by endorsement and delivery.
7. ***Alteration***: Every change or alteration in the cheque requires the full signature of the drawer. Otherwise it will not be paid. If there are more than two alterations, cancel the cheque and draw a fresh cheque without repeating the mistakes.
8. ***Crossing***: Every cheque to be sent through the post, must be crossed. Crossing minimizes the chances of committing frauds. Crossing is a warning on the face of the cheque not to pay cash across the counter. General crossing may be enough to give protection to a cheque against wrong payment. Preferably issue "Account Payee" crossed cheque. It will give maximum safety to your cheques.

20.6 | Advantages of Cheques

1. It is a convenient and cheaper medium of exchange.
2. It is a very popular method of payment.
3. It facilitates the settlement of monetary transactions.
4. It can be sent to distant places by crossing it without fear of loss.
5. It can be made for any amount.
6. Collection of money through cheques is safe and saves a lot of time.

20.7 | Date of Cheque

1. **Stale cheque :** When a cheque is in circulation for a long time, it becomes a stale cheque. The bank considers a cheque as stale if it is not presented for payment within six months from the date of the cheque. A stale cheque is not paid by the bank unless it is confirmed by the drawer.

2. **Anti-dated cheque :** It is a cheque drawn bearing the date earlier than that on which it is issued. The banker pays money on the cheque on presentation.
3. **Post-dated cheque:** If a cheque carries a future date, it is called a post-dated cheque. Bankers do not honour post-dated cheques. For example, a cheque dated 30th August, 1998 is presented to the banker on 20th August, 1998, the banker refuses payment. It is a warning on the face of the cheque that it should not be paid before 30th August, 1998. However, if the cheque is presented on 30th August, the banker honours it.

20.8 | Crossing of Cheques

Cheques may be open or crossed. Open cheque is one which is not crossed. It is paid across the bank's counter. Crossed cheque is a cheque bearing two parallel lines across its face with or without the words "& co.", "Not Negotiable" in between them. The holder of a crossed cheque cannot claim cash across the counter. Crossing is a warning on the face of the cheque not to pay cash across the counter. When a crossed cheque is presented to a banker, he credits the account of the customer with the proceeds of the cheque. If a holder of the crossed cheque has no account, he will get it collected through a person having an account with the bank. Hence it should be remembered that a crossed cheque can be cashed only through an account and not directly.

20.9 | Types of Crossing

There are two kinds of crossing: 1. General Crossing 2. Special Crossing.

1. ***General crossing*:** When two parallel lines with or without the words "& Co.", or "Not Negotiable" are drawn across the face of the cheque, the cheque is said to be crossed generally. Sometimes the words 'A/c Payee' are also written. The following are the examples of general crossing.

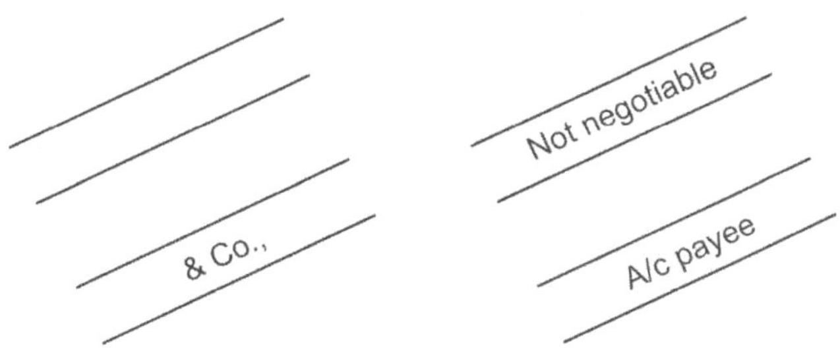

2. ***Special crossing*:** When the cheque bears across its face two parallel lines with the name of a banker, it is said to be crossed specially. In this case, the paying banker pays money only to that bank whose name is specially mentioned in the crossing. The following are the examples of special crossing.

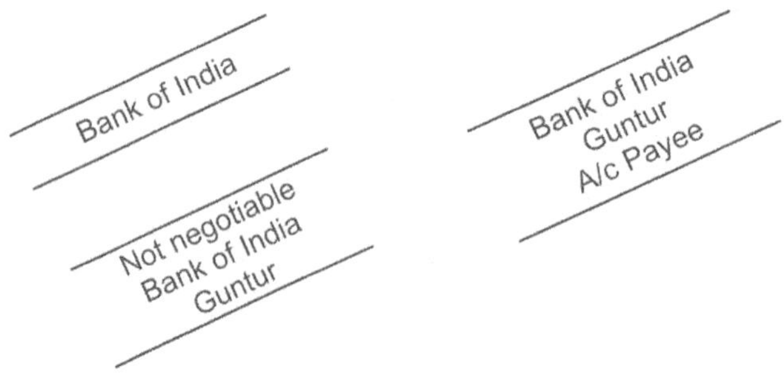

A cheque which is crossed generally will be paid by the banker not in cash at the counter, but always through the intermediary of another banker i.e., through a bank account. If it is crossed specially, the drawee banker will pay it only through the particular banker named in the crossing. *For special crossing parallel lines are optional, but for general crossing parallel lines are compulsory.*

A cheque originally uncrossed may be crossed by any holder. A general crossing can be altered into a special crossing but a special crossing cannot be converted into a general crossing.

Not negotiable crossing: When the words "Not Negotiable" are inserted in between the parallel lines drawn across the cheque, it is called "Not Negotiable" crossing. The effect of this crossing is that the cheque ceases to be a negotiable instrument. Such a cheque is like any stolen goods, the transferee of which does not get a better title than that of a thief. That is, if the transferor has any defective title, the same passes on to the transferee. However, it must be remembered that this crossing does not destroy the negotiability of the cheque. Still it can be transferred by endorsement and delivery. When this type of cheque is presented to a banker he must look to the endorsements and must satisfy himself as to the titles of the endorsees to the cheque. So, "Not Negotiable" crossing gives protection to the drawer or holder against miscarriage or fraud in the course of transit.

A/c. payee crossing: When the words "A/c Payee" are inserted in between the parallel lines drawn across the cheque, it is called "A/c. Payee" crossing. This kind of crossing is a direction to the banker to credit the proceeds of the cheque to the account of the payee only. This type of crossing restricts transferability of the cheque. The payee must have an account with a bank as he cannot transfer his cheque to others.

20.10 | Bearer and Order Cheques

When the contents of the cheque are payable to a person or bearer, it is called a "Bearer Cheque".

Ex: Pay to Srinivas or bearer.

These cheques can be negotiated by mere delivery. They can be passed from hand to hand. The transferee gets title to the contents of the cheque.

When the contents of the cheque are payable to a person or to his order, it is called an 'Order Cheque'

Ex: Pay to Srinivas or bearer.

Order cheques can be negotiated by endorsement and delivery.

20.11 | Advantages of Crossing

1. When a cheque is crossed, a thief would be prevented from getting the payment over the counter of a bank.
2. If the cheque is crossed it is not an easy thing for an unscrupulous person to get payment from a bank.
3. Crossing minimizes the chances of committing frauds.
4. A crossed cheque can be sent to any place without fear in an ordinary post.

20.12 | Who Can Cross a Cheque

Following persons are authorized to cross the cheque :

1. The Drawer of a cheque
2. The Payee can cross the cheque, if it is not already crossed.
3. The Bank in which the cheque is deposited can also cross the cheque.

20.13 | Dishonour of Cheques

There is a legal obligation on bankers to honour cheques which are properly drawn so long as the funds of the customer are sufficient to honour them. If the banker dishonours a cheque without sufficient reason, the customer can claim damages from his bankers. But a banker can dishonour the cheques in the following circumstances :

1. If there is no sufficient money to the credit of the customer.
2. If the cheque is not dated.

3. If the cheque is post-dated.
4. If the cheque becomes stale.
5. If there are material alterations.
6. When the bank receives the notice of death, madness or insolvency of his customer.
7. When the banker receives any garnishee order from the court stopping transactions upon the account.
8. When the cheque is presented after banking hours.
9. When the customer gives a notice that his account is transferred to a third person.
10. If the signature of the drawer differs from his specimen signature.
11. If the drawer of the cheque countermands payment.
12. If the cheque is mutilated. .
13. If the cheque is presented at an office other than the one at which the drawer has an account.
14. If the cheque bears irregular endorsements.
15. If there is a difference in the amount mentioned in words and in figures.
16. If a crossed cheque is not presented through a banker.

20.14 | Blank Cheques

A blank cheque is that which is issued by the drawer without stating the amount. A person who does not know the exact amount which he has to pay may send a blank cheque. The payee fills up the actual amount. To safeguard against fraud the drawer marks on the cheque as "Below Fifty Rupees", "Not over Hundred Rupees", etc.

| Review Questions

Short Answer Questions

1. What are the advantages of a cheque?
2. What is a cheque?
3. Differentiate between a bearer cheque and an order cheque?
4. What is the necessity of crossing a cheque?
5. Define the term 'Endorsement of cheque'?

Long Answer Questions

1. Define a cheque? What are the requirements of a cheque? Write the different types of cheques? Why crossing of a cheque important?
2. Define a cheque? Write its advantages? Explain the points a drawer should keep in his mind while drawing a cheque?

21 Economics

Economics is a social science concerned with the employment of limited resources of society, having alternative uses to produce goods and services. The word "Economics" is derived from two Greek words 'Oikos' (household) and 'Nemein' (management). Hence economics means the management of household in relation to the wants and means of satisfying these wants. A household has innumerable needs and wants but there are limited means to satisfy them. These scarce and limited means are called wealth.

LEARNING OBJECTIVES

- *Principles of Economics*
- *Nature and significance of Economics*
- *Demand and Law of Demand*
- *Demand Schedule*
- *Demand Curve*
- *Classification of goods with reference to demand*
- *Price Elasticity of Demand*
- *Supply and Law of Supply.*

Wealth definition – Adam Smith (classical definition of economics):

The classical economist, Adam Smith defined economics as the science of wealth. Here wealth is in terms of material things. But the definition does not say anything about services. Adam Smith in his treatise, '**WEALTH OF NATIONS**' lays more stress on the ways and means of increasing wealth.

The above definition has a series drawback. It gives the impression that the wealth is the most important part in economics. It lays more emphasis on material (physical) goods. But services are also required for satisfying human wants and needs. Moreover this definition teaches nothing but selfishness.

The neo classical definition of wealth – Alfred Marshall: According to Dr. Marshall, 'Economics is a study of mankind in the ordinary business of life. It examines that part of individual and social action which is most closely connected with the attainment and use of material requisites of well-being. Basically, business is an economic activity. Economic activities are those activities which are concerned with the acquiring and use of wealth.

Alfred Marshall rectified the defect in wealth definition proposed by Adam Smith. He gave more importance to human welfare than wealth. In his famous book captioned "**Principles of Economics**", he defined economics as a study of man's actions in normal business life setting. This definition lays importance on man's activities and enquires how he got income and how he uses it. He defined economics as a social science since it is related to the social aspects of man.

Some important inferences can be drawn from Marshall's definition of economics.

1. Economics is concerned with man's ordinary business of life. It is related to his wealth getting and wealth using activities.
2. Economics is a social science. It is a study of men and how they live and how they think in the ordinary business of life. So economics is a study of man not in isolation but as a member of society or a social group.
3. It is related to those economic activities which promote material welfare.
4. Marshall has given a new dimension to economics. He lifted economics to the realms of a science and divested it from all political influences.

Criticism of the theory proposed by Alfred Marshall

1. Welfare is subjective. It changes according to time, place and person and it cannot be exactly measured. Economics hence cannot be tied up with welfare.
2. According to the definition, economics deals with persons living in society but it does not throw light on all other aspects which may also have an economic perspective.
3. The word 'welfare' cannot be used along with material. There are some goods which do not promote human welfare but still they are studied in economics because they are scarce in relation to demand. So they have some price and they are economic goods. For example liquor and cigarettes etc., are economic goods but they do not promote welfare of the society.
4. All the goods and services which command a price and enter into the circle of exchange are economic aspects whether they are material or non-material. For example teachers, lawyers and actors etc., have their economic aspect because they are scarce and possess value. Hence Marshall's definition is incomplete.

Robbin's scarcity definition: According to Lord Robbin, 'Economics is a science that studies human behavior as a relationship between ends and scarce means which have alternative uses'. Thus according to him, economics is a study of 'means and ends'.

Economics basically deals with how society use their scarce resources to meet their needs and desires.

Lord Robbins who with the publication of his "**Nature and Significance of Economic Science**" in 1932 formulated his own conception of economics. In the words of Robbin 'Economics is the science which studies human behavior as a relationship between ends and scarce means which have alternative uses'. This definition is based on the following postulates which are governed by human behavior.

1. *Unlimited wants:* Human wants are unlimited. We cannot satisfy all our wants. If one want is satisfied another want arises. If human wants are limited there is no economic problem. Multiplicity of wants is the main characteristic feature of the definition.
2. *Limited means:* Human wants are unlimited, but the means, which satisfy human wants, are limited. The economic problem arises because of unlimited wants and limited means.
3. *Means have alternative uses:* The limited means are capable of having alternative uses. For example, coal can be used in factories, Railways and for generation of electricity etc. At a time, the use of a scarce resource for one end prevents its use for any other purpose.
4. *Problem of choice:* All wants cannot be satisfied. Some wants have to be left unsatisfied. Then the problem of choosing which wants to be satisfied and which wants to be given up arises. More urgent wants will be satisfied and less urgent wants will be postponed.

Finally the definition distinguishes economics from technical, political, historical and other related aspects.

Thus economics is essentially a valuation process, which is concerned with multiple ends and scarce means being put to alternative uses in order of their importance.

Criticism of Robbin's definition of economics: Robbin's definition of economics does not offer any solution to the problems of under developed countries. The problems of under developed countries are concerned with the utilization of unused resources.

Robbin has made economics a positive science. But economic is also a normative science. Robbin's definition of economics is sometimes very narrow and sometimes too wide. It is too narrow since it does not include organizational defects which lead to idling of resources.

Economics will be an incomplete body of knowledge without the study of welfare which Lord Robbin has neglected in his definition.

Samuelson's costs and benefits definition of economics: According to Samuelson (Nobel Laureate economist), 'Economics is the study of how people and society end up choosing, with or without the use of money to employ scarce productive resources that could have alternative uses to produce various commodities, over time and distribute them for consumption now, or in the future, among various persons and groups in the society'. It analyses costs and benefits of improving patterns of resource allocation.

A comprehensive definition of economics can be deduced from the above observations which is as follows:

Economics is a science which helps in achieving maximum satisfaction of wants and increasing the welfare as well as economic growth and studying economic activities which are concerned with the efficient consumption, production, exchange and distribution of scarce means having alternative uses.

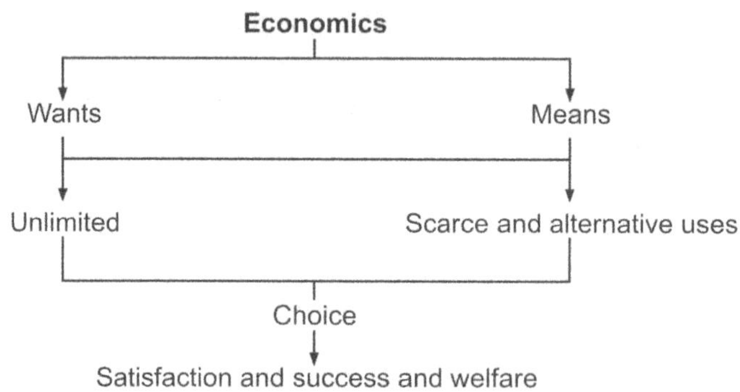

Micro Economics and Macro Economics are the two approaches to the subject of economics. Micro economics is the study of economic actions of individuals and small group of individuals and it is the study of individual economic units. Macro economics is the study of the economy as a whole.

There are three main branches of economics.

1. ***Descriptive economics:*** It is the systematic and scientific study of relevant facts of an economic activity such as foreign trade, industry etc.
2. ***Theory of economics:*** This branch of economics explains the functioning of an economic system and it explains as to how prices of products and services are determined.
3. ***Applied economics:*** This is a very important branch of economics which helps us in ascertaining the causes and significance of economic events. Hence it causes and economic analysis of a situation. The economic theories are tested to find out as to how far they can be beneficially applied in formulating the economic policies.

Different types of economic activities: People are engaged in different kinds of economic activities to earn money which are called occupations. The occupations which are generally adopted by human beings are classified into following three groups:

Business: Business means that economic activity which is primarily done with the purpose of earning profit. It involves the production of goods and services on a regular basis and carries an element of risk and uncertainty. Trading, banking, insurance and manufacturing are business activities.

Profession: Profession means an occupation which involves rendering of personal services of a specialized nature based on professional education, training and knowledge. For example, physician, pharmacist, lawyer, accountant etc. The **professionals** generally charge professional fees from their clients for the services provided to them.

Employment: Employment means a personal services rendered by a person to an organization under a contract of employment or service. An employee is required to perform the duties which are assigned to him by his employer. In lieu of that he receives wages or salary, allowances and other benefit of his services. Employment may be in a Government department or undertaking or in a private organization.

Nature and scope of business economics: Business economics is also called managerial economics. Business economics deals with the use of economic models to analyze business situations. In a business management executive has the prime function of decision making and future planning. Decision making is the process of choosing one action from two or more alternatives available. Future planning means establishing plans for the future. These plans relate to the future program of action by the business unit. The problem of choice arises because of the limited means and the firm has to make the most profitable use of these resources.

A business manager's task is made difficult by the uncertainty which surrounds business decision making. Nobody can predict accurately the future course of business conditions. At the most a business executive can make an intelligent guess of the likely conditions in the future. He prepares the best possible plans for the future depending on past experience and future outlook. The business manager has to continuously take decisions about his output and sales in order to adjust to the uncertainty of the future as it unfolds to him.

Limitations of economics

- Economics encompasses only those human activities which are related to wealth. It is not a comprehensive study of all human activities.
- Economics measures everything in terms of money. There are some areas which cannot be assessed in terms of money like emotions, hopes and aspirations of human beings.
- Economics studies the activities of those human beings who are members of society and only real time activities. It cannot be applied to hypothetical situations.

21.1 | Demand and Law of Demand

Demand means desire. It is the quantity of commodity that the consumer is able and willing to buy at each possible price during a given period of time. A mere desire cannot become demand. A desire which is backed up by an ability to buy and willingness to pay the price is called 'Demand'. There are three elements of demand for a commodity which are as follows:

1. Desire for a commodity,
2. Money to fulfill that desire, and
3. Readiness to part with money.

When we speak of demand we must also state the price. Unless we state the price, the term 'demand' has no meaning. A demand always has a price. Thus the quantity of a commodity purchased at a given price, at a given time, in a given market is called 'demand'.

Demand schedule: Demand schedule is that schedule which express the relation between different quantities of commodity demanded at different prices. According to Samuelson, the table relating price and quantity demanded is called demand schedule.

Demand schedule is of two types:

1. Individual demand schedule
2. Market demand schedule

1. ***Individual demand schedule:*** Individual demand schedule is defined as the quantities of a given commodity purchased by consumer at all possible prices at a given moment other things remaining equal. Table 21.1 indicates the individual demand schedule. It indicates the different quantities of Digene antacid syrup brought by a consumer at different prices at a given time.

   Table 21.1 indicates that as the price of antacid syrup goes on increasing, the quantity demanded goes on falling.

Table 21.1 | Individual demand schedule

Price (Rs.)	Quantity demanded
10	8
20	7
30	6
40	5

2. ***Market demand schedule:*** In every market there are several consumers of a commodity (antacid syrup). Market demand schedule is one that shows total demand of all consumers in the market at different prices of the commodity. So market demand schedule is defined as the quantities of a given commodity which all consumers will buy at all possible prices at a given moment of time.

   Table 19.2 shows that when price of a commodity (antacid syrup) falls, its market demand increases.

Table 21.2 | Market demand schedule

Price of antacid syrup (Rs.)	A's demand	B's demand	Market demand
10	8	5	8 + 5 = 13
20	7	4	7 + 4 = 11
30	6	3	6 + 3 = 9
40	5	2	5 + 2 =7

Demand curve: Demand curve is a graphical representation of demand schedule expressing the relationship between different quantities demanded at different possible prices of a commodity. The demand curve represents the maximum quantities per unit of time that consumers will purchase at various prices.

Demand curve is of two types, 1. Individual demand curve and 2. Market demand curve.

1. ***Individual demand curve:*** Individual demand curve is one that represents different quantities of the commodity demanded by a consumer at different prices. The individual demand curve is represented in Fig. 21.1. In this diagram, the demand

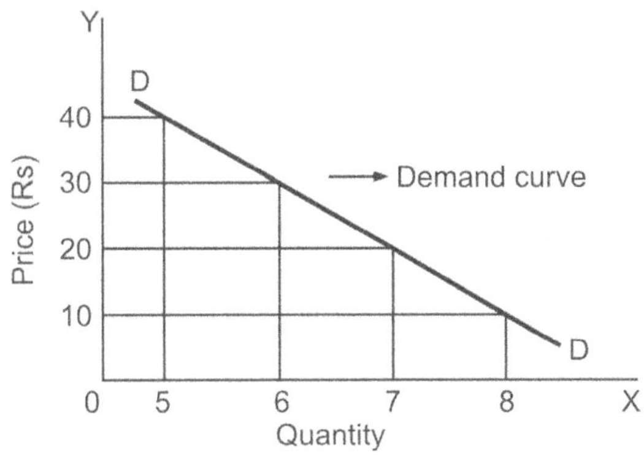

Figure 21.1 | Individual demand curve

of the commodity is shown on *X* axis and price on *Y* axis. DD is demand curve. Every point on the demand curve expresses the relationship between price and demand. When price is Rs. 40 the demand is for 5 units. When price is Rs. 10 demand is for 8 units. Thus slope of demand curve indicates that at higher price, demand is less and at lower price, demand is more

2. ***Market demand curve*:** This curve represents the total of quantities of a commodity demanded by all the consumers in the market at different prices. It is the horizontal summation of the individual demand curves. The market demand curve is shown in Fig. 21.2. The quantity is shown on X axis and price on the Y axis – in Fig 21.2 (i), (ii) and (iii). In Fig 21.2 (i) demand curve of "A", in Fig. 21.2 (ii) demand curve of "B", in fig 21.2 (iii) market demand curve have been shown. By adding the different points on individual demand curves, the market demand curve DD is produced which is shown in Fig 21.2 (iii). Slope of this demand curve is also negative indicating increase relationship between price of commodity and its quantity demanded.

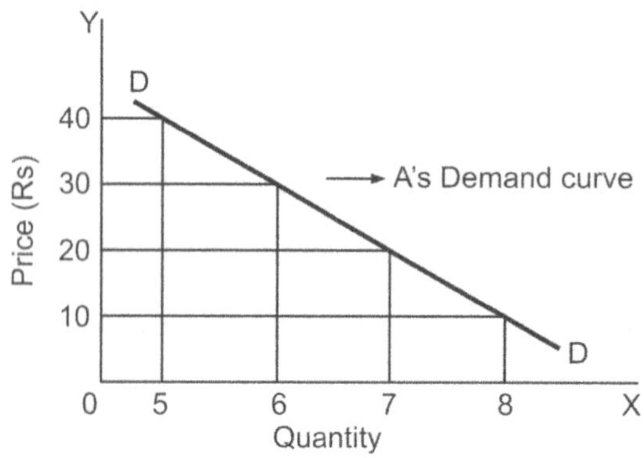

Figure 21.2 | (i) A's demand curve

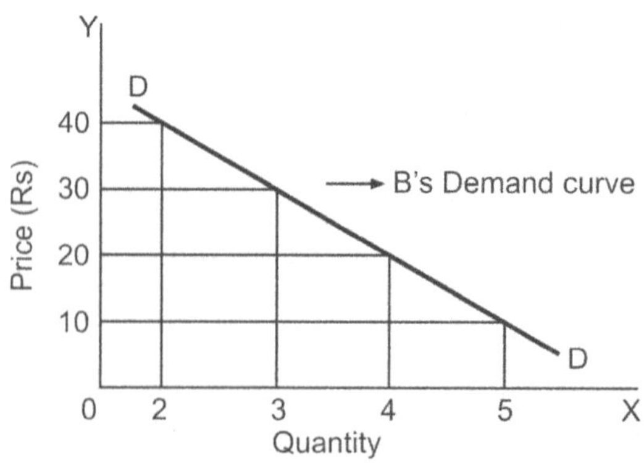

Figure 21.2 | (ii) B's demand curve

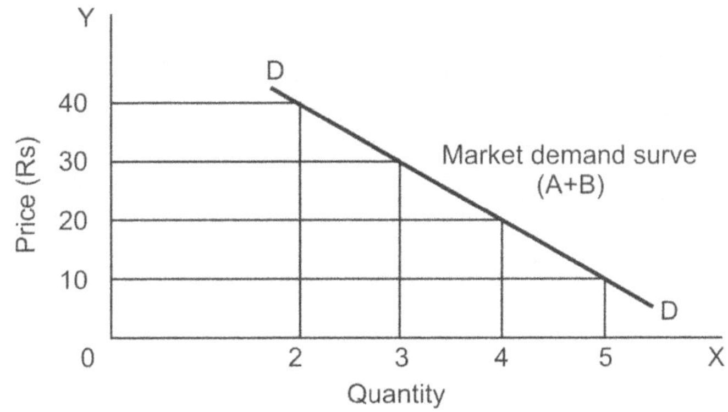

Figure 21.2 | (iii) Market demand curve

In the above Fig. 21.1 (iii) DD curve goes from left side to right side downwards in straight line or in curved form. Price increases, total demand decreases. Price decreases total quantity demand increases. Hence the relationship between price and quantity demand is negative.

Why demand curve goes from left side to right side: The following are the main reasons for the downward sloping demand curve.

1. ***Diminishing marginal utility***: When a consumer buys more units of a commodity the marginal utility of that commodity continuous to decline. Therefore the consumer will buy more units of that commodity only when its price falls. when fewer units are available, utility will be high and the consumer will be prepared to pay more for commodity. This proves that the demand will be more at a lower price and it will be less at a higher price.
2. ***New buyers:*** Every commodity has certain consumers, but when its price falls new consumers start consuming it, as a result demand increases. With the increase in price of that commodity, the consumer reduces or stops its consumption.
3. ***Income effect:*** When the price of commodity falls the real income of the consumers increase because he has to spend less in order to buy the same quantity. On the contrary with the rise in the price of the commodity, the real income of the consumer falls. This is called income effect.
4. ***Substitution effect:*** With the fall in the price of commodity, the prices of its substitutes remaining the same, consumers will buy more of this commodity rather than the substitutes as a result Demand increases.
5. ***Low-income groups:*** In every society majority people are in low-income group. The downward sloping demand curve depends upon this group. Ordinary people buy more when price falls and less when price rises. The rich do not have any effect on the demand curve because they are capable of buying the same quantity even at a higher price.

21.2 | Law of Demand

According to Marshall, 'The Law of Demand states that other things being equal the amount demanded increases with a fall in price and diminishes when price increases'.

Assumptions of law of demand: The main assumptions of the law of demand are as follows:

1. Tastes and preferences of the consumers remain constant.
2. There is no change in the income of the consumer.
3. Prices of the related goods do not change.
4. The wealth of the consumers does not change.
5. Consumers do not expect any change in the price of the commodity in the near future.

***Exceptions to the law of demand*:** In certain cases the demand curve slopes up from left to right i.e., it has positive slope. Under certain circumstances consumers buy more when the price of commodity rises and less when price falls (Fig. 21.3).

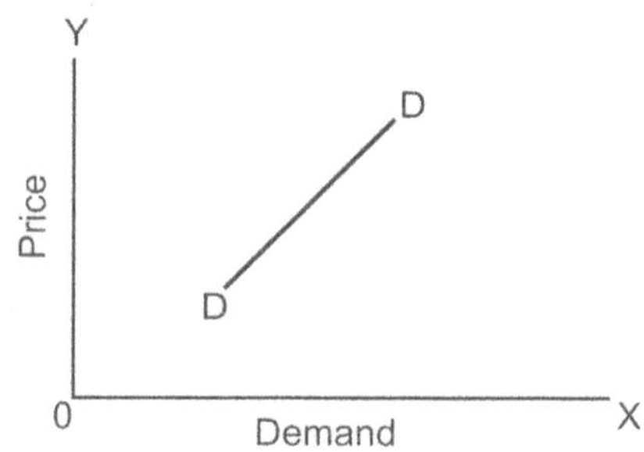

Figure 21.3| Demand curve (exceptional cases)

1. ***War:*** If a shortage is feared in anticipation of war, people may start buying for piling up stocks, for boarding even when the price rises.
2. ***Depression:*** During a depression the prices of commodities are very low and demand for them also less. This is because of the lack of purchasing power with consumers.
3. ***Giffen paradox:*** Sir Robert Giffen in mid 19 century observed that the low paid workers in Britain purchased more bread when its price increased by decreasing the purchase of meat. The increase in demand for bread when the price increased is an exception to the law of demand.
4. ***Conspicuous consumption or Demonstration effect:*** If consumers are affected by the principle of conspicuous consumption or demonstration effect they will like to

buy more of these commodities. For example gold and diamonds, some people buy such goods only if their prices are high.

5. ***Speculation effect:*** When the prices are expected to rise in the future, people buy more for example shares. If they expect a fall in price demand for those share falls.
6. ***Income demand:*** Income demand indicates the relationship between income and the quantity of commodity demanded. It relates to the various quantities of a commodity bought by consumer at various levels of income in a given period of time other things being equal. So with the help of income demand we can say whether a good is superior or inferior.

Classification of goods with reference to demand: With the help of demand, the goods can be classified into five important types. They are :

1. Normal goods or superior goods
2. Inferior goods
3. Giffen goods
4. Complementary goods and
5. Substitutes goods

1. ***Normal goods or superior goods:*** A normal good is that good whose income effect is positive and price effect is negative. A positive income effect means that demand increases due to an increase in income and falls due to fall in income. Negative price effect means that a fall in price results in extension of demand and rise in price results in contraction of demand. The income demand curve for superior goods has a positive slope. The law of demand applies in case of normal goods. (Fig. 21.4).

Figure 21.4 | Demand curve for normal goods

2. ***Inferior goods:*** An inferior good is that good whose income effect is negative. It means that an increase in consumer's income results in decrease in demand for that goods and a decrease in consumer's income results in an increase in demand for that good. The main difference between normal goods and inferior goods is that the income effect of normal goods is positive while that of inferior goods is negative. Law of demand does not apply in this case (Fig. 21.5).

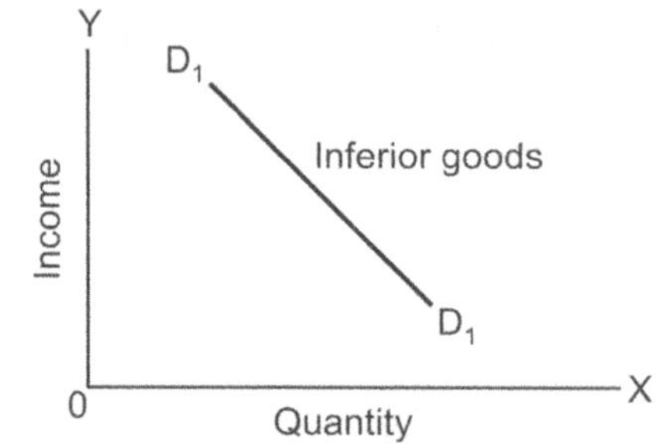

Figure 21.5 | Demand curve for Inferior goods

3. ***Giffen goods:*** These are those inferior goods whose income effect is negative but price effect is positive. In other words, the demand for these goods rises due to an increase in price and falls due to decrease in price. Giffen goods are exception to the law of the demand.

   Cross demand: Generally the demand for a commodity changes when its price changes. We also find that the demand for a commodity changes when prices of other related goods change. This is called 'Cross Demand'. There are two versions in it.

   I. Substitutes goods and II. Complementary goods

4. ***Complementary goods:*** In the case of complementary goods, with the increase in price of one commodity, the quantity demanded of another commodity falls. These are those related goods which jointly satisfy a particular want. Pen and ink are complementary goods. Similarly sugar and syrup are complementary goods. If the price of pen increases, the quantity demand for ink falls. The demand curve for these goods slopes downwards from left to right (Fig. 21.6).

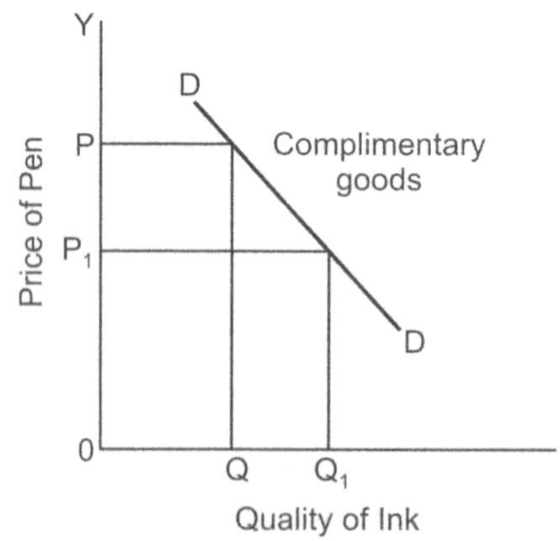

Figure 21.6 | Demand curve for complementary goods

5. ***Substitutes goods:*** In the case of these goods, other things remaining the same, the raise in the price of a commodity may increase the demand for the other commodity. These are those goods which can be used in place of each other. In other words substitutes are those goods; the demand of one is positively related with the price of the other. For example coffee and tea are substitutes. Coffee price rises, tea demand increases as it becomes relatively cheaper. Therefore demand curve for substitutes goes upward from left to right (Fig. 21.7).

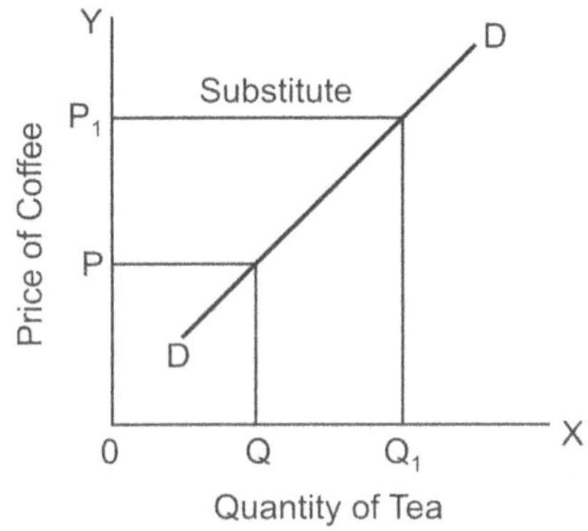

Figure 21.7 | Demand curve for substitutes goods

21.3 | Price Elasticity of Demand

When price changes demand changes. But it seldom happens that price changes lead to uniform changes in demand. Sometimes demand varies much, at other times little due to even small change in price. The credit goes to Marshal who offered a solution by formulating the concept of price elasticity of demand

"The elasticity of demand in a market is great or small according as amount demanded increases much or little for a given fall in price and diminishes much or little for a given rise in price".

Price elasticity of demand is the ratio of percentage change in amount demanded to a percentage change in price.

Price elasticity of demand may be unity, greater than unity, less than unity, zero or infinite.

Price elasticity of demand measures the responsiveness of demand to change in price. There are various types in it.

1. **Perfectly elastic demand:** When an infinite small change in price leads to an infinite large change in the amount demanded.

2. **Perfectly inelastic demand:** When whatever the change in price there is absolutely no change in demand.
3. **Relatively elastic demand:** If the proportion of change in demand is more than the proportionate change in price level.
4. **Relatively inelastic demand:** If the proportionate change in demand is less than the proportionate change in price.
5. **Unitary elasticity of demand:** If the proportionate change in demand is equal to proportionate change in price level.

21.4 | Income Elasticity of Demand

The concept of income elasticity of demand expresses the responsiveness of a consumer demand for any goods to the change in his income. Income elasticity of demand may be defined as the ratio of the percentage change in the quantity demanded of a good to the percentage change in income.

The income elasticity of demand is positive for all superior goods because the consumer demand for goods changes in the direction of the change in his income. However it is negative in case of inferior goods.

***Importance of price elasticity of demand*:** The concept of price elasticity of demand is of great practical importance in the formulation and understanding of a number of economic policies and problems. Some of the important applications are :

1. ***Monopoly price determination:*** A monopolist while fixing the price for his product takes into consideration its elasticity of demand. If the demand for his product is elastic, he will profit more.
2. ***Determination of price under discriminating monopoly:*** Under monopoly discrimination, the problem of pricing the same commodity in two different markets also depends on price elasticity of demand in each market.
3. ***Determination of prices of public utilities :*** When the demand for public services is inelastic, a high price is charged. e.g., : Electricity
4. ***Determination of wages:*** Price elasticity of demand is important in the determination of wages of a particular type of labour. If the demand for labour is elastic, there is no use in rising wages.
5. ***Important to the finance minister:*** Based on the elasticity of demand of a product, the finance minister imposes taxes on the products.
6. ***International trade:*** The concept of elasticity of demand has got great practical importance in analyzing some of the complex problems of international trade such as exports, imports and balance of payments etc.

21.5 | Supply and Law of Supply

The concept of supply occupies an important place in economic theory. Supply of a commodity influences price as does the demand. The supply of goods is the quantity offered for sale in a given market at a given time at various prices. It is also defined as the quantity of commodity offered for sale at a given price in a given market at a given time.

The following are the factors differentiating the supply of a commodity.

1. Supply depends upon the aim of the industry
2. Technical progress is useful in lowering the cost of production
3. *Substitution prices:* A fall in the price of a substitute commodity and its fall in production may also cause the supply of the commodity to increase.
4. *Change in cost of production:* A change in the cost of production may affect the position of supply. A rise in cost will decrease supply.

Generally the terms supply and stock are considered synonymous. But in economics they have different meanings. The amount of a commodity that a seller is willing to supply at a given price is known as 'Supply'. A quantity which a seller can place in the market for sale when demanded is termed as 'Stock'.

Types of supply: There are two types of supply.

1. ***Individual supply:*** It refers to the supply of a commodity by an individual firm in the market.
2. ***Market supply:*** It refers to the supply of a commodity by all the firms in the market producing / selling that particular commodity.

Supply schedule: Supply schedule is a systematic and tabular presentation of a various quantities of a commodity offered for sale at different possible prices. It has two versions.

1. Individual supply schedule 2. Market supply schedule.

1. ***Individual supply schedule:*** It expresses the different quantum of goods supplied by a company at different prices.
2. ***Market supply schedule:*** It refers to the supply schedule of all the firms in the market producing, supplying and selling a particular good. Sum total of the firms producing a particular commodity is called 'Industry'. Thus market supply schedule refers to the supply schedule of the industry as a whole.

21.6 | Law of Supply

Law of supply states that, other things remaining constant, there is positive relationship between price of a commodity and its quantity supplied. Thus more is supplied at higher price and less at the lower price and higher the price, the greater the quantity supplied.

Assumptions of the law of supply:

1. There is no change in the prices of the factors of production
2. There is no change in the technique of production
3. There is no change in the goal of the firm
4. There is no change in the prices of related goods.
5. Producers do not expect change in the price of commodity in the near future.

Exceptions to the law of supply: The following are the exceptions to the law of supply:

1. The law of supply does not apply rigorously to agricultural products whose supply is governed by natural factors. For example, if due to natural calamities the production of wheat is very less, then its supply will not increase in spite of high price.
2. Supply of goods having social distinction will remain limited even if their price may rise high.
3. Seller may be willing to sell more units of perishable goods although their price may be falling.

Elasticity of supply: Elasticity of supply of a commodity measures the responsiveness of the quantity supplied to a change in price. It measures the degree to which the price is effective in calling forth or holding back the quantity. Price elasticity of supply is percentage change in supply of a commodity per unit of time resulting from a given percentage change in price.

There are five types of elasticity of supply.

1. ***Perfectly elastic supply:*** A slight change in the price is attended by an infinite change in supply.
2. ***Perfectly inelastic supply:*** In which supply is completely non-responsive to change in price.
3. ***Relatively elastic supply:*** A relatively elastic supply is the one in which a given change in price produces more than proportionate change in quantity supply.
4. ***Relatively inelastic supply:*** Is the one in which a given change in price is attended by a less than proportionate change in quantity supplied.
5. ***Unitary elastic supply:*** Is the one in which supply equals the proportionate change in price.

Factors affecting supply of commodity: The following factors affect the supply of commodity:

1. ***The commodity price:*** There is a direct relationship between the price and its quantity supplied. If the price is less, quantity supplied is also less.
2. ***Prices of related goods:*** Related goods may be substitutes or goods of joint supply. If the price of substitutes increases, its supply should accordingly increase.
3. ***Prices of all other goods:*** The supply of a good depends upon the prices of all other goods. An increase in the prices of other goods makes them more profitable for the firms. They will increase their supply. On the other hand, the supply of the goods, the price of which has not changed, will become relatively less profitable. The supply of such goods may decrease.
4. ***Number of firms:*** If more number of firms are there, the market supply increases. Similarly decrease in the number of firms will decrease in market supply of a commodity.
5. ***Change in technology:*** Introduction of new technology leads to improvement in the techniques of production which leads to decrease in cost of production. Hence profits tend to increase inducing an increasing supply.

Review Questions

1. Define the term 'Economics'. What are the main branches of economics?
2. Explain the term 'Demand'. How goods are classified with reference to demand?
3. What is demand curve? Why does demand curve slope downwards?
4. What is meant by demand? Mention the factors which influence the demand for a commodity?
5. Define supply? Discuss the law of supply?
6. What is meant by supply? Give the various factors which affect the supply of commodity?
7. Explain the law of supply with the help of supply schedule and supply curve?
8. Explain the different types of goods with reference to demand?

22 Trade

22.1 | Theory of International Trade

LEARNING OBJECTIVES

- *Theory of International Trade*
- *Advantages and Importance of International Trade*
- *Adam Smith and theory of Absolute Cost Advantage*
- *David Ricardo and the theory of Comparative Costs*
- *The Heckscher-Ohlin theory of International trade*
- *Balance of Payments*
- *Balance of Trade*
- *General Agreement on Trade and Tariffs (GATT)*
- *The World Trade Organization (WTO)*
- *Trade related Intellectual Property Rights*
- *Export and Import Procedures.*

Trade may be in internal trade and international trade. Internal trade means place within the geographical boundaries of a nation. International trade takes place among different nations across the political boundaries of a country.

Advantages and importance of international trade

1. It helps countries specialization in production of certain goods at cheap rate due to natural advantages and skills of people.
2. Some countries would have remained only agricultural countries. India depended on foreign countries for her industrial expansion.
3. International trade helps countries to get goods at cheap rates.
4. In times of war and famine, trade helps the nations to overcome the difficulties.
5. International Trade promotes economic development
6. International Trade is a source of income and national income can increase if nations' trades carefully maintaining a favorable balance of payments.

1. **Adam Smith and the Theory of Absolute Cost Advantage:** Adam smith theory of absolute cost advantage in international trade was evolved is a strong reaction to the restrictive and mercantilist views on international trade. He advocated in this theory the necessity of free trade. In his view, this was the main guarantee for progressive expansion of trade and prosperity of nations. Free trade, according to Smith, promotes international division of labor because in it every country tends to specialize in the production of that commodity which it can produce most cheaply. Slogans of self-reliance and protectionism have been raised from time to time, nations have tried it, yet it has eluded all the countries. Smith had therefore propagated the view that free and unfettered international trade will make the countries specialize in the production and exchange of such commodities in which they command absolute advantage over the other participating countries. International trade allows the raising of net output of the countries which participate in it.

   When countries specialize on the basis of absolute advantage in costs, they stand to gain through international trade. A tailor does not make his own shoes and shoemaker does not stitch his own cloths. Both gain by exchanging shoes and cloths. We can illustrate this proposition with the help of an example.

   Suppose there are two countries, A and B which produce two commodities x an y. The cost of producing these commodities is measured in terms of labor involved in their production, the respective outputs in two countries can be shown through the table given below.

Absolute cost difference in two countries

	Countries	Commodities
	x	y
A	12	6
B	6	12

The table given above shows that the two countries A and B have absolute cost advantages. In country A, 1 man-day of labor can produce 12 units of x and 6 units of y. In country B, 1 man-day of labour can produce 6 units of x and 12 units of y. It signifies that country A has an absolute advantage in producing x while country B enjoys absolute advantage in producing commodity y. Ratio exchange is 1:1.

If country A specialize in the production and export of commodity x, while country B specialize in the production and export of commodity Y, both the countries stand to gain.

Adam Smith has emphasized that specialization on the basis of absolute cost advantage would lead to maximization of world production. If both the countries produce two commodities, the aggregate production will be 18 units in each country. If the available labor units are employed in production of x by country A, it can produce 24 units of x. Similarly country B specializing in production of y will be able to produce 24 units of y. The total production in the absence of specialization could be only 36 units of both the commodities taken together, while specialization can yield a total output 48 unit.

Smith argument had certain weakness.

1. This theory assumed that each exporting country had an absolute cost advantage in the production of specific commodities. This assumption may not hold true when a country has no line of production in which it has an absolute superiority.

   Secondly Smith simply indicated the fundamental basis on which international trade rests– the absolute cost advantage and failed to explore in a comprehensive manner the factors influencing trade between two or more countries.

2. **David Ricardo and the Theory of Comparative Costs:** David Ricardo believed that international trade is governed by the comparative cost advantage rather than the absolute advantage. A country will specialize in the line of production in which it has greater relative cost advantage than other countries and the country will import from abroad all such commodities in which it has relative cost advantages.

   Ex: If India can produce computers at an excessively high cost while Japan can produce rice at an excessively high cost, it will surely be beneficial for both to exchange rice and computers.

   Ricardo's comparative cost analysis based on the following assumptions:

   1. There is no intervention by the Government in the economic system.
   2. There is a state of perfect competition in both commodity market and factor market.
   3. There are static conditions in the economy.
   4. Production function is homogeneous of the first degree. It implies that output changes exactly in the same ratio in which the factor inputs changed.
   5. Labor is the only factor of production. Cost of producing a commodity is expressed in labor units.
   6. Labor is perfectly mobile within the country but perfectly immobile between countries.
   7. Transport costs are absent.
   8. There are only two countries and two commodities.

This two country - two commodity model can be analyzed through the table given below.

Labor cost of production

Labor cost per unit of commodity in man hours

Country	Commodity x	Commodity y
A	16	18
B	24	20

The above table indicates that country A has an absolute advantage in producing both x and y commodities as it can produce both the commodities through smaller inputs of labor than in country B. In relative terms, however, country A has comparative advantage in the production and export of commodity x, while country B enjoys an advantage in the production and export of commodity y.

1. In country A, domestic x-y exchange ratio 16:18;

   1 unit of x = 16/18 = 9.89 units of y

   Alternatively 1 unit of y = 18/16 = 1.13 units of x.

2. In country B, domestic x-y exchange ratio 24:20; .

   1 unit of x = 24/20 = 1.2 units of y

   Alternatively 1 unit of y = 20/24 = 0.81 units of x.

The comparative cost ratio for commodity X is 16/24 = 0.67 and it is 18/20 = 0.90 for commodity y.

In country A, one unit of commodity x can be produced through 0.67 x 100: 67% of the effort involved in producing 1 unit of commodity x in country B.

Further, country A can produce 1 unit of commodity y through 0.90 x 100 = 90% of the effort involved in producing it in country B. Still country B has comparative advantage in producing commodity y.

While it requires 24/16 = 150% of effort required in country A in producing a unit of x, it requires only 20/18 x 100: 111% of the effort in country B in producing a unit of y. Thus country B will have a comparative advantage in producing y, similarly country A will have a comparative advantage in turning commodity x.

Ricardo's comparative cost principle underlines the fact that each country will stand to gain through trade so long as the cost ratios for two countries are not equal. Country A specialize in the production of x and country B specialize in the production of y. Country A is willing to give up 1 unit of x for having 0.89 units of y. Country B is willing to give up 1 unit of y for having 0.81 units of x. Suppose A and B agree to exchange 1:1 gain A is worth 0.11 unit of y and that B amounts 0.19 unit of x. So the comparative cost principle confers gains from trade on both the countries. The quantum of gain is determined fundamentally by actual exchange ratio that is settled between the two countries.

Criticism

1. The weakest spot in the Ricardo's theory is its supposition that exchange of goods is determined on the basis of comparative labor costs. In fact output is not the result of labor services alone. Other factors also make a significant contribution in production. So the total cost should include both labor and non-labor costs. The exchange of goods among countries should be determined on the basis of money costs rather than labor cost.
2. The theory is basically of a static character. When we find that there are changes in these circumstances, the theory breaks down.
3. The theory lays too much emphasis on supply conditions and overlooks the impact of demand conditions on prices of goods, their import and export.
4. A very serious defect in this theory is absence of transport costs.
5. The assumption that factors of production have perfect mobility within the country is not true, Ohlin in his view states that factor mobility is very limited even within different regions of the same country .
6. This theory has a severe operational limitation in that it is concerned only with the two commodities, two country situation. In the present day multilateral trade realities, this theory is rather too simplistic.

3. **The Heckscher-Ohlin Theory of International Trade:** The structure of modern theory of international trade rests mainly upon the theory developed by Heckscher and Ohlin. The theory has replaced the classical and neo-classical theories of international trade. There is no conflict between the Heckscher and Ohlin approach, as it supplements the traditional approach. It goes a step further than the comparative cost doctrine to investigate the basic cause of the relative differences in costs. Heckscher and Ohlin have traced the cause of cost differences to relative factor endowments and relative factor intensities. According to this theory, countries which are abundant in labor will export labor intensive goods and those which are rich in capital will export capital intensive goods.

Assumption of the theory

1. This theory considers a two country, two commodities and two factors case. (labor, capital)
2. The factors of production are perfectly mobile within the countries, but they are perfectly mobile between the countries.
3. There is a state of perfect competition both in the product and factor markets.
4. There is full employment of factors of production in both the countries.
5. The production is governed by constant returns to scale.
6. Techniques of production in both countries remain unchanged.
7. Demand functions for different goods are identical in both countries.

8. The factors of production is homogeneous in the two countries.
9. There is absence of transport cost.

1. ***Explanation of the theory:*** The whole basis of differences in comparative costs according to Heckscher-Ohlin theory rests upon two crucial differences between the countries, factors endowments and factor intensities.

Factors endowments

It is an indisputable fact that regions or countries differ from one another in respect of resource endowments or availability of productive factors. Country A may have an abundance of capital while labor may be scarce. On the opposite, there may be an abundance of labor in country B while capital may be scarce. The term relative factor abundance has two different concepts.

1. ***Physical criterion***

According to this criterion a country is said to be relatively capital abundant. The country A can be called relatively capital abundant if the following condition is satisfied

$$\frac{\bar{K}A}{\bar{L}A} < \frac{\bar{K}B}{\bar{L}B}$$

where K and L refers to capital and labor respectively. Bars over K and L signify the fixed factor quantities in each country.

Similarly scarcity of labor in physical terms in country A can be expressed,

$$\frac{\bar{L}A}{\bar{K}A} < \frac{\bar{L}B}{\bar{K}B}$$

For country B relative labour – Abundance

$$\frac{\bar{L}B}{\bar{K}B} > \frac{\bar{L}A}{\bar{K}A}$$

Capital scarcity in B country

$$\frac{\bar{K}B}{\bar{L}B} < \frac{\bar{K}A}{\bar{L}A}$$

Given the above factor proportions the theory states that country A will produce capital- intensive, while B country produce labor intensive commodity (See Fig.). If both the countries produce machines and cloths in the same proportion, and production occurs along OR. The country A would be producing at C and country B producing at D. The points C and D lie on the respective production possibility curve PQ and P, Q, of these two countries. Since at point C the slope of country

A's production possibility curve is steaper than the slope of the production possibility curve of country B at D. This will imply that marginal cost of producing cloth in country A is higher than the marginal cost of producing cloth in country B. Thus if production takes place at points C D, machines can be produced more cheaply in country A and cloth can be produced more cheaply in country B.

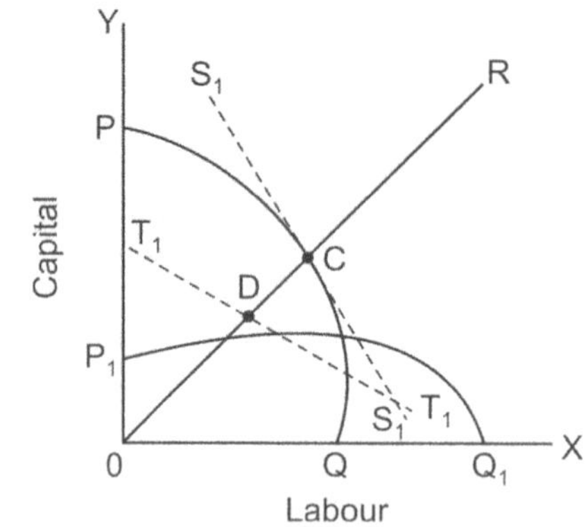

The Heckscher-Ohlin theorem can however, be valid on the basis of physical criterion and the above conclusion only if the consumption pattern in both the countries is identical and if the income elasticity of demand for each commodity equals unity, if the demand conditions are different in the two countries. So the capital abundant countries export capital insensitive commodity and vice-versa.

2. ***Price criterion:*** Another criterion for defining relative factor abundance is the price criterion. The criterion lays down that country having relatively cheap capital and relatively costly labor is capital abundant and vice versa. Country A can be called relatively capital abundant if,

$$\frac{P_k A}{P_L A} > \frac{P_k B}{P_L B}$$

P: Price, K and L signify capital and labor respectively for A and B countries.

Similarly country B can be regarded labor abundant and capital scarce.

$$\frac{P_L A}{P_K A} > \frac{P_L B}{P_K B}$$

Now if country A is capital abundant and labours scarce, the interest rate would be relatively low and wages rates relatively higher when compared with interest rates and wage rates in country B. Therefore country A would decide to produce and export capital intensive commodity and import labor intensive commodity. This generalization can be proved with the help of a graph.

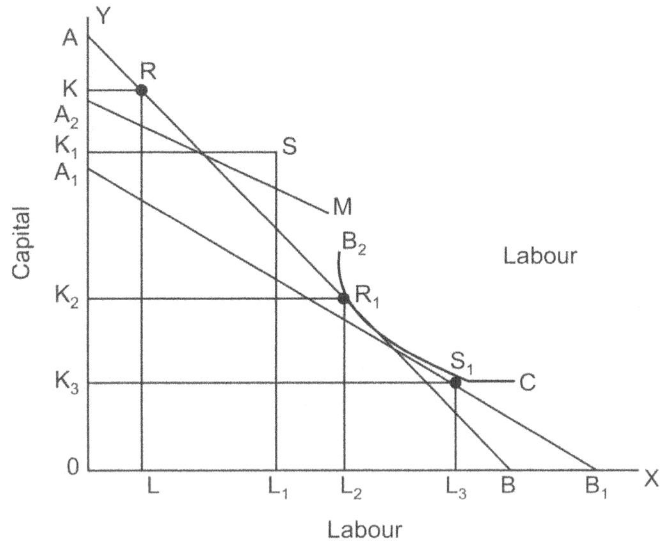

A B is the factor price line for country A and A_1 B_1 is the factor price line for country B. As the slope A B is greater than that of A_1 B_1, capital is relatively cheap in country A and labour is relatively cheap in country B. In other words the cost of producing one unit of machine in country A in terms of capital is OA_1.

The factor price line A_2 B_2 of country B which is parallel to A_1 B_1 is the tangent to the isoquant M at S. It shows that country B can produce one machine by employing OK_1 units of capital and OL_1 units of labour. It means that A_2 K_1 units of capital are equal to OL_1 units of labour and the total cost of producing one unit machine in country B is OA_2

Similarly in the production of same units of cloth in country A, OL_2 units of labour and OK_2 units of capital are employed at R_1 which is the point of tangency between A's factor price line A B and the isoquant C for cloth. Given the factor combination represented OK_2 unit of capital or B_2 L_2 units of labour and the cost of producing the units of cloth represented by the isoquant of cloth in country A in terms of labour OB. If B country employs OK_3 units of capital and OL_3 units of labour producing the given units of cloth, we can easily infer from the diagram that the quantity of capital OK_3 equals B1 L_3 units of labour. The cost producing one unit of cloth in labour terms OB_1 in country B. So B country exports cloths to A country and A country export machines to B country.

2. ***Factor intensities:*** Means the relative proportion in which the two factors say labour and capital are combined at each point on a given isoquant. Differing factors proportions result in different slopes of isoquant for two countries,

Criticism

1. This is only partial equilibrium analysis.

2. This theory based on highly simplifying assumptions of perfect competition, full employment etc.
3. This theory is a static analysis.
4. This theory discusses only identical factors but in the real world quantitative factor differences exist.
5. This theory neglects the by-products.

22.2 | Balance of Payment

Balance of payments is a systematic record of all economic transactions within a particular year between one country and the rest of the countries and its total receipts from them. Balance of payment is a statement of payments and receipts on account of international transactions. International accounts are of three kinds (a) Visible items (b) Invisible items and (c) Capital transfers.

Benham states that "Balance of payments of a country is a record of the monetary transactions over a period with the rest of the world".

Balance of trade: Balance of trade refers to the export and import of visible items, i.e., material goods. It is the difference between the value of visible exports and imports.

Visible items are those items which are recorded in the customs returns. Ex : material goods exported and imported. If the value of visible exports is greater than value of visible imports, balance of trade is favourable trade. If the value of visible exports and imports are equal balance of trade is in equilibrium.

Balance of payments is comparatively a more comprehensive concept because it covers visible items and invisible items. Invisible items are those which are not recorded in the customs returns. Ex: Services (Transportation, banking, Insurance etc.), capital flows, purchase and sale of gold etc. Thus balance of payments is a broad term than balance of trade.

22.3 | General Agreement on Trade and Tariffs [G. A. T. T]

This is an organization of countries which is concerned with regulation and promotion of world trade. GATT was established in 1948, main head quarter at Geneva. It is a result of the desire on the part of 23 countries to work together to reduce the tariffs which were considered to be excessive. The member countries would meet in Geneva and negotiate multilaterally on matters of trade policy. It was also to act as a forum for the settlement of disputes between nations.

The objectives of the GATT

There seem to have been three basic objectives behind the establishment of GATT.

1. It was to provide a frame work for the conduct of trade relations.
2. It was to provide a frame work for the progressive elimination of trade barriers.
3. It was to provide a set of rules that would inhibit countries from taking unilateral action.

The principle of the GATT

1. ***Non-discrimination***: The basic principle of GATT was that of non-discrimination. This principle is contained in what has been known as the "Most Favoured Nation" (MFN) clause.

   This means that a country agrees not to give better treatment to any single nation than it gives to all the contracting parties of GATT. If any country gives preferential tariff treatment to any country then that concession must be extended immediately to all other countries, so that all contracting parties benefit to the same extent.
2. ***Reciprocity***: The reciprocity obligation requires that a country receiving a concession from another should offer an "equivalent concession" in return.
3. ***Transparency***: The GATT forbade the use of direct control on trade, particularly quantitative restrictions, except under special circumstances such as a balance of payments crisis.
4. ***The MFN clause and discrimination against countries***: In the face of it MFN clause seems fair enough but in reality it also involves a hidden discrimination among different countries.

Exceptions to the GATT

1. GATT members were allowed to apply for quantitative import restrictions in order to deal with severe balance of payments problem.
2. Another major exception to the MFN principle is that the member countries can establish free trade areas and custom unions. The most common regional grouping has been the free trade areas.
3. Tariff preference for specific groups of countries are another exception to the MFN principle. The GATT did not object to various preferential arrangements between developed countries and their present territories.
4. ***Dumping:*** Dumping of goods takes place when a country sells its goods in another country at less than the cost of production and transport, GATT allowed discriminatory action. Unfortunately, charges of dumping are difficult to disprove, so this provision in the GATT rules has often been misused.

   President Kennedy of the U.S took the initiative to start a dialogue on further reduction of tariff with the major trading nations of the world. The Kennedy

Round tariff reductions by developing countries have been estimated at about 36-39% and affected 75% of the world trade. Agricultural products were generally excluded from the Kennedy round of agreements.

Another round talks was at Japan during 1973 -79 and is known as the Tokyo round. Once again the concessions were concentrated in manufactured goods and agricultural commodities being treated differently. Moreover, textiles and clothing, leather, footwear and travel goods received lower Tariff cuts and often none at all. In 1989 the 'Geneva accord' was signed, However the United States and European community failed to reach any agreement on agricultural policy.

The Dunkel draft was the final act to be ratified by member nations of the GATT and was tabled at the end of 1991. Dunkel was the secretary general of GATT. This set of rules for the WTO was not immediately acceptable to the different blocks in world trade. Agriculture continued to be main bone of contention between U.S and European community. Another point of disagreement among the contracting parties was export of textiles. But some countries did not agree with Dunkel draft particularly about textiles.

Yet another issue before the member nations pressed by the United States was that of services – insurance, transport, engineering etc. It was one of the new issues of the Uruguay Round.

After extensive discussions and compromises on various issues the Dunkel draft was accepted by the USA and European community and Japan. Other member nations were asked to ratify the draft as it is at an early date, and the 132 member nations ratified the draft one after the other. The WTO was a reality on January 1, 1995.

22.4 | The World Trade Organization (WTO]

The WTO began its operation on January, 1995 and was created to replace the GATT. WTO is a chartered trade organization, not a just secretariat as GATT. However, the WTO continues the work of GATT to limit harmful trade practices. WTO covers services including TRIPS and it has more compelling dispute settlement function. By 2001 there were 142 members in it.

Structure of WTO

The ministerial conference (MC) is at the top of the structural organization of the WTO. It is the supreme governing body which takes ultimate decisions on all matters. It is constituted by representatives of all the member countries [minister of Trade].

The General council is the real engine of the WTO which acts on behalf of the Ministerial conference. It also acts as the dispute settlement body and as the trade policy review body.

Further there are 3 committees, Viz.

1. The committee on Trade and Development [CTD]
2. The committee on Balance Of Payments Restrictions [CBOPR]
3. Committee on Finance, Budget and Administration (CFBA)

   The WTO is conducted by the secretariat which is headed by the Director General (DG) appointed by the MC for the tenure of four years.

Objectives and function of the WTO

The purpose and objectives of the WTO are spelled out in the preamble to the agreement.

1. To ensure the reduction of Tariffs and other barriers to the trade.
2. To eliminate discriminatory treatment in international trade relations;
3. To facilitate higher standards of living, full employment, a growing volume of real income and effective demand and an increase in production and trade in goods and services of the member nations.
4. To make positive effect, which ensures developing countries, especially the least developed to secure a level of share in the growth of international trade that reflects the needs of their economic development.
5. To facilitate the optimal use of the world's resources for sustainable growth.
6. To promote an integrated, more viable and durable trading system incorporating all the resolutions of the Uruguay Round multilateral trade negotiations.

Functions of the WTO

1. To lay down a substantive code of conduct aiming at reducing trade barriers including tariffs and eliminating discrimination in international trade relations.
2. To provide the institutional frame work for the administration of the substantive code, norms governing the conduct of member countries in the global trade.
3. To provide an integrated structure of the administration, thus to facilitate the implementation, administration and fulfillment of the objectives of the WTO Agreement and other multilateral trade agreements.
4. To ensure the implementation of the substantive code.
5. To act as a forum for the negotiation of further trade liberalization.
6. To cooperate with the IMF and WB and its associates for establishing a trade policy-making.
7. To settle the trade-related disputes.

Importance of WTO

WTO is a permanent institution. It is expected to play the role of a watch dog in the sphere of trade, investment etc.

22.5 | Trade Related Intellectual Property Rights

This agreement is related to the following areas of Trade related aspects.

1. Copy right and related right
2. Trade marks
3. Geographical indications
4. Industrial designs.
5. Patents
6. Lay-out design of integrated circuits
7. Protection of units closed information
8. Control of anti-competitive practices in contractual licenses.

All WTO members are required to amend their patent laws, so as to provide protection to intellectual property. Indian Patents Act 1974 provided process patents instead of product patents. WTO provisions require this to be reversed. All the nations have to amend their patent laws by 2005. India couldn't amend its Indian Patents Act, 1974 in time.

22.6 | Trade Related Investment measures

These relate to investment policies of member countries. The member nations have to accept the following obligations.

(a) To notify the WTO about the operation of such investment measures.

(b) To make a commitment to eliminate such investment measures within a specified period which is two years for developing countries and five years for under-developed countries

The Uruguay Round agreement do not affect our country's investment policies. It is entirely up to us to decide in which areas we permit foreign investment and in which areas this is not to be permitted.

Trade services

Under the General Agreement on Trade in Services (GATS), markets shall be opened for banking, insurance and other financial services including legal and medical services. An agreement to this effect was reached and 102 WTO members made commitments. They opened up their financial markets from March 1999.

Some issues under WTO

1. ***Export subsides***: In the case of prohibition of Red subsidies (income tax exemption on export profit, and interest subsidy on export credit) are not applicable as per capita income less than $1000.
2. ***Support to agriculture***: The Agreement on Agriculture (AOA) came in force January 1995. It was stipulated a reduction 20% in subsidies to agriculture by developed countries and 13% reduction in developing countries over 6 years.
3. ***Impact on Industry***: Under WTO stipulations quantitative restrictions (QRs) on imports had to be phased out by 2003. In April 2001 the remaining 714 items will be freed.
4. ***Textiles and Multi fibre Agreement (MFA)***: The MFA is being phased out over 10 years period starting in 1997. The abolition of Quota restrictions would help to increase exports of textiles and garments, a major item of exports from India.

22.7 | India and the WTO

India was the one of the 23 countries which signed the GATT document in 1948. The 50th year of the founding WTO was celebrated in 1998. India's minister of commerce participated in the celebrations.

India's view point was that the developed countries must first practice what they preach.

2nd the WTO has to give enough time to the developing countries to enable them to adjust to the new WTO rules, especially those regarding Quantitative restrictions and trade related TRIPS

India is very much worried about the conditions of removal of quantitative restrictions on imports by 1999. Both US and E.C. community have asked India to lift the ban on imports because its balance of payments position is now sound, all the same India has to go slow in liberalization of trade.

After amending the export & import policy 1998 the Government of India has shifted 340 items from the restricted list of imports to the open general license and balance 2400 items can be shifted OGL category by end of 2000.

22.8 | Export Procedures

Export is selling the goods and merchandise to other countries crossing the geographical frontiers of the country. The foreign trade requires the services of export and import agents. A good example of export is India selling goods to USA and England. Export earns a country lot of foreign exchange and helps in tilting the balance of payments.

22.9 | Export Procedure

The export of goods to other countries involves several recognized procedures and systematic steps. The important procedures are given below.

1. **Receipt of indent:** Receipt of Order from the foreign importer. This is called indent. There are two types of indents. 1. Open Indent and 2. Closed Indent. Open indent consists of the written request for goods required. But closed indent consists of not only the written order for goods but also related instructions regarding the goods like type of packing, mode of transport, insurance etc.
2. **Receipt of license for export:** For exporting goods outside India, a license is required. The license for export is issued by the Controller of Exports. Prescribed format is available for this purpose. The person who intends to export has to fulfill all the conditions by filling the application for the purpose.
3. **Procurement of goods:** The goods required for export are purchased by the exporter in the local market. The specifications listed in the indent, sent by the importer have to be kept in mind by the exporter while procuring the merchandise.
4. **Packing and labeling:** The contents are packed according to the specifications issued in the indent letter. If no specifications are given, then the goods are packed according to the exporter's norms. After packing the goods, labeling should be properly done so that the goods is recognized by the importer.
5. **Appointment of forwarding agents:** Forwarding agent is appointed for the shipment of the goods and other ancillary services. Forwarding agents collect the goods from Railways and other transport services and they help in arranging for the shipment, payment of export duty, insurance, loading and fulfilling other formalities of shipment.
6. **Dispatch of goods:** Forwarding agents do the delivery of goods by showing letter from the exporter which they already received by post. Then arrangement is made for the shipment of goods.
7. **Foreign customs permit:** The forwarding agent has to get the return permission for export from the Government. This is called customs permit. For this, he has to fill the requisite application providing particulars like quantity of goods, nature of goods and it's value etc. Generally the permission for export is given expect for the goods which are banned by the Government for export.

8. **Shipping order:** Once the customs permit is received, necessary arrangements for sending the goods in ship and freight etc., has to be decided with the shipping company. Shipping order is prepared which is usually of two types, 1. Ready Order and 2. Forward Order. Ready order is given for the goods to be transported immediately and the name of the ship is specified. The goods which is to be transported at a later date and the name of the ship is not mentioned in Forward order. After receiving the shipping order the goods will be sent.

9. **Export duty and shipment bill:** Forwarding agent fills up the shipping bill or customs house challan in triplicate. The detail of goods, name of the ship, name of the exporter and his address etc., is specified in it. The customs authorities keep one copy of the shipping bill and return two copies after receiving the customs duty.

   The shipping bill is of three types:

   (i) Duty Free (ii) Dutiable (iii) Coastal

   Duty free is applicable to goods on which duty is not payable whereas dutiable is used for goods on which duty is payable. Coastal is used for goods which are sent from one port to another port within the country.

10. **Dock dues or challan:** For sending the goods in to the port, permission has to be taken from the Dock authorities. For obtaining the permission Dock Challan is filled in duplicate and presented to the Dock authorities along with the copies of the shipping order, shipping bill and the Dock charges. One copy of the dock challan is returned to forwarding agent. The Dock authorities make necessary arrangements for loading the goods in to the ship.

11. **Loading the goods:** Dock officials usually load the goods into the ship. Inspection by the customs officials is done at the time of loading of the goods and their approval specified on the shipping bill.

12. **Mate's receipt:** Once the goods is loaded on to the ship, the Captain of the ship gives an acknowledgment receipt to the forwarding agent. This is called the Mate's receipt. It is of two types, (I) Clean and (II) Foul. If the packing of the goods is satisfactory, the Captain gives a clean receipt and if it not satisfactory or defective, he gives a foul receipt.

13. **Bill of lading:** The forwarding agent gets the bill of lading by showing the mate's receipt. A revenue stamp is affixed on every copy of bill of lading. It is a proof that freight has been paid.

14. **Marine insurance:** Marine insurance is done to cover the goods against sea perils (dangers) for an amount 10-15% higher than the value of goods. Insurance should be done from the same company as specified in the indent.

15. **Forwarding agents advice:** The forwarding agent will send an account of expenses occurred adding his commission and along with the copies of bill of lading, insurance policy bill, dock challan etc., to the exporter.

16. **Preparation of export invoice:** Based on the specifications of the indent, the exporter will prepare the export invoice, the consular invoice and certificate of Origin (the place from where the goods originated) and sends it to the importer.
17. **Payment:** Payment depends upon the terms and conditions between the exporter and the importer. Usually Bank drafts, Bill of exchange and sometimes documents against acceptance bill and documents against Payment bill are utilized.
18. **Advice to importer:** When once the whole process is completed and the ship sails, the exporter will inform in advance regarding the dispatch to the importer. Information is sent to the importer for getting the necessary documents related to the shipment ready.

22.10 | Import Procedures

When a country purchases goods from other countries and brings the merchandise into the country crossing the geographical borders of the country, it is called an Import. Usually, the goods and services which are deficient and falling short are usually brought from outside. In India, we import electronic goods, software accessories and other sunrise products.

22.11 | Import Procedure

The following recognized steps are there in the process of Import.

1. **Obtaining import license:** Ministry of Commerce usually issues the Import License. The importer has to get an import license by applying in a prescribed application to the controller of imports, Government of India.
2. **Foreign exchange:** Since the goods are purchased in another country, payment has to be made in the currency of country of origin of goods. In such cases permission has to be obtained from Reserve Bank of India to get the necessary foreign exchange.
3. **Placing the indent:** The importer prepares the detailed specifications of the items to be imported and hand it over to any import agent. The importer can send the indent direct to the export agent of that country, if it is known to importer.
4. **Dispatch of goods by export agent:** On receiving the indent, the export agent will purchase the required goods from the producers of wholesalers, packs them as per specification, get them insured and sends them to the importer. He also sends all the documents of title of goods to the importer.

5. **Obtaining shipment documents:** Export agent also sends shipment document like bill of lading along with other documents. On the receipt of these documents, the importer starts process of getting the goods cleared from the port.
6. **Appointment of clearing agent:** The importer appoints a clearing agent at the port to get the possession of his goods. He endorses all his documents in favor of clearing agent.
7. **Endorsement of delivery:** After getting the documents, the clearing agent visit the office of shipping company for the endorsement of delivery on the bill of landing or a delivery order in his favor. If any balance freight is due, it is paid off and the delivery of goods is received by clearing agent.
8. **Payment of the import duty:** The clearing agent, visit the customs office to get three forms known as bill of entry. These forms are in three different colors i.e., black, blue and sky blue. Black form is used for the goods on which octroi is payable, blue form is for the goods to be sold or used within the country and sky blue for the goods meant for re-export. On receiving this form, the customs authorities inspect the goods and charge customs duty. One copy of the form is kept by the customs department while other two copies are handed over to the agent.
9. **Dock dues:** The goods can be taken out from the Dock only after paying the Dock Dues. After paying the customs duty the agent pays the dock dues by filling the necessary forms in duplicate.
10. **Taking delivery of goods:** Before taking the delivery of goods, the condition of the goods is checked by the agent. If the goods are not in a good condition, he prepares a report to fix the responsibility for the damage. Demurrage (fine) has to be paid if the goods are not cleared from the dock within a specified period.
11. **Keeping goods in warehouse:** If the importer is unable to pay customs charges, due to any reason, the goods are kept in the 'bonded warehouse'. A special entry bill is filled for this purpose. The customs authorities give a receipt called 'dock warrant' to the importer. The importer can take delivery of goods only after the payment of the import duty.
12. **Dispatch of goods by clearing agent:** After getting the delivery of goods from dock, the clearing agents send it to the importer by rail. He gets the railway receipt (R/R) from the railway authorities and sends it to the importer, so that the importer can get the delivery of goods from the railways.

13. **Receipt of documents:** The agent sends the documents like R/R, vouchers of expenses and his commission bill to the importer by post.
14. **Taking the delivery:** The importer gets the delivery of goods from the railway or the transporter company, by showing the relevant documents. The goods are transferred to the godowns of the importer.

Review Questions

Short Answer Questions

1. Write a short note on import procedure.
2. Explain trade related intellectual property rights?

Long Answer Questions

1. Explain in detail the process of Export and Import procedures.
2. Explain the importance of GATT agreement in modern world.
3. Explain the concept - TRIPS.

23 Insurance

23.1 | Introduction

LEARNING OBJECTIVES

- *Definition and importance of Insurance*
- *Principles of Insurance*
- *Types of Insurance-Life Insurance and General Insurance*
- *Re-insurance*

Business is a complex human activity and is intricately woven with several hazards. Businessman should be careful and carryout his business activities with foresight and caution so that he can earn profits. There are innumerable risk in the business activity. Hence the businessman should be able to avoid some and some risks can be shifted by him to agencies or persons who are qualified and willing to share the risks. Insurance is a means of shifting the un-avoidable risks in the business activity to a insurer in consideration of a nominal cost called premium. Insurance helps the businessman in carrying on the business with confidence and peace of mind.

23.2 | Definition

Insurance is a contract or agreement under which one party agrees in return of a consideration to pay an agreed amount of money to another party to make good for a loss, damage, injury something of value in which the insured has pecuniary interest in case of an un-expected event.

The agency which is a party to insurance agreement is known as 'Insurer' or 'Insurance Company'. The person who gets his life or property insured is known as 'Insured' or 'Assured'. The contract in writing is known as 'Policy'. Periodic payments by the insured in lieu of the insurance coverage by the insurer is known as 'Premium'.

23.3 | Principles of Insurance

Irrespective of the category of Insurance, generally Insurance contracts have the following fundamental principles.

(a) **Utmost Good faith:** An Insurance contract requires absolute and utmost good faith on the part of the parties concerned. Each party must reveal to the other party all informations influencing the contract. Failure to reveal material information or suppression of the facts or misrepresentation regarding the contract gives the affected party the right to regard the contract as null and void.

While making the proposal and while continuing it till the completion of the contract, the insured has to disclose all material facts and information related to the contract. If this is not done, the insured has no obligation against that contract.

The insurance contracts are different from the ordinary business contracts. In business contracts, the buyer should be beware and is expected to take necessary care to satisfy himself regarding the genuineness and quality of goods he intends to purchase. The businessman will not be disclosing all the information regarding the goods being sold. But in case of insurance contracts both the parties are under an obligation to make the fullest disclosure of all such facts which may have some bearing on the decision of the other party to enter into such contract. This binding applies particularly to the insured party who is naturally in possession of all material facts relating to his life or property.

(b) **Insurable Interest:** No person can enter into a valid contract of insurance unless he has some interest in the matter of insurance. Without the interest, the contract will be a gamble and it will become null and void. Insurable interest is an interest in the preservation of a thing, or continuation of a life, recognized by law. Whoever has such interest in a thing or life may insure that thing or that life. Insurable interest is in the nature of pecuniary or financial interest in a life or thing. One can have an insurable interest only when one stands to benefit financially by the continuance of the life or object insured. The loss caused by the risk insured against must be capable of estimation in terms of money. Insurable interest must be present both at the time of making the contract and at the time of loss of the subject matter. In all types of insurance the insured has to establish his insurable interest in the insured object at the time when the loss is paid to him on the happening of the event insured against.

(c) **Indemnity:** All insurance contracts other than life insurance are contracts of indemnity (Security against loss or compensation). The basic purpose of insurance is to shift the loss of a person or object to the insurance company which can easily spread it over a large number of policy holders. A person gets the same amount as he has lost due to the loss of his goods or damage to his property in insurance settlement. Insurance contract is not a business contract and hence the insured cannot be permitted to make a profit out of his loss.

If an insurance company agrees to pay a fixed sum higher than the amount of loss which the insured may suffer, the insured is in a constant temptation to destroy his goods or property intentionally and obtain a profit out of the insurance contract. Hence it is a well established principle of insurance that an insured should be paid only the cash value of his loss in the event of the occurrence of loss and nothing more.

For example if a person insures his goods against fire for Rs. 50,000/- and in the course of the time, if the goods are destroyed and the actual loss is found to be Rs. 20,000/-, the owner of the goods will be indemnified only to the extent of Rs. 20,000/- . Contrary if the goods or property is insured for a smaller sum than the actual cash value of the actual loss, the insurance company is bound to pay the amount of the policy and not the actual loss. It is because by under insuring his goods, the insured has expressed his intention of transferring only a part of his actual loss to the insurance company. The remaining loss will have to be met by the insured himself. This is not applicable to life insurance and other personal insurances where a fixed sum is undertaken to be paid either on the death of a person or after the expiry of a fixed period. Hence life insurance contracts are called as 'contracts of indemnity'.

(d) Subrogation: The doctrine of subrogation is an extension and a corollary of the principle of indemnity. According to it, the insurer steps into the shoes of the insured and becomes entitled to all rights of the insured regarding the subject-matter of insurance after the claim of the insured has been fully and finally settled. In some cases, there may be a possibility of his getting something in addition to that which he has received from the insurance company. The goods may have been partially damaged or the property may not have been fully destroyed. In such a case, the insured may try to obtain the value of scrap in addition to the money received in settlement of the claim. This will, however, be contrary to the principle of indemnity because the insured will be able to get more than what he has really lost. The doctrine of subrogation comes into operation here. The scrap, or whatever is left of the damaged or destroyed goods or property will automatically pass into the hands of the insurance company after the payment of the claim under this doctrine.

The important characteristics of this principle are:

1. The insured has to surrender all his rights to the insurer who have paid the claim, to the extent of the amount paid by the insurer.
2. The insurance company will have the same right which the insured had against the third party.

3. On this issue, the insurance company can file a case in the court of law to obtain the benefits in the name of insured.
4. The insurance company will get this right only when compensation has been already made to the insured.

(e) Contribution: In some cases a person may insure his goods with more than one insurer which is known as 'Double Insurance'. In the event of a loss, the insured will be indemnified only against the actual amount of loss incurred through the risk insured against. In this situation, the companies which are a party to the agreement will follow the principle of contribution.

Each company will contribute that proportion of the loss which the policy issued by it bears to the total amount for which insurance has been effected with all the companies. The insured can take two or more than two policies for the same property but he shall not be entitled to claim from each insurer more than the ratable proportion of the loss to which one is liable.

Example: Suppose say A.S.N. Pharmacy College, Tenali has insured the college building for Rs. 1,00,00,000 with Andhra Bank for Rs. 80,00,000 and with State Bank of India for Rs. 1,00,00,000. A loss of Rs. 50,00,000 occurs for the building. The liability of Andhra Bank and State Bank of India will be calculated as follows.

Liability of Andhra Bank = × loss

= × 50,00,000

= Rs. 22.00,000/-

Liability of S.B.I = × loss

= × 50,00,000

= Rs. 28,00,000/-

Thus, all insurance companies are legally liable to contribute their proportionate share towards the payment of risk.

(f) Mitigation of Loss: When a mishap or accident occurs, it is the prime responsibility of the insured to take all possible steps to minimize the loss or damage to the property as would have been taken by anybody who is not insured. The rationale behind this principle is that the insured should not become careless and lethargic in the event of the mishap because the property which is getting damaged is already insured. But he should act like any un-insured intelligent person. This does not imply that he should risk his life in saving the property which is being destroyed. The meaning of the clause is that all possible and reasonable efforts should be done by the insured in protecting and saving his property in the event of an accident.

(g) Causa Proxima: Causa Proxima means the direct or the most nearest cause. In the case where the accident insured against is the outcome of a several events, the insurance company will meet the loss only if it is caused by the nearest event covered by the policy. The meaning is that an insured person can recover the loss only when the accident is caused by any of the nearest risks insured against it. For example a consignment is being sent in a wagon in a train. The goods is insured for transportation in the train. Suppose during the trans-shipment, the goods are unloaded and kept in a station for further action. Now if the goods are damaged due to fire, the insurance company is not responsible and will not honour the contract because the risk took place due to a reason which does not come under the purview of the contract and the cause is remote.

Causes of loss are of two types

(a) Insured accidents

(b) Excepted or un-insured accidents

An insured may recover damages if the cause has been immediate or near cause to the loss and the insurer will not be liable to compensate for excepted or un-insured accidents arising due to direct or indirect reasons.

23.4 | Types of Insurance

The subject of insurance is broadly classified into two categories based on the fact that whether the insurance is for life or for inanimate objects.

(a) Life Insurance

(b) General Insurance

(a) ***Life Insurance***: Life insurance is a contract for payment of a sum of money to the person assured (or falling him/her, to the person entitled to receive the same) on the happening of the event insured against. Usually the contract provides for the payment of an amount on the date of maturity or at specified dates at periodic intervals or at unfortunate death, if it occurs earlier. Among other things, the contract also provides for the payment of premium periodically to the Corporation by the assured. Life insurance is universally acknowledged to be an institution which eliminates 'risk', substituting certainty for uncertainty and comes to the timely aid of the family in the unfortunate event or the death of the breadwinner. By and large, life insurance is civilization's partial solution to the problems caused by death. Life insurance, in short, is concerned with two hazards that stand across the life-path of every person; that of dying prematurely leaving a dependent family to fend for itself and that of living to old age without visible means of support.

The following schemes of Life Insurance are very popular.

1. Individual Schemes
2. Group Schemes

1. ***Individual Schemes:*** The common individual Life Insurance policies are given below

(i) *Whole Life Assurance Plan*: A low cost insurance plan where the Sum Assured is payable on the death of the life assured and premiums are payable throughout life.

(ii) *Endowment Assurance Plan*: Under this plan the Sum Assured is payable on the date of maturity or on death of the life assured, if earlier.

(iii) *Convertible Term Assurance Plan*: It provides term assurance for 5 to 7 years with an option to purchase a new Limited Payment Whole Life Policy or an Endowment Assurance Policy at the end of the selected term provided the policy is in full force.

(iv) *Joint Life–last Survivor–Annuity–cum–Assurance Plan (for husband and wife)*: In this type of Policy the claim amount is payable partly in lump sum and partly in the form of an annuity with return of balance sum assured on the death to the survivor.

(v) *Children Policy*: This policy provides benefits to a minor and takes care of his education, health, marriage and future needs. LIC has various children's deferred assurance plans like Komal Jeevan, Jeevan Kishore, Jeevan Balya etc.

(vi) *Woman's Policy*: This policy provides benefits to women and even covers diseases specific to women. Jeevan Bharati, LIC's money back plan, has been designed for women in the age group of 18 to 50 years. This policy provides for accident benefit and disability benefit up to an overall limit of Rs. 25 lakhs and covers woman specific diseases like cancer in the breast, ovarian, cervical and vagina.

(vii) *Pension Policy*: This policy provides for either immediate or deferred pension for life after retirement. The pension payments are made till the death of the annuitant (unless the policy has provision of guaranteed period).

2. **Group Schemes:** Group Insurance schemes offer Life Insurance to various groups such as employer-employee, professionals, co-operatives, weaker sections of the society etc. The scheme also provides insurance coverage to people under certain approved occupations at subsidized rates under social security group schemes. Besides providing insurance coverage, it also offers group schemes to employers which provide funding of gratuity and pension liabilities of the employers.

   The main features of this group schemes are as follows:

   - Low Premium
   - Simple Insurability conditions
   - Premium Decision based on age, combination of members, occupations and working conditions of the groups.

The following group schemes are available:

- *Group Superannuation Plan :* This plan allows employer and an employee to make a certain fixed regular contribution to a fund. The accumulated amount is utilized to provide various benefits on employee's retirement, death or on withdrawal.
- *Group term Plan:* This plan provides for life cover to members of a group. The benefit is paid to the beneficiary nominated by the members on death.
- *Group Gratuity Plan:* This plan helps employers to fund their statutory gratuity obligation under the payment of Gratuity Act. Every employer is under the obligation to pay half-month salary for every completed year of service to each of his employee on their exit. At the end of the accumulation period, the policy holder has an option to choose pension for self only or pension for self and spouse.

Some important terms and their definition in life insurance:

- *Surrender Value:* If a policy holder decides to surrender his policy (i.e., discontinue it) before its maturity the insurer pays him the surrender value. A policy, however, acquires surrender value after it has run for at least three years. Such value is based on the actual premium paid, though it is only a fraction of the total amount paid by way of premium.
- *Paid–up Value:* If the policy holder discontinues the payment of the premium on the life policy, he may get it paid up. In such a case, he will be entitled to the paid-up value of the policy. Such a value will, however, be paid only at the maturity of the policy.
- *Automatic Non-Forfeiture:* Generally, if the premium on a policy is not paid at the due time, it lapses. It can be revived only after paying up the arrears of premium. In some cases, the policy may include an automatic non-forfeiture clause. Under it, if the payment of the premium is discontinued after it acquires surrender value the premium will be automatically received from the surrender value. When, however, the surrender value is fully exhausted, the policy lapses.
- *Assignment:* The assignment of a policy means the transfer of the rights and liabilities of the assured to the third party. "It is, however, possible to assign the policy itself without assigning the right under it", assignment must be in writing and may be made on a separate piece of paper or as an endorsement on the back of the policy itself. The notice of assignment must be given to the insurer who will register it.
- *Nomination:* When the Policy holder mentions the name of a person in the policy or endorses it thereon, with the object of enabling him to get the amount of the policy after his (Policy holder's) death, it is called nomination. The person so named is called a nominee. If the policy becomes due for payment within the life-time of the assured, the money will be paid to him; otherwise, it will be paid to the

nominee. A nomination may be cancelled or changed before the maturity of the policy.

(b) ***General Insurance*:** General Insurance is the insurance coverage given to movable and immovable assets. It provides risk cover to movable assets like shops, godowns, goods during transportation, vehicles etc. Insurance coverage to immovable assets includes factories, houses, shops and other establishments. General insurance is an important risk cover for business community. Usually all businessman buy general insurance based upon their exigencies. Some of the important insurance covers under the general insurance scheme are as follows:

Fire Insurance: Fire insurance is a contract of indemnity under which insurance company or the insurer, in consideration of the premium paid, undertake to compensate the insured for any loss that may result due to the occurrence of the fire. It is a yearly contract and automatically lapses at the end of the year, unless it is renewed. The premium may be paid either in lump sum or by installments. The document of the contract is known as 'Fire Insurance Policy'.

For taking out a fire policy, the owner of the goods or property has to fill proposal form giving details of the property, its location, its contents, etc. The insurer then assesses the risk through surveyors who may make on the spot enquiries about the property and determine the risk involved in its insurance against risks of fire. Generally, the insurer gives his acceptance of the proposal submitted by the insured subject to the payment of premium. In such cases, the risk will commence only when the premium has been paid. Before the policy in its final form can be prepared; the insurer will issue a cover note which is in the nature of an interim protection note. If a fire occurs in the meanwhile, the cover note will cover the risk and the insurer will be liable under it. Finally a fire insurance policy duly stamped and containing the terms and conditions of insurance will be issued by the insurer to the insured.

The following are the important types of fire policies :

(a) *Comprehensive Policy*: It is also called as 'All Insurance Policy'. This type of policies are issued to cover risks like fire, explosion, lightening, thunderbolt, riots, strikes, burglary etc.

(b) *Blanket Policy*: It covers all assets – fixed as well as current – of the insured under one blanket.

(c) *Specific Policy*: A Specific Policy is the one which insures a risk for specific sum. In case of any loss to the property insured under such a policy, the insurer will pay the whole loss of the insured, provided that it does not exceed the specified sum mentioned in the Policy.

(d) *Floating Policy*: It covers one or several kind of goods lying in different localities under one sum and for one premium.

(e) *Valued Policy*: In this policy, the value of the property is ascertained or agreed upon and the insurer undertakes to pay his agreed value in the event of the destruction of property by fire.

(f) *Reinstatement Policy*: In this policy, the insurer pays the amount which is required to reinstate the asset or property destroyed. While calculating the amount of claim, depreciation is not deducted from the original value of the assets.

Marine Insurance: In marine insurance, the risk covered are loss or damage to the insured vessel, cargo or passengers during transportation on the high seas. Marine insurance is a contract under which the insurer undertakes to indemnity the insured against the losses incidental to marine adventure. Sea perils include risk of loss by piracy, capture, seizure, jettison, barberry etc. A marine policy may be taken for a particular period or for a particular voyage.

The following types of marine policies are common:

(a) *Time Policy*: This is a policy whereby the insurance is made for a specified period of time. It is suitable for hull insurance though it may be taken out also for movables and other goods when small quantities are involved.

(b) *Voyage Policy*: The policy is meant to insure the subject matter in transit from one place to another. The subject matter insured is generally cargo which is exposed to marine risks in the course of transit.

(c) *Mixed Policy*: It is also known as time and voyage policy. It seeks to insure the subject matter (hull or ship) on a particular voyage for a specific period of time.

(d) *Floating Policy*: It is used by the cargo-owners who make regular shipments of cargoes to insure the shipment expected to be made during a certain period of one policy. A policy may be taken for a fixed amount. Whenever some cargo is shipped, the insured makes a declaration about the value of the shipment and total value of the policy is reduced by that amount. Such declarations are made from time to time till the total value is exhausted and the policy is run off.

(e) *Blanket Policy*: It is taken for a certain amount but the premium is paid on the whole of it in the beginning of the policy and is re-adjusted at the end of the term of the policy in accordance with the actual amounts and risk as shown by records of the insured.

(f) *Fleet Insurance Policy*: It is designed to insure a whole fleet of liners or steamers.

(g) *Port Policy*: It covers the ship when it is anchored in some port.

Miscellaneous Insurance: In addition to the above risk factors, there are some minor inherent risks also like theft, damage to the vehicle, recovery of loan etc. So in order to cover this type of risks, the general insurance companies have introduced the following miscellaneous insurance policies.

(a) ***Motor Insurance***: A motor insurance covers the following risks.

- Damage to the vehicle by fire or accident or theft
- Injury to the owner of the vehicle
- Injury or death of some other party due to an accident in which the vehicle of the insured is involve.

A Policy covering all the above aspects is called as 'Comprehensive Policy'.

(b) ***Third Party Insurance***: This policy covers the risk because of damage to the property of a third party in addition to that arising out of personal bodily injury caused to a third party. Examples are house owners liability to tenants etc.

(c) ***Fidelity Insurance***: This Policy is done by an owner of business to cover the risks arising out of fraud and dishonesty done by his employees. This is a type of precaution on the part of the owner to protect himself in case his employees cheat him of goods or cash.

(d) ***Credit Insurance***: This policy consists of indemnifying the policy holder (a businessman) against the risks arising from the insolvency of a debtor. It implies that the insurer guarantees the credit worthiness and solvency of the debtors.

(e) ***Burglary, Theft and Robbery Insurance***: This is the policy, a comprehensive policy which covers the risks of theft and other things like burglary. For this type of policy the insured has to provide the necessary details like value and information regarding the safe in which the valuables are kept etc.

23.5 | Advantages of Insurance

- Insurance provides safety and security to individuals thereby the ability of a person to work increases and he can concentrate on his work.
- Life Insurance is a form of compulsory savings and it will be helpful during old age and in difficult circumstances.
- Insurance guards against theft and burglary which are a common phenomena now-a-days.
- Insurance provides security against risk of loss to a businessman.
- Insurance leads to stability in the business because the business is protected against the risks of loss and damage.
- Insurance companies mobilize the savings of the public and invest them in the stock market.
- Insurance creates lot of job potential.

23.6 | Re-Insurance

Sometimes an insurer wants to distribute some of his liability to another insurer. When the liability is more than what he can conveniently bear, he can transfer the excessive part of such risks to another insurer. For this he will insure that part of the risk with another insurer. This is called as 'Re-Insurance'.

Re-Insurance is of two types

1. **Facultative Re-Insurance:** The re-insurance of particular risk by agreement with another insurer.
2. **Treaty Re-Insurance:** Re-Insurance under a treaty by which the re-insurers agree to accept a certain proportion of all risks beyond a certain limit under written by the insurers.

| Review Questions

Short Answer Questions

1. Explain the concept 'Insurance'?
2. Briefly explain the doctrine of subrogation?
3. Explain briefly the marine insurance policy?
4. What are the advantages of Insurance?
5. Explain the concept of Life Insurance?

Long Answer Questions

1. Explain the various principles of Insurance?
2. Explain the concept 'General Insurance'? What are the various types of General Insurance?
3. Explain the individual and group schemes of Life Insurance Policy?

24 Labour Welfare

24.1 | Definition

Labor Welfare can be defined as creation of minimum required standards of the provision of facilities like health, food, clothing, housing, medical assistance, education, insurance, job security, recreation etc., which enable the worker and his family to lead a good working life, family life and social life.

Labor Welfare is anything done for the intellectual, physical, moral and economic betterment of the workers by the employers or the government or other agencies over and above what is laid down by law.

LEARNING OBJECTIVES

After studying the chapter the students familiarize themselves with the following concepts:

- *Important features of Labor Welfare*
- *Objectives of Labor Welfare*
- *Principles of Labor Welfare*
- *Types of Labor Welfare*
- *Benefits of Labor Welfare*
- *Labor Welfare in India*
- *Agencies of Labor Welfare in India*
- *Labor Welfare-Factories Act 1948*

24.2 | Characteristic Features of Labor Welfare

1. Welfare measures and amenities are provided not only to the employees but also to their family members.
2. There is a wide variation in the facilities and amenities provided which depend on the historical, cultural and societal conditions prevailing.
3. The contributors to Labor Welfare are the employers, government, trade unions and other outside agencies.

4. Labor Welfare measures do not include those facilities which are statutory or obligatory under any contract between the employer and the employee. They are only optional and voluntarily provided.

24.3 | Need for Labor Welfare

India is a developing country which is aiming for rapid economical and social development. Hence the concept of labor welfare is more important to our country. Labor welfare measures have immense beneficial effects on the work force. The important benefits are:

1. It has a humanistic approach and enables the workers to enjoy fuller and richer life.
2. It is economical as it improves the efficiency of the workers.
3. It has a civic approach in the sense that it develops a sense of responsibility and dignity among the workers.
4. It builds up a stable work force by reducing absenteeism.
5. It helps in winning the employees loyalty and to combat trade unionism .
6. It improves the morale of the workers and motivates them to work more.
7. It enhances the image of the organization and creates an atmosphere of goodwill between the labor and the management and also between management and the public.

24.4 | Objectives of Labor Welfare

The following are the important objectives of labor welfare:

1. To provide a congenial working atmosphere where the work force can excel.
2. To boost the morale of workers and to reduce the sense of frustration among them.
3. To relieve the workforce from their personal and family worries.
4. Helping the employees in maintaining good health.
5. To provide the employee a means of self expression and gratification.

24.5 | Principles of Labor Welfare

While formulating the objectives of labor welfare measures, the following principles to be kept in mind.

1. ***Right spirit***: The welfare activities should be undertaken in the right spirit. They are not substitute for low wages and other allowances. Nor they should be provided to undermine the influence of the trade unions.

2. **Should serve the real need of the workers:** The scheme so formulated must serve the real need of the employees concerned. Special classes of workers require special type of welfare services. Depending on the nature of the work and industry, the industrialist should assess the actual need of the workers and the priorities should be determined.
3. **Co-operation of the workers:** No welfare scheme could succeed without the active support of the workers. The workers should be allowed to participate in the formulation and administration of any welfare scheme to achieve the real objectives of the scheme.
4. **No compulsion:** There should be no compulsion for workers to avail of these facilities. In other words, labour welfare should be voluntary and the workers should be free to take advantage of such facilities (However, some compulsion must be imposed on the employers).

24.6 | Types of Labor Welfare

The Labor Welfare measures which are provided to the workforce can be broadly classified into the following categories.

1. **Intramural facilities:** Facilities provided within the four walls of the organization or factory. These facilities include canteen, provision of safety measures for the workers, good lighting conditions, first aid kit etc. These facilities are required to be provided by law.
2. **Extramural facilities:** Facilities offered to the workers outside the factory. They include accommodation, recreation facility, educational facility, sports facility etc. These facilities are not obligatory but are provided by the organization for the general welfare of workers.
3. **Statutory facilities:** These are the facilities which are to be provided under the provisions of law and labor legislation. These facilities may be either intramural or extramural facilities. They cannot be ignored as they are enforceable by law. For example provision of potable drinking water, provision of clean latrines and bathrooms.
4. **Mutual facilities:** These are the facilities which are not obligatory but done voluntarily by the workers themselves for their own interest. Hence the management or the employer has no role in it.
5. **Voluntary:** The facilities provided by the organization on its own and which are not obligatory come under this category. This type of facilities boosts the morale of employees.

24.7 | Benefits of Labor Welfare

Labor Welfare measures provide several benefits for the development of workers. The important benefits are :

1. ***Improvement in morale***: Welfare measures help in securing the willing co-operation of the workers which leads to decrease in anti social and wrong activities on the part of the employees. Hence this leads to increased morale and motivation.
2. **Harmonious industrial relations:** Strikes, Harthals, conflicts by the workers are minimized and a feeling of oneness with the organization is created.
3. **Improvement in the general efficiency and economy:** Welfare measures will improve the efficiency and productivity of the employees because they are relieved from the domestic problems like poor housing, insanitary conditions etc.
4. **Creation of permanent workforce:** When the organization looks after the employees well by providing them all necessary amenities and facilities, employees will not look for a change and stick on to the jobs for a longer period which helps in the stabilization of workforce.
5. **Social benefits:** The increase in the efficiency of the workers leads to an increase in production, rate of profit and the earnings of the organization. The increased earning leads to better salaries of the workers which leads to their happiness. Hence the standard of living of the society is raised.

24.8 | Labor Welfare in India

During the First and Second World War there were only isolated instances of labor welfare work in our Country. In the post war period and due to industrial revolution there was industrial expansion and the process of large scale production led to the rise of the working class as a source of power. After the independence, more teeth were given to factories act and the first two five year plans laid more emphasis on effective implementation of various statutory provisions.

24.9 | Agencies of Labor Welfare in India

Labor Welfare work in India is usually carried out by four main agencies namely,

1. The Employers
2. The Worker's Associations
3. The Central Government and
4. The State Government.

1. **Employers Role in Welfare Work:** Employer is in direct contact with the workforce. Hence he can play a important role in providing facilities required by the employees in addition to the what is laid down by law. Many organizations

like Infosys, Satyam Computers, Tata Corp., Reliance are providing excellent benefits to the employees in the form of welfare measures. The important welfare amenities provided by them are educational facilities, crèches, housing facilities, sponsoring trips to the family abroad, gifts on the marriages of children etc.

2. **Labor Welfare Work by Worker's Associations:** These are the activities provided by the Unions for the benefits of their members by means of funds mobilized by them. Several unions have done a good deal of work in this regard. Some of them worth mentioning are Mazdoor Union, Textile Labor Association etc. Welfare activities provided by these associations include schools, libraries, maternity homes, dispensaries, co-operative societies and free legal aid etc.
3. **Labor Welfare Work by Central Government:** The Central Government after independence has enacted several labor laws for the benefit of the workers. Some of the important acts are factories act, 1948, Coal Mines Labor Welfare Fund Act, 1947, etc.

   In five year plans also, The Central Government has spent huge amounts towards labour welfare. For example in 1st Five year plan, Rs. 29 crores, in 2nd Plan Rs. 71.08 crores and in 6th Five Year Plan, Rs. 350 crores.
4. **Labor Welfare work by State Governments:** Several State Governments and Union Territories have provided welfare centers which provide educational, recreational and health services to the workforce. These centers also provide library, gymnasium, training in handicrafts and tailoring classes for women workers etc. The main sources of finances for these funds are realized from employees only in the form of fines, voluntary donations, unclaimed and forfeited sums in Provident Fund Account and any Fund transferred from any other sources.

24.10 | Labor Welfare under Factories Act, 1948

The Factories Act, 1948 contains the following provisions relating to Labor Welfare:

1. **Washing Facilities:** In every factory (a) adequate and suitable facilities shall be provided and maintained for the use of workers; (b) separate and adequately screened facilities shall be provided for the use of male and female workers; (c) such facilities shall be easily accessible and shall be kept clean.
2. **Facilities for storing and drying clothing:** In every factory provision for suitable place should exist for keeping clothing not worn during working hours and for the drying of wet clothing.
3. **Facilities for sitting:** In every factory, suitable arrangements for sitting shall be provided and maintained for all workers who are obliged to work in a standing position so that the workers may take advantage of any opportunity for rest which

may occur in the course of work. If in any factory workers can efficiently do their work in a sitting position, the Chief Inspector may require the occupier of the factory to provide such seating arrangements as may be practicable.

4. **First aid appliance:** Under the Act, the provision for first-aid appliances are obligatory. At least one first-aid box or cupboard with the prescribed contents should be maintained for every 150 workers. It should be readily accessible during all working hours. Each first-aid box or cupboard shall be kept in the charge of a separate responsible person who holds a certificate in the first-aid treatment recognized by the State Government and who shall always be readily available during the working hours of the factory.

   In every factory wherein more than 500 workers are ordinarily employed there shall be provided and maintained an ambulance room of the prescribed size containing the prescribed equipment. The ambulance room shall be in the charge of properly qualified medical and nursing staff. These facilities shall always be made readily available during the working hours of the factory.

5. **Canteens:** In every factory employing more than 250 workers, the State Government may make rules requiring that a canteen or canteens shall be provided for the use of workers. Such rules may provide for (a) the date by which the canteen shall be provided, (b) the standards in respect of construction, accommodation, furniture and other equipment of the canteen; (c) the foodstuffs to be served therein and charges which may be made thereof; (d) the constitution of a managing committee for the canteens and representation of the workers in the management of the canteen; (e) the items of expenditure in the running of the canteen which are not to be taken into account in fixing the cost of foodstuffs and which shall be borne by the employer; (f) the delegation to the Chief Inspector, of the power to make rules under clause (c).

6. **Shelters, rest rooms and lunch rooms:** In every factory wherein more than 150 workers are ordinarily employed, there shall be a provision for shelters, rest room and suitable lunch room where workers can eat meals brought by them with provision for drinking water. Where a lunch room exists, no worker shall eat any food in the work room. Such shelters or rest rooms or lunch rooms shall be sufficiently lighted and ventilated and shall be maintained in a cool and clean condition.

7. **Crèches:** In every factory wherein more than 30 women workers are ordinarily employed there shall be provided and maintained a suitable room or rooms for the use of children under the age of six years of such women. Such rooms shall provide adequate accommodation, shall be adequately lighted and ventilated, shall be maintained in clean and sanitary conditions and shall be under the charge of women trained in the care of children and infants.

The State Government may make rules for the provision of additional facilities for the care of children belonging to women workers including suitable provision of facilities:

(a) for washing and changing their clothing (b) of free milk or refreshment or both for the children and (c) for the mothers of children to feed them at the necessary intervals.

8. **Welfare officers:** In every factory wherein 500 or more workers are ordinarily employed, the occupier shall employ in the factory such number of welfare officers as may be prescribed under Sec. 49(1). The State Government may prescribe the duties, qualifications and conditions of service of such officers.

Review Questions

Short Answer Questions

1. Explain the provisions of the Indian Factories Act, 1948 with respect to the welfare of the workers?
2. Define the term 'Labor Welfare'? Give a brief account of the welfare activities organized by different agencies in India?

25 Materials Management and Control

25.1 | Introduction and Definition

LEARNING OBJECTIVES

- *General introduction and definition of Materials Management*
- *Drugs store management*
- *Tenders*
- *Contract*
- *Codification*
- *Methods of Codification*
- *Lay out and facilities*
- *Inventory Control*
- *Scrap and Surplus disposal*

It is the science that deals with the raw materials procurements, obtaining machines and equipment which are necessary for the production process and it also includes the upkeep and maintenance of the plant and making available the spare parts required for the machinery in the plant.

Every manufacturing enterprise requires raw materials and semi-finished goods as inputs for obtaining the products desired. Hence the success of an enterprise depends to a large extent on the efficient and judicious use and procurement of raw materials and other inputs. Materials Management is a fundamental tool of the Business which adds value directly to the product itself. Materials Management is the planning, directing, controlling the activities which are related with the materials and inventory requirements from the point of their inception to their introduction into the manufacturing process. It deals with the regulating and controlling the flow of materials in relation to the changes in the variables like demand, price, availability, quality, delivery schedule etc.

25.2 | Objectives of Materials Management

1. It maintains the continuity of production by providing regular uninterrupted supply of raw materials.
2. It helps in procuring best quality items at the most reasonable price.
3. It leads to minimizing waste and economy thereby leading to high productivity.
4. Due to efficient management of production inputs, cost of production is lowered which leads to enhancement of profits.
5. It helps in maintaining optimum stocks and minimizes the storage and stock control costs.

25.3 | Functions of Materials Management

1. Procurement of raw materials and other inputs required for production.
2. Maintaining stores and stock levels.
3. Receiving and issuing of the materials.
4. Transportation and material handling.
5. Disposal of scrap and surplus material.

25.4 | Organization of a Materials Management Department

Every manufacturing organization has a separate materials management department, functioning directly under the President. The main role of this department is planning, directing, controlling and co-ordination of all the activities related to the materials and machinery in an organization.

The department is usually under the control of a materials manager. He is assisted by managers of each function separately. Usually he is assisted by a inventory control manager, purchasing control manager, traffic control manager and production control manager.

25.5 | Importance of Materials Management

The important inputs in a manufacturing organization are men, material and machinery. About 80% of the capital is invested in the above categories. A well designed material management operations lead to considerable saving in the capital expenditure. Thus materials management department plays a very vital role in the success of an organization. A good materials management has the following advantages :

1. Continuity in the production process due to uninterrupted supply of raw materials.
2. Continuous monitoring on the input costs and transportation costs.
3. Due to efficient store and stock control, minimization of waste.
4. Optimum utilization of men, material and machinery.
5. Helps in production of good quality goods.
6. Helps in reducing the steps involved in the manufacturing process.
7. Over storage of raw materials is avoided.
8. Helps in the elimination of shortages and provides continuous supply of goods.

25.6 | Importance of Purchasing

Purchasing is defined of the Procurement of Materials, Supplies, Machinery, tools, Implements, equipment and Services, which are necessary for the production of certain goods which includes the planning and policy activities, research and development and selection of source of supply etc.

Purchasing is a very important function of materials management. It consist of a exploration of market to obtain goods and services of desired quality, quantity at lowest price and at the desired time. Supplier who can provide standard items at a reasonable rate is chosen.

A success of any business organization depends on the effective buying. It is a managerial activity and includes R & D for the selection of right material and right source, timely delivery, ensuring inspections to control quality and quantity, receiving, store keeping and accounting operations related to purchases.

25.7 | Objectives of Purchasing

1. **Right Source:** The source from which the material is to be procured should be dependable and capable of supplying items of uniform quality.
2. **Right Quality:** Prior assessment of the quality should be done, then only the order should be placed with the supplier for his purchase.
3. **Right Quantity:** While deciding the right quantity, factors such as price structure, discounts, and availability of items are to be taken into consideration.
4. **Right Price:** The goods should be purchased at right price. For determination of the right price the cost structure of the product has to be taken into consideration.

5. **Right Time:** For determining the right time of purchase, the lead time information is taken into consideration. The lead time means the total time consumed between the recognition of the need of an item, till its receipt for use.
6. **Right place of Delivery:** The goods should be delivered at the place of the business. A supplier should deliver the goods at the place where they are required.

25.8 | Functions of Purchase Department

Buying incorporates not only the purchase of goods but also the entire gamut of purchase procedure. The important functions are:

1. Calculating and estimating the total material requirement.
2. Deciding the economic order quantity i.e., the optimum number of units or quantity that must be purchased less than one order.
3. Market survey to know the right person who can supply right goods at right price.
4. Calling for quotations and tenders.
5. Placing order for real quantity on the basis of quotations or tenders according to the terms and conditions laid there in.
6. Receiving the goods and an inspection of quality and quantity.
7. Distributing the goods to store.
8. Checking of the bill and making the payment.
9. Disposal of the items which are not useful.
10. Avoiding duplication of purchase and monitoring so that materials are not wasted or damaged by the user department.
11. Setting of disputes arising out of purchase of materials.
12. Maintenance of records pertaining to suppliers, products available with them.

25.9 | Purchasing Procedure

Various steps involved in the purchase of goods is known as purchasing procedure. A systematic procedure has to be developed by every organization for its smooth running. The purchase procedure involves the following steps:

1. Purchase Requisition,
2. Selection of the suppliers,
3. Inviting Quotations or tenders,
4. Placing the order,
5. Receiving and checking the material,
6. Checking of invoice or bill,

7. Recording of bills in books,
8. Releasing the payment to the supplier.

1. **Purchase Requisition:** When the existing stocks are depleted and come to a minimum, the stores in charge fills in the replenishment form and sends it to the purchase department. The purchase requisition indicates the type, quantity and quality of items to be purchased.
2. **Selection of the Suppliers:** A list of suppliers is collected from market survey journals, newspapers and trade guides. The suppliers are selected based on their credibility and who can provide timely service and in required quantity. Their past experience and their nature of service etc., is assessed.
3. **Inviting Quotations or Tenders:** Quotations are invited from suppliers with the list of requirements. If the Quantum of goods is large, tenders can be invited by giving list of requirements in leading newspapers. A last date is given for the tenders to reach the purchase department.
4. **Placing the Order:** Based on the quotations received the lowest quoted price order is selected. After selection of the supplier, the order is placed in the standard purchase order form called 'Supply Order'. The supply order contains the detailed order, the specifications of the items, quantity required, the price and other terms and conditions of the supply. It is signed by the authorized person. The supply order is a legal document. Generally 5 - 6 copies of supply orders are prepared. Two copies are sent to the suppliers who are expected to sign one copy as an acknowledgment and return it to the supply department. One copy is to be sent to the stores in charge. One copy goes to Accounts department, and another copy remains with the purchase manager.
5. **Receiving and Checking the Material:** The material sent by the supplier is received by the store keeper. Each and every item is physically checked, Quantity verified and specifications are cross checked with the invoice or "bill sent by the supplier". If the goods required doesn't confirm with any specifications or any damage is noticed, the matter is recorded on the challan form or bill and the supplier must be informed immediately so as to rectify the mistakes by the supplier.
6. **Checking the Invoice or Bill:** If the goods are received in satisfactory condition the invoice is checked before it is approved for payment. The rates of various items charged in the bill and the other terms and conditions are thoroughly checked and compared with the supply order.
7. **Recording of the Bills in Books:** The bills are sent to Accounts Section where the bills are entered into Account books. Any errors in bills are immediately informed to higher authorities for necessary action.
8. **Releasing the Payment to the Supplier:** According to terms and conditions of the supply order, the payment is done by Accounts Section to the supplier.

25.10 | Drug Store Management

Methods of Purchasing

Each organization adopts its own method of purchasing. The method adopted depends upon the classification of products in the production system, policy of the organization and behavior of the market. Some of the important methods of purchasing are:

(a) **Purchasing by requirement:** When there is a requirement for the goods, material, then only an order is placed. This method is suitable for items not in regular or continuous use but used in production process.

(b) **Market purchasing:** This method involves purchasing when goods price is low or fluctuating. This method provides obtaining the items at lower prices and economy for the organization. This method is useful in situations where major price variations are prominent,

(c) **Speculative purchasing:** Excessive purchasing is done when prices are low with the idea of earning profit by selling the items purchased in excess at a higher price. By this method, it is possible to get more profits and protection against strategies, but the organization has to meet financial commitments.

(d) **Contract purchasing:** The organization enters into the agreement with different suppliers for supply of items for a definite period of time. This is done when the prices are low.

(e) **Scheduled purchasing:** The purchasing is done according to the requirements of various departments of the organization. This is the most scientific method of purchasing. Proper balance is made between amount procured and amount required.

25.11 | Modes of Purchasing

The goods may be purchased in any one of the following ways:

1. By Inspection,
2. By Sample or Pattern,
3. By Description or brand,
4. By Grading.

1. **By Inspection:** Purchasing by inspection is the oldest mode of purchasing and still widely used in retail and wholesale transactions. In this method the customer comes to the premises of the seller for the inspection of the goods which are to be purchased. It is an ordinary method and has limited scope and utility because consumers living in the local area can go to the sellers show room for inspection and it is not possible for the customers living in very distant places to come for personal inspection.

2. **By Sample:** By sampling method consist of examining the sample of goods. A sample is specimen of goods usually of raw materials, food grains etc. It is a representative of the bulk sample. Its quality will reflect to a large extent the quality of the whole lot. While purchasing goods samples have to be carefully examined by the intending purchaser. That will give a idea about the quality of the bulk. Similarly a pattern is a specimen of standard Manufacture and it reveals the varieties of shade and texture. The code number given in the pattern has to be stated about the type of the goods and the order is placed.
3. **By Description:** Certain products become popular by advertisement because of brand name or trade names. Such type of goods can be purchased by simply specifying a particular brand or particular number in the catalogue to order the goods that he intends to purchase.
4. **By Grading:** Purchasing of standard items is done by looking at a grade. These grades are usually given by standard organization like Indian Bureau of Standards. These grades stand for quality. These grades help the trader in purchasing uniform and standard products.

25.12 | Selection of Suppliers

The prospective suppliers are contracted through their sales representatives, catalogues and sample of items, through the advertisements appearing in news papers, trade journals, trade shows and trade conference. When a new item is required for the first time and the source of supply is not known, the best way is to advertise for the demand. A number of suppliers may respond to these advertisements. Among these the most suitable one is selected.

Factors to be considered for the Selection of Prospective Suppliers

1. His past history and performance.
2. The financial position of the supplier.
3. His capacity to provide after sales service and technical assistance.
4. Response to the quotations invited.
5. The price is lowest or reasonable as compared to the competitors.
6. His general behavior and attitude when the goods are returned by the purchaser and his reputation in the market.

Considering all the above factors, a suitable list of suppliers is prepared which can be used for the purchases required for the organization. Usually the suppliers for different categories of items are prepared because no single supplier can supply all the items required.

25.13 | Credit Information

Credit (loan) is a medium through which goods can be purchased or sold without cash payment. Credit is useful to the wholesalers and retailers, credit helps the retailers to store the stock and sell the goods in large quantity. Credit helps the wholesalers to carry on their business with less capital. Though credit helps to store the stock and increases the sales, it involves risks such as bad debts and delayed payments. A sound credit policy, selection of good parties (parties indicate either wholesalers or retailers or customers) and prompt collection of loan are essential for the successful functioning of credit system.

Before giving credit, the following information must be ascertained about the parties.

1. **Character of the Parties:** Before giving credit to any parties, the business organization should find out their character. Character includes honesty, reliability, trust worthiness, morale and prompt payment of the parties.
2. **Capacity of the Parties:** The business organization should find out whether the parties have adequate business experience and whether they can be able to repay the loan amount in time etc.
3. **Capital of the Parties:** The business organization should gather information about the assets of the parties, the market value of their assets and the liabilities of the parties and the ratio between their assets and liabilities.
4. **Conditions of the Parties:** Before giving the credit to the concerned parties, the owner or organization must ascertain whether the parties can able to sell the goods efficiently or not.

The above 4 factors should be carefully considered before giving credit to any parties.

25.14 | Tenders

Tenders - Definition

Tenders are otherwise known as quotations. Tender is a tool used by business organization e.g., Public marketing, Govt. Departments, Private sector etc.) to execute their work at least cost. The business organizations sometimes invite tenders to purchase or sell the materials. They prefer lowest bidder while placing orders (i.e. while receiving goods from the suppliers) and highest bidder while supplying goods to the purchasers.

Methods of Obtaining Tenders

Usually tenders are invited when huge amount is involved. The different methods of obtaining tenders are:

1. Open tender,
2. Limited tender,
3. Single tender,
4. Oral tender, and
5. Closed tender.

1. **Open Tender:** Some tenders are invited by advertisement. Such type of tenders is known as open tenders. Open tenders are advertised when the suppliers are many and the value is large. The lowest tender is generally accepted but not in all cases. Open tenders are costly and time consuming.
2. **Limited Tender:** Some tenders are invited from a limited number of firms directly. Such types of tenders are known as limited tenders. When the value of tender is moderate, limited tender system is used.
3. **Single Tender:** Some tenders are invited from only one firm. Such tenders are known as single tender. Single tender is invited when a repetitive order is placed within a short period.
4. **Oral Tender:** In case, when the requirement is minimum and urgently needed, one man is deputed to purchase the required items from open market. He has to enquire the prices from two or three suppliers and purchase the materials from the supplier who quotes the minimum price. Such type of tenders is known as oral tenders.
5. **Closed Tender:** Closed tenders are also invited by advertisements. The business organizations invite sealed (closed) tenders from the reputed firms in a prescribed form. The tender forms are issued on payment of prescribed amount. The tenders will be opened in front of all the bidders on the particular date. The organization selects lowest bidder while placing orders and highest bidder while supplying orders.

25.15 | Contracts

Contract is a legal agreement between the supplier and the buyer. When the large quantity of material is required to be supplied at regular period of time or a big job is to be finished in a considerable length of time, then contracts are preferred. The contractor supplies the material, according to the terms and conditions laid down in the contract. The contract agreement is signed by both the parties, the contracture and the contractor and this signed agreement serves as legal document.

There are different types of contracts. Contracts related to purchasing are known as purchase contract. Purchase contract is also known as purchase order.

Purchase order contains the following particulars.

1. Order no., date and the reference number
2. Supplier's name and address.
3. Description of the items and quantity required
4. Rate and the amount
5. Method of delivery by road or rail or post
6. Date of delivery
7. Packing and forwarding instructions

8. Cash discount and other terms of payment
9. Signature of the officer.

25.16 | Price Determination or Pricing of Materials

Systematic pricing of prescriptions is very important because it is beneficial to the pharmacist and the patient and it will improve the public relations.

The cost of the drug should not be either too high or too low. The price charged for the prescription should be fair and reasonable.

Irrational and haphazard methods of calculations lead to the dissatisfaction and criticism from the customers. The price charged for a medication must cover the cost of ingredients, containers, time required for compounding and dispensing, professional services (packing, labeling, entering in the register etc.) over head expense and an additional net profit.

In hospital pharmacy, some pharmaceutical preparations are manufactured and stored in the drug store. Then these preparations are sold to the patients against prescription of the registered medical practitioners. The price of these preparations is to be fixed and charged from the patients. The price can be calculated by any one of the following methods:

1. First in - First out method. (FIFO)
2. Last in - First out method (LIFO)
3. Average cost method
4. Replacement price method
5. Inflated price method
6. Standard price method

1. **First in-first out method (FIFO):** The preparations which are received first are to be sold first. Such preparations are priced at the cost price when it is received (at the time of receiving) and sold at the price till the stock is exhausted. As soon as the oldest lot is exhausted. The preparations are priced at the cost price of the next oldest lot in the sequence. The method is useful when the prices are stable and purchase issues are less.
2. **Last in-first out method (LIFO):** In this method, the price of the latest consignment in stock is used for calculating the value of issues until that consignment is exhausted, then the next lot of pricing is used and so on through the successive lots.
3. **Average cost method:** In this method, when a new stock of goods is received, the total value of goods in stock is calculated. It is divided by the total quantity in hand and this will give the average price. All the preparations are sold at this price until a new consignment is received.

4. **Replacement price method:** This method is also known as market price method. In this method the materials are priced at the prevailing market price as the date of issue. The main advantage of this method is that it considers the current market price which is more significant for the purpose of Pricing Policies.
5. **Inflated price method:** When some drugs are stored for a long time like volatile drugs, menthol, etc., these goods are subject to some wastage. In such cases the price is fixed by the following method.

   Price of the drug = Cost of the quantity of materials/
   The quantity of the materials expected to be finally
   Available after wastage.

   For example, the total cost of Anaesthetic Ether is rupees 3000/- (60 bottles, each bottle cost about Rs. 50/-). The expected wastage may be 20% of the total quantity.

   For 100 bottles the wastage is 20 bottles.

   For 60 bottles = 12 bottles

   - The materials left after wastage = 60 – 12 = 48 bottles
   - Cost of 1 bottle is Rs. 50/-
   - Cost of 48 bottles = 48 × 50 = 2400/-
   - as per the above formulae the price of each bottle is
   - = Rs. 57.50/-
   - The cost of each bottle is priced and sold at the Rate of Rs. 57.50/-.
6. **Standard price method:** In this method the material issued are charged at a pre-determined or estimated price which reflects a normal or an affected future price. The standard price is generally fixed after careful examinations of the current market price, trend of the price and market conditions etc. The standard price is made applicable for a definite period, say a month or a quarter or a year. The standard price should be revised periodically to avoid discrepancies which go beyond a particular limit.

25.17 | Legal Requirements

1. **Legal Requirements in purchasing:** Law of contract is an agreement between two or more persons during business transaction (between buyer and seller). There must be lawful proposal by one party and lawful acceptance by the other party. As the result two parties can enter into the agreement. A person cannot enter into the agreement during purchasing if he is a lunatic or minor etc.

   The form of agreement may be oral or in writing. When the agreement is in writing, it must comply with the necessary legal formalities. If there is a breach of contract, the affected party has all rights to reject the contract and he is eligible to claim damages.

2. **Legal Requirements involved in payment of price:** There are three legal aspects involved in payment of price namely time of payment, place of payment and mode of payment. The buyer has to pay the due amounts in time. The seller has to make all measures to prevent the deterioration of goods during transit. If the buyer fails to inspect the goods within the reasonable time and find out whether all the items are in good condition and whether they confirm, with their terms and conditions, then the buyer is responsible for damage or loss of any item.
3. **Legal Requirements in pricing of bulk drugs:** The drug price control order, 1987 authorizes the Central Govt. to fix the maximum sale price of bulk drugs. While fixing prices of bulk drugs, the following points should be taken into consideration:
   (i) a post tax return of 14% on net worth,
   (ii) a return of 22% on capital employed,
   (iii) an internal rate return of 12% based on long term marginal costing in respect of new plant.
4. **Legal Requirements in Pricing Drug Formulations:** The drug price control order, 1987 authorized the Central Govt. to fix the maximum sale price of drug formulations. The retail price of drug formulations is fixed based on the following formula.

$$RP = (MC + CC + PM + PC) \times ED$$

Where	RP	=	Retail price
	MC	=	Material cost
	CC	=	Conversion cost
	PM	=	Cost of packaging materials
	PC	=	Packaging charges
	MAPE	=	Maximum allowable post-manufacturing expenses
	ED	=	Excise duty

25.18 | Codification of Various Items in Drug Store

Usually manufacturers, distributors and wholesalers have large merchandise in the stores. It is difficult to locate the items in the store unless some system is evolved to store them. There should be place for everything and everything should be in its right place. Therefore code numbers are allotted to various items to facilitate easy identification. Codification is the process of assigning a code number or code symbol to a particular material for easy identification.

25.19 | Advantages of Codification

1. It helps in easy identification of items.
2. It helps in grouping the similar items together.
3. The ambiguity in description of the materials can be avoided.
4. The detailed description of the materials is minimized.
5. The coding system maintains the secrecy of the items.
6. It helps in avoiding duplication of items.
7. It helps in physical counting.
8. It helps in computerization of store records and accounting.
9. It helps in inspection of materials.

25.20 | Methods of Codification

1. Alphabetical order method
2. Mnemonic method
3. Numerical method
   (a) Decimal system (b) Block system
4. Combination method or Alpha-numerical method or random method
5. Location coding
   (a) Fixed location (b) Random location (c) Zonal location

1. ***Alphabetical order method***: This method is also known as 'letter code system'. In this system all items are given code number alphabetically. Alphabet consists of 26 letters. For example code 'C' represents capsules and code 'T' represents 'Tablets'. This method is suitable when the storage space is less. But this type of coding system is not useful when stores consist of a large number of items.
2. ***Mnemonic method***: In this method, coding letters assigned to each items so that they can be very easily identified. For example APC represents Aspirin, Paracetamol and Caffeine tablets. The main disadvantages are that the items cannot be identified without referring code index book.
3. ***Numerical method***: This method is also known as 'Sequence System method'. Under this method, separate numbers are assigned to different classification of store items. Each time a new type of material is acquired the next higher number in sequence is assigned to it. The method has the following two sub-systems.
   (a) ***Decimal System***: In this system, the numbers are assigned in such a way that each digit represents the separate name under same heading. For example let the code number 10 represent Tablets, under this heading 'Tablets', 10.1 represents paracetamol tablets, 10.2 represents Analgin tablets, 10.3 represents

Disprin tablets and so on. The main advantage of this system is that numbers can be expanded to maximum to include number of new items. But the method is tedious.

(b) ***Block System*:** In this method the numbers are reserved for specified items. For example, let the number 10 to 50 is allotted to various types of tablets and the numbers 51 to 100 is allotted to various types of capsules. For example 10.1, 10.2, 10.3, 10.4, 10.5 and so as represents antipyretic, analgestic tablets, anti inflammatary, cold remedies so on. Number 11.1, 11.2, 11.3, 11.4, and so on represents anti hypertensive tablets. Number 51.1, 51.2, 51.3, 51.4 and so represents multivitamin group of capsules.

4. ***Combination method*:** In this method, both mnemonic and numerical methods are combined to assign a code to different items of the store. For example, code no. CPC Y1 is allotted to chloramphenicol Capsules and code number PAT 11 is allotted to paracetamol with analgin tablets.

   This method is used when store items are quite large. The method is flexible and at the same it aids in memorizing the codes for different stores items.

5. ***Location Coding*:** In a large organization there are a large number of stores and each store may be quite large in size. So the store rooms are divided in blocks and each block is identified by lateral block letter and a longitudinal block letter. Within each block every row is divided vertically into columns and horizontally into shelves. Each and every shelf is given a particular number. The location of item can be identified from warehouse number, block number, row number, column number, rack number and shelf number etc. Location of any item inside the store rooms can also be done in the following manner.

   (a) ***Fixed location*:** In this method each and every group of items is allotted a fixed place inside the store according to either (a) supplier wise (b) item wise or (c) according to the utility of the item.

   (b) ***Random Location*:** This is most widely used in almost all kinds of retail shops but each group of items are stored in a particular shelf for its easy location. In this system the retailer should be very efficient in remembering the location of each item.

   (c) ***Zonal Location*:** According to this system, available space is divided into different zones and each zone is allotted to different kind of items. The zones can be named as:

      (a) bulk zone
      (b) reserve stock zone
      (c) consumable item zone and
      (d) Spare parts zone etc.

25.21 | Drug Store Management

Handling of drug stores and other hospital supplies: Storage facilities in drug store is the medicines which are received from the distributors are stored in drug stores. The drug store should have adequate space for storage of drugs with proper lighting, ventilation and temperature controls. Special locked storage space is provided to meet the legal requirements for storage of narcotics, alcohol and prescribed drugs. The drugs are stocked in containers such as boxes and kept on flexible racks and shelves etc. The drugs are stored in such a way that they should not be damaged due to high temperature.

Arrangements of drugs in drug store: The drugs may be arranged in the following manner:

1. ***According to manufactures:*** The drugs are arranged in a drug store, manufacturer-wise. For example, the drugs manufactured by Glaxo (India) Ltd. are placed in one cup-board.
2. ***According to pharmacological action:*** The drugs may be arranged according to the pharmacological action. For example, all analgesic drugs are placed in one cupboard. All multi-vitamin preparations are kept in another cupboard and so on.
3. ***Alphabetical order:*** The drugs may also be arranged alphabetically. The drugs starting with first letter 'A' are placed in one row of a cupboard. Drugs starting with letter 'B' are placed in another row of the same cupboard and so on.
4. ***As per old stock and date of expiry:*** The drugs are stored in such a way that the older stock must be sold first. The drugs having date of expiry may be arranged in such a way that these drugs can be sold before their date of expiry. So the old stock is stored in the front row and the fresh stock is stored on the backside.

Handling of drug stores and other hospital supplies in drug stores: It is a place where the drugs are preserved for distribution to hospital wards and other user-departments. The store in maintained by competent and legally qualified pharmacist assisted by trained personnel.

Objectives

1. Maintenance of record pertaining to receipt and issue of drugs.
2. To procure drugs for clinical trials and research work going on in hospital.
3. To maintain the stocks of all drugs and surgical requirements required in the hospital.
4. To procure drugs from different sources.
5. To carry out all the operations regarding drugs economically to save revenue.

25.22 | Layout and Facilities

1. The medical store or pharmacy ideally, should be centrally located in a spacious and well ventilated place.
2. There should be sufficient number of shelves and drawers in the pharmacy for placing drugs.
3. A refrigerator of good quality should be provided in pharmacy.
4. A mobile trolley should be available for sending heavy bottles and containers to medical wards.
5. Drugs should be stored in the pharmacy in such a way that the pharmacist can supervise the procedure.
6. All the procurements made by pharmacy should directly reach pharmacy in an unopened state.
7. All the stock received should be physically checked and cross verified with the receiving order or purchase order. The material received must be entered in the receipts register.
8. The fast moving items must be kept handy near the counter. The slow moving drugs or drugs which are not used frequently may be kept on the upper shelves; the bulky items should be kept on the bottom shelves.
9. Surgical instruments, rubber goods and sutures should be stored separately on racks specially reserved for the purpose.
10. Drugs should be arranged according to their categories or according to the companies who have supplied the drugs.
11. The drugs should be stored in such a way that the older stocks are sold first.
12. The drugs having date of expiry should be sold before the actual date of expiry. Otherwise the old stocks and expired drugs will remain unsold resulting in financial loss to the drug store.
13. Hence old stock should be placed in the first rows and the fresh stock on the back rows.
14. The expired drugs should be stored in a separate cupboard meant for storing the expired drugs.
15. Poisonous medications are handled with caution and kept in locked cabinet and separated from other medications.
16. Medications are released from the drug store on the written order of the physician.
17. Only after making necessary entries in the register, the medications and other surgical items should be issued from the store.
18. Surgical instruments, sutures, surgical dressings and other surgical accessories should be handled very carefully with aseptic precautions for the welfare of the patients under-going surgery.

25.23 | Inventory Control

Definition: Inventory means all the raw materials, spare parts, tools, fuels, lubricants, semi processed materials and finished goods etc., recorded in the books of any organization at any given point of time. On an average about 30% of the working capital is spent on inventories. Hence for the smooth working of the business organization, a sound inventory should be maintained. It should be neither excessive nor inadequate but of maximum level. Inventory management is essential to maintain a large size inventory for smooth and efficient production and also for sales operation. It also minimizes a firm's investment in inventory with a view to gain maximum profit.

Some of the important definitions of inventory are:

- Inventory is a list of names, quantities and or monetary values of all or any group of items.
- Inventories are the supplies of raw materials and finished goods in the warehouse.
- All the materials, parts and in process or finished products recorded in the books by any organization and kept in its stores, warehouses and plants are known as inventories.
- Inventory is a comprehensive list of movable items necessary to manufacture and product and to maintain the equipment and machinery in good working order.

25.24 | Objectives of Inventory Control

The main objectives of inventory control are:

1. To maintain sufficient inventory so as to avoid production held up which leads to customer dissatisfaction, loss of revenue and increase in cost.
2. To avoid excess investment in inventory.
3. To improve the customer service.
4. To keep plant (equipment) costs low. The overall plant costs are kept low by stable production which is possible only by having sufficient inventories.

Functions of inventory control

1. Men, machines and materials are properly utilized.
2. The products can be supplied to the consumers at a short notice as and when the demand is received.
3. Wastage of materials and theft of materials can be checked.

4. To assess the material requirement systematically.
5. To obtain and supply the required quantity of the materials at the lowest cost and in proper time.
6. To keep the inventories as low as possible which leads to consistent price of market conditions.
7. To maintain proper records and to assess the stock position of the materials. If the stock position is properly maintained, the material can be supplied regularly and accurately.

25.25 | Modern Techniques of Inventory Control

The following techniques are commonly used to control the inventory:

1. ABC Analysis or ABC method
2. VED Analysis
3. Perpetual inventory control system
4. Lead time method
5. Safety stock method
6. Minimum and maximum stock levels
7. Economic order quantity (EOQ) method

1. **ABC Analysis or ABC method:** ABC method means 'Always Better Control' method. This is a selective analysis based on annual inventory value which is found out as follows - the number of units of each material/part used during the past year is multiplied by its unit cost. Then the inventory items are divided into three groups A, B and C in the order of their annual value. The method is based on the concept - "Thick on the best and thin on the rest'.

In any organization, it becomes essential to have stock and keep track of large number of items of different kind. The investment in such items is substantial and record keeping is expensive.

Thus for better and more economic control of items in inventory, the items should be classified according to their significance or priority for reordering.

The inventory of high value items (in terms of annual usage) is to be controlled carefully due to high turnover and heavy investment. This can lead to substantial savings due even a small percentage decrease in inventory. For the lower value items (in terms of annual usage), the cost of inventory management is significant and should be controlled because it may be more than the possible inventory savings.

Hence, this technique with a selective approach concentrates time and attention upon the items in terms of their monetary turnover. According to this approach, the items are classified into three main categories

1. A Class 2. B Class 3. C Class

(a) ***A Class Items:***

1. These items cover 10% of the total inventories
2. It consumes about 70% of total budget
3. Hence these items require strict monitoring
4. They require either no safety stocks or low safety stocks
5. They need maximum follow up
6. The items must be handled by senior officers.

As seen from the above, tight control measures are envisaged at all stages which include:

1. Determination of purchase schedules
2. Demand forecast for consumption
3. Safety stock fixation
4. Receipts and inspection procedure establishment.

Following important measures can be adopted to exercise control over items in this category.

1. Purchase on exact requirement basis
2. Waste control measures should be adopted
3. Cheaper substitutes should be discovered (if possible)
4. Frequent periodical checking for material issued and in store
5. Only the required amount of material should be issued
6. Order should be placed after technical and commercial inquiry
7. Pilferage preventive measures
8. Low safety stocks should be maintained
9. Exact cost of individual items should be taken into account.

(b) ***B Class Items:***

1. It covers 20% of the total inventories
2. It consumes 20% of total budget
3. It requires moderate control
4. It requires low safety stocks
5. It needs periodic follow up
6. It can be handled by middle management.

The following steps are required:

1. Purchases should be based on exact requirement
2. Costing should be done on average basis per accounting
3. The store keeper should check personally the stock and periodical check-up should be done.

(c) ***C Class items:***

1. This class of items cover 70% of the total inventories
2. It consumes 10% of total expenditure of inventories
3. It may require loose control
4. It requires high safety stocks
5. It needs close follow up
6. It can be handled by any official of the organization.

Some of the important measures to be adopted for this category of items are:

- Visual quantity control is sufficient rather than paper control
- Purchases should be based on estimated usage
- Costing should be done on average basis for accounting
- Infrequent checking of the level of ordering should be clear and counter - checking by store keeper would be sufficient.

Advantages of ABC method of inventory control

1. It ensures better control over costly items
2. It helps in developing scientific method of controlling inventories
3. It helps in maintaining the stock in a better way
4. It helps in reducing the storage costs
5. It helps in maintaining enough stocks of group A, B and C items

Application of ABC analysis

ABC analysis can be applied at various stages of material management. The stages are:

1. Stores lay out
2. Value Analysis
3. Stock Records
4. Priority treatment to different items
5. Determination of safety stock limits
6. To evolve useful re-ordering strategy
7. Information of items which require higher degree of control.

2. **VED Analysis:** VED Analysis means Vital, Essential and Desirable Analysis. This system is based on the utility of the materials. Based on the usage, the items or materials are divided into three categories vital, essential and desirable items.

   Vital material is the most essential items for production. Without this material, production is stopped for a period of several days or even months. Since the cost of material is high and so it takes longer time to purchase and replace the material. Essential items are the one which are very essential for production. Without this material, production is stopped only for few hours or a day. Since the material is not so costly and hence it can be purchased and replaced easily.

   Desirable items, these are needed by an organization but do not cast any effect on its performance.

   In a drug store, VED Analysis is very useful in controlling and maintaining the stock of various types of formulations of a particular group of drugs. The older the brand, the greater will be its requirement. The past trends are not useful in calculating the requirements of a particular brand.

   For example, Acetyl Salicylic acid is available as disprin tablets, anacin tablets and APC tablets. Disprin tablets have huge demand followed by anacin with moderate and APC less demand. Hence Disprin tablets are vital, Anacin – essential and APC–desirable. In a drug store, there should be maximum stock of disprin tablets, followed by anacin and then of APC tablets.

   VED technique of inventory control is very useful in controlling and maintaining the stock of various spare parts or raw materials used in production process.

3. **Perpetual inventory control system:** Proper examination with regard to receipt, issue and balance of material in hand is done every time when the stock is handled and moreover the entire stock is rechecked. Hence this enables the manufacturer to know about the material available without physical stock verification.

   The Perpetual inventory system consists of:

   1. Bin Card 2. Stores ledger 3. Continuous stock-taking

   (a) ***Bin Card:*** Record of all items of materials and goods in the store is recorded in this document. Hence this card serves the purpose of ready reckoner. It shows quantities of each material received, issued and in stock.

   Every item has a separate bin card. Each receipt, issue or return is recorded in the bin in a serial order and the latest balance is shown after each receipt and issue.

   A typical format of Bin Card is shown below:

GVS Co. Ltd.

Bin Card

Description :
Code :
L.F. No. :

Bin No :
Normal Qty to order :
Max Stock level :
Reorder Stock level :

	Receipt			Issue	
Date	G.R. No.	Quantity	S.R. No.	Qty	Balance quantity

(b) ***Store ledger:*** It is maintained by cost accounting department. It is prepared in the loose bound form so that the leaves can be easily removed and inserted.

(c) ***Continuous stock-taking:*** Periodically limited numbers of items are physically checked and data compared with that of bin card and ledger record to verify the correctness.

Advantages of the system

1. It helps to detect clerical errors.
2. It helps to check the store items in a methodical manner.
3. Timely action can be taken on serious shortages.
4. It helps in the preparation of profit and loss account and balance sheet.
5. Possibility of verification of maximum and minimum stock levels. Hence over stocking and under stocking is avoided.
6. It serves as a moral check on the staff, this serves as an indication to dishonesty.
7. Capital investment in materials will be under control.
8. On account of continuous stock verification the balance in stock can be known at anytime during the year.
9. It is helpful in formulating proper purchase policies since position of stock is known.

10. It makes available correct stock figures for claims to be lodged with the insurance company in case of damage.

4. ***Lead time method*:** The time interval between the placing the order for purchase of certain items to the time, the materials are actually received in the stores. It has two important components.
   (a) Administrative or servicing lead time
   (b) Supplier's lead time
   (a) ***Administrative or servicing lead time*:** It is also known as internal lead time and it is the time taken by the organization for placing the order which includes time taken for calling the quotations, preparing comparative statements, inspecting the material and then placing the orders.
   (b) ***Supplier's lead time*:** The time gap between the placements of order to the receipt of goods in the store is known as suppliers lead time.

   The lead time should be kept minimum to keep the investment in inventories within limits. The longer the lead time, the larger is the safety stock required resulting in excess investment in inventories. It is not possible to decrease supplier's lead time since it is in the hands of external source, hence internal lead time can be conveniently reduced. Hence lead time is an important factor to be looked into in both retail and wholesale business of drugs.

5. ***Safety stock method***
   1. A firm has to keep adequate safety stock as well as ordinary stock. Over-stocking goods are known as safety stock.
   2. Inventories are generally divided into "Working stock" (quantity of the inventories that are ordered) and 'safety stock' (overstocking of goods).
   3. If the demand is stationary or if there is no much variation in demand, there is no need for stocking of inventories (goods). When the demand increases, safety stock level can also be increased. Depending on the demand one can decide whether the goods can be stocked or overstocked.
   4. If there is more demand on particular goods, then such goods can be stocked. The safety stock of an item depends upon its lead time, usage value and its carrying cost. If the lead time is longer, then it is necessary to stock the inventories. If the value is high, the safety stock level of the item is kept at minimum. Depending upon the carrying cost also, one can decide whether the goods can be stocked or not.

6. ***Minimum and maximum stock levels***

   (a) ***Minimum stock level*:** The stock of any item should not be allowed to fall below the lower limit. This is known as minimum stock level, the particular item should not go out of stock. If the items are out of stock, it is not possible to supply the materials in time to the consumers. So minimum stock level should be maintained. This level is determined by considering the following factors :

1. Rate of consumption of the material
2. Reorder level
3. Time taken to receive fresh supplies from the producers or from the distributors.

Minimum stock level is determined by using the formula

Minimum stock level =

Reorder level – normal consumption per week

(b) ***Maximum stock level*:** The stock of any item should not be allowed to raise beyond the upper limit. This is known as maximum stock level. Any item should not be stocked too much. If the stock level is beyond the upper limit, the company has to invest large amounts and same times the company may incur loss if there is no demand on particular items. So stock level of the goods should always be maintained at optimum level.

The maximum stock level is determined by considering the following factors:

(i) Rate of consumption of the materials
(ii) Reorder level
(iii) Time taken to receive fresh supplies from the producers or from the distributors
(iv) Amount of capital needed and available
(v) Storages space available
(vi) Market trend
(vii) Nature of the material and
(viii) Government restrictions.

Maximum stock level is determined by using the formula.

Maximum stock level = Reorder level – Minimum consumption per week

(c) ***Re-order level*:** Reorder level is the stock position between minimum and maximum stock level. The re-order level is always slightly more than the minimum stock level. When the stock of any item reaches at re-order level, the process for the purchase of material should be started.

The re-order level is determined by using the formula.

Reorder level = Minimum consumption per week × Maximum time taken to receive fresh supplies

7. **Economic Order Quantity (EOQ) method:** EOQ method is used to find out how much of the inventories (goods) are to be ordered. The correct quantity to be ordered is determined by considering the following factors:

(i) Ordering cost, and (ii) The inventory carrying cost.

The ordering cost consist of the cost of paper, typing, postage, filling etc., the cost of salaries of staff and other miscellaneous cost.

The inventory carrying cost consist of storage cost, cost of insurance and taxes, salaries of store-keeper and losses in stores due to pilferage, wastage, breakage etc.

Methods of determination of EOQ: Tabular column method and algebraic formula method are used to determine EOQ

1. ***Tabular column method:*** The purchasing details are written in a tabular column. This arrangement may help the company to find out the number of orders needed weekly or quarterly or monthly or yearly. For example, let the order cost is Rs. 100/- per order, inventory carrying cost is 10% and annual usage is Rs, 60,000/-. Suppose the particular item was ordered every month, the annual order cost would be Rs. 1200/- (Rs. 100 × 12).
   The annual inventory carrying cost would be Rs. 500/- i.e.,
   The total annual cost would be
   Rs. 1700/- (1200 + 500 = 1700/-)
   Suppose the particular item was ordered once in two months (i.e. 6 times in a year) the annual order cost would be Rs. 600/- (Rs. 100 × 6).
   The annual inventory carrying cost would be Rs. 1000/- i.e.,
   The total annual cost would be 600 + 1000 = 1600/-
   The above data would be represented in tabular column as follows.

S.No.	No. of orders per year	Annual ordering Cost Rs.	Annual Inventory Carrying Cost	Total Annual Cost Rs.
1	12	1200/-	500/-	1700/-
2	6	600/-	1000/-	1600/-

   Total annual cost = Annual Ordering Cost + Annual Inventory Carrying Cost.
   Thus if the purchasing detail is represented in a tabular column, it is easier to find out an approximate EOQ.

2. ***Algebraic Method:***

   EOQ can also be determined by using formula:

$$EOQ = \sqrt{\frac{2ab}{CS}}$$

a = Annual consumption

b = Buying cost per order

C = Cost per unit of material

S = Storage and other inventory carrying cost

For example, annual consumption of the particular item is 2000 kg (a), let the item was ordered 5 times per year.

Buying cost, (i.e., cost to handle the order) is Rs. 10/- per order (b). The cost of material is Rs 5/- per kg (C).

The storage and other inventory carrying cost Rs. 100/- per year (S).

Then EOQ is determined by the following way:

Buying Cost for one order is Rs. 10/-

∴ Buying cost for 5 orders = 10 × 5 = 50/-

$$EOQ = \sqrt{\frac{2 \times a \times b}{C \times S}}$$

$$= \sqrt{\frac{2 \times 2000 \times 10 \times 5}{5 \times 100}}$$

$$= \sqrt{400}$$

$$= 20 \text{ Units.}$$

Establishing an effective purchase procedure: By means of an effective purchase procedure and maintaining register, inventory control can be properly maintained. Effective purchase procedure means various steps involved in purchasing of materials. The first step in effective purchase procedure is to find out the requirement of the goods needed. Then the requirement is written in the requisition form. The supplier is selected and order is placed. The goods are received, checked thoroughly and payment is made. The purchase transaction is recorded in a proper register. Effective purchase procedure and inventory control are interlinked.

25.26 | Scrap and Surplus Disposal

Definition: Scrap is the residue – obtained from certain type of manufacturing operations. Scrap is most commonly obtained in engineering industries. Example for scrap : Small metal particles during drilling and turning in engineering industry ; wood particles in carpentry; powders and fine granules during processing and packing of tablets.

Classification

Scrap may be classified into:

1. Legitimate Scrap; 2. Administrative Scrap and 3. Defective Scrap

1. **Legitimate scrap:** The scrap which can be anticipated in advance during certain manufacturing operations. For example: Scrap is obtained in the form of powders and fine granules during tablet manufacturing process.
2. **Administrative scrap:** This type of scrap is obtained when same type of material becomes obsolete due to change in design.
3. **Defective scrap:** This type of scrap is obtained from sub-standard raw materials and poor workmanship in handling such materials.

Control of scrap: The Scrap can be controlled by effective management of raw materials during its manufacture. The scrap can be controlled by the following methods :

1. By providing careful attention during designing the product.
2. By selecting the right materials and equipments during production.
3. By appointing right type of personnel with experience, so that they can handle the materials and equipments properly.

Disposal of scrap: There are two methods of disposal of scrap :

1. The scrap can be disposed by selling, if the scrap is fit for reprocessing, in such case the scrap can be used for subsequent production.
2. Scrap may be sold to scrap dealers through auction.

25.27 | Surplus

Definition: The surplus items are those items which are not required by the firm or organization. Example for surplus items – spoiled raw materials, rejected components, defective parts, obsolete materials, and equipment in a drug store. Expiry date goods come under surplus material.

Disposal of Surplus: There are two methods of disposal of surplus:

1. The surplus can be disposed by selling if the surplus cannot be reprocessed into useful materials.
2. If the surplus is fit for reprocessing it can be used for subsequent production.

Review Questions

Short Answer Questions

1. Give an account of
   (a) Credit information
   (b) Contracts
2. What is meant by the term "Supply order".
3. Define "purchase Procedure".
4. What are the advantages of codification?
5. How is an order placed with a supplier?
6. Write three factors responsible for the success of a drug store ?
7. What are the merits and demerits of opening a drug store in rural or small town?
8. Write three factors responsible for the success of a drug store.
9. Write the formula for calculation of retail price of a drug formulation.
10. What are the various documents needed to open a retail drug store?
11. What is inventory and inventory control?
12. Describe the various functions of the inventory control?
13. Give the various methods of finding EOQ?
14. How is re-order level of inventory calculated?
15. Define the terms Scrap and Surplus?

Long Answer Questions

1. What do you understand from the term purchasing? Describe importance and objectives of purchasing?
2. Explain the term 'codification'? Explain the various methods of codification of drugs?
3. Describe in detail about handling of drug stores and other hospital supplies?
4. What are the different methods of arrangement of drugs in a drug store?
5. What are the legal requirements in pricing of bulk drugs and drug formulations?
6. What do you understand from the term 'drug house management'? Discuss the factors which should be taken into consideration for the selection of site of a retail drug-store?
7. Describe layout design of a drug store along with its flow diagram?
8. A pharmacist is interested to start a drug store. Discuss the legal requirements for the same.
9. What is a tender? Describe in detail about the various methods of obtaining tenders.
10. What are the factors to be considered to select a supplier?
11. Explain the term "inventory control"? Discuss the ABC Analysis? Write the main differences between A, B and C types of inventories?
12. What do you know about EOQ? Discuss the various methods for determining the EOQ?
13. Write in detail about various levels of inventory which required in maintains to control it?
14. How maximum stocks, minimum stock level and re-order level of inventories are calculated?
15. Discuss in brief the various techniques of inventory control?
16. What is perpetual inventory system? How it is useful in inventory control? What are the advantages of the system?

26 Financial Management

26.1 | Financial Management

Financial Management means planning, organizing, directing and controlling the financial activities such as procurement and utilization of funds of the enterprise. It means applying general management principles to financial resources of the enterprise.

LEARNING OBJECTIVES

- *Scope and objectives of Financial Management*
- *Functions of Financial Management*
- *Objectives of Financial Planning*
- *Finance Functions*
- *Role and functions of a Financial Manager*
- *Meaning and factors determining Capital structure*
- *Capitalization in Finance*
- *Over Capitalization*
- *Under Capitalization*
- *Financial goals - Profit vs. Wealth*
- *Profit Maximization*
- *Financial Intermediaries - Meaning, Role and Importance*
- *Recent trends*

Scope/Elements

1. Investment decisions includes investment in fixed assets (called as capital budgeting). Investments in current assets are also a part of investment decisions called as working capital decisions.
2. Financial decisions: They relate to the raising of finance from various resources which will depend upon decision on type of source, period of financing, cost of financing and the returns thereby.
3. Dividend decision: The finance manager has to take decision with regards to the net profit distribution. Net profits are generally divided into two:
    (a) Dividend for shareholders: Dividend and the rate of it has to be decided.
    (b) Retained profits: Amount of retained profits has to be finalized which will depend upon expansion and diversification plans of the enterprise.

26.2 | Objectives of Financial Management

The financial management is generally concerned with procurement, allocation and control of financial resources of a concern. The objectives can be:

1. To ensure regular and adequate supply of funds to the concern.
2. To ensure adequate returns to the shareholders: this will depend upon the earning capacity, market price of the share, expectations of the shareholders.
3. To ensure optimum funds utilization. Once the funds are procured, they should be utilized in maximum possible way at least cost.
4. To ensure safety on investment, i.e., funds should be invested in safe ventures so that adequate rate of return can be achieved.
5. To plan a sound capital structure: There should be sound and fair composition of capital so that a balance is maintained between debt and equity capital.

26.3 | Functions of Financial Management

1. **Estimation of capital requirements:** A finance manager has to make estimation with regards to capital requirements of the company. This will depend upon expected costs and profits and future programs and policies of a concern. Estimations have to be made in an adequate manner which increases earning capacity of enterprise.

2. **Determination of capital composition:** Once the estimation have been made, the capital structure have to be decided. This involves short- term and long- term debt equity analysis. This will depend upon the proportion of equity capital a company is possessing and additional funds which have to be raised from outside parties.

3. **Choice of sources of funds:** For additional funds to be procured, a company has many choices like:
   (a) Issue of shares and debentures
   (b) Loans to be taken from banks and financial institutions
   (c) Public deposits to be drawn like in form of bonds.

   Choice of factor will depend on relative merits and demerits of each source and period of financing.
4. **Investment of funds:** The finance manager has to decide to allocate funds into profitable ventures so that there is safety on investment and regular returns is possible.

5. **Disposal of surplus:** The net profits decisions have to be made by the finance manager. This can be done in two ways:
   (a) Dividend declaration: It includes identifying the rate of dividends and other benefits like bonus.
   (b) Retained profits: The volume has to be decided which will depend upon expansion, innovational, diversification plans of the company.
6. **Management of cash:** Finance manager has to make decisions with regards to cash management. Cash is required for many purposes like payment of wages and salaries, payment of electricity and water bills, payment to creditors, meeting current liabilities, maintenance of enough stock, purchase of raw materials, etc.
7. **Financial controls:** The finance manager has not only to plan, procure and utilize the funds but he also has to exercise control over finances. This can be done through many techniques like ratio analysis, financial forecasting, cost and profit control, etc.

26.4 | Financial Planning

Financial Planning is the process of estimating the capital required and determining it's competition. It is the process of framing financial policies in relation to procurement, investment and administration of funds of an enterprise.

Objectives of Financial Planning

Financial Planning has got many objectives to look forward to:

(a) Determining capital requirements: This will depend upon factors like cost of current and fixed assets, promotional expenses and long- range planning. Capital requirements have to be looked with both aspects: short- term and long- term requirements.
(b) Determining capital structure: The capital structure is the composition of capital, i.e., the relative kind and proportion of capital required in the business. This includes decisions of debt- equity ratio- both short-term and long- term.
(c) Framing financial policies with regards to cash control, lending, borrowings, etc.
(d) A finance manager ensures that the scarce financial resources are maximally utilized in the best possible manner at least cost in order to get maximum returns on investment.

26.5 | Importance of Financial Planning

Financial Planning is process of framing objectives, policies, procedures, programs and budgets regarding the financial activities of a concern. This ensures effective and adequate financial and investment policies. The importance can be outlined as:

1. Adequate funds have to be ensured.
2. Financial Planning helps in ensuring a reasonable balance between outflow and inflow of funds so that stability is maintained.
3. Financial Planning ensures that the suppliers of funds are easily investing in companies which exercise financial planning.
4. Financial Planning helps in making growth and expansion programs which help in long-run survival of the company.
5. Financial Planning reduces uncertainties with regards to changing market trends which can be faced easily through enough funds.
6. Financial Planning helps in reducing the uncertainties which can be a hindrance to growth of the company. This helps in ensuring stability and profitability in concern.

26.6 | Finance Functions

The following explanation will help in understanding each finance function in detail

Investment Decision

One of the most important finance functions is to intelligently allocate capital to long term assets. This activity is also known as capital budgeting. It is important to allocate capital in those long term assets so as to get maximum yield in future. Following are the two aspects of investment decision

(a) Evaluation of new investment in terms of profitability

(b) Comparison of cut off rate against new investment and prevailing investment.

Since the future is uncertain therefore there are difficulties in calculation of expected return. Along with uncertainty comes the risk factor which has to be taken into consideration. This risk factor plays a very significant role in calculating the expected return of the prospective investment. Therefore while considering investment proposal it is important to take into consideration both expected return and the risk involved.

Investment decision not only involves allocating capital to long term assets but also involves decisions of using funds which are obtained by selling those assets which become less profitable and less productive. It is wise decisions to decompose depreciated assets which are not adding value and utilize those funds in securing other beneficial assets. An opportunity cost of capital needs to be calculating while dissolving such assets. The correct cut off rate is calculated by using this opportunity cost of the required rate of return (RRR).

Financial Decision

Financial decision is yet another important function which a financial manger must perform. It is important to make wise decisions about when, where and how should a business acquire funds. Funds can be acquired through many ways and channels. Broadly speaking a correct ratio of an equity and debt has to be maintained. This mix of equity capital and debt is known as a firm's capital structure. A firm tends to benefit most when the market value of a company's share maximizes; this not only is a sign of growth for the firm but also maximizes shareholders wealth. On the other hand the use of debt affects the risk and return of a shareholder. It is more risky though it may increase the return on equity funds. A sound financial structure is said to be one which aims at maximizing shareholders return with minimum risk. In such a scenario the market value of the firm will maximize and hence an optimum capital structure would be achieved. Other than equity and debt there are several other tools which are used in deciding a firm capital structure.

Dividend Decision

Earning profit or a positive return is a common aim of all the businesses. But the key function a financial manger performs in case of profitability is to decide whether to distribute all the profits to the shareholder or retain all the profits or distribute part of the profits to the shareholder and retain the other half in the business. It's the financial manager's responsibility to decide an optimum dividend policy which maximizes the market value of the firm. Hence an optimum dividend payout ratio is calculated. It is a common practice to pay regular dividends in case of profitability another way is to issue bonus shares to existing shareholders.

Liquidity Decision

It is very important to maintain a liquidity position of a firm to avoid insolvency. Firm's profitability, liquidity and risk all are associated with the investment in current assets. In order to maintain a tradeoff between profitability and liquidity it is important to invest sufficient funds in current assets. But since current assets do not earn anything for business therefore a proper calculation must be done before investing in current assets. Current assets should properly be valued and disposed of from time to time once they become non profitable. Currents assets must be used in times of liquidity problems and times of insolvency.

26.7 | Role of a Financial Manager

Financial activities of a firm is one of the most important and complex activities of a firm. Therefore in order to take care of these activities a financial manager performs all the requisite financial activities.

A financial manger is a person who takes care of all the important financial functions of an organization. The person in charge should maintain a far sightedness in order to ensure that the funds are utilized in the most efficient manner. His actions directly affect the Profitability, growth and goodwill of the firm.

Following are the main functions of a Financial Manager

1. ***Raising of Funds*****:** In order to meet the obligation of the business it is important to have enough cash and liquidity. A firm can raise funds by the way of equity and debt. It is the responsibility of a financial manager to decide the ratio between debt and equity. It is important to maintain a good balance between equity and debt.
2. ***Allocation of Funds*****:** Once the funds are raised through different channels the next important function is to allocate the funds. The funds should be allocated in such a manner that they are optimally used. In order to allocate funds in the best possible manner the following point must be considered
   - The size of the firm and its growth capability
   - Status of assets whether they are long term or short tem
   - Mode by which the funds are raised.

   These financial decisions directly and indirectly influence other managerial activities. Hence formation of a good asset mix and proper allocation of funds is one of the most important activity.
3. ***Profit Planning*****:** Profit earning is one of the prime functions of any business organization. Profit earning is important for survival and sustenance of any organization. Profit planning refers to proper usage of the profit generated by the firm. Profit arises due to many factors such as pricing, industry competition, state of the economy, mechanism of demand and supply, cost and output. A healthy mix of variables and fixed factors of production can lead to an increase in the profitability of the firm. Fixed costs are incurred by the use of fixed factors of production such as land and machinery. In order to maintain a tandem it is important to continuously value the depreciation cost of fixed cost of production. An opportunity cost must be calculated in order to replace those factors of production which has gone thrown wear and tear. If this is not noted then these fixed cost can cause huge fluctuations in profit.
4. ***Understanding Capital Markets*****:** Shares of a company are traded on stock exchange and there is a continuous sale and purchase of securities. Hence a clear understanding of capital market is an important function of a financial manager. When securities are traded on stock market there involves a huge amount of risk

involved. Therefore a financial manger understands and calculates the risk involved in this trading of shares and debentures. It is on the discretion of a financial manager as to how distribute the profits. Many investors do not like the firm to distribute the profits amongst share holders as dividend instead invest in the business itself to enhance growth. The practices of a financial manager directly impact the operation in capital market.

26.8 | Capital Structure - Meaning and Factors Determining Capital Structure

Meaning of Capital Structure

Capital Structure is referred to as the ratio of different kinds of securities raised by a firm as long-term finance. The capital structure involves two decisions:

(a) Types of securities to be issued are equity shares, preference shares and long term borrowings (Debentures).

(b) Relative ratio of securities can be determined by process of capital gearing. On this basis, the companies are divided into two

  (i) Highly geared companies: Those companies whose proportion of equity capitalization is small.

  (ii) Low geared companies: Those companies whose equity capital dominates total capitalization.

26.9 | Factors Determining Capital Structure

1. **Trading on Equity:** The word "equity" denotes the ownership of the company. Trading on equity means taking advantage of equity share capital to borrow funds on reasonable basis. It refers to additional profits that equity shareholders earn because of issuance of debentures and preference shares. It is based on the thought that if the rate of dividend on preference capital and the rate of interest on borrowed capital is lower than the general rate of company's earnings, equity shareholders are at advantage which means a company should go for a judicious blend of preference shares, equity shares as well as debentures. Trading on equity becomes more important when expectations of shareholders are high.
2. **Degree of control:** In a company, it is the directors who are so called elected representatives of equity shareholders. These members have got maximum voting rights in a concern as compared to the preference shareholders and debenture holders. Preference shareholders have reasonably less voting rights while debenture

holders have no voting rights. If the company's management policies are such that they want to retain their voting rights in their hands, the capital structure consists of debenture holders and loans rather than equity shares.

3. **Flexibility of financial plan:** In an enterprise, the capital structure should be such that there is both contractions as well as relaxation in plans. Debentures and loans can be refunded back as the time requires. While equity capital cannot be refunded at any point which provides rigidity to plans. Therefore, in order to make the capital structure possible, the company should go for issue of debentures and other loans.
4. **Choice of investors:** The Company's policy generally is to have different categories of investors for securities. Therefore, a capital structure should give enough choice to all kind of investors to invest. Bold and adventurous investors generally go for equity shares and loans and debentures are generally raised keeping into mind conscious investors.
5. **Capital market condition:** In the lifetime of the company, the market price of the shares has got an important influence. During the depression period, the company's capital structure generally consists of debentures and loans. While in period of boons and inflation, the company's capital should consist of share capital generally equity shares.
6. **Period of financing:** When company wants to raise finance for short period, it goes for loans from banks and other institutions; while for long period it goes for issue of shares and debentures.
7. **Cost of financing:** In a capital structure, the company has to look to the factor of cost when securities are raised. It is seen that debentures at the time of profit earning of company prove to be a cheaper source of finance as compared to equity shares where equity shareholders demand an extra share in profits.
8. **Stability of sales:** An established business which has a growing market and high sales turnover, the company is in position to meet fixed commitments. Interest on debentures has to be paid regardless of profit. Therefore, when sales are high, thereby the profits are high and company is in better position to meet such fixed commitments like interest on debentures and dividends on preference shares. If company is having unstable sales, then the company is not in position to meet fixed obligations. So, equity capital proves to be safe in such cases.
9. **Sizes of a company:** Small size business firms capital structure generally consists of loans from banks and retained profits. While on the other hand, big companies having goodwill, stability and an established profit can easily go for issuance of shares and debentures as well as loans and borrowings from financial institutions. The bigger the size, the wider is total capitalization.

26.10 | Capitalization in Finance

What is Capitalization

Capitalization comprises of share capital, debentures, loans, free reserves,etc. Capitalization represents permanent investment in companies excluding long-term loans. Capitalization can be distinguished from capital structure. Capital structure is a broad term and it deals with qualitative aspect of finance. While capitalization is a narrow term and it deals with the quantitative aspect.

Capitalization is generally found to be of following types-

- Normal
- Over
- Under

26.11 | Overcapitalization

Overcapitalization is a situation in which actual profits of a company are not sufficient enough to pay interest on debentures, on loans and pay dividends on shares over a period of time. This situation arises when the company raises more capital than required. A part of capital always remains idle. With a result, the rate of return shows a declining trend. The causes can be-

1. **High promotion cost:** When a company goes for high promotional expenditure, i.e., making contracts, canvassing, underwriting commission, drafting of documents, etc. and the actual returns are not adequate in proportion to high expenses, the company is over-capitalized in such cases.
2. **Purchase of assets at higher prices:** When a company purchases assets at an inflated rate, the result is that the book value of assets is more than the actual returns. This situation gives rise to over-capitalization of company.
3. **A company's floatation in boom period:** At times company has to secure it's solvency and thereby float in boom periods. That is the time when rate of returns are less as compared to capital employed. This results in actual earnings lowering down and earnings per share declining.
4. **Inadequate provision for depreciation:** If the finance manager is unable to provide an adequate rate of depreciation, the result is that inadequate funds are available when the assets have to be replaced or when they become obsolete. New assets have to be purchased at high prices which prove to be expensive.
5. **Liberal dividend policy:** When the directors of a company liberally divide the dividends into the shareholders, the result is inadequate retained profits which are very essential for high earnings of the company. The result is deficiency in company.

To fill up the deficiency, fresh capital is raised which proves to be a costlier affair and leaves the company to be over- capitalized.

6. **Over-estimation of earnings:** When the promoters of the company overestimate the earnings due to inadequate financial planning, the result is that company goes for borrowings which cannot be easily met and capital is not profitably invested. This results in consequent decrease in earnings per share.

Effects of Overcapitalization

1. ***On Shareholders*:** The over capitalized companies have following disadvantages to shareholders:
    (a) Since the profitability decreases, the rate of earning of shareholders also decreases.
    (b) The market price of shares goes down because of low profitability.
    (c) The profitability going down has an effect on the shareholders. Their earnings become uncertain.
    (d) With the decline in goodwill of the company, share prices decline. As a result shares cannot be marketed in capital market.
2. ***On Company*:**
    (a) Because of low profitability, reputation of company is lowered.
    (b) The company's shares cannot be easily marketed.
    (c) With the decline of earnings of company, goodwill of the company declines and the result is fresh borrowings are difficult to be made because of loss of credibility.
    (d) In order to retain the company's image, the company indulges in malpractices like manipulation of accounts to show high earnings.
    (e) The company cuts down it's expenditure on maintenance, replacement of assets, adequate depreciation, etc.
3. ***On Public*:** An overcapitalized company has got many adverse effects on the public:
    (a) In order to cover up their earning capacity, the management indulges in tactics like increase in prices or decrease in quality.
    (b) Return on capital employed is low. This gives an impression to the public that their financial resources are not utilized properly.
    (c) Low earnings of the company affects the credibility of the company as the company is not able to pay it's creditors on time.
    (d) It also has an effect on working conditions and payment of wages and salaries also lessen.

26.12 | Undercapitalization

An undercapitalized company is one which incurs exceptionally high profits as compared to industry. An undercapitalized company situation arises when the estimated earnings are very low as compared to actual profits. This gives rise to additional funds, additional profits, high goodwill, and high earnings and thus the return on capital shows an increasing trend. The causes can be:

1. Low promotion costs
2. Purchase of assets at deflated rates
3. Conservative dividend policy
4. Floatation of company in depression stage
5. High efficiency of directors
6. Adequate provision of depreciation
7. Large secret reserves are maintained.

Effects of Under Capitalization

1. ***On Shareholders***
   (a) Company's profitability increases. As a result, rate of earnings go up.
   (b) Market value of share rises.
   (c) Financial reputation also increases.
   (d) Shareholders can expect a high dividend.
2. ***On company***
   (a) With greater earnings, reputation becomes strong.
   (b) Higher rate of earnings attract competition in market.
   (c) Demand of workers may rise because of high profits.
   (d) The high profitability situation affects consumer interest as they think that the company is overcharging on products.
3. ***On Society***
   (a) With high earnings, high profitability, high market price of shares, there can be unhealthy speculation in stock market.
   (b) Restlessness in general public is developed as they link high profits with high prices of product.
   (c) Secret reserves are maintained by the company which can result in paying lower taxes to government.
   (d) The general public inculcates high expectations of these companies as these companies can import innovations, high technology and thereby best quality of product.

26.13 | Financial Goal - Profit vs. Wealth

Every firm has a predefined goal or an objective. Therefore the most important goal of a financial manager is to increase the owner's economic welfare. Here economics welfare may refer to maximization of profit or maximization of shareholders wealth. Therefore shareholders wealth maximization (SWM) plays a very crucial role as far as financial goals of a firm are concerned.

Profit is the remuneration paid to the entrepreneur after deduction of all expenses. Maximization of profit can be defined as maximizing the income of the firm and minimizing the expenditure. The main responsibility of a firm is to carry out business by manufacturing goods and services and selling them in the open market. The mechanism of demand and supply in an open market determine the price of a commodity or a service. A firm can only make profit if it produces a good or delivers a service at a lower cost than what is prevailing in the market. The margin between these two prices would only increase if the firm strives to produce these goods more efficiently and at a lower price without compromising on the quality.

The demand and supply mechanism plays a very important role in determining the price of a commodity. A commodity which has a greater demand commands a higher price and hence may result in greater profits. Competition among other suppliers also effect profits. Manufacturers tends to move towards production of those goods which guarantee higher profits. Hence there comes a time when equilibrium is reached and profits are saturated.

According to Adam Smith - **business man in order to fulfill their profit motive in turn benefits the society as well**. It is seen that when a firm tends to increase profit it eventually makes use of its resources in a more effective manner. Profit is regarded as a parameter to measure firm's productivity and efficiency. Firms which tend to earn continuous profit eventually improvise their products according to the demand of the consumers. Bulk production due to massive demand leads to economies of scale which eventually reduces the cost of production. Lower cost of production directly impacts the profit margins. There are two ways to increase the profit margin due to lower cost. Firstly a firm can produce at lower cost but continue to sell at the original price, thereby increasing the revenue. Secondly a firm can reduce the final price offered to the consumer and increase its market thereby superseding its competitors.

Both ways the firm will benefit. The second way would increase its sale and market share while the first way only tend to increase its revenue. Profit is an important component of any business. Without profit earning capability it is very difficult to survive in the market. If a firm continues to earn large amount of profits then only it can manage to serve the society in the long run. Therefore profit earning capacity by a firm and public motive in some way goes hand in hand. This eventually also leads to the growth of an economy and increase in National Income due to increasing purchasing power of the consumer.

26.14 | Profit Maximization

Many economists have argued that profit maximization has brought about many disparities among consumers and manufacturers. In case of perfect competition it may appear as a legitimate and a reward for efforts but in case of imperfect competition a firm's prime objective should not be profit maximization. In olden times when there was not too much of competition selling and manufacturing goods were primarily for mutual benefit. Manufacturers didn't produce to earn profits rather produced for mutual benefit and social welfare. The aim of the single producer was to retain his position in the market and sustain growth, thereby earning some profit which would help him in maintaining his position. On the other hand in today's time the production system is dominant by two tier system of ownership and management. Ownership aims at maximizing profit and management aims at managing the system of production thereby indirectly increasing the income of the business.

These services are used by customers who in turn are forced to pay a higher price due to formation of cartels and monopoly. Not only have the customers suffered but also the employees. Employees are forced to work more than their capacity. They is made to pay in extra hours so that production can increase.

Many times manufacturers tend to produce goods which are of no use to the society and create an artificial demand for the product by rigorous marketing and advertising. They tend to make the product so tempting by packaging and labeling that it is difficult for the consumer to resist. These happen mainly with products which aim to target kids and teenagers. Ad commercials and print ads tend to provide with wrong information to artificially hike the expectation of the product.

In case of oligopoly where the nature of the product is more or less same exploit the customer to the max. Since they form cartels and manipulate prices by giving very less flexibility to the consumer to negotiate or choose from the products available. In such a scenario it is the consumer who becomes prey of these activities. Profit maximization motive is continuously aiming at increasing the firm's revenue and is concentrating less on the social welfare.

Government plays a very important role in curbing this practice of charging extraordinary high prices at the cost of service or product. In fact a market which experiences a high degree of competition is likely to exploit the customer in the name of profit maximization, and on the other hand where the production of a particular product or service is limited there is a possibility to charge higher prices is greater. There are few things which need a greater clarification as far as maximization of profit is concerned

Profit maximization objective is a little vague in terms of returns achieved by a firm in different time period. The time value of money is often ignored when measuring profit.

It leads to uncertainty of returns. Two firms which use same technology and same factors of production may eventually earn different returns. It is due to the profit margin. It may not be legitimate if seen from a different stand point.

26.15 | Financial Intermediaries - Meaning, Role and its Importance

A financial intermediary is a firm or an institution that acts an intermediary between a provider of service and the consumer. It is the institution or individual that is in between two or more parties in a financial context. In theoretical terms, a financial intermediary channels savings into investments. Financial intermediaries exist for profit in the financial system and sometimes there is a need to regulate the activities of the same. Also, recent trends suggest that financial intermediaries role in savings and investment functions can be used for an efficient market system or like the sub-prime crisis shows, they can be a cause for concern as well.

Financial Intermediation

Financial intermediaries work in the savings/investment cycle of an economy by serving as conduits to finance between the borrowers and the lenders. In the financial system, intermediaries like banks and insurance companies have a huge role to play given that it has been estimated that a major proportion of every dollar financed externally has been done by the banks. Financial intermediaries are an important source of external funding for corporate. Unlike the capital markets where investors contract directly with the corporate creating marketable securities, financial intermediaries borrow from lenders or consumers and lend to the companies that need investment.

Role of the Financial Intermediaries

The reason for the all-pervasive nature of the financial intermediaries like banks and insurance companies lies in their uniqueness. As outlined above, Banks often serve as the "intermediaries" between those who have the resources and those who want resources. Financial intermediaries like banks are asset based or fee based on the kind of service they provide along with the nature of the clientele they handle. Asset based financial intermediaries are institutions like banks and insurance companies whereas fee based financial intermediaries provide portfolio management and syndication services.

Need for regulation

The very nature of the complex financial system that we have at this point in time makes the need for regulation that much more necessary and urgent. As the sub-prime crisis has shown, any financial institution cannot be made to hold the financial system hostage to its questionable business practices. As the manifestations of the crisis are being felt and it is now apparent that the asset backed derivatives and other "exotic" instruments are amounting to trillions, the role of the central bank or the monetary authorities in reining in the rogue financial institutions is necessary to prevent systemic collapse.

As capital becomes mobile and unfettered, it is the monetary authorities that have to step in and ensure that there are proper checks and balances in the system so as to prevent losses to investors and the economy in general.

Recent trends

Recent trends in the evolution of financial intermediaries, particularly in the developing world have shown that these institutions have a pivotal role to play in the elimination of poverty and other debt reduction programs. Some of the initiatives like micro-credit reaching out to the masses have increased the economic well being of hitherto neglected sectors of the population.

Further, the financial intermediaries like banks are now evolving into umbrella institutions that cater to the complete needs of investors and borrowers alike and are maturing into "financial hyper marts".

Financial intermediaries have a key role to play in the world economy today. They are the "lubricants" that keep the economy going. Due to the increased complexity of financial transactions, it becomes imperative for the financial intermediaries to keep re-inventing themselves and cater to the diverse portfolios and needs of the investors. The financial intermediaries have a significant responsibility towards the borrowers as well as the lenders. The very term intermediary would suggest that these institutions are pivotal to the working of the economy and they along with the monetary authorities have to ensure that credit reaches to the needy without jeopardizing the interests of the investors. This is one of the main challenges before them.

Financial intermediaries have a central role to play in a market economy where efficient allocation of resources is the responsibility of the market mechanism. In these days of increased complexity of the financial system, banks and other financial intermediaries have to come up with new and innovative products and services to cater to the diverse needs of the borrowers and lenders. It is the right mix of financial products along with the need for reducing systemic risk that determines the efficacy of a financial intermediary.

Review Questions

Short Answer Questions

1. Explain the objectives of Financial Planning?
2. List out the major differences between over capitalization and under capitalization?
3. Who are financial intermediaries? Explain their importance?
4. Give a note on role of capitalization in financial management?
5. Throw light on recent trends in financial planning?

Long Answer Questions

1. Financial planning is the heart of any business. Explain?
2. Explain the factors determining the capital structure?
3. Explain the role and functions of a financial manager?

27 Entrepreneurship Development

27.1 Meaning and Definition of Entrepreneur

The word entrepreneur has come from the France word “entreprendra”which means to undertake, to pursue opportunities to fulfill needs and wants through innovation to undertake business.

In the year 1725 the word entrepreneur was first brought into economics by a social scientist named Richard cantilion and the expert who invented the theory of entrepreneurship was David mc Cellion in 1961.

Entrepreneur is a person who organizes, operates and assumes the risk for business venture.

Entrepreneur is a person 1. who exercise the function or 2. initiating coordinating controlling or institute major change in a business enterprise and or 3. bearing those risk of operation which arise from the dynamic nature of society and imperfect knowledge of the future which can cast through transfer calculation or elimination

Entrepreneur is the agent who purchases the means of production for combination into marketable product.

So we can say that entrepreneur a person who takes risk for establishing a new venture or business in order to create utility for the welfare of human being as well as for him or herself. She or he is always a person who seeks out opportunities and takes on challenges.

LEARNING OBJECTIVES

- *Meaning and definition of entrepreneur*
- *Characteristics of an entrepreneur*
- *Qualities of a successful entrepreneur*
- *Relation between entrepreneur and entrepreneurship*
- *Distinction between entrepreneur and a manager*
- *Different types of entrepreneurs*
- *Factors of entrepreneurship development*
- *Causes of success and failure of entrepreneur*
- *Prospects of entrepreneurship development*
- *Problems of entrepreneurship development*
- *Steps for removing the problems of entrepreneurship development*

27.1.1 Meaning and Definition of Entrepreneurship

Entrepreneurship is considered as of assuming the risk of an entrepreneur.

Entrepreneurship is the capacity for innovation, investment and expansion in new markets product and techniques.

Entrepreneurship as economic venture organizing and risk taking capabilities.

Entrepreneurship is the force of creative destruction whereby established way of doing things is destroyed by the creating of new and better ways to get things done

From the functional view point entrepreneurship is defined as the combination of activities such as perception of market opportunities gaining command over scarce resources purchasing input producing and marketing of product responding to competition and maintaining relation with political administration and public bureaucracy for concession, licenses and taxes etc.

Characteristics of an entrepreneur

An entrepreneur is a person who initiates a business venture. There are some essential features of an entrepreneur which are describing below.

- **Risk taking capability:** Every business has risk of time, money etc., so an entrepreneur must have the risk taking capability.

  ***Creativity and innovation*:** An entrepreneur has an initiator possesses creativity and innovative power.

  ***Need for achievement*:** The entrepreneur has strong desire to achieve the goal of business. He is always driven by the needs for achievement.

  ***Need for autonomy*:** An entrepreneur does not like to be under anybody. it is the need for autonomy which drives a person to be an entrepreneur.

  ***Internal locus of control*:** An entrepreneur believes in him and his work.

  ***External locus of control*:** He also believes in fate for ultimate result.

  ***Self confident*:** An entrepreneur has confidence in him.

  ***Leadership capability*:** An entrepreneur must have leadership capability to lead works under him.
- **Industriousness:** A successful entrepreneur must have leadership capability to lead workers working under him.
- **Decision making capability:** The entrepreneur has capability to take quick decision.
- **Adaptability:** He has the capacity to adapt with any kind of situation that arise in the enterprise.
- **Foresightness:** The entrepreneurs have a good foresight to know about future business environment.
- **Others:** The other feature are dynamism, ambition, education and training, long term involvement, future orientation.

Qualities of successful entrepreneur

To become a successful as an entrepreneur in its business life, a businessman should possess a quite a number of essential qualities. Those are noted below:

1. ***Moderate risk taking***: An entrepreneur always takes calculated risk to operate the organization.
2. ***Hard work***: An entrepreneur is very much hard worker, he or she always busy with various types work.
3. ***Accountability***: A successful entrepreneur is accountable well as his associates always accountable to him.
4. ***Educated in real sense***: successful entrepreneur is educated. In real sense .he tries to implement his organizational objectives through his education.
5. ***Analytical mind***: A successful entrepreneur is analytical minded. He scrutinizes every activity on the organization.
6. ***Dynamic leadership***: A successful entrepreneur is always dynamic to operate the organization.
7. ***Presence of mind***: A successful entrepreneur is always at present of mind he is always aware of activities that to happening in the organization and around him.
8. ***Accommodative***: A good entrepreneur has the capacity to make his own place at every sector
9. ***Courageous and tactful***: Techniques is very much essential for a successful entrepreneur.
10. ***Maker of right decision***: A successful entrepreneur makes right decision in right time in right place.
11. ***Foresighted***: A successful entrepreneur foresights the future and take decision accordingly.
12. ***Right perception of things***: A successful entrepreneur thinks in a right way.
13. ***Enjoy simple life***: A successful entrepreneur always deals a simple life a general people of the society.
14. ***Strong desired to success***: A successful entrepreneur have a strong desire to success. He is driven by the desire to success.
15. ***Innovation***: Innovation is the process of making new something. A successful entrepreneur is innovative.
16. ***Self confidence***: A successful entrepreneur is self confidence does not rely on other for decision or fate.
17. ***Goal setting***: A successful entrepreneur set the goal.
18. ***Keen observation***: A successful entrepreneur always observes the origination.
19. ***Sociable***: A successful entrepreneur is sociable person.
20. ***Loves to work***: A successful entrepreneur is very much addicted to work.
21. ***Loves new ideas***: A successful entrepreneur loves new ides of the organization.
22. ***Team builder***: A successful entrepreneur builds a suitable team.

23. ***Clean understanding*:** A successful entrepreneur clearly understands every thing.
24. ***Ability to conceptualize*:** A successful entrepreneur is able to conceptualize the reality.
25. ***Other*:** The other qualities are patience, optimistic, strategist, etc.

Relationship between Entrepreneur and entrepreneurship

The relationship between entrepreneur and entrepreneurship are discussed below:

Entrepreneur

Entrepreneurship

1. Entrepreneur is a person.
   Entrepreneurship is a process.
2. Entrepreneur is an organizer.
   Entrepreneurship is an organization.
3. Entrepreneur is an innovator.
   Entrepreneurship is an innovation.
4. Entrepreneur is a risk bearer.
   Entrepreneur is a risk bearing.
5. Entrepreneur is a motivator.
   Entrepreneur is a motivation.
6. Entrepreneur is a creator.
   Entrepreneur is a creation.
7. Entrepreneur is a visualizer.
   Entrepreneur is a vision.
8. Entrepreneur is a leader.
   Entrepreneurship is a leadership.
9. Entrepreneur is an imitator.
   Entrepreneurship is an imitation.

Distinction between an entrepreneur and a manager

Sometimes the word entrepreneur and manager are used as synonyms. In fact there are some differences between them. They are described below:

Subject matter ----------- **Entrepreneur** ------------ **Manager**

1. **Motive:** Thinking function. His main motive is to start a new venture by setting up an enterprise.
   Doing function. His main motive is to render service to the organization already established.
2. **Status:** Entrepreneur is the owner of the enterprise.
   Manager is the service holder or servant of the enterprise.

3. **Risk bearing:** Being owner of the enterprise assume all risk and uncertainty involved in the enterprise.
   As the servant don't take or bear risk and uncertainty involved in the organization.
4. **Reward:** Reward is profit which is highly uncertain.
   Get salary as a reward which is fixed and certain.
5. **Innovation:** An entrepreneur is an innovator.
   A manager is not an innovator in that sense he implements the plan prepared by the entrepreneur.
6. **Qualification:** They are not highly qualified but have extraordinary experience forecasting.
   They are highly qualified (institutional education).

After the above discussion we can say that at a time an entrepreneur can be a manager but a manager cannot be an entrepreneur.

Different types of entrepreneurs

On the basis of nature ***Clarence Danhof*** classified entrepreneurs into four categories. These are:

1. ***Innovative entrepreneurs*:** An innovative entrepreneur in one, who introduces new goods, inaugurates new method of production, discovers new market and recognizes the enterprise. It is important to note that such entrepreneurs can work only when a certain level of development is already achieved and people look forward to change and improvement.
2. ***Imitative entrepreneurs*:** These types of entrepreneurs creatively imitate the innovative technical achievement made by another firm. Imitative entrepreneurs are suitable for underdeveloped countries as it is hard for them to bear the high cost of innovation.
3. ***Fabian entrepreneurs*:** Fabian entrepreneurs are characterized by very great caution and skepticism to experiment any change in their enterprises. They usually do not take any new challenge. They imitate only when it becomes perfectly clear that failure to do not so would result in a loss of the relative position in the enterprise.
4. ***Drone entrepreneurs*:** They are characterized by a refusal to adopt any change even at cost of severely reduction of profit.

Some other types of entrepreneurs

(i) ***Solo operators*:** These are the entrepreneurs who essentially work alone and if needed at all employ a few employees. In the beginning most of the entrepreneurs start their enterprises like them.

(ii) ***Active partners*:** Active partners are those entrepreneurs who start or carry on an enterprise as a joint venture. It is important that all of them actively participate in the operations of the business.

(iii) ***Innovators*:** Such entrepreneurs with their competence and creativity innovate new products. Their basic interest lies in research and innovative activities.

(iv) ***Buyers' entrepreneurs*:** These are the entrepreneurs who do not like to bear much risk. They do not take the risk of production but take the risk of marketing a product i.e., wholesaler and retailer.

(v) ***Life timers*:** These entrepreneurs believe business as an integral part of their life. These entrepreneurs actually inherit their family business i.e., goldsmith, potter etc.

(vi) ***Challengers*:** These are the entrepreneurs who initiate business because of the challenges it presents. They believe that 'No risk, No gain'. When one challenge seems to be met, they begin to look for new challenges.

Beside these, there are Govt. and Non-govt. entrepreneurs.

Factors of Entrepreneurship development:

(A) Personal factors

1. Ability to cope with the situation
2. Age
3. Education
4. Personality
5. Intrapersonal communication ability
6. Achievement motivation
7. Self-confidence
8. Competence
9. Emotion
10. Understanding capacity

(B) Environmental factors

1. Socio-cultural factors

- Religion
- Values
- Rural-urban orientation
- Marginality
- Education
- Tradition

2. Political and legal factors

- Govt. legal bindings
- Govt. policies
- Rules and laws related to the industry and business

(C) Institutional factors

1. Financial institution

2. Training and development institution
3. Consulting firms
4. Incubators organization (old & pioneer)
5. Research organization

(D) Micro factors

1. Enterprise itself
2. Suppliers
3. Intermediaries
4. Customers
5. Competitors
6. Public

(E) Macro factors

1. Demographic factors
2. Economic factors
3. Physical factors
4. Technological factors
5. Cultural/social factors

(F) Others

1. Venture capital
2. Experience entrepreneurs
3. Technically skilled labor force
4. Supplier's accessibility
5. Proximity to universities
6. Availability of land facilities
7. Accessibility of transportation
8. Favorable loan and financial policies
9. Decepted population
10. Availability of supportive
11. Attractive living condition
12. Capital intensiveness
13. Research and development activities
14. Capital incentive ness
15. Proximity to corporate head quarters
16. Competitive situation

Causes of success and failure of entrepreneur

An entrepreneur may sometime become successful and sometime becomes failure. There are some causes of such success and failure. They are noted below:

1. ***Selection of business***: It is an important aspect. That means an entrepreneur has to determine what type business he is going to start. From various points of view the feasibility of the business should be tested.
2. ***Proper planning***: Proper planning is also important. For planning, planning premises like political, economic, social premised should be considered first. The steps of planning should be followed properly.
3. ***Initial capital***: if the initial capitals are not an optimal level the organization would fall. So whether the enterprise is big or small the initial capital should be sufficient enough.
4. ***Determination of market demand***: Through research the demand in the market should be identified. Both for long term and short term it should be considered.
5. ***Marketing of product***: If the promotion policy, channel of destitution, transportation is not good the enterprise would fall.
6. ***Education and experience***: One of the important tasks of the entrepreneurs is to select right person for the right post because the success of an enterprise depends on the right selection of employees.
7. ***Joint initiative***: One may have much money and another may have more merit. Through joint initiative it can be balanced. But sometime for joint initiative misunderstanding arise, or sometimes corruption occur which may result in fall of enterprise.
8. ***Employment***: Recruitment and appointment should be properly done. Those who have specialized skill should be appointed to that specialized job. Inefficient, corrupted employees may be responsible for fall of business.
9. ***Location of business***: Site selection is an important factor. While starting a new business, an entrepreneur should think about the location of the business. In this case, many factors should be considered such as availability of raw materials, proper communication system, availability of labor, marketing facilities and so on.
10. ***Qualities of management***: The management must have a minimum quality to success otherwise it would fall.

These are the common causes for which one enterprise may become successful and another may fall.

The opportunities or prospects of entrepreneurship development

1. ***Availability of human resources***: India has its vast population of about 150 million. So there is a great possibility of developing entrepreneurship and entrepreneurs in India. HR is the fundamental factors of production that is available in vast amount. So production that is available in vast amount. Therefore, entrepreneurs can easily use them on payment that may encourage them to be

entrepreneur. Therefore, abundance of HR is the great opportunity in creating entrepreneurs in India.

2. ***Industrial innovative sensation*:** People of India have industrial innovative sensation. They may get involved largely in industrial initiative if they get favorable opportunity. Already they established many small and cottage industries with the help of NGOs and other financing institution.
3. ***Mobility of profession*:** A considerable number of villagers now replaced their agriculture-based profession into petty businesses and many other small and cottage industry. Many of them transferred into city area. Thus, way here creates a mobility of profession. That is another prospect of developing entrepreneurship in India.
4. ***No religious hindrances on mobility of profession*:** In India, there are any religious and cultural hindrances on mobility of profession. Most of the people are changing their work, profession day by day. In past, certain religious people belong to certain profession. But now people get engaged in their desired profession without religious and cultural hindrance. That is another prospect of creating entrepreneurs.
5. ***Large number of educated unemployed*:** In our country, there are many educated unemployed people, but there is a limited scope of employment. For this reason, educated unemployed people will take new initiative to do something new themselves. As there is a close connection of education and entrepreneurship there is a possibility of developing entrepreneurship.
6. ***Tendency toward industries work*:** Industrials work bears more salary, status, facilities for living in city area and so on. For this reason people tending towards industrial work. Thus, industrial sector will be developed in future. Such mentality and tendency is helpful in developing entrepreneurs. Therefore, it is another prospect of developing entrepreneurs.
7. ***Preference in establishing agro-based industry in Government planning*:** As our country is agro-based, there is a greater possibility of establishing agro-based industry. Besides, most of the raw materials of industry come from agricultural sector. So our resourceful agriculture sector is helpful in developing entrepreneurship. Nowadays, Govt. announces preference in agro-based industry that is also greater opportunity to develop entrepreneurs.
8. ***Liberalization of Govt. industrial policy*:** With the aim of rapid industrialization, govt. adopted liberalization in industrial policy and encourages entrepreneurs to come ahead in industrial sector with their large capital. For this reason, investors are investing their capital in industrial sector.
9. ***Disbursement of micro-credit by different NGO's*:** In our country there are large numbers of NGOs providing micro-credit to the village poor people. That is helpful in forming small and cottage industry. NGOs also provide training facilities, advice, investment, consultancy, raw materials etc to its loaner.

Problems of entrepreneurship development

As a third world country, in India there is no abundant facilities for developing entrepreneurship rather exist a large number of obstacles, which are liable for not developing entrepreneurs in India described below:

1. ***Improper publicity of Govt. facilities*:** For developing entrepreneurs in limited basis. Those have not informed properly to the remote villagers. Therefore, these facilities cannot work well. Some urban centered people accept the facilities that are not enough for developing entrepreneurs' ass over the country. So this is one of the fundamental obstacles.
2. ***Insufficient arrangement of pre-investment advice*:** For this reason most of entrepreneur can't study market feasibility for the product and business demand for the product in market, possibility of gaining profit etc. For the lack of this study most of the entrepreneur can't operate their activities successfully. Many of them fail in their initial activities.
3. ***Lack of required financing*:** This is the fundamental problem of developing entrepreneurship. Here, entrepreneurs faces problem in collecting required working capital and fixed capital, most of the financing organization demand for supporting papers and apply rigid condition. As a result most of the entrepreneurs cannot get rise capital to operate their activities smoothly. Working capital, fixed capital and capital for expansion of business.
4. ***Scarcity of raw materials and other factors of production*:** In our country, there is an immense shortage of basic raw materials to operate industrial activities smoothly such as skilled manpower, technology, capital and so on. For this reason they has to import basic raw materials and supplementary factors of production that increase the cost of production. As a result, entrepreneur can't take initiatives to establish industrial organization smoothly.
5. ***Problem in marketing produced product*:** Now-a-days marketing of the product has become an important task in business. In open market economy, product of the home and foreign countries compete with each other in same market. Usually quality products capture the market. Because of different problem and lack of factors of production, our entrepreneur can't produce or hardly produce quality product as developed country. For this reason, now a days they face marketing problem greatly for every product.
6. ***Lack of training*:** Training is essential to work efficiently and effectively in any field. Training is a practical experience regarding job that is necessary to increase efficiency and productivity. In our country, there is no available training centre to provide training in developing entrepreneurs. As a result, people cannot come ahead to take initiative that is an obstacle to develop entrepreneurship.
7. ***Lack of package help*:** In developed country, Govt. and non-govt. sector provide package help for developing industrial sector. In includes, technical help, raw materials, and working capital and so on. These are helpful in creating entrepreneurship as well as industry. But in our country there is no abundance package help that is very essential for developing entrepreneurship in our country.

So it is another problem of developing entrepreneurs and entrepreneurship in India.

8. ***Lack of knowledge regarding technology and management*:** In developed country most of the business and industries are technology oriented and they follow modern management technique. Those are helpful in developing dynamic entrepreneurs. Nevertheless, in our country there is little scope of technology and modern management. Besides, we also have no proper knowledge regarding those matters.

Suggestions for removing the problems of entrepreneurship development

1. ***Making specific policy*:** To perform any activities some policies should be maintained. We all shall recognize that some effective policies should be made to develop entrepreneurship. Relating organization and officials should make some specific policies for developing it.
2. ***Involving entrepreneurial knowledge in text book*:** As our education system is theoretical based so entrepreneurial knowledge should be included in textbook. So that students can achieve entrepreneurial knowledge that will be beneficiary for developing entrepreneurship in future.
3. ***Offering package help*:** After providing training, trainee should be provided necessary help for developing industrial sector. Necessary help including fixed capital, working capital, technical men, technology, and raw material and so on. This is helpful in creating entrepreneurship.
4. ***Formal arrangement of training*:** People who are engaged in entrepreneurial work or people who are willing to take new initiative have suggested providing training in the respective field that will be helpful for them to take initiative and operates industry smoothly. Govt. and non-govt. organization can arrange this program.
5. ***Increasing govt. facilities and its extensive publicity*:** Govt. facilities for developing entrepreneurship are not sufficient. So govt. should provide abundant facilities for developing entrepreneurship. Govt. should also arrange extensive publicity of it's given facilities. So that rural centered people can get these facilities. That will be very helpful in developing entrepreneurship in India.
6. ***Encouragement in industrialization*:** Govt. and non govt. organization may encourages people towards industrialization by providing different facilities including tax redemption or tax holiday, EPZ facility, BSCIC industrial state, providing raw material, capital, technical assistance etc. with unqualified condition.
7. ***Establishment of supplementary industry*:** Entrepreneurship may be developed by establishing supplementary industry extensively. Some of them produce industrial product that are reproduced large industry and some of them use by product of large industry. They are also essential to develop large-scale industry.
8. ***Increasing loan facilities*:** Most of the people establish small or large-scale industry with loan facility. Financing institution should provide sufficient loan to the entrepreneur with flexible condition and supporting paper. This program will be helpful in establishing and operating new industries and businesses.

9. ***Exhibition of industrial product*:** To increase demand for industrial product govt. and non-govt. organization may arrange exhibition. Industrial fair in domestic country will be helpful in creating demand for industrial product. Industrial product may introduce in abroad. It is an important recommendation to develop entrepreneurs and entrepreneurship.
10. ***Reduction of tax and duty*:** Govt. may encourage industrialization by lessening duty rate of industrial product. That will also lessen cost of industrial product, which is helpful in capturing market. Thus, way industrialization or entrepreneurship will be developed duty on importing raw materials have suggested to reduce.
11. ***Favorable import and export policy*:** Most of the basic raw materials used in industry have been imported from foreign countries. Some industrial products have produced to export as a whole. So for developing industrialization and entrepreneurship proper authority should make obvious and flexible export-import policy.

Review Questions

Short Answer Questions

1. Explain factors of entrepreneurship development?
2. Explain different types of entrepreneurs?

Long Answer Questions

1. Explain the major differences between a entrepreneur and entrepreneurship?
2. Explain the qualities of a successful entrepreneur?
3. Explain the reasons for success or failure of entrepreneurship?

28 Time and Space Management

The term time management is a misnomer. You cannot manage time; you manage the events in your life in relation to time. You may often wish for more time but you only get 24 hours, 1,440 minutes or 86,400 seconds each day. How you use that time depends on skills learned through self analysis, planning, evaluation, and self-control. Much like money, time is both valuable and limited: it must be protected, used wisely, and budgeted. People who practice good time management techniques often find that they:

- Are more productive,
- Have more energy for things they need to accomplish,
- Feel less stressed,
- Are able to do the things they want,
- Get more things done,
- Relate more positively to others, and
- Feel better about themselves.

Finding a time management strategy that works best for you depends on your personality, ability to self- motivate and level of self- discipline.

Keeping a time log is a helpful way to determine how you are using your time. Start by recording what you are doing for 15-minute intervals for a week or two. Evaluate the results. Ask if you did everything that was needed; determine which tasks require the most time; determine the time of day when you are most productive; and analyze where

LEARNING OBJECTIVES

- *Meaning of Time and Space Management*
- *Personal Digital Assistant*
- *Benefits of Space Management*
- *Ten Space Management Commandments*
- *Developing a Space Management strategy*

most of your time is devoted – job, family, personal, recreation, etc. Identifying your most time-consuming tasks and determining whether you are investing your time in the most important activities can help you to determine a course of action. In addition, having a good sense of the amount of time required for routine tasks can help you be more realistic in planning and estimating how much time is available for other activities.

Managing your time effectively requires a distinction between what is *important* and what is *urgent.* Experts agree that the most important tasks usually aren't the most urgent tasks. However, we tend to let the urgent dominate our lives. Covey, and Merrill (1994) categorize our activities into four quadrants in their *Time Management Matrix*: urgent, not urgent, important and not important. While activities that are both urgent and important must be done, Covey et.al. suggests that we spend less time on activities that are not important (regardless of their urgency) in order to gain time to focus on activities that are not urgent but important. Focusing on these important activities allows you to gain greater control over your time and possibly reduce the number of important tasks that do become urgent. A daily, weekly or monthly list depends on your lifestyle. Just be careful not to allow the list-making to get out of control and do not keep multiple lists at the same time. Rank the items on your "to do" list in order of priority (both important and urgent). You may choose to group items in categories such as high, in mind that your goal is not to mark off the most items; rather you want to mark off the highest priority items. Having a prioritized "to do" list allows you to say "no" to activities that may be interesting or provide a sense of achievement but do not fit your basic priorities.

Time management experts recommend using a personal planning tool to improve your productivity. Examples of personal planning tools include electronic planners, pocket diaries, calendars, computer programs, wall charts, index cards and notebooks. Writing down your tasks, schedules, and memory joggers can free thoughts instead. The key is to find one planning tool that works for you and use that tool consistently. Some reminders when using a planning tool are:

- Always record your information on the tool itself. Jotting notes elsewhere that have to be transferred later is inefficient.
- Review your planning tool daily.
- Carry your planning tool with you.
- Remember to keep a list of your priorities in your planning tool and refer to it often.
- Synchronize electronic planners with your computer and recharge the batteries in your planner on a regular basis.
- Keep a back-up system

28.1 | Personal Digital Assistant

Capabilities of PDAs vary by the model and some users include Wi-Fi or cellular technology on their handheld device. Some suggestions for using your PDA to its capacity are:

- Assign a different color for each calendar item so that you can distinguish personal appointments from business meetings, for example.
- Use the task application feature to manage projects. Most PDAs allow the user to group tasks under separate headings, prioritize tasks and assign deadlines.
- Use the repeat function for recurring dates such as birthdays, anniversaries, and regularly scheduled meetings.
- Investigate additional software and hardware that is compatible with your PDA. You may be able to enter information more quickly using a portable, detachable keyboard rather than a stylus, for example. Or, you may want the ability to access the Internet for retrieving files or checking other calendars.
- Place a notebook the size of your PDA in your carrying case for writing down "to dos" if you have difficulty recording them with your PDA's task application feature.

Most people find that disorganization results in poor time management. Professional organizers recommend that you first get rid of the clutter. A frequently used method is to set up three boxes (or corners of a room) labeled "Keep" – "Give Away" – "Toss." Separate the clutter by sorting items into these boxes. Immediately discard items in your "Toss" box. Your "Give Away" box may include items you want to sell, delegate, or discontinue so find a method to eliminate these items such as a yard sale, charitable donation, or gifts to friends or family members outside your home. With the clutter gone, the next step is to implement a system that allows you to handle information (e.g., tasks, papers, e-mail, etc.) less, only once, when possible. You have 5 options for handling information:

1. Throw it away, delete it, or otherwise get rid of it.
2. Delegate it: give it to someone else to do, file, or respond.
3. Act on it yourself. Then throw it away or file it
4. File it temporarily until it needs action or until additional information is received. Follow-up: a "tickler" file can be useful for holding temporary information.
5. File it permanently where you can easily find it later.

Even the busiest people find time for what they want to do and feel is important. Scheduling is not just recording what you *have* to do (e.g., meetings and appointments), it is also making a time commitment to the things you *want* to do. Good scheduling requires that you know yourself. Using your time log, you should have determined those times during the day when you are most productive and alert. Plan your most challenging tasks for when you have the most energy. Block out time for your high priority activities first and protect that time from interruptions.

If you know you will have waiting time or commuting time, schedule small tasks such as writing a letter, jotting down a shopping list, reading or listening educational audiotapes to capitalize on the time loss. Try to limit scheduled time to about 3/4th of your day, leaving time for creative activities such as planning, dreaming, thinking, and reading.

Block out time for your high priority activities first and protect that time from interruptions.

Delegation means assigning responsibility for a task to someone else, freeing up some of your time for tasks that require your expertise. Delegation begins by identifying tasks that others can do and then selecting the appropriate person(s) to do them. You need to select someone with the appropriate skills, experience, interest, and authority needed to accomplish the task. Be as specific as possible in defining the task and your expectations, but allow the person some freedom to personalize the task. Occasionally check to determine how well the person is progressing and to provide any assistance, being careful not to take over the responsibility. Finally, don't forget to reward the person for a job well done or make suggestions for improvements if needed.

Another way to get help is to "buy" time by obtaining goods or service that save you a time investment. For example, paying someone to mow your lawn or clean your house, using a computerized system, or joining a carpool to transport your children to their extracurricular activities can allow you free time to devote to other activities. Delegation begins by identifying tasks that others can do and selecting the appropriate person(s) to do them.

You may be putting off tasks for a variety of reasons. Perhaps the task seems overwhelming or unpleasant. Try breaking down the task into smaller segments that require less time commitment and result in specific, realistic deadlines. If you're having trouble getting started, you may need to complete a preparatory task such as collecting materials or organizing your notes. Also, try building in a reward system as you complete each small segment of the task

Your time may be impacted by external factors imposed by their people and things. You can decrease or eliminate time spent in these activities by implementing some simple tips listed below.

Use voice mail and set aside time to return calls.

- Avoid small talk. Stay focused on the reason for the call.
- Stand up while you talk on the phone. You are more likely to keep the conversation brief.
- Take any necessary action immediately following the call.
- Set aside times of the day for receiving calls and let others know when you are available.
- Keep phone numbers readily available near the telephone.
- Establish blocks of time when you are available for visits.
- Tell the visitor politely that you cannot meet with them at this time and schedule the visit for a more convenient time.
- Set a mutually agreeable time limit for the visit.
- When someone comes to the door, stand up and have your meeting standing.

Know the purpose of the meeting in advance.

- Arrive on time.
- Start and end the meeting on time.
- Prepare an agenda and stick to it. Use a timed agenda, if necessary.
- Don't schedule meetings unless they are necessary and have a specific purpose or agenda.

Set aside a specific time to view and respond to your mail and e-mail, but don't let it accumulate to the point that it becomes overwhelming to sort.

- Turn off instant messaging features on e-mail.
- Handle each item only once, if possible. Practice the options for dealing with.
- Sort mail near a garbage can and delete junk e-mail immediately from your electronic mailbox.
- Answer written messages by responding on the margins or bottom of the page.

Establish a master calendar for each family member to post their time commitments.

- Make each family member responsible for consulting the master calendar for potential conflicts.
- Create a central area for posting communications such as appointment, reminders, announcements, and messages.

Recent psychological studies have shown that multi-tasking does not actually save time. In fact, the opposite is often true. You lose time when switching from one task to another, resulting in a loss of productivity. Routine multi-tasking may lead to difficulty in concentrating and maintaining focus when needed.

The care and attention you give yourself is an important investment of time. Scheduling time to relax, or do nothing, can help you rejuvenate both physically and mentally, enabling you to accomplish tasks more quickly and easily. Learn to manage time according to your biological clock by scheduling priority tasks during your peak time of day, the time your energy level and concentration are at their best. Poor time management can result in fatigue, moodiness, and more frequent illness. To reduce stress, you should reward yourself for a time management success. Take time to recognize that you have accomplished a major task or challenge before moving on to the next activity.

28.2 | Space Management

Most organizational processes are closely tied to spaces; space optimization pays off, big time! 9 benefits of Space Management:

1. ***Identify under-utilized spaces*:** Almost 45% of space portfolio is vacant at any point in time. This implicates that the organization pays a vast amount for NOT occupying space. This is absolutely ridiculous. We only want to pay for something we actually use, not for anything we don't use.

   The organization can directly impact the bottom line by reducing under-utilized space. To reduce under-utilized space, we need to identify which spaces are under-utilized. Without an automated solution this is impossible.

2. ***Align workplace initiatives with business goals*:** Over the last few years most organizations have created vision documents including sustainability goals. Your organization is going to do more, using fewer resources.

   Although this has a direct impact on the bottom line, it creates a challenge. Without a firm grip on space occupancy; organizations can't align their workplace initiatives to their business goals. Effective space management is a fundamental requirement for impacting bottom line result.

3. ***Forecast Future Space Requirements*:** Today's economical climate is extremely dynamic. Since we want to reduce under-utilized space, we also need to be able to forecast future space requirements. This is challenging as future space requirements have a direct relation with organizational growth or contraction.

   Space management helps you to create reliable forecasts about future space requirements. In addition to that, allow you to create what-if scenarios and compare associated costs based on business evolution variables.

4. ***Simplify Chargeback Process*:** From time to time organizational disputes about charged space usage occur. These disputes are frustrating for many stakeholders. You need to solve them quickly. Space Management can help you analyze historical space usage and create accurate chargeback reports.

   What's more important, when departments are held accountable for their actual space usage, they tend to be more defensive in their space usage which will have a direct impact on your bottom line.

5. ***Simplify space analysis*:** Space analysis using spreadsheets = misery.

   Particularly historical data is extremely hard to capture in spreadsheets, let alone the analysis of it. Space Management using an IWMS helps you to analyze your actual space usage, compare it with the planned space usage and make informed decisions that will impact your bottom line.

6. ***Streamline the move process*:** Moves are expensive and move costs quickly grow out of control. Due to the nature of the move, moves have a large impact on every organization. Just think of the organizational impact of a departmental move, in terms of resources.

   If you want to impact your bottom line through effective space management, you also need effective move management. This means streamlining the entire move process from request to completion in order to optimize churn rates and reduce costs.

7. ***Compare actual with planned space utilization***: Although you have carefully planned your future space requirements, real life can always throw surprises at you. Therefore it's very important to constantly compare planned space utilization with actual space utilization.

   By using dashboards and business intelligence reports, you need to monitor the actual space utilization, and make changes in usage accordingly. Closely monitoring actual space usage helps you to intervene when necessary.

8. ***Increase efficiency***: Your organizational goals and business needs ensure individuals or departments have to cooperate with each other. These affiliations (or the lack of) have a big impact on your bottom line. Let me explain.

   Suppose two departments are depending on each other (e.g. Accounts Payable and Accounts Receivable). What do you think will be the impact on organizational effectiveness if they were:

   - Located on the same floor in the same building close to each other?
   - Located on separate floors in the same building?
   - Located on separate floors in separate buildings?

   Most Integrated Workplace Management Systems can graphically create scenarios based on interdepartmental relations. These scenarios are used to increase efficiency which has a direct impact on your bottom line.

9. ***Utilize Building Information Modeling***: Building Information Modeling (BIM) is the process of generating and managing building data during its life cycle. Typically it uses three-dimensional, real-time, dynamic building modeling software to increase productivity in building design and construction.[2] The process produces the Building Information Model (abbreviated as BIM), which encompasses building geometry, spatial relationships, geographic information, and quantities and properties of building components.

   A lot of information required for Building Information Modeling is already available which will in the near future be the dominant management approach for generating and managing a building.

28.3 | Ten Space Management Commandments

1. Have reliable, comprehensive, accurate and up-to-date information, accessible on a database – data is a key platform for improving space management – if you can't measure it you can't manage it.
2. Carry out regular space utilization and management surveys – the process of obtaining and managing data, and an on-going understanding of what users are doing, needs to be an integral part of the space management process.

3. Develop effective communication and management systems - communication is a key vehicle for success – or failure.
4. Effective leadership is essential – a 'space champion' is needed if real progress is to be made.
5. Effective and appropriate management systems are required – available techniques – such as space charging and computerized timetabling – need to be carefully reviewed and implemented as appropriate, and regularly monitored. These are the instruments for change.
6. Understanding of user needs is the key to success – if you do not know what users want you cannot effectively satisfy their needs. This is vital.
7. Engage academics and other users of the estate – the mechanics and management support are important prerequisites for change, but real academic involvement is absolutely vital if real change is to be made.
8. Plan flexibly and for the long-term – quick fix measures are a false economy.
9. Relate to strategic plan – space management is intended to serve the needs of the institution – not the other way round. However, effective space management will always positively support strategic plans. 10. Fund appropriately – the estate is the 'shop window' for an institution, as well as where most of the institutions' activity takes place. Therefore inadequate funding can lead to loss of investment elsewhere

28.4 | Developing A Space Management Strategy

A Space Management Strategy (SMS) should be a clear statement on how space is to be managed in the institution. It should describe the course of action that the institution will pursue in managing space. A list of policies needs to be included within the strategy documentation, along with the measures that are to be used in pursuing these policies. The SMS should form a seamless link with the Estate Strategy and should be based upon the conclusions of the Estate Strategy – in other words helping to put the Estate Strategy into practice. As the Estate Strategy will be based upon the Institutional Strategy, it follows that the SMS should be in accord with the corporate objectives of the institution. In developing a SMS it is vital that the objectives to be achieved by developing and implementing such a strategy are clearly understood. These objectives might include making effective and efficient use of existing space, and reducing space whilst meeting occupier's needs. If the objectives of the SMS are not made clear, then users of the estate can become confused as to what the SMS policies and measures are intended to achieve. The SMS needs to be dynamic. Although the strategy needs to be based upon key strategic drivers (e.g., the Estate Strategy and Institutional Strategy), it also needs to be developed around users needs and feedback. This is important to help ensure maximum 'buy-in' to the strategy. This in turn requires that an ongoing monitoring process is in place to update and revise the strategy. The SMS also needs to be the 'responsibility' of a senior group within the institution. This should be a Space Management Committee (SMC) or equivalent. This SMC should also have responsibility for co-coordinating and developing other space management initiatives so as to ensure the SMS is achieved and not in conflict with other measures or policies.

In developing a SMS document there are a number of broad issues that should be considered by an institution. These are summarized below:

What is the SMS to focus upon? It is essential that institutions look at the advantages and disadvantages of the various space management measures, specifically in terms of how they assist in achieving the objectives of the SMS. A regular review of the strategy should take place. This may be annually in terms of evaluating overall performance. Review on a 2 to 3 year basis may be necessary in order to consider if the overall strategy should be changed.

Below is a list of key guidelines to help in updating or producing a SMS. The list is not necessarily comprehensive, but it should be a useful starting point for an institution in assessing the suitability of their policies.

***Brevity*:** Keep the main policy document short – detail should be put in an appendix. As a guide, the main policy document should be under 10 pages. (Appendices will be in addition to this).

***Readability*:** The policy document should be capable of being read and understood by any member of the institution.

***Accessibility*:** The policy should ideally be available to anyone. This should be agreed with senior management. A realistic means of making it available should be put in place (e.g. on a website/intranet site, publishing note of its existence, identifying how to get hold of a copy, etc).

***Relationships*:** The relationship of the document (and policies contained within it) with other policy documents (e.g., Estate Strategy, etc) should be clearly spelt out. This will help ensure all policies within the institution are mutually supportive – and not working in opposition. Check that the policies in the SMS do support the other policies of the institution. Ideally a statement to this effect should be included within the document.

***Responsibility*:** Specify the purpose of the strategy and lines of responsibility. Specify the ultimate decision-makers, and those charged with final responsibilities.

***Coverage*:** Specify all areas covered by the policy (e.g., all space, including departmental space, space costing, etc.). Also consider specifying what is not covered by the policy. This can clarify any confusion.

***Documentation*:** Detail any appropriate documents that need to be consulted in implementing the SMS (e.g., Estate Strategy, Timetabling request forms etc).

***Procedures*:** Detail the steps that need to be undertaken in managing space, such as requesting or releasing space or booking ‘central’ space. This should be in an appendix to the document. This should include worked examples as appropriate.

Approval: Ensure that the senior management and governing body have approved the SMS. Ideally, the policy should be consulted upon within the institution.

In summary, the SMS should cover the following:

Responsibility: Make clear who is responsible for space management from a management perspective (the Space Management Committee) and from a user perspective (all users!).

Purpose: Provide a clear and realistic set of policies that support the strategy, including details of the objective behind the strategy.

Communication: Indicate how information and requests will be disseminated, including key delivery and decision dates.

Implementation: Provide details of the measures that will be used in implementing the policies (e.g. space charging, space allocation process, timetabling process), and how they are to be used.

Feedback: Describe the process to be used in obtaining feedback and input.

Review Questions

Short Answer Questions

1. Write a note on Personal digital assistant?
2. Explain ten space commandments?
3. Explain the benefits of Space management?

Long Answer Questions

1. Explain the steps for developing a successful space management strategy?
2. Space management optimization is the key to success of an organization- Explain?

29 Prescribing Habits of Physicians

Nothing can be taken for granted in today's marketing era. A marketer can succeed if they manage to create a difference. It is essential that a product has multiple reasons for being purchased which is different from other available products. And it becomes more challenging in the industry wherein the customer who takes decision is not the ultimate consumer. As in case of prescription drug markets in India where the ultimate consumers (patients) have little say and are dependent upon the intermediate customers (doctors). It is estimated that India's $12 billion drug market is growing 14 percent annually and companies are expected to triple sales forces by 2020 to capture this growing market. Hence to sustain in this cut throat competitive business, a viable strategy is needed. The most important part of this strategy is to study the prescribing behavior of the doctors which is seen as a cognitive activity wherein pros and cons of the behavior are weighed before a drug choice is made.

LEARNING OBJECTIVES

- *Physician's prescribing behavior*
- *Data sources for pharm. companies*

The physicians' prescribing behavior can be influenced and multiple factors are involved in physicians' decision to change their prescribing habits. Non medical factors are important predictors of total prescribing volume among physicians. Factors like reading to involvement of professional colleagues were affecting GPs decision to change their prescribing behavior. Tangible rewards to doctors given by pharmaceutical companies, visits by PSR lead to physician loyalty to prescribe. Promotional tools used by the pharmaceutical companies on different doctors revealed that private sector doctors attached more importance to personal selling and educational promotional tools while DMs attached more importance to scientific promotional tools as compared to MD and PG Diploma doctors.

Doctors get influenced in their prescription behavior due to Psychosocial Factors. A good number of studies have also concluded that the physicians have a positive attitude towards the pharmaceutical sales representatives (PSR) also known as MR (medical representatives) and they have an impact on the prescribing behavior of the physicians. Doctors have positive attitude towards the interaction by the pharmaceutical companies which starts as early in medical school and till the practice lasts. The frequent contact of the doctors with the PSR was significantly associated with the greater willingness to prescribe the new drugs. PSR visits influence doctors prescribing behavior and while most doctors value the information they receive from the PSR. Both the studies also revealed that the doctors were less critical and found less susceptible to any influence by the promotional activities than their colleagues.

Pharmaceutical companies firmly reject the idea that using physician prescribing data is inappropriate or increases the cost of health care. They argue that using physician prescribing data increases efficiency in conveying information, because sales representatives can provide physicians with the most current information about available medications, including the risks and benefits. If access to physician prescribing data were blocked, say the companies, physicians would see an increase in the number of sales calls, less targeted educational information, and fewer or less relevant drug samples.

Not all physician prescribing data are detrimental; if used properly, such data can benefit physicians by enabling them to self-evaluate by comparing their prescribing habits with evidence-based guidelines. Data can also be used to increase the efficiency of drug recalls and to monitor and assess benefits and risks after drugs have received marketing approval from the U.S. Food and Drug Administration. Prescribing information is also useful for public health agencies involved in studies about drug interactions, prescribing trends, long-term effects of medication, and preventing medical errors.

The data enables pharmaceutical sales representatives to see what drugs physicians prescribe – and how much they are prescribing. Before sales representatives enter an orthopedic office, they already know which non steroidal anti-inflammatory medications the orthopedic surgeon is prescribing (celecoxib vs. meloxicam vs. naproxen vs. ibuprofen). They can also see usage trends and determine whether a physician is increasing the use of one drug and decreasing the use of another.

Armed with this information, sales representatives can tailor their pitches and make their drug compare extremely well to those most often prescribed. They can also target those physicians within a group who are not using their drug and spend less time and energy with those who do use it.

How do they know?

Drug companies can get physicians' prescribing data relatively easily. When a patient gets a prescription filled at a major pharmacy, a record of each prescription, minus the patient's name, is sold to a data management company, which bundles information from multiple pharmacies. This bundled information is then sold to the pharmaceutical companies, who provide it to their sales representatives. Most physicians we polled were unaware that their prescribing data is entered into a nationwide database and sold to pharmaceutical companies.

Anyone with access to the Internet can go to one of several online Web sites and purchase specific physician prescribing information. In addition, most of these Web sites also sell other types of data about physicians and their practices, including state medical license numbers, Unique Provider Identification Number/National Provider Identification numbers, and physician Drug Enforcement Agency number etc.

Other data sources

Local pharmacies and online Web services aren't the only ones selling physician information. Since the early 1990s, pharmaceutical companies have purchased information about physicians from the American Medical Association (AMA). As the nation's largest physician organization, the AMA maintains the most inclusive physician Masterfile in the United States, with information on more than 820,000 living physicians. Although the AMA data files contain large amounts of data about individual physicians, they do not contain individual physician prescribing information. In 2005, the AMA received $44.5 million – about 15 percent of its total revenue – from the sales of database products.

Physicians prescribe more broadly than commonly perceived. Although most physicians have a "favorite" drug, they are not reluctant to try new therapies. Physicians who prescribe broadly see more patients with varied comorbidities and formulary designs. Prescribing fewer drugs is associated with lower rates of medication adherence and higher out-of-pocket costs, but the effects are small and inconsistent across classes. Broad prescribing may be due to:

- The increasing number of drugs in a class.
- Pharmaceutical marketing, particularly direct-to-physician promotions.
- The role of pharmacy managers and third-party payers.

In 2004, pharmaceutical firms spent more than $57 billion on marketing in the United States, roughly twice their expenditure on research and development. Most of this spending targeted physicians through sales representatives (detailing), sampling (provision of drugs at no cost), physician meetings, and advertisements in medical journals. For example, industry-sponsored promotional events increased from 120,000 in 1998 to 371,000 events in 2004. There has also been a significant increase in the frequency and size of federal and state penalties for illegal promotion of drugs and pricing irregularities.

These trends have raised the concern that pharmaceutical companies might have undue influence on the prescribing behavior of physicians. In particular, there is concern that a significant percentage of physicians might be prescribing a narrow range of heavily promoted drugs, or might be exclusively prescribing branded drugs to the detriment of patient welfare. However, empirical evidence on the prescribing behavior of physicians and its consequences for patients is limited. Some studies suggest that physicians exhibit narrow prescribing behavior, particularly general practitioners, but much of this evidence is decades old. More recent work finds that the prescribing patterns of physicians are substantially more concentrated than the aggregate market in each class, and that physicians differ in their preferred drug within a class.

While theory suggests that habitual prescribing can be both clinically suboptimal and economically wasteful, the appropriateness of broad versus narrow prescribing is likely to depend on the composition of the drug class. Narrow prescribing patterns may be optimal when one drug is clearly superior to the others, or if all the drugs in the class act in a similar way. For example, prescribing only a generic or low-cost brand in a largely homogeneous class may be beneficial given that lower patient cost-sharing is associated with improved adherence. In addition, most generics are inherently safer than newer drugs because of their longer track record in clinical practice and known side effects. Alternatively, some drug classes are characterized by heterogeneous effects, where a specific drug provides therapeutic benefit to some patients and little to others, or has known side effects that are problematic for a subset of patients. If the heterogeneous benefits and side effects of these drugs are known ex-ante, a better informed physician will engage in broader prescribing behavior, taking into account the specific medical characteristics of each patient. Levine-Taub and colleagues found that psychiatrists have broader prescribing patterns than general practitioners within the a typical antipsychotic class, but they cannot determine how much of the difference is explained by variation in the case mix of patients seen by psychiatrists versus non specialists.

Beyond the challenge of predicting a drug's therapeutic value for a new patient, an unrelated factor further complicates the prescribing decision; plan formularies. Most modern drug classes include an array of similar products that compete for essentially the same population of patients, and health plans typically choose a small subset of these products to offer at low cost-sharing rates. In addition, direct-to-consumer advertising has emboldened patients to request specific treatments. How these factors have affected physicians' choice of drug therapies is uncertain.

Review Questions

Short Answer Questions

1. Enlist the data sources for collecting the physician details?

Long Answer Questions

1. Explain the role of psychology and peer influence on the drug prescribing patterns of physicians?

30 Pharma Inventory Management

30.1 | Selection of Pharm. Stockist and Distributor

Distributor basically distributes the goods in a bulk quantity to the respective parties, which comprises of retailers and suppliers. Their supply of services includes the product information, estimates, technical supports, after-sales services and credits to the customers, through a channel management system. These channels are interdependent organizations generally designed by firms with the help of proper path-orientation.

They are defined as 'an entity that buys non-competing products or product lines, warehouses them, and resells them to retailers or directly to the end users or customers'. They supply goods directly to the stores or other businesses, which are then sold to the consumers. They provide services with strong manpower and cash support to the supplier or manufacturer's promotional efforts. They are supposed to maintain an exclusive buying agreement, which limits their participants and enable them to cover a certain territory.

A stockist is 'a retailer that stocks goods for a particular type of sale'. Stockist is also a distributor, who depends upon some factors like time and place. They store goods in the form of stocks, and then distribute them to the respective users.

LEARNING OBJECTIVES

- *Meaning of Stockist and Distributor*
- *Criteria for selecting Stockist and Distributor*
- *Drug discovery*
- *Target Validation*
- *Lead Optimization*
- *Preclinical testing*
- *Investigational new drug application and safety*
- *Current status of drug research in India*
- *Market challenges*
- *Market opportunities*
- *Government initiatives*
- *Future outlook*
- *Drug marketing research*
- *Direct to consumer advertising*
- *Unethical recruitment of physicians*

They store bulk amount of goods and products. The link between the manufacturer and the stockist is maintained by the manufacturer's employees, who manage all the distribution, purchases, labor management, and supervises the delivery process. They handle all the relations with the distributor and sometimes push the stock onto the distributor to meet their sales targets and basically perform one type of business at the regular intervals of time. They make available of the products at the time of shortage of resources. It is observed that the general store managers stock the goods in their storage chambers in order to sell the products at a specified fixed time.

Who are they?

- A distributor is a person who distributes and supplies the products to the other respective authorities. A stockist is one who stocks the goods.

Dependency on factors

- Distributor is not dependent on any factors.
- Stockist is dependent on the factors such as season, time and place.

Functions

- He is a basic distributor who supplies the products to their respective user.
- Stockist is also suppliers, but he first stores the goods, and then distributes.

Roles

- Distributor can be manufacturers
- A stockist can be retailers and distributors.

Time factor

- He supplies the products at regular intervals, and in continuity.
- He make the products available at the time of shortage.

Criteria for Selecting Pharm. Stockist and Distributor

First and the most important step in appointing right distributor is that only person at supervisory level should search for distributor of a company (be it new distributor or replacement of old ineffective distributor). Under no circumstances front level field staff should be allowed to do survey in market.

There should be synergy of distribution in their company's products and products which are being sold by the distributor. Synergy of distribution means that outlets being serviced by a distributor should be same at least 90% with the outlets in which your products will be sold.

For example sales staff of a company which manufactures and markets Biscuits should avoid appointing distributor of Asian paints or Fevicol, or a distributor which deals in medical products, as in this case outlets which sell or deal in Fevicol or Asian paints or pharma products do not sell biscuits. Similarly an outlet selling biscuit will not sell Fevicol, or Asian paint or pharma products.

So when a FMCG sales staff sets out for finding distributor for his company then as a first step he must carefully select only those distributors who reach service and sell products in outlets where his products will be sold. So sales staff of a company which manufactures Confectionery should shortlist those distributors who distribute biscuits, or wafers or other confectionery items as these distributors will help in making his products available at right kind of outlets in less time.

So the next step in the direction of appointing right party as distributor is to find and select five or six of such parties who have synergy of distribution with products of a company. We will refer to such parties with synergy of distribution as **RELEVANT DISTRIBUTORS.**

After short listing five or such relevant distributors, **the next step for staff of FMCG Company is to take feedback of these parties from the retailers and wholesalers who sell his company's products.** Feedback of all these relevant distributors should be taken on following parameters:

(a) Financial position of the distributor: Very important as distributor with good finance can invest in company's stock and invest in credit in market.

(b) Relations of distributor in market: In today's competitive market with very little difference in quality and pricing of different companies manufacturing same products, relations of distributors in market play an important role in ultimate success of any company's products in market.

(c) Does he extend credit in market: Simple. If a distributor extends credit to his customers as is being provided by distributors of competitor's products then sales will grow faster.

(d) Distributor's own involvement in market: Here again if a distributor's involvement in market is good then his relations in market will also be good. The more he is involved in business of a company's products the better are chances for the sales growth of that company.

Company's sales staff then should visit the market and do survey in market of all the five or six relevant distributors selected by him.

To make his market survey (for new distributor or replacement of an old distributor) effective, he should take feedback of all selected relevant distributors from at least 30% of total outlets in a town or area of a large town or minimum 30 outlets. So for example if he is looking for a distributor in a town with up to 40 outlets then he should take feedback of relevant distributors from at least 30 outlets of that town.

But if he is searching for a distributor in a town with more than 200 outlets then he should take feedback about relevant distributors from at least 30% of outlets i.e., 60 outlets. The larger the sample size (more the no of retailers or wholesalers from whom he takes feedback) for his survey the better are his chances of finding right distributor for his company.

Again to make his market survey for distributor appointment, company sales staff should cover small outlets (C class outlets who purchase very less quantity of his products, give payment to distributor after more than 25 days), medium class outlets (B class outlets who sell maximum of his products, who give payment in two weeks) and A class outlets (Who purchase in good quantity, give payment in a week). Inclusion all types of outlets in his survey (to take feedback about selected relevant distributors) will give him fair idea about distributors who cover all types of outlets. There will always be distributors who cover only C class outlets or who cover only A class outlets. The success of any company depends on a distributor who covers and sells company's products at all types of outlets.

Again to fully fortify his survey the company staff must ensure that he covers some of outlets of each type in different markets or different areas of a town. This type of coverage of outlets in most of parts of town or most of markets of town will result in identification of distributors who cover all markets or all areas of a town.

In this market survey he should take feedback of all relevant distributors from retailers and wholesalers of a market on above parameters. He should ask retailers and wholesalers to rank all shortlisted five or six relevant distributors on a scale of 1 to 10 separately on each of above parameters.

After doing full market survey for all the selected relevant distributors the company staff should do total of total scores of all relevant distributors as per marks given by different wholesalers and retailers to different relevant distributors on a scale of 1 to 10.

On basis of total scores of these relevant distributors his **next step should be to shortlist at least three distributors** (Top three relevant distributors with maximum scores). He must shortlist minimum three distributors as a safeguard in case his top choice refuses to take distributorship of his company because of whatever reason. Then in such a case he can choose from the remaining two shortlisted distributors. We will call them **Shortlisted Distributors**.

Now the role of supervisory sales staff ends with short listing of at least three distributors.

The responsibility of appointing the right distributor out of three shortlisted distributors should lie with senior managerial level minimum RSM. An RSM with his experience and past mistakes can always select best of the three shortlisted parties.

Next step: Before approaching shortlisted distributors for purpose of appointing one of the shortlisted distributors as his company's distributors the RSM should have done thorough homework on the following factors:

(i) Estimated business or sales that the company expects from the distributor.

(ii) The investment that the company wants or expects from its distributor in town,

(iii) The infrastructure requirement i.e., godown space, supply units, salesmen etc from its distributor.

(iv) The support that the company will provide to distributor to generate sales in market or town i.e., no. of days sales staff working, scheme, support etc.

He should have concrete, specific and to the point answers and clarity on all the above parameters. His clarity on above factors will help him convince the shortlisted distributor on most of their queries.

The first question that RSM should ask each of shortlisted distributor is whether the shortlisted distributor is ready to expand his business or whether shortlisted distributor would be interested in taking distributionship of products of his company. Only if shortlisted distributor agrees to the same then RSM should proceed with next step of evaluation of the shortlisted distributor.

If the distributor is ready to expand his business then the next step for the RSM or concerned manager should be do the thorough **Need Analysis** of prospective Distributor. Need analysis is done to understand in detail the real reasons why the prospective party wants to expand his business or wants to start a new business. If the need of prospective distributor is long term in nature and is not short term or is not impulsive only then the prospective distributor should be considered for taking the discussion forward. To further throw light on this factor if a distributor wants to settle down his son in business then his interest in business will be more serious as compared to a person who wants to get into business just because he has taken VRS and now wants to do business. His interest will be more fickle. So more serious and longer term the need for business of prospective distributor better he will be as a business associate.

Then on next step, RSM should judge and evaluate all the shortlisted distributors on following criteria **financial position.** Asking and checking (if shortlisted distributor agrees) to bank statements of shortlisted distributors. Checking his purchase and payment record with other companies in which the shortlisted distributors deal.

Checking his infrastructure: He should check whether infrastructure like office or godown or supply vehicles of shortlisted distributor is owned or rented. If owned he can always ask for property papers (if shortlisted distributor agrees for the same). He can check RC of supply vehicles of distributors.

If a distributor owns supply vehicles then his chances of remaining in distribution line are more as compared to distributors who operate through rented supply vehicles or who hire vehicles from market to supply stocks.

He can always informally ask the staff of distributor like salesmen, godown keeper, accountant etc., about their association with distributor, since when they are working with distributor etc. These informal discussions with distributors staff yield great insights and information about the shortlisted distributor.

He should also take feedback of each of shortlisted distributor from sales staff of other companies whose distributionship is being held or managed by shortlisted distributor.

After satisfying himself on above parameters the RSM should take final decision of appointing distributor of company.

The last and most important step in appointment of right distributor is to brief the shortlisted distributor (who has agreed to take distributorship of products of his company) about the following facts:

(i) History of company.

(ii) Management of company.

(iii) Distributor margin in % age.

(iv) Margin of retailers in terms of % age.

(v) Minimum Number of days stock that he needs to maintain in his godown. Here most of sales staff lie. And this incorrect briefing to distributor in the beginning result into long term problems in the times to come.

(vi) Minimum investment from him in company's business. Here correct estimate of investment should be given to distributor so that he can plan his funds and infrastructure accordingly. With objective of getting yes from shortlisted distributor most of sales staff lie here.

(vii) Requirement of godown space for keeping stocks of company.

(viii) Minimum sales he will get from company in a month or in a year as the case may be. Here genuine sales figure should be given to earn distributor's faith in the long run. If sales staff give higher sales figure and actual sales is less than the committed or promised sales figure then distributor's faith in company sales staff will be reduced. And this is one area where most of sales staff gives wrong information deliberately just to trap unsuspecting distributors.

Sales support provided by company (in terms of company's sales staff working in his town or market).

Sales promotion support being provided by company (schemes, support which leads to sales growth in his market).

Damage policy of company i.e., how the company settles claims related to unsold, expired or unsalable products of company lying in market and at godown of distributor.

Minimum order in quantity or value that distributor needs to place to company or its SS or its CFA.

After briefing the shortlisted distributor on above factors, if the shortlisted distributor agrees to join hands with his company as a distributor, RSM should go ahead and appoint the shortlisted distributor as his company's distributor.

30.2 | Drug Discovery, Development and Marketing Research

For the first time in history, scientists are beginning to understand the inner workings of human disease at the molecular level. Recent advances in genomics, proteomics and computational power present new ways to understand illness. The task of discovering and developing safe and effective drugs is even more promising as our knowledge of disease increases. As scientists work to harness this knowledge, it is becoming an increasingly challenging undertaking.

It takes about **10-15 years to** develop one new medicine from the time it is discovered to when it is available for treating patients. The average cost to research and develop each successful drug is estimated to be **$800 million** to **$1 billion**. This number includes the cost of the thousands of failures: For every 5,000-**10,000** compounds that enter the research and development (R&D) pipeline, ultimately only one receives approval.

These numbers defy imagination, but a deeper understanding of the R&D process can explain why so many compounds don't make it and why it takes such a large, lengthy effort to get one medicine to patients. Success requires immense resources the best scientific minds, highly sophisticated technology and complex project management. It also takes persistence and, sometimes, luck. Ultimately, though, the process of drug discovery brings hope and relief to millions of patients.

Target Validation

Test the target and confirm its role in the disease. After choosing a potential target, scientists must show that it actually is involved in the disease and can be acted upon by a drug. Target validation is crucial to help scientists avoid research paths that look promising, but ultimately lead to dead ends. Researchers' demonstrate that a particular target is relevant to the disease being studied through complicated experiments in both living cells and in animal models of disease.

Drug Discovery

Find a promising molecule (a "lead compound") that could become a drug. Armed with their understanding of the disease, scientists are ready to begin looking for a drug. They search for a molecule, or "lead compound," that may act on their target to alter the disease course. If successful over long odds and years of testing, the lead compound can ultimately become a new medicine.

There are a few ways to find a lead compound:

Nature: Until recently, scientists usually turned to nature to find interesting compounds for fighting disease. Bacteria found in soil and moldy plants both led to important new treatments, for example. Nature still offers many useful substances, but now there are other ways to approach drug discovery.

De novo: Thanks to advances in chemistry, scientists can also make molecules from scratch. They can use sophisticated computer modeling to predict what type of molecule may work.

***High-throughput Screening*:** This process is the most common way that leads are usually found. Advances in robotics and computational power allow researchers to test hundreds of thousands of compounds against the target to identify any that might be promising. Based on the results, several lead compounds are usually selected for further study.

***Biotechnology*:** Scientists can also genetically engineer new drug entities.

***Early Safety Tests*:** Perform initial tests on promising compounds

Lead compounds go through a series of tests to provide an early assessment of the safety of the lead compound. Scientists test Absorption, distribution, Metabolism, **E**xcretion and **Tox**icological (ADME/Tox) properties, or "pharmacokinetics," of each lead. Successful drugs must be:

- absorbed into the blood stream,
- distributed to the proper site of action in the body,
- metabolized efficiently and effectively,
- Successfully excreted from the body and
- demonstrated to be not toxic

These studies help researchers prioritize lead compounds early in the discovery process. ADME/Tox studies are performed in living cells, in animals and via computational models.

Lead Optimization

Alter the structure of lead candidates to improve properties

Lead compounds that survive the initial screening are then "optimized," or altered to make them more effective and safer. By changing the structure of a compound, scientists can give it different properties. For example, they can make it less likely to interact with other chemical pathways in the body, thus reducing the potential for side effects.

Hundreds of different variations or "analogues" of the initial leads are made and tested. Teams of biologists and chemists work together closely: The biologists test the effects of analogues on biological systems while the chemists take this information to make additional alterations that are then retested by the biologists. The resulting compound is the candidate drug.

Even at this early stage, researchers begin to think about how the drug will be made, considering formulation (the recipe for making a drug, including inactive ingredients used to hold it together and allow it to dissolve at the right time), delivery mechanism (the way the drug is taken by mouth, injection, inhaler) and large.

Preclinical Testing

Lab and animal testing to determine if the drug is safe enough for human testing with one or more optimized compounds in hand, researchers turn their attention to testing them extensively to determine if they should move on to testing in humans. Scientists carry out *in vitro* and *in vivo* tests. *In vitro* tests are experiments conducted in the lab, usually carried out in test tubes and beakers ("vitro" is "glass" in Latin) and *in vivo* studies are those in living cell cultures and animal models ("vivo" is "life" in Latin). Scientists try to understand how the drug works and what its safety profile looks like. The U.S. Food and Drug Administration (FDA) require extremely thorough testing before the candidate drug can be studied in humans.

During this stage researchers also must work out how to make large enough quantities of the drug for clinical trials. Techniques for making a drug in the lab on a small scale do not translate easily to larger production. This is the first scale up. The drug will need to be scaled up even more if it is approved for use in the general patient population.

At the end of several years of intensive work, the discovery phase concludes. After starting with approximately 5,000 to 10,000 compounds, scientists now have winnowed the group down to between one and five molecules, "candidate drugs," which will be studied in clinical trials.

The Drug Development Process

Investigational New Drug (IND) Application and Safety File IND with the FDA before clinical testing can begin; ensure safety for clinical trial volunteers through an Institutional Review Board

Before any clinical trial can begin, the researchers must file an Investigational New Drug (IND) application with the FDA. The application includes the results of the preclinical work, the candidate drug's chemical structure and how it is thought to work in the body, a listing of any side effects and manufacturing information. The IND also provides a detailed clinical trial plan that outlines how, where and by whom the studies will be performed.

The FDA reviews the application to make sure people participating in the clinical trials will not be exposed to unreasonable risks.

In addition to the IND application, all clinical trials must be reviewed and approved by the Institutional Review Board (IRB) at the institutions where the trials will take place. This process includes the development of appropriate informed consent, which will be required of all clinical trial participants.

Statisticians and others are constantly monitoring the data as it becomes available. The FDA or the sponsor company can stop the trial at any time if problems arise. In some cases a study may be stopped because the candidate drug is performing so well that it would be unethical to withhold it from the patients receiving a placebo or another drug.

Finally, the company sponsoring the research must provide comprehensive regular reports to the FDA and the IRB on the progress of clinical trials.

In Phase 1 trials the candidate drug is tested in people for the first time. These studies are usually conducted with about 20 to 100 healthy volunteers. The main goal of a Phase 1 trial is to discover if the drug is safe in humans. Researchers look at the pharmacokinetics of a drug: How is it absorbed? How is it metabolized and eliminated from the body? They also study the drug's pharmacodynamics: Does it cause side effects? Does it produce desired effects? These closely monitored trials are designed to help researchers determine what the safe dosing range is and if it should move on to further development.

In Phase 2 trials researchers evaluate the candidate drug's effectiveness in about 100 to 500 patients with the disease or condition under study, and examine the possible short-term side effects (adverse events) and risks associated with the drug. They also strive to answer these questions: Is the drug working by the expected mechanism? Does it improve the condition in question? Researchers also analyze optimal dose strength and schedules for using the drug. If the drug continues to show promise, they prepare for the much larger Phase 3 trials.

In Phase 3 trials researchers study the drug candidate in a larger number (about 1,000-5,000) of patients to generate statistically significant data about safety, efficacy and the overall benefit-risk relationship of the drug. This phase of research is key in determining whether the drug is safe and effective. It also provides the basis for labeling instructions to help ensure proper use of the drug (e.g., information on potential interactions with other medicines).

Phase 3 trials are both the costliest and longest trials. Hundreds of sites around the United States and the world participate in the study to get a large and diverse group of patients. Coordinating all the sites and the data coming from them is a monumental task.

During the Phase 3 trial (and even in Phases 1 and 2), researchers are also conducting many other critical studies, including plans for full- scale production and preparation of the complex application required for FDA approval.

Once all three phases of the clinical trials are complete, the sponsoring company analyzes all of the data. If the findings demonstrate that the experimental medicine is both safe and effective, the company files a New Drug Application (NDA) which can run 100,000 pages or more with the FDA requesting approval to market the drug. The NDA includes all of the information from the previous years of work, as well as the proposals for manufacturing and labeling of the new medicine.

FDA experts review all the information included in the NDA to determine if it demonstrates that the medicine is safe and effective enough to be approved (see sidebar "How does the FDA decide to approve a new drug?"). Following rigorous review, the FDA can either 1) approve the medicine, 2) send the company an approvable letter requesting more information or studies before approval can be given, or 3) deny approval.

Review of an NDA may include an evaluation by an advisory committee, an independent panel of FDA-appointed experts who consider data presented by company representatives and FDA reviewers. Committees then vote on whether the FDA should approve an application, and under what conditions. The FDA is not required to follow the recommendations of the advisory committees.

Going from small-scale to large-scale manufacturing is a major undertaking. In many cases, companies must build a new manufacturing facility or reconstruct an old one because the manufacturing process is different from drug to drug. Each facility must meet strict FDA guidelines for Good Manufacturing Practices (GMP).

Making a high-quality drug compound on a large scale takes great care. Imagine trying to make a cake, for example, on a large scale making sure the ingredients are evenly distributed in the mix, ensuring that it heats evenly. The process to manufacture most drugs is even more complicated than this. There are few, if any, other businesses that require this level of skill in manufacturing.

Research on a new medicine continues even after approval. As a much larger number of patients begin to use the drug, companies must continue to monitor it carefully and submit periodic reports, including cases of adverse events, to the FDA.

In addition, the FDA sometimes requires a company to conduct additional studies on an approved drug in "Phase 4" studies. These trials can be set up to evaluate long-term safety or how the new medicine affects a specific subgroup of patient.

Current Status of Drug Research in India

Indian pharmaceutical companies' entry into the drug discovery and development field dates back to the early 1990s when India announced the signing of the World Trade Organization (WTO) agreement that introduced a product patent system from Jan. 1, 2005. Changes in the regulatory environment in the same year led to other developments with the emergence of the country as a favorite destination for "chemistry" outsourcing followed by "collaborative drug discovery as contract agencies where in-house strengths in chemistry of local companies was augmented with focus biology".

Over the past few years, Indian pharmaceutical companies have been attempting to re-orientate their efforts toward developing new innovative medicines. However, the transition by Indian generic-drug makers will remain slow given the high risk levels associated with drug discovery. Despite this, local companies made headway in this sector. In May 2012, Ranbaxy Laboratories launched Synriam (arterolane maleate plus piperaquine phosphate), a new drug for the treatment of uncomplicated Plasmodium falciparum malaria. Similarly, Cadila Healthcare launched Lipaglyn (saroglitazar) in June 2013, for the treatment of diabetes. Saroglitazar is claimed to be the first new chemical entity (NCE) discovered and developed by an Indian pharmaceutical company.

Local Companies in Drug Discovery

Recently, Indian companies such as Bugworks in Bengaluru and Vitas Pharma in Hyderabad have ventured into drug discovery. The move of Indian start-ups into the drug discovery space will present a new source of innovative medicines to the Indian pharmaceutical sector. However, their impact will come primarily through collaborations.

The Indian business environment will remain highly challenging for start-ups due to low levels of intellectual property protection, pricing uncertainties, and delays in receiving clinical trial approvals. In addition, venture capital and private equity have not been actively supporting such biopharmaceutical start-ups, leaving such companies to turn towards larger multinational pharmaceutical companies and domestic drug manufacturers for funding. According to a study into life-sciences venture capital published in 2013, only 32 out of a surveyed 170 biotechnology firms in India were backed by venture capital.

Market Challenges

Pharmaceutical companies operating in India face distinct challenges like insufficient innovation, limited access to high risk funding, short supply of skilled professionals, and specialized equipment.

Low levels of intellectual protection continue to be a problem. India registers a low score on BMI's Pharmaceutical Risk/Reward Index (RRI)'s measure of Patent Respect (an index providing a globally comparative and numerically based assessment of a market's attractiveness for innovative drug makers) compared to its Asian counterparts such as China and Indonesia. The low score is driven by the frequent threats to patents through compulsory licenses being revoked or rejected by the patent office.

The clinical-trial segment also faces challenges such as regulatory uncertainty regarding conduct of trials, unethical practices, and approval delays. It is estimated that it takes one year in India to gain regulatory approval of trials as compared with just 28 days in the United States. This is further compounded by regulatory uncertainty following the US Supreme Court's ruling in 2013 to suspend 157 previously approved clinical trials.

As a result, Indian pharmaceutical companies have begun to move their operations outside of the country, despite the potentially higher cost. Lupin Pharmaceuticals has set up two research and development plants in the United States while Cipla said in July 2014 that it will invest $150 million in the United Kingdom for research and clinical trials. Clinical trials in India declined from 264 in 2009 to 174 by 2013.

India's pricing regulation continues to undergo significant changes that create high levels of uncertainty in launching new drugs. In September 2014, the government rescinded guidelines issued the previous May that would have given the National Pharmaceutical Pricing Authority (NPPA) the power to set prices of non-essential medicines. In December 2014, however, the NPPA announced that it will bring an additional 52 new drugs under price control. Consequently, drug makers have cut back on the number of medicines launched; data from the Central Drugs Standard Control Organization highlights a decline from 270 in 2008 to 56 as of November 2014.

Market Opportunities

Despite these challenges, industry players can still explore opportunities in the local business environment. Driving these prospects includes the country epidemiological transition with the burden of non-communicable diseases growing while the burden of communicable disease continues to decline, according to BMI's Burden of Disease Database (BoDD). In addition, drug-discovery companies in India are supported by a large pool of human resources with 14% of graduates in 2012 coming from science-related backgrounds. Furthermore, tertiary education remains strong, which drives the country's score of 73.6 on BMI's Operational Risk's measure of Tertiary Education above the Asia Pacific's average.

Government Initiatives

The government has taken many initiatives in accordance with India's Department of Pharmaceuticals Pharma Vision 2020, which is designed to make India a hub for end-to-end drug manufacturing. To encourage greater participation from industry players, the government may want to consider dialog and collaboration between the government policy makers, senior leadership of Indian pharmaceutical industry and key opinion leaders from research institutes and academia on ways to better support novel drug discovery in India. The regulatory guidelines should be amended to encourage global pharmaceutical companies to not only continue outsourcing their research and development activities to Indian companies but also work on end-to-end solution starting from drug discovery to commercialization in India.

There is a need for speeding the regulatory processes at all stages of drug development starting from seeking licenses for initiating drug discovery, conducting clinical trials in India to obtaining regulatory approval for commercialization. Other areas to look into include speeding up the patent approval process and addressing issues such as the definition of patentability and compulsory licensing.

Future outlook

The development of new drug discovery in India has the potential to improve the overall healthcare system in the country. The introduction of new medicines will help alleviate the burden of diseases as it provides greater access to innovative medicines through the clinical trials conducted in India. The growth of the local pharmaceutical research and development sector can serve as a key driver of economic growth, and this will help increase income levels and improve the access to healthcare services.

Drug Marketing Research

Marketing research of drugs can be arranged into five categories:

1. Physicians-targeted promotions,
2. Direct to-consumer advertising,
3. unethical recruitment of physicians,
4. researchers' conflicts of interest and
5. data manipulation in clinical trials.

Drug companies' promotions subconsciously influence physicians' prescription patterns. Heavy advertising to consumers results in more prescriptions being written, whether or not the new drug is in the best interests of patients, and therefore strongly correlates with sales increases for the promoted new drug. The pharmaceutical industry's public relation firms unethically recruit physicians to endorse their companies' clinical studies. Researchers' financial conflicts of interest often influence results in the corresponding studies; in many cases, the employed researchers receive extra financial benefits, such as stock options and funding for future projects, from the drug company for which they are conducting clinical trials. Pharmaceutical companies manipulate research data to prevent negative data from leaking to the public. Much evidence suggests that the pharmaceutical industry's economic influence on the medical field is substantial. Despite the threats these activities pose to the reliability of medical care and the integrity of research, the reputation for quality in healthcare is not yet lost; the continuing quality of healthcare will depend primarily on the morality of next generation's scientists and doctors.

Physicians-Targeted Promotions

Drug companies' promotions subconsciously influence physicians' prescription patterns. In 2014, the pharmaceutical industry in India spent $ 5.63 billion on promotions, which include free office supplies, all-expenses-paid events, sales representatives, and awards to physicians. The number of prescriptions written for two promoted drugs before and after the physicians attended the seminar; it was found that the numbers of prescriptions for those two drugs, when compared against the national average, significantly increased after the seminar.

Promotion-induced subconscious influence is a widely studied phenomenon. An ideal physician provides his or her patients the best available care for the most economical price; however, despite physicians' reassurances, studies show that promotions influence how they prescribe. If doctors under subconscious influence prescribe the promoted drug and it is a more expensive alternative, thereby causing patients to incur higher treatment costs, in theory at least, the patients are still receiving quality care.

Direct-To-Consumer Advertising

Heavy direct-to-consumer (DTC) advertising strongly correlates with increased sales for the promoted drugs but, in terms of both money and health, may not be in the best interest of patients. The advertisements may have prompted those who previously had no need for the drug to imagine that their conditions were more serious and needed the help of the drug.

If DTC advertising only motivated certain patients to see their doctors more often, its harmful effects would be debatable. The larger and more important problem of DTC advertising concerns potential health risks posed by new drugs. New drugs are not time tested; their long-term effects are unknown; many patients who can be just as effectively treated with less expensive, older drugs are risking their health whenever drugs.

Rofecoxib, a COX-2 inhibitor, is a case in point. COX-2 inhibitors were intended to replace non-steroidal anti-inflammatory drugs (NSAIDs), such as ibuprofen, as a superior temporary pain reliever that does not have the side effect of gastrointestinal bleeding. Arthritic patients have long relied on NSAIDs to temporarily relieve pain, but when NSAIDs are taken on a long-term basis, they can seriously damage the gastrointestinal lining and, with no advance warning, can cause life-threatening internal bleeding. This side effect is an even greater danger to those who had previously suffered serious gastrointestinal conditions such as ulcers, because in these patients, life-threatening side effects can occur even if the drug is taken for only a short period of time. For arthritic patients who are suffering or have previously suffered serious gastrointestinal conditions such as ulcers, or who are allergic to NSAIDs, or who had been using NSAID on a long-term basis, the arrival of COX-2 inhibitors, which includes Celecoxib was welcome news, as this new drug was reported to be safer than NSAIDs for the gastrointestinal system. However, as with any new drug, there is the potential for side effects that had remained un-discovered during clinical trials (which focus on short-term efficacy and side effects); prescriptions for the new class of drugs should only have been written for those at risk from NSAIDs.

Unethical Recruitment of Physicians

Another problem lies in the pharmaceutical industry's public relations firms recruiting physicians to endorse the company's clinical studies. Given the substantial investment that pharmaceutical companies earmark for promotions, it would not be surprising for them to decide to make the offer more enticing. If that were to happen and more physicians were to take up the offer, then the reputation of medical professionals and the reliability of medical information would be placed at substantial risk.

Researchers' Conflicts of Interest

Researchers' financial conflicts of interests (COI) have the potential to influence results in the corresponding studies. COI includes "consultancy, employment, stock ownership, patent licensing, and honoraria and excludes financial relationships based on grants, awards, fellowships, free drugs or equipment, and authors serving as speakers or on an advisory board".

Privately funded studies rarely report negative findings. These data suggest that either authors with COI have a better eye for research with positive outcomes or are predisposed to find positive outcomes because of the vested interests they hold. If researchers are influenced financially to manipulate experimental data, doctors and patients run the risk of not finding out the real negatives of a drug until it has been used on patients, often on large scale.

Data Manipulation

Evidence suggests that pharmaceutical companies manipulate clinical data to prevent negative results reaching the public. In 2000, Searle announced that its newest arthritis drug, Celebrex (celecoxib), the first of the COX-2 inhibitors, was safer on the gastrointestinal system than the older NSAIDs such as ibuprofen. This claim was important both for the patients and the marketer because gastrointestinal complications from using the older arthritis drugs account for approximately 7000 hospitalizations annually. Celebrex was heavily marketed and soon cost patients $2 per pill. But in 2004, when Group Health Cooperative of Seattle reviewed the protocol of the study that Searle had conducted for FDA approval and that was kept in FDA's public information database, the agency found that Searle had reported only the six-month results, which showed that Celebrex produced fewer gastrointestinal problems than the older drugs, instead of the results for the entire 2-month study, which revealed no such difference.

The pharmaceutical industry's economic influence on the medical field is substantial. Of the five marketing tactics discussed in this study, physicians-targeted promotions and direct-to-consumer advertising present the least potential harm to patients because, although there is the possibility of being exposed to unnecessary health risks, the quality of patient care generally remains the same, only patient's end up spending more on expensive drugs and extra doctor visits. Pharmaceutical companies' unethical recruiting of doctors potentially poses a greater risk, the extent of which depends on the individual doctor's morality. The greatest harm that could come from this marketing practice is the reporting of unreliable data, either because of researchers' conflict of interests or the manipulation of data; ethical doctors cannot make sound judgments about the most effective treatments for their patients if the information that they receive is skewed. Should this trend continue, patients could end up suffering from unreliable or even dangerous treatments and drug therapies

There is, however, time to correct these problems. Despite the evidence of the unhealthy and unethical influence of the pharmaceutical industry in the medical field, which threatens the reliability of medical care and the integrity of research, the reputation for quality health care is still intact. To prevent the degrading or collapse of our highly regarded health system, the Government should require drug companies to publish the results of all Phase II and III drug trials in a national public registry thereby preventing the non-reporting of controversial data in unpublished trials. Moreover, for-profit drug companies should not be allowed to contract out clinical studies but should instead be required to give the funding to the FDA for it to contract out the studies. The debate over medical ethics is gaining momentum and is slowly being incorporated into the curricula in some medical schools and graduate programs in fields of study involving medical research. However, the quality of healthcare will ultimately depend on the morality of this and the coming generations of scientists and doctors.

30.3 | Economic and Competitive Aspects of Pharmaceutical Industry

The analysis of the economic and financial performances is a frequently debated matter in the economic media from the last decades, covering a very large spectrum, comprising various meanings and tendencies which will continuously capture the interest of the economists, the accountants and the IT specialists. A firm's performance measurement has been the subject matter of discussion for decision makers.

Overview on global pharmaceutical industry

The global pharmaceutical industry has proved a rapid growth over the years and emerged as one of the fastest growing industries in the world. However, world pharmaceutical production and consumption is still unevenly dispersed around the world with the developed countries as the leading producers and consumers of pharmaceuticals.

World pharmaceutical market was valued at US$ 875 billion with a growth rate of 4.1% over the previous year at the constant exchange rate. The volume of pharmaceutical industry has surged from USD 647 billion in 2005 to USD 875 billion in 2010, corresponding to an increase of 35.2%. During this period, the industry's growth rate has witnessed a declining trend from 7.2% in 2005 to 4.1% in 2010. This decline is mainly associated with the slowdown in economic activity, especially in the developed countries which consume a large quantity of global pharmaceutical products. In 2008, economic slowdown in developed countries culminated into one of the worst global financial and economic crisis since the Great Depression. The negative effects were felt across the globe and the pharmaceutical sector experienced the same situation. However, in 2009, the negative effects of the crisis subsided and global economy has started to recover.

Both in terms of production and consumption, global pharmaceutical market is highly concentrated in the developed regions like North America (38%), Europe (29%) and Japan (12%) which in 2010 accounted for nearly 80% of global market. Developing regions like Asia, Africa, Australia and Latin America with a share of nearly 85% of world population are accounted for only 21% of global pharmaceutical consumption in 2010. A breakdown of pharmaceutical market in developing world reveals that Asia, Australia and Africa represent nearly 15% whereas Latin America accounts for 6% of the global pharmaceutical market.

Pharmaceutical industry, like IT industry, relies heavily on research and development (R&D) activities. Hence proper R&D facilities should be built and researchers and technicians should be provided with necessary financial resources to develop an innovative pharmaceutical industry in the competitive economies.

Besides economies of scale in manufacturing, clinical trials and marketing, bigger companies can allow investments in more research and development (R&D) projects that diversify their future drugs portfolio and make them much more stable in the long term. As the result, top-companies in the industry were active participants of mergers and acquisitions (M&A), new joint ventures and spin-offs of non-core businesses.

Generics drugs are usually produced by a manufacturer who is not the inventor of the original product, and are marketed when intellectual property protection rights are exhausted. Original drugs, the branded ones, are those which revolutionize a certain market segment when they are launched, opening a new therapeutic area or providing a new treatment for a disease.

Global pharmaceutical companies are trying hard to stave off the R&D crisis through mergers and acquisitions, geographic expansion and diversification into new areas such as consumer health. As a consequence, pharmaceutical companies will face significant operating challenges as the expiration of significant drug patents is set to erase record levels of revenues and earnings, R&D is costly but if successful, it pays off. The market for pharmaceutical products is global and most (western) countries spend a large share of their income on health (around 6 to 10%). The national budgets that are spent on pharmaceuticals range from around 1% to 2% of GDP.

The pharmaceutical industry is the high technology sector with the highest value-added per person employed, well ahead of the average value for high-tech and manufacturing industries. The pharmaceutical industry is also the sector with the highest ratio of R&D investment to net sales. After a decade of strong US market dominance, which led to a significant shift of economic and pharmaceutical research activity towards the US during the period 1995-2005, Europe is now also facing increasing competition from emerging economies. For 2011-2012 China, India and Brazil are predicted to be the fastest growing regions among developing countries for the pharmaceutical industry.

India now ranks 3rd worldwide in volume and 13th in value and exporting to more than 200 countries around the globe including the highly regulated markets of US, Europe, Japan and Australia. In the same time, several studies show that China is predicted to be the second largest pharmaceutical market after the United States by 2015. Due to the evolution of the markets, within the next decade, Asia is expected to overtake Europe in pharmaceutical sales, driven by growth in key emerging markets. Owing to their rapid growth, most of the important pharmaceutical companies are focusing on the emerging markets of Brazil, Russia, India, China, Mexico, and Turkey (BRIC-MT) to increase global and regional drug sales.

SWOT analysis on Indian Pharmaceutical Market

Strengths	**Weaknesses**
1. Produces original drugs 2. Relatively cheap labor force makes a potential threat to suppliers in developing countries	1. Focused on the production of generic medicine. 2. Is one of the smallest exporters of pharmaceutical products in the EU. 3. Whilst the large population creates demand for pharmaceuticals, the low GDP per capita means that patients are unlikely to be able to afford the most expensive drugs and will settle for the cheaper alternatives.
Opportunities	**Threats**
3. Generic medicines dominate market, which points toward positive prospects for exporters in developing countries. 4. India will be the fourth largest pharmaceutical market in Central & Eastern Europe in 2016	4. The economic crisis is affecting the consumption of pharmaceutical products in the country, especially regarding non prescription products.

The performance of an organization remains a central challenge for management research. In many diagnosis analyses, built around the main object of activity, there are direct links to items of financial performance. However, comparative economic data are not always available and they are subjective during a performance assessment. Due to these considerations, a greater attention has been given in the last years to the financial performance which generated a big impact over the performance management system.

Financial statements contain a wealth of information which, if properly analyzed and interpreted, can provide valuable insights into a firm's performance and position on the market. Several studies that approach the performance issue at the microeconomic level prove the special importance of financial management aspects, on the improvement of which depend the outcomes and the companies' competiveness.

What interests us in a particular way, taking into account the specific of economic activity is the financial performance, through which we understand the capacity of a firm to generate new resources from day to day operations in a certain period of time. Information regarding performance represents evidence about financial performance that are collected and systematically used. Evidence may relate to efficacy or effectiveness of activities in this case talking about outcomes, factors that may affect the results and measures that can be taken to improve financial performance.

Performance can be measured through several indicators or financial ratios. So far the literature has analyzed the performance of companies from various countries and economy sectors through different accounting based measures with great impact including return on assets (ROA), return on equity (ROE) and gross profit margin (GPM), net operating profitability (NOP), return on total assets (ROTA) , return on invested capital (ROIC), return on assets (ROA). Performance at microeconomic level has been studied depending also on liquidity such as current ratio and liquid ratio, risks factors identified through leverage and cash flow per liabilities. Other researches highlight performance assessment expressed by earnings before interests and taxes (EBIT) or expressing it though economic value added (EVA), return on equity (ROE), operating profit margin (OPM).

In the financial analysis, the wide use of financial ratios is an answer to the high amount of data contained in a set of financial statements and to the issue of comparing companies of different sizes. Financial ratios may be used individually or in groups, in order to compare companies among themselves or against industry benchmarks. In most cases, the result of such analyses depends to a high extent on the financial analyst's skills and expertise.

A performance measure to determine the financial state of a company should not be sensitive to the choices of accounting methods and procedures, but it must assess the current management decisions, the risks of investment decisions and not punish managers for circumstances that are beyond their control.. Under these circumstances a better choice could be EVA or any other performance measure that would consider "adding" value through previous investments. Nevertheless, ROE is often used in econometric analyses with financial data.

Growth dynamics factors:

- **EBITDA or EBIT Margin:** EBITDA margin is calculated as EBIDTA (Earnings before Interest, Taxes, Depreciation and Amortization) divided by Total Sales and EBIT Margin as EBIT (Earnings Before Interest and Taxes) divided by total revenue.
- Net **Profit Margin:** The ratio reveals the overall profitability of the concern, that's why it is very useful to the owners and prospective investors. It also indicates management efficiency in manufacturing, managing and selling of the products.
- Earnings **per Share (EPS):** It is an important financial performance measure.
- Together with other ratios, EPS can provide insightful information on a firm's growth and financial condition.

Liquidity factors

- **Current Ratio:** Going further than the usually employed models which are supposing liniar relations in only one sense, between ROE and various factors of financial ratios type, we will propose testing the hypotesis regarding the existence of non-linear relations between the financial ratios and ROE specific to various industries. According to Mramor and Marmor-Kosta ROE should rise fairly quickly, with the positive evolution of liquidity from zero until at some level of liquidity reaches a maximum level of ROE. ROE beyond that level starts to decrease slightly as the current liquidity continues to grow. Companies with low liquidity problems are estimated to meet its short term obligations, problems which have a negative impact on the rate of return. Once reached the optimum level of liquidity ratio, additional liquidity costs outweigh the benefits and the rate of return fades. In this case the function is estimated to have a quadratic form of logarithmic type as described before. (Mramor et al., 1997).

- **Quick Ratio:** (immediate liquidity) - Evolution of ROE based on immediate liquidity and current liquidity is similar, with the observation of faster growth and achieving the maximum faster in case of the immediate liquidity.

Risk factor

- Leverage **under the expression of Debt to Total Assets (DTTA)** - Financial structure leverage or simply leverage, calculated as ratio between debt and total assets (the version used in our model) or the ratio between liabilities and total assets. Financial structure leverage measures how the company's total assets are financed by debt or equity.

Company Size Factors

- **Book value (BV):** A company's common stock equity as it appears on a balance sheet, equal to total assets minus liabilities, preferred stock, and intangible assets such as goodwill.

30.4 | Marketing of Generic Drugs

A generic drug (generic drugs, short: generics) is a drug defined as "a drug product that is comparable to a brand/reference listed drug product in dosage form, strength, quality and performance characteristics, and intended use". It has also been defined as a term referring to any drug marketed under its chemical name without advertising to the chemical makeup of a drug rather than to the advertised brand name under which the drug is sold.

Although they may not be associated with a particular company, generic drugs are subject to the regulations of the governments of countries where they are dispensed. Generic drugs are labeled with the name of the manufacturer and the adopted (nonproprietary name) of the drug.

A generic drug must contain the same active ingredients as the original formulation. According to the U.S. Food and Drug Administration (FDA), generic drugs are identical or within an acceptable bioequivalent range to the brand-name counterpart with respect to pharmacokinetic and pharmacodynamic properties. By extension, therefore, generics are considered (by the FDA) identical in dose, strength, route of administration, safety, efficacy, and intended use. The FDA's use of the word "identical" is very much a legal interpretation, and is not literal. In most cases, generic products are available once the patent protections afforded to the original developer have expired. Generic drugs are in general less effective than the original formulation due to a weaker placebo effect and a stronger placebo effect. When generic products become available, the market competition often leads to substantially lower prices for both the original brand name product and the generic forms. The time it takes a generic drug to appear on the market varies. In most countries of the world, patents give 20 years of protection. However, many countries/regions, e.g., the European Union and the USA may grant up to 5 years of additional protection for drugs ("patent term restoration") if manufactures meet specific goals such as conducting clinical studies for pediatric patients. Manufacturers, wholesalers, insurers, and drugstores can each increase prices at various stages of production and distribution.

Prescriptions may be issued for drugs specifying only the chemical name, rather than a manufacturer's name; such a prescription can be filled with a drug of any brand meeting the specification. For example, a prescription for lansoprazole can be filled with generic lansoprazole, Paracetamol, Helicid or Aspirin.

Biopharmaceuticals such as monoclonal antibodies are different from small molecule drugs because of their biological nature. Generic versions of these drugs, known as biosimilars, are typically regulated under an extended set of rules.

Generic drugs are usually sold for significantly lower prices than their branded equivalents. One reason for the relatively low price of generic medicines is that competition increases among producers when drugs no longer are protected by patents. Companies incur fewer costs in creating generic drugs (only the cost to manufacture, rather than the entire cost of development and testing) and are therefore able to maintain profitability at a lower price. The prices are low enough for users in many less-prosperous countries to afford them. For example, Thailand has imported millions of doses of a generic version of the blood-thinning drug Plavix (used to help prevent heart attacks), at a cost of 3 US cents per dose, from India, the leading manufacturer of generic drugs.

In the UK, generic drug pricing is controlled only by the reimbursement price. Beneath this, the price paid by pharmacists and doctors is determined mainly by the number of license holders, the sales value of the originator brand and the ease of manufacture. A typical price decay graph will show a 'scalloped' curve, which usually starts out on the day of generic launch at the brand price, and then falls as competition intensifies. After some years, the graph typically flattens out at approximately 20% of the originator brand price. In about 20% of cases, the price 'bounces', which means some license holders, withdraw from the market when the selling price dips below their cost of goods. The price then rises for a while until they re-enter the market with new stock.

Generic manufacturers do not incur the cost of drug discovery. Sometimes, reverse-engineering is used to develop bioequivalent versions to existing drugs. Generic manufacturers also do not bear the burden of proving the safety and efficacy of the drugs through clinical trials, since these trials have already been conducted by the brand name company (See the Approval and regulation section, below, for more information about the approval process.). The average cost to brand-name drug companies of discovering and testing a new innovative drug (with a new chemical entity) has been estimated to be as much as $800 million.

Generic drug companies may also receive the benefit of the previous marketing efforts of the brand-name drug company, including media advertising, presentations by drug representatives, and distribution of free samples. Many drugs introduced by generic manufacturers have already been on the market for a decade or more, and may already be well known to patients and providers (although often under their branded name).

For as long as a drug patent lasts, a brand name company enjoys a period of "marketing exclusivity" or monopoly, in which the company is able to set the price of the drug at a level which maximizes profitability. The profit often greatly exceeds the development and production costs of the drug (This is partially offset by research and development of other drugs which do not make a profit.). The advantage of generic drugs to consumers comes in the introduction of competition, which prevents any single company from dictating the overall market price of the drug. Competition is also seen between generic and name-brand drugs with similar therapeutic uses when physicians or health plans adopt policies of preferentially prescribing generic drugs as in step therapy. With multiple firms producing the generic version of a drug, the profit-maximizing price generally falls to the ongoing cost of producing the drug, which is usually much lower than the monopoly price.

Pharmaceutical companies that market generic products generally are not regarded as innovators, but rather as companies that produce copies of originator products to be launched at patent expiration. However, many generics companies have developed excellent scientific innovative skills in an effort to circumvent the defense patents of originator companies. More patents per product, in terms of both drug substances (process patents and polymorph patents) and formulations, are issued to generics companies than to companies that are traditionally considered to be 'innovators'. This quantity of issued patents highlights the technical knowledge and skill sets that are available in generics companies. In order to adopt a completely innovative model (i.e., the development of NCEs), a generics company would require a completely new set of skills in several fields, including a sufficient knowledge base, project and risk management experience, and capability for clinical data evaluation. However, with relatively little investment, generics companies should be able to progress into the so-called 'supergeneric' drug space - an area of innovation that reflects the existing competencies of both innovative and generics companies.

Indian drug companies have evolved to become one of the top players in the global generic market. The evolution is attributed to patent and regulatory changes in the Indian pharmaceutical sector over the last few decades. One of the most important development is the introduction of the Indian Patents Act, recognizing process patents in 1970. During the process patent regime which prevailed in India for around 35 years, country saw an exponential increase in the number of pharm. companies. It is understood that, under the protected regime, India strengthened its capabilities to reverse engineer and develop generic versions of new drugs. Post 2005, with the introduction of the product patent régime, the foreign innovator drug industry discovered a market in India. With the advent of the product patent regime, the Indian pharmaceutical companies positioned themselves in a way that they could portray dominance in the global generic market. India has now emerged as one of the world's top exporters in generic medicines.

Marketing Strategies Need to be Adopted by Generic Drug Manufactures

When the generic drug companies launch a generic version of the patented drug in the market, they face an indirect but strong opposition from the lobby of innovator drug companies, so far as to delay and disincentivise, as much as possible, the launch of generic drugs in market. A tool box of strategies is created and employed by almost each of the innovator drug companies so as to achieve their goal of extending their revenue streams and in turn making it difficult for the generic drug companies to do their business.

Delay in generic launch also causes serious problem to the public at large, as needy patients are forced to purchase expensive brands for a longer duration, when they can have easy access to generic and cheaper versions of such drugs

A patent owner has a right to exclude others from using its patented technology for a particular period only, subsequent to the expiry of which period, the patented technology falls in the public domain. After the expiry of the patent and the related exclusivities, innovator drug companies cannot restrain others from manufacturing generic versions of their drugs. As soon as a generic version of an innovator drug enters the market, a decline in the sales of the innovator drug is generally witnessed. Due to better pricing for generics, the market share of the innovator drug generally reduces drastically in the following years after patent expiry.

Therefore generic drug manufacturers face tremendous opposition from innovator drug manufacturer when they start manufacturing generic versions of the innovators breakthrough drugs. The innovators desire to control the phenomenon and aim to prevent generic manufacturers from developing and bringing into market the generic versions of their drugs has led to a mix of strategies which help to delay the launch of generic drugs thereby prolonging revenue streams of innovator drug companies.

***Following strategies may serve well for increasing generic drug utilization*:**

1. Generic substitution
2. Plan benefit design
3. E-prescribing
4. Education
5. Pharmacist/Prescriber incentives
6. Drug pricing/reimbursement

7. Prescription Pads
8. Regular patent monitoring
9. Legislation.

1. **Generic substitution:** The generic drug companies should motivate physicians to take affirmative steps before prescribing brand name drugs. This can be mandatory generic substitution and secondly step therapy. Mandatory generic substitution means generic version of a drug must be dispensed when available. Step therapy means initiating therapy with the most cost effective generic drug and progressing to more costly brand name drugs.
2. **Plan Benefit Design:** Health plans giving more discounts for generic drug usage.
3. **E-prescribing:** Electronic prescribing is a system that allows physicians to generate prescriptions with the use of a personal computer or handheld device. E-prescribing can provide physicians who may not be aware of generic availability with immediate access to formulary information allowing them to discuss generic drug options at the time of prescribing.
4. **Education:** Companies should go for broad based media campaigns, signs or information provide through pharmacies regarding the benefits of generic drugs.
5. **Pharmacist/Prescriber Incentives:** Giving bonuses and pay for performance to doctors, pharmacists.
6. **Drug pricing reimbursement:** The insurance companies can limit the amount reimbursed to medical stores and pharmacy managers' for certain drugs in order to promote generic utilization.
7. **Prescription Pads:** Prescription pads for physicians with a format suggesting dispense as written mandate.
8. **Regular patent monitoring:** It is necessary that a regular check on new patents being done is keenly watched.
9. **Legislation:** The governments should enact laws to encourage generic drug prescription.

Challenges with Generic Drug Brand Prescribing

1. Lack of generics for biological drugs. The regulatory authority currently lacks a statutory pathway that would allow it to approve generic or bioequivalent version of biological drug.

   The savings associated with utilization of low cost generic prescription drugs make them an obvious choice in the struggle to contain health care costs. However the policy makers and scientists should address the questions surrounding the therapeutic equivalence of generic drugs and create a pathway for the approval of generic biologic drugs.

2. Some professional organizations and patent advocates argue that switching from a brand name drug to a generic drug could be problematic for some patients. No doubt this argument lacks scientific backing.
3. Efforts to increase generic utilization may also stymied by consumers who prefer brand name drugs to generic drugs and are willing to pay for them. The phenomenon may be due to deep seated tendencies. Some patients associate a higher price with increased value.

30.5 | Patient Motivation

While the doctor's diagnostic and therapeutic skills help to restore hope and relieve some of the patient's emotional stress, technologic approach is not always enough. A patient's emotions and frame of mind must also be considered as a component of a patient's holistic state of health. The state of rapport between patient and doctor can be just as important as the technical care provided, and this rapport is established on a foundation of sincerity, understanding, kindness, and personalized care.

A doctor has moral obligations and professional responsibilities for each patient's health. Thus, the physician should anticipate possible patient stress by questioning the scope of everyday activities. This questioning and the resulting consideration, however, do not mean to conclude with blunt condemnations. The alert doctor will be aware that typical patients are not interested in the technical aspects of their conditions. They are interested in the removal of pain, discomfort, immobility, and how the condition affects their life-style. Therefore, it is important that the patient's everyday activities, hobbies, work and personal habits be considered along with the clinical aspects of the patient's condition. Patient interrogation should continue throughout the examination to qualify and substantiate information gathered within the case history. Many doctors conduct a case history systems review while the examinations are in process.

Patients have the right to know what you are going to do to them and why you are going to do it. Inform as you perform. To assure clear motivational communications, tell the patient what you are going to do and what you hope it will reveal. Explain what you are doing again as you do it, and relate it to benefits. As you examine and test, briefly explain:

1. What you have found that is normal
2. What you have found that is abnormal, and
3. What you hope the procedure will reveal when correlated with other findings.

People have a thirst for knowledge when it comes to their own bodies. Almost the same goals can be obtained indirectly, if you wish, by dictating into a recorder in the presence of the patient.

Conditioning patient before hand relieves fear of the unknown. Explanation during the procedures assures the patient that you know what you are doing. Post procedural reinforcement of what you have done thoroughly justifies the procedure. These procedures of dynamic communications hold the patient's attention, make the patient feel as if he is part of the process rather than an object, and deepen the doctor patient rapport.

"Off-the-cuff" diagnostic judgments should never be offered during your examination, nor should the patient's condition be minimized or inflated. In other words, don't give out clinical information piecemeal that is best delivered within your "Report of Findings." Keep your clinical opinions to yourself until all the facts have been evaluated. It will prevent possible embarrassment if initial impressions cannot be substantiated. However, it is good procedure to make notes of a patient's apprehensions and cover them in detail in your report.

When all tests have been completed, inform the patient that you feel you have all the facts necessary to properly evaluate the disorder(s). State that after you study the findings of the physical, orthopedic, neurologic, and laboratory tests and analyze the films taken, you will have a definite answer for the patient. Advice the patient when you wish him to return for your report, and ask him to present the visit slip at the exit counter and arrange for an appointment.

It is good policy that each patient entering the practice be presented with a packet of pertinent materials at this time. This packet typically consists of several pieces of literature such as an overview of chiropractic health care, basic office policies, general health tips, an illustration depicting the effects of spinal misalignments, etc.

The typical patient initially has eight major questions that silently beg to be answered. For review, these are:

1. What is wrong with me?
2. What caused it?
3. What can you do to help?
4. Will it hurt?
5. How long will it take to get better?
6. How much will it cost?
7. What should I avoid and for how long?
8. Will there be any lasting effects?

These priority questions should be answered even if the subjects are not brought up by the patient. However, more detailed answers should be given to those that are vocalized by a prospective patient. When these and related questions are answered to the patient's satisfaction, the patient will have faith that you know what you are doing and place his health care in your hands with confidence. If these questions are not answered satisfactorily, the patient's fears will motivate him to seek answers elsewhere.

Briefly explain pertinent spinal anatomy. To answer the above questions, the report is usually constructed along these lines:

1. Discuss each examination's findings, positive and negative, significant and insignificant, via a systems review that is keyed to the patient's presenting complaints, point by point.
2. Explain your diagnostic impressions, the disorder's etiology and typical progression, and probable precipitating causes of symptoms, neural physiology, and chiropractic philosophy.
3. Outline your recommended treatment plan and check points.
4. Describe the degree of anticipated discomfort.
5. Render a qualified prognosis (eg, in percentages).
6. Explain the office's fee policy, and agree on arrangements.
7. Thoroughly explain the patient's responsibilities and cooperation necessary (e.g,, home therapy, exercises, activity restrictions, rest, diet, supplements, etc).
8. Discuss all anticipated benefits according to typical case histories, national statistics, etc, if your recommendations are followed with sincere cooperation.
9. Obtain informed consent to proceed with therapy.

It is usually good to avoid pointing out probable consequences of nontreatment unless the patient is reluctant to follow your recommendations. However, these opinions may be discreetly discussed after the patient is well on the way to recovery.

The presentation should be constructed so that it is well correlated, flows smoothly from point to point, and is stated in terms acceptable to the patient's level of understanding. Patients respect honesty; thus, voice your honest reservations if you have any, but do not belabor the subject of inconclusive findings. The use of charts, diagrams, pictures, textbooks, scaled plastic models, visualizers, and marked x-ray films are quite helpful in showing normals and explaining the progression of the disorder involved.

Keep in mind that people will remember things they are shown much more readily than things they are told. Talk in terms that will enable the patient to "visualize" what you mean. Use analogies to make a point: "It's just like...." By all means, keep your presentation simple, to the point, and encourage questions. A typical comprehensive presentation need not take longer than 15-20 minutes.

Several authorities agree that the five most common mistakes made during a report are as follows:

1. The doctor talks too long and explains details too much. If a patient's level of confidence is not high after your initial consultation and examination, the report itself will not save the relationship. Take the time to answer the patient's questions, and get started with therapy as soon as the patient is ready.
2. The doctor attempts to talk extemporaneously, without the aid of a case resume. This results in rambling, poor coordination, and confusion that most people will notice.
3. The doctor tends to exaggerate the facts and paint a brighter picture than can

logically be expected under the circumstances in an attempt to relieve a patient's fears and gain a reputation of getting people well quickly. However, many disorders require considerable time to heal. When patients are not told that improvement will take time, they may become discouraged.

4. The doctor fails to differentiate the differences and benefits of palliative therapy, corrective therapy, rehabilitative therapy, and maintenance care. Each has distinct goals. When this is not done, most patients will discontinue therapy on the first signs of improvement.
5. The doctor makes critical remarks regarding previous case management, failing to realize that this is an obvious indirect criticism of the patient's selection.

Most of us have found that even personal motivation is difficult at times. Thus, it comes as no surprise that the task of motivating patients on a long- term basis to alter entrenched habits that are destructive to health is sometimes exasperating.

The problem is how to transfer patient agreement in the office to patient agreement in other environments such as daily activities at home, at work, at recreation, and at the dinner table.

Behavioral scientists have expended considerable effort to provide us with greater understanding of the dynamics of motivation that are practical in the doctor-patient relationship. Granted, behaviorists are sometimes accused of developing good theories that don't work in practical situations. However, logic mandates that there is no such thing as a "good" theory that doesn't work. Either the theory is poor or the application is poor. To focus attention on this, we will explore a few basic motivational theories and describe some common observations of application.

Basic Behavioral Frameworks

The core of motivational theory is based on the premise that human energy is the result of internal tensions or needs begging for fulfillment. The goal of most behavior is the reduction of these tensions for the promise of pleasure or the avoidance of pain. Consistent human action (behavior) is thus witnessed as a means of reducing stress by attempting to attain goals that promise to satisfy activated needs. This path-goal framework suggests that patients, as people in general, will behave in a manner that will lead to the attainment of a goal that they value and which they expect they can achieve. Such a framework identifies for the doctor and his assistants three basic criteria that are vital in the motivational process:

1. *Goal availability*: With some disorders, some goals may not be perceived as available to the patient; i.e, the prognosis may not indicate complete recovery. This will often require a high degree of psychic adaptability and adjustment on the part of the patient involved.
2. *Perceived effort-reward probability*: How likely is it that a given amount of effort (e.g., case management, patient time, finances, personal contribution) will result in

the attainment of the patient's priority goals? Does the case management consistently reward the behavior the doctor involved deserves from the patient?

3. *Goal value*: How likely is it that the reward offered within the prognosis provides the means to satisfy the goal valued most by the patient? This factor, goal value, is often the most overlooked factor in patient communications.

It is obvious that the goals (*e.g*, health, strength, locomotion, etc) a patient selects depend on what needs are activated.

Thus, we could conceivably identify an array of anxieties, but such a list would have little practical value in the average office setting. What the typical practitioner and office staff need is a basic framework that offers specific direction to identify, examine, and understand the particular needs of a particular patient that will produce healthy goal-directed behavior. Both the work of Maslow and Herzberg offer such a framework to the doctor even though their work has been primarily employee oriented.

A professional understanding of human nature and why people think and act as they do requires some appreciation of psychologic theory. The reason for this will become more apparent as this chapter progresses.

The Need Hierarchy of Maslow

Put in the simplest terms, Maslow's framework groups all needs into five basic categories:

2. safety
3. social
4. self-esteem
5. self-actualization

Maslow stated that these categories are related to each other in the form of an orderly hierarchy in which one category of needs becomes activated only after its sublevel is relatively satisfied.

The lowest level in the hierarchy, the foundation stone, is physiologic and concerns a person's needs for food, water, and shelter necessary for self- preservation. When these needs become urgent, people don't think about nonskid carpets (safety) or having a new suit recognized (self-esteem). The highest level concerns creativity and self-actualization: the development of latent human potential.

The Dual-Factor Theory of Herzberg

Although not as popular as Maslow's hierarchy of human needs, Herzberg offers a framework that makes two important contributions to a doctor's or assistant's skill in motivating patient attitudes. First, it more explicitly provides the link between a person's needs and performance. Second, the framework provides a model that helps the doctor and assistant apply basic concepts. And third, it identifies two basic fact affecting patient motivation:

1. The conditions extrinsic to the task at hand These would include, for example, office procedures, payment policies, interpersonal relations, insurance benefits, and other "environmental" or "atmospheric" conditions. These factors are important to a satisfactory doctor patient relationship and have a distinct impact on the optimal results that can be achieved.
2. The task itself. This factor presents such questions as: Do the doctor's services and counsel provide a sense of achievement and recognition for that achievement? Are the tasks recommended of primary interest to the patient? Do the tasks provide a challenge that can lead to a sense of accomplishment? Such task conditions are called "motivator factors" by Herzberg because it is their presence or absence that largely determines whether or not individuals will be motivated toward high performance or cooperation.

Conditions extrinsic to the task at hand generally consist of the lower levels of the Maslow need hierarchy such as the physiologic, safety, and social needs. Esteem and self-actualization levels comprise the needs concerning motivator factors.

It is important for doctors and assistants to understand that satisfaction of higher-level needs is a greater spur to typical patient cooperation than satisfaction of lower-level needs in our society. Lower level needs tend to be taken for granted unless threatened. These factors focus attention on two fundamental implications in case management:

1. The doctor must create an atmosphere in which the patient is able to satisfy lower-level needs so that higher-level needs will seek satisfaction. For instance, the patient is likely to become fixated emotionally at the lower levels during the relationship unless progress is guided emotionally as well as physically.
2. The doctor must be sure that his instructions are sufficiently challenging and interesting so that they will serve as a means to the satisfaction of higher-level needs. Otherwise, the patient whose higher-level needs are active will have to look elsewhere to the benefits of "total" health, life enrichment, and the quality of life. The objective of such a program is to design the tasks of case management so that patient performance (cooperation) readily leads to satisfaction of the higher-level needs.

An understanding of patient motivation necessitates a basic understanding of the interaction between patient needs and goals.

This is the path-goal framework, and its importance is being magnified by ever increasing medicolegal responsibilities (i.e., red tape).

Thus far in this section, we have examined the basic formation of the pathgoal framework and have viewed two basic frameworks (Maslow's and Herzberg's) that provide an effective way of looking at patient needs and their relationship to patient cooperation. However, successful application of these theories requires consideration of several areas that are often neglected in practical application.

Basic Application Considerations

The path-goal theory emphasizes the importance of the linkage between motivation, performance, and goal attainment. According to this popular concept, the important variables in the motivation process are:

1. The availability of the rewards perceived as important by the patient (attainment of pleasure or avoidance of pain). Do the rewards exist in fact? Does prognosis show good promise for attainment? Is the patient convinced?

2. The probability of achieving these rewards by following the doctor's instructions. Can a high degree of patient cooperation be linked to the rewards – the attainment of pleasure or the avoidance of pain?

Most practitioners do a fairly good job in communicating these two areas. Those who are lax in the area of communicating the availability of rewards are characterized by their preoccupation with lower-level needs rather than providing patients with opportunities to satisfy higher-level needs (e.g., Herzberg's motivators). Thus, many rewards necessary to insure the fulfillment of the patient's goals do not exist. Hidden Motives. The most common fault lies in the doctor's acceptance of the patient's presenting complaint as the "real" complaint that spurred professional attention. As research has adequately established the relationship between goal fulfillment and human performance, practitioners must spend adequate time identifying just exactly what the patient is seeking in terms of health care. This requires some degree of diplomatic interrogation during the initial and especially subsequent office visits when tension has been reduced. Patient needs and related health goals must be isolated if strategic problem solving is to be achieved.

***Word Usage*:** Diplomatic interrogation also relates to the subject of semantics that was introduced in the last chapter. Ten doctors taken at random will define the simple word health in ten different ways. We can expect no less from lay people. The word health is an abstraction, and a generalization can never be an attainable goal. Both the doctor and the patient must be in agreement as to what the starting point is and what the goal is. This is true for any task that requires cooperation.

The Need for Explicitness. "Better locomotion in Mrs. Smith's arthritic body" is not a goal. What does "better locomotion" mean? "A 10% increase in the flexion of Mrs. Smith's left knee in 4 weeks" is a goal. There is no question what this means.

Naturally, any goal agreed upon must be within the realm of the doctor's clinical judgment and the patient's needs.

Nevertheless, without specific task goals, neither the patient nor the doctor would know when a task is completed. When a specific task is set and achieved, both doctor and patient are motivated to achieve higher specific goals. When specific task goals are not established, patients self-dismiss and doctors register for another "practice building" seminar.

Communicating Reward Availability

Aside from the identification of the patient's needs and goals, the alert doctor must spend some time in identifying the rewards available and in determining how best to use them. Eventually, through linking patient goals and probable rewards, the doctor can motivate high levels of confidence and cooperation. Thus, reward identification and usage, as well as goal identification, become prerequisites in the process of motivation. Once rewards are identified, the doctor must be sure that he has conveyed to the patient what rewards are probable in a certain period of time according to the patient's history, the examination findings, the doctor's experience, and the doctor's clinical judgment. The promise of rewards is a necessary condition of motivation.

However, the most important aspect of reward availability in patient relations is not what the doctor says is probable but what the patient perceives and believes will be available.

***Defining the Path*:** It is also important that the doctor clearly identify the means (path) necessary to achieve the rewards available (i.e., the treatment plan). In addition to the clinical procedures conducted at the office, this path may include dietary regimens, therapeutic exercises, and habit alterations that are solely under the control of the patient.

Achievement and Behavior: Consideration must also be given to the second basic aspect: the probability of achieving rewards through prescribed behavior. What is the linkage between patient cooperation and the attainment of desired results? When a cooperative patient perceives that chances of achieving a particular reward are no better than that of an insincere patient, the doctor may have created a motivational problem. This will most likely result in reduced performance- related behavior because it is not rewarded subjectively or from the doctor or assistants by recognition (self-esteem motivator). Any doctor who feels that he can bring about health by attending to a patient a few minutes once or twice a week when the patient is not cooperating is living in a fantasy world, regardless of his expertise. The attainment of health is not found in a technique, it is found in cooperative goal attainment founded on intelligent actions.

The importance of the relationship between patient goals, the availability of rewards, and the probability of achievement of specific objectives cannot be overemphasized in motivational relationships.

Encouraging Patient Motivation

Maslow has suggested that people tend to aspire to higher and higher levels of need as the lower level needs become fulfilled. Herzberg states that personal achievement is one of the motivators that must be fulfilled if one person desires to motivate another person to higher levels of performance. In addition, research has brought forth two important considerations involved in any form of achievement motivation:

1. It is important to establish feedback as to how one is doing; and
2. It is important to establish well-defined, achievable task objectives. In the doctor-patient relationship, especially, these must be mutually agreed upon.

The concepts of the behaviorist concerning the higher-level needs such as personal achievement provide guidelines to action for health-care personnel in the area of patient-cooperation evaluation and feedback. The provision of identifiable task objectives and feedback as to patient performance toward these objectives is lacking in many offices that operate far below their potential. Unfortunately, the doctors involved frequently seek external solutions to these internal problems.

It has been said that the only reason a doctor fails to reach his potential is that the unsuccessful practitioner refuses to do what the successful practitioner is doing. These unfortunates are a benefit to you, however, for they show you what to avoid. Following are some examples of poor application of good theory:

1. Failure to communicate explicitly. For example, a patient may communicate to a friend: "Dr. Brown is a fine person, but you never know where you stand. I'm not sure what is expected of me, what I can do to speed recovery, and I only get vague comments as to how I am doing under treatment." Statements by patients similar to this imply a failure of the part of the attending physician. We can readily see that two important elements in the motivational process are missing:
   (a) well-defined achievable task objectives, and
   (b) specific feedback as to the progressive accomplishments toward the objectives.
2. Failure to link task objectives with patient responsibilities. Too often health practitioners place a low priority on this aspect of communications, which results in the objective never being accomplished because one of the prerequisites to achievement motivation did not exist in the relationship. If a pretentious doctor wants to take all the credit for a patient's recovery, he will also have to take all the blame if the results obtained are not optimal.
3. Failure to mutually set achievable task objectives with the patient. This responsibility is avoided by some doctors because they believe this is an infringement upon "the doctor's" prerogatives. Any patient who has a doctor with this set of outdated beliefs is likely to be denied the opportunity to fulfill higher-level needs and adapt to "first aid" benefits only: "When I'm really sick, I go to a real doctor."

When a patient presents an uncooperative attitude, the odds have it that the doctor has failed to recognize the importance of establishing objectives and achieving performance feedback as motivational instruments within case management.

Enriching the Doctor-Patient Relationship

Job enrichment and similar programs, if they are implemented by people who fully understand the purpose and if they are conducted in a well- planned manner, have tremendous potential for solving many of the motivational problems that exist in industry today. These same principles, but on a much less complex level, can be utilized within the doctor-patient relationship with exciting results. Patient motivation through enrichment essentially involves adding meaningful tasks and removing tasks that may cause patient boredom. There is no law that states that you must do the same thing to the same patient in the same way on every visit.

The implementation of a program of this positive nature requires a challenging emphasis in the doctor's role. Some physicians will resist this because they see an usurpation of professional prerogatives – rights that exist only in some physicians' minds. They cannot identify with a situation where doctor and patient have entered a partnership toward achieving health goals. The doctor who is inflexible, who cannot see the advantages of such a relationship of shared responsibilities, and who cannot see that such a relationship frees him to tasks that require his specialized attention should alter his thinking. If not, such a doctor knowingly or unknowingly may become a deterrent to the health program, and his contribution will diminish.

Administering to Basic Needs

It should be readily appreciated at this point that positive relations based on a sound understanding of human relations has both clinical and economic benefits. Numerous studies have shown that a patient with a positive mental attitude will heal quicker than one with a negative attitude. On the other hand, a positive mental attitude in the doctor and assistant enhances professional skills. From a practice standpoint, it keeps established patients loyal to the practice and encourages voluntary testimonials that attract new patients to the practice.

Gaining the Competitive Edge

As undoubtedly there will be equally competent and equally equipped offices in your area, it will be the human relations factors that will differentiate your office from others that offer similar services. Competent health service can be found most anywhere, but competent humanize service is more difficult to find. People will go where their thirst for personalized attention can be satisfied to some degree, if all other factors are equal. This is why some doctors fail to draw sufficiently from their local community while others draw patients from a several hundred mile radius. Without a knowledge of or priority of positive human relations, many doctors and assistants can literally force some patients out of the practice simply by failing to nourish emotional hungers.

We are living in a highly technological-oriented society. We are classified by codes and numbers, our lives appear to be manipulated by computers and indifferent "red tape," and our inner needs for individuality often go begging for recognition and attention. Thus, the average person today is not looking for professional competency, sophisticated technology, or efficient case administration. These factors are taken for granted. The quest is for warmth, reassurance, and personal recognition.

Just as a business that has an abundance of excellent technology can operate in the red, so can a health practice. On the other hand, it is not unusual for a business or a health practice to double its income in a few years once it recognizes the importance of serving people's inner as well as outer needs.

If a patient becomes discouraged, seek some sign of improvement and congratulate the patient on that progress. Discouraged people need hope, support, and reinforcement. Remember, behavior that is rewarded tends to be repeated.

Another important aid is to give the discouraged patient something special to do; e.g., an exercise, a diet, a regimen of some sort to get the patient into the act of active participation and expectation. Once the patient cooperates even a little, let them know that you are proud of them: e.g., "I'm proud of you for the way you are taking care of yourself. Now I know I can count on you." These are powerful motivators. Gratitude from a doctor for improvement is not an expected thing. Then give special service, and let the patient know it is special service especially for them.

Analyzing Patient Complaints

During your initial interview with a patient entering your practice, you may learn that the patient has been switching from the practice to another for the same condition. This is a clue that emotional needs may be begging for attention. The reasons patients give for changing from doctor to doctor are almost endless, but rarely will they be the real reasons that motivated the self-dismissals. Following are just a few of the more common reasons that patient have great difficulty in openly expressing:

- "My complaints were belittled and made light of."
- "I was consistently kept waiting for long periods, as if my time was unimportant. Then I was hurried here and there, and nobody had the time to listen to me."
- "I couldn't understand what they were doing or why they wanted to do it. When I asked, they talked in highly technical language that confused me. I was treated like a child told to obey instructions without explanation."
- "I was just another case to him. I wasn't a human being. I was the 2 o'clock insurance whiplash."
- "His assistant played favorites, I wasn't one of them, and I found this insulting."

If we analyze these and scores of similar complaints, we will come to one conclusion. All involve insults to the patient's ego. They all said in unspoken words, "You don't count," "You're not important." Any complaint, however, is serious to the patient involved, and every patient should be provided with concentrated, undivided attention. Within the hospitable environment, people are escorted, not directed. Alert health personnel will take the time to establish a personal rapport with each patient before giving impersonal instructions; and personalized attention will be offered freely, without favoritism. Even if an assistant may be responsible for the primary procedure or therapy on a particular visit, the patient should never leave the office without visiting with the doctor for at least a few moments.

Model Question Papers

Model Question Paper-I

1. What do you understand by decision making? Explain the various steps involved in the process of decision-making?
2. Define personnel Management. What are the important functions of personnel management?
3. What do you mean by Sales Promotion? What are advantages and limitations of sales promotion?
4. Define Retail Trade. Give its characteristics. What is the difference between retailer and wholesaler in relation to pharmaceutical marketing?
5. What is the procedure to be employed while selecting the employees for a large size drug organization?
6. What is a Trial Balance? Why is it prepared and what are the ways of preparation of it?
7. Write short notes on the following:
   (a) Principles of materials management
   (b) Demand Curves
   (c) Marshalling of Balance Sheet.
8. Enter the following transactions into a 3-column cash book:

1998		Rs.
Jan 1	Balance of Cash in hand	400
	Cash at Bank	8,000
	Fresh Capital introduced	6,000
Jan 3	Deposited into Bank	5,000
Jan 4	Sold goods for cash	400

Jan 6	Received from Mohan	1,980	
	Discount allowed to him	20	
Jan 9	Electricity bill paid by cheque	110	
Jan 11	Machinery purchased	1,200	
Jan 14	Goods purchased from Prasad for cash		2,000
Jan 17	Paid to Rajesh	490	
	Discount received from him	10	
Jan 19	Withdrew from Bank for Office use	400	
Jan 21	Withdrew from bank for Private use	600	
Jan 22	Paid rent by cheque	200	
Jan 26	Received from Raja	780	
	Discount allowed	20	
Jan 27	Received cheque from Pratap	390	
	Discount allowed	10	
Jan 29	Cheque received from Pratap		
	Sent to bank	170	
Jan 30	Deposited into Bank	170	
Jan 31	Paid salaries	600	

Model Question Paper-II

1. Explain the concept of Management. Add a note on the principles of management.
2. Define financial management. What are its main functions?
3. What are the factors to be kept in mind while selecting an advertising medium? Explain briefly about press advertising and outdoor advertising.
4. What is meant by channels of distribution? Enumerate the important channels of distribution in pharmaceutical marketing.
5. What do you understand by Marketing Research? Discuss in detail the marketing research procedure.
6. Write short notes on the following:
   (a) Performance evaluation technique
   (b) Principles of economics
   (c) Differentiate between Trading account and Profit and Loss Account?
7. What is cash book? Why is it kept? Explain various types of cash book.
8. Prepare Trading, Profit and Loss Account of Gopi Medical store for the year ended 31st December 1997 from the following particulars :

Particulars	Rs.	Rs.
Opening Stock	10,000	
Rent	300	
Trade Expenses	600	
Returns inward	600	
Sales	84,000	
Purchases	50,000	
Purchase returns		300
Carriage inwards	200	
Wages	500	
Discount	40	
Discount received		50
Commission	20	
Salaries	2,000	
Legal Expenses	50	
Audit fees	70	
Bank charge	50	
Sales Tax	60	
Interest in drawings		100
Interest on investments		200
Repairs and renewals	260	
Closing Stock Rs. 5,000		

Model Question Paper-III

1. Discuss the export procedures in detail. What do you mean by 'Documentary bill' used for payment in export-import operation?
2. What is the effect of endorsement of bill of exchange? Explain the term 'Noting of a bill'.
3. A pharmaceutical company is interest in promoting an analgesic tablet. Outline the nationwide promotion campaign using all promotion tools.
4. Give an ideal compensation plan which a prospective pharmacist will like to have. Compare it with management's expectations.
5. Discuss the services rendered by wholesaler to manufacturer and retailers.
   (a) Name the errors which do not affect the trial balance.
   (b) Explain errors of commission. Give two examples for such errors
6. Give the functioning of departmental store and multiple shop business for drug distribution. What should be the structure of mail order business?
7. Enter the following transactions in the double column cash book of Mr. X and balance it:

1999	Particulars	Rs.
May 1	Opening Balance	
	Cash in hand	1,350
	Cash in bank	4,000
May 2	Paid to Petty Cash	500
May 2	Sold goods for cash	1,200
May 2	Paid to Srinath by Cheque	2,000
May 3	Received Cheque from Shyam	1,500
May 4	Received Cheque from Mr. Chari	4,000
May 5	Goods purchased for cash	1,500
May 10	Sold goods for cash	800
May 12	Withdrew cash from bank	1,000
May 15	Purchased stationery for cash	400
May 20	Deposited cash in bank	7,000
May 20	Sold goods for cash	8,000
May 25	Withdrew cash from bank	500
May 31	Paid salaries in cash	1,200

Model Question Paper-IV

1. Discuss the principles of Sales Promotion. How advertisement plays an important role in it?
2. Describe the nature and types of marketing channels and intermediaries required for pharmaceuticals marketing.
3. What type of basic information services should be planned for market research? How will you plan training program for pharmacist?
4. Discuss level and elements of compensation to the pharmacist. How will you evaluate their performance?
5. How will you distinguish between a promissory note and bill of exchange? What are the essential requirements of bill of exchange?
6. Describe procedure of importing goods to India. State the nature of documents required for the same.
7. Prepare a check list of questions for rating a prospective applicant for pharmaceutical distributorship.

8. The following particulars relate to business of Mr. Chatterjee on May 31, 1999.

	Rs.
Balance as shown by Cash Book	1,000
Balance as shown by Bank Pass-Book	1,200
Cheque issued but not presented for Payment	1,300
Cheque deposited but payment yet not collected	1,100

Prepare Bank reconciliation statement of Mr. Chatterjee on May 31, 1999.

Model Question Paper-V

1. What criteria should be considered while planning for a literature for retailing. How it can be successfully implemented.
2. Why export documentation is necessary? Mention important shipping documents used in export trade.
3. What is trial balance? How it is prepared? How will you rectify trial balance errors?
4. Consider statements, critically comment on them?
   (a) 'The purpose of advertisement is to promote sales'
   (b) 'The purpose of advertisement is to improve buyer's disposition towards company's produce'
5. Discuss the concept of management. How will you manage administration of departmental store?
6. What incentives one should plan to stimulate average pharmacist to better their usual performance?
7. What is law of demand and supply? How price of a commodity is determined in perfect market?
8. The Bank Pass Book of M/s Monarch Pharma showed a balance of Rs. 22,500 on May 31, 1999, but cheques issued prior to it amounting to Rs. 12,970 had not been presented for encashment. Two cheques of Rs. 1950 and Rs. 1,178 were deposited into bank on May 31, 1999, but credited by bank in June, 1999.

   Prepare a bank reconciliation statement as on May 31, 1999.

Model Question Paper-VI

1. Discuss the nature and importance of management in modern pharmaceutical organization.
2. Distinguish product layout and process layout.
3. Briefly explain the importance and methods of employee training.

4. What are the various sales promotion techniques adopted by a pharmaceutical organization?
5. Explain the principles of costing and estimating.
6. Write short notes on :
   (a) Drug store management
   (b) Inspection of materials
7. (a) Explain the advantages of Double Entry Book Keeping
   (b) Prepare a profit and loss account from the following information.

Particulars	Rs.
Gross Profit	16,000
Interest received	2,600
Discount earned	1,000
Office rent paid	1,000
Bad debts	1,000
Depreciation	1,000
Printing and stationery	1,500
Postage	500
Advertising	1,200
Office Insurance	200
Lighting and heating	600
Carriage outwards	500
Furniture	2,000

***Adjustments*:**

(a) Prepaid office rent Rs. 200
(b) Depreciated furniture by 10%
(c) Outstanding lighting and heating charges Rs. 150.

Model Question Paper-VII

1. Classify the site for opening a pharmacy and discuss the various factors effective in selection of a site for pharmacy.
2. Write in detail about sales promotion and market research for a retail pharmacy.
3. Define production Management. Discuss the various types of production systems. Write the objectives of production planning and control.

4. What is marketing research? Discuss the nature, significance of market research in modern business with a special reference to pharmaceutical industry. Explain briefly the method of conducting a market research.
5. Discuss the nature and functions of personnel management in a pharmaceutical industry.
6. From the following balance extracted at the close of the year ended 31st December 2001, prepare profit and loss account as on that date :

Particulars	Rs.
Gross Profit	2,65,350
Rent 7,400	
Commission Paid	4,250
Salaries	9,750
Taxes 9,750	
Trade expenses	1,457
Bank expenses	1,850
Printing and stationary	7,825
Carriage outward	5,500
Discount allowed	4,750
Discount given	3,550
Bad debts	2,358
Depreciation on Machinery	3,950

7. Journalize the following transactions. Ram Mohan with a capital of Rs. 1,00,000 started the business.

2001 Particulars	Rs.	
August 1	Bought goods from Ravi	15,000
August 3	Sold goods to Vasu	18,500
August 6	Cash Purchase	18,000
August 8	Paid Salaries	5,000
August 10	Cash Sales	12,000
August 11	Bought furniture by paying through Cheque	1,800
August 11	Paid Cash to Ravi	13,500
	Discount received	1,500
August 13	Received Cash from Vasu	16,500
	Discount paid	1,500
August 15	Deposited in Bank	10,000
August 18	Paid towards advertisement through cheque	500

August 20	Stationary expenses	700
August 21	Sold old furniture	1,500
August 25	Received cheque towards interest	500
August 31	Owners personnel drawing	1,000

The following adjustments are required :

(a) Closing stock as on 31st March 2003 was Rs. 57,000.

(b) Depreciation on plant and machinery @ 10%, Fixtures and Fittings @ 5%

(c) Prepaid Insurance Rs. 500

(d) Prepaid Salary Rs. 600

(e) Outstanding interest on overdraft Rs. 2,500.

Model Question Paper – VIII

1. Distinguish between management and organization. Explain the functions of management.
2. What are the factors affecting location of an industry? Discuss the additional factors that are to be taken into consideration while establishing a pharmaceutical unit.
3. What is meant by production planning and control? Explain the steps to be taken to ensure good quality in a pharmaceutical industry.
4. Discuss various methods of selection. Explain the job evaluation methods suitable for pharmaceutical industry.
5. What are the approaches to the study of marketing? Explain the importance of the retailers in marketing pharmaceutical products.
6. Examine the sales promotional policies suitable to pharmaceutical product marketing.
7. From the under mentioned Trial Balance of Mitra and Co., prepare a Trading account, a Profit and Loss Account and a Balance sheet.

Trial Balance as on 31-03-2003

Particulars	Dr Rs.	Cr Rs.
Opening Stock	45,000	
Plant and Machinery	85,000	
Capital A/c		90,000
Sundry Creditors		40,000

Fixtures and Fittings	7,500	
Discount received		3,500
Freehold premises	75,000	
Bank overdraft		20,000
Purchases	1,50,000	
Provision for bad debts		3,000
Salaries	14,000	
Purchase returns		1,500
Sundry debtors	55,000	
Sales (net)		3,37,070
Manufacturing expenses	15,000	
Manufacturing wages	30,000	
Carriage inwards	2,000	
Carriage outwards	2,100	
Administrative expenses	10,000	
Bad debts	750	
Interest and bank charges	625	
Discount allowed	750	
Insurance	1,500	
Cash at Bank	695	
Cash in hand	150	
	4,95,070	4,95,070

Model Question Paper – IX

1. Describe briefly the selection procedure followed in a Large scale organization for its employees?
2. Discuss the need for production planning and control in the present competitive world.
3. Define the term marketing. State and explain the functions of marketing
4. How does co-ordination help in smooth running of an enterprises.
5. Explain Taylor's principles of scientific management.
6. Define and explain the process of communication
7. What do you mean by job evaluation? Discuss the various methods of job evaluation.
8. What is the significance of Marketing Research? Briefly examine the principal methods employed for the purpose.

Model Question Paper – X

1. Distinguish between administration and management and explain briefly the universality of the principles of management.
2. Explain briefly four techniques of labour welfare in India.
3. What do you understand by Insurance? Explain the general principles of Insurance.
4. Outline the functions of the personnel department in a large organization.
5. What do you understand by Oligopoly? Explain the concept of Law of Demand and Supply.
6. Define the concept organizing? Explain the different types in it?
7. Explain the procedure for the recruitment and selection of personnel in an organization.
8. What do you understand by inventory control? Briefly explain the different techniques of inventory control?

Index

Q

R

S

www.ingramcontent.com/pod-product-compliance
Lightning Source LLC
Chambersburg PA
CBHW080929240926
51849CB00003BA/418
9789352300259